YOU HAVE KILLER ME

by JAMIE S. RICH *&* JOËLLE JONES

lettered by DOUGLAS E. SHERWOOD

designed by KEITH WOOD

edited by JAMES LUCAS JONES *&* JILL BEATON

PUBLISHED BY ONI PRESS, INC.

JOE NOZEMACK *founder & chief financial officer*

JAMES LUCAS JONES *publisher*

CHARLIE CHU *v.p. of creative & business development*

BRAD ROOKS *director of operations*

RACHEL REED *marketing manager*

MELISSA MESZAROS MACFADYEN *publicity manager*

TROY LOOK *director of design & production*

HILARY THOMPSON *graphic designer*

KATE Z. STONE *junior graphic designer*

ANGIE KNOWLES *digital prepress lead*

ARI YARWOOD *executive editor*

ROBIN HERRERA *senior editor*

DESIREE WILSON *associate editor*

ALISSA SALLAH *administrative assistant*

JUNG LEE *logistics associate*

Special thanks to Terry and Satoka for their assistance
with the tones, which were all applied by hand.
Their aid was a big help in completing the process.

onipress.com
facebook.com/onipress
twitter.com/onipress
onipress.tumblr.com
instagram.com/onipress

First Edition: June 2009
Softcover Edition: February 2018

ISBN 978-1-62010-436-1
eISBN 978-1-62010-075-2

Printed in China.

Library of Congress Control Number: 2017946445

1 2 3 4 5 6 7 8 9 10

CHAPTER 1

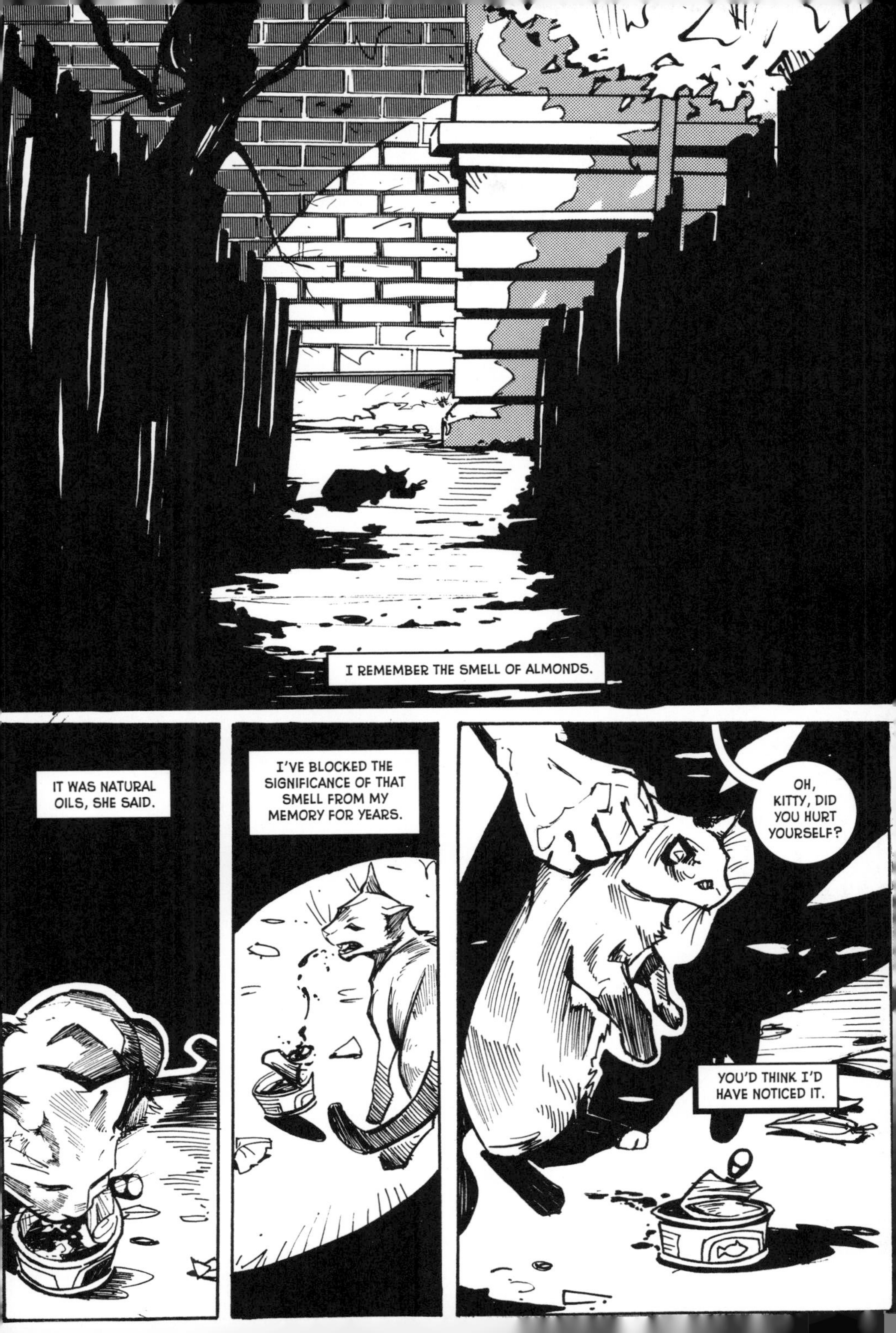
I REMEMBER THE SMELL OF ALMONDS.
IT WAS NATURAL OILS, SHE SAID.
I'VE BLOCKED THE SIGNIFICANCE OF THAT SMELL FROM MY MEMORY FOR YEARS.
OH, KITTY, DID YOU HURT YOURSELF?
YOU'D THINK I'D HAVE NOTICED IT.

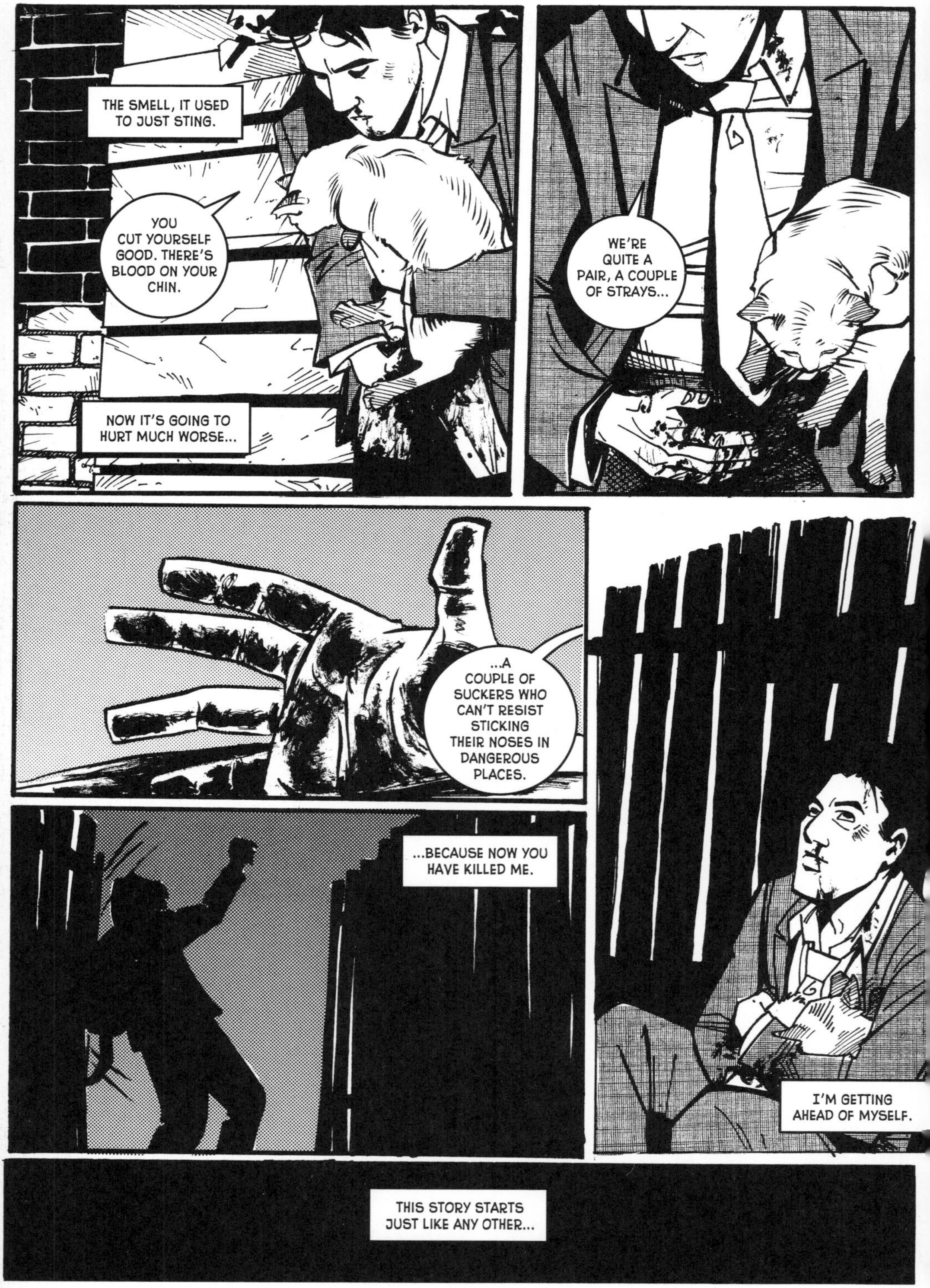
THE SMELL, IT USED TO JUST STING.
YOU CUT YOURSELF GOOD. THERE'S BLOOD ON YOUR CHIN.
NOW IT'S GOING TO HURT MUCH WORSE...
WE'RE QUITE A PAIR, A COUPLE OF STRAYS...
...A COUPLE OF SUCKERS WHO CAN'T RESIST STICKING THEIR NOSES IN DANGEROUS PLACES.
...BECAUSE NOW YOU HAVE KILLED ME.
I'M GETTING AHEAD OF MYSELF.
THIS STORY STARTS JUST LIKE ANY OTHER...

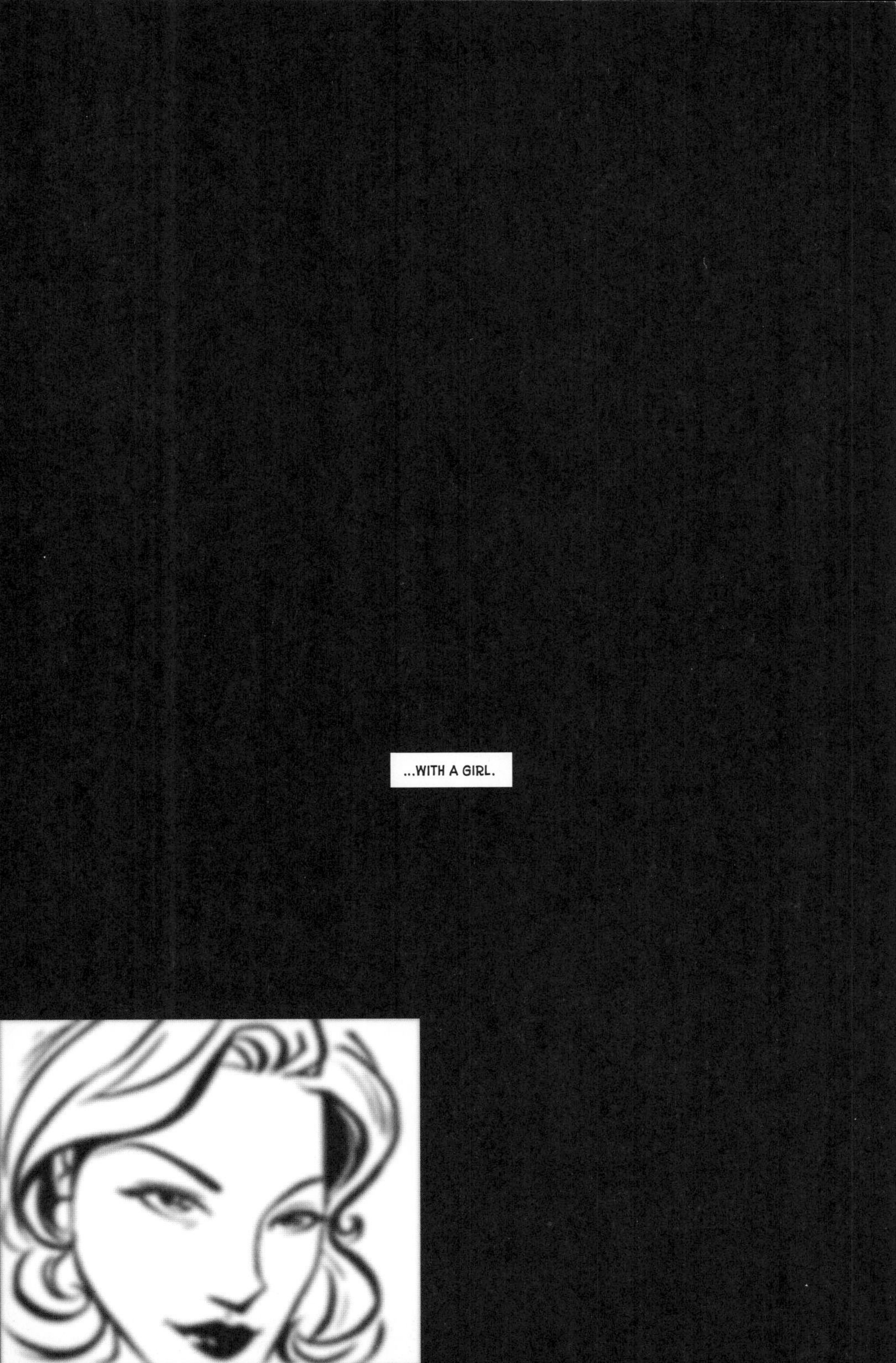
...WITH A GIRL.

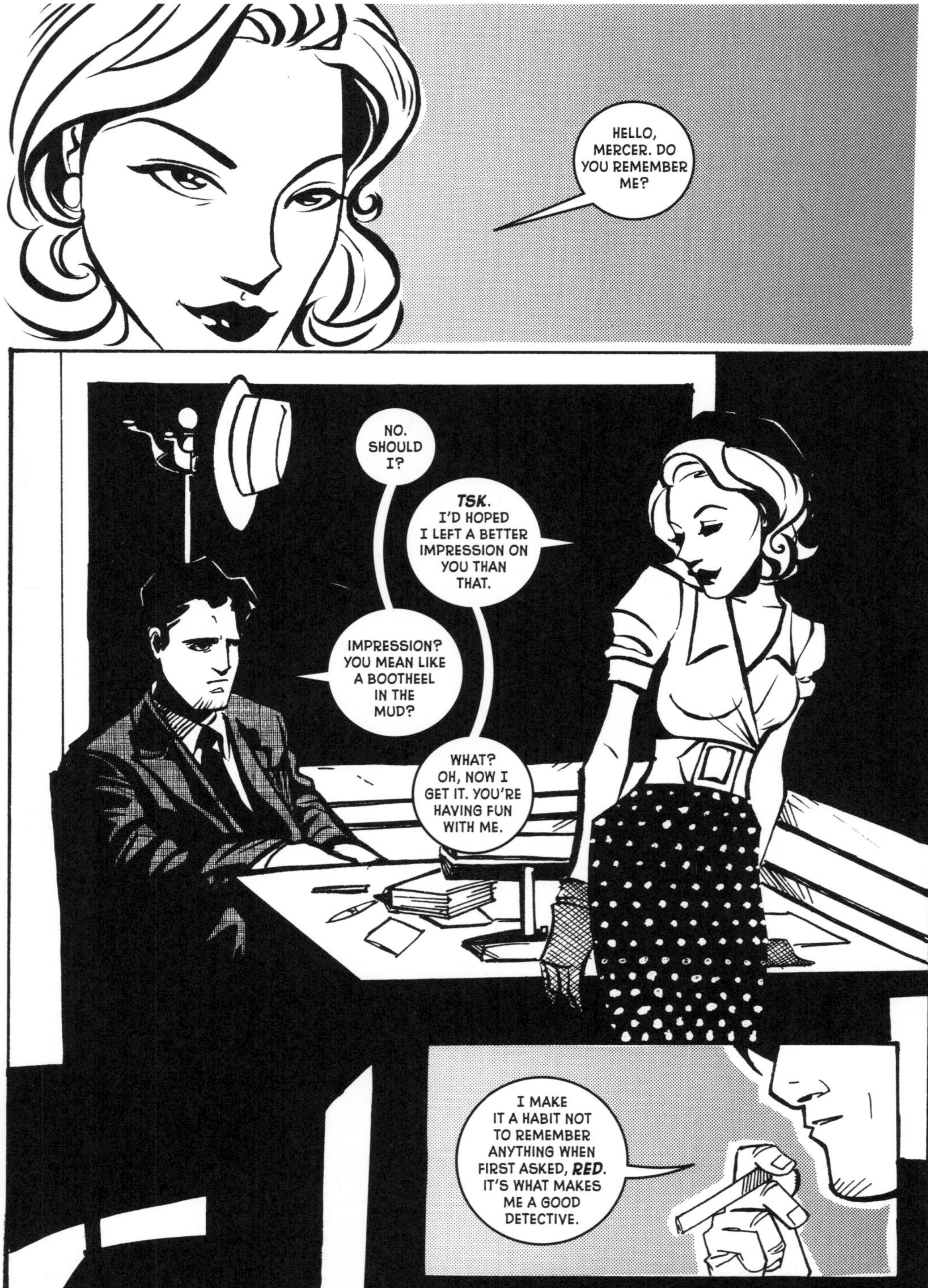

HELLO, MERCER. DO YOU REMEMBER ME?
NO. SHOULD I?
TSK. I'D HOPED I LEFT A BETTER IMPRESSION ON YOU THAN THAT.
IMPRESSION? YOU MEAN LIKE A BOOTHEEL IN THE MUD?
WHAT? OH, NOW I GET IT. YOU'RE HAVING FUN WITH ME.
I MAKE IT A HABIT NOT TO REMEMBER ANYTHING WHEN FIRST ASKED, RED. IT'S WHAT MAKES ME A GOOD DETECTIVE.

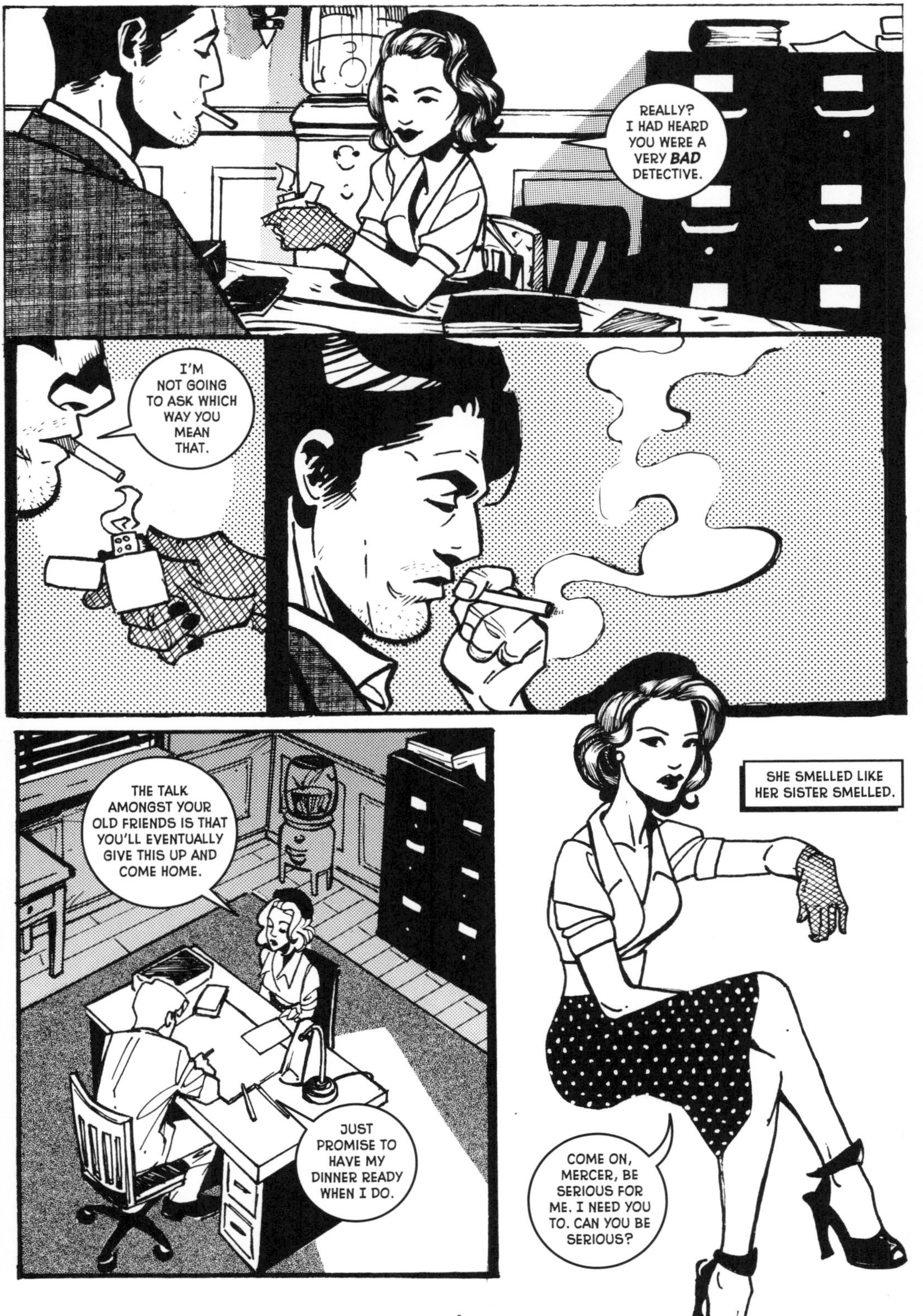
REALLY? I HAD HEARD YOU WERE A VERY BAD DETECTIVE.
I'M NOT GOING TO ASK WHICH WAY YOU MEAN THAT.
THE TALK AMONGST YOUR OLD FRIENDS IS THAT YOU'LL EVENTUALLY GIVE THIS UP AND COME HOME.
JUST PROMISE TO HAVE MY DINNER READY WHEN I DO.
SHE SMELLED LIKE HER SISTER SMELLED.
COME ON, MERCER, BE SERIOUS FOR ME. I NEED YOU TO. CAN YOU BE SERIOUS?

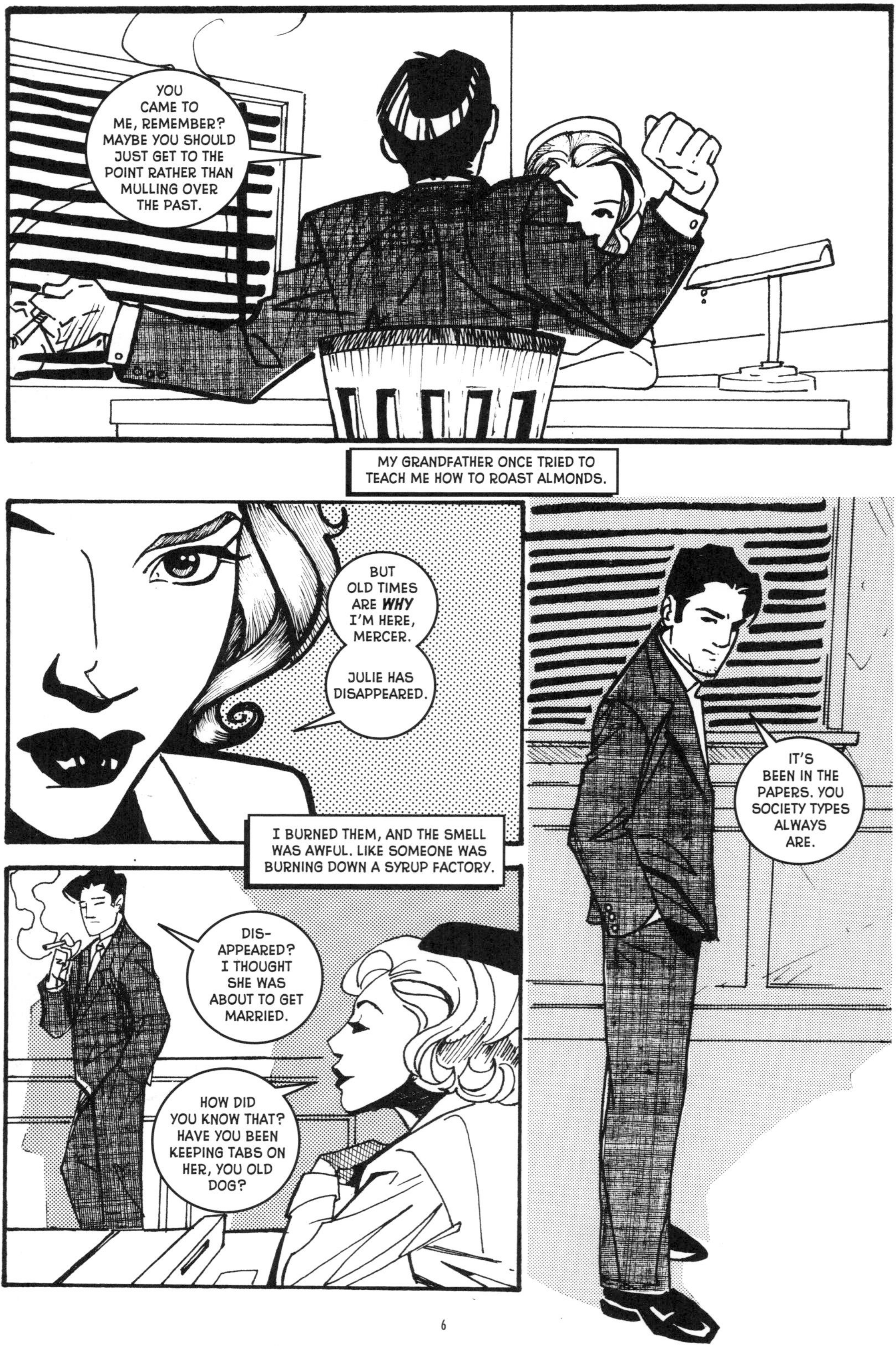
YOU CAME TO ME, REMEMBER? MAYBE YOU SHOULD JUST GET TO THE POINT RATHER THAN MULLING OVER THE PAST.
MY GRANDFATHER ONCE TRIED TO TEACH ME HOW TO ROAST ALMONDS.
BUT OLD TIMES ARE *WHY* I'M HERE, MERCER.
JULIE HAS DISAPPEARED.
I BURNED THEM, AND THE SMELL WAS AWFUL. LIKE SOMEONE WAS BURNING DOWN A SYRUP FACTORY.
DIS-APPEARED? I THOUGHT SHE WAS ABOUT TO GET MARRIED.
HOW DID YOU KNOW THAT? HAVE YOU BEEN KEEPING TABS ON HER, YOU OLD DOG?
IT'S BEEN IN THE PAPERS. YOU SOCIETY TYPES ALWAYS ARE.

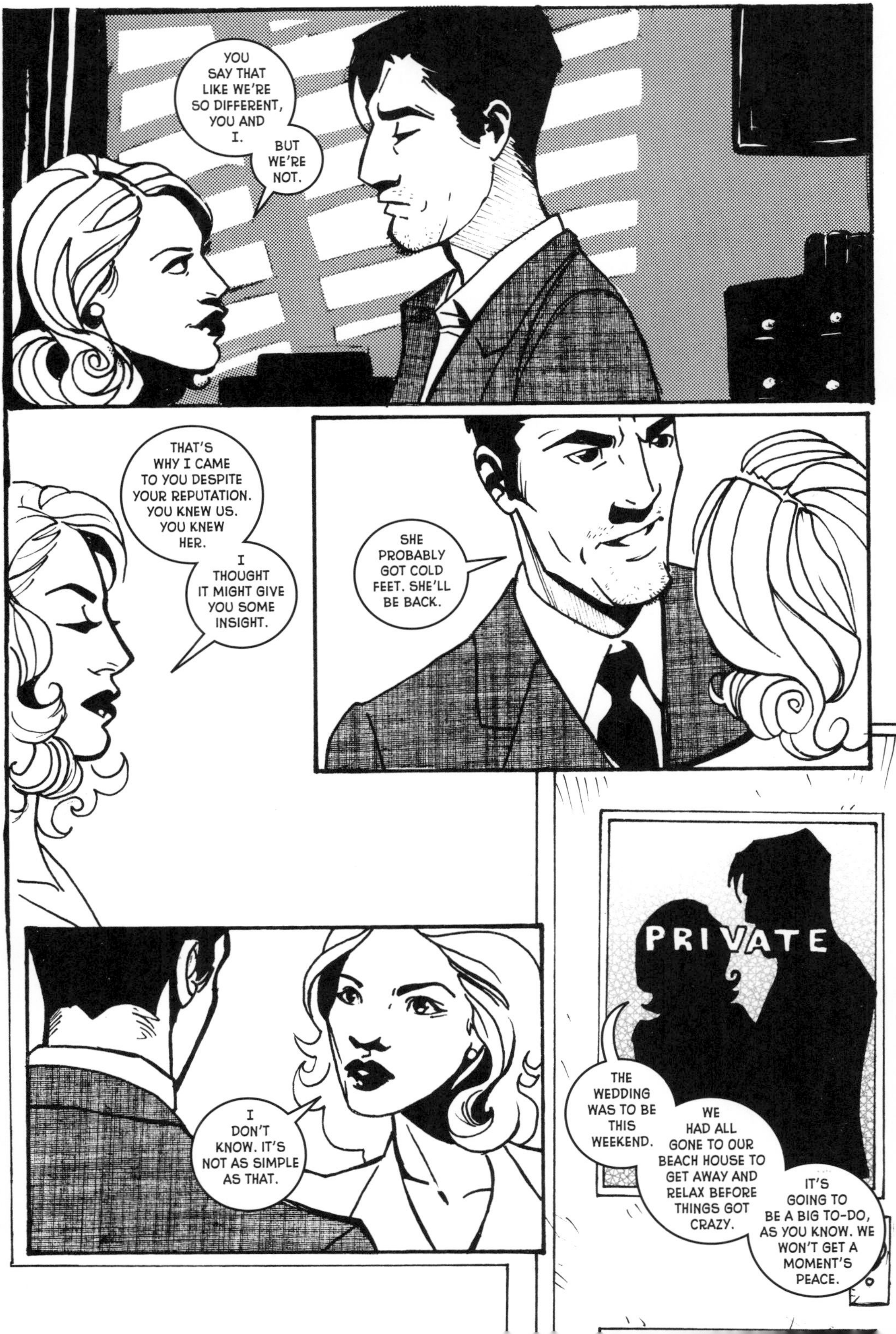
YOU SAY THAT LIKE WE'RE SO DIFFERENT, YOU AND I.
BUT WE'RE NOT.
THAT'S WHY I CAME TO YOU DESPITE YOUR REPUTATION. YOU KNEW US. YOU KNEW HER.
I THOUGHT IT MIGHT GIVE YOU SOME INSIGHT.
SHE PROBABLY GOT COLD FEET. SHE'LL BE BACK.
I DON'T KNOW. IT'S NOT AS SIMPLE AS THAT.
PRIVATE
THE WEDDING WAS TO BE THIS WEEKEND.
WE HAD ALL GONE TO OUR BEACH HOUSE TO GET AWAY AND RELAX BEFORE THINGS GOT CRAZY.
IT'S GOING TO BE A BIG TO-DO, AS YOU KNOW. WE WON'T GET A MOMENT'S PEACE.

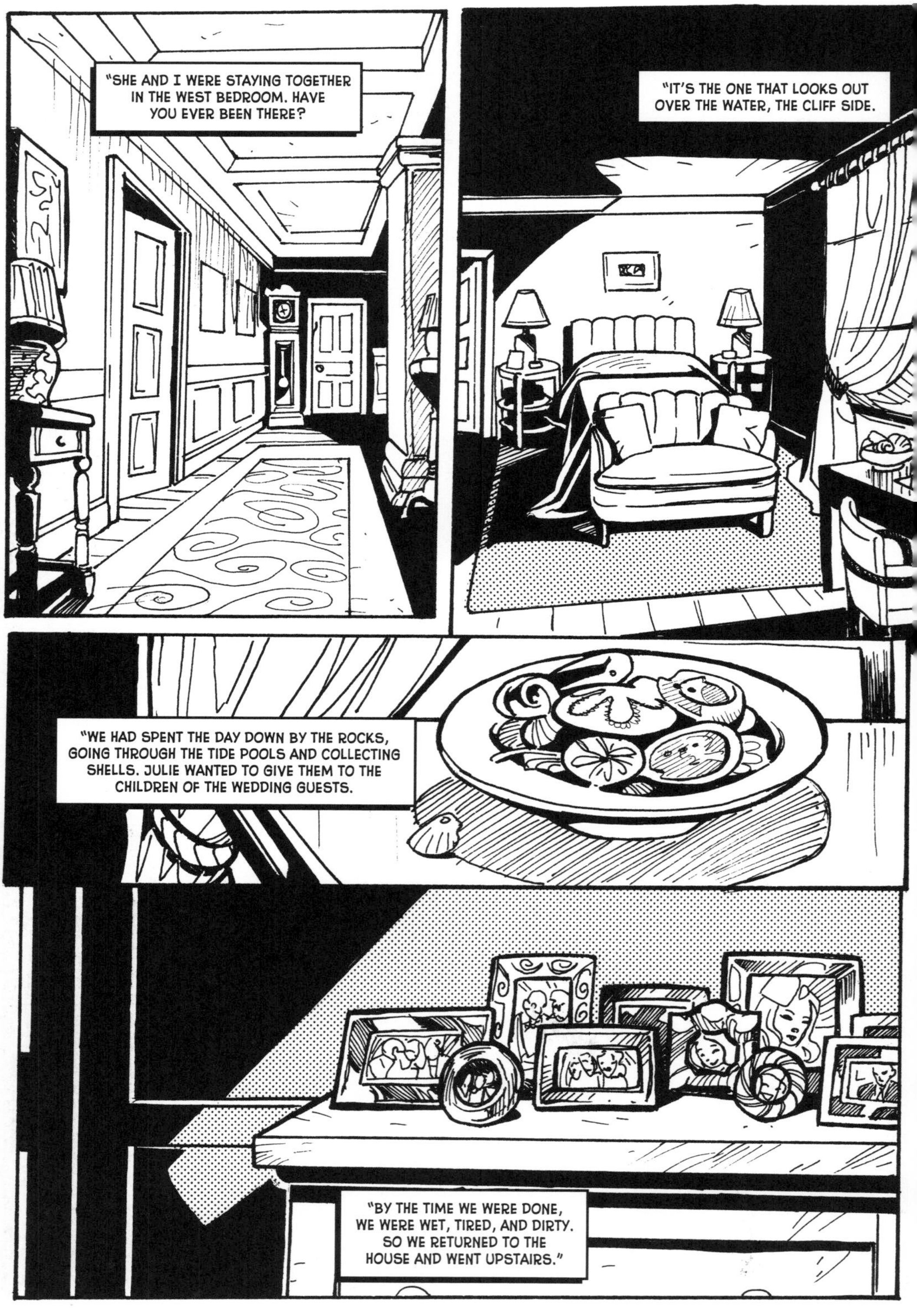
"SHE AND I WERE STAYING TOGETHER IN THE WEST BEDROOM. HAVE YOU EVER BEEN THERE?
"IT'S THE ONE THAT LOOKS OUT OVER THE WATER, THE CLIFF SIDE.
"WE HAD SPENT THE DAY DOWN BY THE ROCKS, GOING THROUGH THE TIDE POOLS AND COLLECTING SHELLS. JULIE WANTED TO GIVE THEM TO THE CHILDREN OF THE WEDDING GUESTS.
"BY THE TIME WE WERE DONE, WE WERE WET, TIRED, AND DIRTY. SO WE RETURNED TO THE HOUSE AND WENT UPSTAIRS."

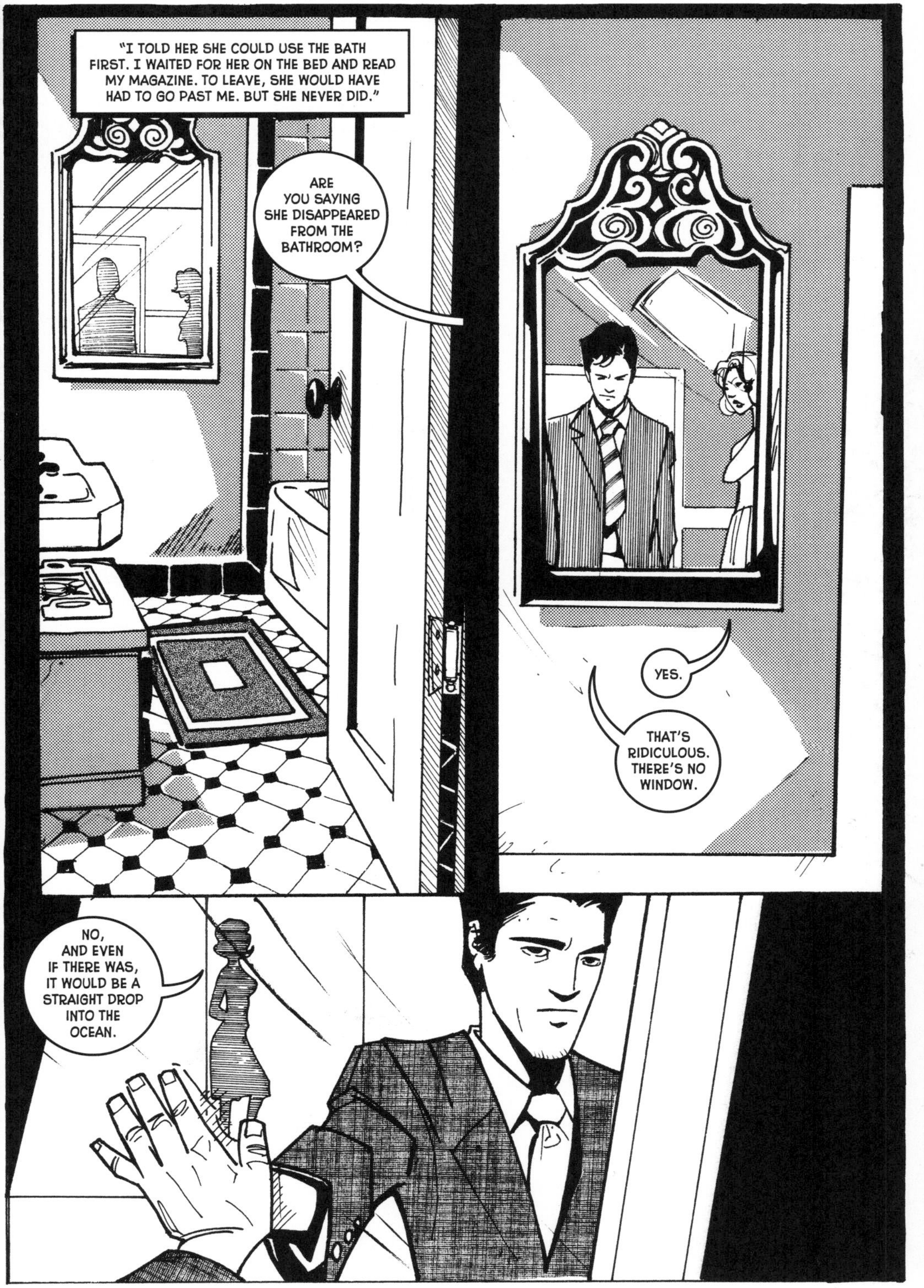
"I TOLD HER SHE COULD USE THE BATH FIRST. I WAITED FOR HER ON THE BED AND READ MY MAGAZINE. TO LEAVE, SHE WOULD HAVE HAD TO GO PAST ME. BUT SHE NEVER DID."
ARE YOU SAYING SHE DISAPPEARED FROM THE BATHROOM?
YES.
THAT'S RIDICULOUS. THERE'S NO WINDOW.
NO, AND EVEN IF THERE WAS, IT WOULD BE A STRAIGHT DROP INTO THE OCEAN.

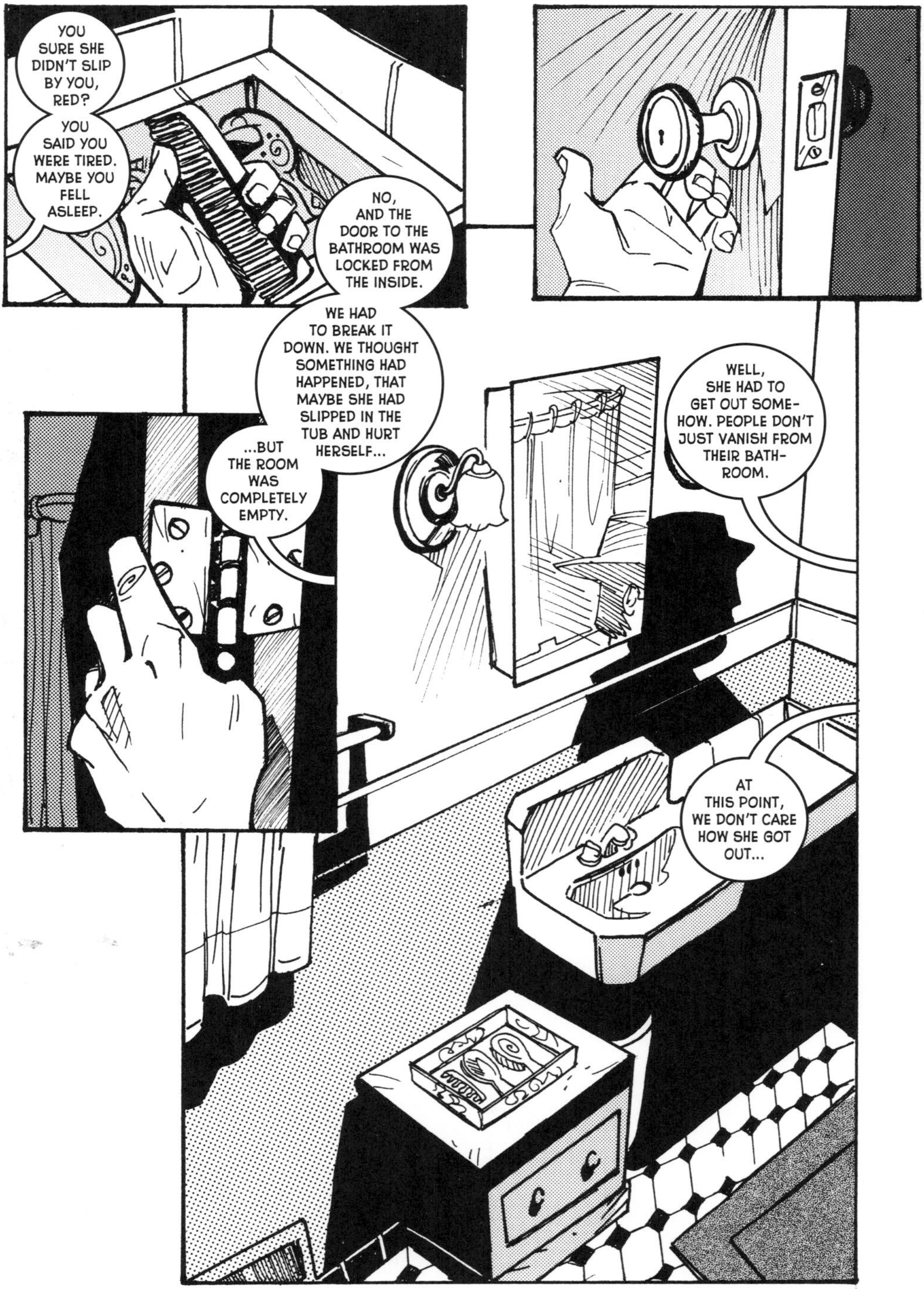
YOU SURE SHE DIDN'T SLIP BY YOU, RED?
YOU SAID YOU WERE TIRED. MAYBE YOU FELL ASLEEP.
NO, AND THE DOOR TO THE BATHROOM WAS LOCKED FROM THE INSIDE.
WE HAD TO BREAK IT DOWN. WE THOUGHT SOMETHING HAD HAPPENED, THAT MAYBE SHE HAD SLIPPED IN THE TUB AND HURT HERSELF...
...BUT THE ROOM WAS COMPLETELY EMPTY.
WELL, SHE HAD TO GET OUT SOME-HOW. PEOPLE DON'T JUST VANISH FROM THEIR BATH-ROOM.
AT THIS POINT, WE DON'T CARE HOW SHE GOT OUT...

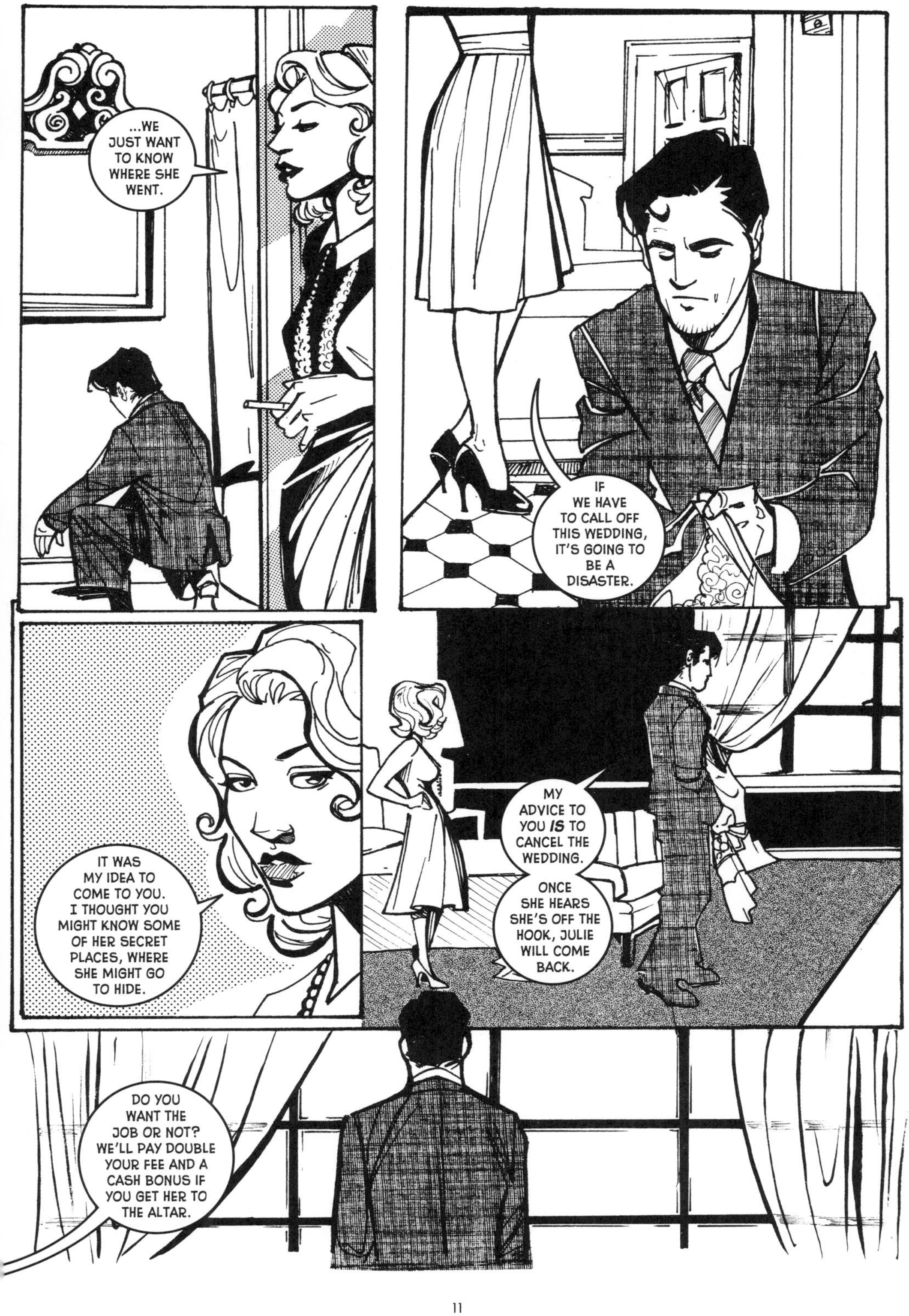
...WE JUST WANT TO KNOW WHERE SHE WENT.
IF WE HAVE TO CALL OFF THIS WEDDING, IT'S GOING TO BE A DISASTER.
IT WAS MY IDEA TO COME TO YOU. I THOUGHT YOU MIGHT KNOW SOME OF HER SECRET PLACES, WHERE SHE MIGHT GO TO HIDE.
MY ADVICE TO YOU ***IS*** TO CANCEL THE WEDDING.
ONCE SHE HEARS SHE'S OFF THE HOOK, JULIE WILL COME BACK.
DO YOU WANT THE JOB OR NOT? WE'LL PAY DOUBLE YOUR FEE AND A CASH BONUS IF YOU GET HER TO THE ALTAR.

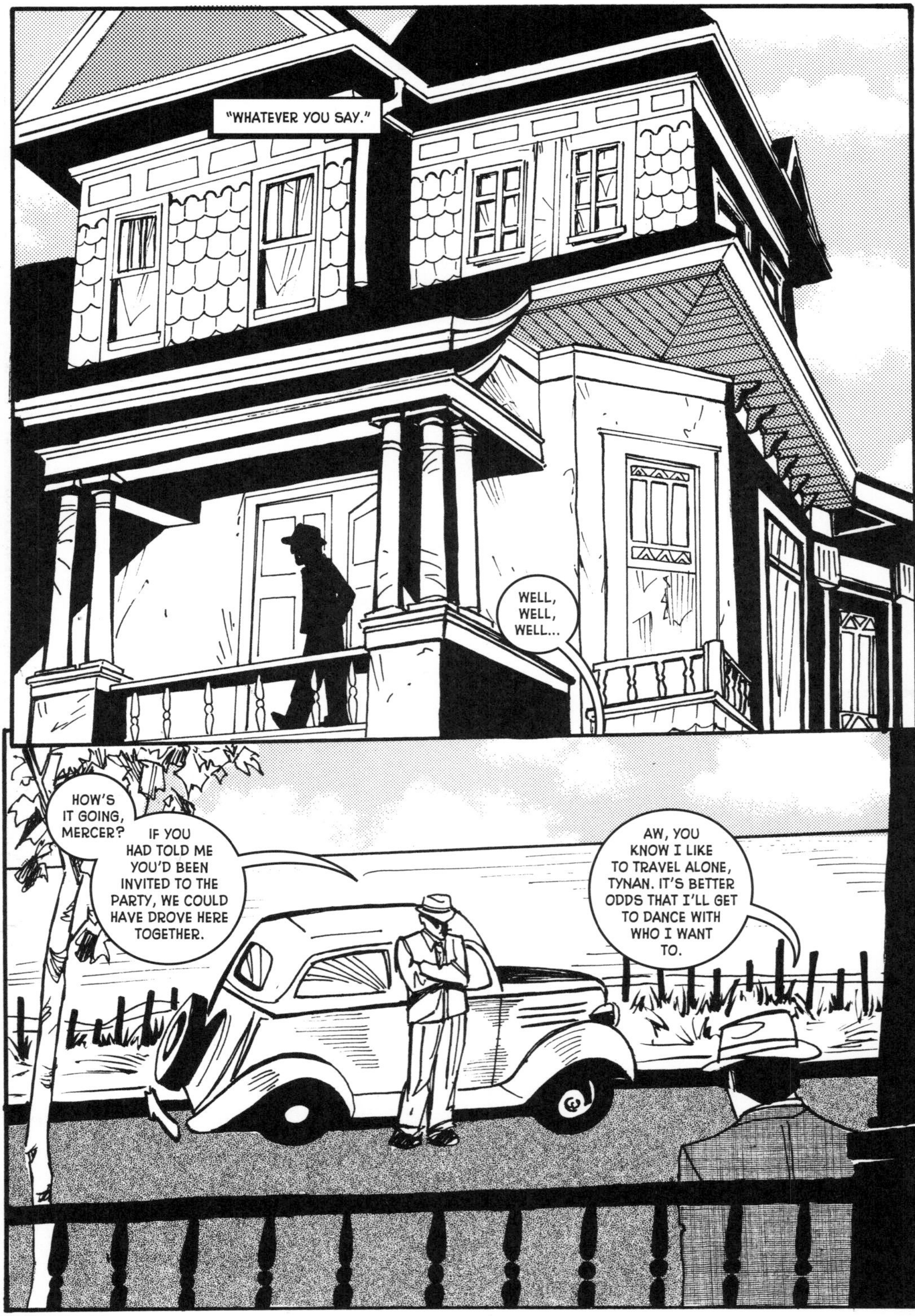
"WHATEVER YOU SAY."
WELL, WELL, WELL...
HOW'S IT GOING, MERCER?
IF YOU HAD TOLD ME YOU'D BEEN INVITED TO THE PARTY, WE COULD HAVE DROVE HERE TOGETHER.
AW, YOU KNOW I LIKE TO TRAVEL ALONE, TYNAN. IT'S BETTER ODDS THAT I'LL GET TO DANCE WITH WHO I WANT TO.

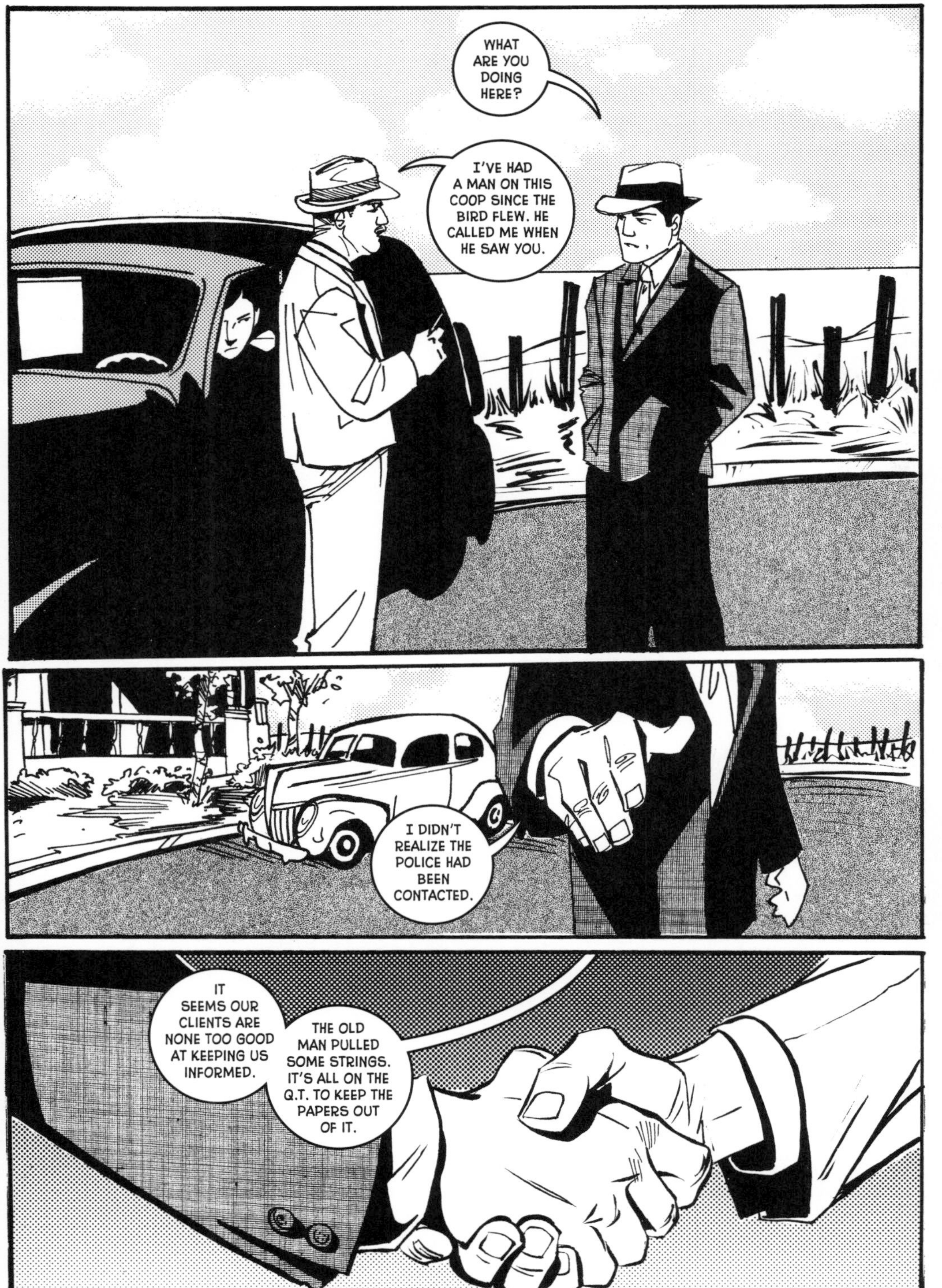
WHAT ARE YOU DOING HERE?
I'VE HAD A MAN ON THIS COOP SINCE THE BIRD FLEW. HE CALLED ME WHEN HE SAW YOU.
I DIDN'T REALIZE THE POLICE HAD BEEN CONTACTED.
IT SEEMS OUR CLIENTS ARE NONE TOO GOOD AT KEEPING US INFORMED.
THE OLD MAN PULLED SOME STRINGS. IT'S ALL ON THE Q.T. TO KEEP THE PAPERS OUT OF IT.

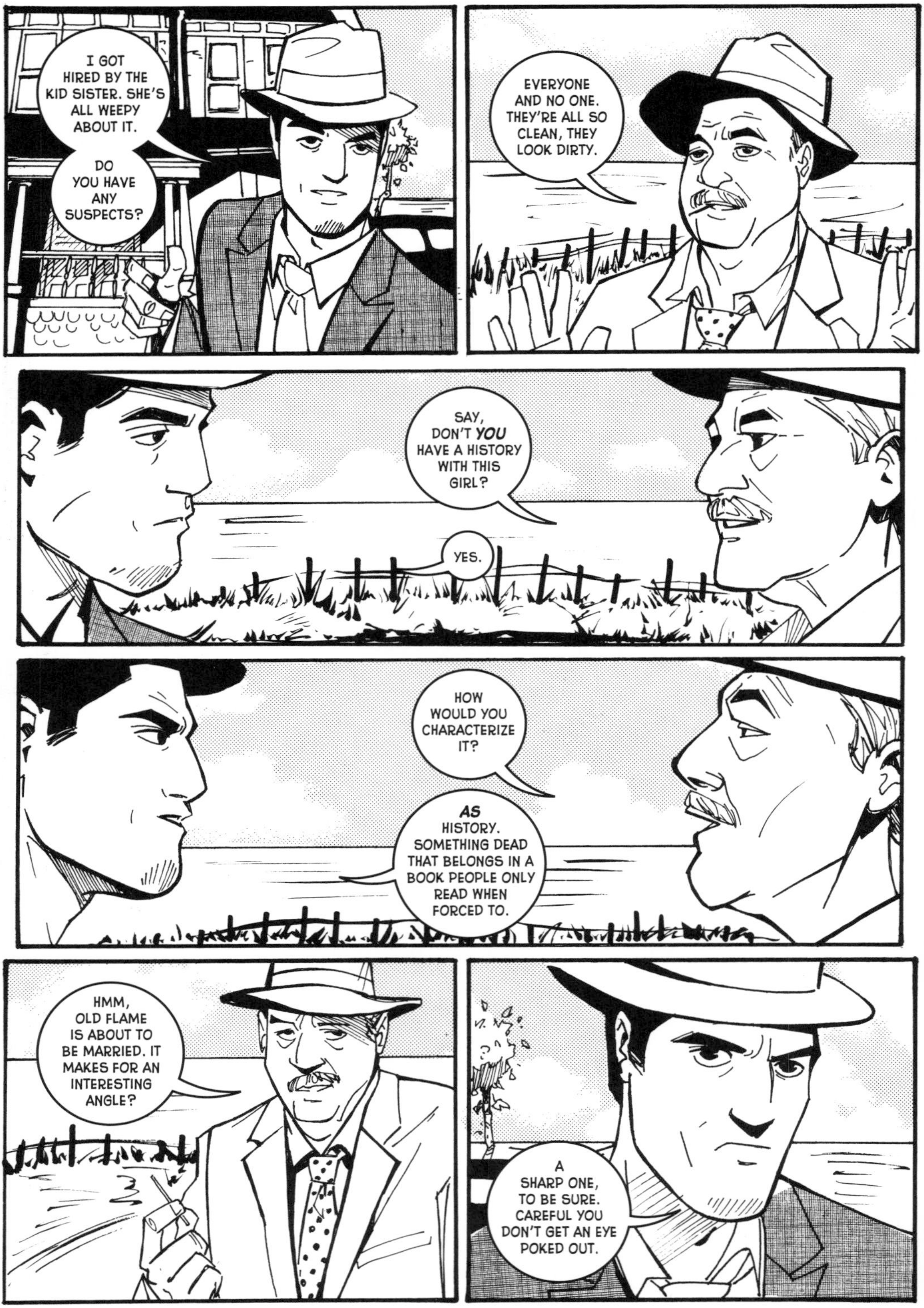
I GOT HIRED BY THE KID SISTER. SHE'S ALL WEEPY ABOUT IT.
DO YOU HAVE ANY SUSPECTS?
EVERYONE AND NO ONE. THEY'RE ALL SO CLEAN, THEY LOOK DIRTY.
SAY, DON'T *YOU* HAVE A HISTORY WITH THIS GIRL?
YES.
HOW WOULD YOU CHARACTERIZE IT?
AS HISTORY. SOMETHING DEAD THAT BELONGS IN A BOOK PEOPLE ONLY READ WHEN FORCED TO.
HMM, OLD FLAME IS ABOUT TO BE MARRIED. IT MAKES FOR AN INTERESTING ANGLE?
A SHARP ONE, TO BE SURE. CAREFUL YOU DON'T GET AN EYE POKED OUT.

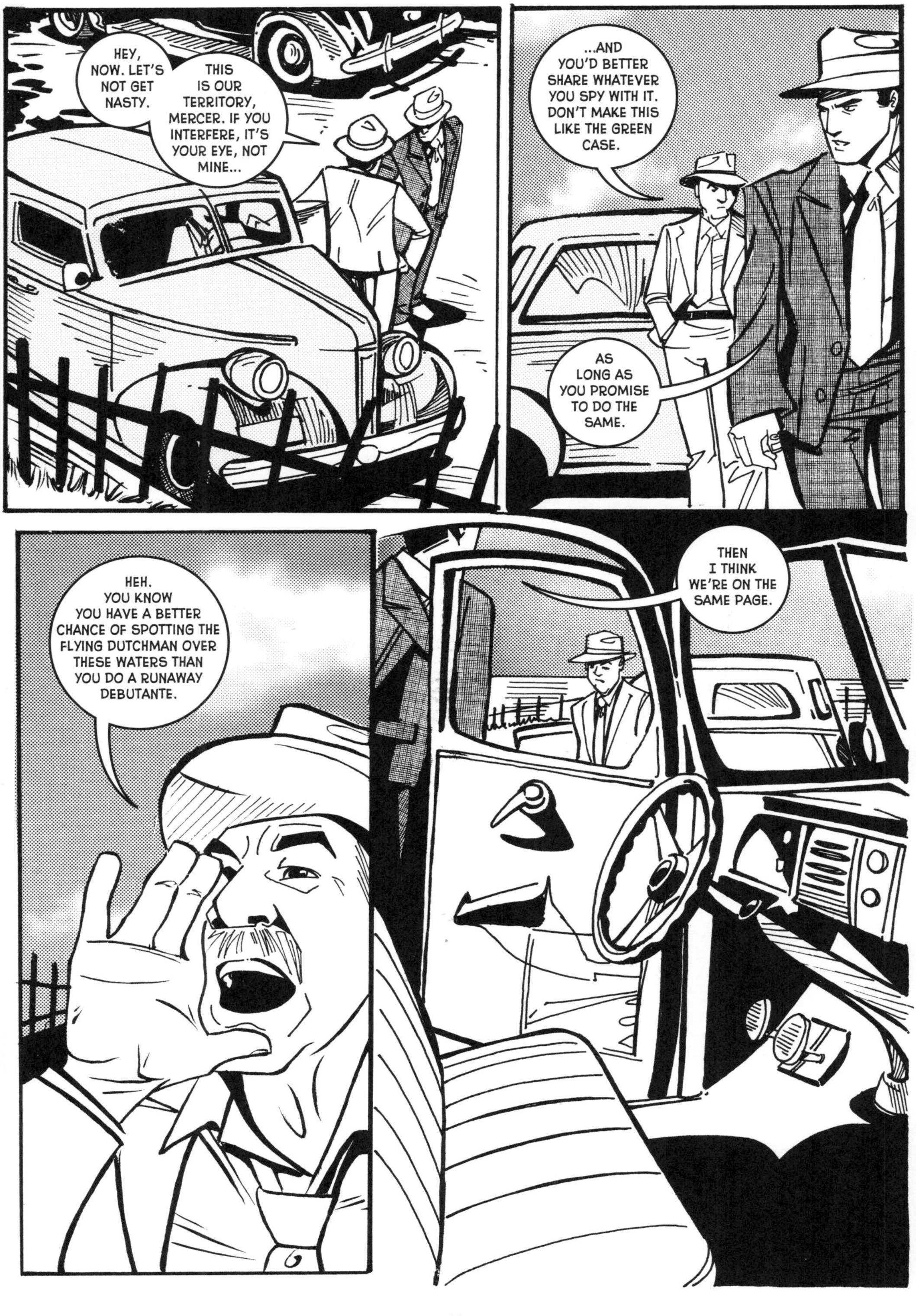
HEY, NOW. LET'S NOT GET NASTY.
THIS IS OUR TERRITORY, MERCER. IF YOU INTERFERE, IT'S YOUR EYE, NOT MINE...
...AND YOU'D BETTER SHARE WHATEVER YOU SPY WITH IT. DON'T MAKE THIS LIKE THE GREEN CASE.
AS LONG AS YOU PROMISE TO DO THE SAME.
HEH. YOU KNOW YOU HAVE A BETTER CHANCE OF SPOTTING THE FLYING DUTCHMAN OVER THESE WATERS THAN YOU DO A RUNAWAY DEBUTANTE.
THEN I THINK WE'RE ON THE SAME PAGE.

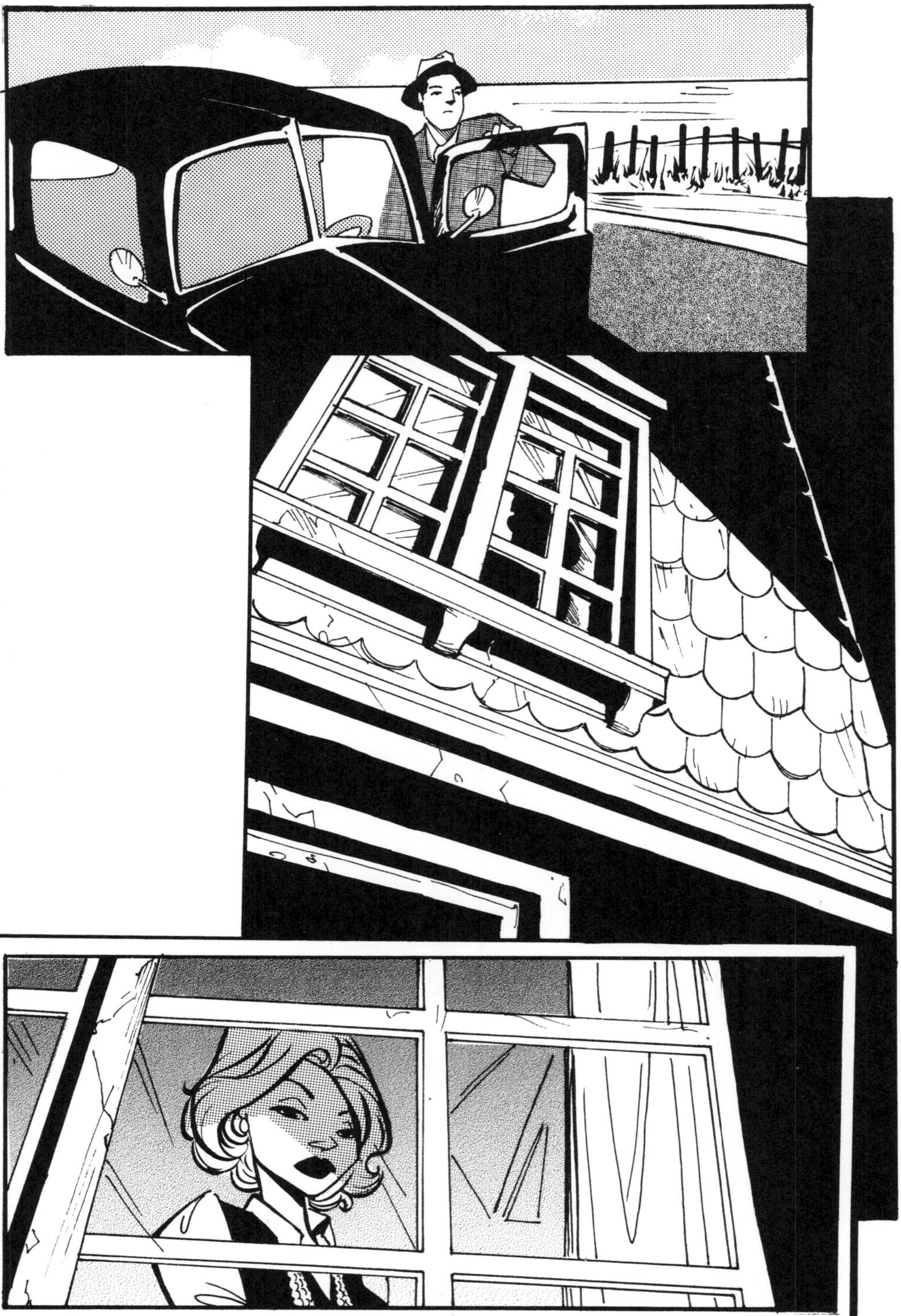

CHAPTER 2

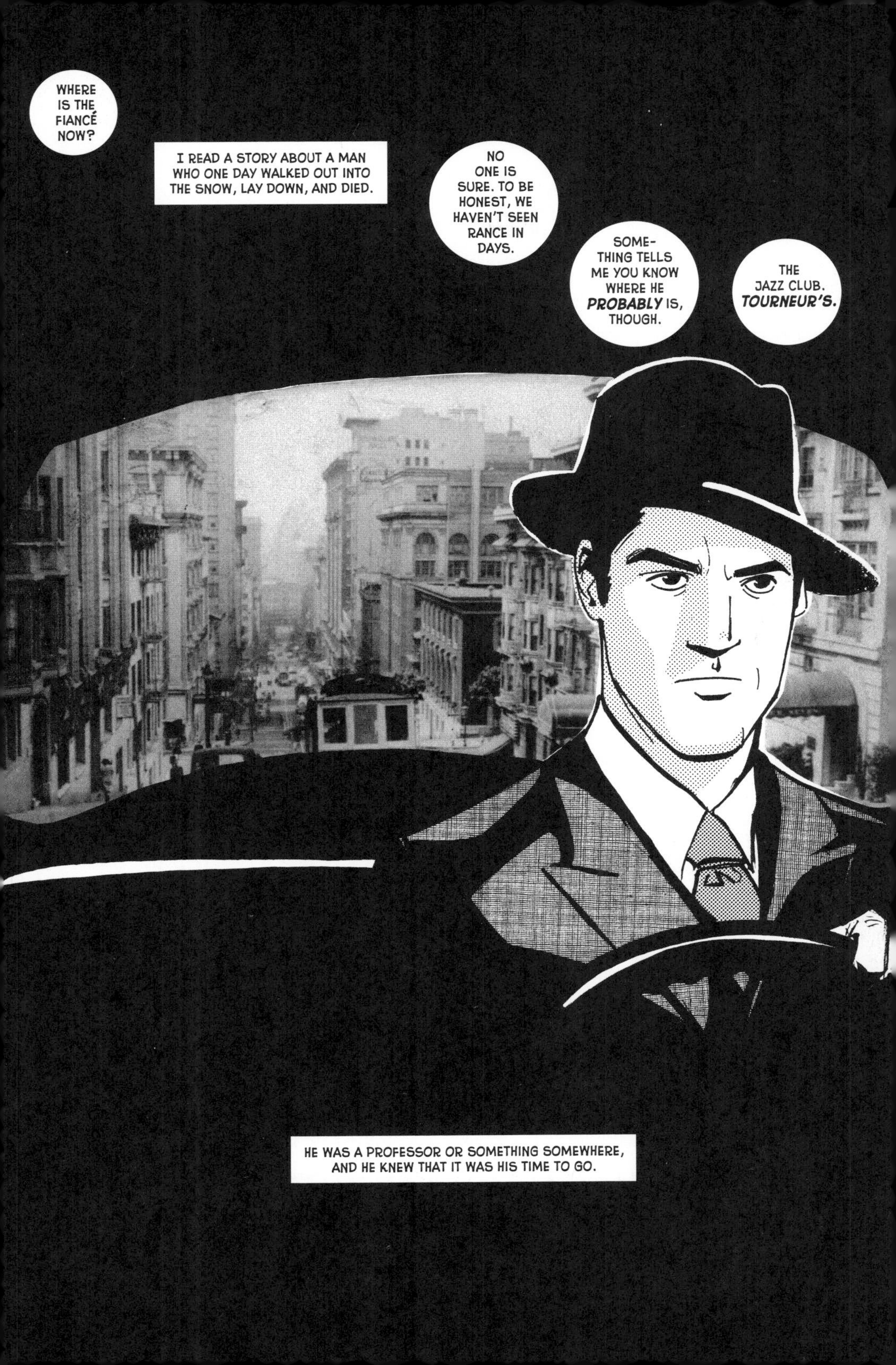
WHERE IS THE FIANCÉ NOW?
I READ A STORY ABOUT A MAN WHO ONE DAY WALKED OUT INTO THE SNOW, LAY DOWN, AND DIED.
NO ONE IS SURE. TO BE HONEST, WE HAVEN'T SEEN RANCE IN DAYS.
SOME-THING TELLS ME YOU KNOW WHERE HE *PROBABLY* IS, THOUGH.
THE JAZZ CLUB. *TOURNEUR'S.*
HE WAS A PROFESSOR OR SOMETHING SOMEWHERE, AND HE KNEW THAT IT WAS HIS TIME TO GO.

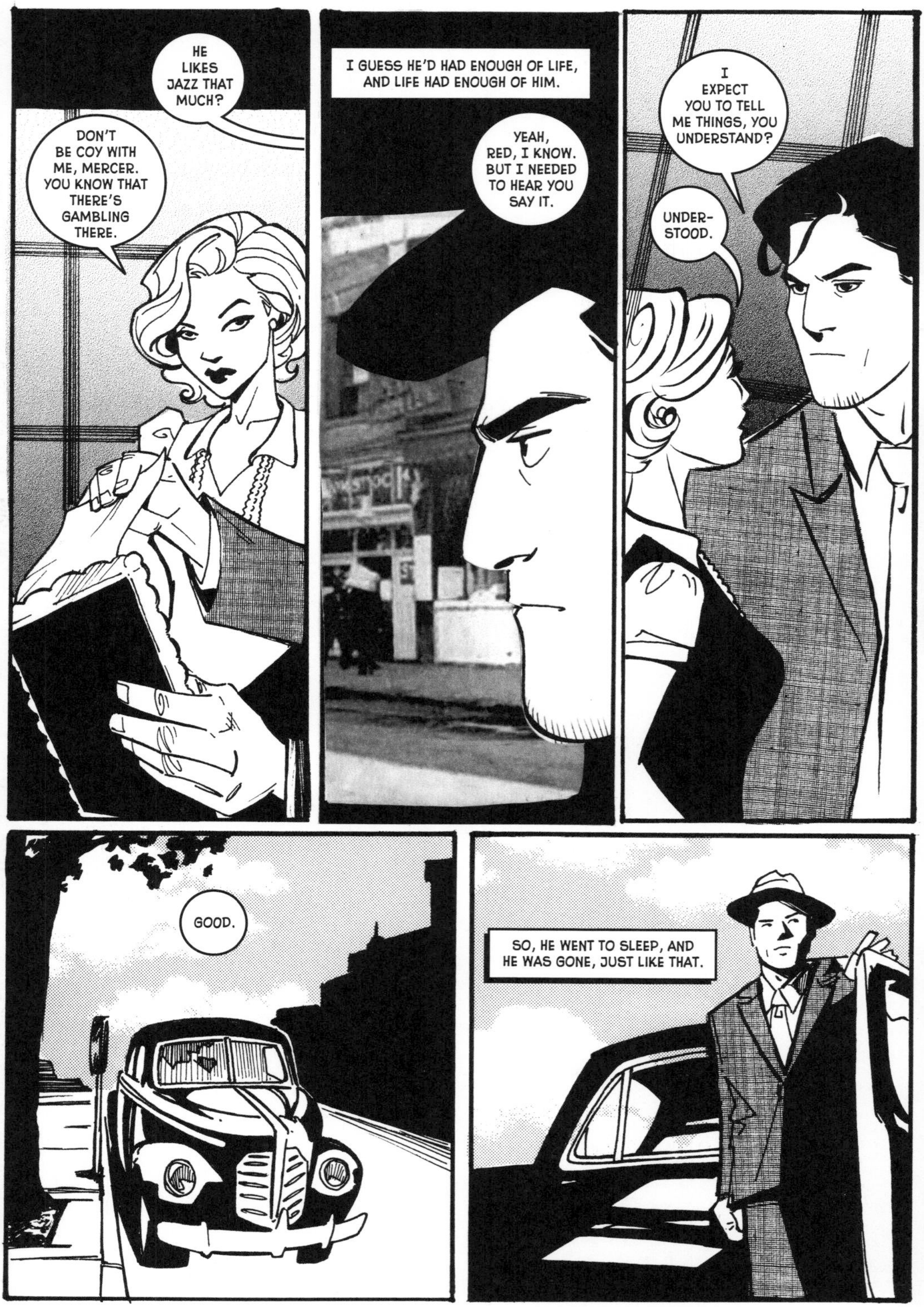

HE LIKES JAZZ THAT MUCH?
DON'T BE COY WITH ME, MERCER. YOU KNOW THAT THERE'S GAMBLING THERE.
I GUESS HE'D HAD ENOUGH OF LIFE, AND LIFE HAD ENOUGH OF HIM.
YEAH, RED, I KNOW. BUT I NEEDED TO HEAR YOU SAY IT.
I EXPECT YOU TO TELL ME THINGS, YOU UNDERSTAND?
UNDER-STOOD.
GOOD.
SO, HE WENT TO SLEEP, AND HE WAS GONE, JUST LIKE THAT.

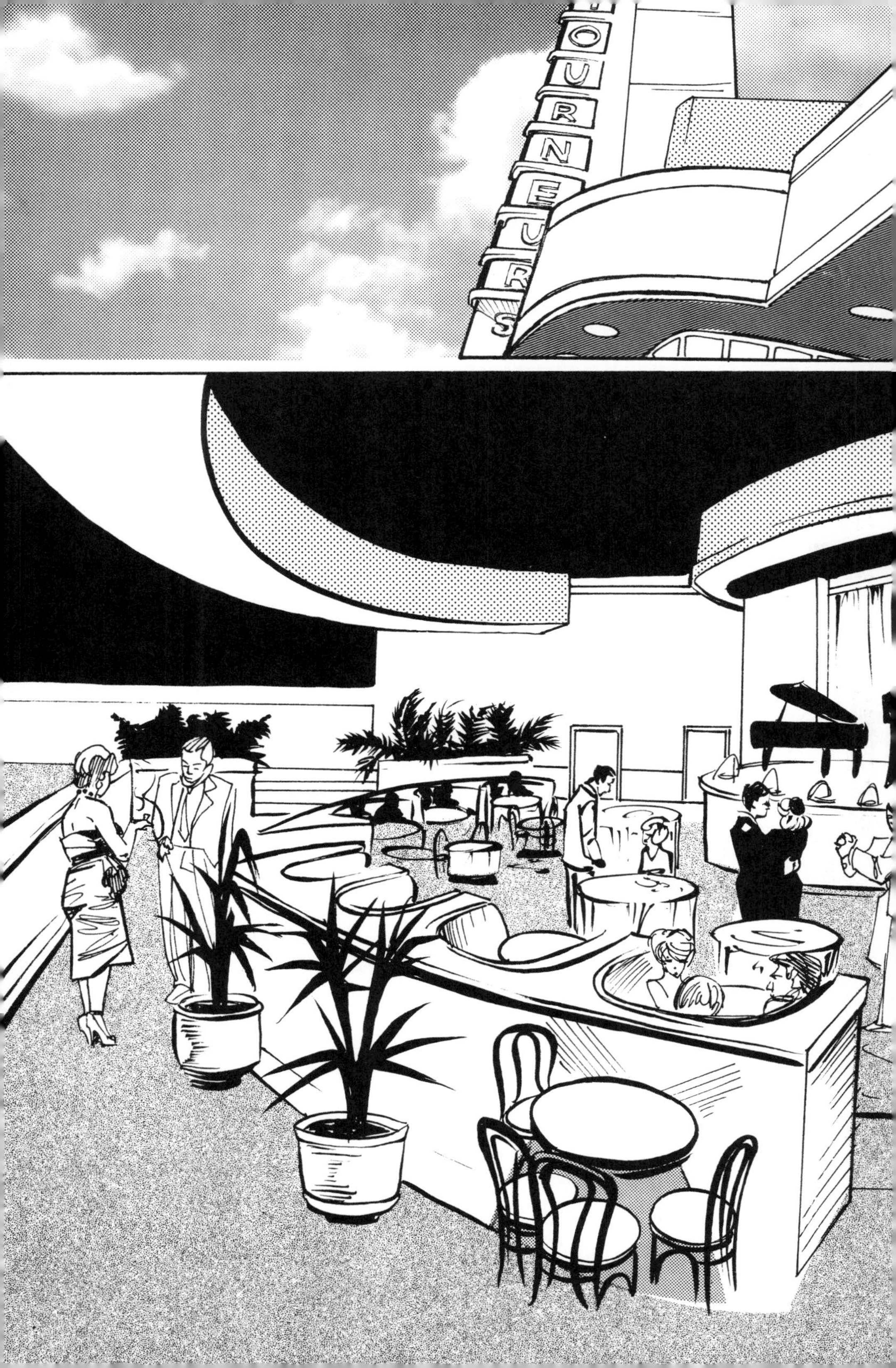
OURNEURS

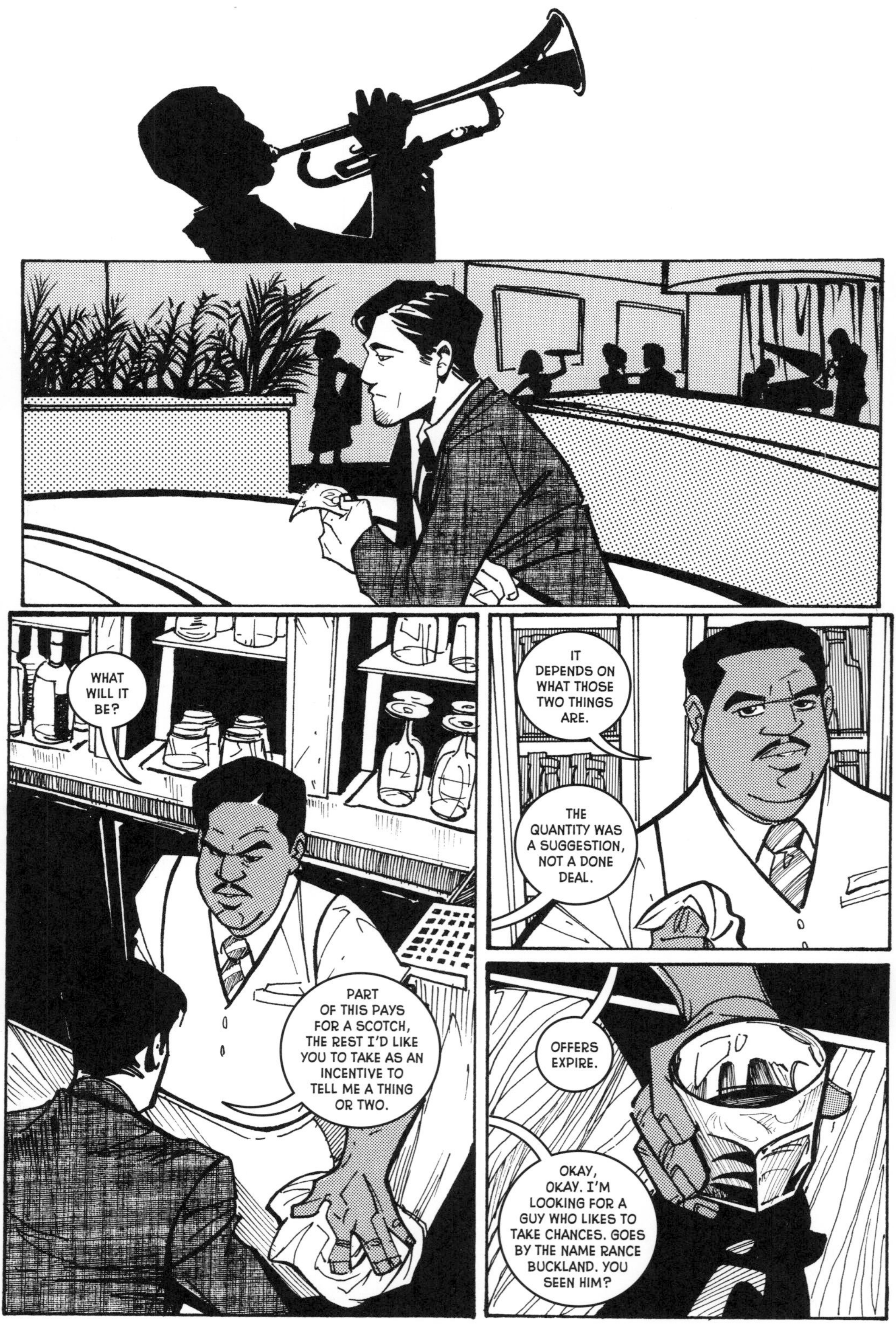
WHAT WILL IT BE?
PART OF THIS PAYS FOR A SCOTCH, THE REST I'D LIKE YOU TO TAKE AS AN INCENTIVE TO TELL ME A THING OR TWO.
IT DEPENDS ON WHAT THOSE TWO THINGS ARE.
THE QUANTITY WAS A SUGGESTION, NOT A DONE DEAL.
OFFERS EXPIRE.
OKAY, OKAY. I'M LOOKING FOR A GUY WHO LIKES TO TAKE CHANCES. GOES BY THE NAME RANCE BUCKLAND. YOU SEEN HIM?

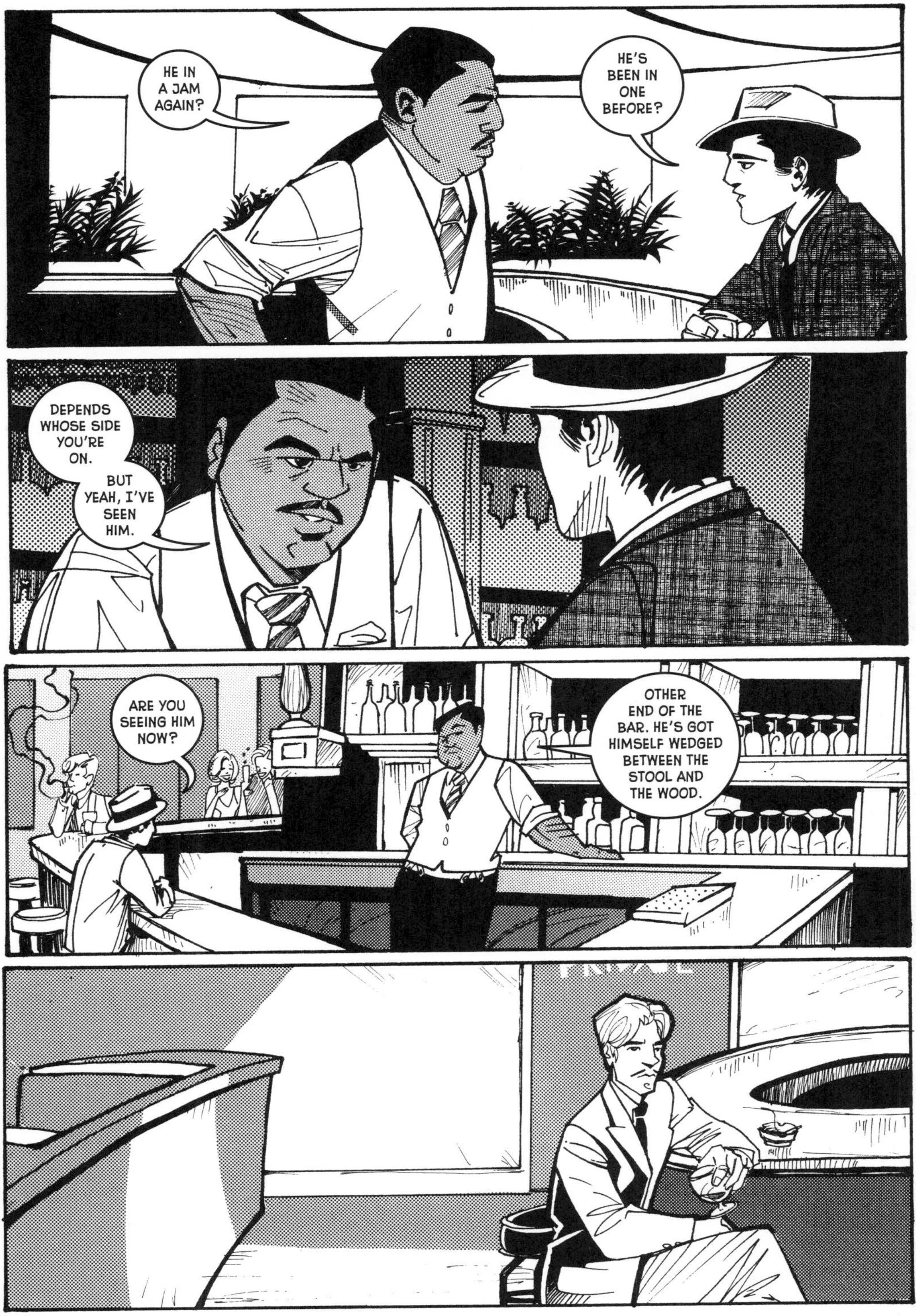
HE IN A JAM AGAIN?
HE'S BEEN IN ONE BEFORE?
DEPENDS WHOSE SIDE YOU'RE ON.
BUT YEAH, I'VE SEEN HIM.
ARE YOU SEEING HIM NOW?
OTHER END OF THE BAR. HE'S GOT HIMSELF WEDGED BETWEEN THE STOOL AND THE WOOD.

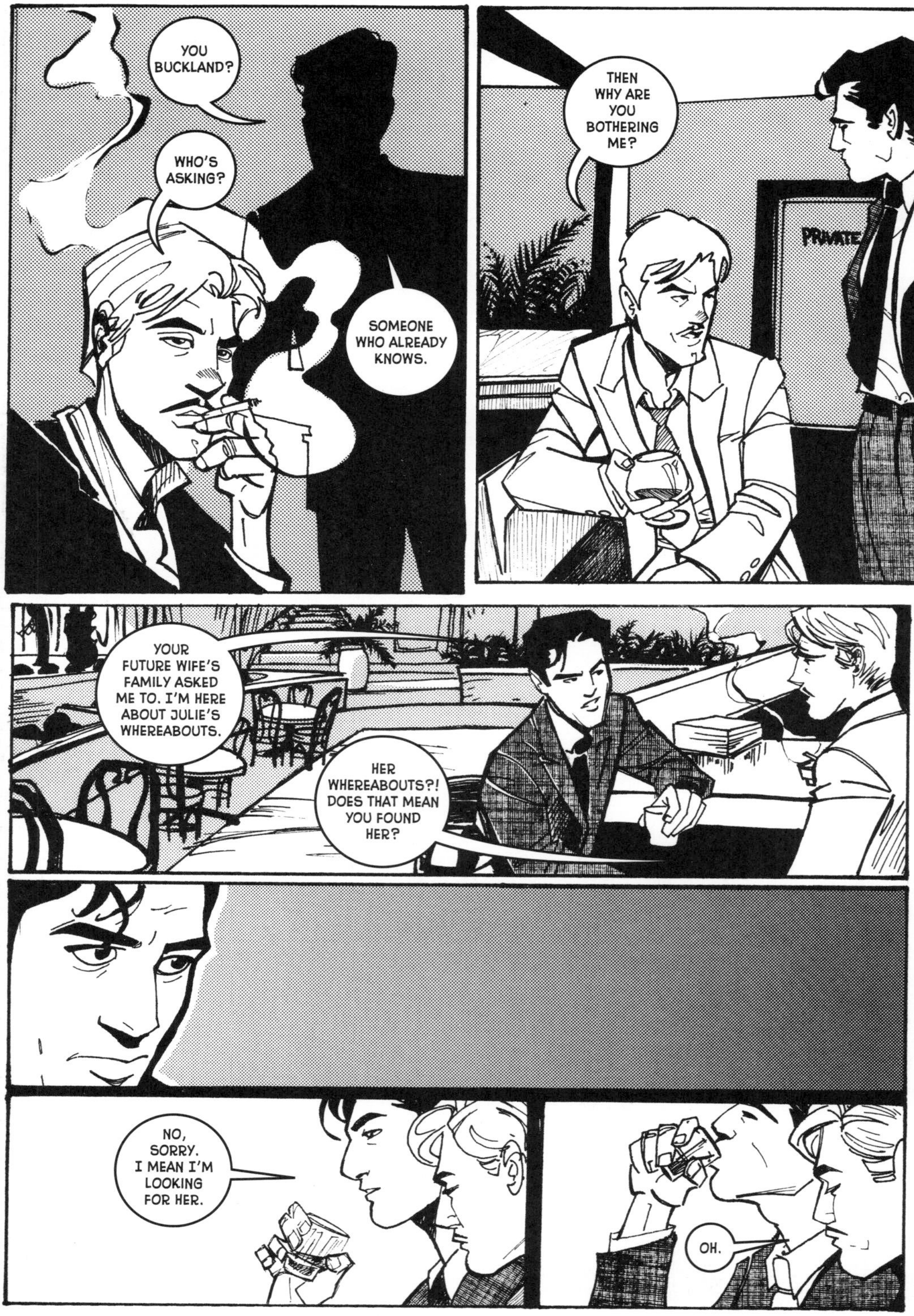
YOU BUCKLAND?
WHO'S ASKING?
SOMEONE WHO ALREADY KNOWS.
THEN WHY ARE YOU BOTHERING ME?
PRIVATE
YOUR FUTURE WIFE'S FAMILY ASKED ME TO. I'M HERE ABOUT JULIE'S WHEREABOUTS.
HER WHEREABOUTS?! DOES THAT MEAN YOU FOUND HER?
NO, SORRY. I MEAN I'M LOOKING FOR HER.
OH.

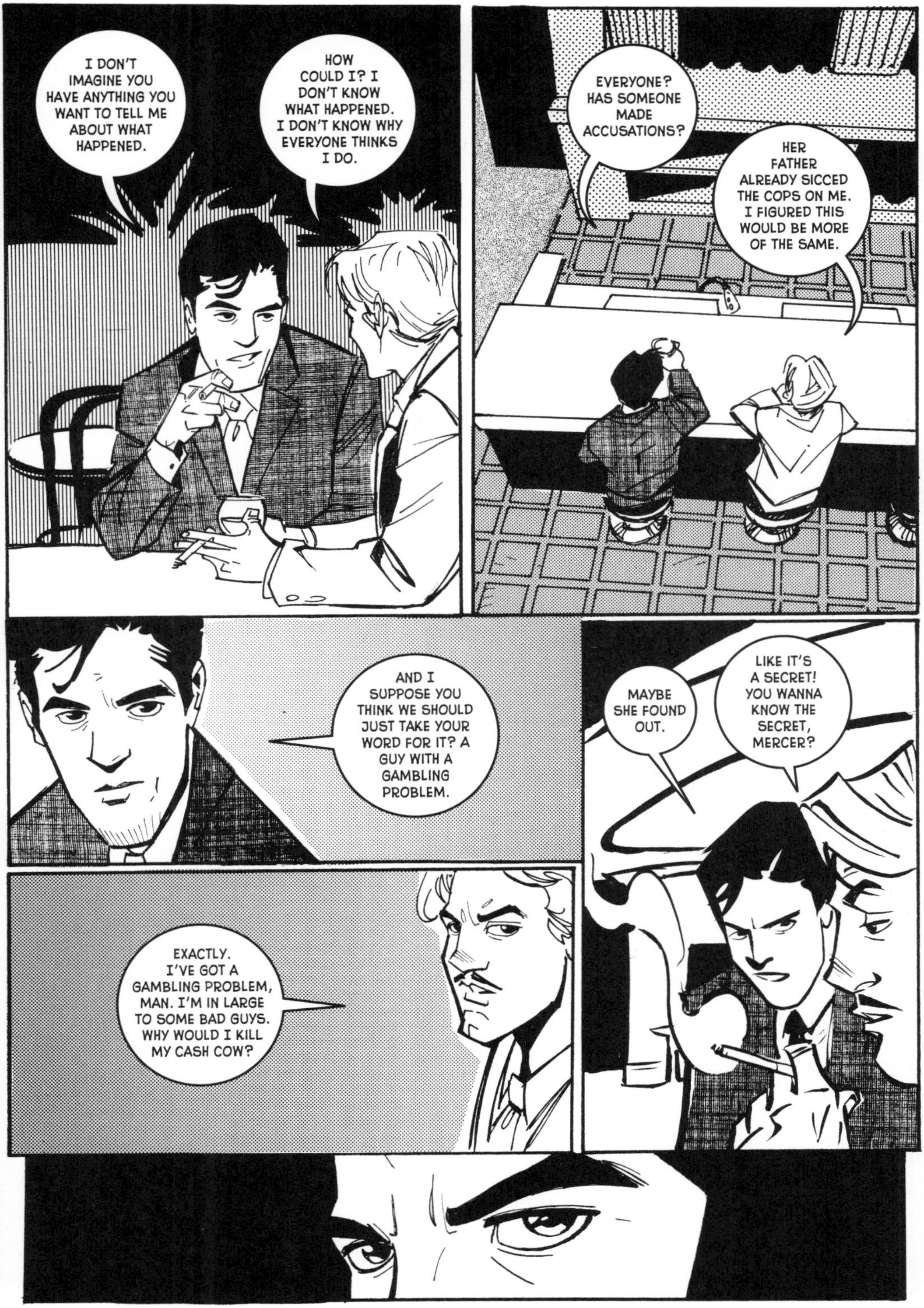
I DON'T IMAGINE YOU HAVE ANYTHING YOU WANT TO TELL ME ABOUT WHAT HAPPENED.
HOW COULD I? I DON'T KNOW WHAT HAPPENED. I DON'T KNOW WHY EVERYONE THINKS I DO.
EVERYONE? HAS SOMEONE MADE ACCUSATIONS?
HER FATHER ALREADY SICCED THE COPS ON ME. I FIGURED THIS WOULD BE MORE OF THE SAME.
AND I SUPPOSE YOU THINK WE SHOULD JUST TAKE YOUR WORD FOR IT? A GUY WITH A GAMBLING PROBLEM.
EXACTLY. I'VE GOT A GAMBLING PROBLEM, MAN. I'M IN LARGE TO SOME BAD GUYS. WHY WOULD I KILL MY CASH COW?
MAYBE SHE FOUND OUT.
LIKE IT'S A SECRET! YOU WANNA KNOW THE SECRET, MERCER?

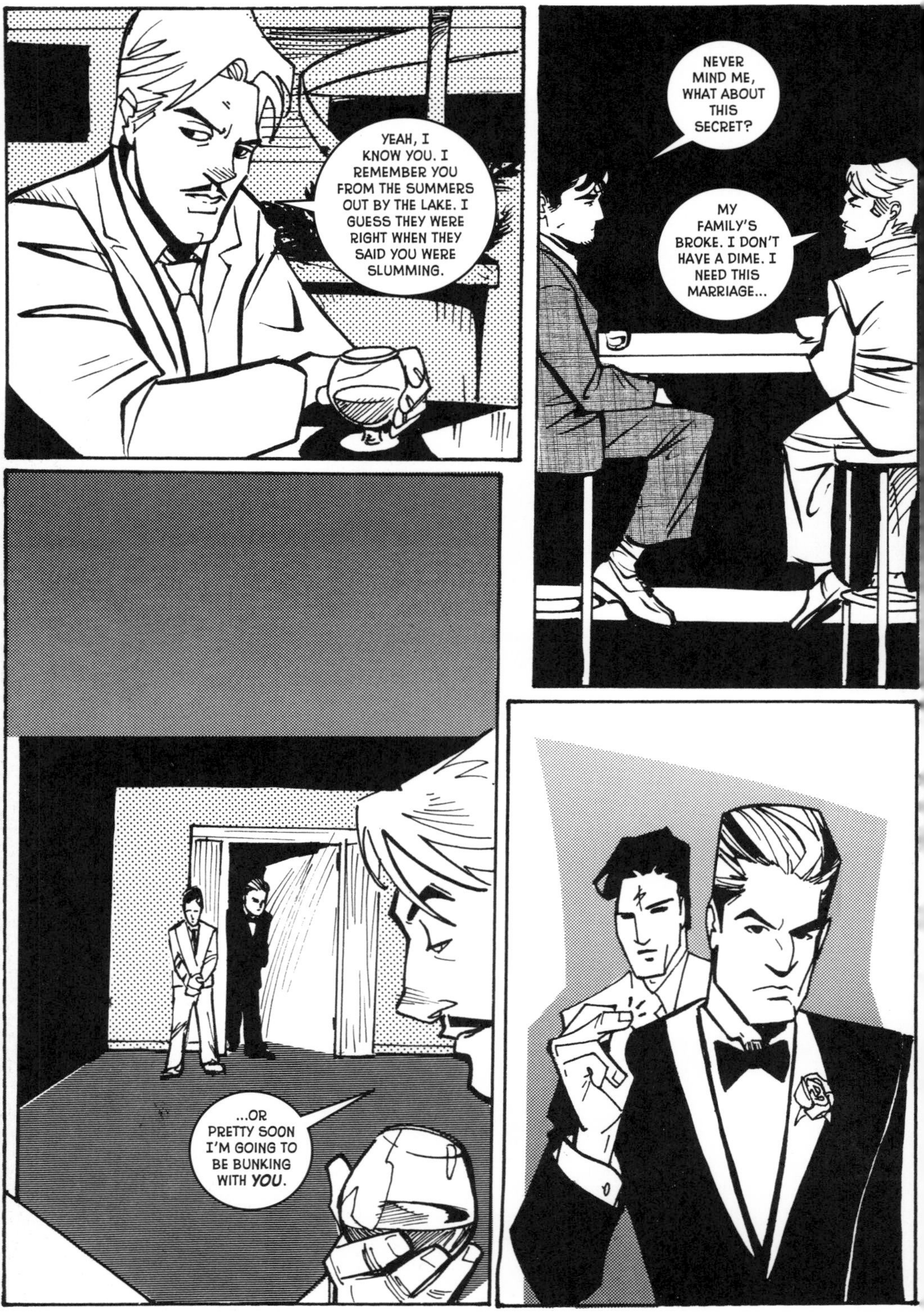
YEAH, I KNOW YOU. I REMEMBER YOU FROM THE SUMMERS OUT BY THE LAKE. I GUESS THEY WERE RIGHT WHEN THEY SAID YOU WERE SLUMMING.
NEVER MIND ME, WHAT ABOUT THIS SECRET?
MY FAMILY'S BROKE. I DON'T HAVE A DIME. I NEED THIS MARRIAGE...
...OR PRETTY SOON I'M GOING TO BE BUNKING WITH *YOU*.

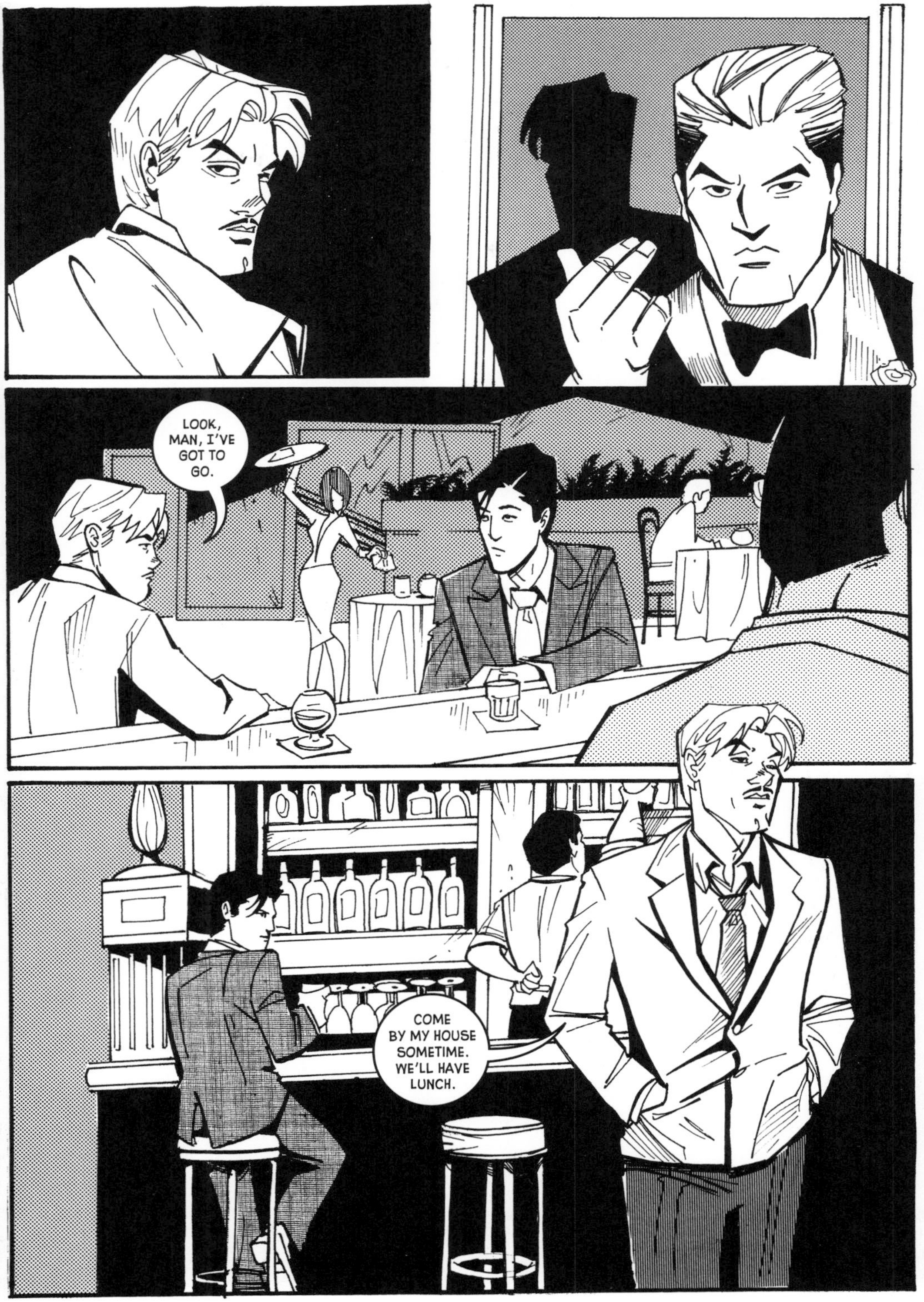
LOOK, MAN, I'VE GOT TO GO.
COME BY MY HOUSE SOMETIME. WE'LL HAVE LUNCH.

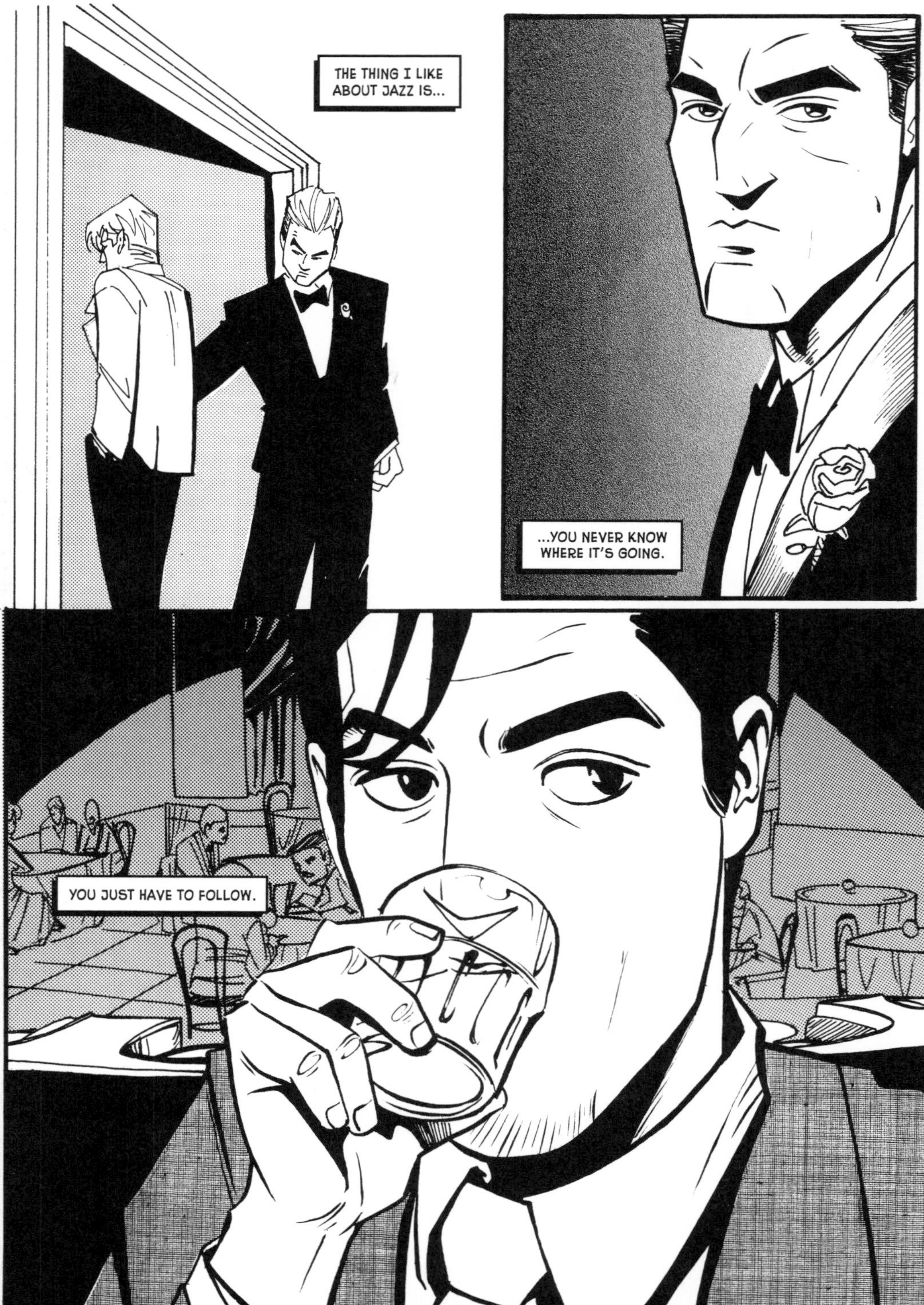
THE THING I LIKE ABOUT JAZZ IS...
...YOU NEVER KNOW WHERE IT'S GOING.
YOU JUST HAVE TO FOLLOW.

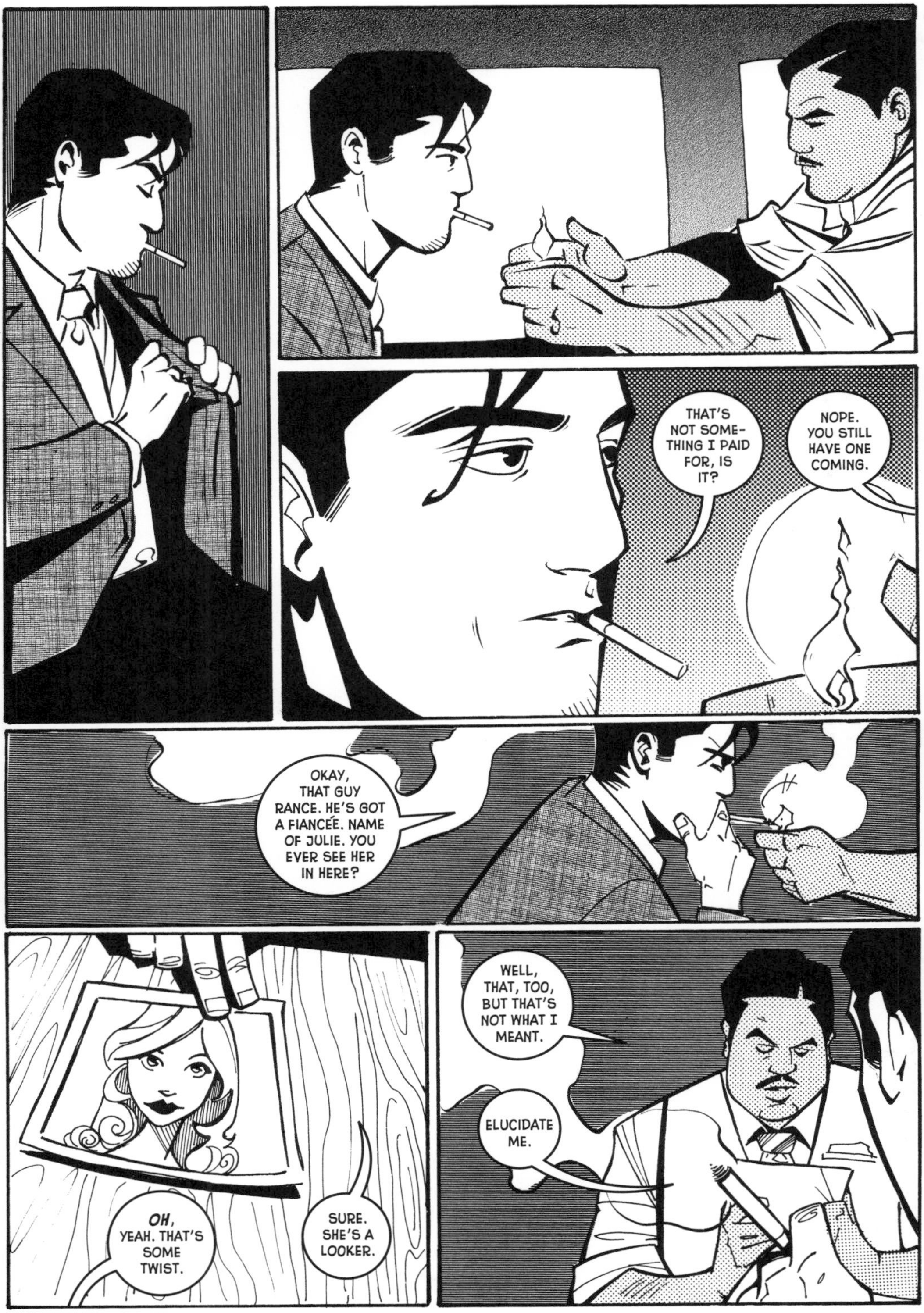
THAT'S NOT SOME-THING I PAID FOR, IS IT?
NOPE. YOU STILL HAVE ONE COMING.
OKAY, THAT GUY RANCE. HE'S GOT A FIANCÉE. NAME OF JULIE. YOU EVER SEE HER IN HERE?
OH, YEAH. THAT'S SOME TWIST.
SURE. SHE'S A LOOKER.
WELL, THAT, TOO, BUT THAT'S NOT WHAT I MEANT.
ELUCIDATE ME.

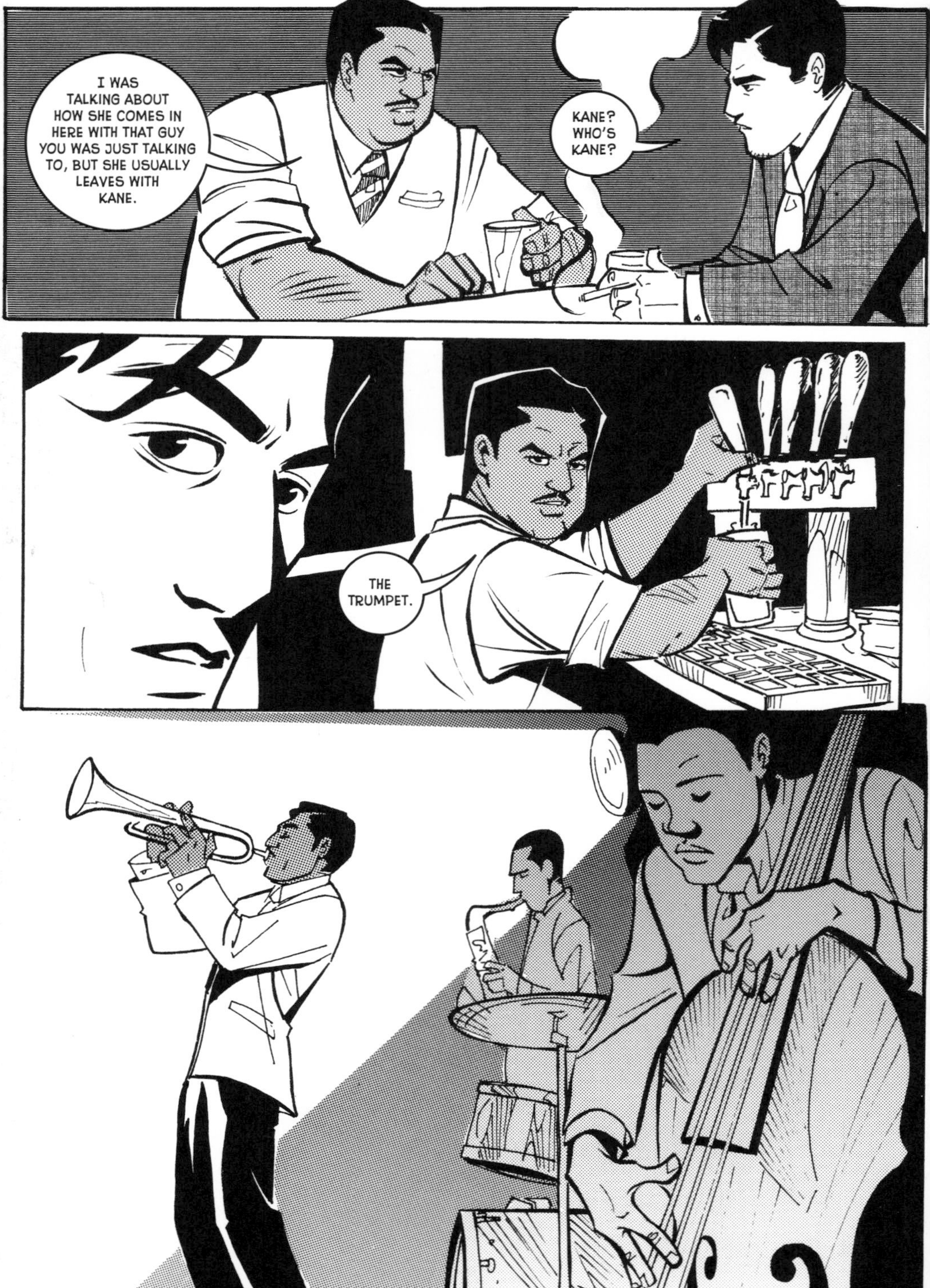
I WAS TALKING ABOUT HOW SHE COMES IN HERE WITH THAT GUY YOU WAS JUST TALKING TO, BUT SHE USUALLY LEAVES WITH KANE.
KANE? WHO'S KANE?
THE TRUMPET.

CHAPTER 3

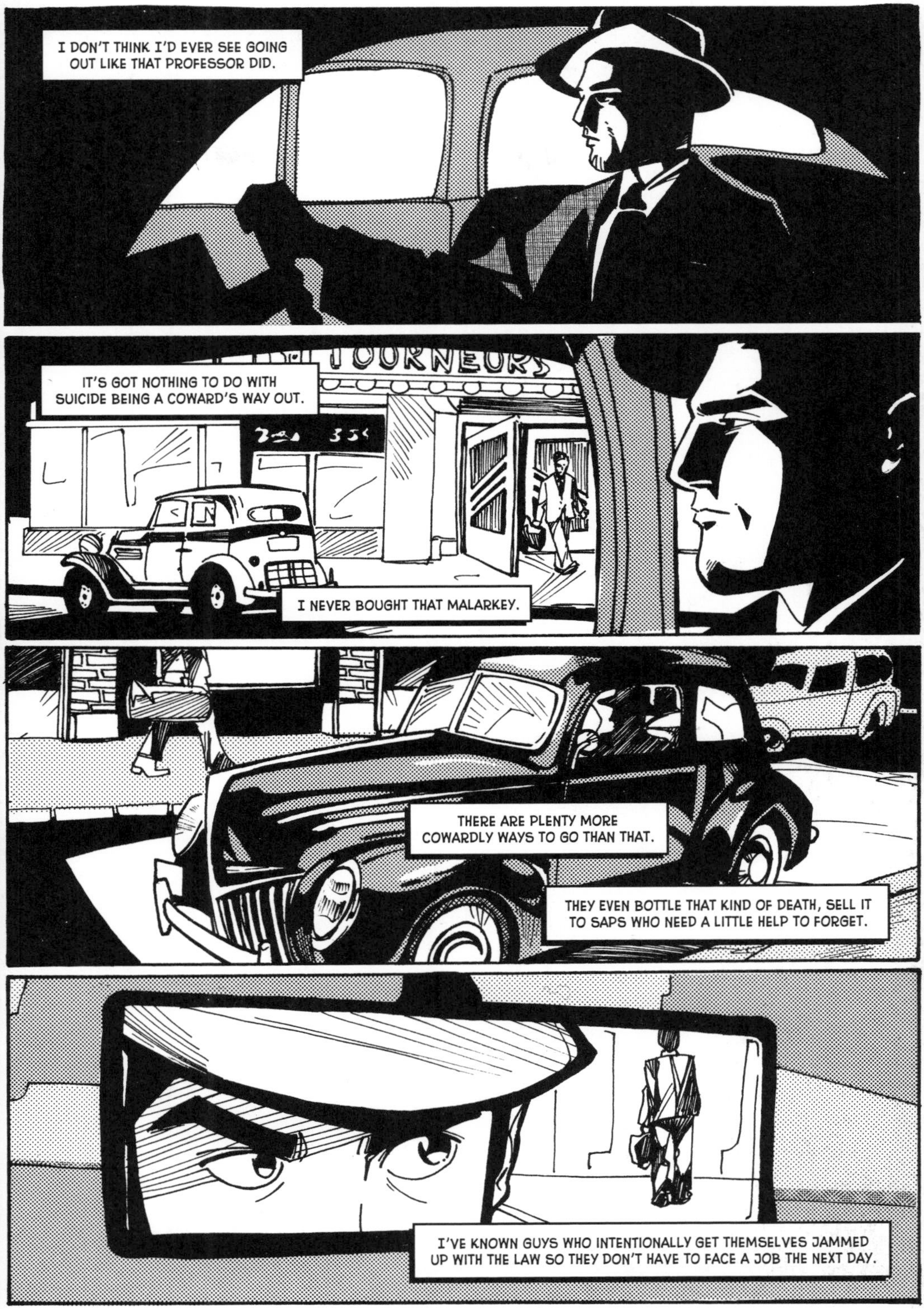
I DON'T THINK I'D EVER SEE GOING OUT LIKE THAT PROFESSOR DID.
TOURNEURS
IT'S GOT NOTHING TO DO WITH SUICIDE BEING A COWARD'S WAY OUT.
I NEVER BOUGHT THAT MALARKEY.
THERE ARE PLENTY MORE COWARDLY WAYS TO GO THAN THAT.
THEY EVEN BOTTLE THAT KIND OF DEATH, SELL IT TO SAPS WHO NEED A LITTLE HELP TO FORGET.
I'VE KNOWN GUYS WHO INTENTIONALLY GET THEMSELVES JAMMED UP WITH THE LAW SO THEY DON'T HAVE TO FACE A JOB THE NEXT DAY.

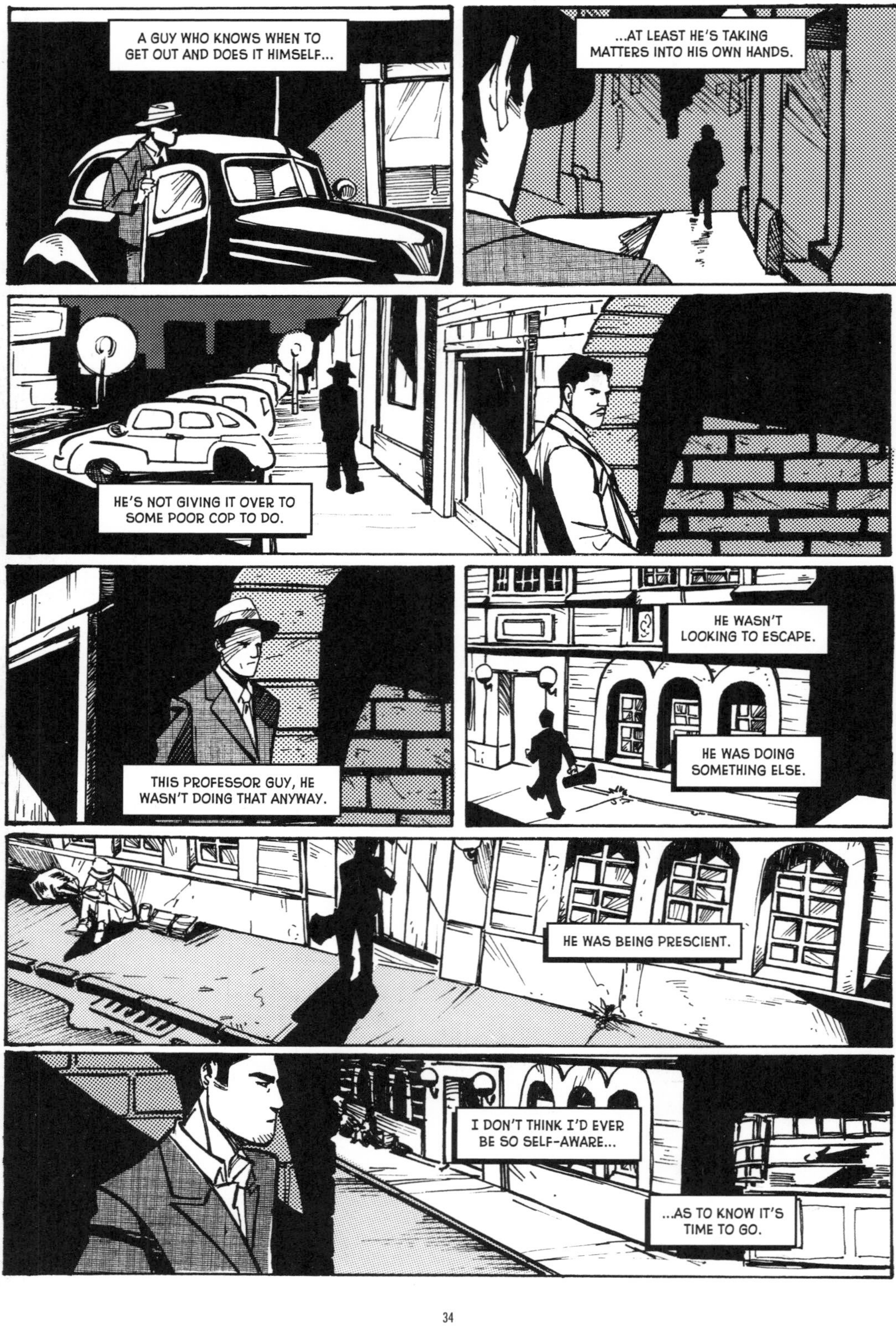
A GUY WHO KNOWS WHEN TO GET OUT AND DOES IT HIMSELF...
...AT LEAST HE'S TAKING MATTERS INTO HIS OWN HANDS.
HE'S NOT GIVING IT OVER TO SOME POOR COP TO DO.
THIS PROFESSOR GUY, HE WASN'T DOING THAT ANYWAY.
HE WASN'T LOOKING TO ESCAPE.
HE WAS DOING SOMETHING ELSE.
HE WAS BEING PRESCIENT.
I DON'T THINK I'D EVER BE SO SELF-AWARE...
...AS TO KNOW IT'S TIME TO GO.

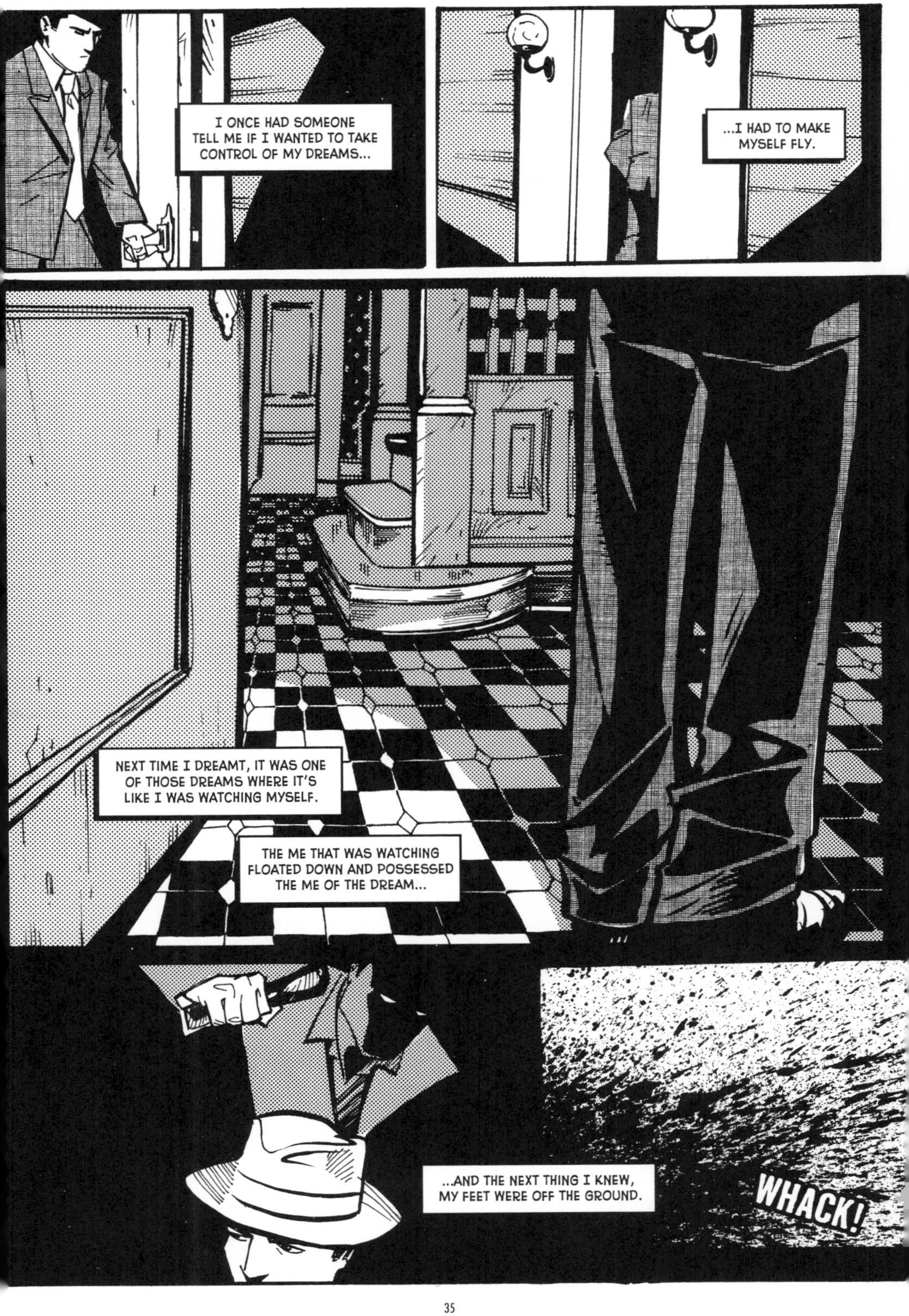
I ONCE HAD SOMEONE TELL ME IF I WANTED TO TAKE CONTROL OF MY DREAMS...
...I HAD TO MAKE MYSELF FLY.
NEXT TIME I DREAMT, IT WAS ONE OF THOSE DREAMS WHERE IT'S LIKE I WAS WATCHING MYSELF.
THE ME THAT WAS WATCHING FLOATED DOWN AND POSSESSED THE ME OF THE DREAM...
...AND THE NEXT THING I KNEW, MY FEET WERE OFF THE GROUND.
WHACK!

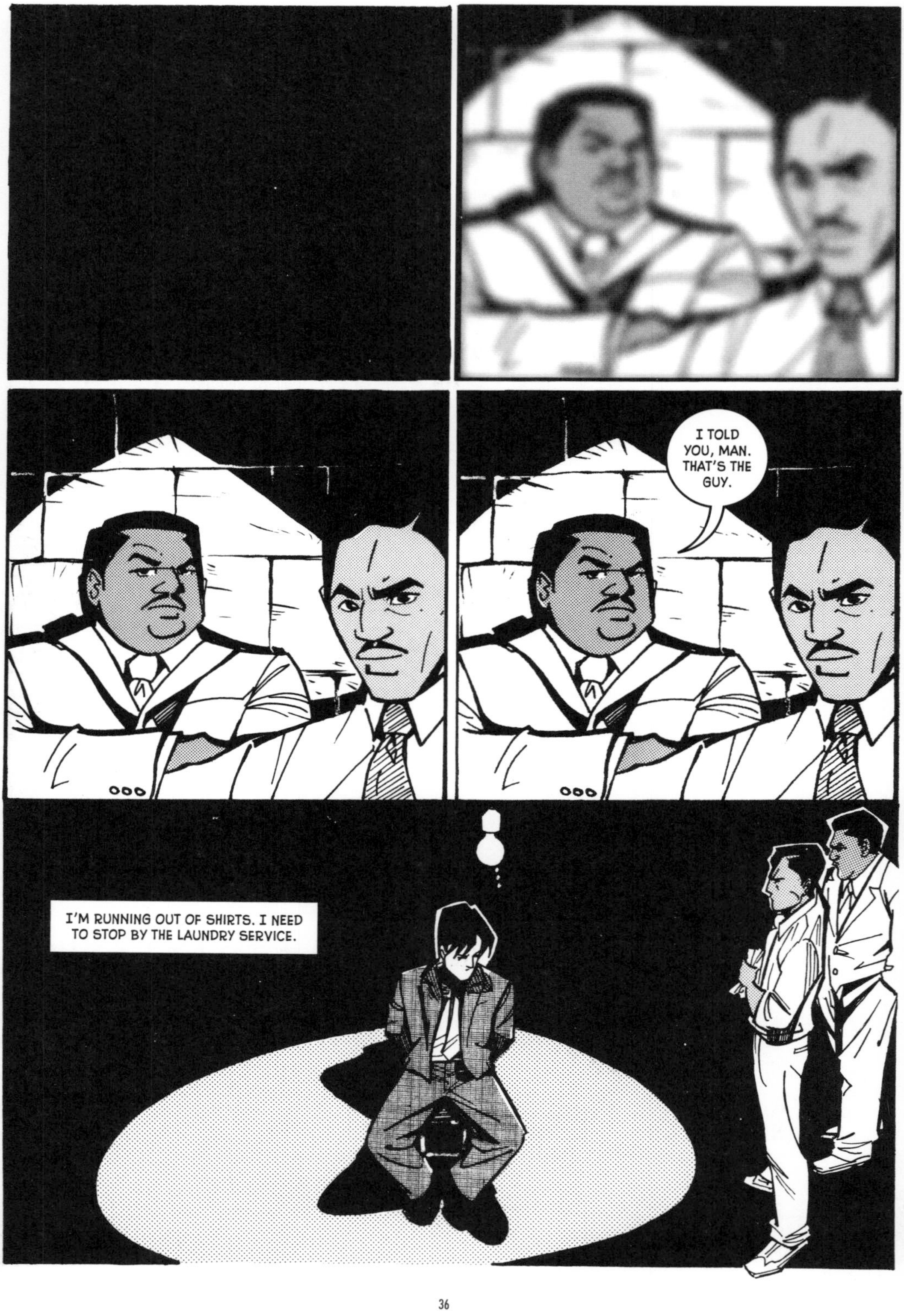
I TOLD YOU, MAN. THAT'S THE GUY.
I'M RUNNING OUT OF SHIRTS. I NEED TO STOP BY THE LAUNDRY SERVICE.

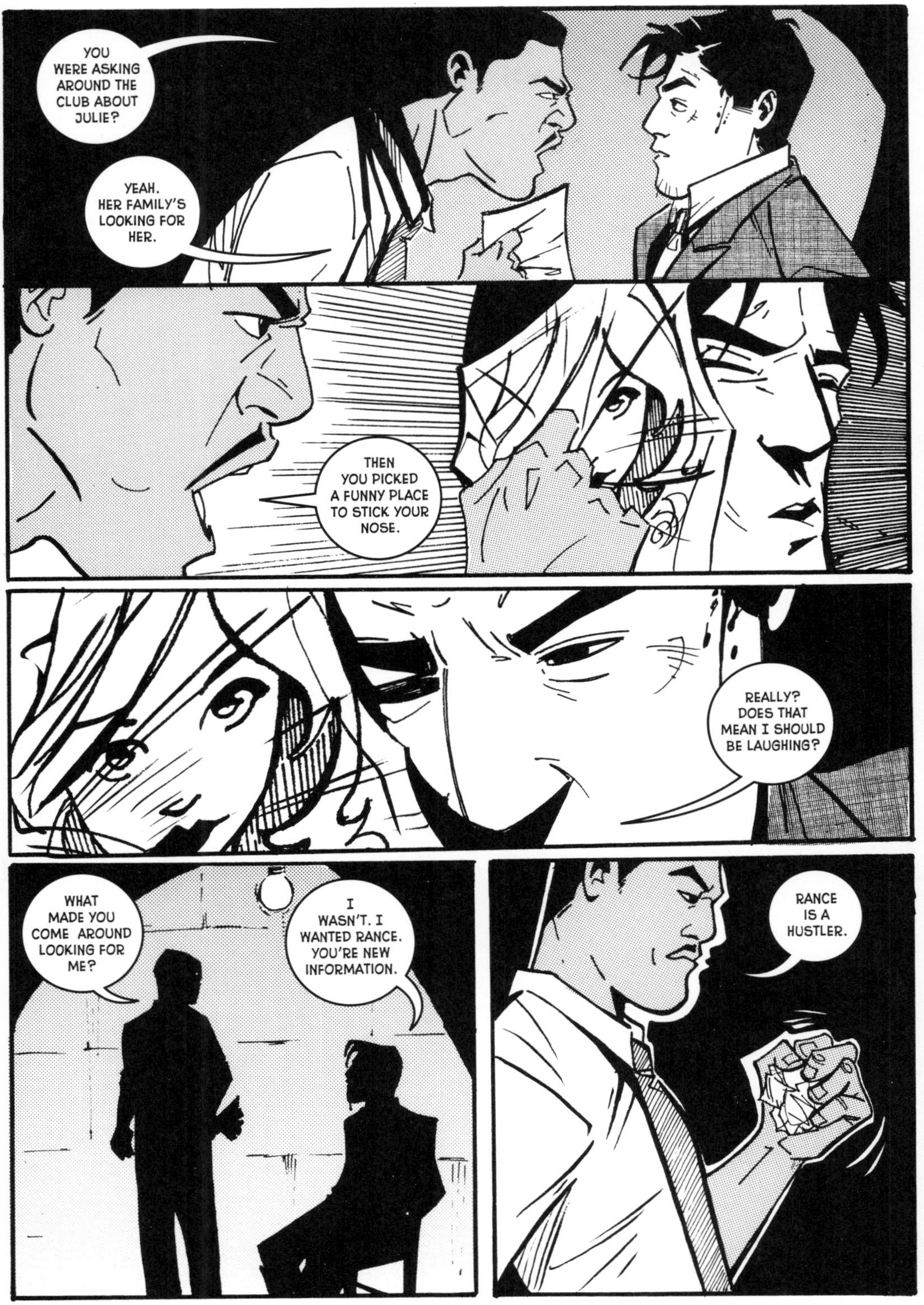
YOU WERE ASKING AROUND THE CLUB ABOUT JULIE?
YEAH. HER FAMILY'S LOOKING FOR HER.
THEN YOU PICKED A FUNNY PLACE TO STICK YOUR NOSE.
REALLY? DOES THAT MEAN I SHOULD BE LAUGHING?
WHAT MADE YOU COME AROUND LOOKING FOR ME?
I WASN'T. I WANTED RANCE. YOU'RE NEW INFORMATION.
RANCE IS A HUSTLER.

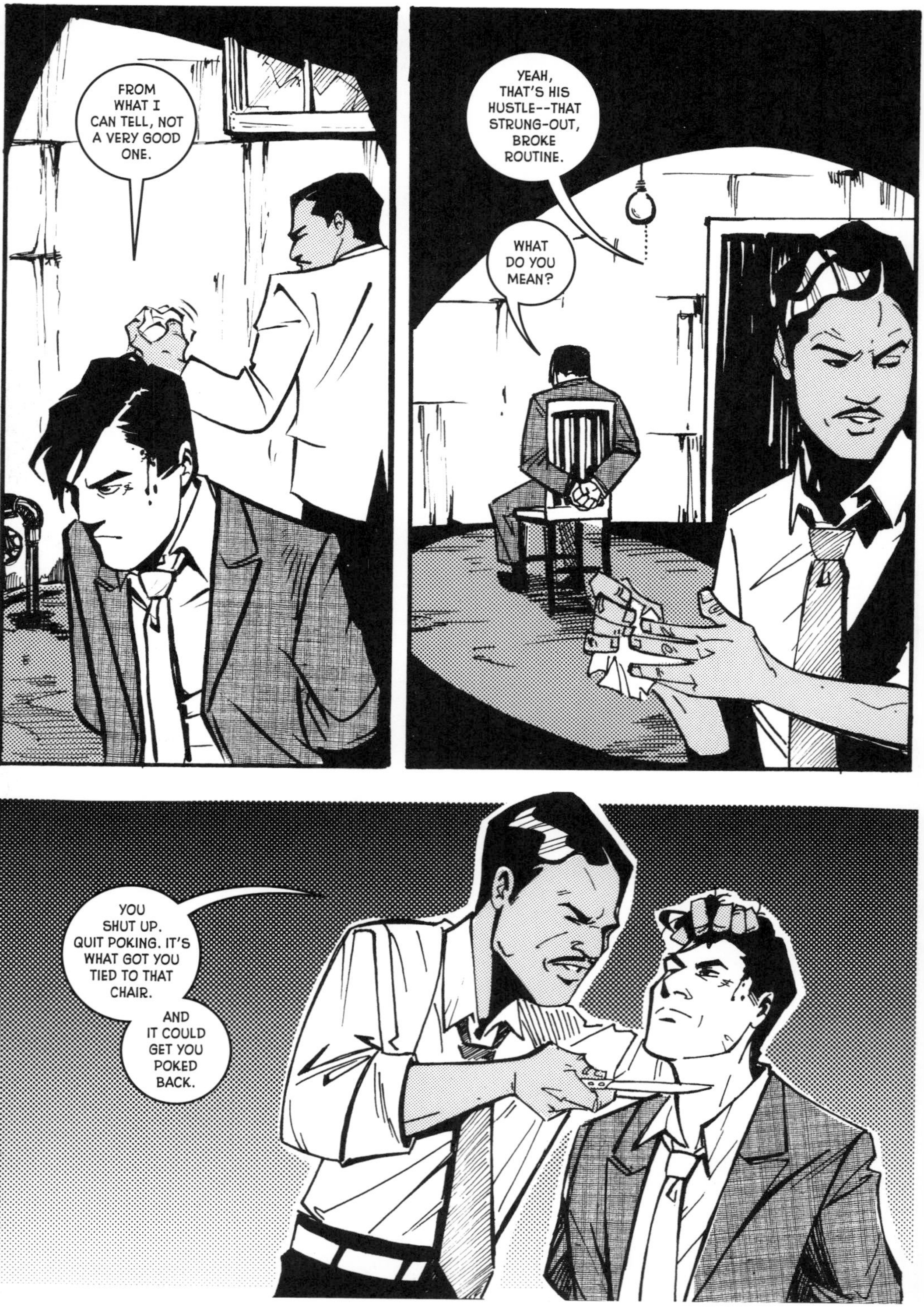
FROM WHAT I CAN TELL, NOT A VERY GOOD ONE.
YEAH, THAT'S HIS HUSTLE--THAT STRUNG-OUT, BROKE ROUTINE.
WHAT DO YOU MEAN?
YOU SHUT UP. QUIT POKING. IT'S WHAT GOT YOU TIED TO THAT CHAIR.
AND IT COULD GET YOU POKED BACK.

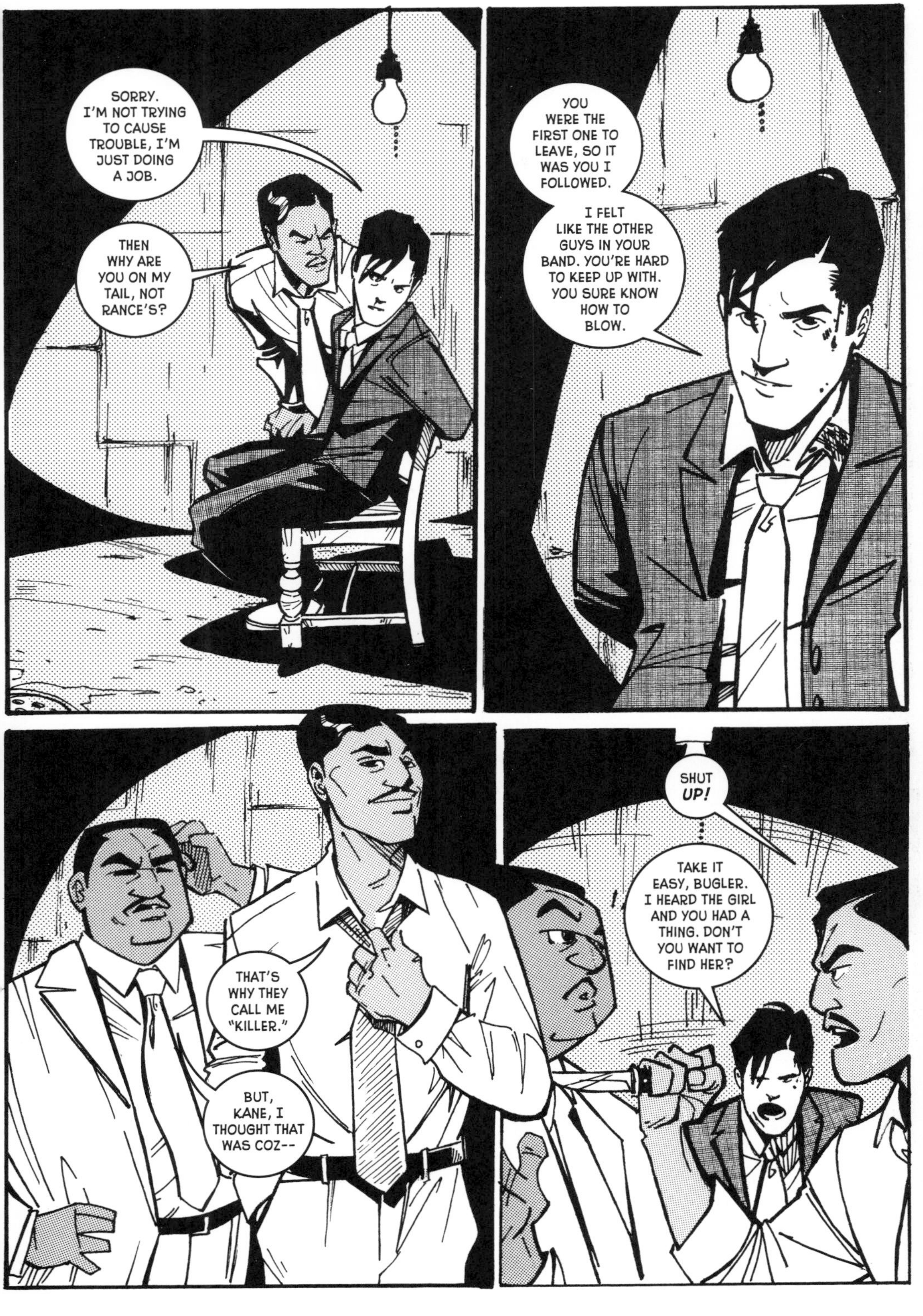
SORRY. I'M NOT TRYING TO CAUSE TROUBLE, I'M JUST DOING A JOB.
THEN WHY ARE YOU ON MY TAIL, NOT RANCE'S?
YOU WERE THE FIRST ONE TO LEAVE, SO IT WAS YOU I FOLLOWED.
I FELT LIKE THE OTHER GUYS IN YOUR BAND. YOU'RE HARD TO KEEP UP WITH. YOU SURE KNOW HOW TO BLOW.
THAT'S WHY THEY CALL ME "KILLER."
BUT, KANE, I THOUGHT THAT WAS COZ--
SHUT *UP!*
TAKE IT EASY, BUGLER. I HEARD THE GIRL AND YOU HAD A THING. DON'T YOU WANT TO FIND HER?

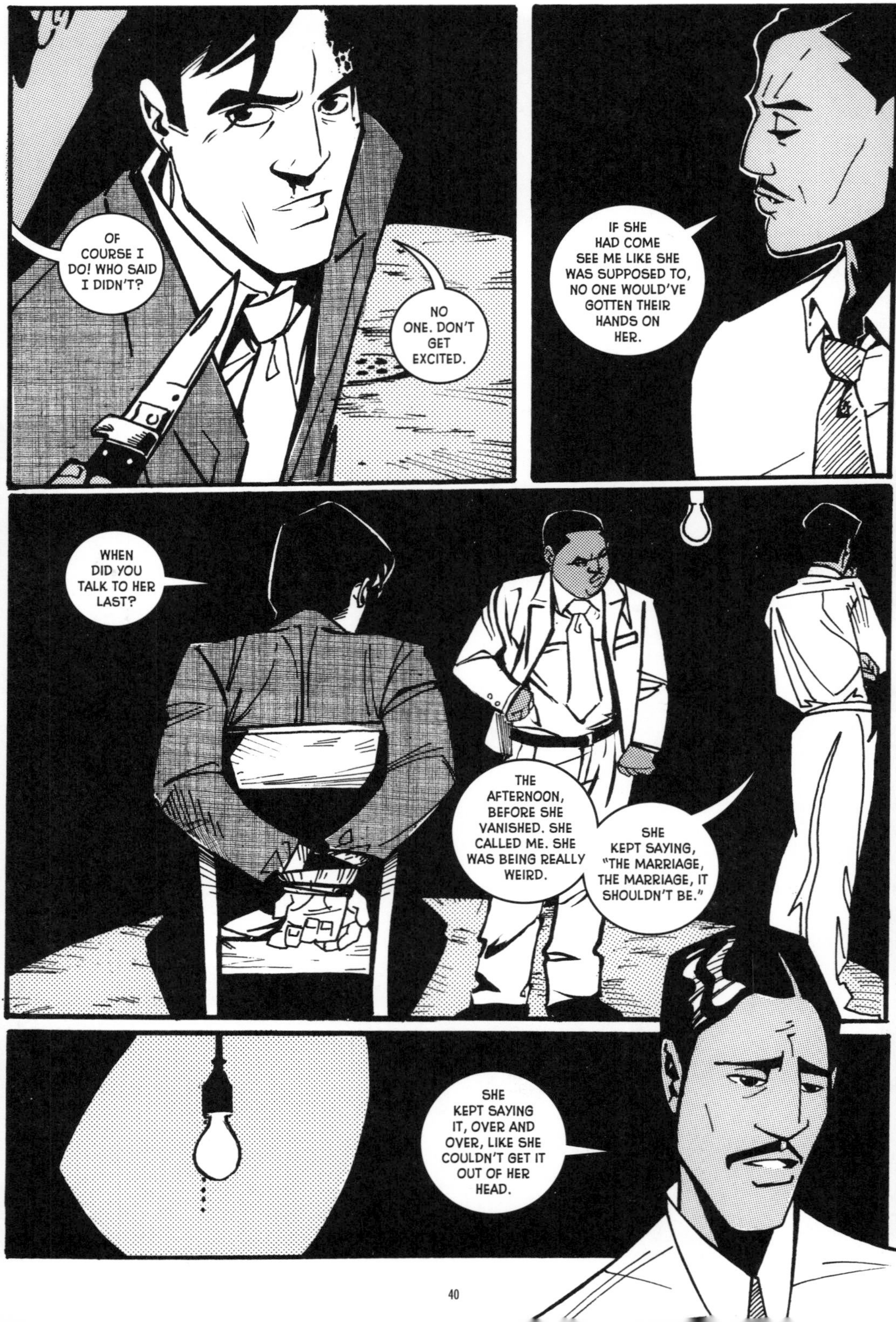
OF COURSE I DO! WHO SAID I DIDN'T?
NO ONE. DON'T GET EXCITED.
IF SHE HAD COME SEE ME LIKE SHE WAS SUPPOSED TO, NO ONE WOULD'VE GOTTEN THEIR HANDS ON HER.
WHEN DID YOU TALK TO HER LAST?
THE AFTERNOON, BEFORE SHE VANISHED. SHE CALLED ME. SHE WAS BEING REALLY WEIRD.
SHE KEPT SAYING, "THE MARRIAGE, THE MARRIAGE, IT SHOULDN'T BE."
SHE KEPT SAYING IT, OVER AND OVER, LIKE SHE COULDN'T GET IT OUT OF HER HEAD.

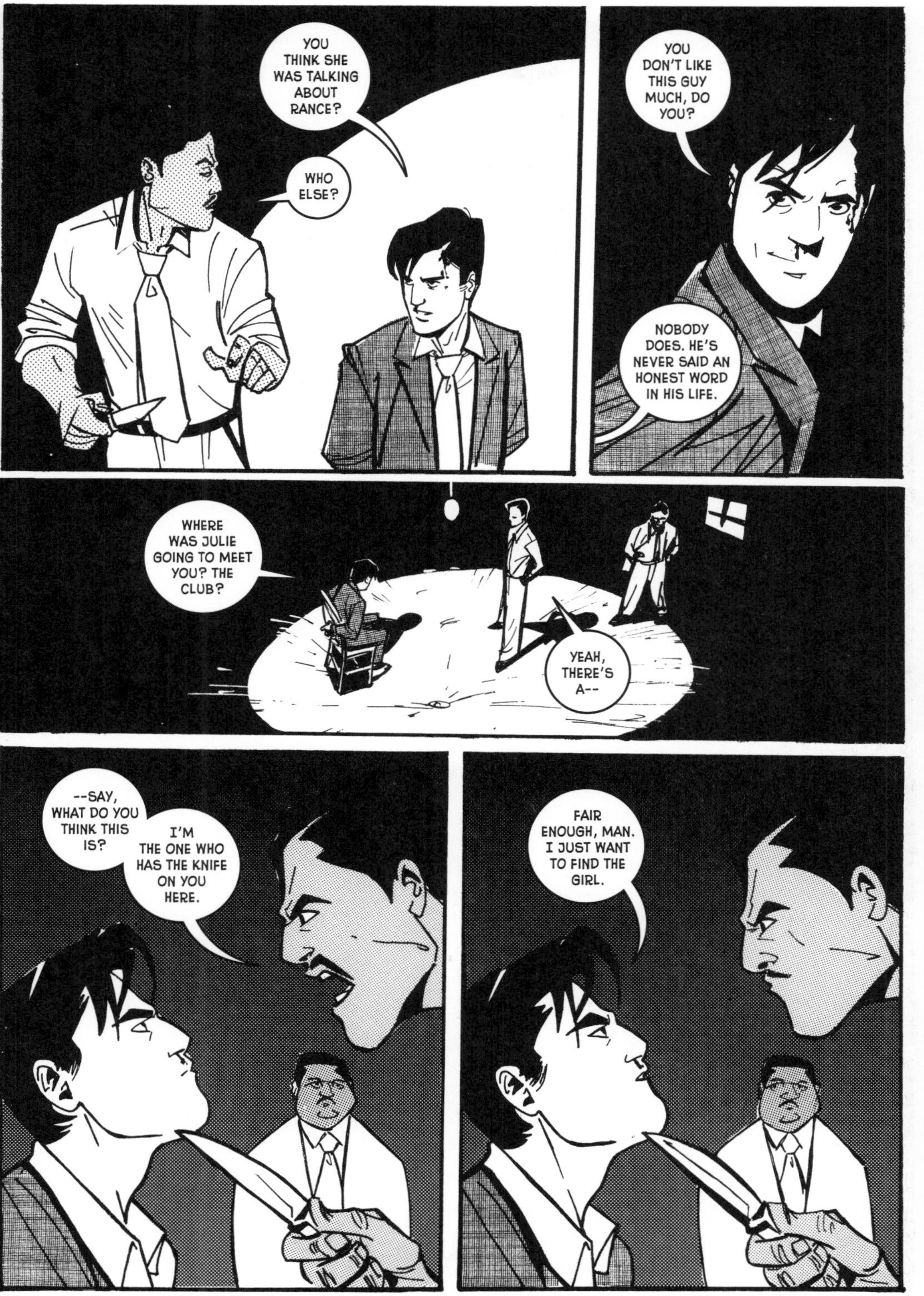
YOU THINK SHE WAS TALKING ABOUT RANCE?
WHO ELSE?
YOU DON'T LIKE THIS GUY MUCH, DO YOU?
NOBODY DOES. HE'S NEVER SAID AN HONEST WORD IN HIS LIFE.
WHERE WAS JULIE GOING TO MEET YOU? THE CLUB?
YEAH, THERE'S A--
--SAY, WHAT DO YOU THINK THIS IS?
I'M THE ONE WHO HAS THE KNIFE ON YOU HERE.
FAIR ENOUGH, MAN. I JUST WANT TO FIND THE GIRL.

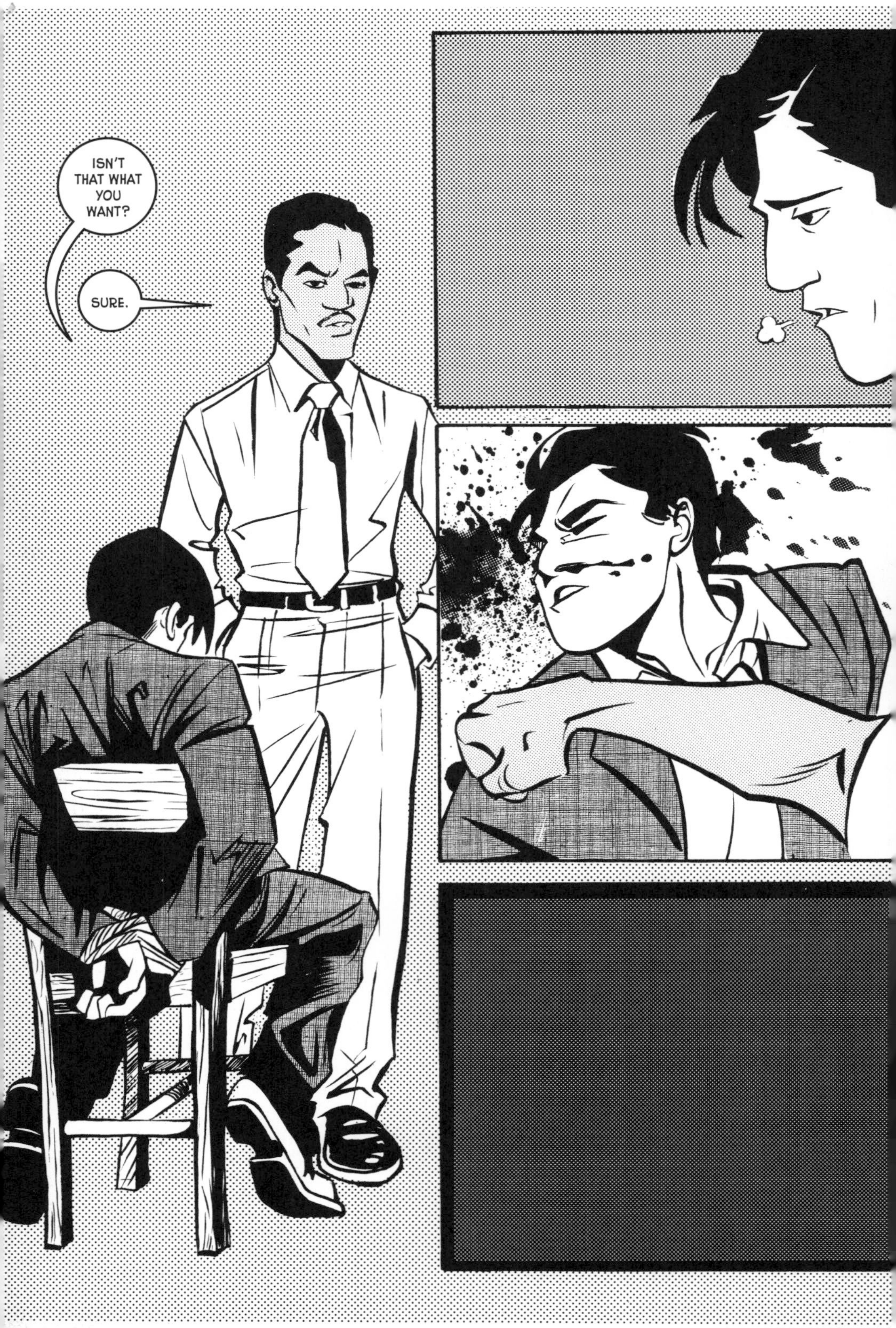
ISN'T THAT WHAT YOU WANT?
SURE.

CHAPTER 4

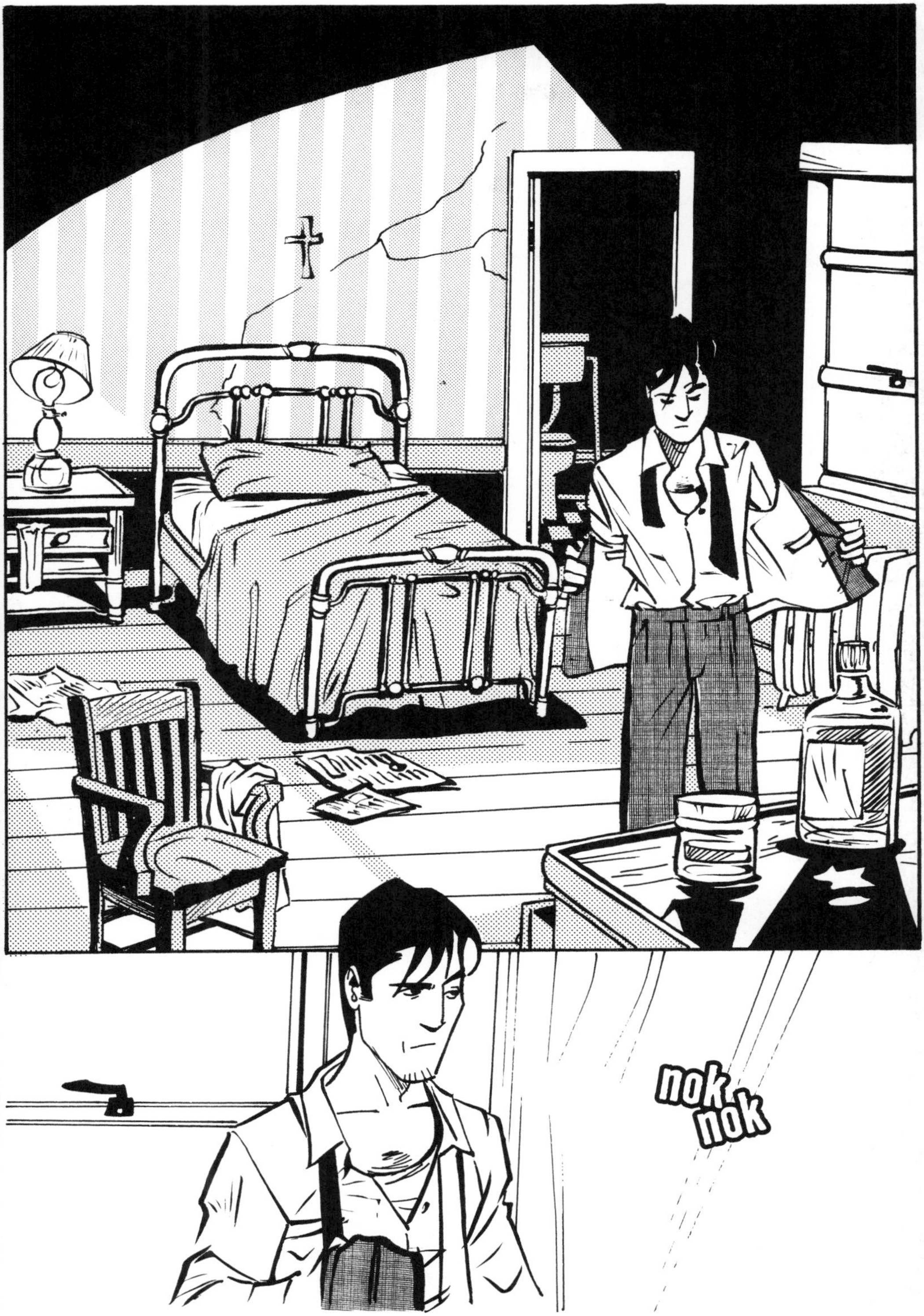
nok nok

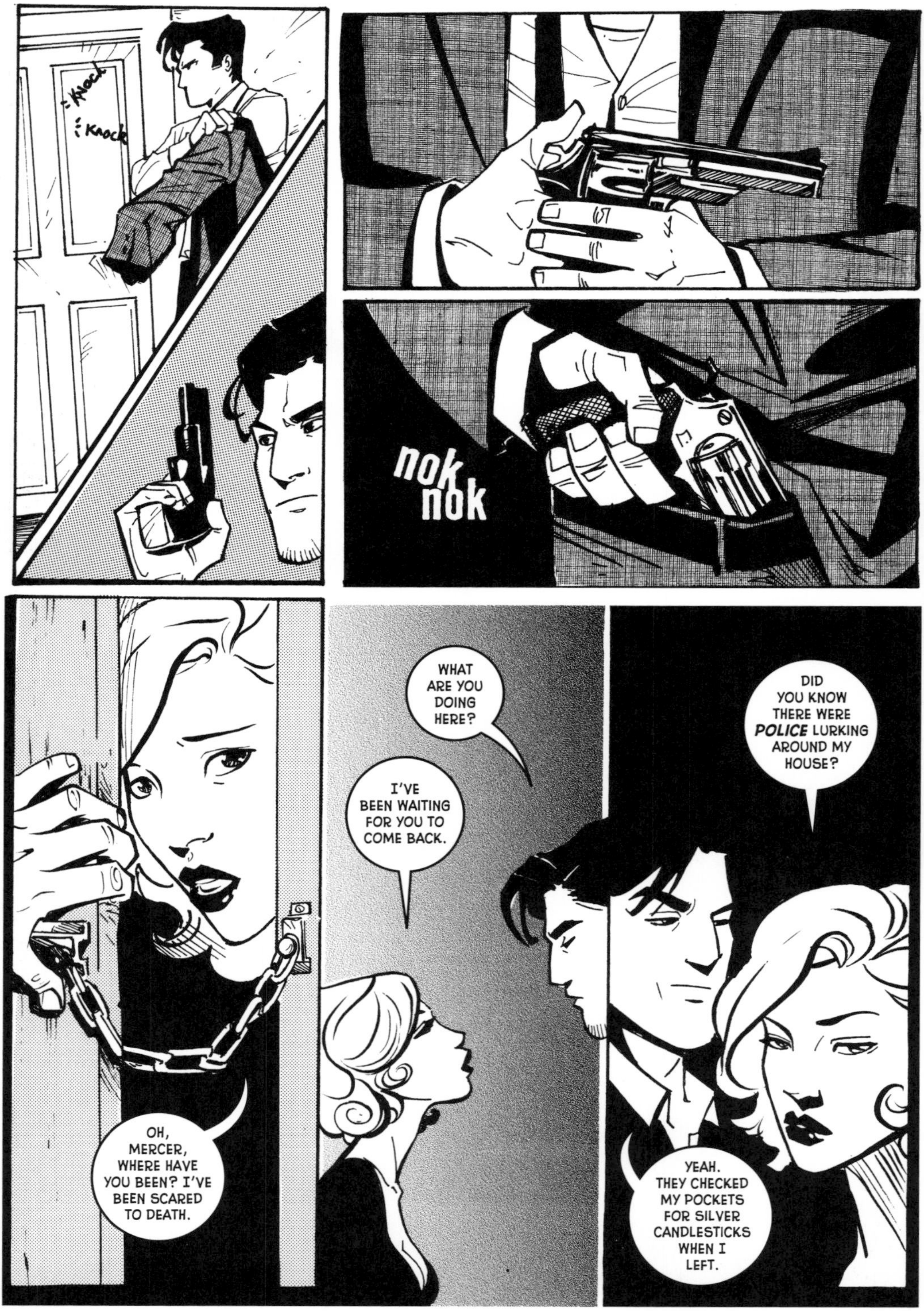
KNOCK
KNOCK
nok nok
OH, MERCER, WHERE HAVE YOU BEEN? I'VE BEEN SCARED TO DEATH.
WHAT ARE YOU DOING HERE?
I'VE BEEN WAITING FOR YOU TO COME BACK.
DID YOU KNOW THERE WERE POLICE LURKING AROUND MY HOUSE?
YEAH. THEY CHECKED MY POCKETS FOR SILVER CANDLESTICKS WHEN I LEFT.

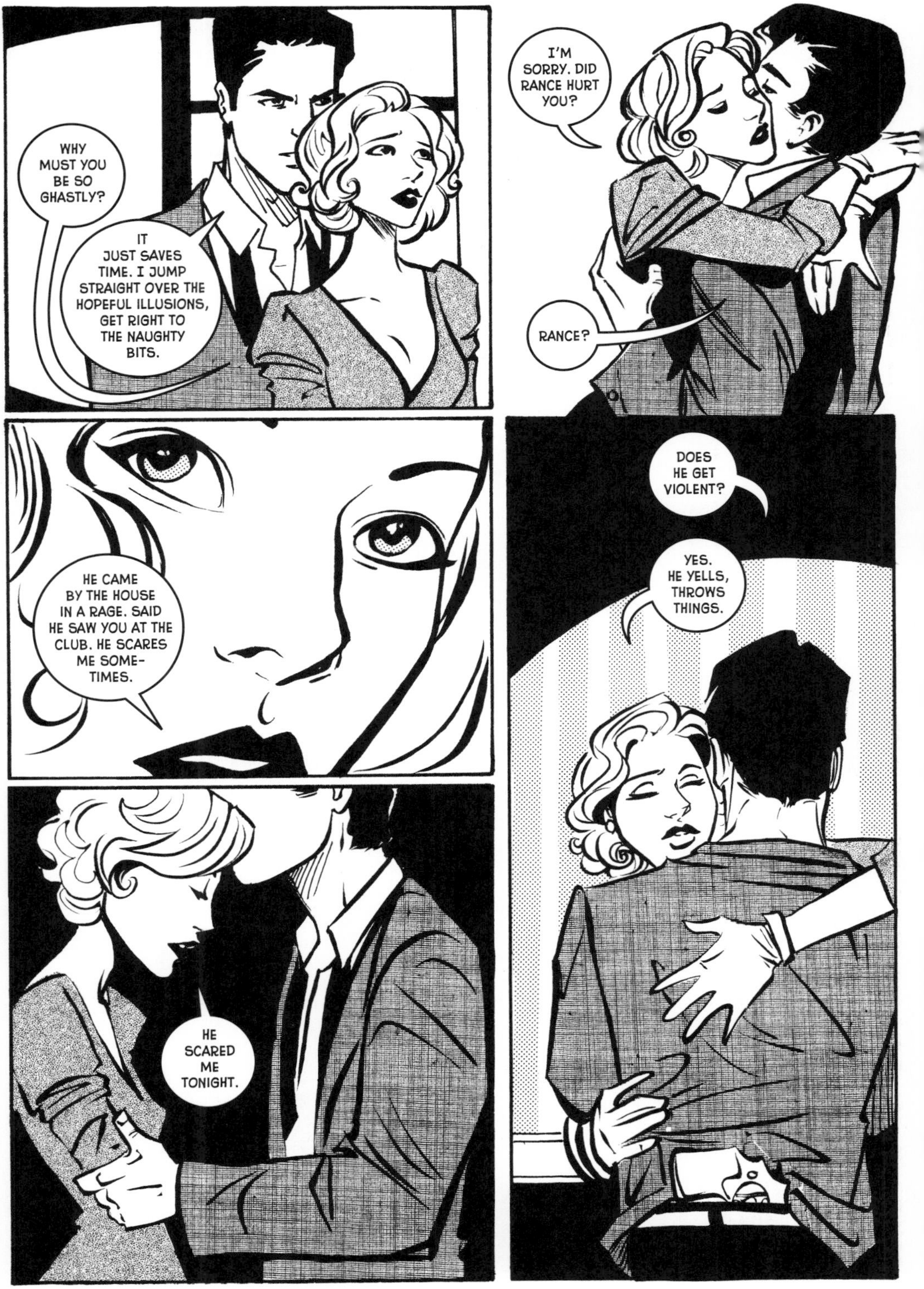

WHY MUST YOU BE SO GHASTLY?
IT JUST SAVES TIME. I JUMP STRAIGHT OVER THE HOPEFUL ILLUSIONS, GET RIGHT TO THE NAUGHTY BITS.
I'M SORRY. DID RANCE HURT YOU?
RANCE?
HE CAME BY THE HOUSE IN A RAGE. SAID HE SAW YOU AT THE CLUB. HE SCARES ME SOME-TIMES.
HE SCARED ME TONIGHT.
DOES HE GET VIOLENT?
YES. HE YELLS, THROWS THINGS.

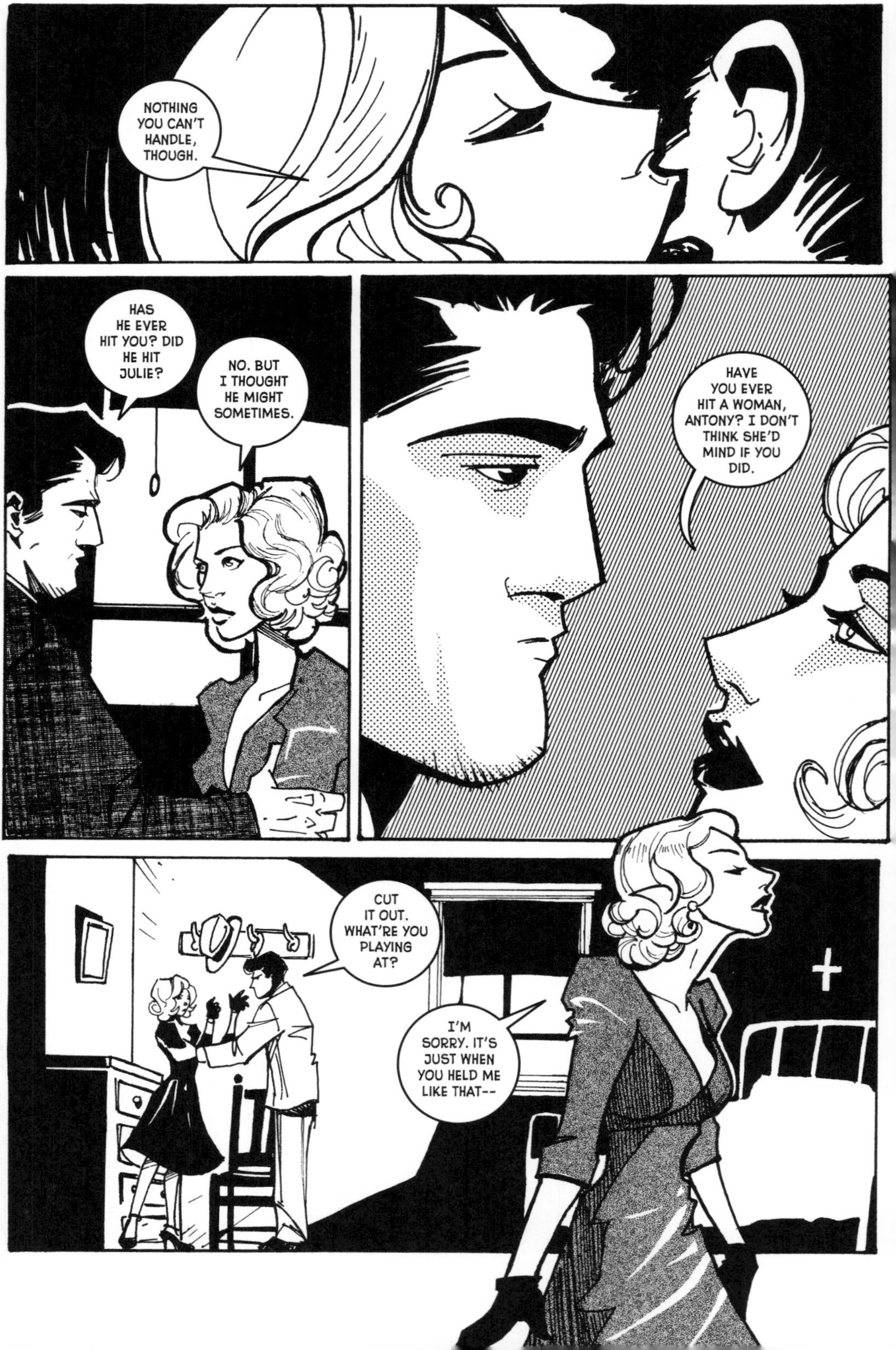
NOTHING YOU CAN'T HANDLE, THOUGH.
HAS HE EVER HIT YOU? DID HE HIT JULIE?
NO. BUT I THOUGHT HE MIGHT SOMETIMES.
HAVE YOU EVER HIT A WOMAN, ANTONY? I DON'T THINK SHE'D MIND IF YOU DID.
CUT IT OUT. WHAT'RE YOU PLAYING AT?
I'M SORRY. IT'S JUST WHEN YOU HELD ME LIKE THAT--

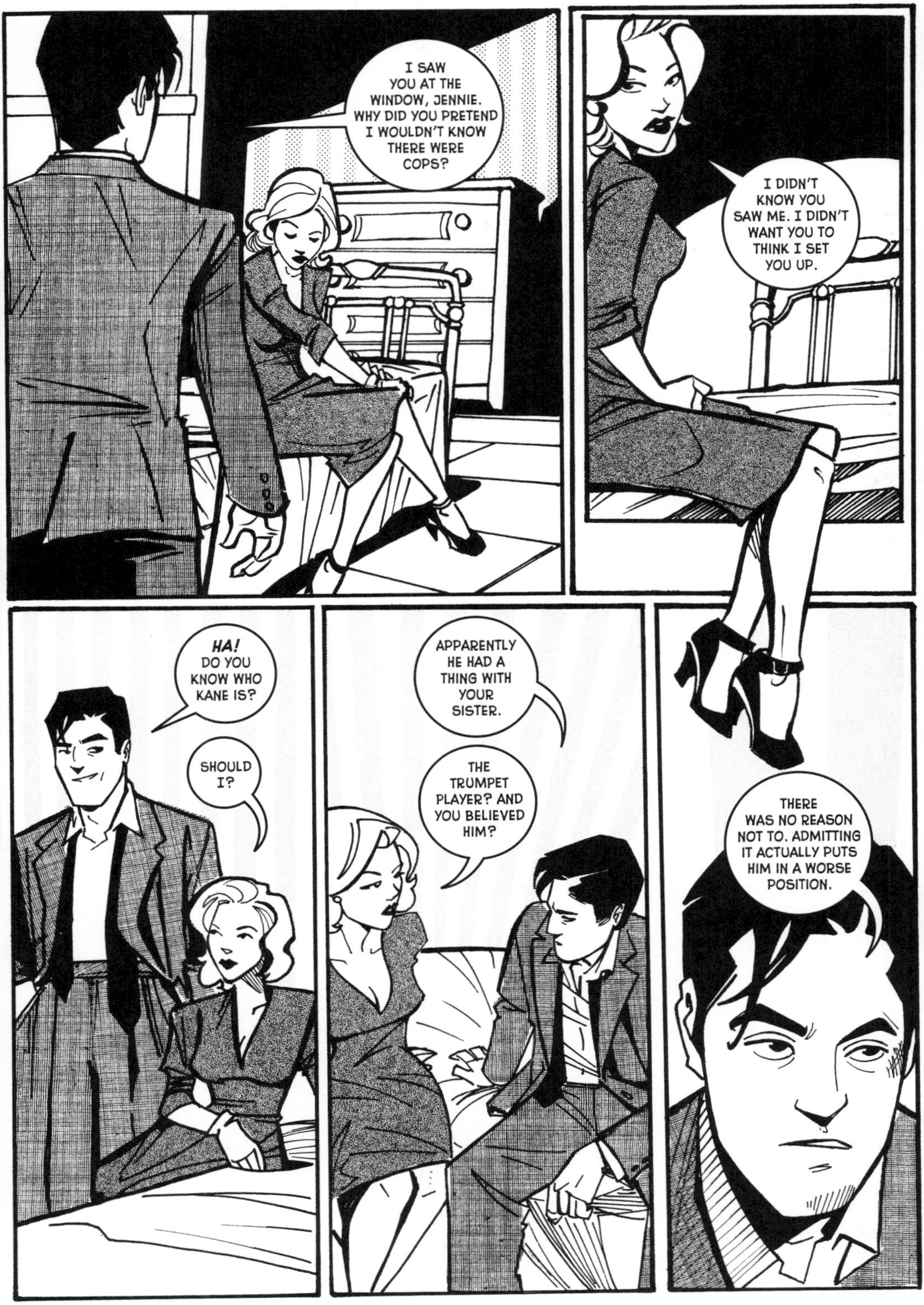
I SAW YOU AT THE WINDOW, JENNIE. WHY DID YOU PRETEND I WOULDN'T KNOW THERE WERE COPS?
I DIDN'T KNOW YOU SAW ME. I DIDN'T WANT YOU TO THINK I SET YOU UP.
HA! DO YOU KNOW WHO KANE IS?
SHOULD I?
APPARENTLY HE HAD A THING WITH YOUR SISTER.
THE TRUMPET PLAYER? AND YOU BELIEVED HIM?
THERE WAS NO REASON NOT TO. ADMITTING IT ACTUALLY PUTS HIM IN A WORSE POSITION.

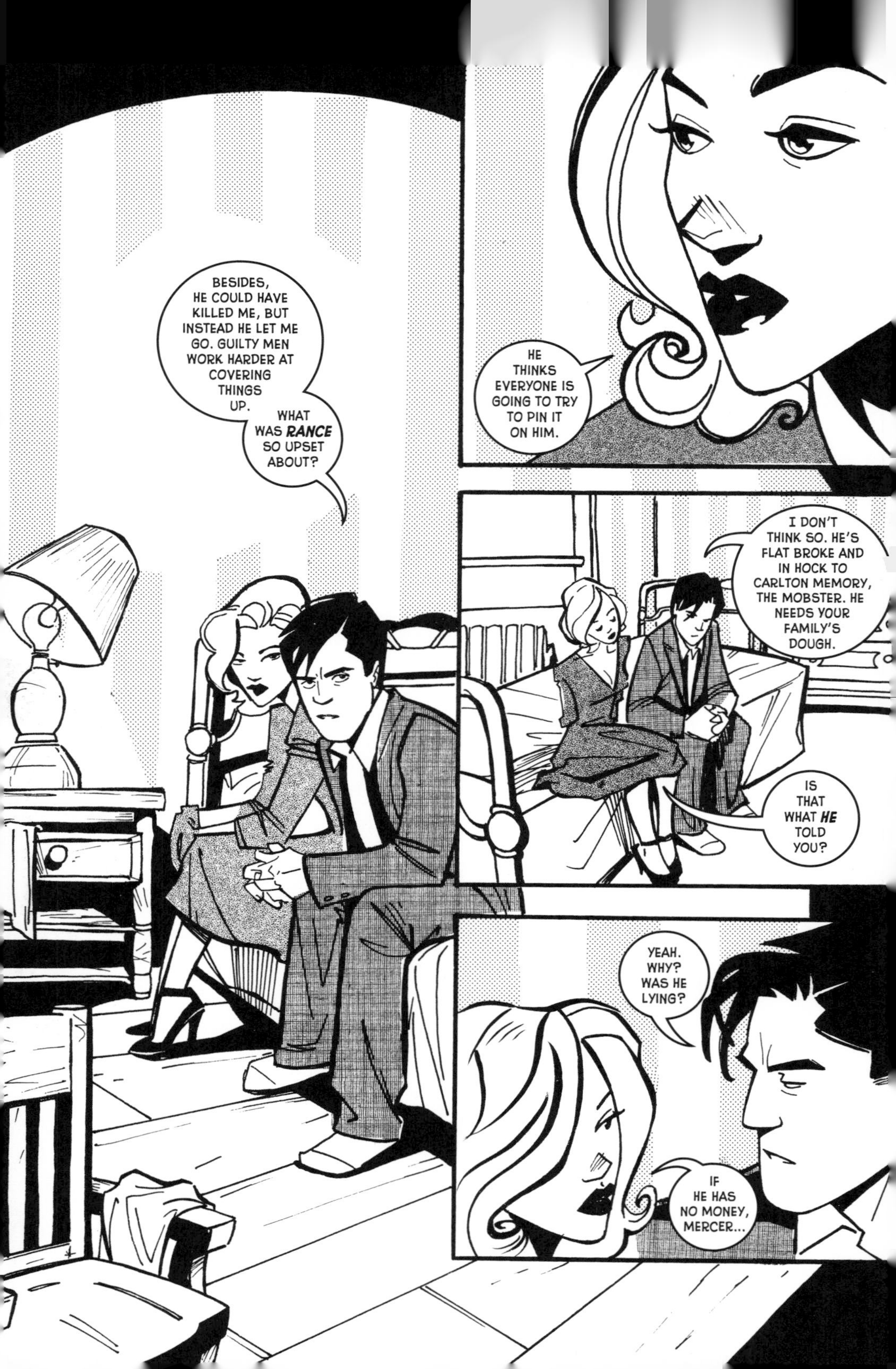
BESIDES, HE COULD HAVE KILLED ME, BUT INSTEAD HE LET ME GO. GUILTY MEN WORK HARDER AT COVERING THINGS UP.
WHAT WAS RANCE SO UPSET ABOUT?
HE THINKS EVERYONE IS GOING TO TRY TO PIN IT ON HIM.
I DON'T THINK SO. HE'S FLAT BROKE AND IN HOCK TO CARLTON MEMORY, THE MOBSTER. HE NEEDS YOUR FAMILY'S DOUGH.
IS THAT WHAT HE TOLD YOU?
YEAH. WHY? WAS HE LYING?
IF HE HAS NO MONEY, MERCER...

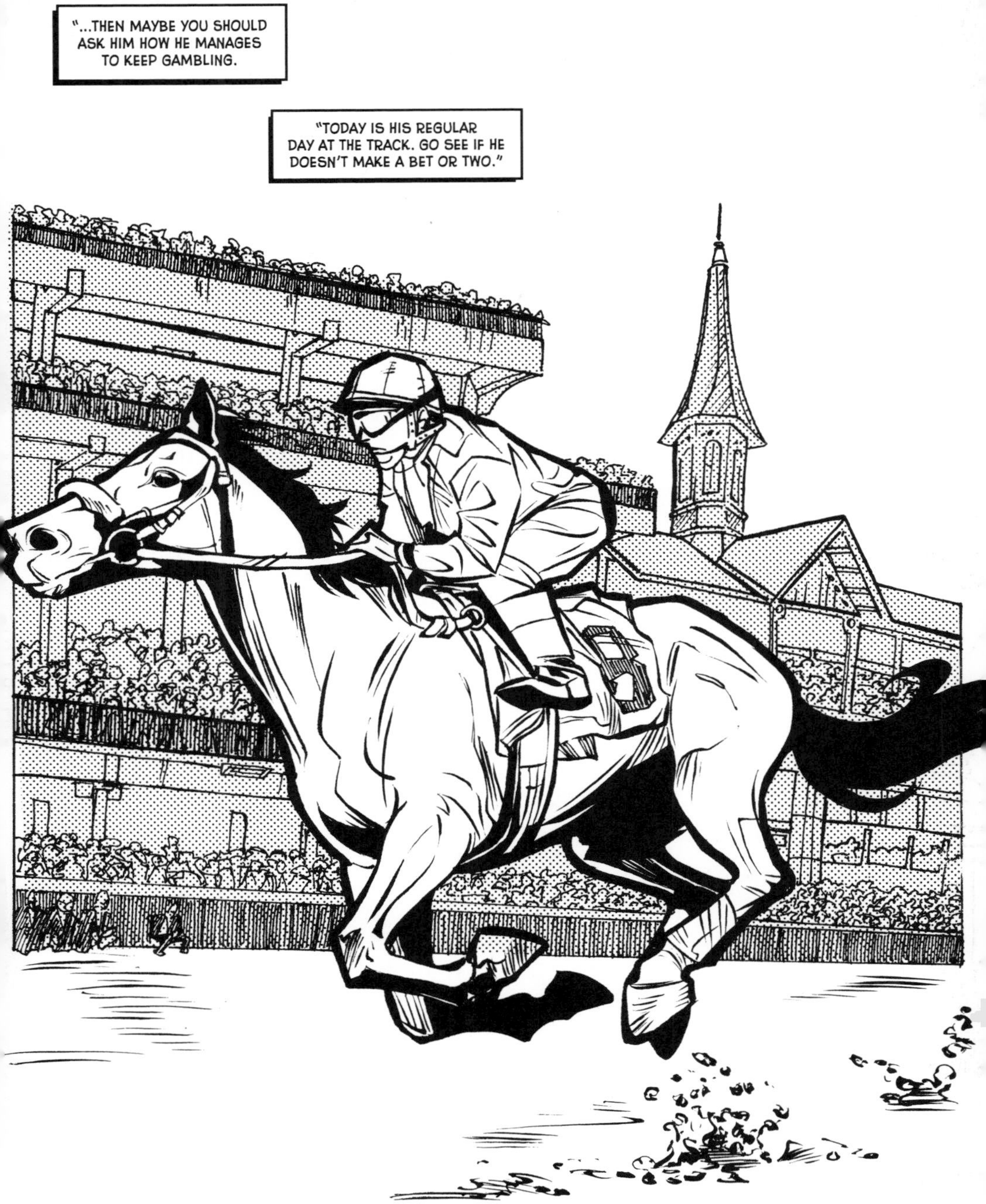
"...THEN MAYBE YOU SHOULD ASK HIM HOW HE MANAGES TO KEEP GAMBLING.
"TODAY IS HIS REGULAR DAY AT THE TRACK. GO SEE IF HE DOESN'T MAKE A BET OR TWO."

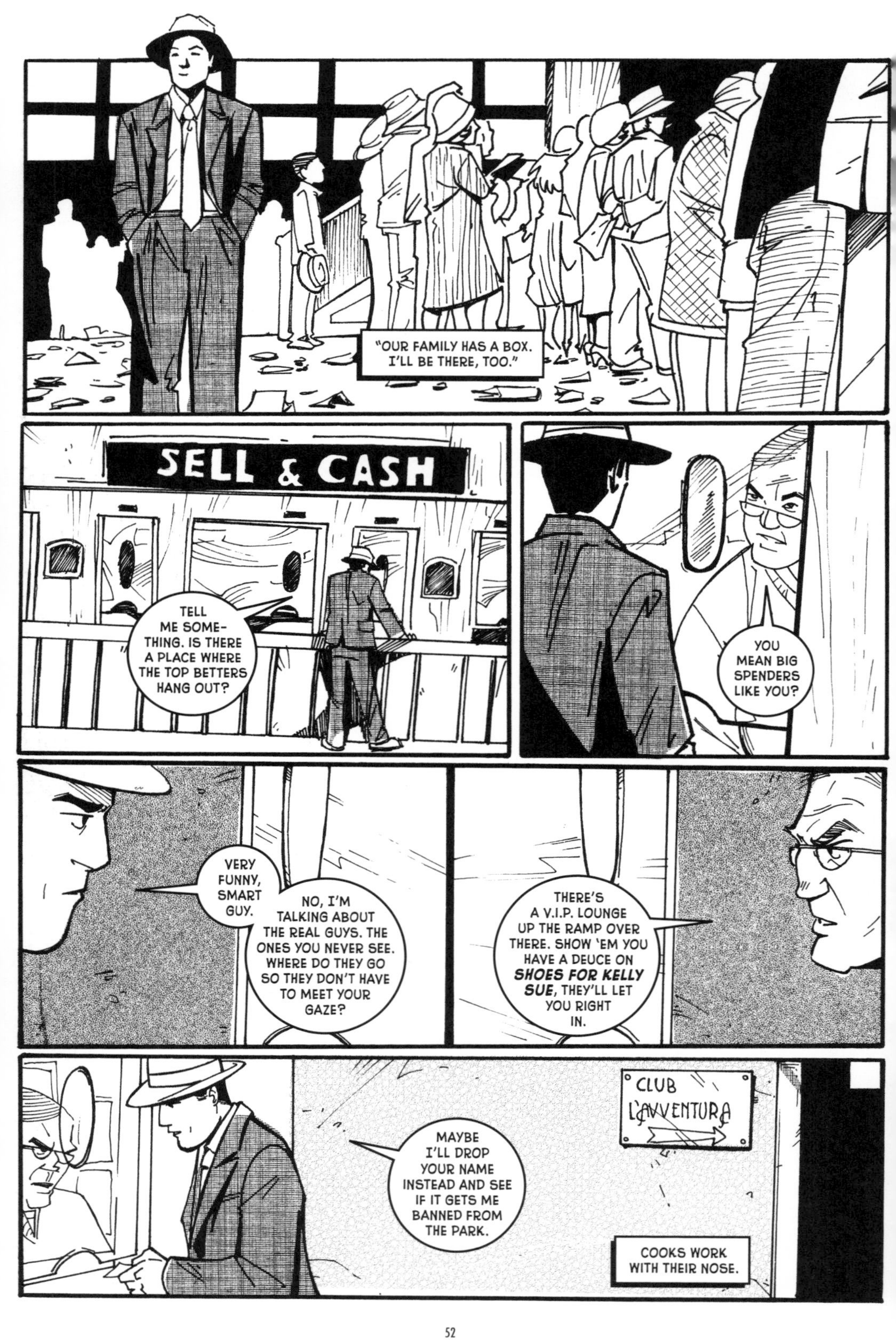
"OUR FAMILY HAS A BOX. I'LL BE THERE, TOO."
SELL & CASH
TELL ME SOME-THING. IS THERE A PLACE WHERE THE TOP BETTERS HANG OUT?
YOU MEAN BIG SPENDERS LIKE YOU?
VERY FUNNY, SMART GUY.
NO, I'M TALKING ABOUT THE REAL GUYS. THE ONES YOU NEVER SEE. WHERE DO THEY GO SO THEY DON'T HAVE TO MEET YOUR GAZE?
THERE'S A V.I.P. LOUNGE UP THE RAMP OVER THERE. SHOW 'EM YOU HAVE A DEUCE ON ***SHOES FOR KELLY SUE***, THEY'LL LET YOU RIGHT IN.
CLUB L'AVVENTURA
MAYBE I'LL DROP YOUR NAME INSTEAD AND SEE IF IT GETS ME BANNED FROM THE PARK.
COOKS WORK WITH THEIR NOSE.

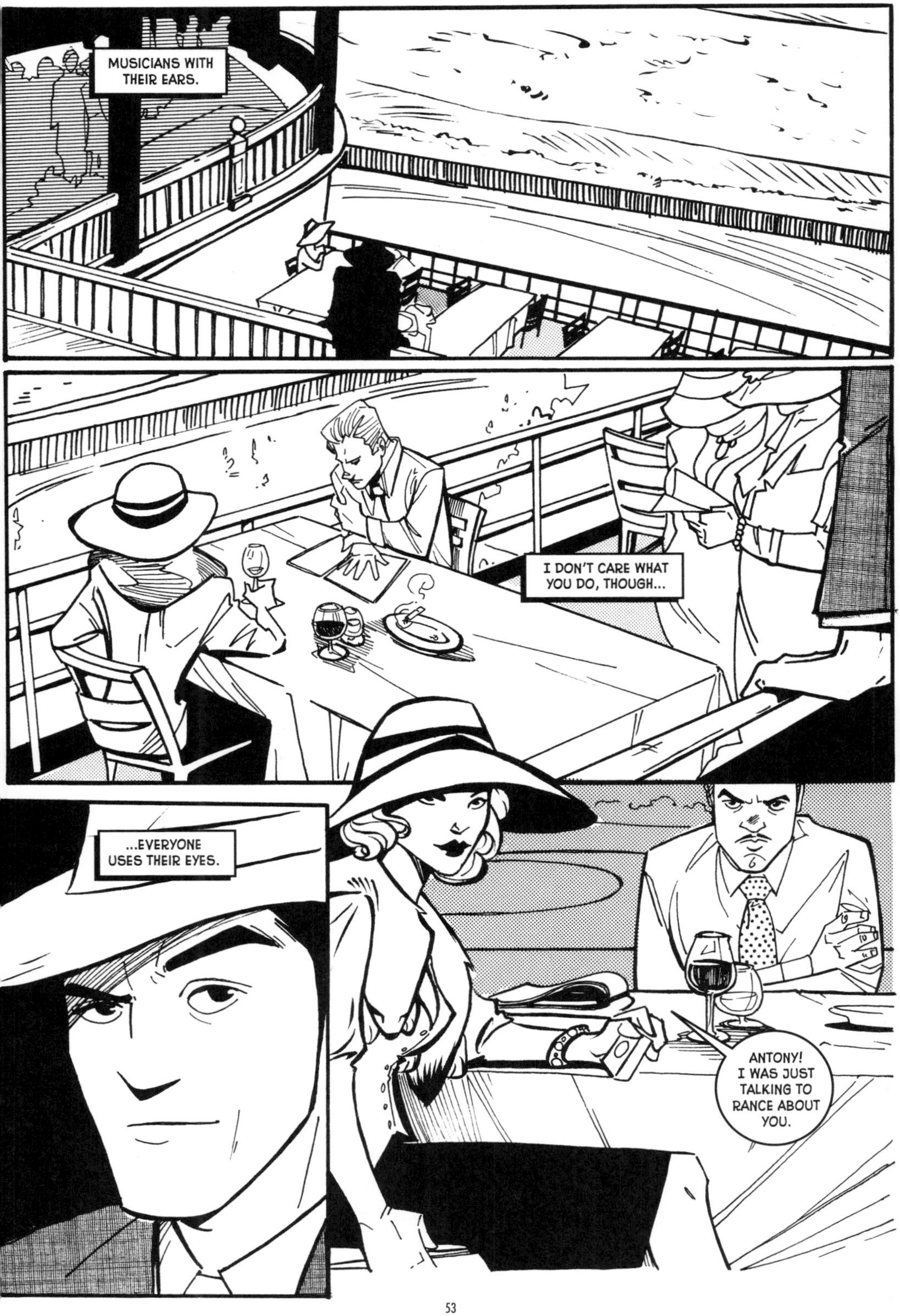
MUSICIANS WITH THEIR EARS.
I DON'T CARE WHAT YOU DO, THOUGH...
...EVERYONE USES THEIR EYES.
ANTONY! I WAS JUST TALKING TO RANCE ABOUT YOU.

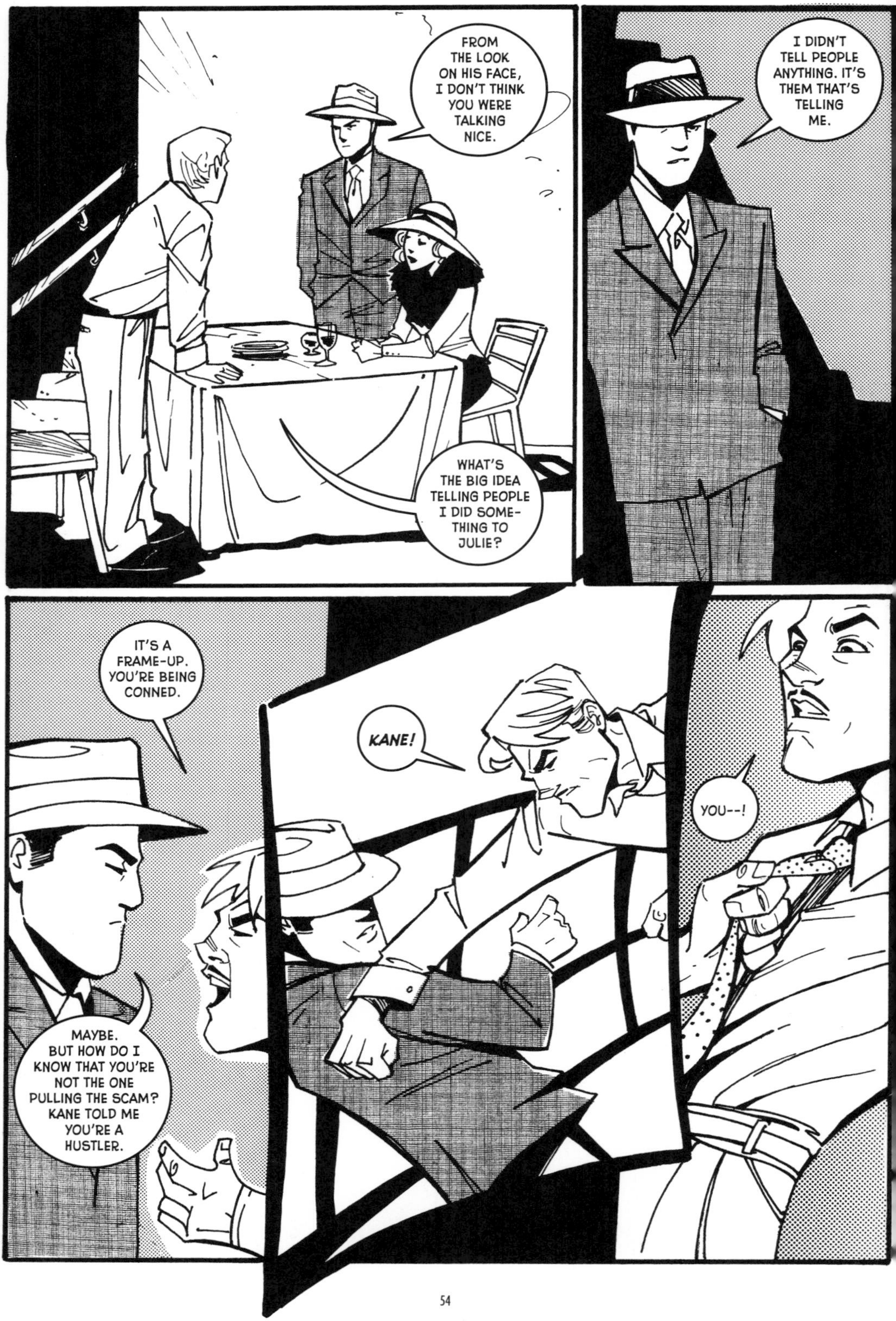
FROM THE LOOK ON HIS FACE, I DON'T THINK YOU WERE TALKING NICE.
WHAT'S THE BIG IDEA TELLING PEOPLE I DID SOME-THING TO JULIE?
I DIDN'T TELL PEOPLE ANYTHING. IT'S THEM THAT'S TELLING ME.
IT'S A FRAME-UP. YOU'RE BEING CONNED.
MAYBE. BUT HOW DO I KNOW THAT YOU'RE NOT THE ONE PULLING THE SCAM? KANE TOLD ME YOU'RE A HUSTLER.
KANE!
YOU--!

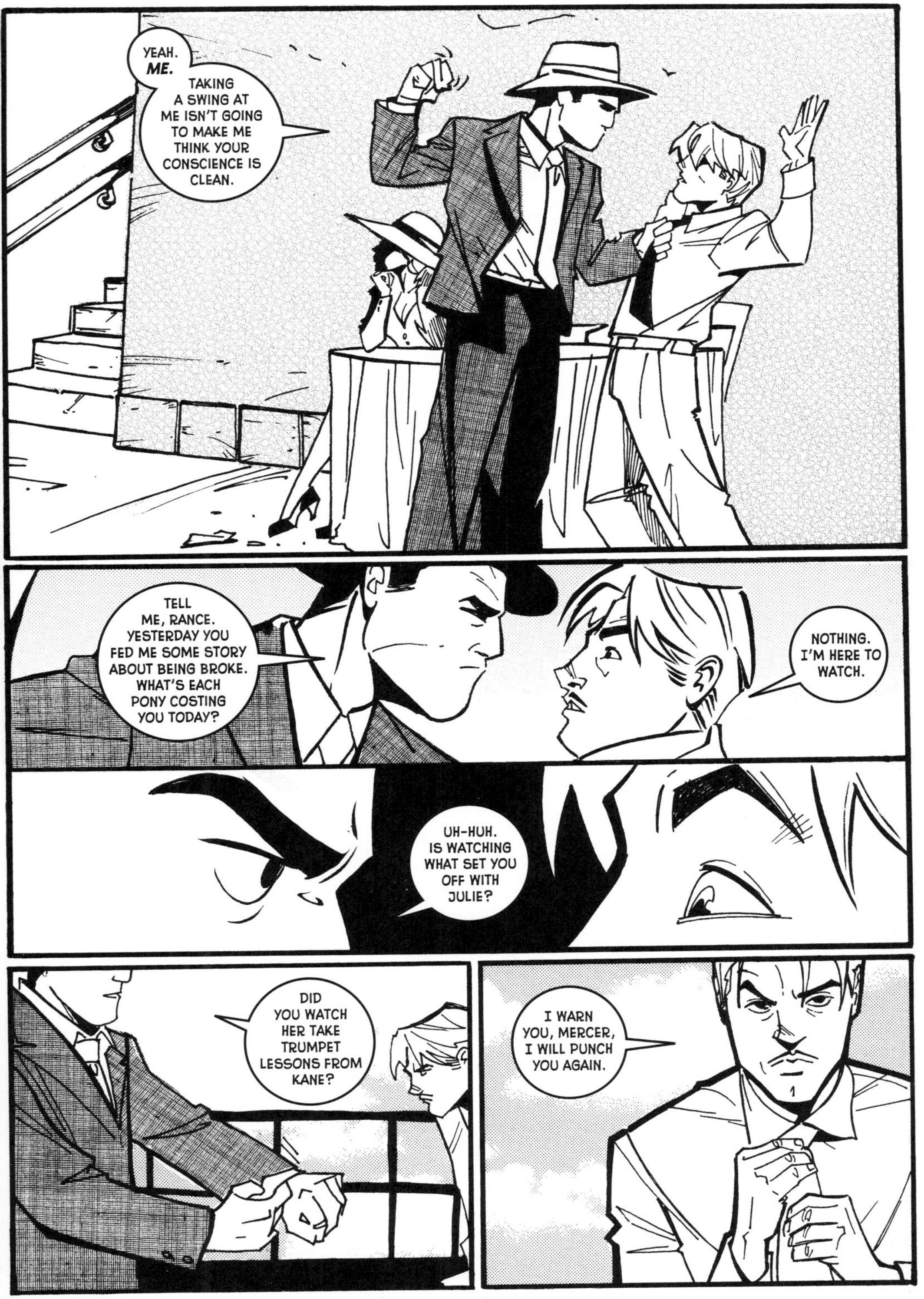
YEAH. **ME.** TAKING A SWING AT ME ISN'T GOING TO MAKE ME THINK YOUR CONSCIENCE IS CLEAN.
TELL ME, RANCE. YESTERDAY YOU FED ME SOME STORY ABOUT BEING BROKE. WHAT'S EACH PONY COSTING YOU TODAY?
NOTHING. I'M HERE TO WATCH.
UH-HUH. IS WATCHING WHAT SET YOU OFF WITH JULIE?
DID YOU WATCH HER TAKE TRUMPET LESSONS FROM KANE?
I WARN YOU, MERCER, I WILL PUNCH YOU AGAIN.

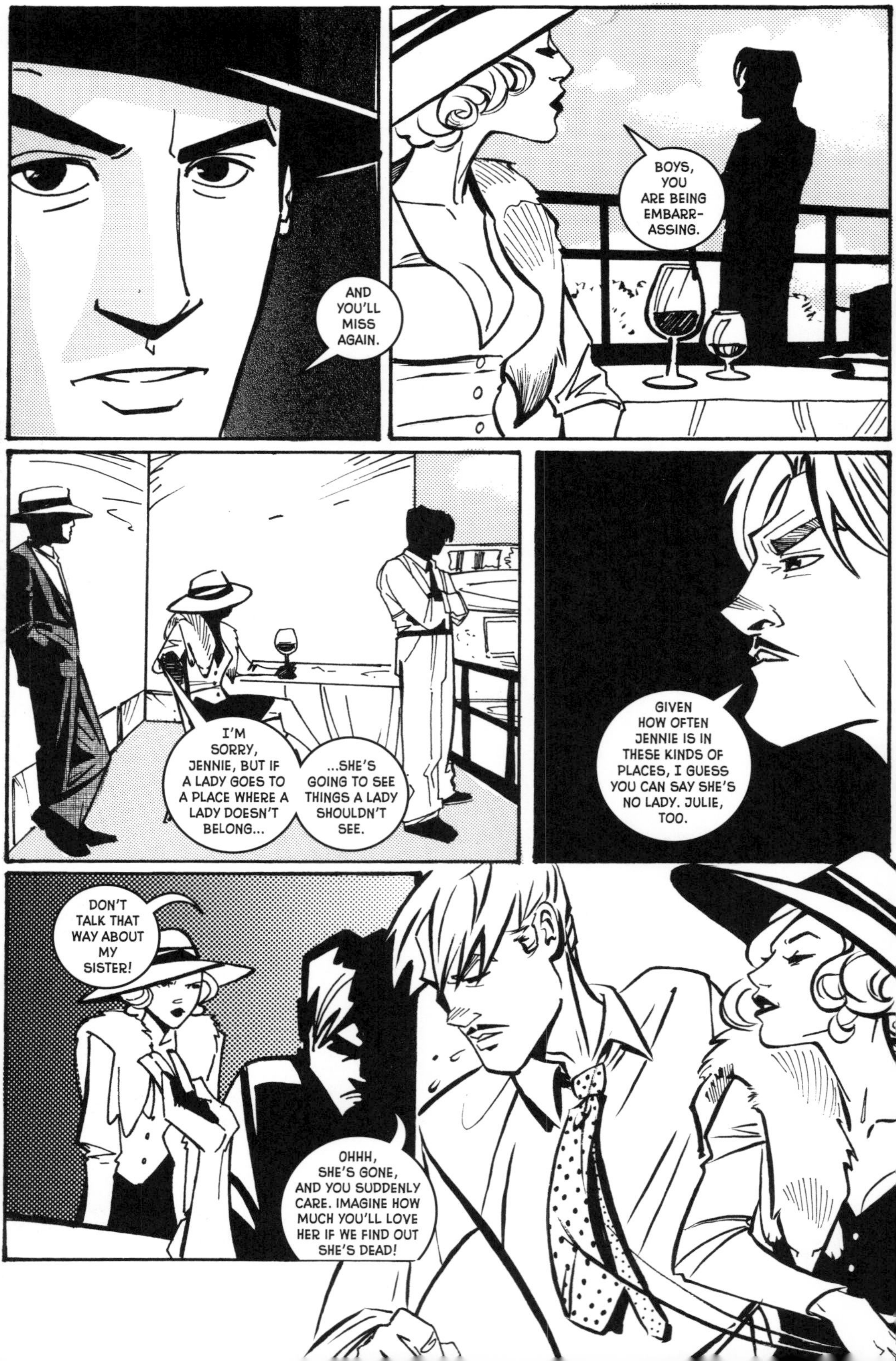
AND YOU'LL MISS AGAIN.
BOYS, YOU ARE BEING EMBARR-ASSING.
I'M SORRY, JENNIE, BUT IF A LADY GOES TO A PLACE WHERE A LADY DOESN'T BELONG...
...SHE'S GOING TO SEE THINGS A LADY SHOULDN'T SEE.
GIVEN HOW OFTEN JENNIE IS IN THESE KINDS OF PLACES, I GUESS YOU CAN SAY SHE'S NO LADY. JULIE, TOO.
DON'T TALK THAT WAY ABOUT MY SISTER!
OHHH, SHE'S GONE, AND YOU SUDDENLY CARE. IMAGINE HOW MUCH YOU'LL LOVE HER IF WE FIND OUT SHE'S DEAD!

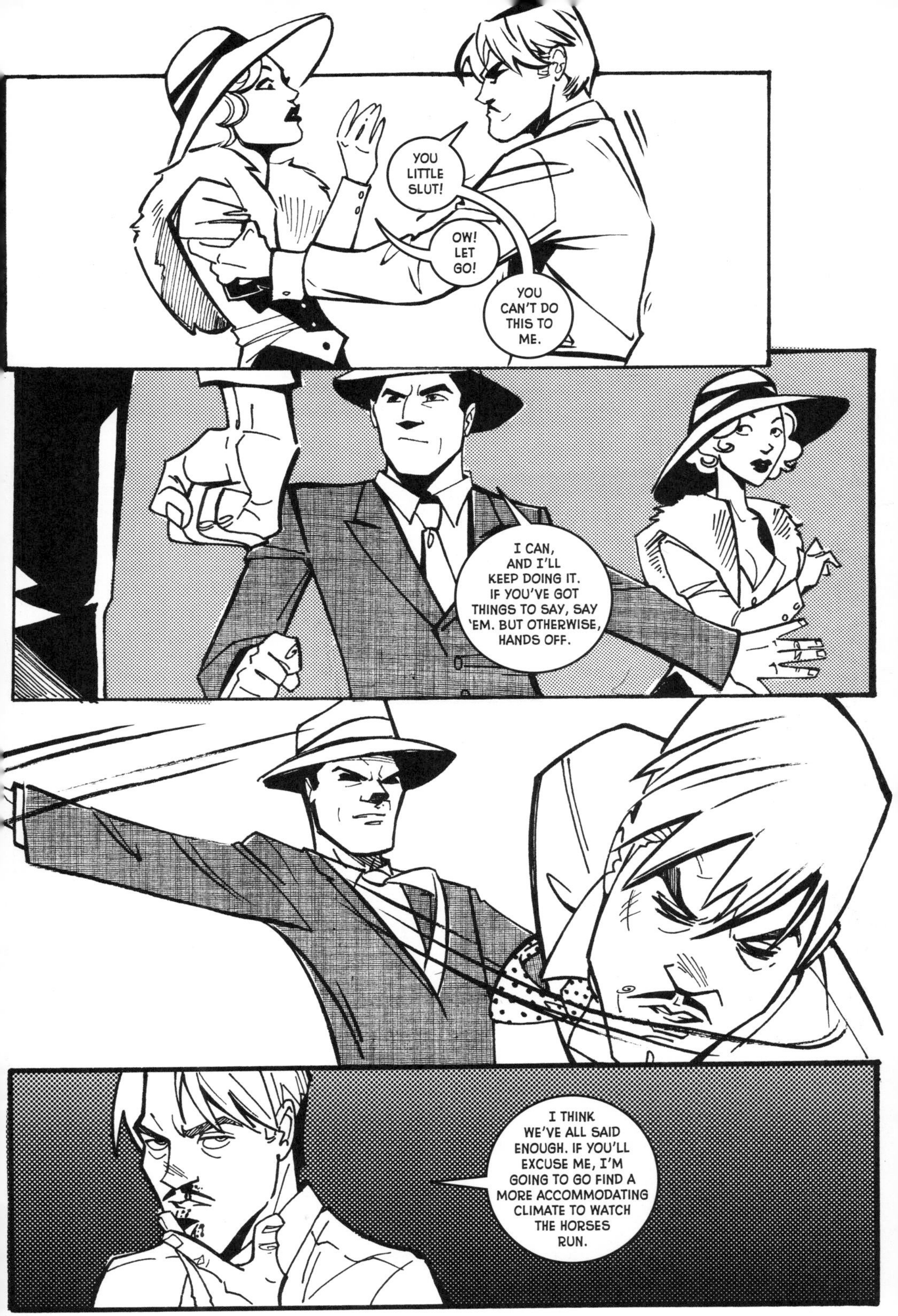
YOU LITTLE SLUT!
OW! LET GO!
YOU CAN'T DO THIS TO ME.
I CAN, AND I'LL KEEP DOING IT. IF YOU'VE GOT THINGS TO SAY, SAY 'EM. BUT OTHERWISE, HANDS OFF.
I THINK WE'VE ALL SAID ENOUGH. IF YOU'LL EXCUSE ME, I'M GOING TO GO FIND A MORE ACCOMMODATING CLIMATE TO WATCH THE HORSES RUN.

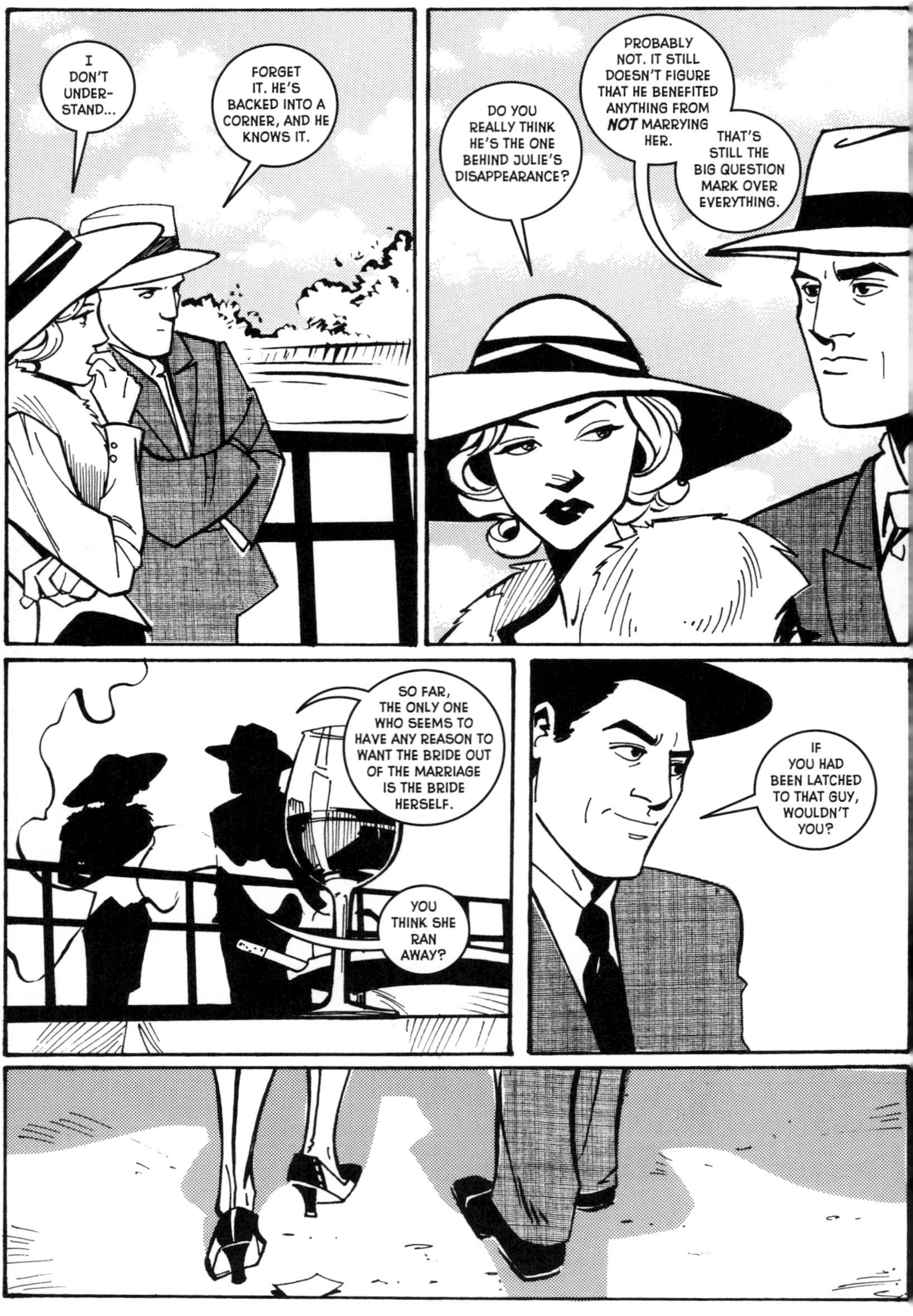
I DON'T UNDER-STAND...
FORGET IT. HE'S BACKED INTO A CORNER, AND HE KNOWS IT.
DO YOU REALLY THINK HE'S THE ONE BEHIND JULIE'S DISAPPEARANCE?
PROBABLY NOT. IT STILL DOESN'T FIGURE THAT HE BENEFITED ANYTHING FROM *NOT* MARRYING HER.
THAT'S STILL THE BIG QUESTION MARK OVER EVERYTHING.
SO FAR, THE ONLY ONE WHO SEEMS TO HAVE ANY REASON TO WANT THE BRIDE OUT OF THE MARRIAGE IS THE BRIDE HERSELF.
YOU THINK SHE RAN AWAY?
IF YOU HAD BEEN LATCHED TO THAT GUY, WOULDN'T YOU?

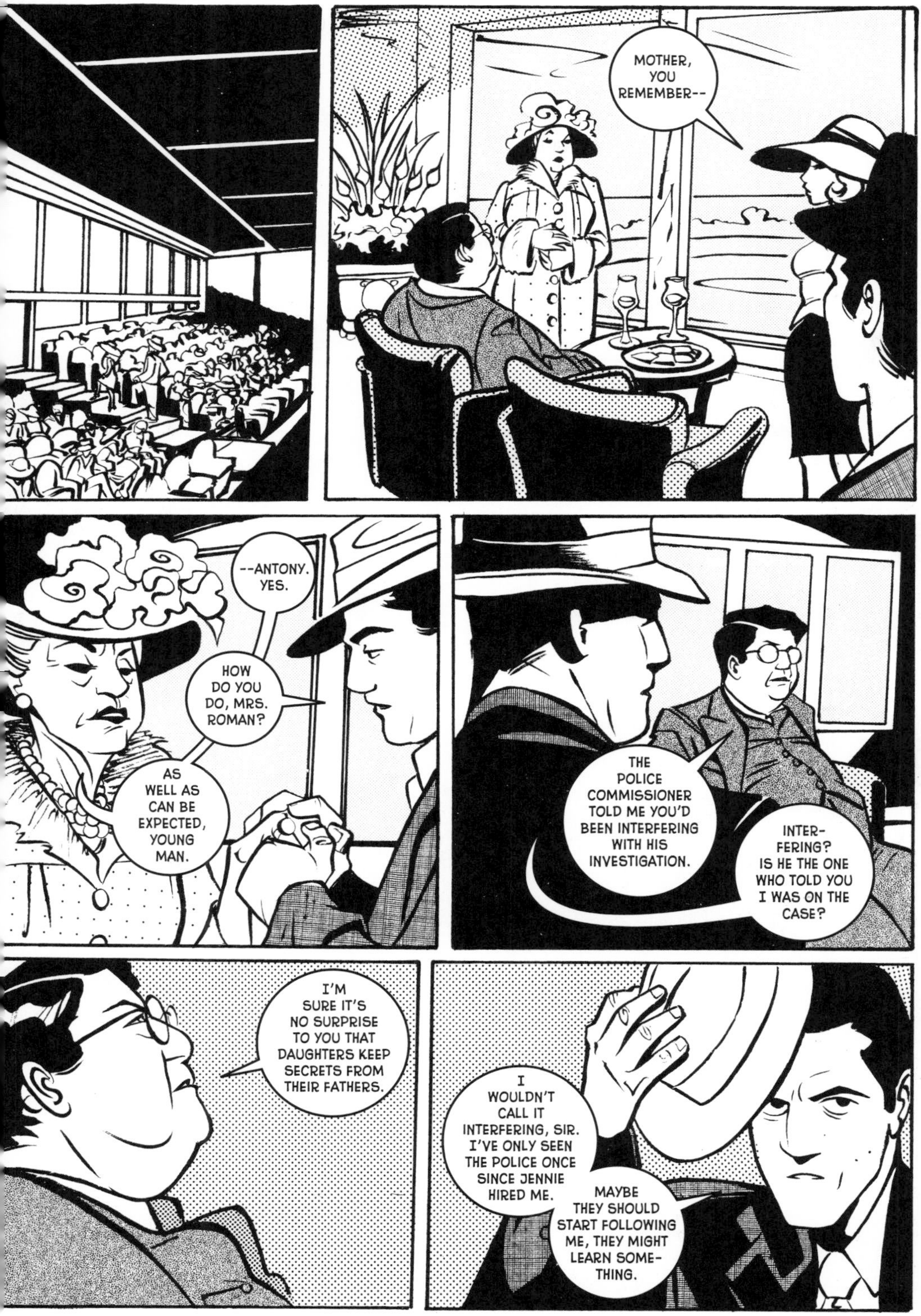
MOTHER, YOU REMEMBER--
--ANTONY. YES.
HOW DO YOU DO, MRS. ROMAN?
AS WELL AS CAN BE EXPECTED, YOUNG MAN.
THE POLICE COMMISSIONER TOLD ME YOU'D BEEN INTERFERING WITH HIS INVESTIGATION.
INTER-FERING? IS HE THE ONE WHO TOLD YOU I WAS ON THE CASE?
I'M SURE IT'S NO SURPRISE TO YOU THAT DAUGHTERS KEEP SECRETS FROM THEIR FATHERS.
I WOULDN'T CALL IT INTERFERING, SIR. I'VE ONLY SEEN THE POLICE ONCE SINCE JENNIE HIRED ME.
MAYBE THEY SHOULD START FOLLOWING ME, THEY MIGHT LEARN SOME-THING.

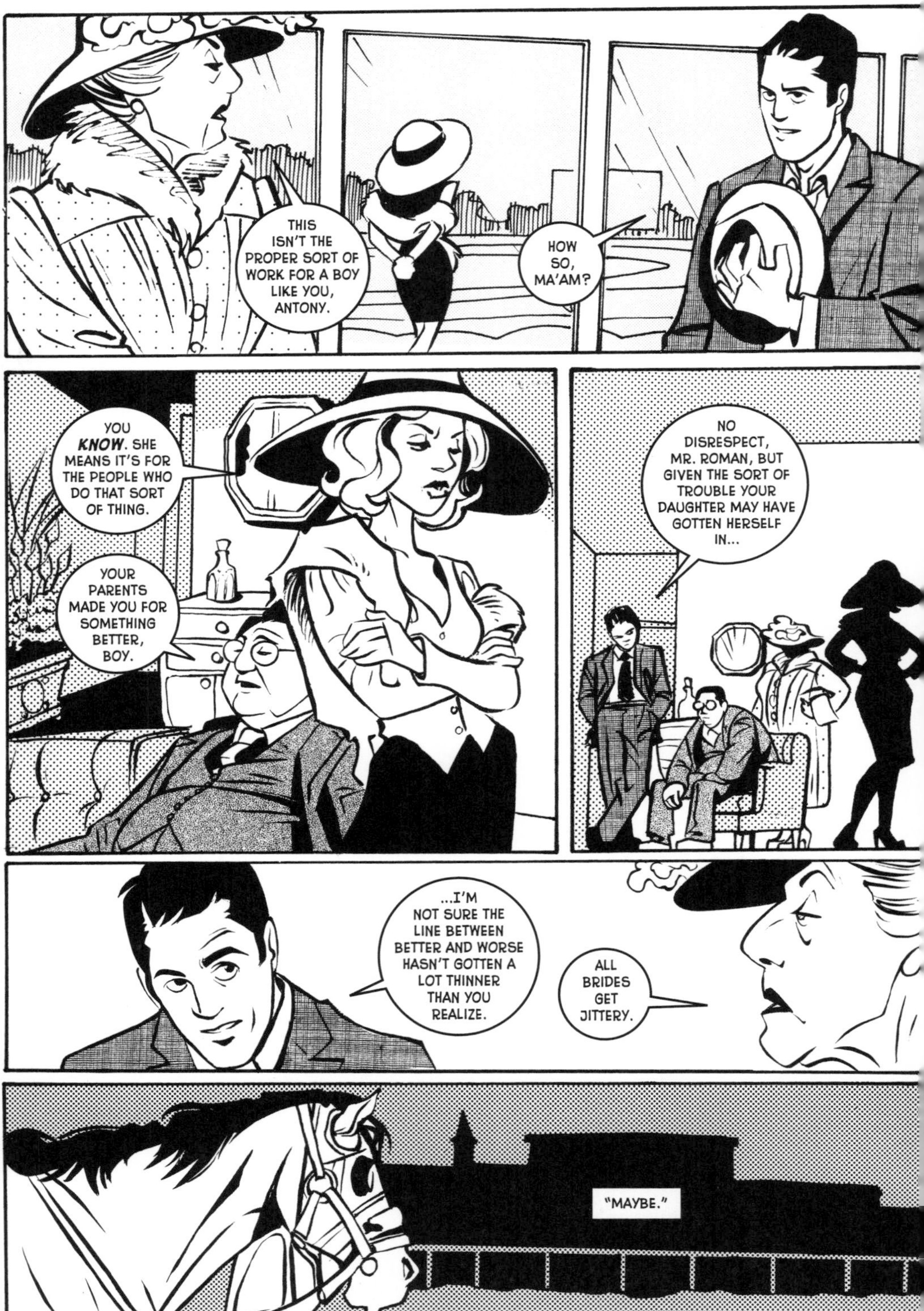
THIS ISN'T THE PROPER SORT OF WORK FOR A BOY LIKE YOU, ANTONY.
HOW SO, MA'AM?
YOU ***KNOW***. SHE MEANS IT'S FOR THE PEOPLE WHO DO THAT SORT OF THING.
YOUR PARENTS MADE YOU FOR SOMETHING BETTER, BOY.
NO DISRESPECT, MR. ROMAN, BUT GIVEN THE SORT OF TROUBLE YOUR DAUGHTER MAY HAVE GOTTEN HERSELF IN...
...I'M NOT SURE THE LINE BETWEEN BETTER AND WORSE HASN'T GOTTEN A LOT THINNER THAN YOU REALIZE.
ALL BRIDES GET JITTERY.
"MAYBE."

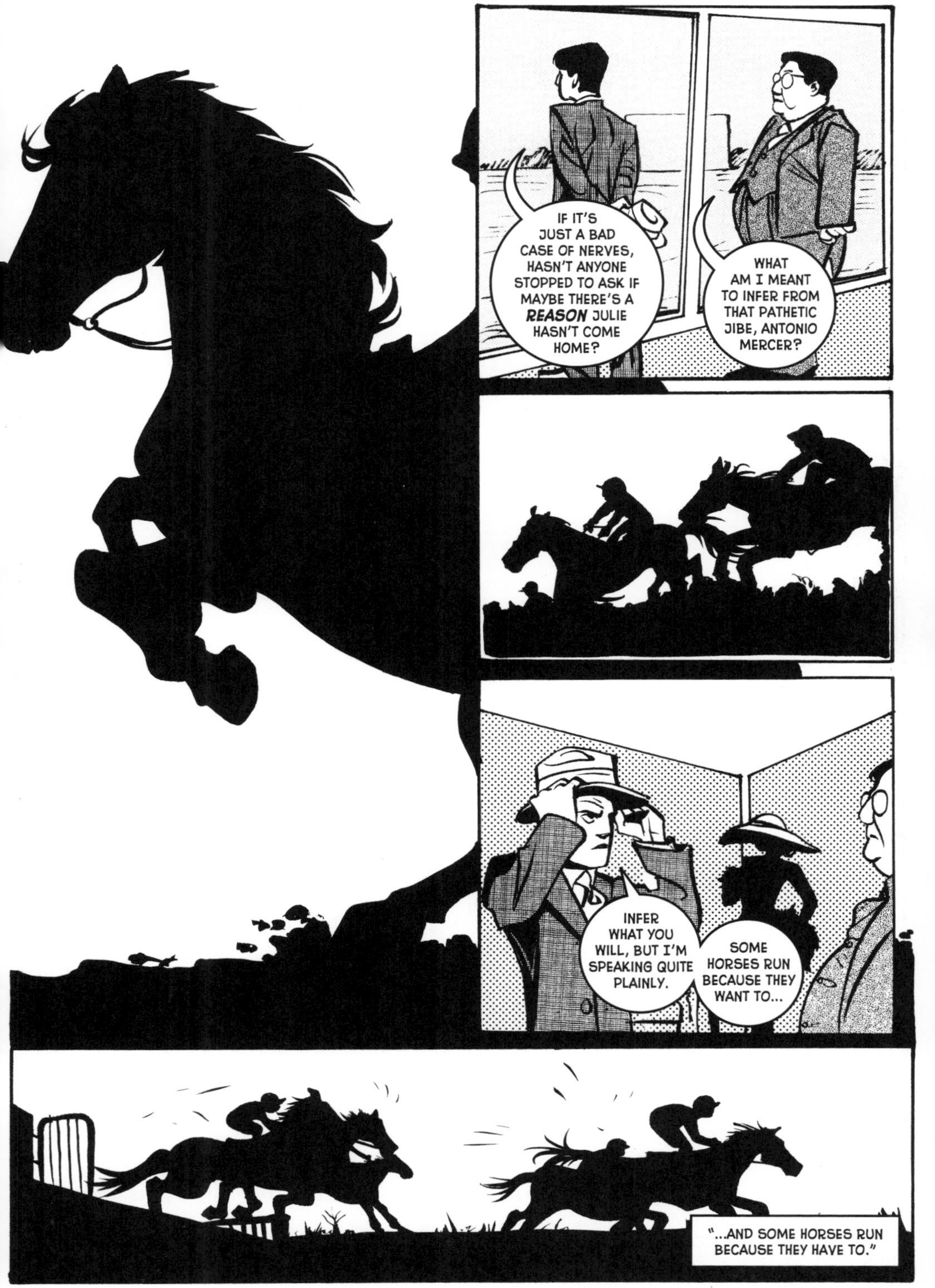
IF IT'S JUST A BAD CASE OF NERVES, HASN'T ANYONE STOPPED TO ASK IF MAYBE THERE'S A **REASON** JULIE HASN'T COME HOME?
WHAT AM I MEANT TO INFER FROM THAT PATHETIC JIBE, ANTONIO MERCER?
INFER WHAT YOU WILL, BUT I'M SPEAKING QUITE PLAINLY.
SOME HORSES RUN BECAUSE THEY WANT TO...
"...AND SOME HORSES RUN BECAUSE THEY HAVE TO."

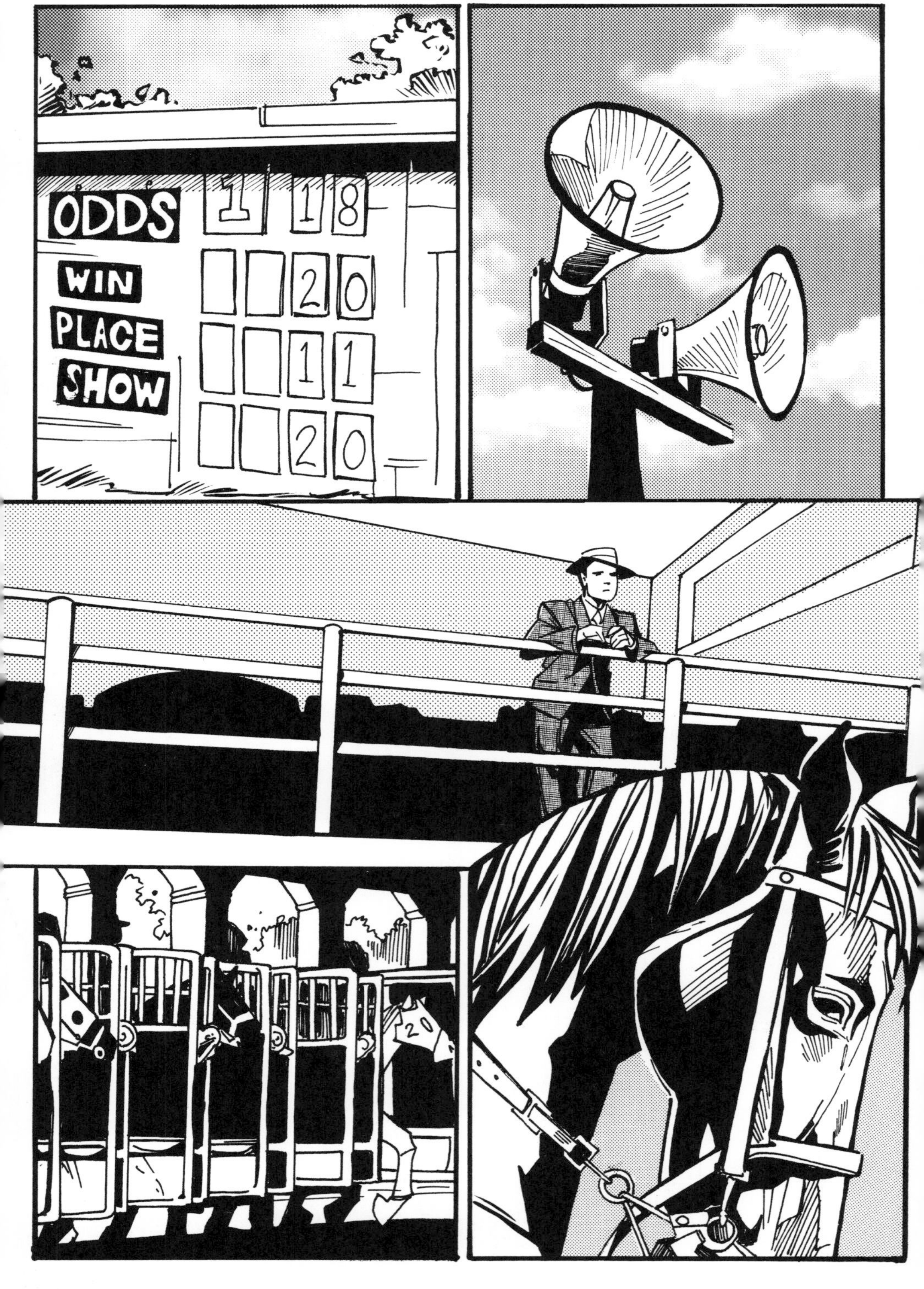
ODDS
1 18
WIN
2 0
PLACE
1 1
SHOW
2 0
20

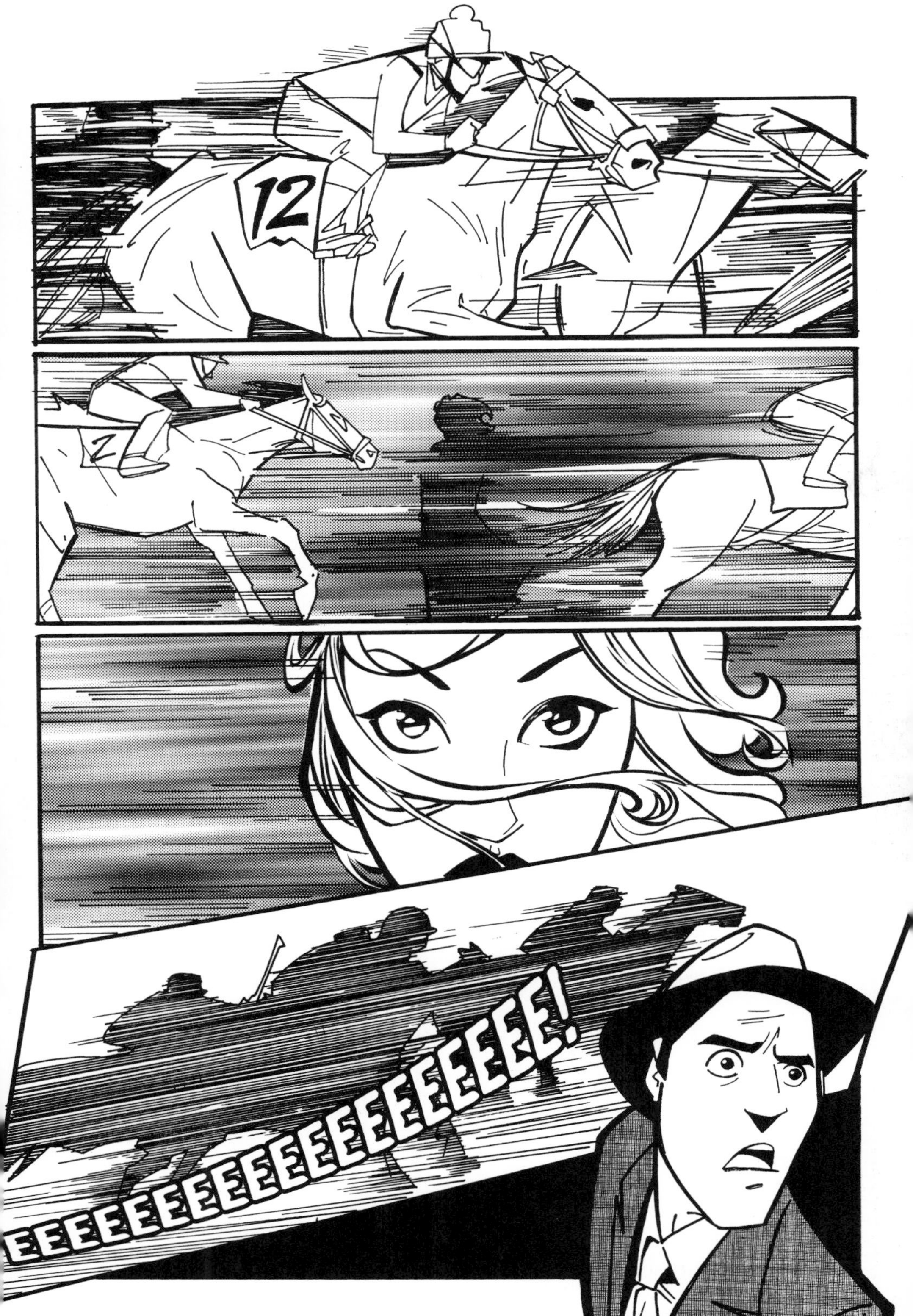

EEEEEEEEEEEEEEEEEEEEE!

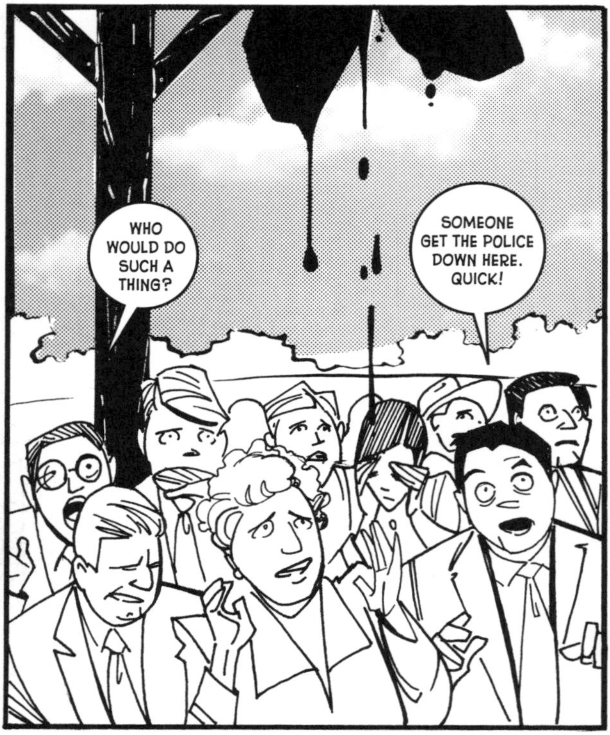
WHO WOULD DO SUCH A THING?
SOMEONE GET THE POLICE DOWN HERE. QUICK!
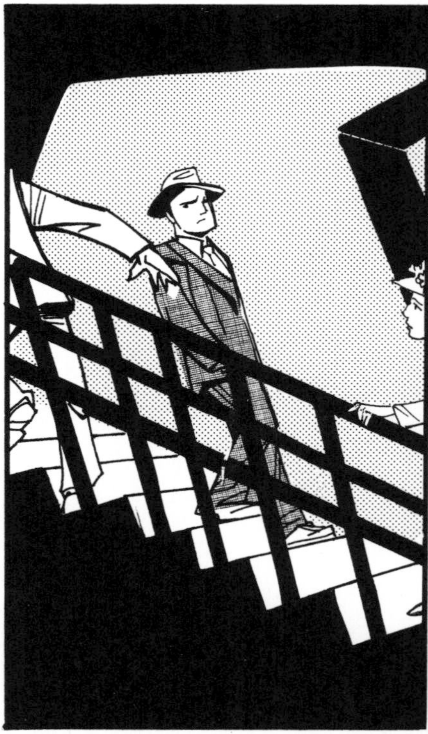
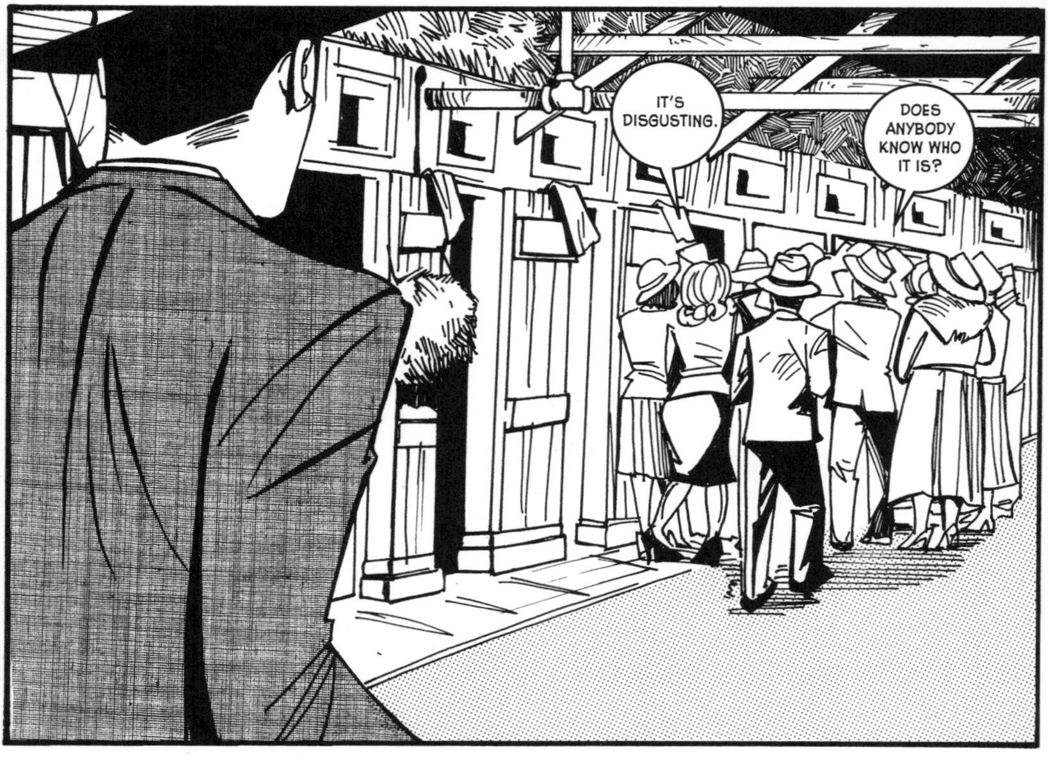
IT'S DISGUSTING.
DOES ANYBODY KNOW WHO IT IS?

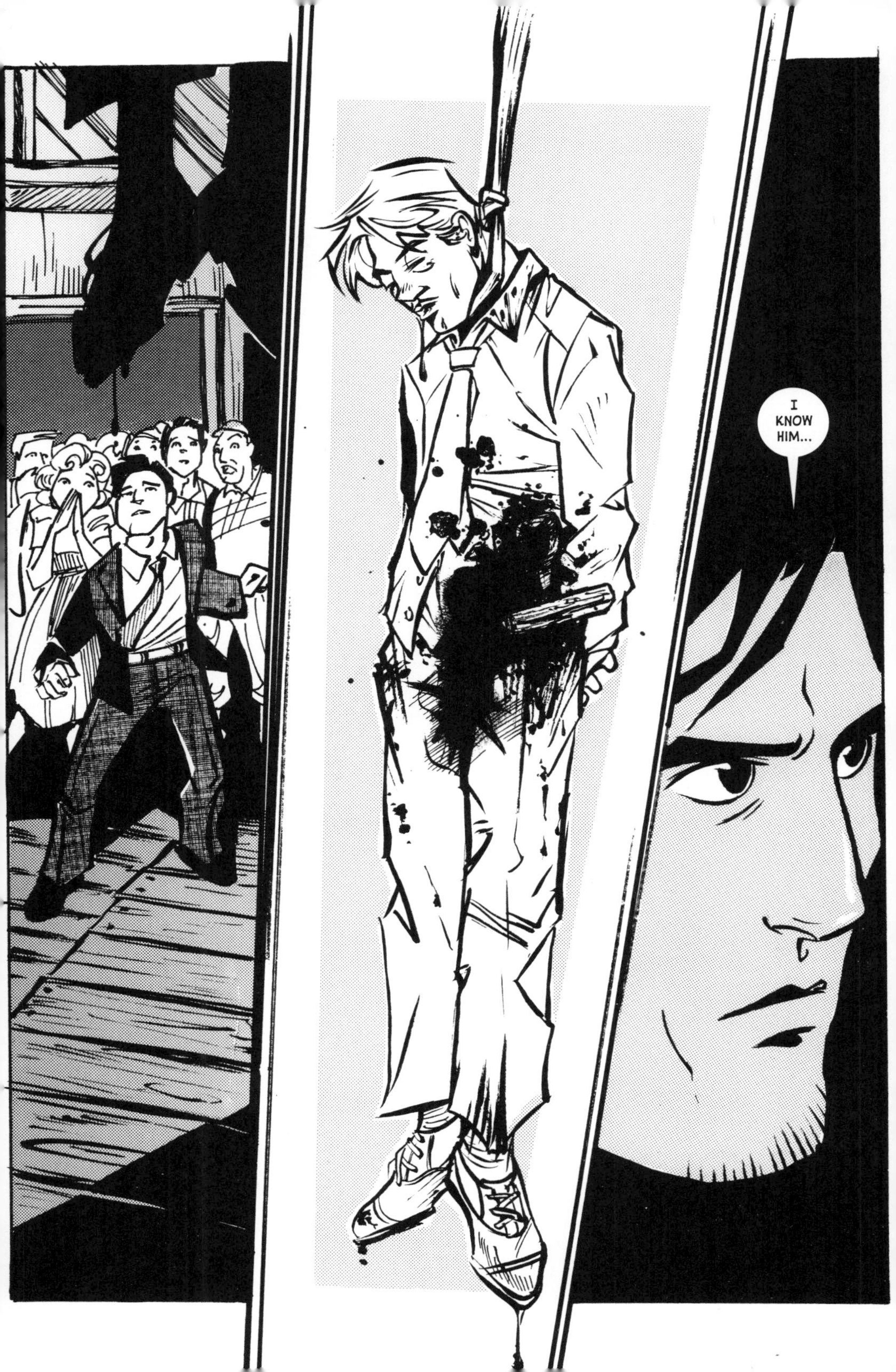
I KNOW HIM...

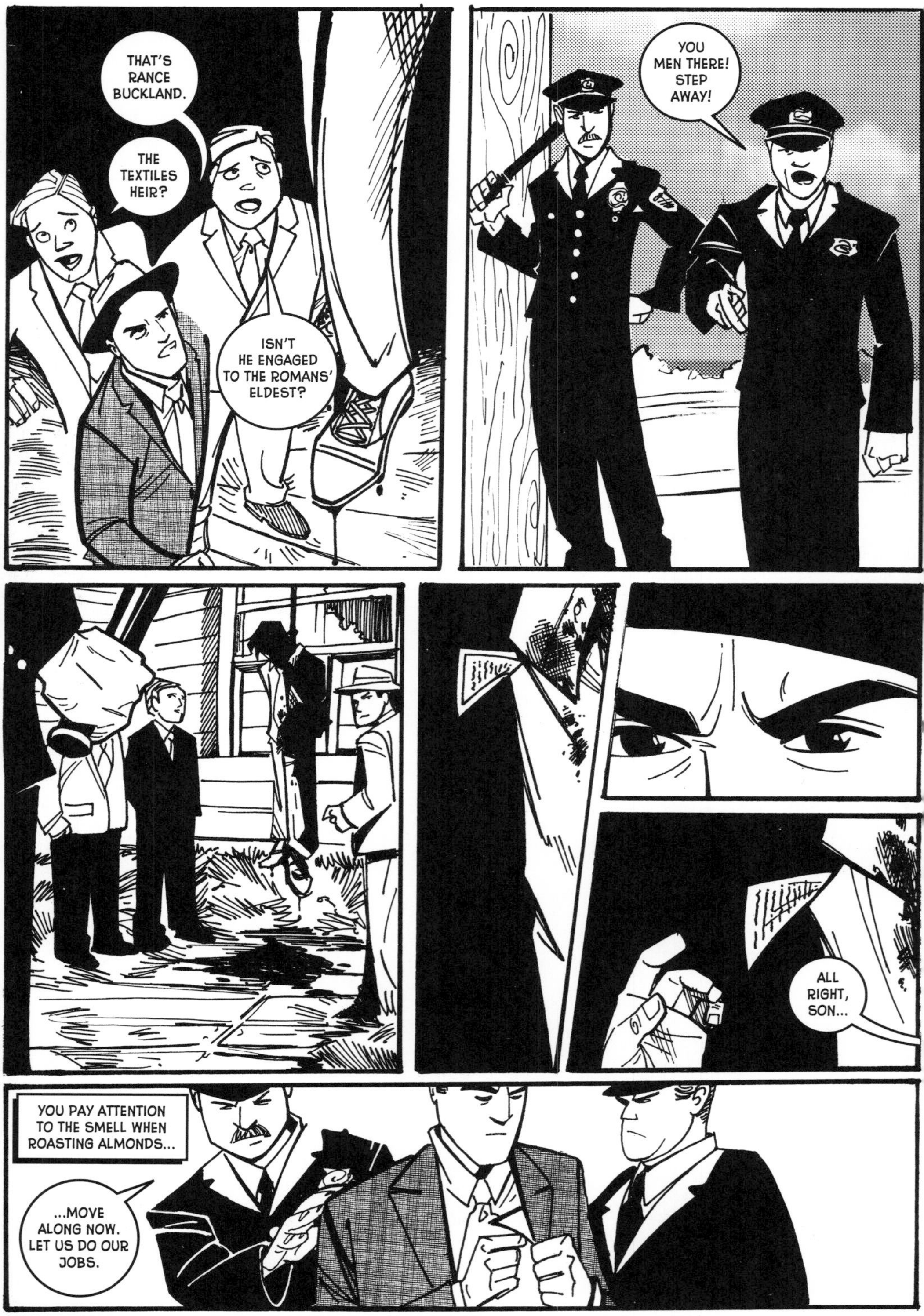
THAT'S RANCE BUCKLAND.
THE TEXTILES HEIR?
ISN'T HE ENGAGED TO THE ROMANS' ELDEST?
YOU MEN THERE! STEP AWAY!
ALL RIGHT, SON...
YOU PAY ATTENTION TO THE SMELL WHEN ROASTING ALMONDS...
...MOVE ALONG NOW. LET US DO OUR JOBS.

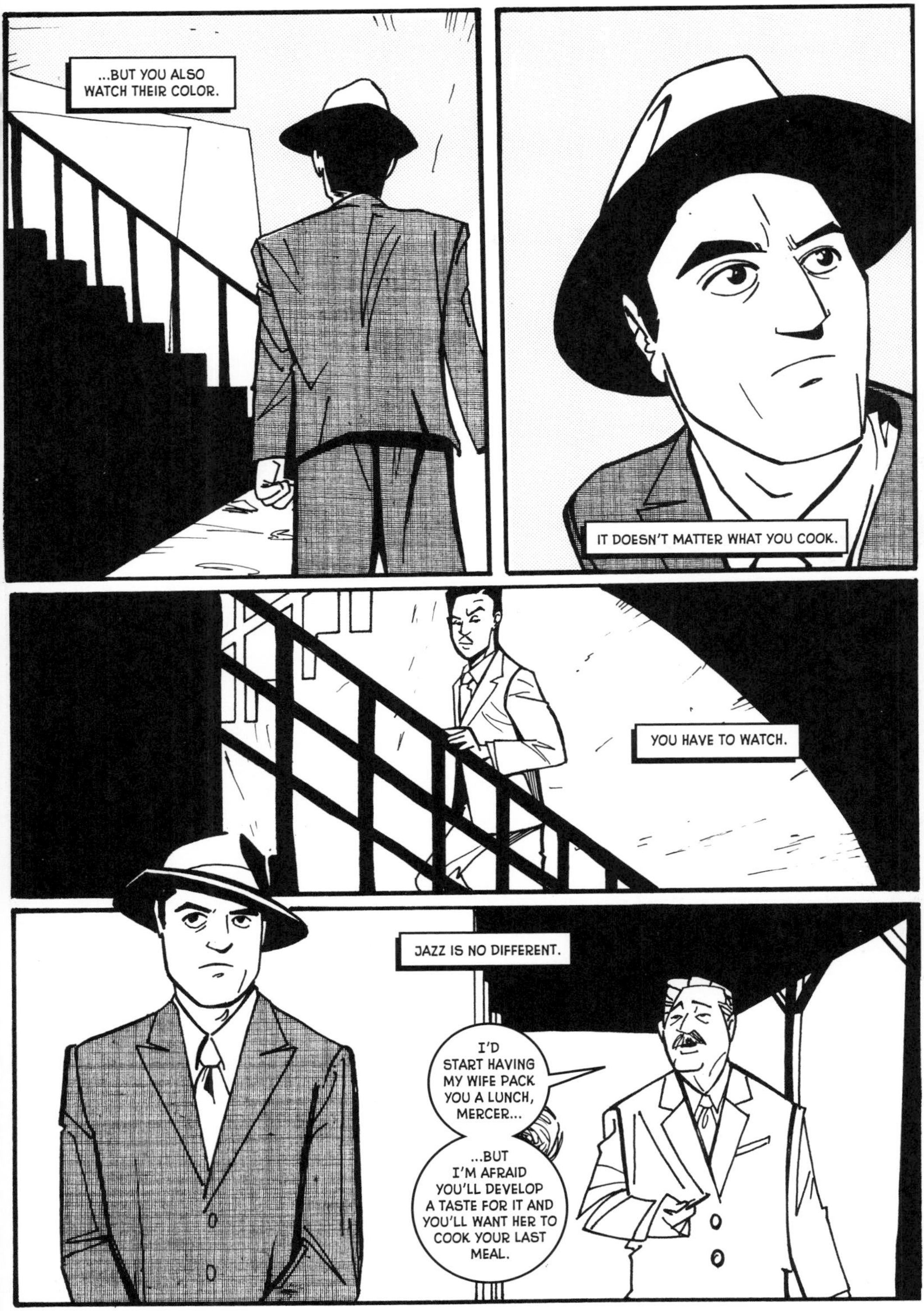

...BUT YOU ALSO WATCH THEIR COLOR.
IT DOESN'T MATTER WHAT YOU COOK.
YOU HAVE TO WATCH.
JAZZ IS NO DIFFERENT.
I'D START HAVING MY WIFE PACK YOU A LUNCH, MERCER...
...BUT I'M AFRAID YOU'LL DEVELOP A TASTE FOR IT AND YOU'LL WANT HER TO COOK YOUR LAST MEAL.

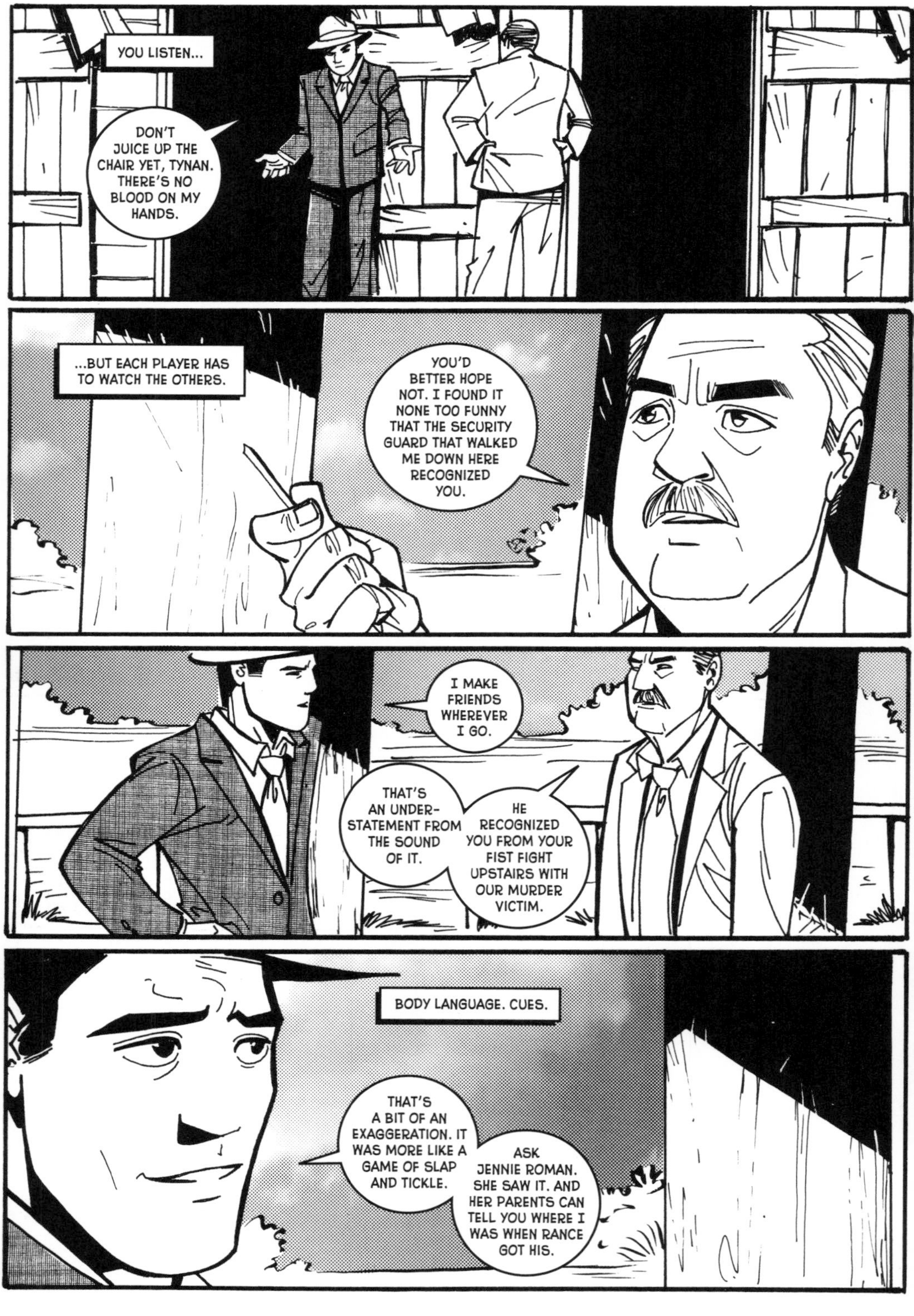
YOU LISTEN...
DON'T JUICE UP THE CHAIR YET, TYNAN. THERE'S NO BLOOD ON MY HANDS.
...BUT EACH PLAYER HAS TO WATCH THE OTHERS.
YOU'D BETTER HOPE NOT. I FOUND IT NONE TOO FUNNY THAT THE SECURITY GUARD THAT WALKED ME DOWN HERE RECOGNIZED YOU.
I MAKE FRIENDS WHEREVER I GO.
THAT'S AN UNDER-STATEMENT FROM THE SOUND OF IT.
HE RECOGNIZED YOU FROM YOUR FIST FIGHT UPSTAIRS WITH OUR MURDER VICTIM.
BODY LANGUAGE. CUES.
THAT'S A BIT OF AN EXAGGERATION. IT WAS MORE LIKE A GAME OF SLAP AND TICKLE.
ASK JENNIE ROMAN. SHE SAW IT. AND HER PARENTS CAN TELL YOU WHERE I WAS WHEN RANCE GOT HIS.

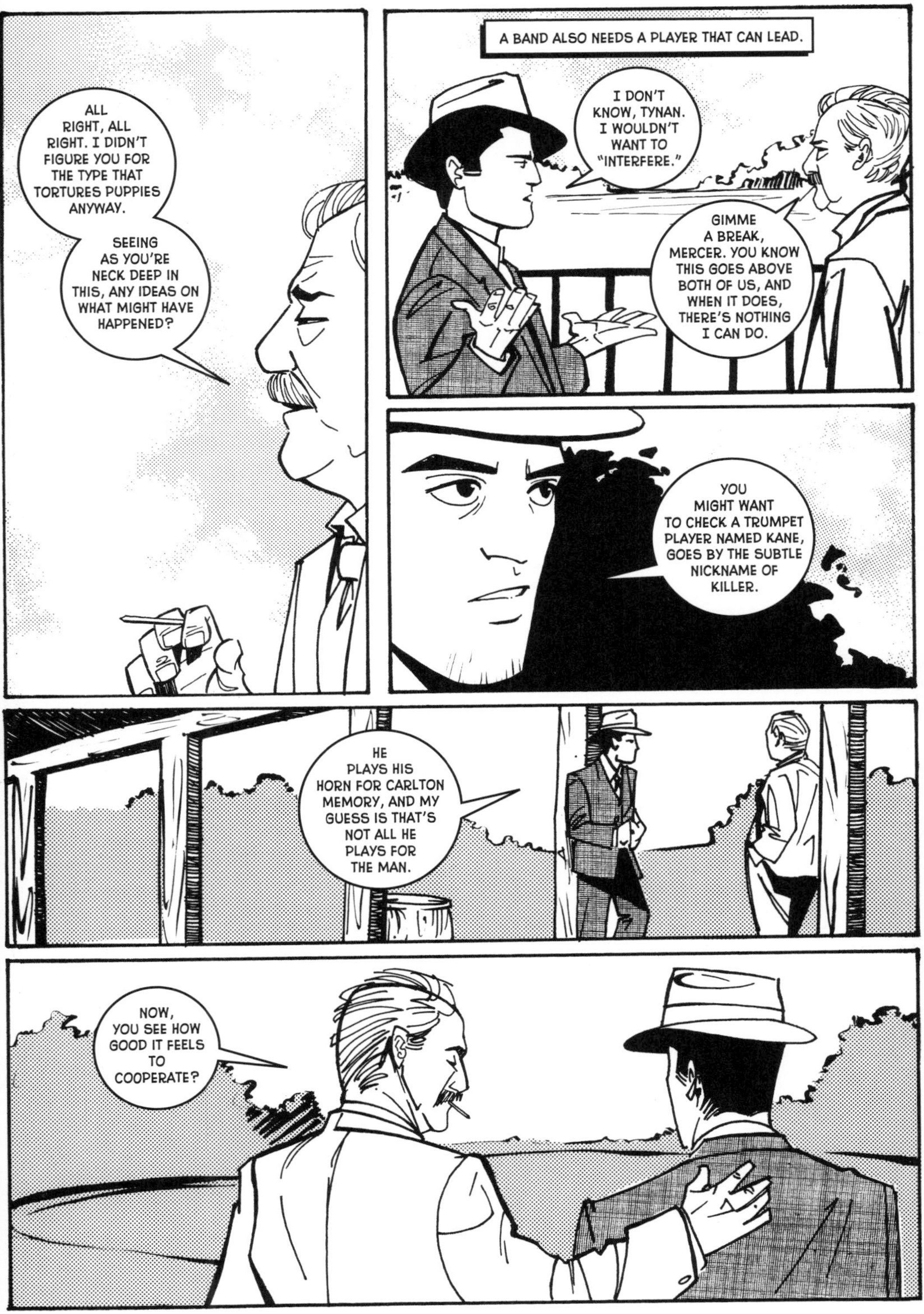
ALL RIGHT, ALL RIGHT. I DIDN'T FIGURE YOU FOR THE TYPE THAT TORTURES PUPPIES ANYWAY.
SEEING AS YOU'RE NECK DEEP IN THIS, ANY IDEAS ON WHAT MIGHT HAVE HAPPENED?
A BAND ALSO NEEDS A PLAYER THAT CAN LEAD.
I DON'T KNOW, TYNAN. I WOULDN'T WANT TO "INTERFERE."
GIMME A BREAK, MERCER. YOU KNOW THIS GOES ABOVE BOTH OF US, AND WHEN IT DOES, THERE'S NOTHING I CAN DO.
YOU MIGHT WANT TO CHECK A TRUMPET PLAYER NAMED KANE, GOES BY THE SUBTLE NICKNAME OF KILLER.
HE PLAYS HIS HORN FOR CARLTON MEMORY, AND MY GUESS IS THAT'S NOT ALL HE PLAYS FOR THE MAN.
NOW, YOU SEE HOW GOOD IT FEELS TO COOPERATE?

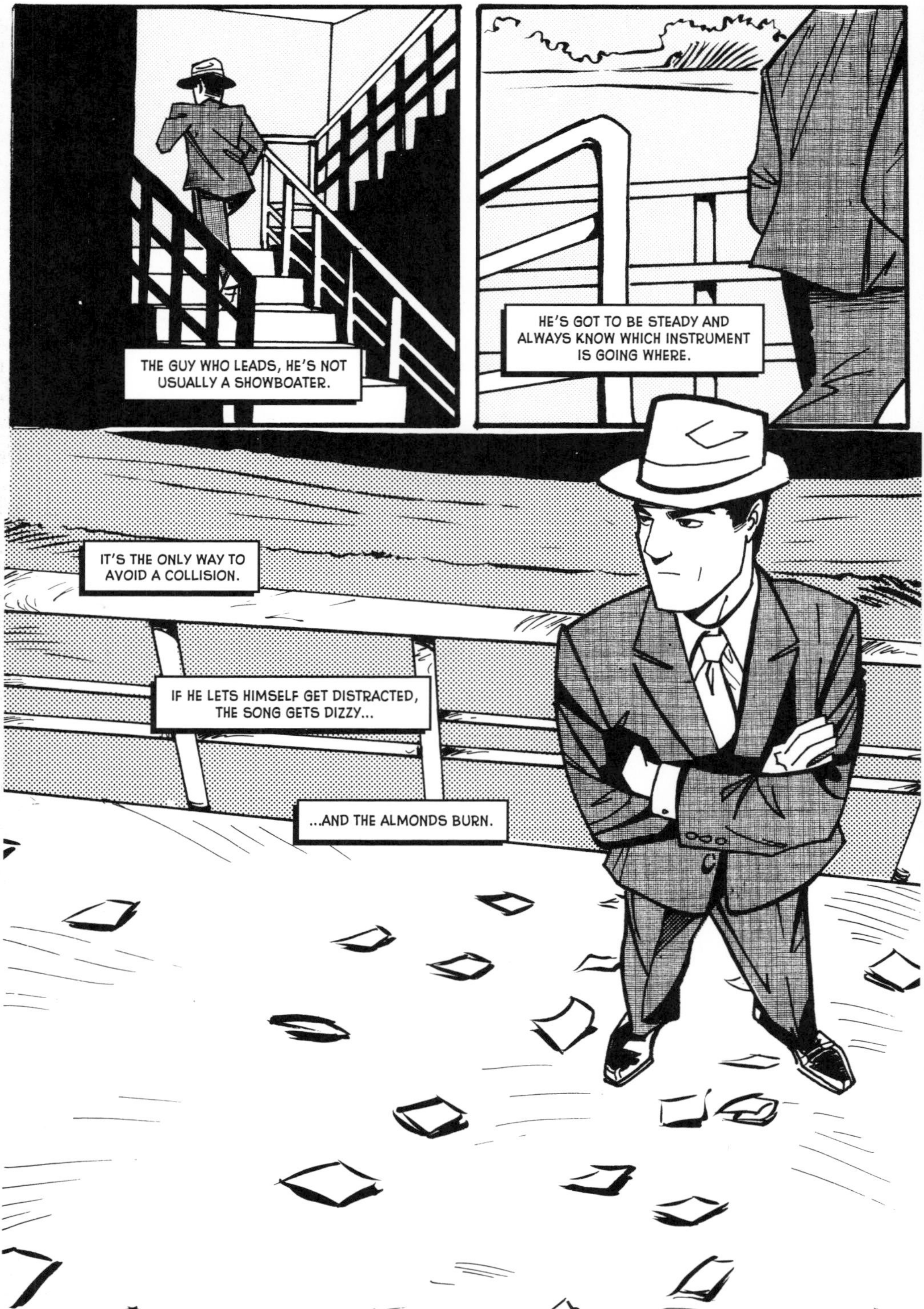
THE GUY WHO LEADS, HE'S NOT USUALLY A SHOWBOATER.
HE'S GOT TO BE STEADY AND ALWAYS KNOW WHICH INSTRUMENT IS GOING WHERE.
IT'S THE ONLY WAY TO AVOID A COLLISION.
IF HE LETS HIMSELF GET DISTRACTED, THE SONG GETS DIZZY...
...AND THE ALMONDS BURN.

CHAPTER 5

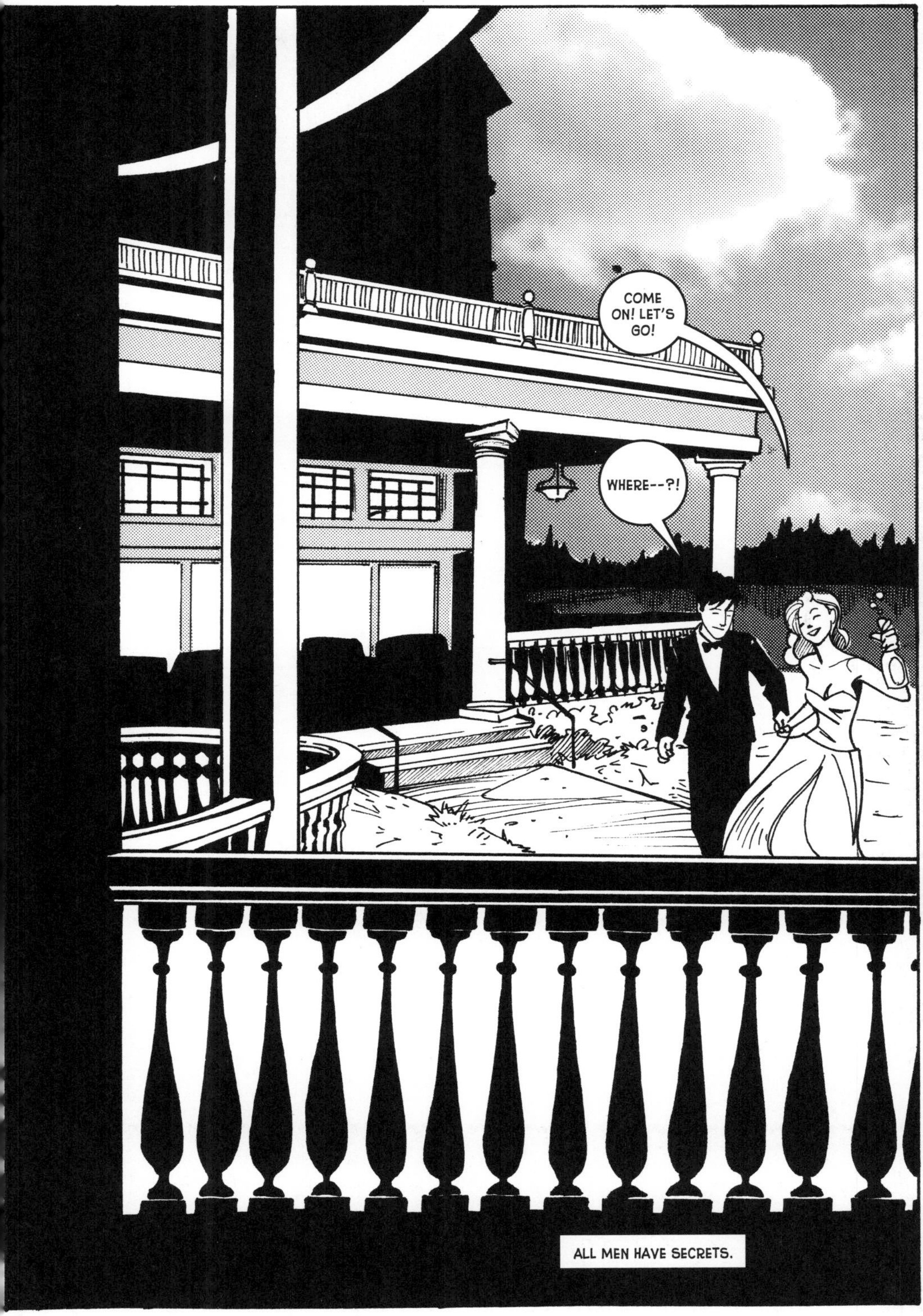
COME ON! LET'S GO!
WHERE--?!
ALL MEN HAVE SECRETS.

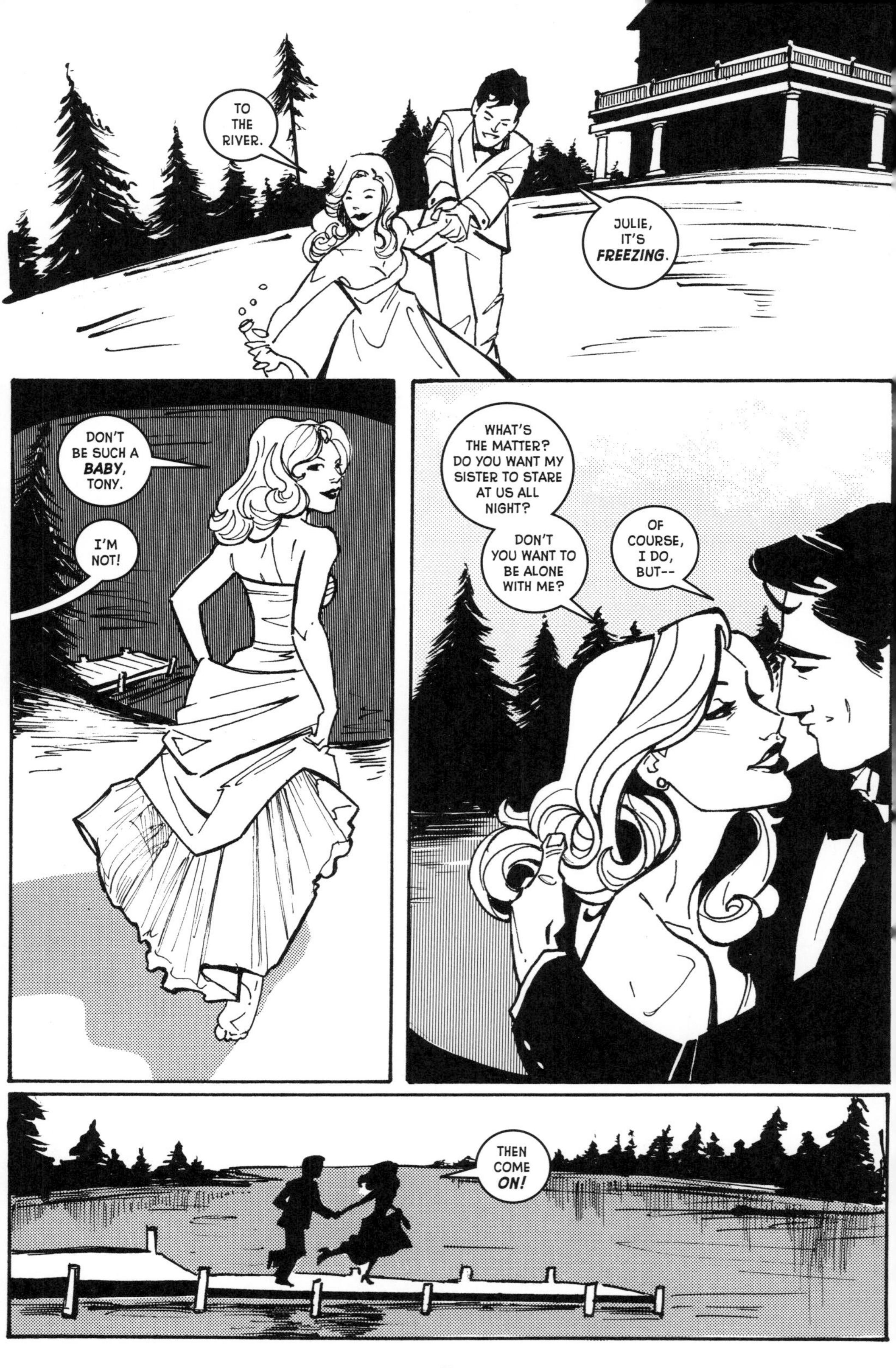
TO THE RIVER.
JULIE, IT'S FREEZING.
DON'T BE SUCH A BABY, TONY.
I'M NOT!
WHAT'S THE MATTER? DO YOU WANT MY SISTER TO STARE AT US ALL NIGHT?
DON'T YOU WANT TO BE ALONE WITH ME?
OF COURSE, I DO, BUT--
THEN COME ON!

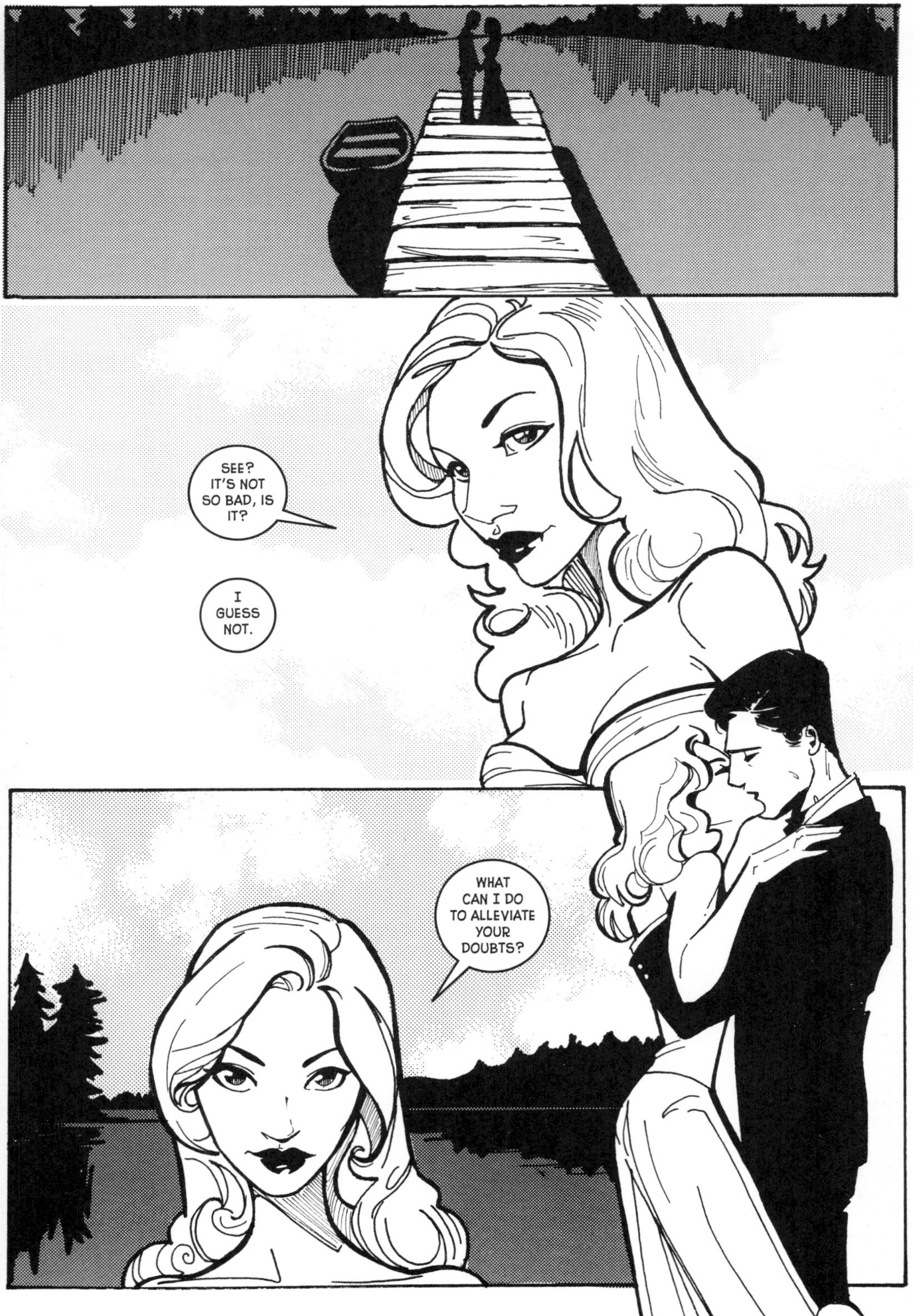
SEE? IT'S NOT SO BAD, IS IT?
I GUESS NOT.
WHAT CAN I DO TO ALLEVIATE YOUR DOUBTS?

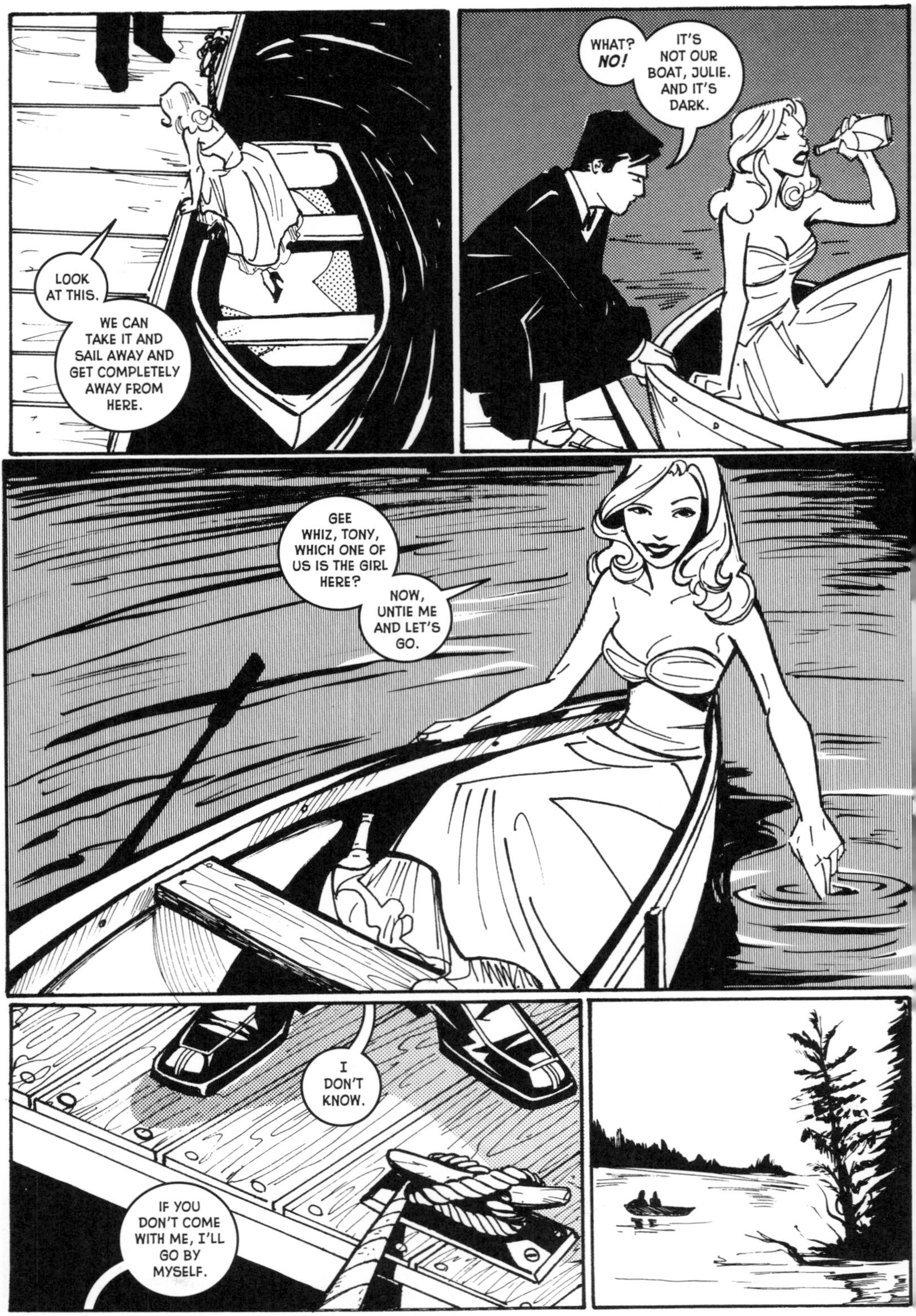
LOOK AT THIS.
WE CAN TAKE IT AND SAIL AWAY AND GET COMPLETELY AWAY FROM HERE.
WHAT? NO!
IT'S NOT OUR BOAT, JULIE. AND IT'S DARK.
GEE WHIZ, TONY, WHICH ONE OF US IS THE GIRL HERE?
NOW, UNTIE ME AND LET'S GO.
I DON'T KNOW.
IF YOU DON'T COME WITH ME, I'LL GO BY MYSELF.

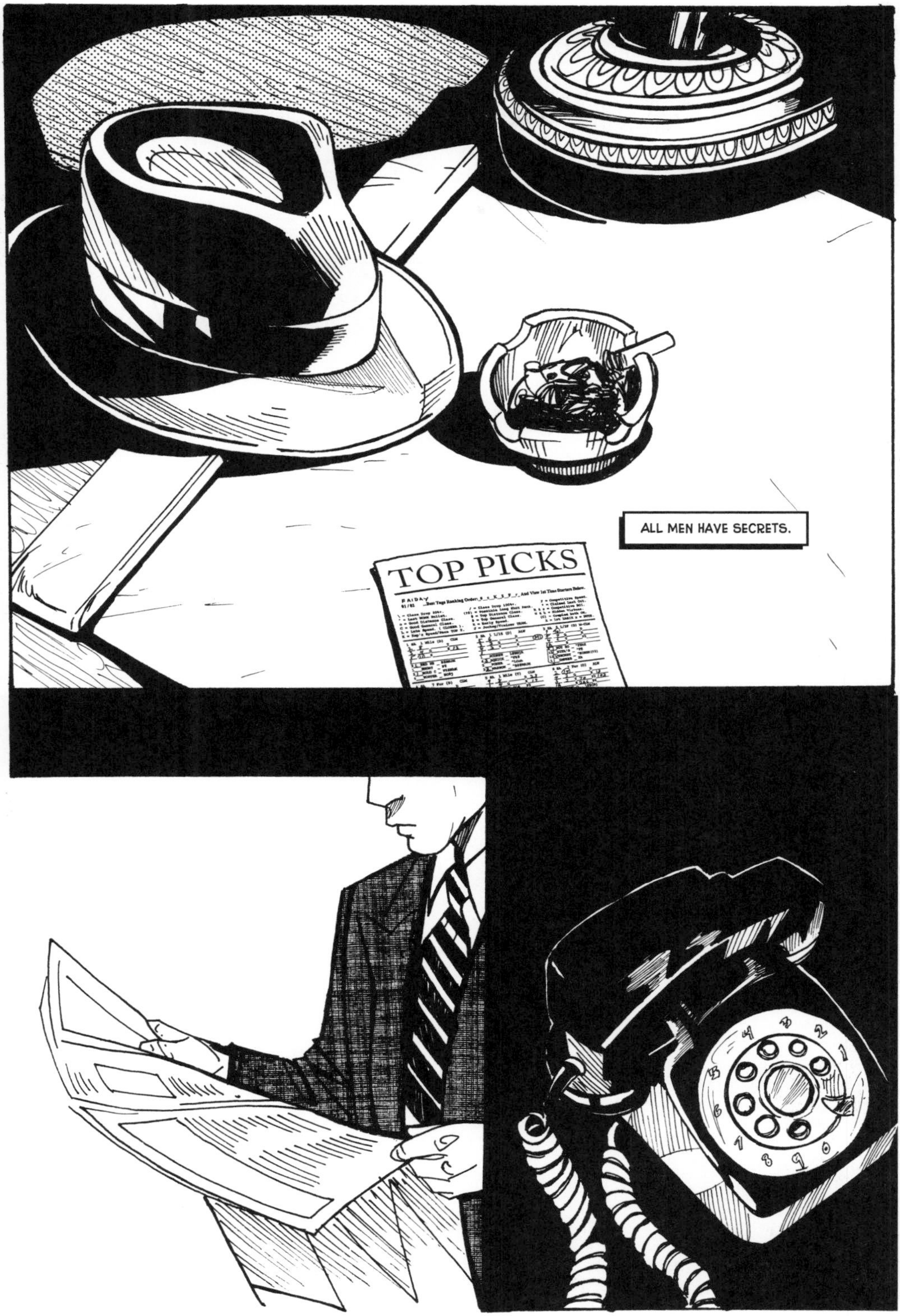
ALL MEN HAVE SECRETS.
TOP PICKS

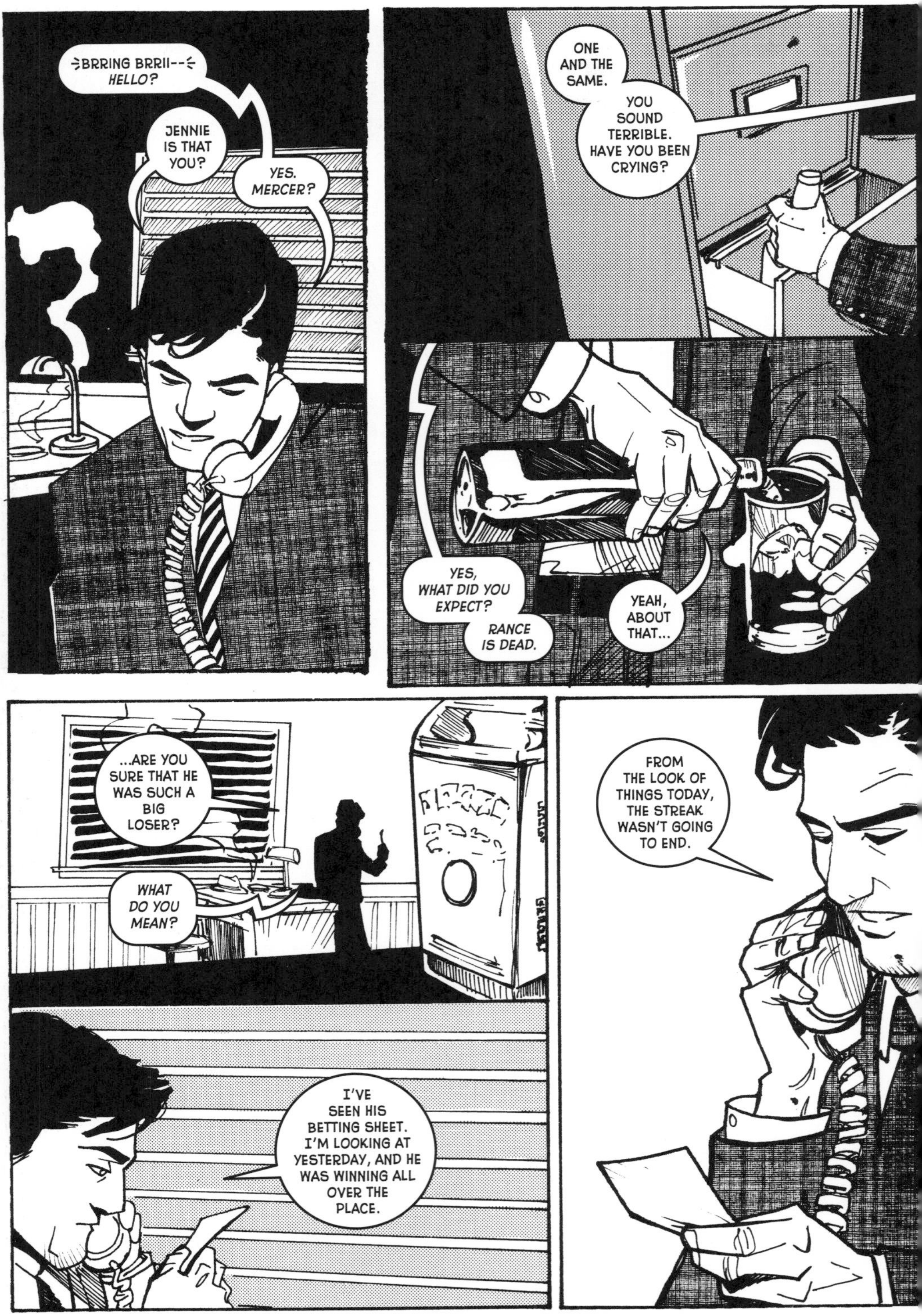
⚟BRRING BRRII--⚞ HELLO?
JENNIE IS THAT YOU?
YES. MERCER?
ONE AND THE SAME.
YOU SOUND TERRIBLE. HAVE YOU BEEN CRYING?
YES, WHAT DID YOU EXPECT?
RANCE IS DEAD.
YEAH, ABOUT THAT...
...ARE YOU SURE THAT HE WAS SUCH A BIG LOSER?
WHAT DO YOU MEAN?
I'VE SEEN HIS BETTING SHEET. I'M LOOKING AT YESTERDAY, AND HE WAS WINNING ALL OVER THE PLACE.
FROM THE LOOK OF THINGS TODAY, THE STREAK WASN'T GOING TO END.

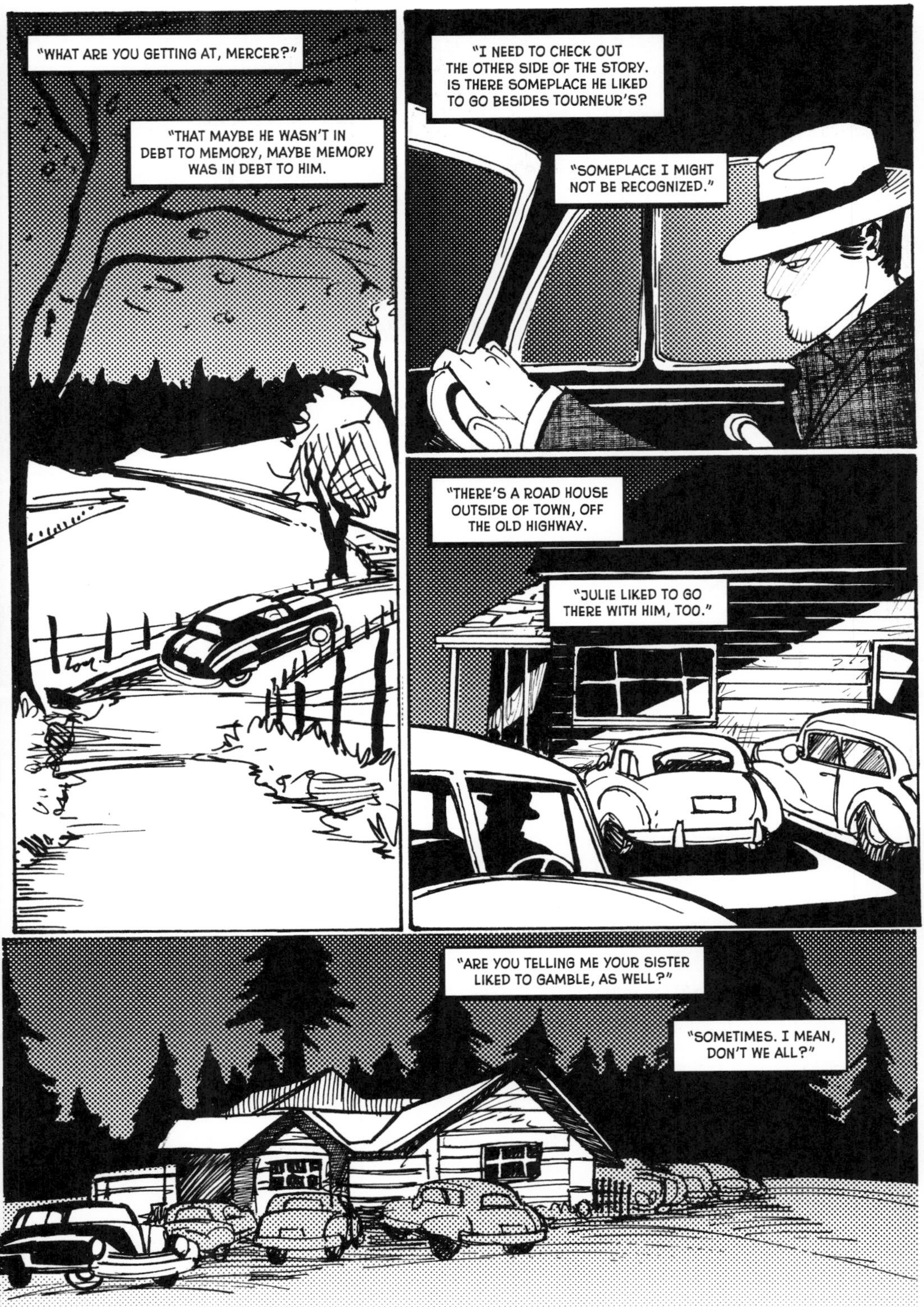
"WHAT ARE YOU GETTING AT, MERCER?"
"THAT MAYBE HE WASN'T IN DEBT TO MEMORY, MAYBE MEMORY WAS IN DEBT TO HIM.
"I NEED TO CHECK OUT THE OTHER SIDE OF THE STORY. IS THERE SOMEPLACE HE LIKED TO GO BESIDES TOURNEUR'S?
"SOMEPLACE I MIGHT NOT BE RECOGNIZED."
"THERE'S A ROAD HOUSE OUTSIDE OF TOWN, OFF THE OLD HIGHWAY.
"JULIE LIKED TO GO THERE WITH HIM, TOO."
"ARE YOU TELLING ME YOUR SISTER LIKED TO GAMBLE, AS WELL?"
"SOMETIMES. I MEAN, DON'T WE ALL?"

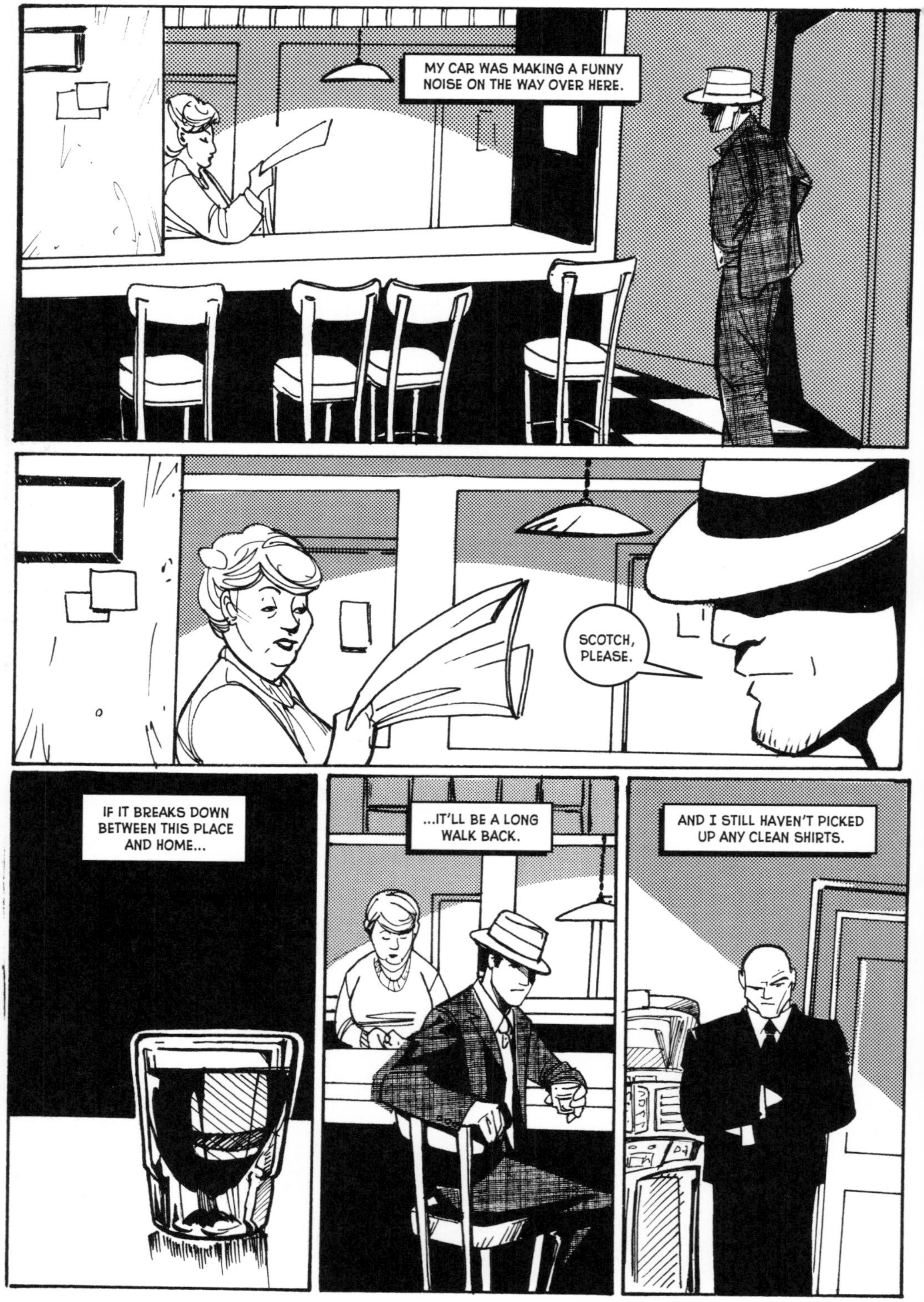
MY CAR WAS MAKING A FUNNY NOISE ON THE WAY OVER HERE.
SCOTCH, PLEASE.
IF IT BREAKS DOWN BETWEEN THIS PLACE AND HOME...
...IT'LL BE A LONG WALK BACK.
AND I STILL HAVEN'T PICKED UP ANY CLEAN SHIRTS.

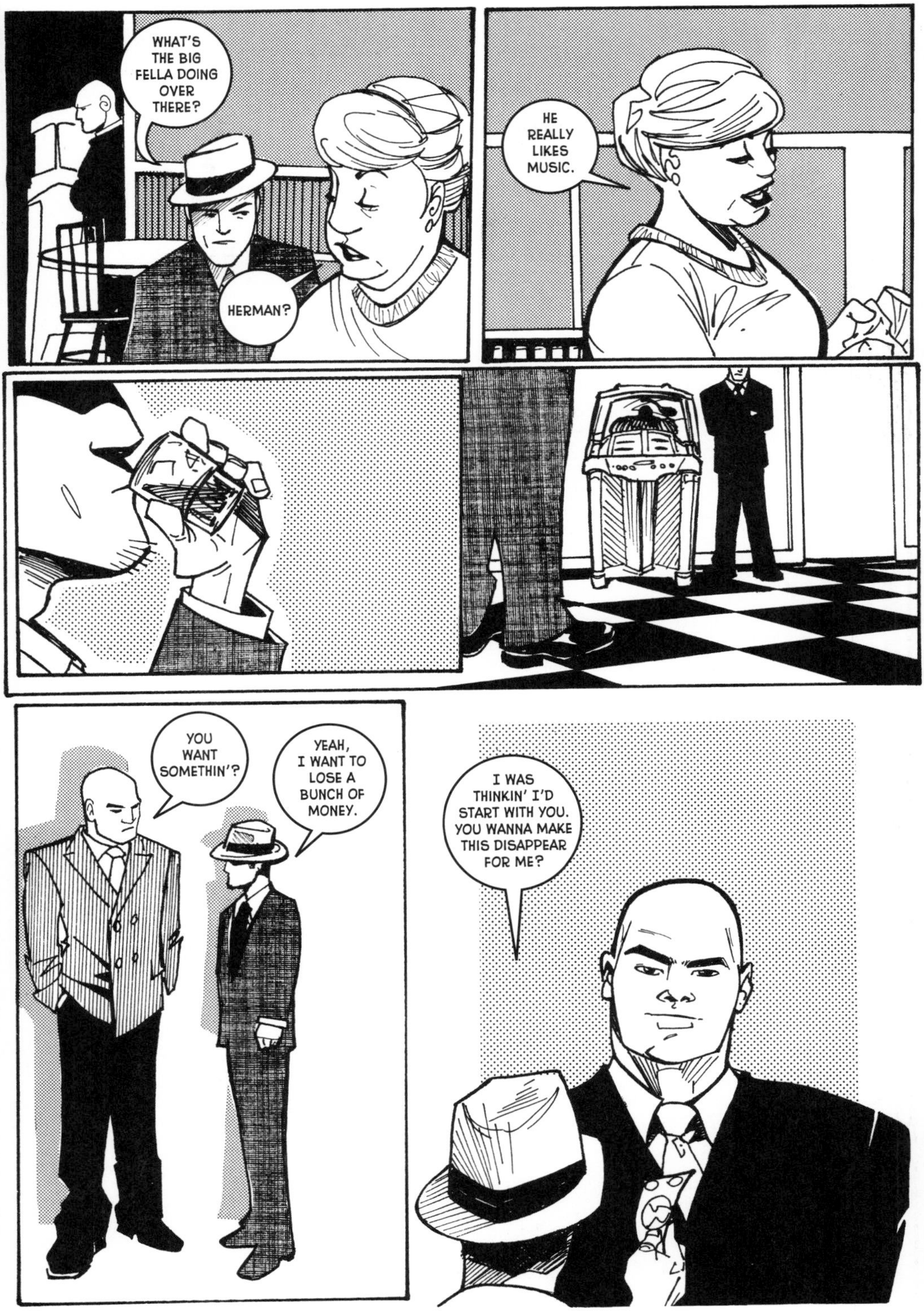
WHAT'S THE BIG FELLA DOING OVER THERE?
HERMAN?
HE REALLY LIKES MUSIC.
YOU WANT SOMETHIN'?
YEAH, I WANT TO LOSE A BUNCH OF MONEY.
I WAS THINKIN' I'D START WITH YOU. YOU WANNA MAKE THIS DISAPPEAR FOR ME?

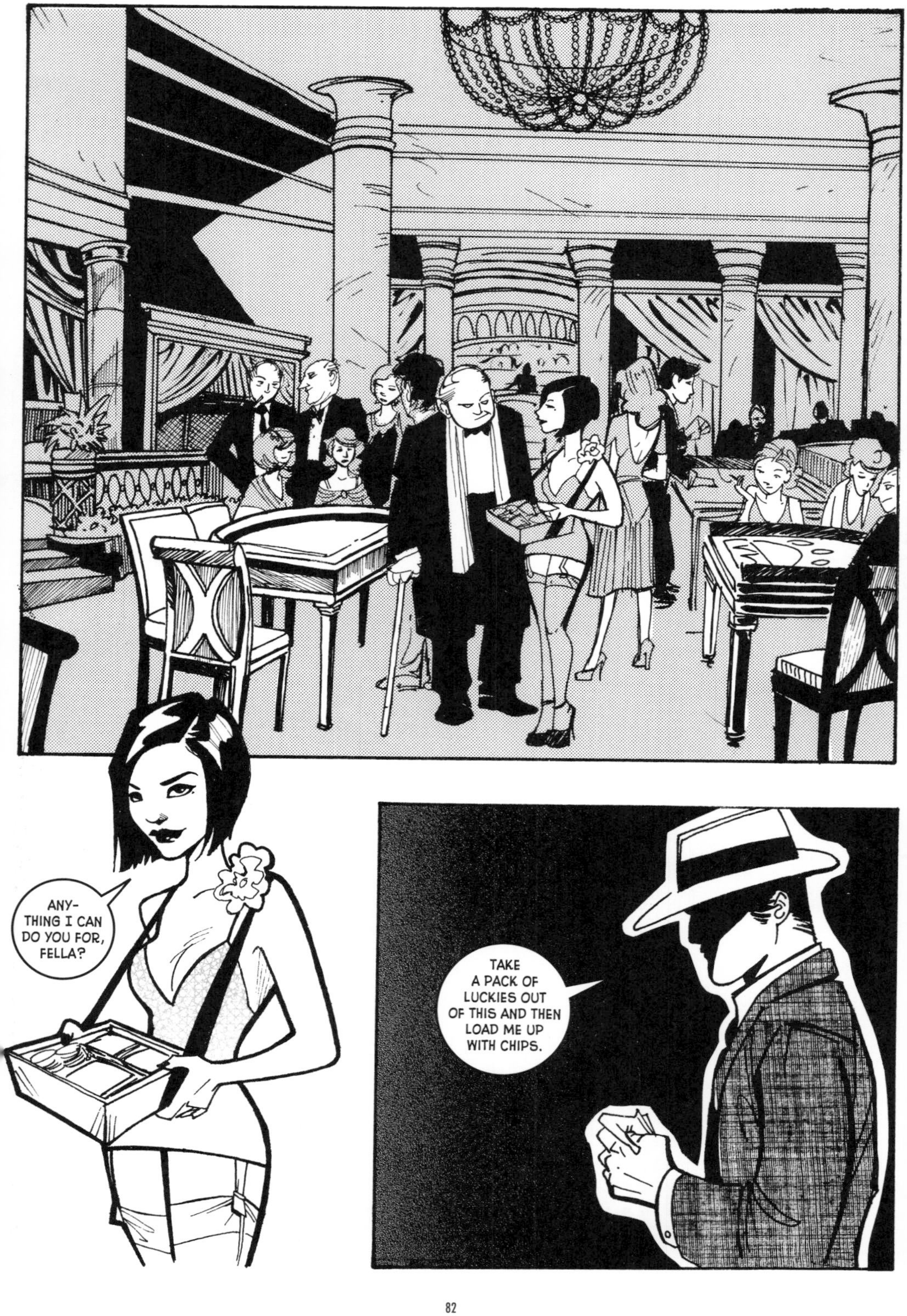
ANY-THING I CAN DO YOU FOR, FELLA?
TAKE A PACK OF LUCKIES OUT OF THIS AND THEN LOAD ME UP WITH CHIPS.

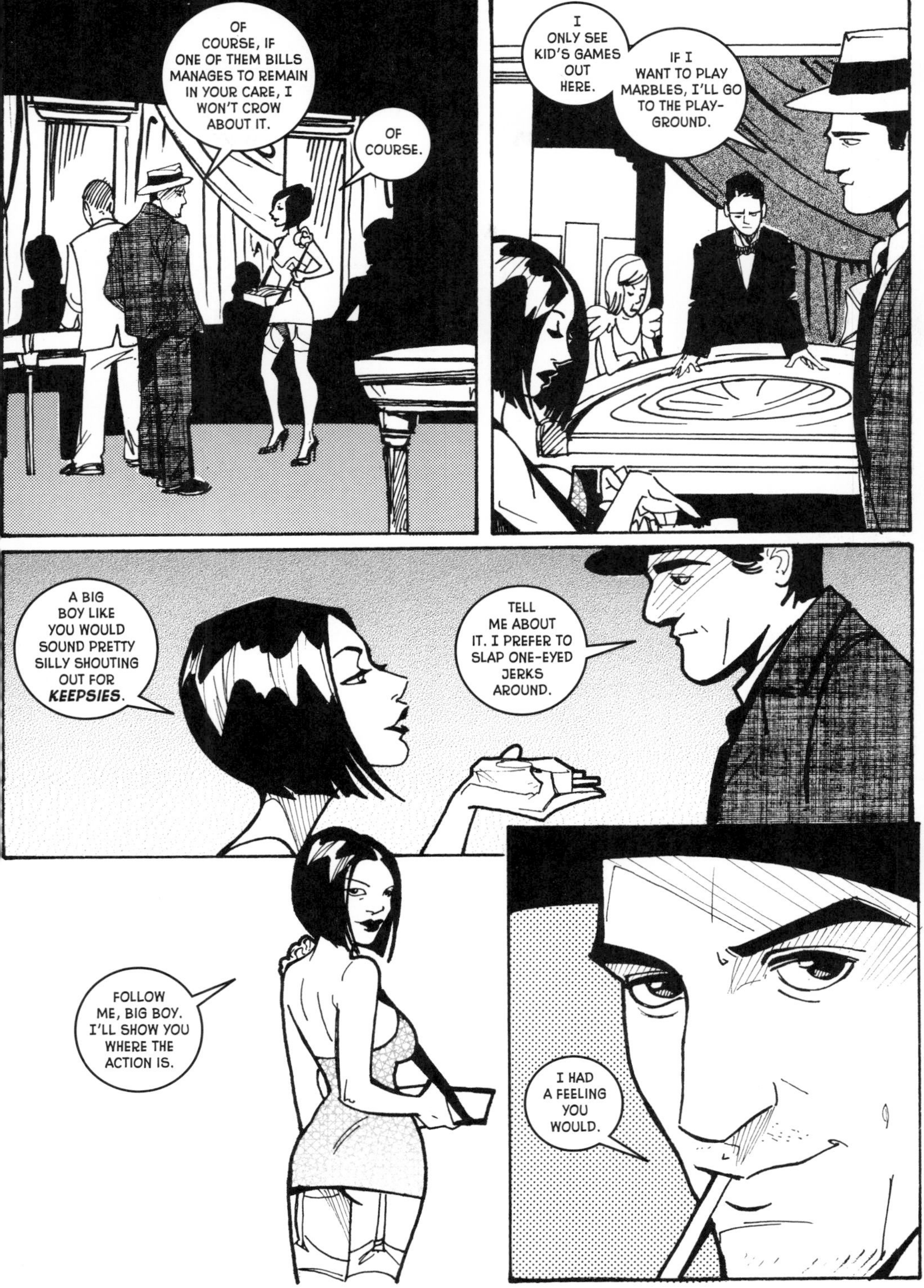
OF COURSE, IF ONE OF THEM BILLS MANAGES TO REMAIN IN YOUR CARE, I WON'T CROW ABOUT IT.
OF COURSE.
I ONLY SEE KID'S GAMES OUT HERE.
IF I WANT TO PLAY MARBLES, I'LL GO TO THE PLAY-GROUND.
A BIG BOY LIKE YOU WOULD SOUND PRETTY SILLY SHOUTING OUT FOR **KEEPSIES**.
TELL ME ABOUT IT. I PREFER TO SLAP ONE-EYED JERKS AROUND.
FOLLOW ME, BIG BOY. I'LL SHOW YOU WHERE THE ACTION IS.
I HAD A FEELING YOU WOULD.

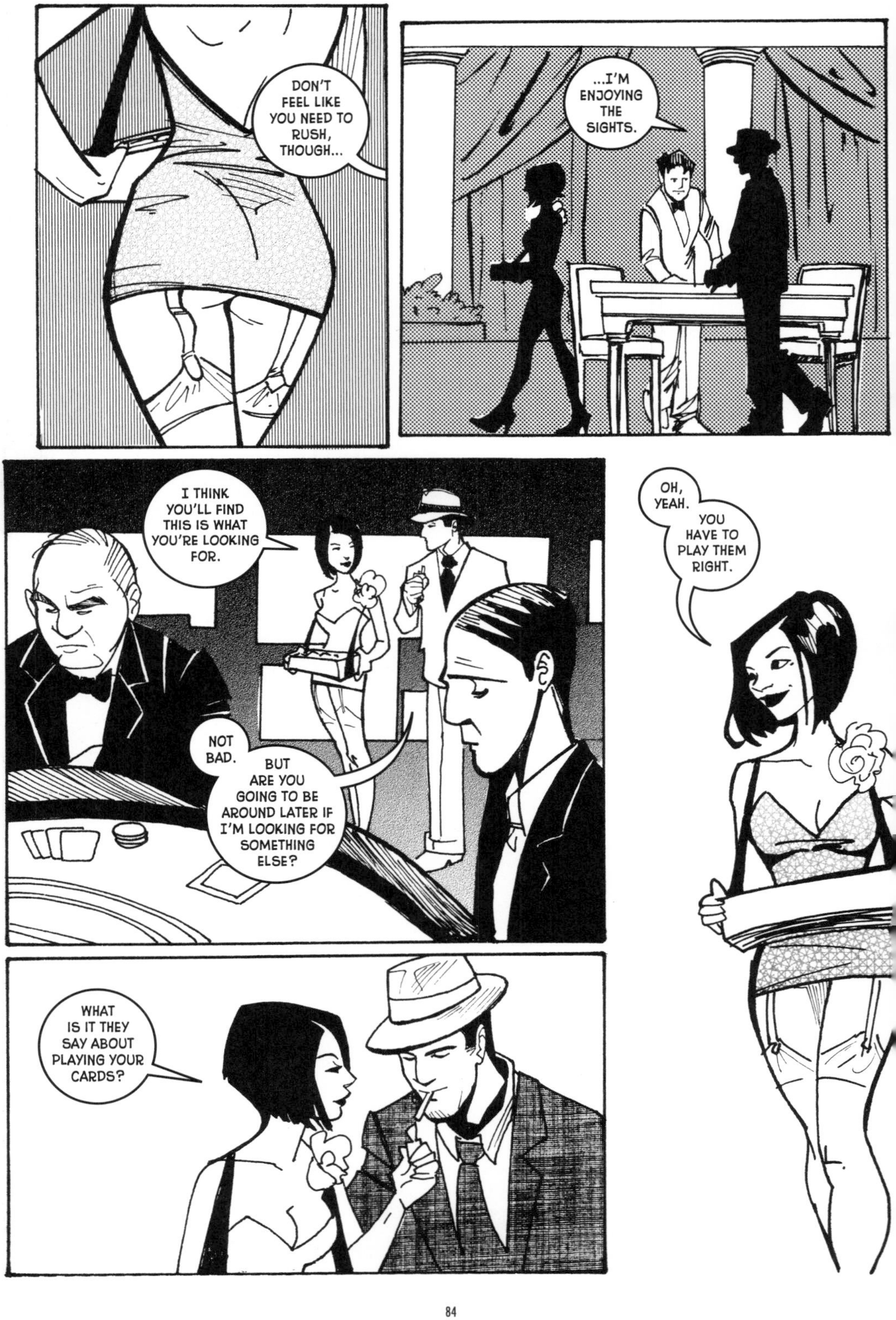
DON'T FEEL LIKE YOU NEED TO RUSH, THOUGH...
...I'M ENJOYING THE SIGHTS.
I THINK YOU'LL FIND THIS IS WHAT YOU'RE LOOKING FOR.
NOT BAD.
BUT ARE YOU GOING TO BE AROUND LATER IF I'M LOOKING FOR SOMETHING ELSE?
WHAT IS IT THEY SAY ABOUT PLAYING YOUR CARDS?
OH, YEAH.
YOU HAVE TO PLAY THEM RIGHT.

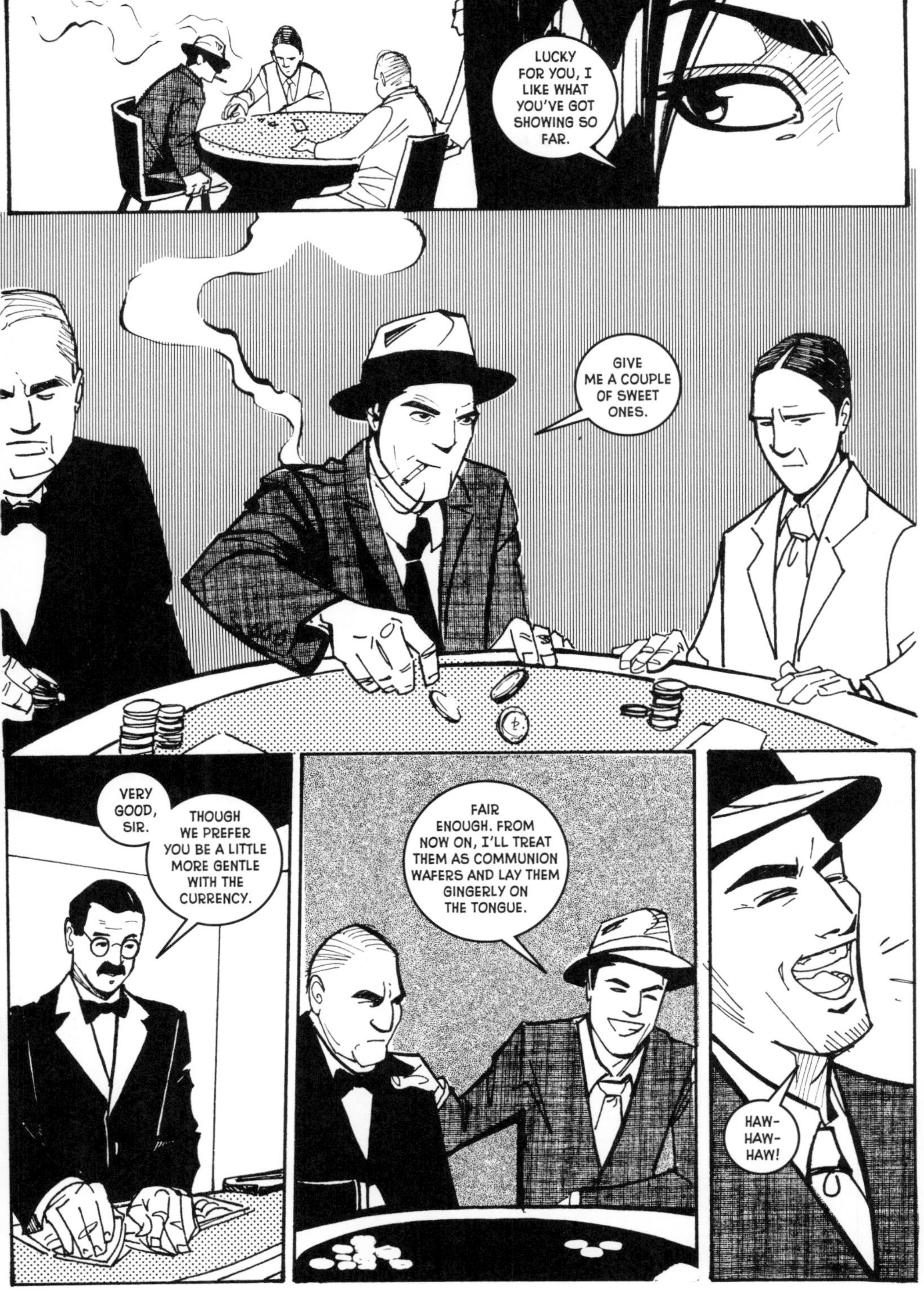
LUCKY FOR YOU, I LIKE WHAT YOU'VE GOT SHOWING SO FAR.
GIVE ME A COUPLE OF SWEET ONES.
VERY GOOD, SIR.
THOUGH WE PREFER YOU BE A LITTLE MORE GENTLE WITH THE CURRENCY.
FAIR ENOUGH. FROM NOW ON, I'LL TREAT THEM AS COMMUNION WAFERS AND LAY THEM GINGERLY ON THE TONGUE.
HAW-HAW-HAW!

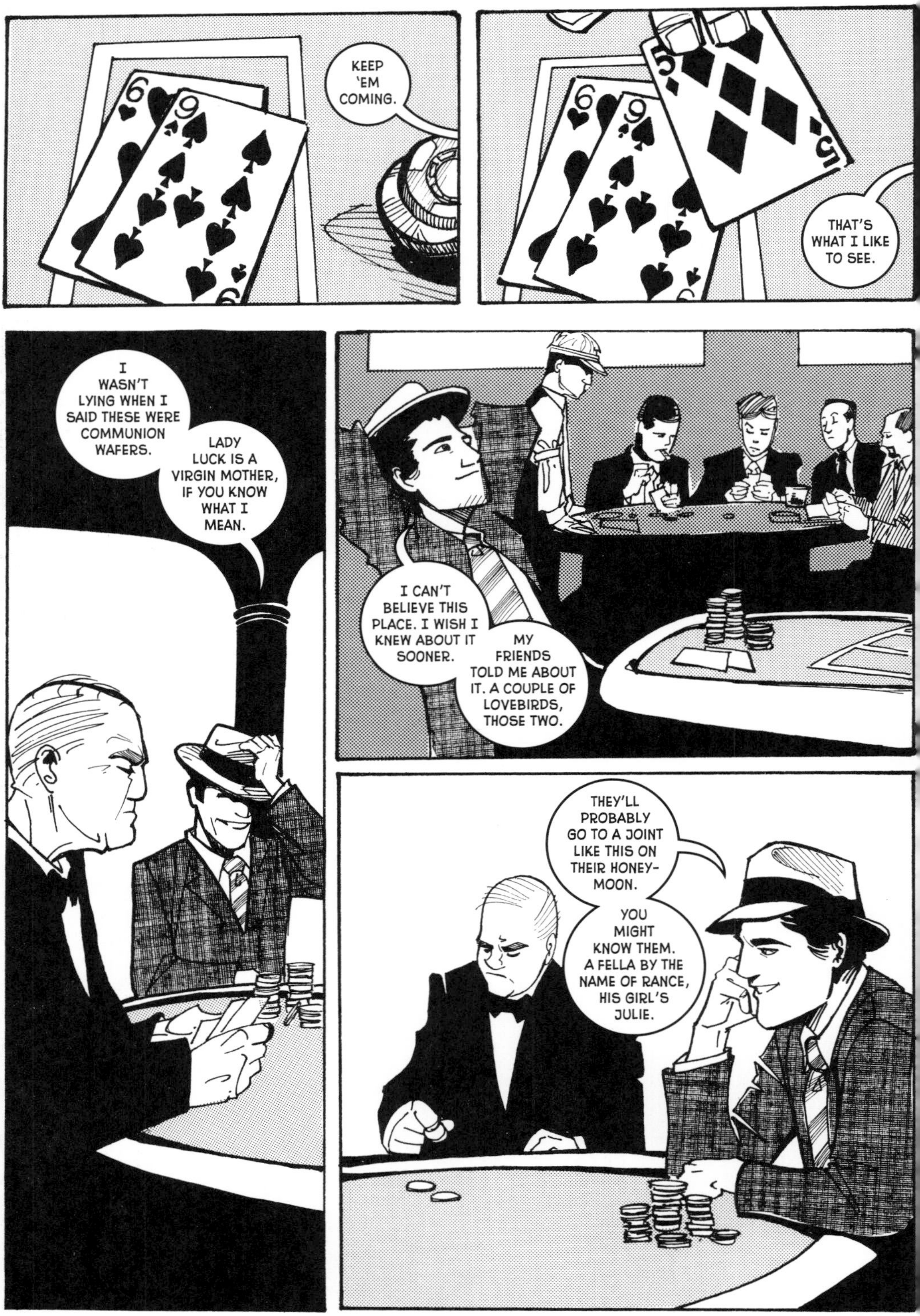
KEEP 'EM COMING.
THAT'S WHAT I LIKE TO SEE.
I WASN'T LYING WHEN I SAID THESE WERE COMMUNION WAFERS.
LADY LUCK IS A VIRGIN MOTHER, IF YOU KNOW WHAT I MEAN.
I CAN'T BELIEVE THIS PLACE. I WISH I KNEW ABOUT IT SOONER.
MY FRIENDS TOLD ME ABOUT IT. A COUPLE OF LOVEBIRDS, THOSE TWO.
THEY'LL PROBABLY GO TO A JOINT LIKE THIS ON THEIR HONEY-MOON.
YOU MIGHT KNOW THEM. A FELLA BY THE NAME OF RANCE, HIS GIRL'S JULIE.

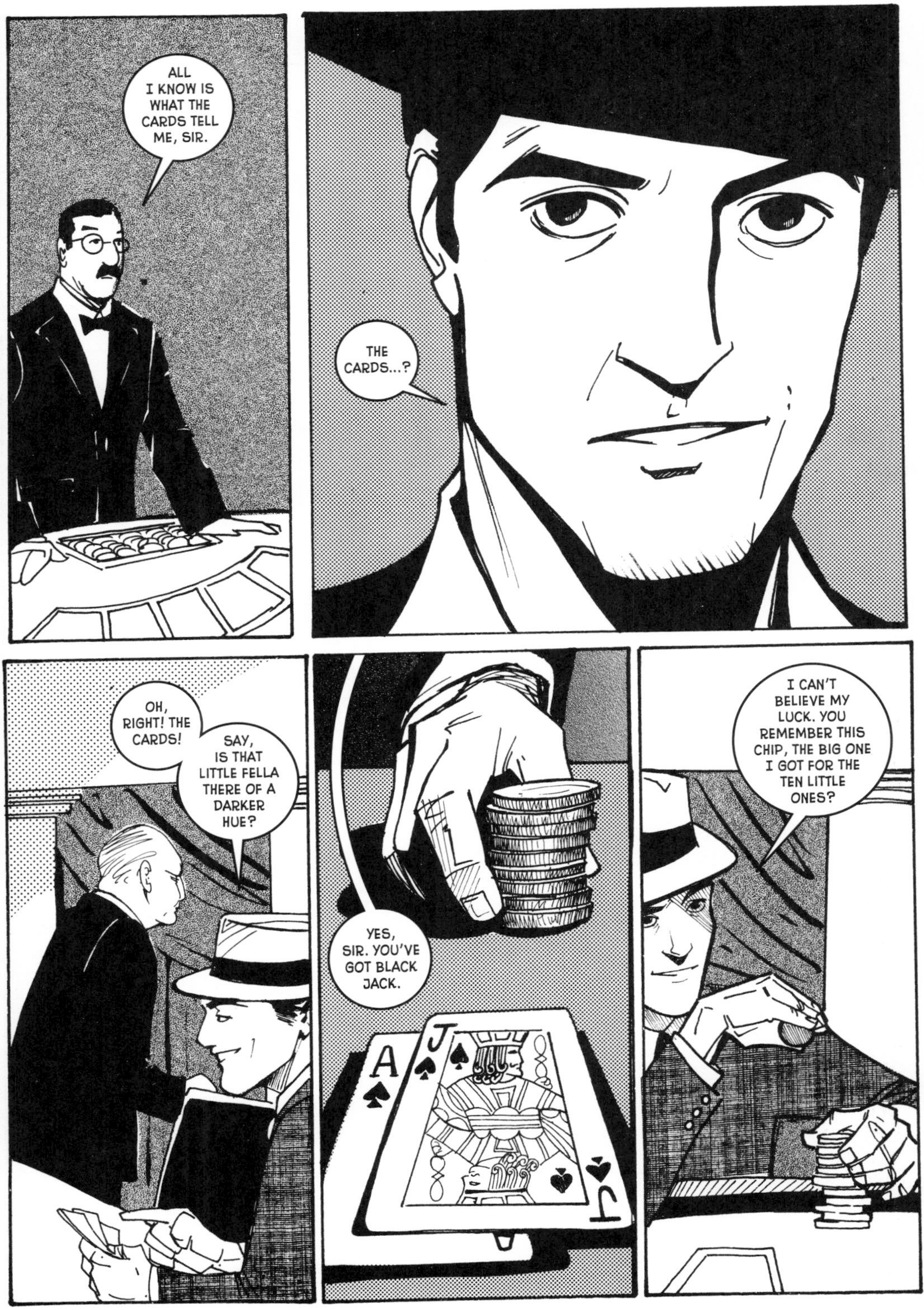
ALL I KNOW IS WHAT THE CARDS TELL ME, SIR.
THE CARDS...?
OH, RIGHT! THE CARDS!
SAY, IS THAT LITTLE FELLA THERE OF A DARKER HUE?
YES, SIR. YOU'VE GOT BLACK JACK.
I CAN'T BELIEVE MY LUCK. YOU REMEMBER THIS CHIP, THE BIG ONE I GOT FOR THE TEN LITTLE ONES?

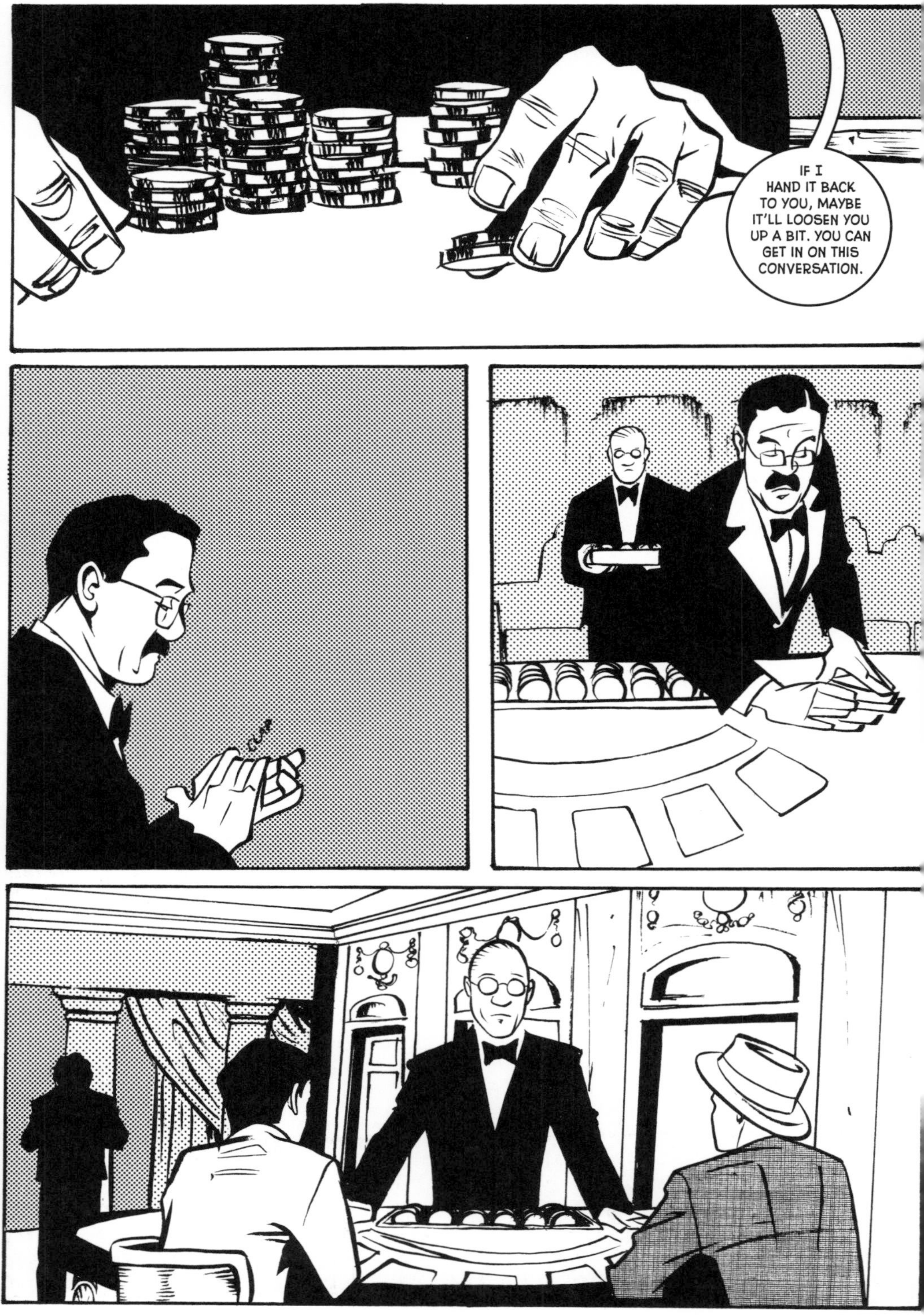
IF I HAND IT BACK TO YOU, MAYBE IT'LL LOOSEN YOU UP A BIT. YOU CAN GET IN ON THIS CONVERSATION.
CLAP

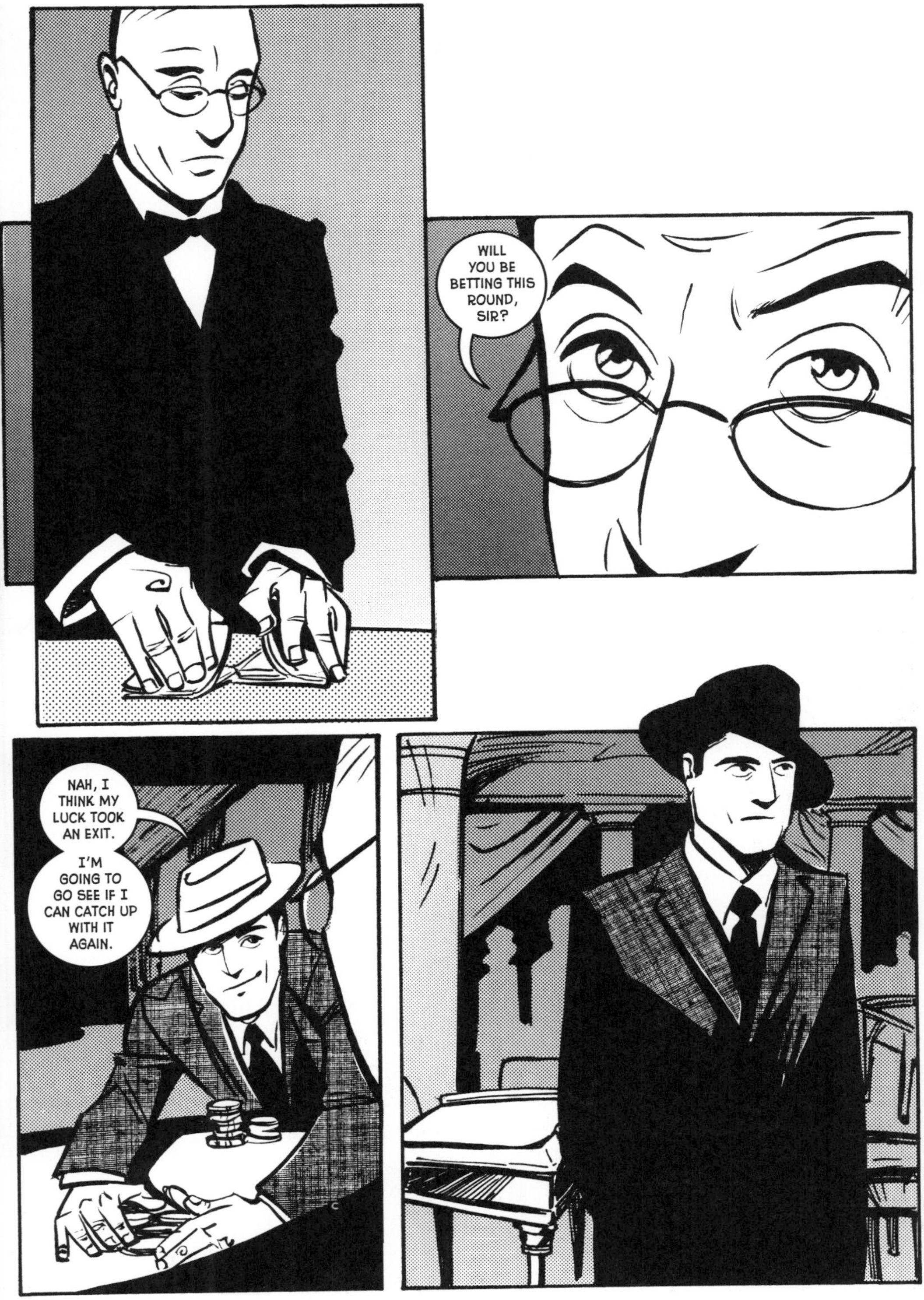
WILL YOU BE BETTING THIS ROUND, SIR?
NAH, I THINK MY LUCK TOOK AN EXIT.
I'M GOING TO GO SEE IF I CAN CATCH UP WITH IT AGAIN.

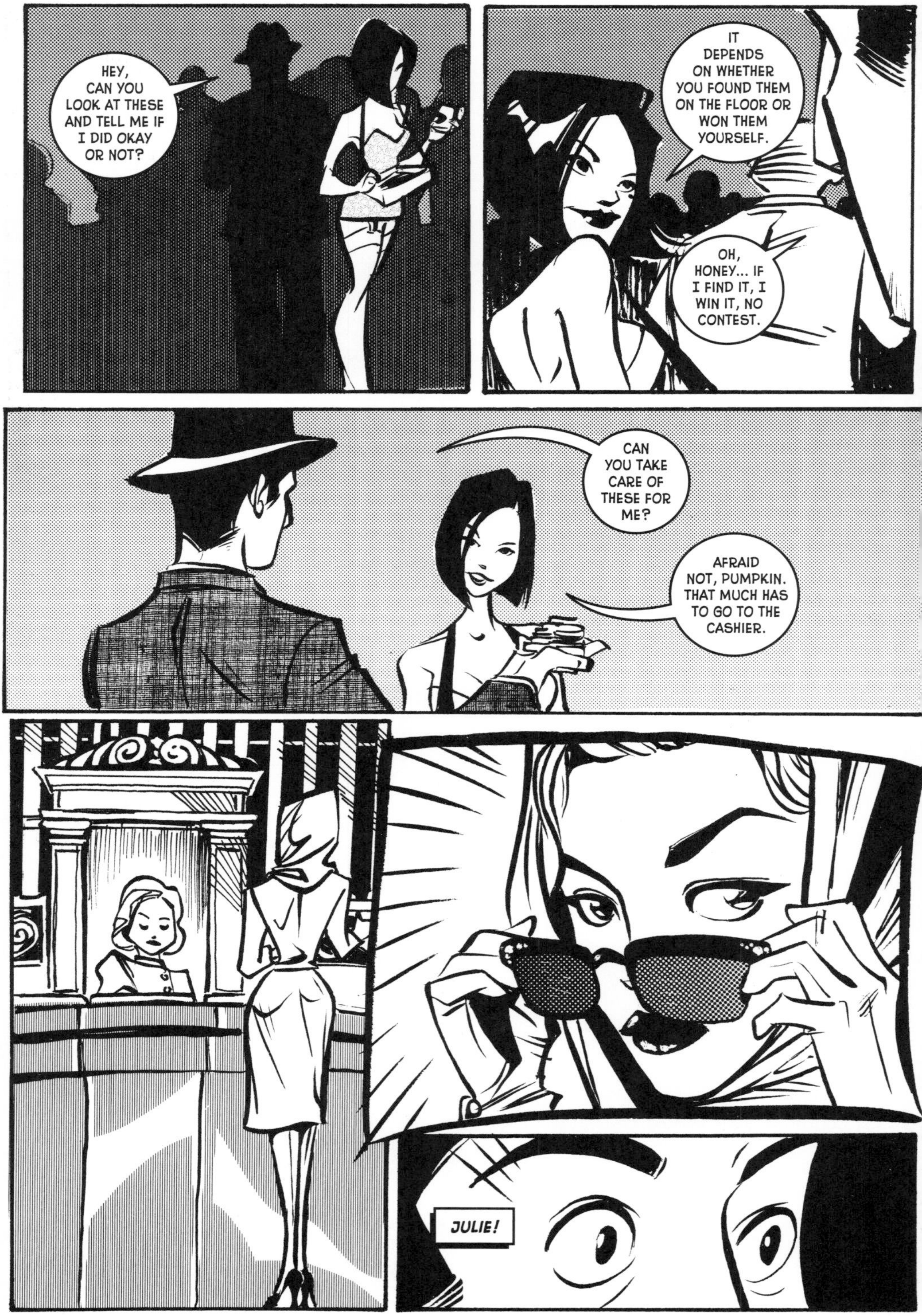
HEY, CAN YOU LOOK AT THESE AND TELL ME IF I DID OKAY OR NOT?
IT DEPENDS ON WHETHER YOU FOUND THEM ON THE FLOOR OR WON THEM YOURSELF.
OH, HONEY... IF I FIND IT, I WIN IT, NO CONTEST.
CAN YOU TAKE CARE OF THESE FOR ME?
AFRAID NOT, PUMPKIN. THAT MUCH HAS TO GO TO THE CASHIER.
JULIE!

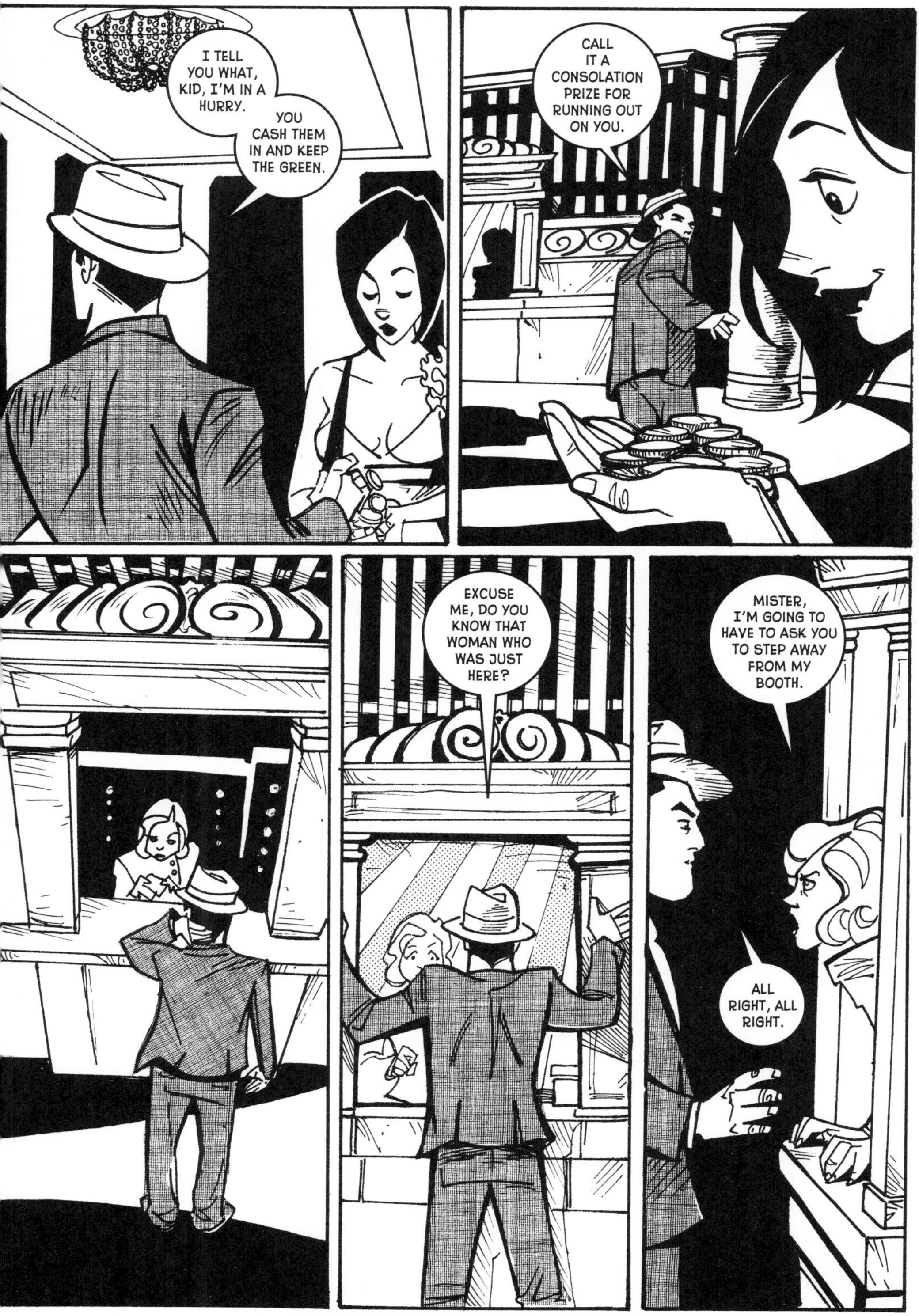
I TELL YOU WHAT, KID, I'M IN A HURRY.
YOU CASH THEM IN AND KEEP THE GREEN.
CALL IT A CONSOLATION PRIZE FOR RUNNING OUT ON YOU.
EXCUSE ME, DO YOU KNOW THAT WOMAN WHO WAS JUST HERE?
MISTER, I'M GOING TO HAVE TO ASK YOU TO STEP AWAY FROM MY BOOTH.
ALL RIGHT, ALL RIGHT.

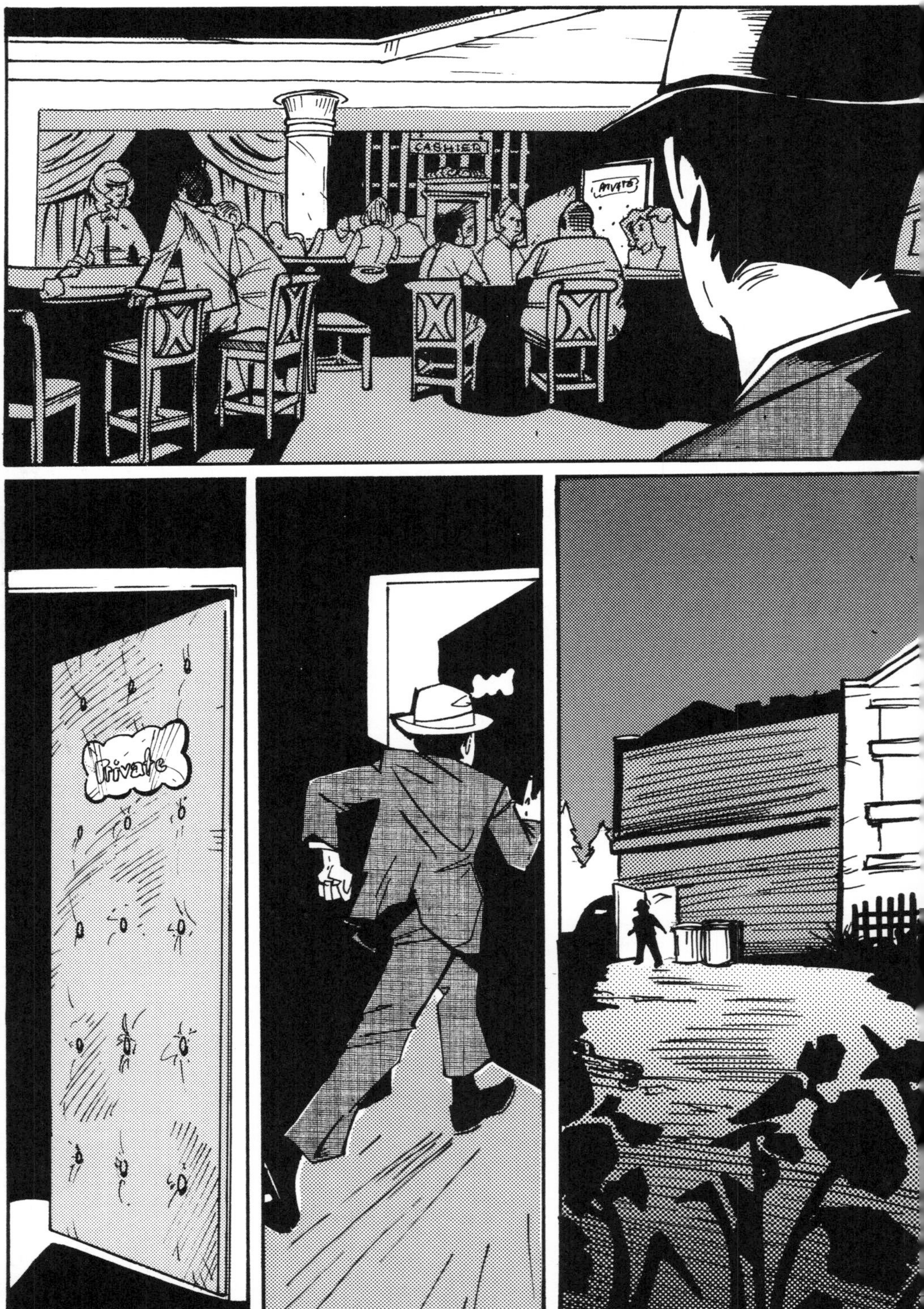
CASHIER
Private
Private

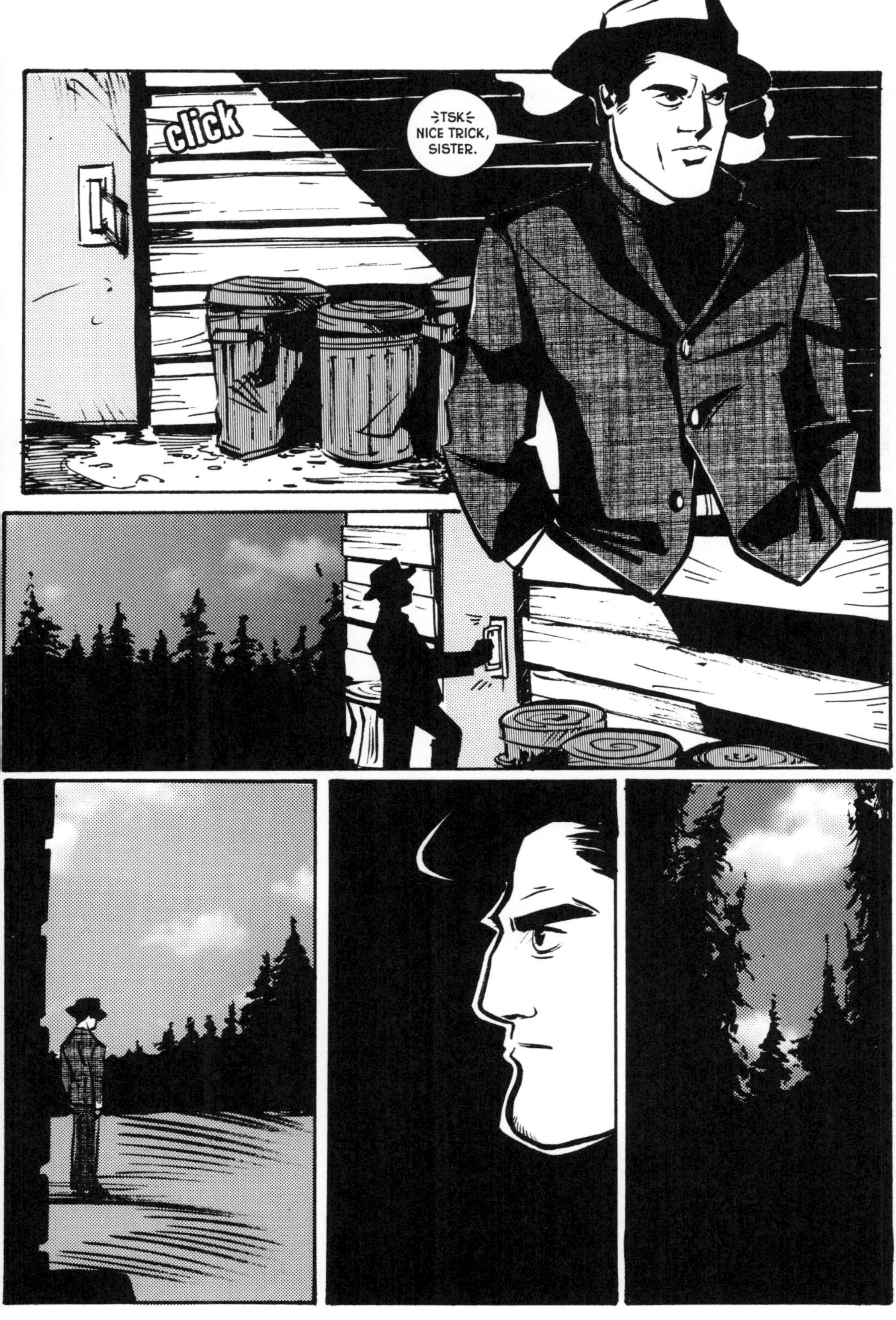
click
TSK
NICE TRICK,
SISTER.

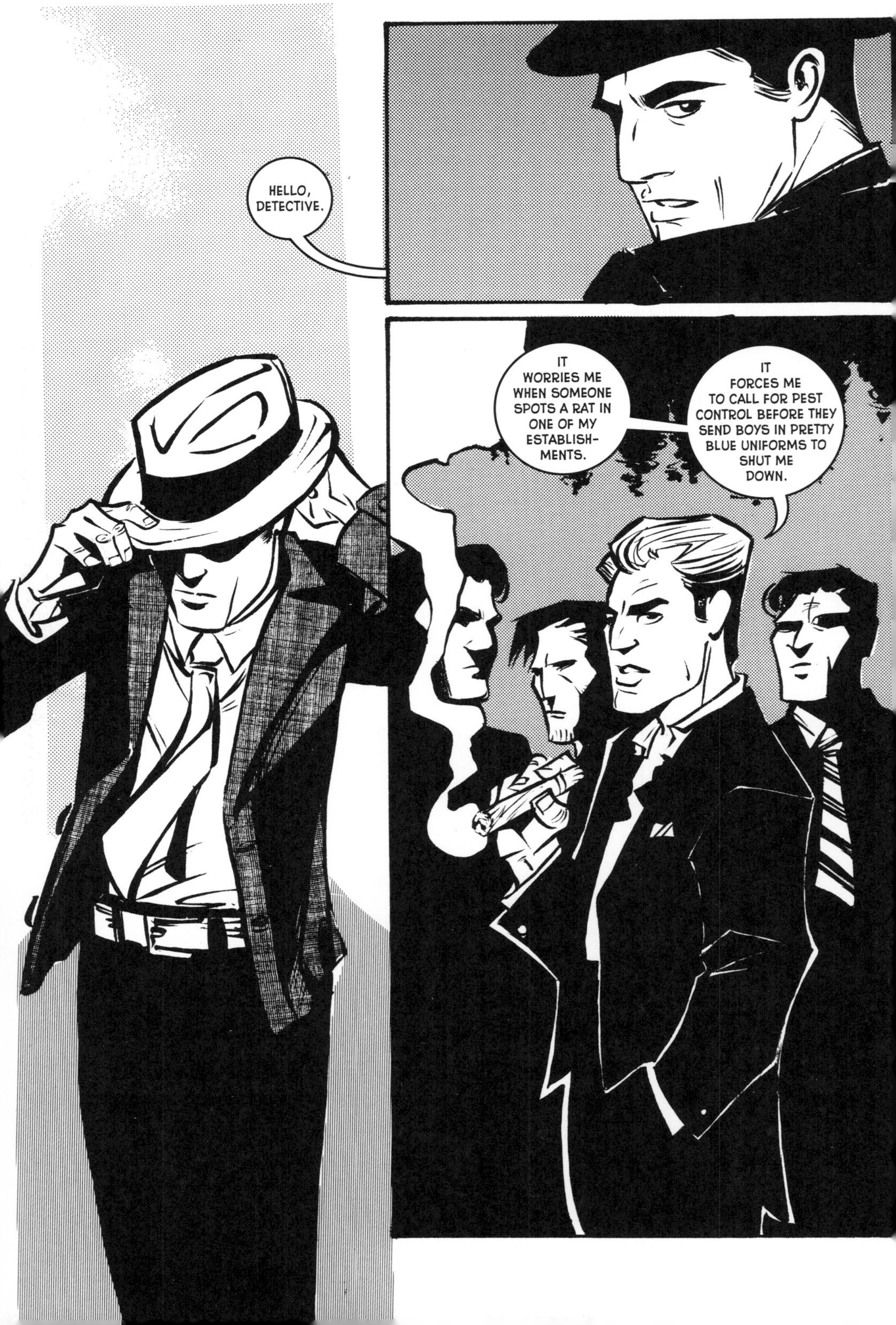
HELLO, DETECTIVE.
IT WORRIES ME WHEN SOMEONE SPOTS A RAT IN ONE OF MY ESTABLISH-MENTS.
IT FORCES ME TO CALL FOR PEST CONTROL BEFORE THEY SEND BOYS IN PRETTY BLUE UNIFORMS TO SHUT ME DOWN.

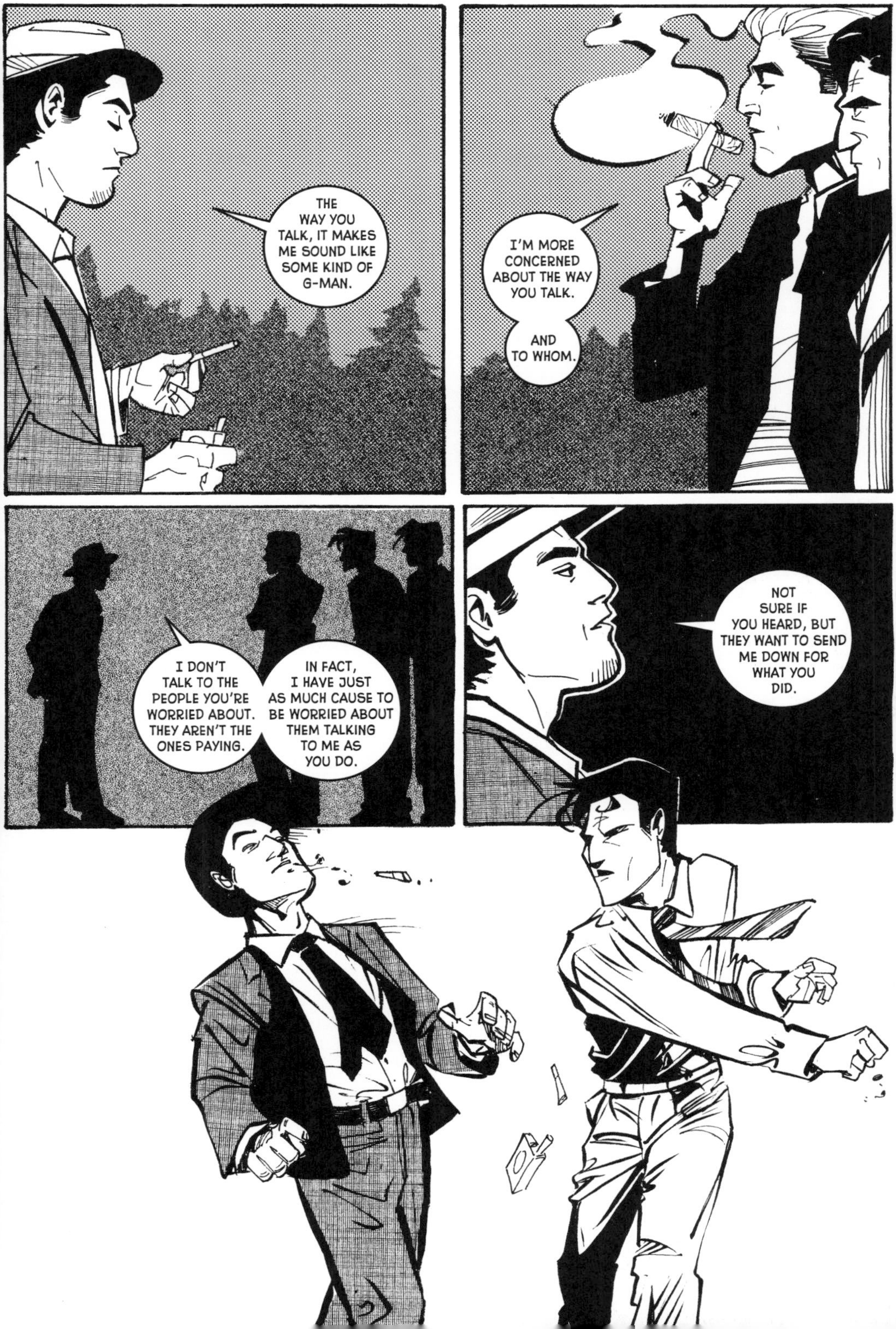
THE WAY YOU TALK, IT MAKES ME SOUND LIKE SOME KIND OF G-MAN.
I'M MORE CONCERNED ABOUT THE WAY YOU TALK.
AND TO WHOM.
I DON'T TALK TO THE PEOPLE YOU'RE WORRIED ABOUT. THEY AREN'T THE ONES PAYING.
IN FACT, I HAVE JUST AS MUCH CAUSE TO BE WORRIED ABOUT THEM TALKING TO ME AS YOU DO.
NOT SURE IF YOU HEARD, BUT THEY WANT TO SEND ME DOWN FOR WHAT YOU DID.

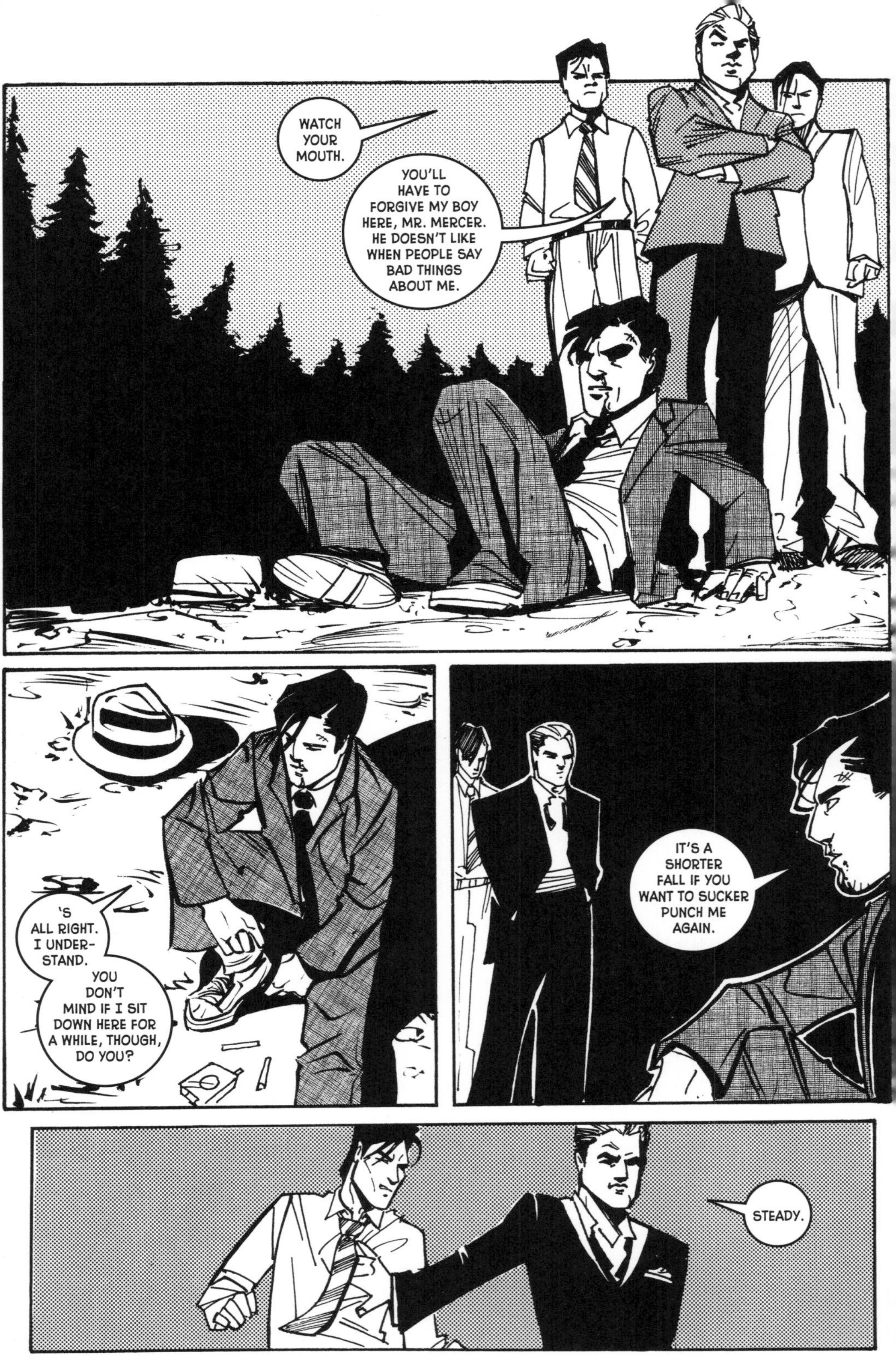
WATCH YOUR MOUTH.
YOU'LL HAVE TO FORGIVE MY BOY HERE, MR. MERCER. HE DOESN'T LIKE WHEN PEOPLE SAY BAD THINGS ABOUT ME.
'S ALL RIGHT. I UNDER-STAND.
YOU DON'T MIND IF I SIT DOWN HERE FOR A WHILE, THOUGH, DO YOU?
IT'S A SHORTER FALL IF YOU WANT TO SUCKER PUNCH ME AGAIN.
STEADY.

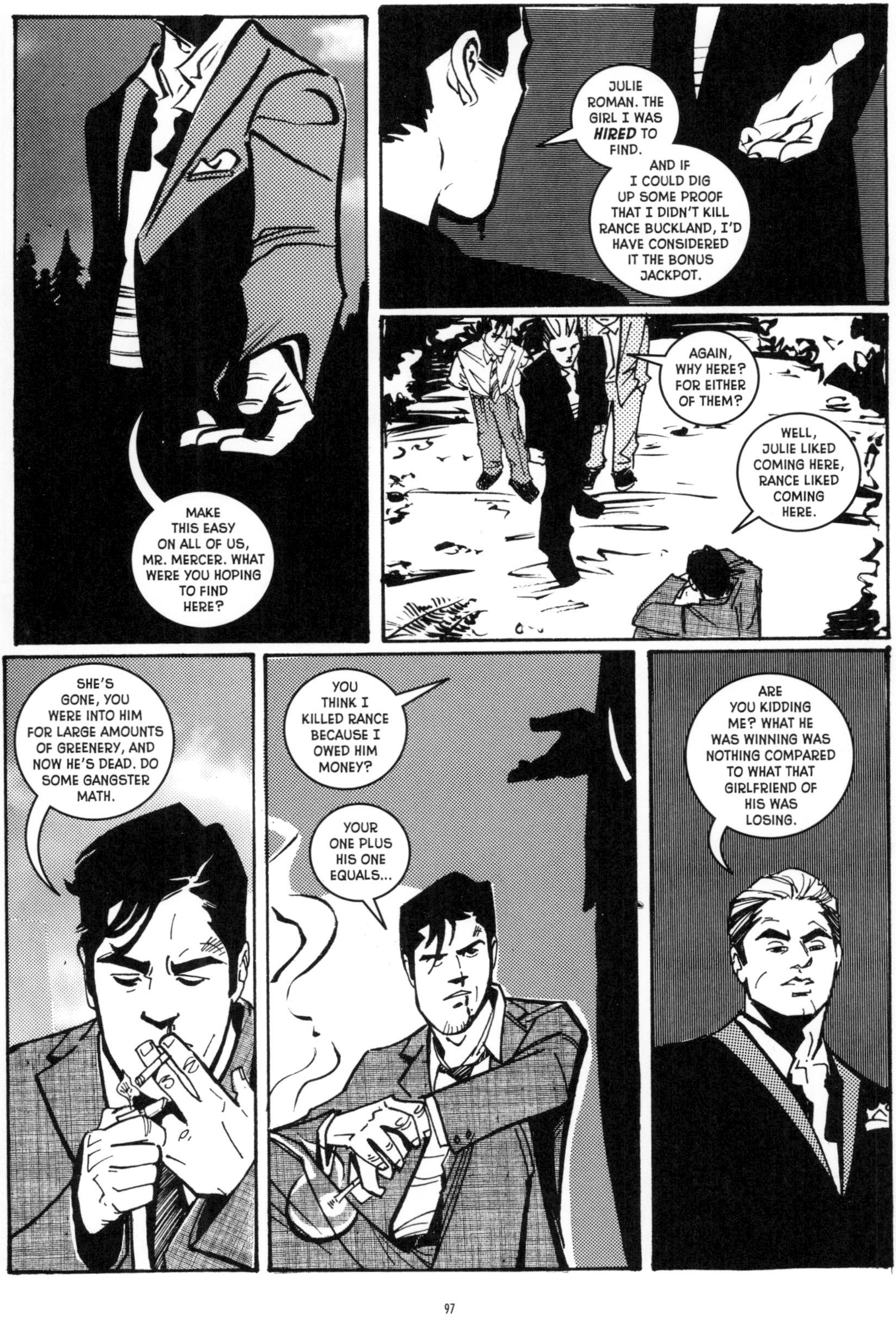

MAKE THIS EASY ON ALL OF US, MR. MERCER. WHAT WERE YOU HOPING TO FIND HERE?
JULIE ROMAN. THE GIRL I WAS HIRED TO FIND.
AND IF I COULD DIG UP SOME PROOF THAT I DIDN'T KILL RANCE BUCKLAND, I'D HAVE CONSIDERED IT THE BONUS JACKPOT.
AGAIN, WHY HERE? FOR EITHER OF THEM?
WELL, JULIE LIKED COMING HERE, RANCE LIKED COMING HERE.
SHE'S GONE, YOU WERE INTO HIM FOR LARGE AMOUNTS OF GREENERY, AND NOW HE'S DEAD. DO SOME GANGSTER MATH.
YOU THINK I KILLED RANCE BECAUSE I OWED HIM MONEY?
YOUR ONE PLUS HIS ONE EQUALS...
ARE YOU KIDDING ME? WHAT HE WAS WINNING WAS NOTHING COMPARED TO WHAT THAT GIRLFRIEND OF HIS WAS LOSING.

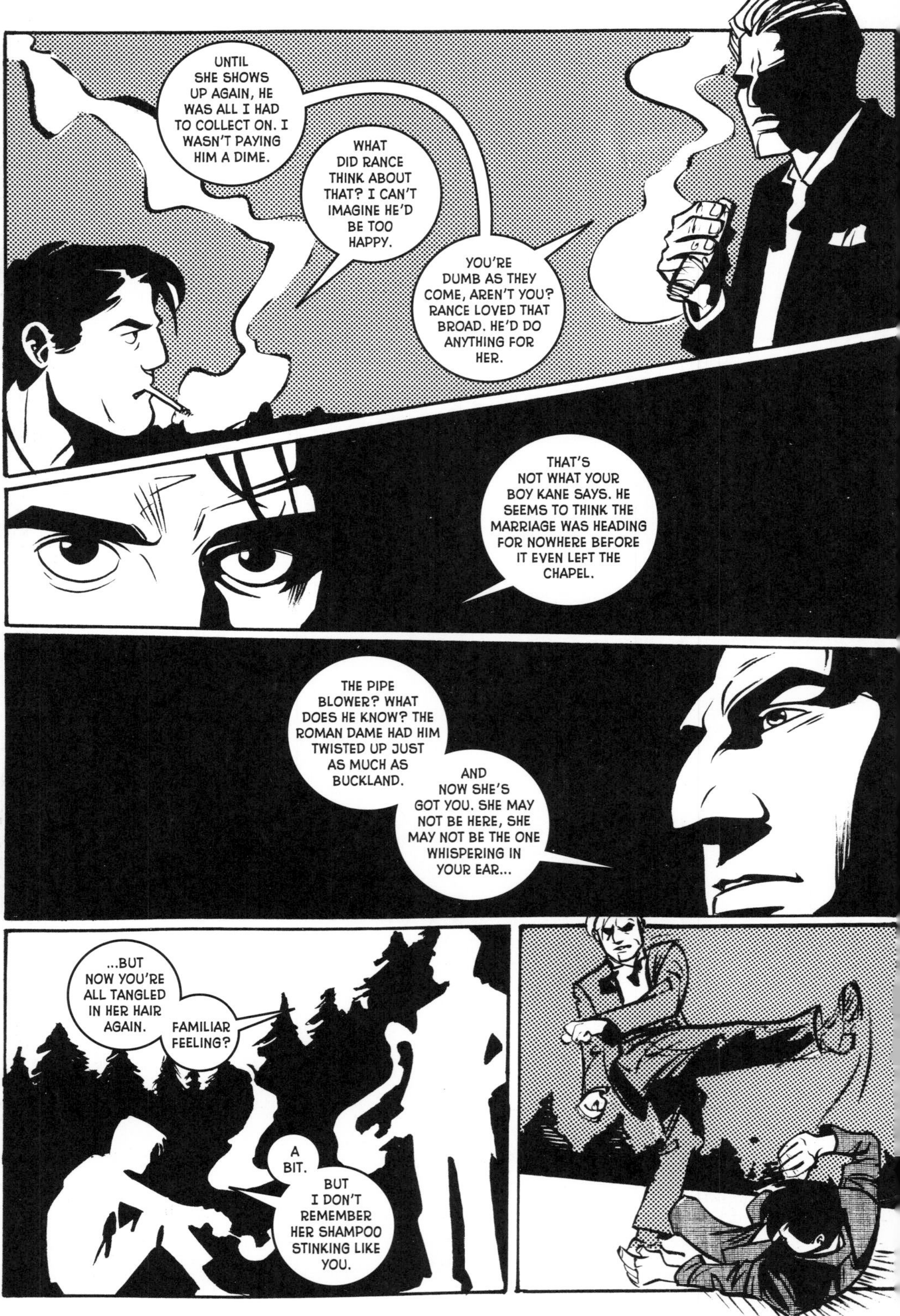
UNTIL SHE SHOWS UP AGAIN, HE WAS ALL I HAD TO COLLECT ON. I WASN'T PAYING HIM A DIME.
WHAT DID RANCE THINK ABOUT THAT? I CAN'T IMAGINE HE'D BE TOO HAPPY.
YOU'RE DUMB AS THEY COME, AREN'T YOU? RANCE LOVED THAT BROAD. HE'D DO ANYTHING FOR HER.
THAT'S NOT WHAT YOUR BOY KANE SAYS. HE SEEMS TO THINK THE MARRIAGE WAS HEADING FOR NOWHERE BEFORE IT EVEN LEFT THE CHAPEL.
THE PIPE BLOWER? WHAT DOES HE KNOW? THE ROMAN DAME HAD HIM TWISTED UP JUST AS MUCH AS BUCKLAND.
AND NOW SHE'S GOT YOU. SHE MAY NOT BE HERE, SHE MAY NOT BE THE ONE WHISPERING IN YOUR EAR...
...BUT NOW YOU'RE ALL TANGLED IN HER HAIR AGAIN.
FAMILIAR FEELING?
A BIT.
BUT I DON'T REMEMBER HER SHAMPOO STINKING LIKE YOU.

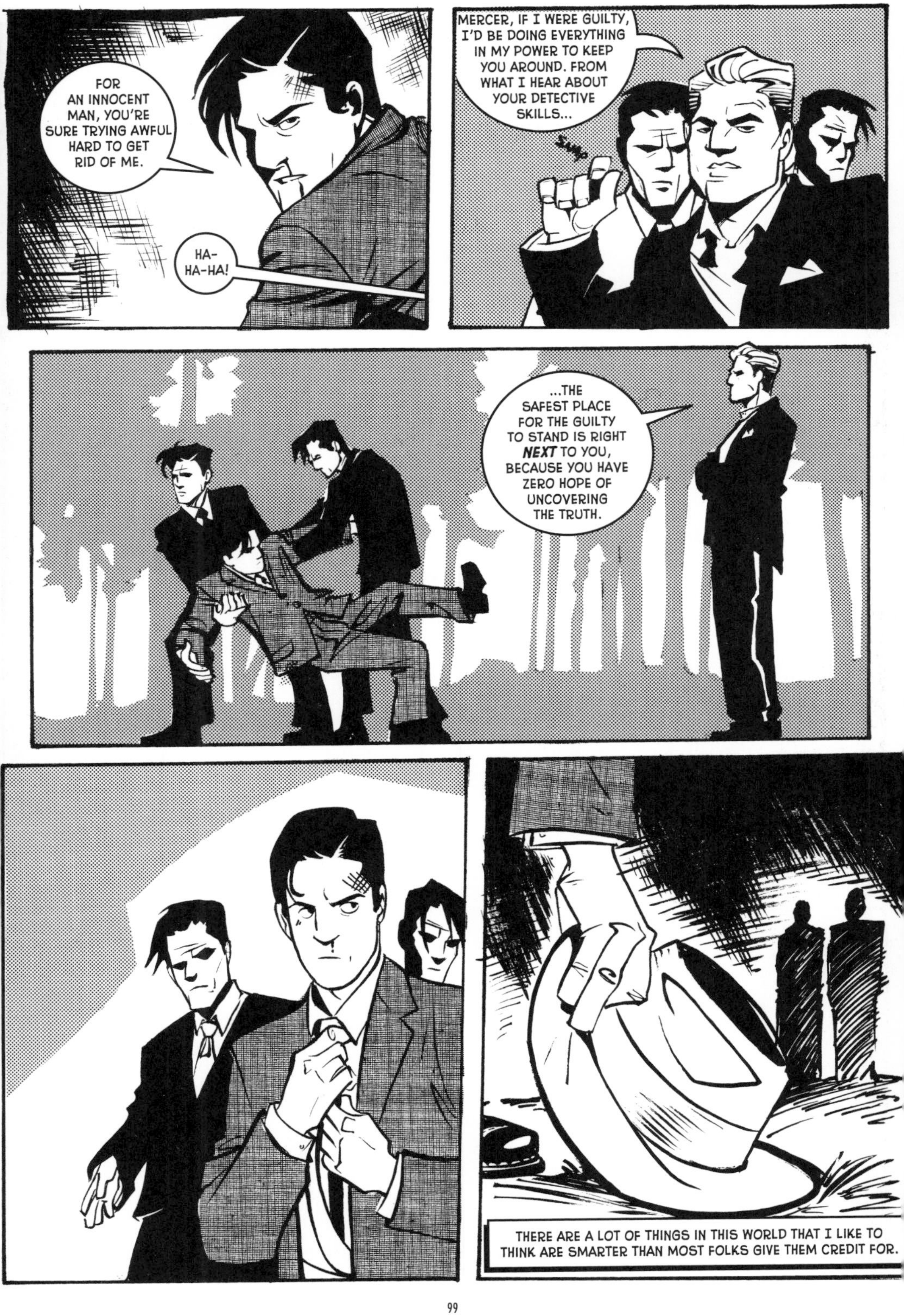
FOR AN INNOCENT MAN, YOU'RE SURE TRYING AWFUL HARD TO GET RID OF ME.
HA-HA-HA!
MERCER, IF I WERE GUILTY, I'D BE DOING EVERYTHING IN MY POWER TO KEEP YOU AROUND. FROM WHAT I HEAR ABOUT YOUR DETECTIVE SKILLS...
...THE SAFEST PLACE FOR THE GUILTY TO STAND IS RIGHT *NEXT* TO YOU, BECAUSE YOU HAVE ZERO HOPE OF UNCOVERING THE TRUTH.
THERE ARE A LOT OF THINGS IN THIS WORLD THAT I LIKE TO THINK ARE SMARTER THAN MOST FOLKS GIVE THEM CREDIT FOR.

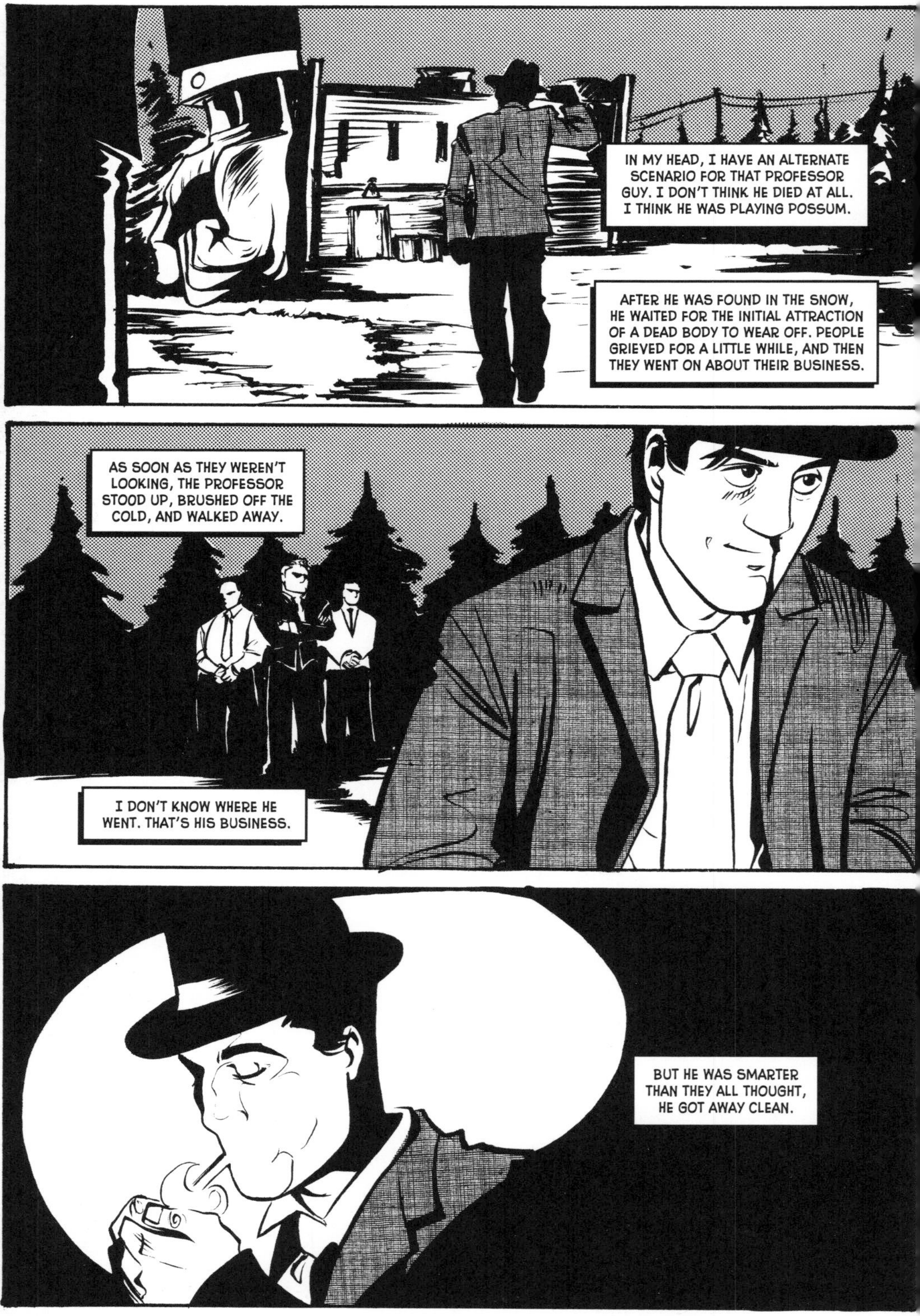
IN MY HEAD, I HAVE AN ALTERNATE SCENARIO FOR THAT PROFESSOR GUY. I DON'T THINK HE DIED AT ALL. I THINK HE WAS PLAYING POSSUM.
AFTER HE WAS FOUND IN THE SNOW, HE WAITED FOR THE INITIAL ATTRACTION OF A DEAD BODY TO WEAR OFF. PEOPLE GRIEVED FOR A LITTLE WHILE, AND THEN THEY WENT ON ABOUT THEIR BUSINESS.
AS SOON AS THEY WEREN'T LOOKING, THE PROFESSOR STOOD UP, BRUSHED OFF THE COLD, AND WALKED AWAY.
I DON'T KNOW WHERE HE WENT. THAT'S HIS BUSINESS.
BUT HE WAS SMARTER THAN THEY ALL THOUGHT, HE GOT AWAY CLEAN.

CHAPTER 6

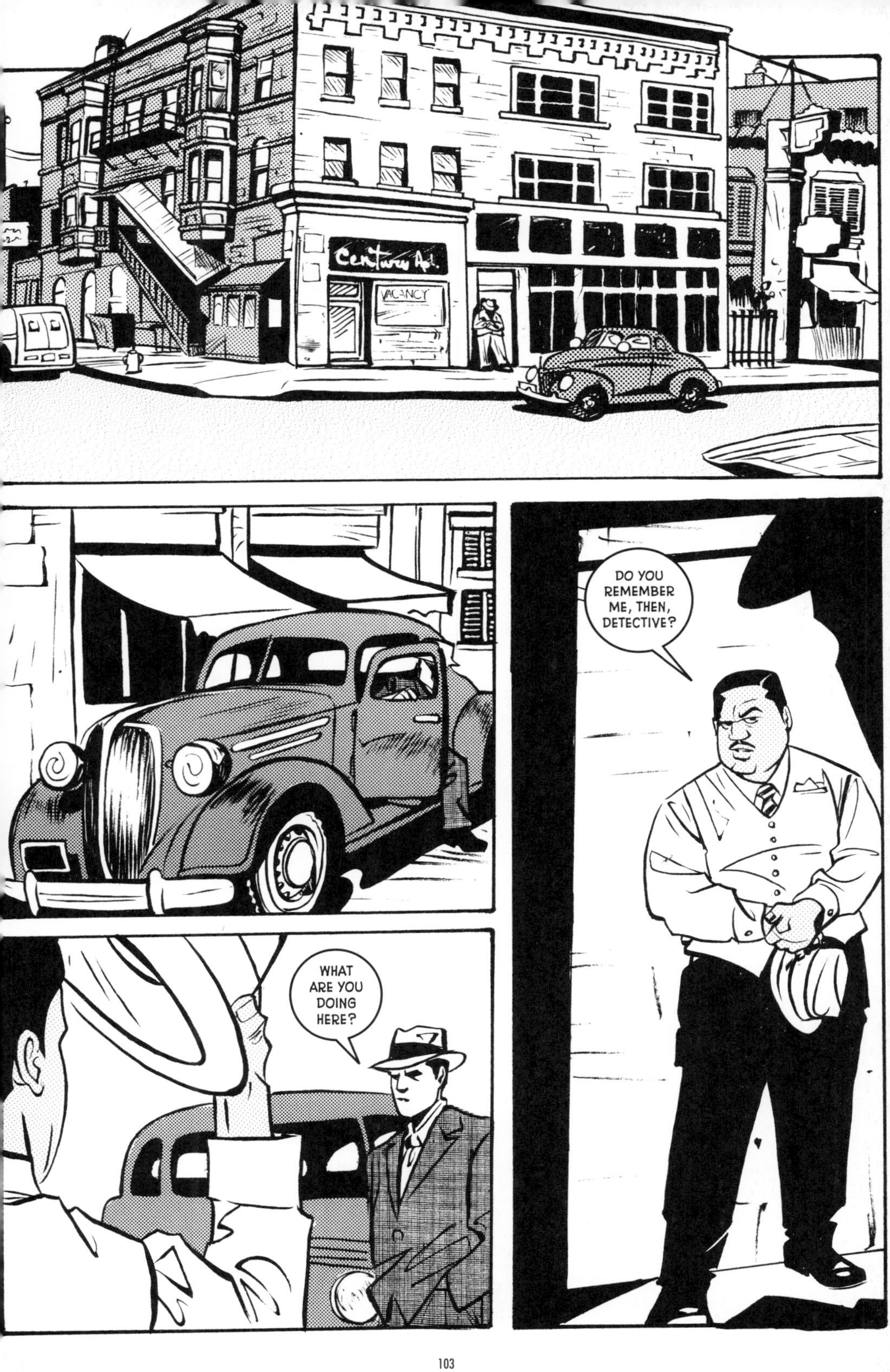
Century Apt.
VACANCY
DO YOU REMEMBER ME, THEN, DETECTIVE?
WHAT ARE YOU DOING HERE?

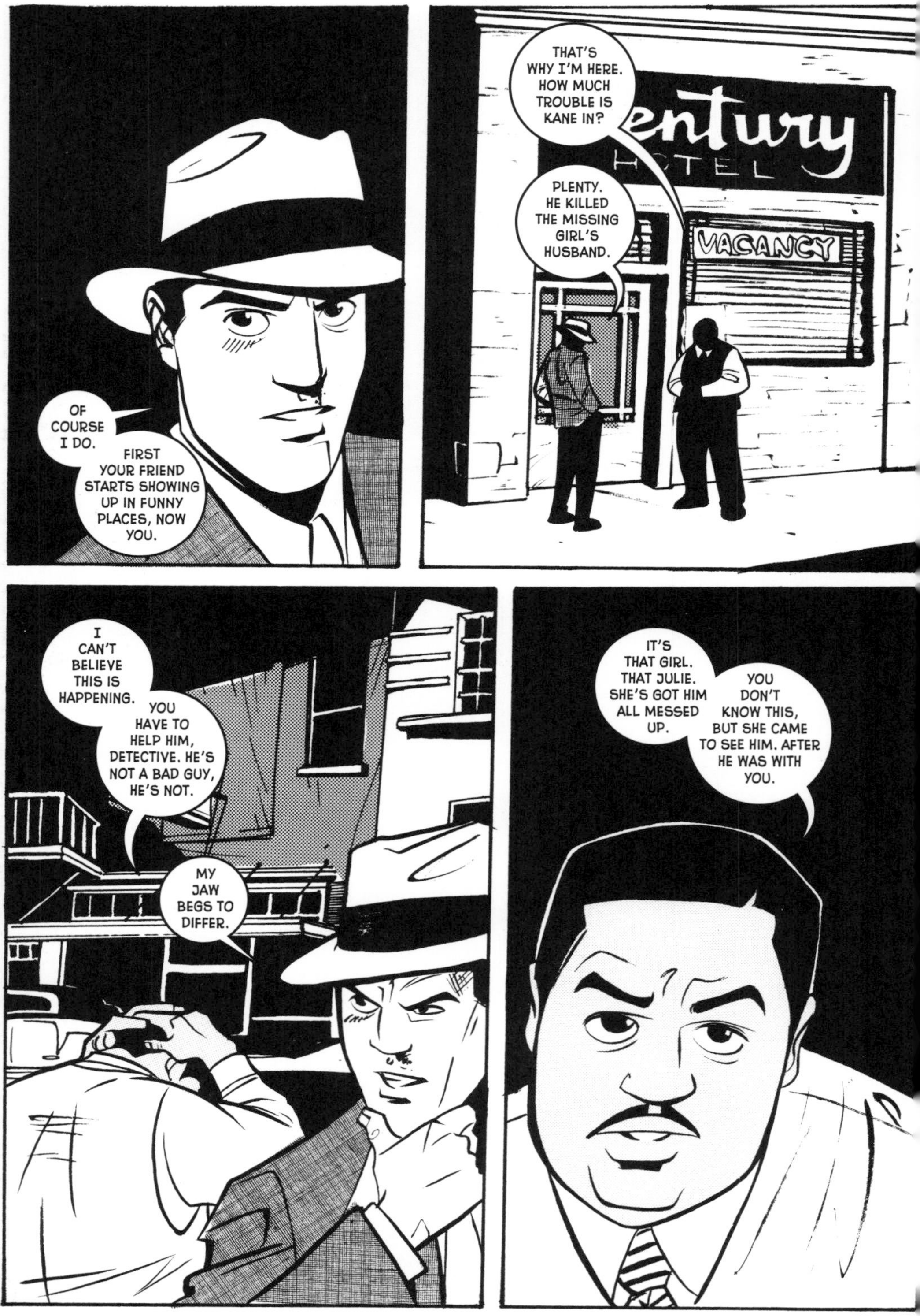
OF COURSE I DO.
FIRST YOUR FRIEND STARTS SHOWING UP IN FUNNY PLACES, NOW YOU.
THAT'S WHY I'M HERE. HOW MUCH TROUBLE IS KANE IN?
entury
HOTEL
PLENTY. HE KILLED THE MISSING GIRL'S HUSBAND.
VACANCY
I CAN'T BELIEVE THIS IS HAPPENING.
YOU HAVE TO HELP HIM, DETECTIVE. HE'S NOT A BAD GUY, HE'S NOT.
MY JAW BEGS TO DIFFER.
IT'S THAT GIRL. THAT JULIE. SHE'S GOT HIM ALL MESSED UP.
YOU DON'T KNOW THIS, BUT SHE CAME TO SEE HIM. AFTER HE WAS WITH YOU.

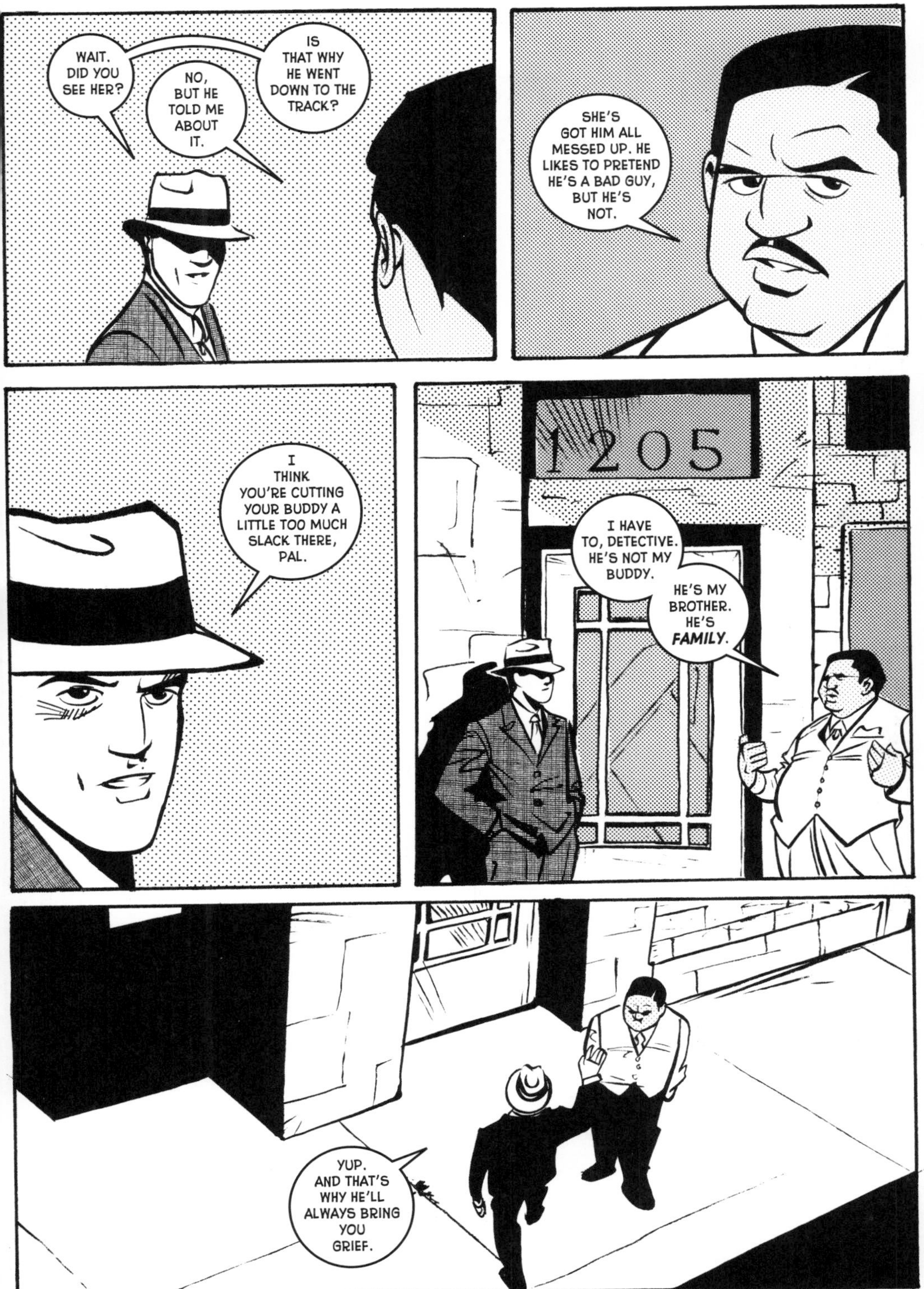
WAIT. DID YOU SEE HER?
NO, BUT HE TOLD ME ABOUT IT.
IS THAT WHY HE WENT DOWN TO THE TRACK?
SHE'S GOT HIM ALL MESSED UP. HE LIKES TO PRETEND HE'S A BAD GUY, BUT HE'S NOT.
I THINK YOU'RE CUTTING YOUR BUDDY A LITTLE TOO MUCH SLACK THERE, PAL.
1205
I HAVE TO, DETECTIVE. HE'S NOT MY BUDDY.
HE'S MY BROTHER. HE'S *FAMILY*.
YUP. AND THAT'S WHY HE'LL ALWAYS BRING YOU GRIEF.

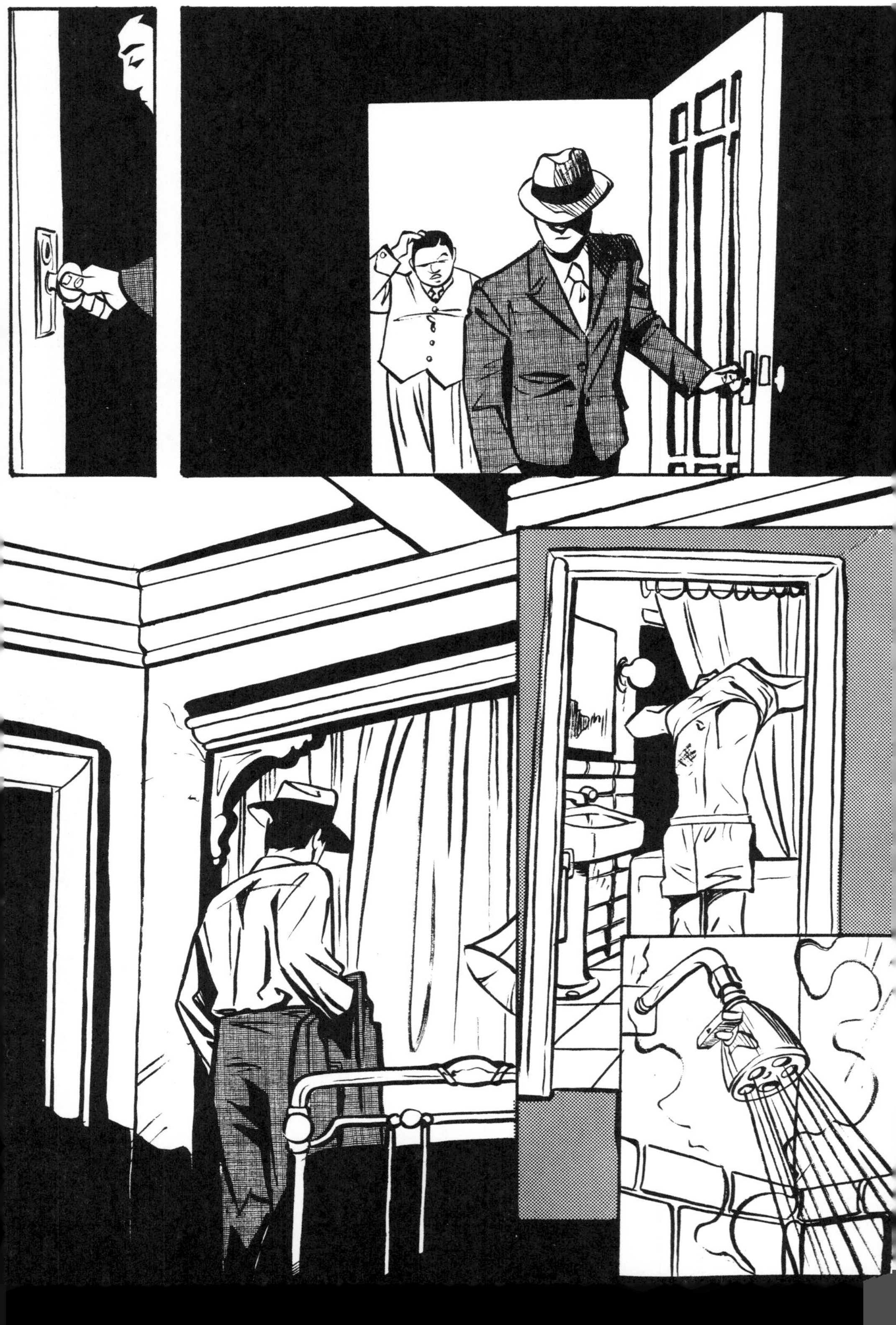

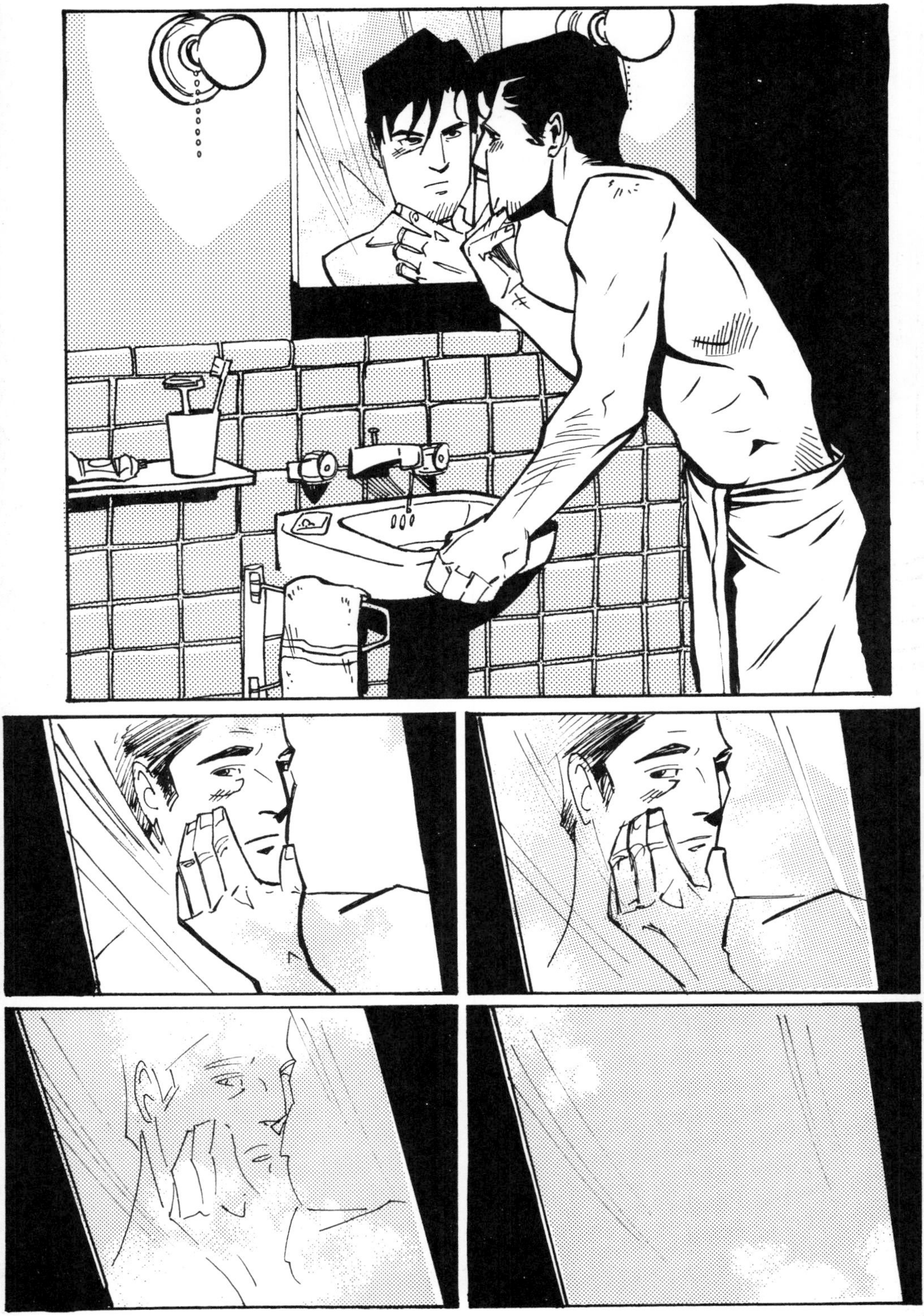

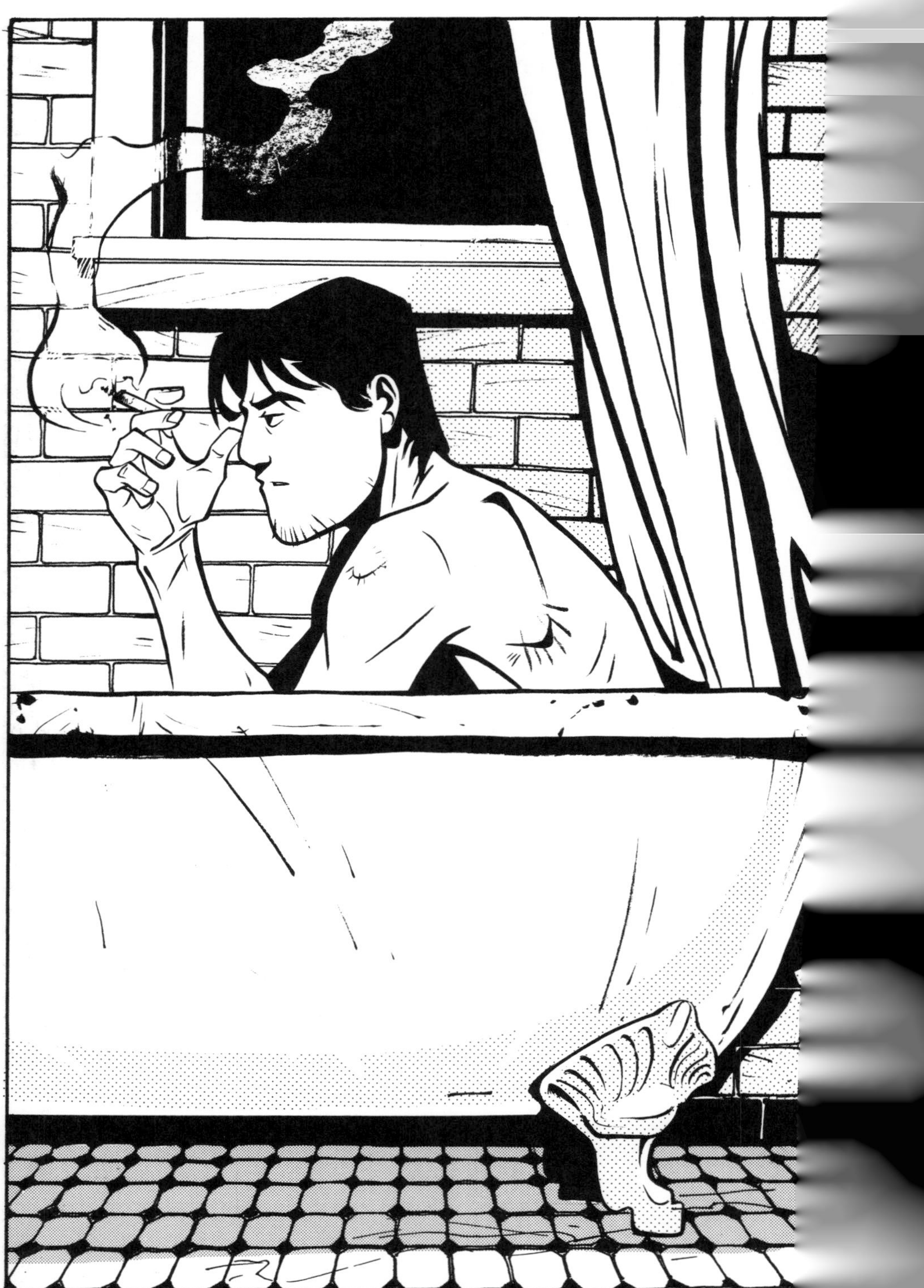

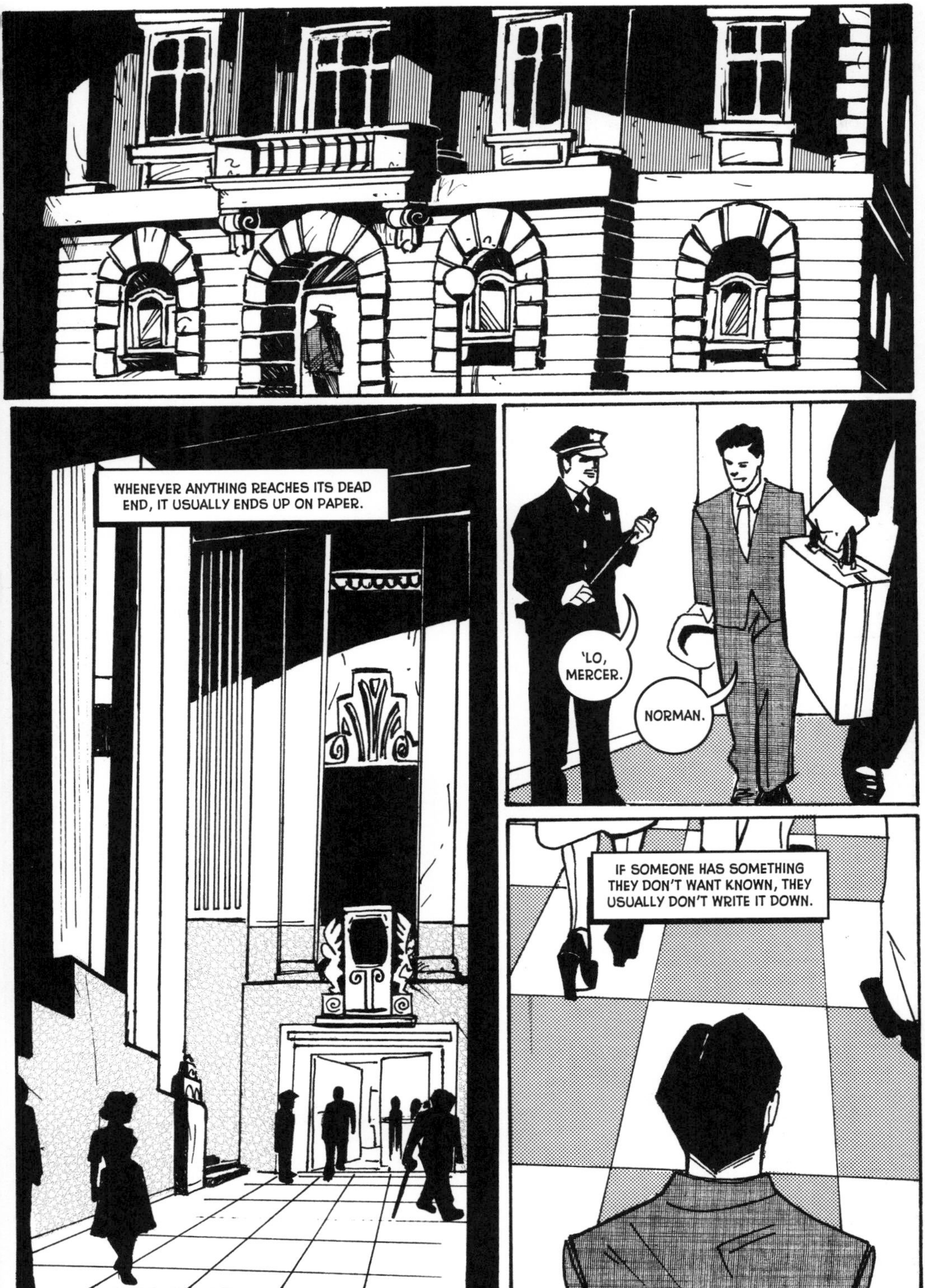
WHENEVER ANYTHING REACHES ITS DEAD END, IT USUALLY ENDS UP ON PAPER.
'LO, MERCER.
NORMAN.
IF SOMEONE HAS SOMETHING THEY DON'T WANT KNOWN, THEY USUALLY DON'T WRITE IT DOWN.

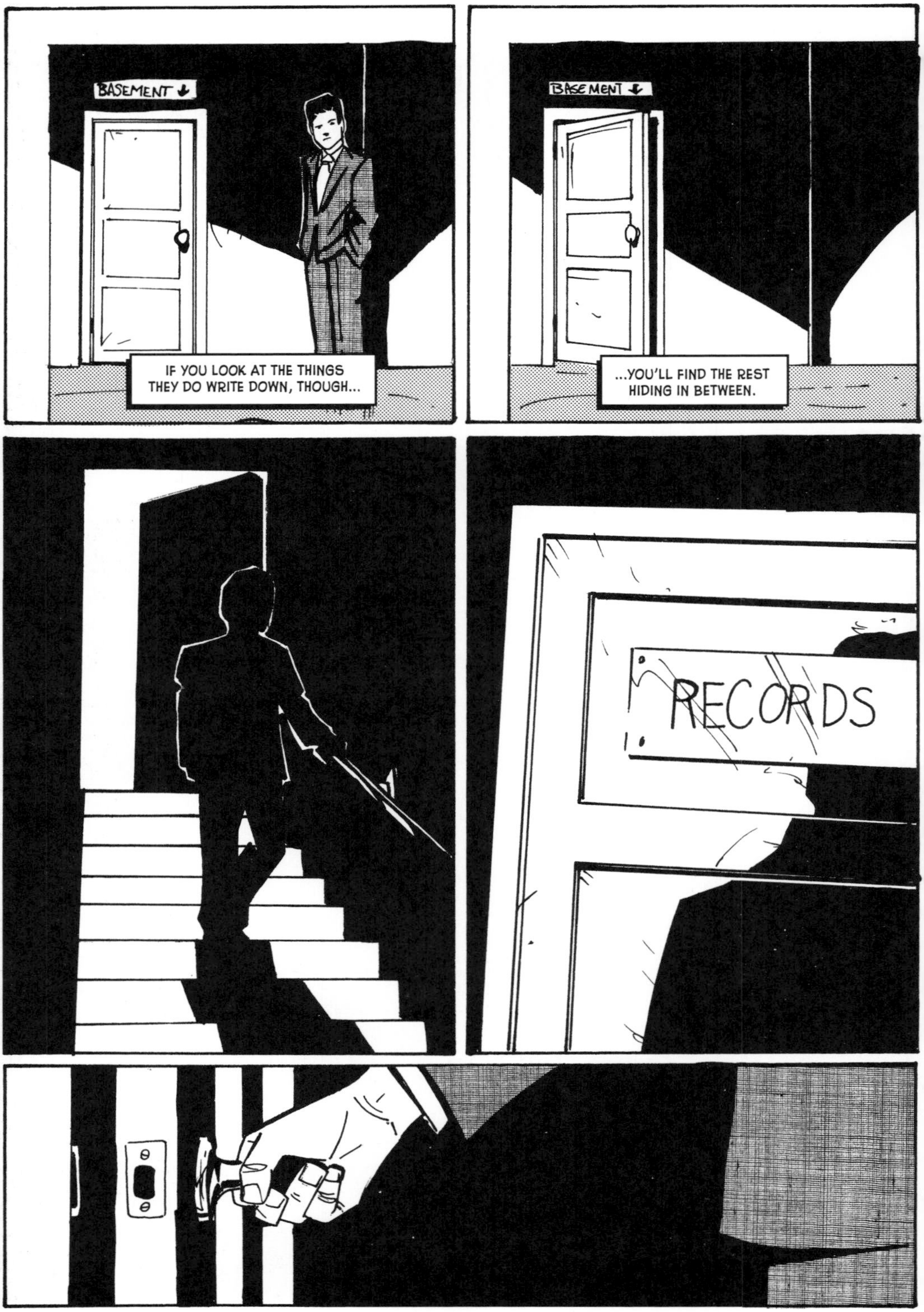
BASEMENT
IF YOU LOOK AT THE THINGS THEY DO WRITE DOWN, THOUGH...
BASEMENT
...YOU'LL FIND THE REST HIDING IN BETWEEN.
RECORDS

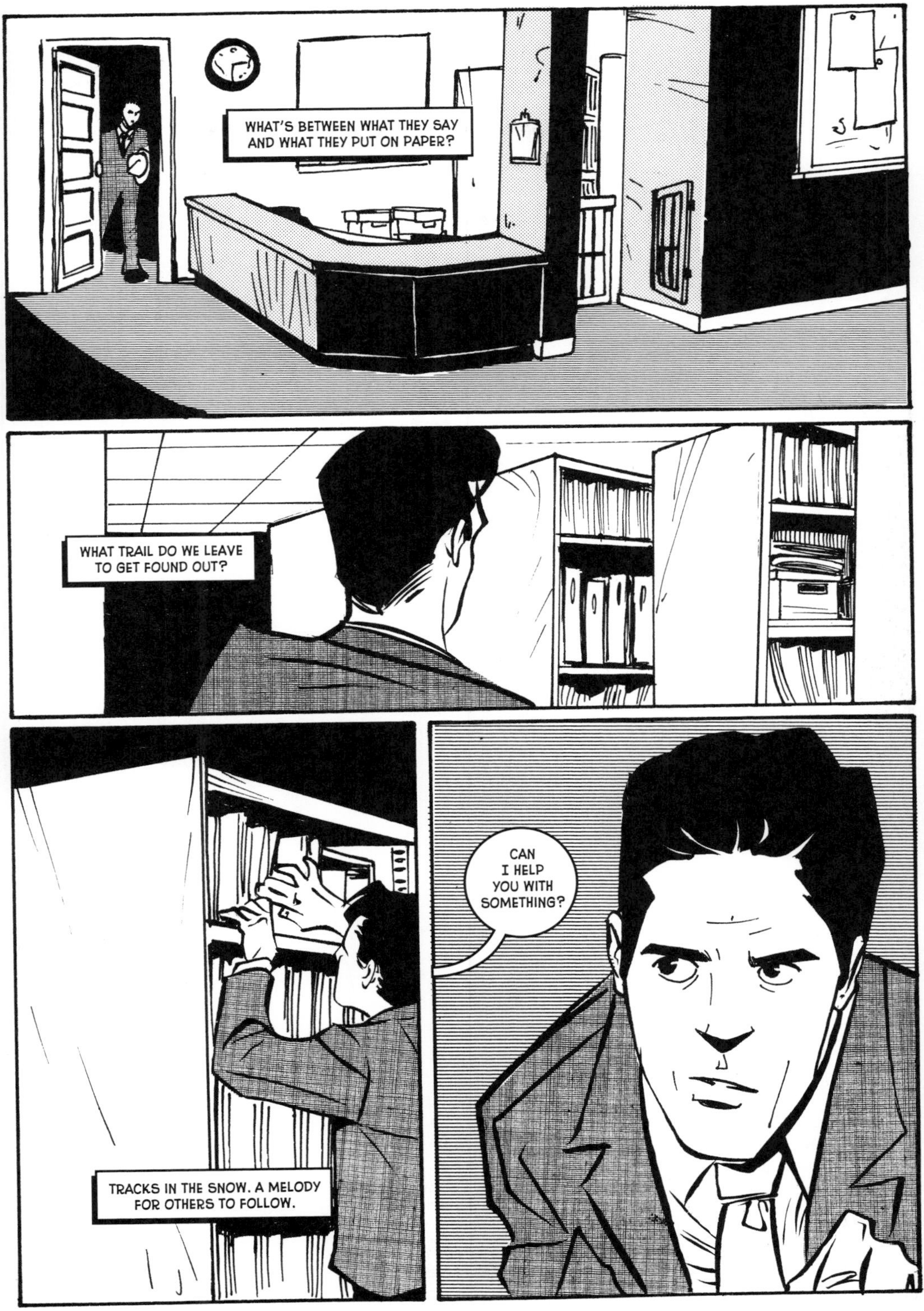
WHAT'S BETWEEN WHAT THEY SAY
AND WHAT THEY PUT ON PAPER?
WHAT TRAIL DO WE LEAVE
TO GET FOUND OUT?
TRACKS IN THE SNOW. A MELODY
FOR OTHERS TO FOLLOW.
CAN I HELP YOU WITH SOMETHING?

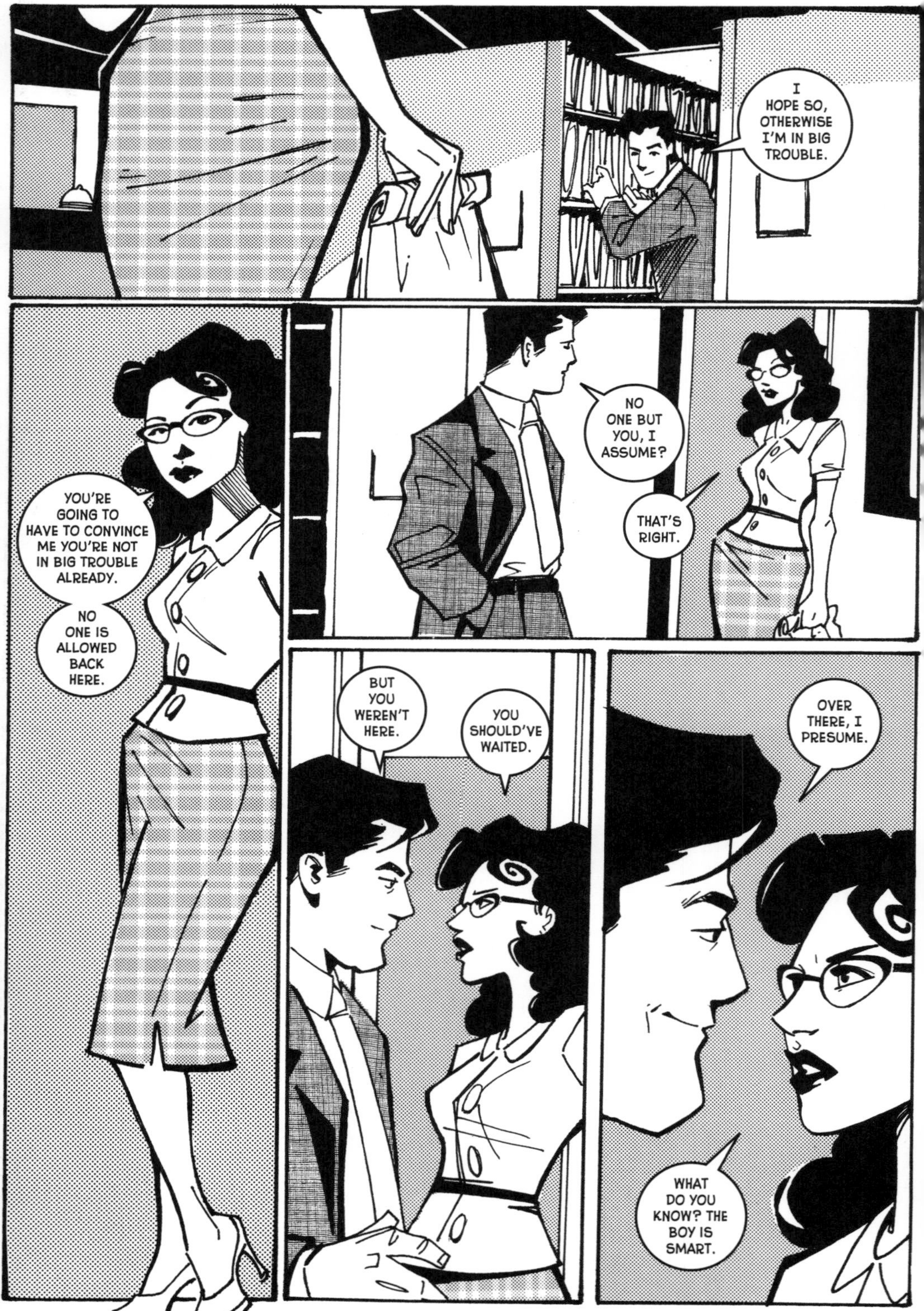
I HOPE SO, OTHERWISE I'M IN BIG TROUBLE.
YOU'RE GOING TO HAVE TO CONVINCE ME YOU'RE NOT IN BIG TROUBLE ALREADY.
NO ONE IS ALLOWED BACK HERE.
NO ONE BUT YOU, I ASSUME?
THAT'S RIGHT.
BUT YOU WEREN'T HERE.
YOU SHOULD'VE WAITED.
OVER THERE, I PRESUME.
WHAT DO YOU KNOW? THE BOY IS SMART.

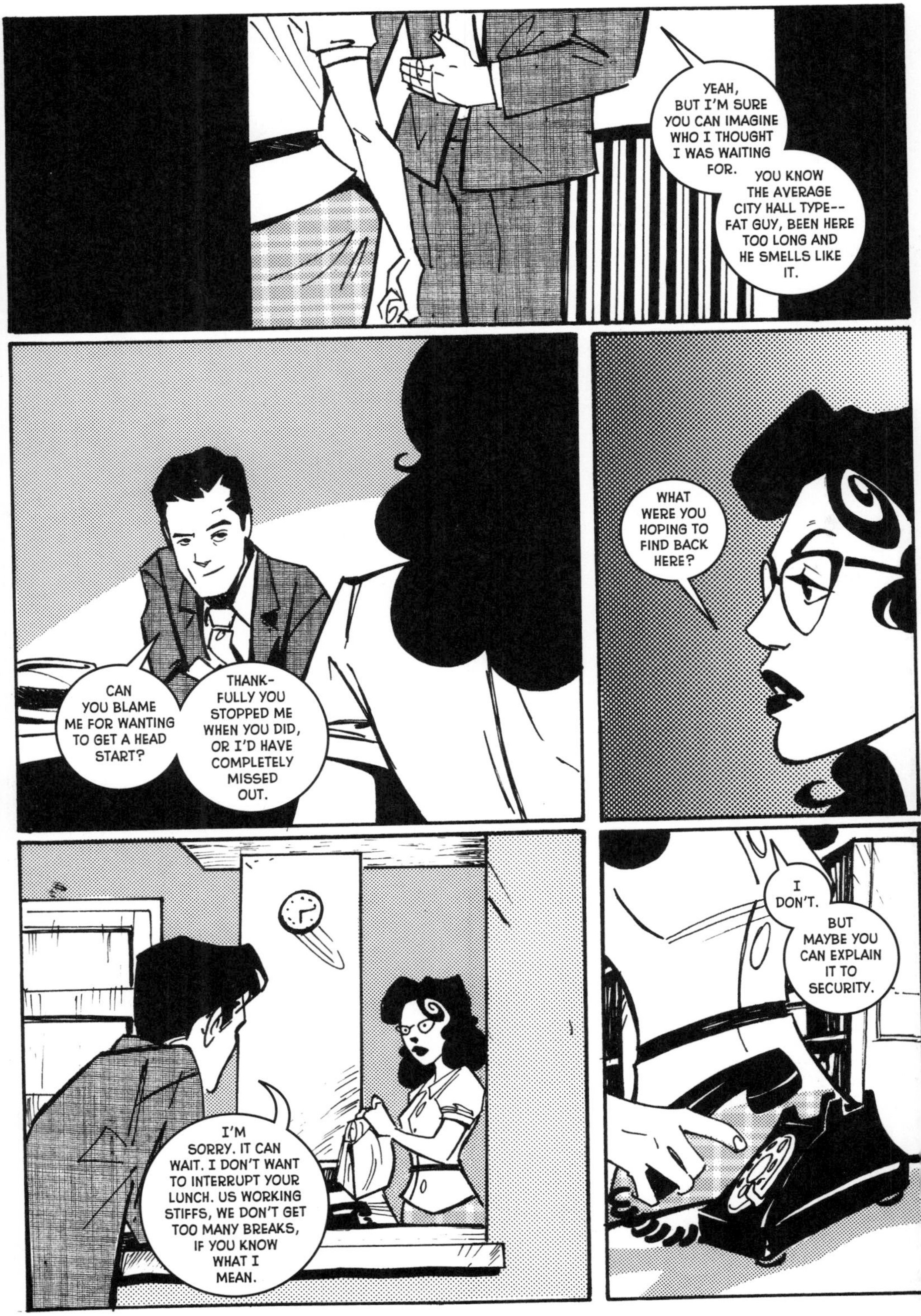
YEAH, BUT I'M SURE YOU CAN IMAGINE WHO I THOUGHT I WAS WAITING FOR.
YOU KNOW THE AVERAGE CITY HALL TYPE-- FAT GUY, BEEN HERE TOO LONG AND HE SMELLS LIKE IT.
CAN YOU BLAME ME FOR WANTING TO GET A HEAD START?
THANK-FULLY YOU STOPPED ME WHEN YOU DID, OR I'D HAVE COMPLETELY MISSED OUT.
WHAT WERE YOU HOPING TO FIND BACK HERE?
I'M SORRY. IT CAN WAIT. I DON'T WANT TO INTERRUPT YOUR LUNCH. US WORKING STIFFS, WE DON'T GET TOO MANY BREAKS, IF YOU KNOW WHAT I MEAN.
I DON'T.
BUT MAYBE YOU CAN EXPLAIN IT TO SECURITY.

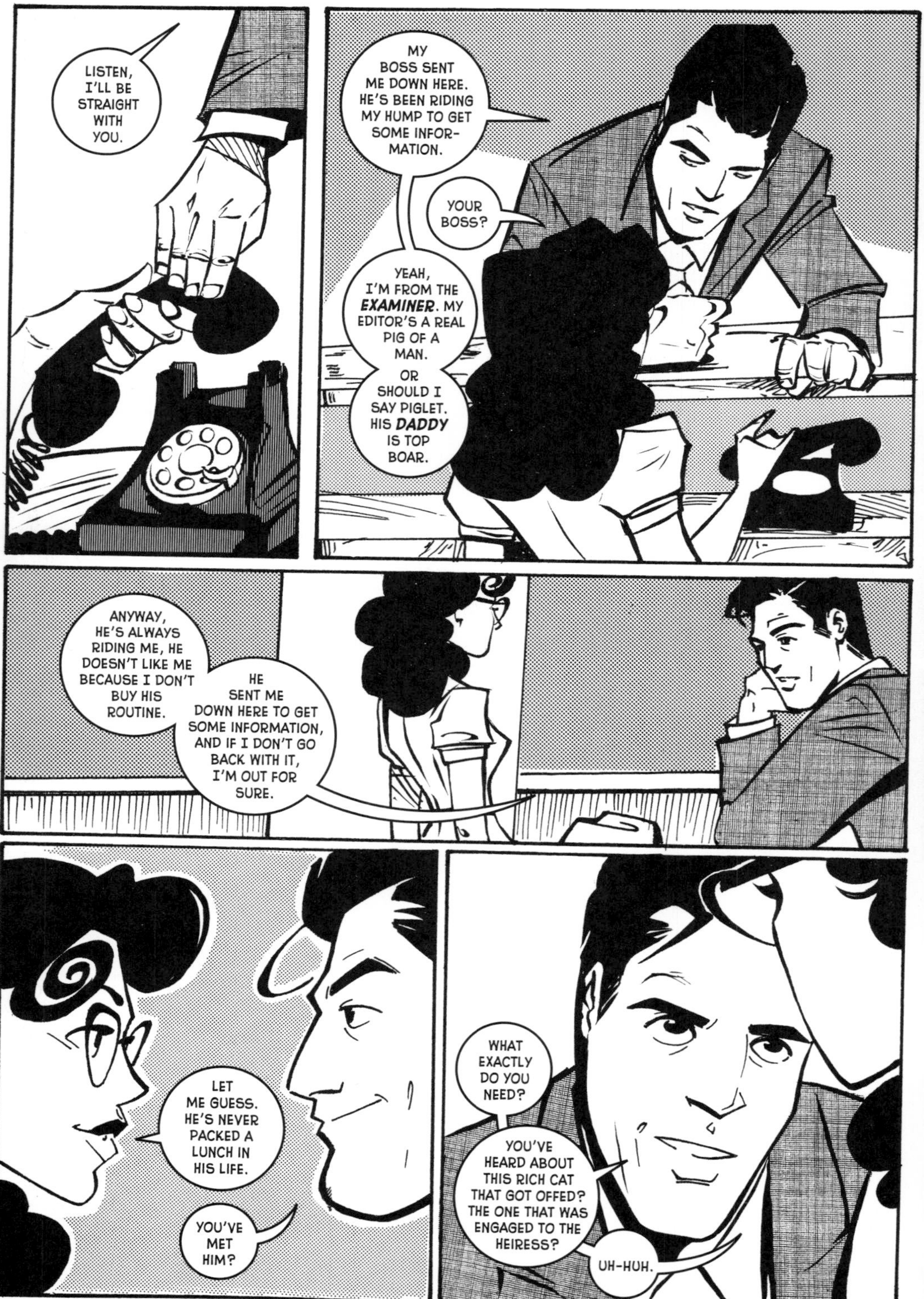
LISTEN, I'LL BE STRAIGHT WITH YOU.
MY BOSS SENT ME DOWN HERE. HE'S BEEN RIDING MY HUMP TO GET SOME INFOR-MATION.
YOUR BOSS?
YEAH, I'M FROM THE **EXAMINER**. MY EDITOR'S A REAL PIG OF A MAN.
OR SHOULD I SAY PIGLET. HIS ***DADDY*** IS TOP BOAR.
ANYWAY, HE'S ALWAYS RIDING ME, HE DOESN'T LIKE ME BECAUSE I DON'T BUY HIS ROUTINE.
HE SENT ME DOWN HERE TO GET SOME INFORMATION, AND IF I DON'T GO BACK WITH IT, I'M OUT FOR SURE.
LET ME GUESS. HE'S NEVER PACKED A LUNCH IN HIS LIFE.
YOU'VE MET HIM?
WHAT EXACTLY DO YOU NEED?
YOU'VE HEARD ABOUT THIS RICH CAT THAT GOT OFFED? THE ONE THAT WAS ENGAGED TO THE HEIRESS?
UH-HUH.

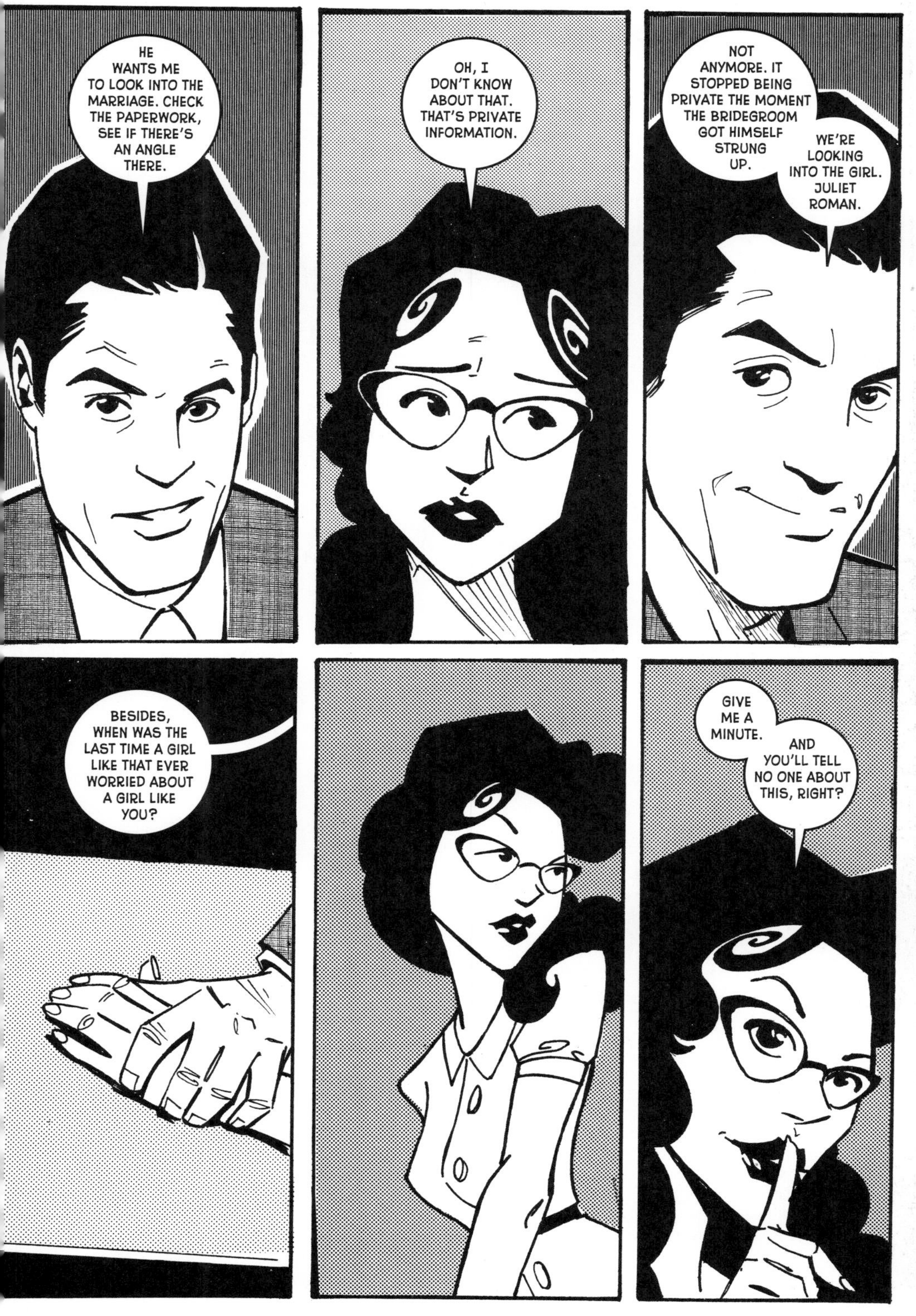
HE WANTS ME TO LOOK INTO THE MARRIAGE. CHECK THE PAPERWORK, SEE IF THERE'S AN ANGLE THERE.
OH, I DON'T KNOW ABOUT THAT. THAT'S PRIVATE INFORMATION.
NOT ANYMORE. IT STOPPED BEING PRIVATE THE MOMENT THE BRIDEGROOM GOT HIMSELF STRUNG UP.
WE'RE LOOKING INTO THE GIRL. JULIET ROMAN.
BESIDES, WHEN WAS THE LAST TIME A GIRL LIKE THAT EVER WORRIED ABOUT A GIRL LIKE YOU?
GIVE ME A MINUTE.
AND YOU'LL TELL NO ONE ABOUT THIS, RIGHT?

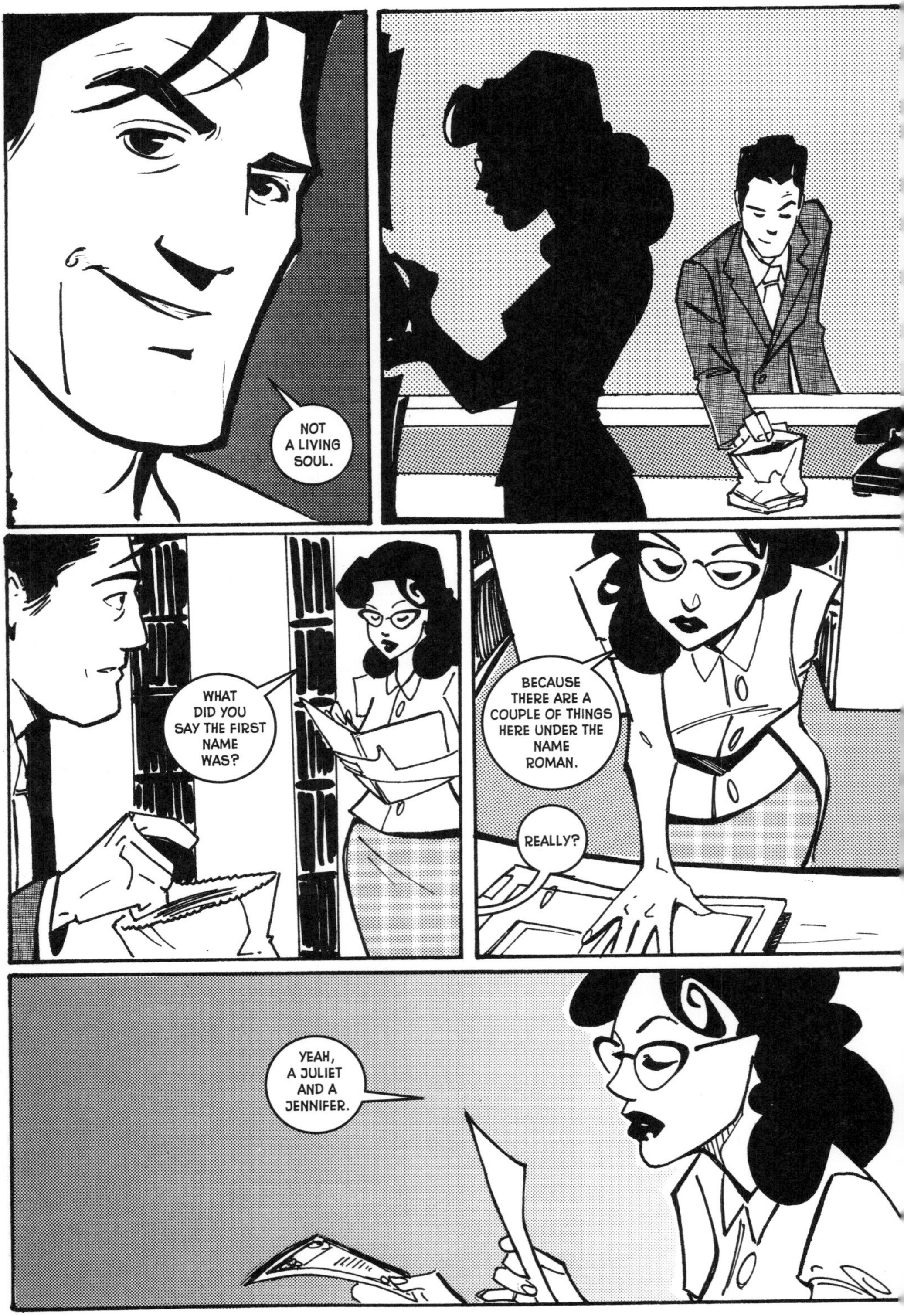
NOT A LIVING SOUL.
WHAT DID YOU SAY THE FIRST NAME WAS?
BECAUSE THERE ARE A COUPLE OF THINGS HERE UNDER THE NAME ROMAN.
REALLY?
YEAH, A JULIET AND A JENNIFER.

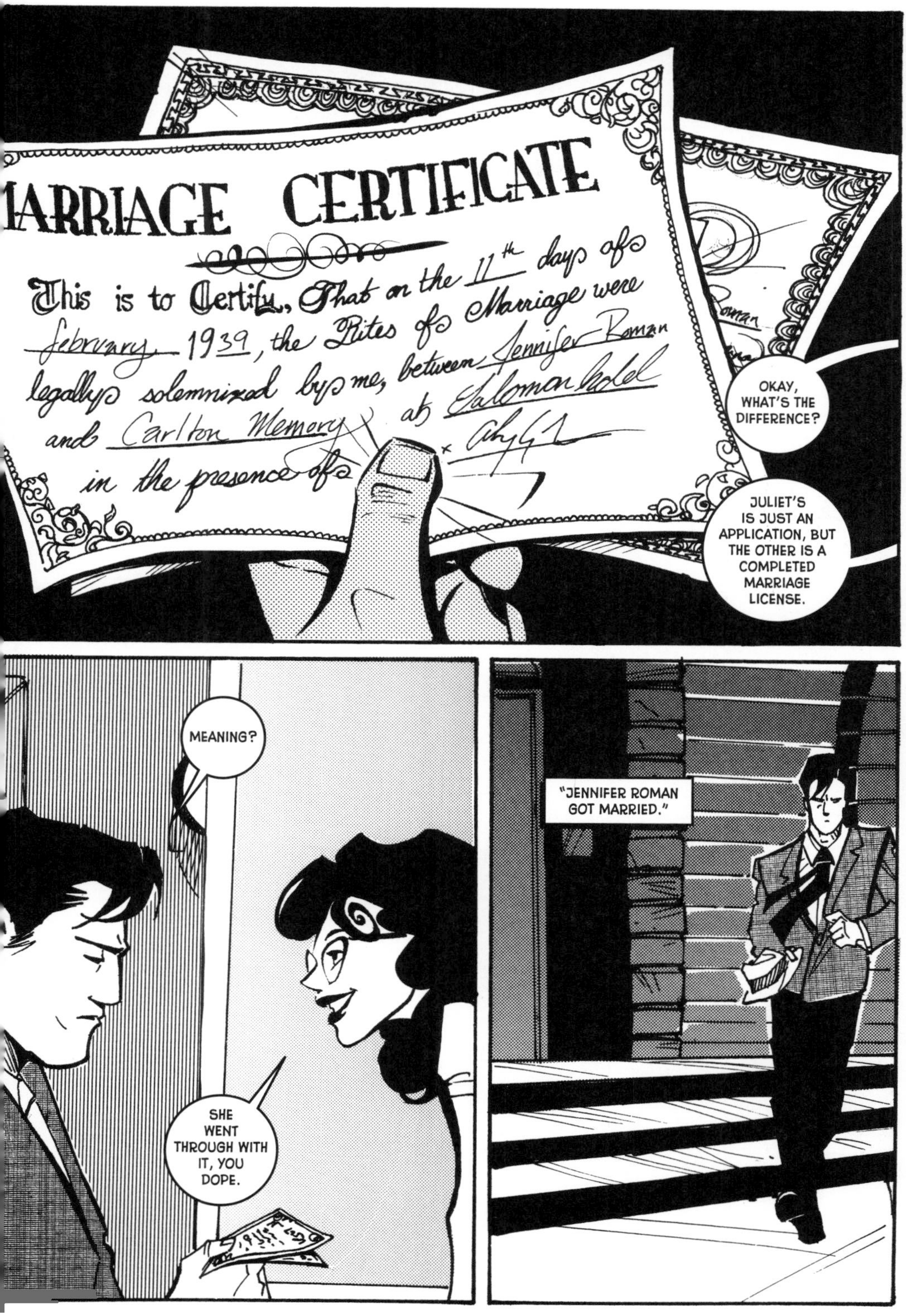
ARRIAGE CERTIFICATE
This is to Certify, That on the 11th day of
February 1939, the Rites of Marriage were
legally solemnized by me, between Jennifer Roman
and Carlton Memory at
in the presence of
OKAY, WHAT'S THE DIFFERENCE?
JULIET'S IS JUST AN APPLICATION, BUT THE OTHER IS A COMPLETED MARRIAGE LICENSE.
MEANING?
SHE WENT THROUGH WITH IT, YOU DOPE.
"JENNIFER ROMAN GOT MARRIED."

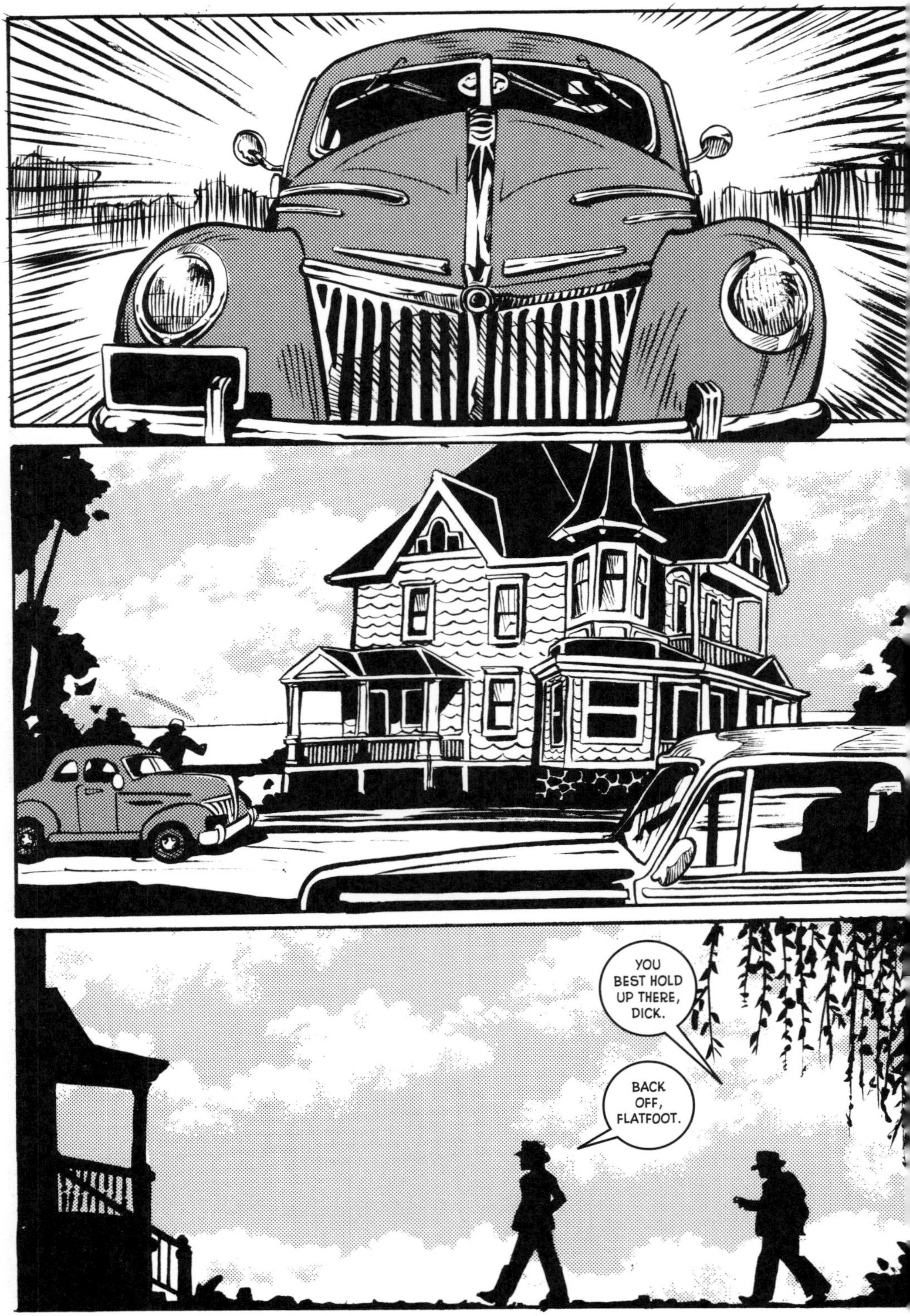
YOU BEST HOLD UP THERE, DICK.
BACK OFF, FLATFOOT.

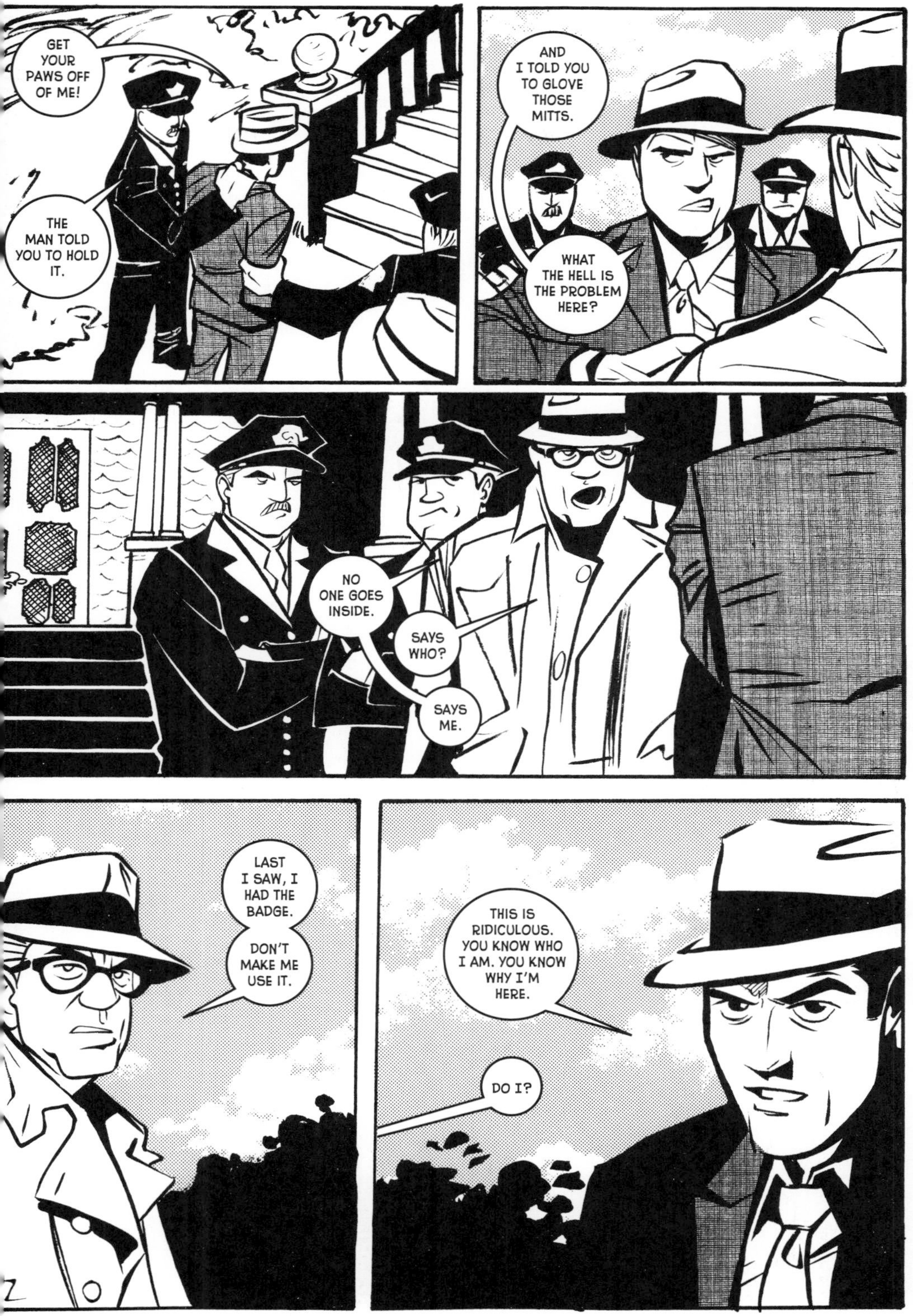
GET YOUR PAWS OFF OF ME!
THE MAN TOLD YOU TO HOLD IT.
AND I TOLD YOU TO GLOVE THOSE MITTS.
WHAT THE HELL IS THE PROBLEM HERE?
NO ONE GOES INSIDE.
SAYS WHO?
SAYS ME.
LAST I SAW, I HAD THE BADGE.
DON'T MAKE ME USE IT.
THIS IS RIDICULOUS. YOU KNOW WHO I AM. YOU KNOW WHY I'M HERE.
DO I?

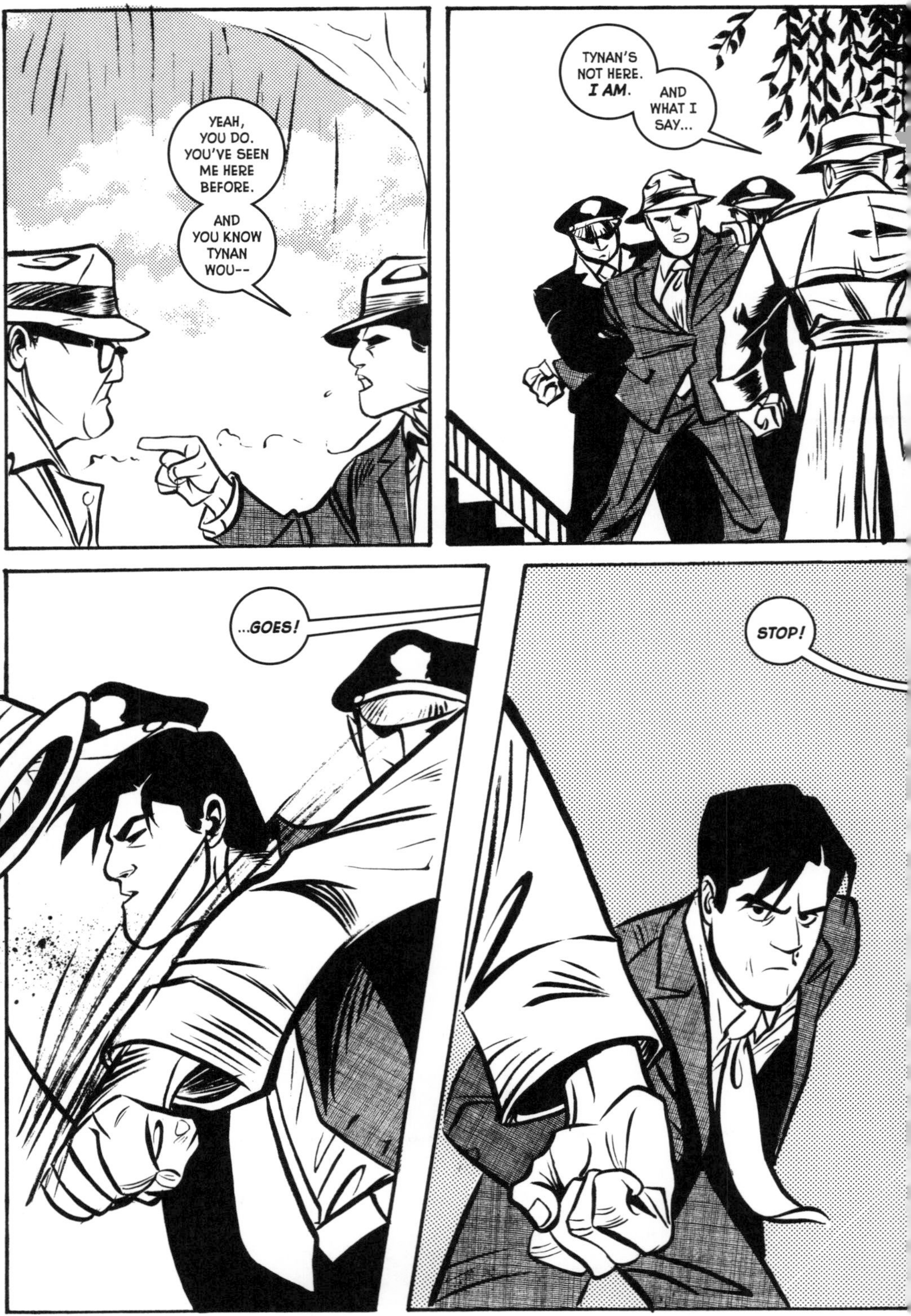
YEAH, YOU DO. YOU'VE SEEN ME HERE BEFORE.
AND YOU KNOW TYNAN WOU--
TYNAN'S NOT HERE. I AM.
AND WHAT I SAY...
...GOES!
STOP!

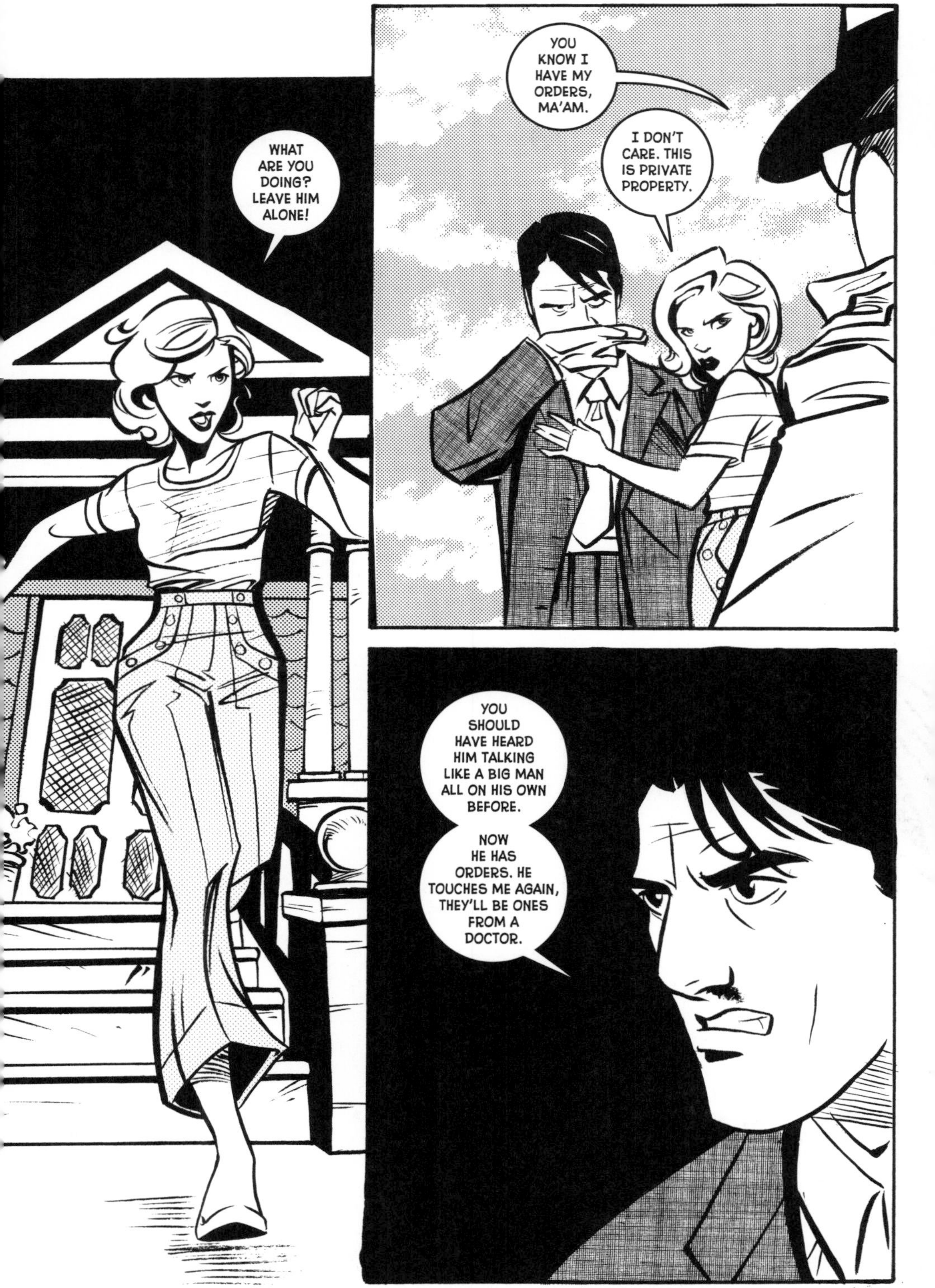
WHAT ARE YOU DOING? LEAVE HIM ALONE!
YOU KNOW I HAVE MY ORDERS, MA'AM.
I DON'T CARE. THIS IS PRIVATE PROPERTY.
YOU SHOULD HAVE HEARD HIM TALKING LIKE A BIG MAN ALL ON HIS OWN BEFORE.
NOW HE HAS ORDERS. HE TOUCHES ME AGAIN, THEY'LL BE ONES FROM A DOCTOR.

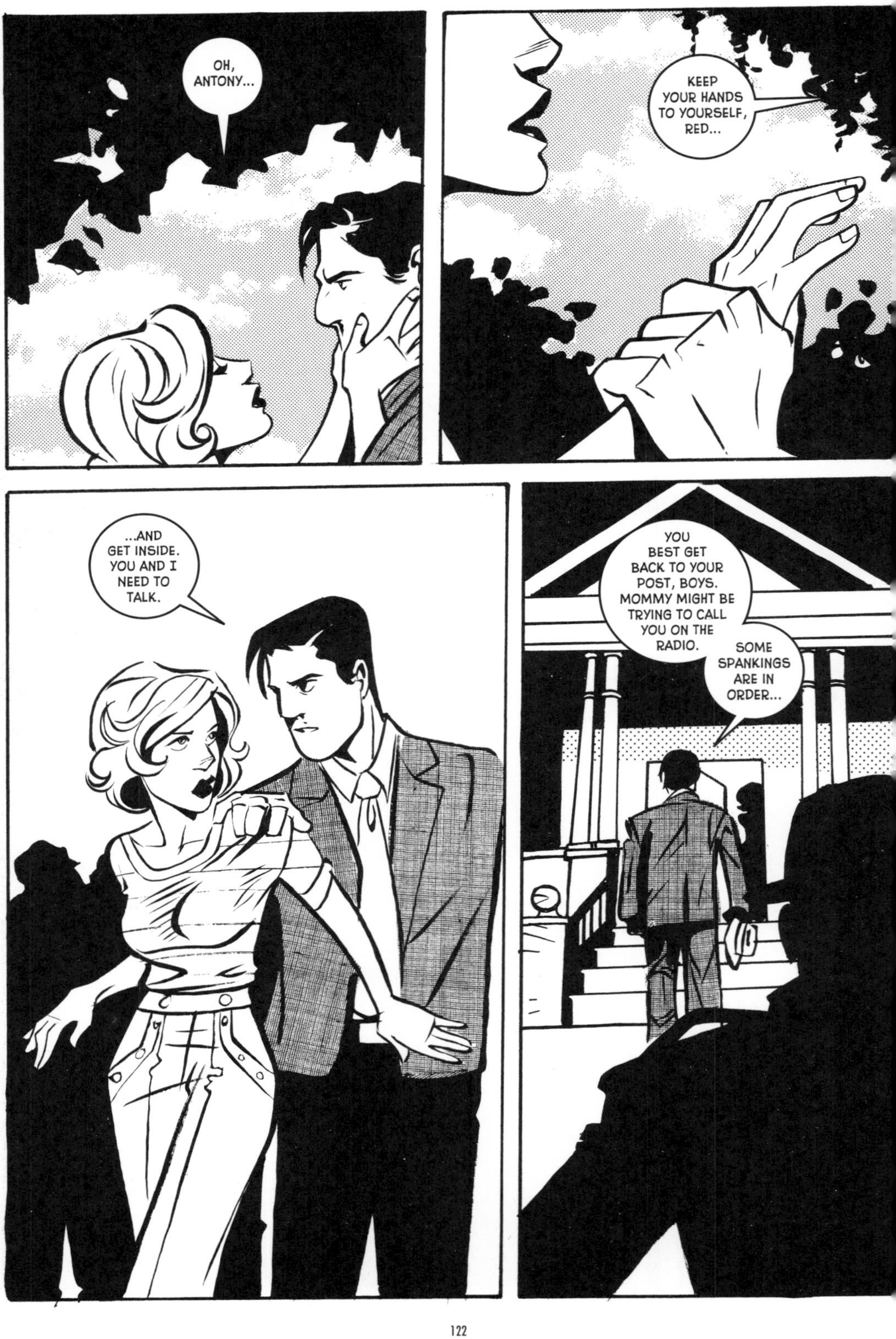
OH, ANTONY...
KEEP YOUR HANDS TO YOURSELF, RED...
...AND GET INSIDE. YOU AND I NEED TO TALK.
YOU BEST GET BACK TO YOUR POST, BOYS. MOMMY MIGHT BE TRYING TO CALL YOU ON THE RADIO.
SOME SPANKINGS ARE IN ORDER...

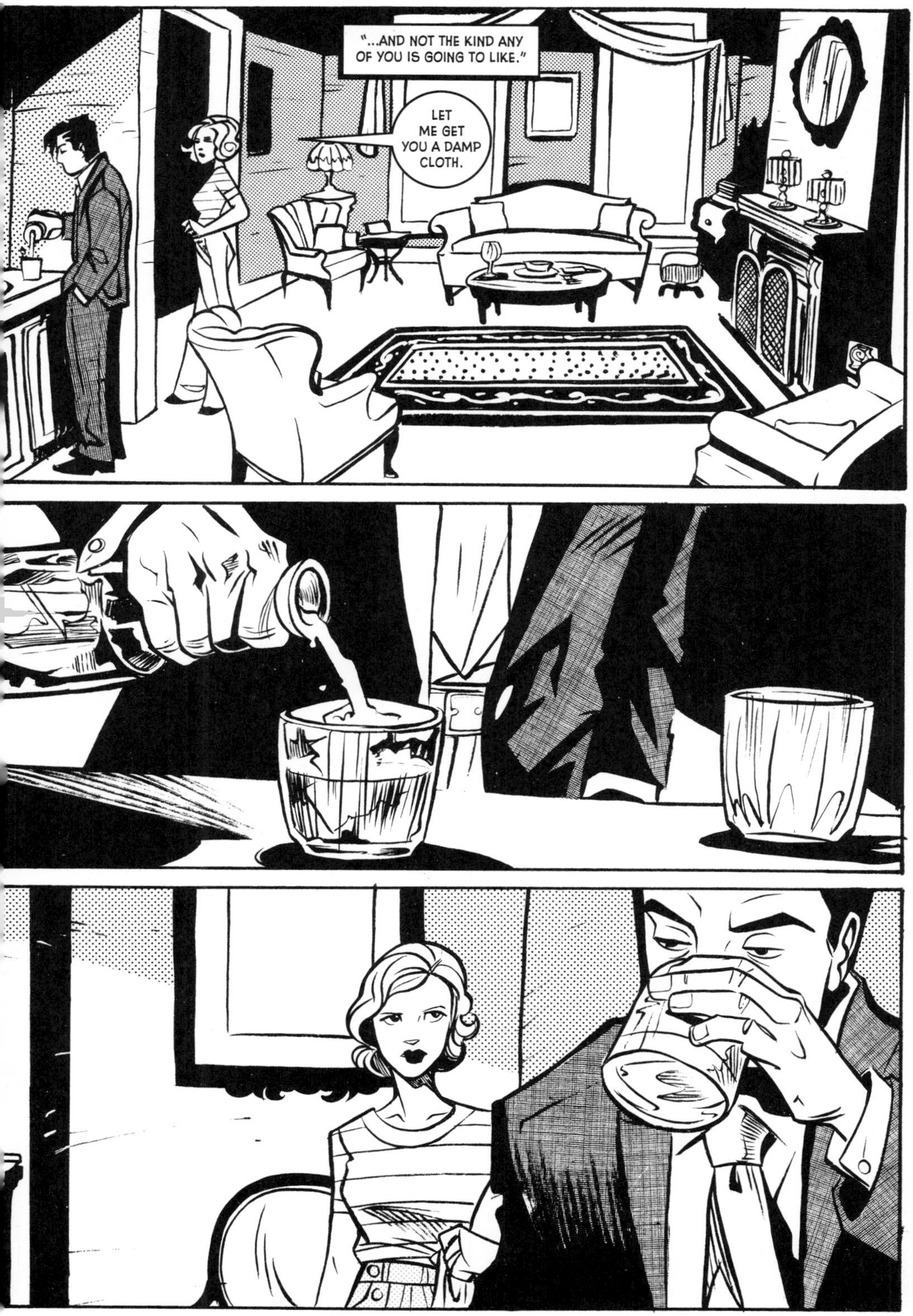
"...AND NOT THE KIND ANY OF YOU IS GOING TO LIKE."
LET ME GET YOU A DAMP CLOTH.

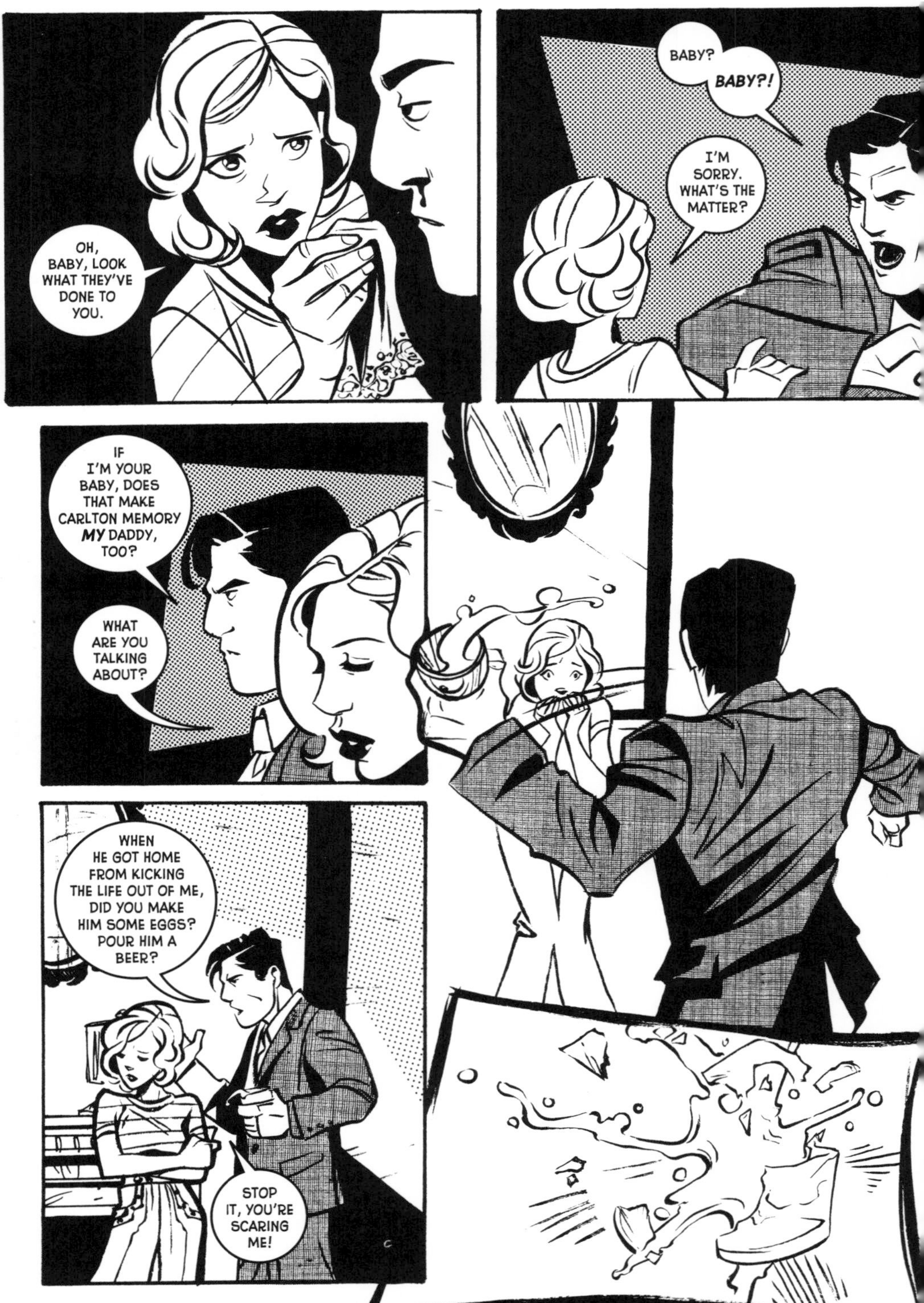
OH, BABY, LOOK WHAT THEY'VE DONE TO YOU.
BABY?
BABY?!
I'M SORRY. WHAT'S THE MATTER?
IF I'M YOUR BABY, DOES THAT MAKE CARLTON MEMORY MY DADDY, TOO?
WHAT ARE YOU TALKING ABOUT?
WHEN HE GOT HOME FROM KICKING THE LIFE OUT OF ME, DID YOU MAKE HIM SOME EGGS? POUR HIM A BEER?
STOP IT, YOU'RE SCARING ME!

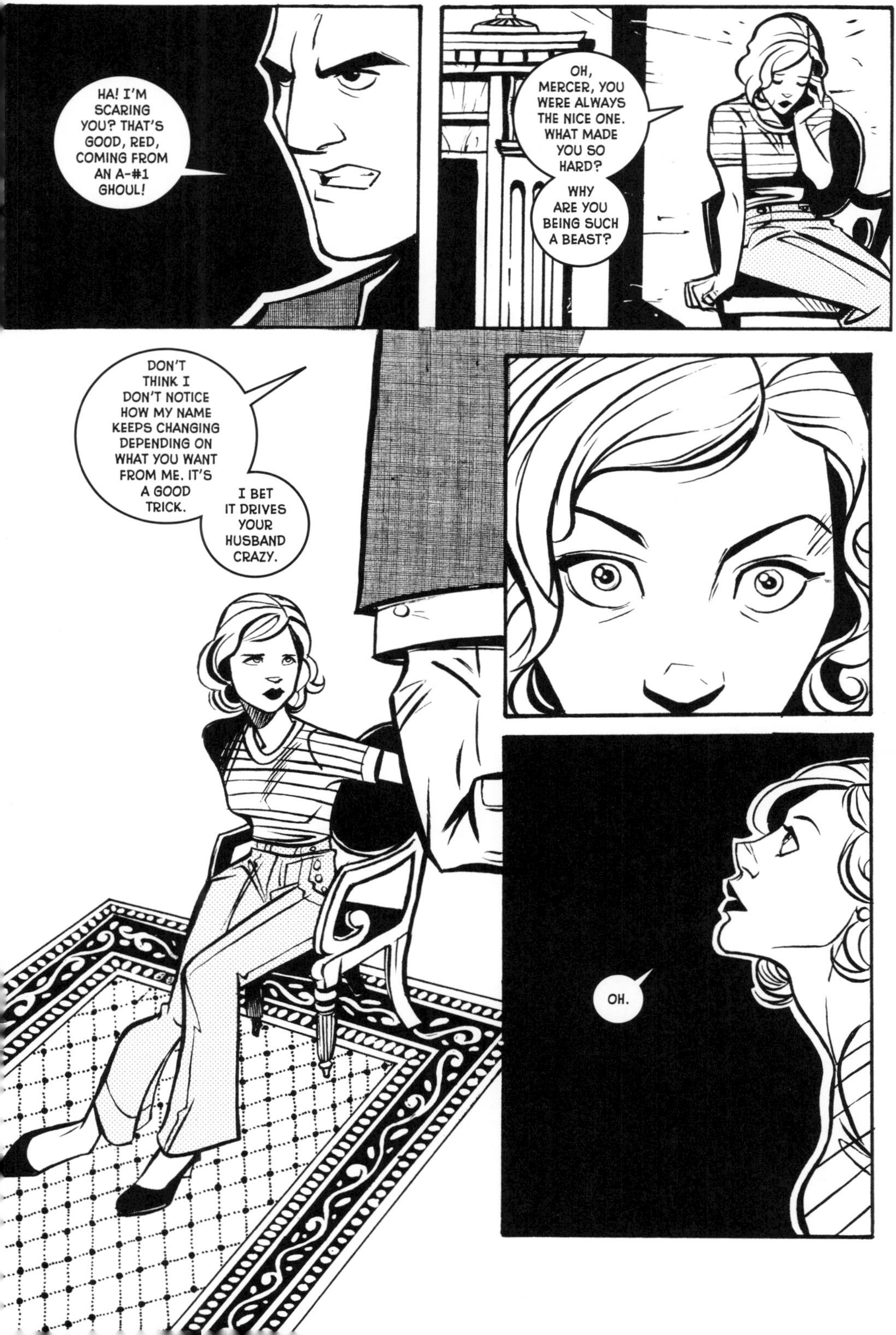
HA! I'M SCARING YOU? THAT'S GOOD, RED, COMING FROM AN A-#1 GHOUL!
OH, MERCER, YOU WERE ALWAYS THE NICE ONE. WHAT MADE YOU SO HARD?
WHY ARE YOU BEING SUCH A BEAST?
DON'T THINK I DON'T NOTICE HOW MY NAME KEEPS CHANGING DEPENDING ON WHAT YOU WANT FROM ME. IT'S A GOOD TRICK.
I BET IT DRIVES YOUR HUSBAND CRAZY.
OH.

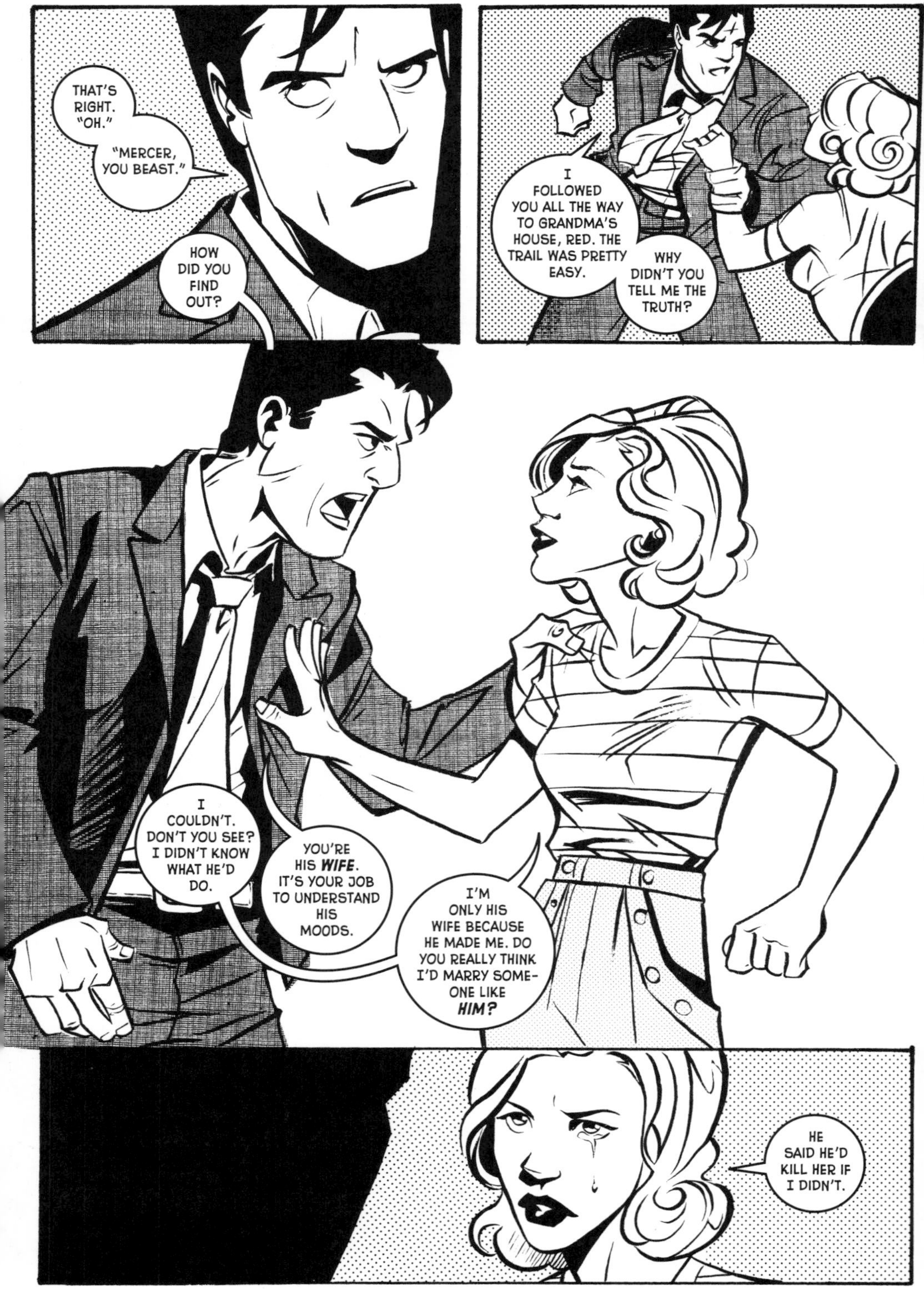
THAT'S RIGHT. "OH."
"MERCER, YOU BEAST."
HOW DID YOU FIND OUT?
I FOLLOWED YOU ALL THE WAY TO GRANDMA'S HOUSE, RED. THE TRAIL WAS PRETTY EASY.
WHY DIDN'T YOU TELL ME THE TRUTH?
I COULDN'T. DON'T YOU SEE? I DIDN'T KNOW WHAT HE'D DO.
YOU'RE HIS **WIFE**. IT'S YOUR JOB TO UNDERSTAND HIS MOODS.
I'M ONLY HIS WIFE BECAUSE HE MADE ME. DO YOU REALLY THINK I'D MARRY SOME-ONE LIKE **HIM?**
HE SAID HE'D KILL HER IF I DIDN'T.

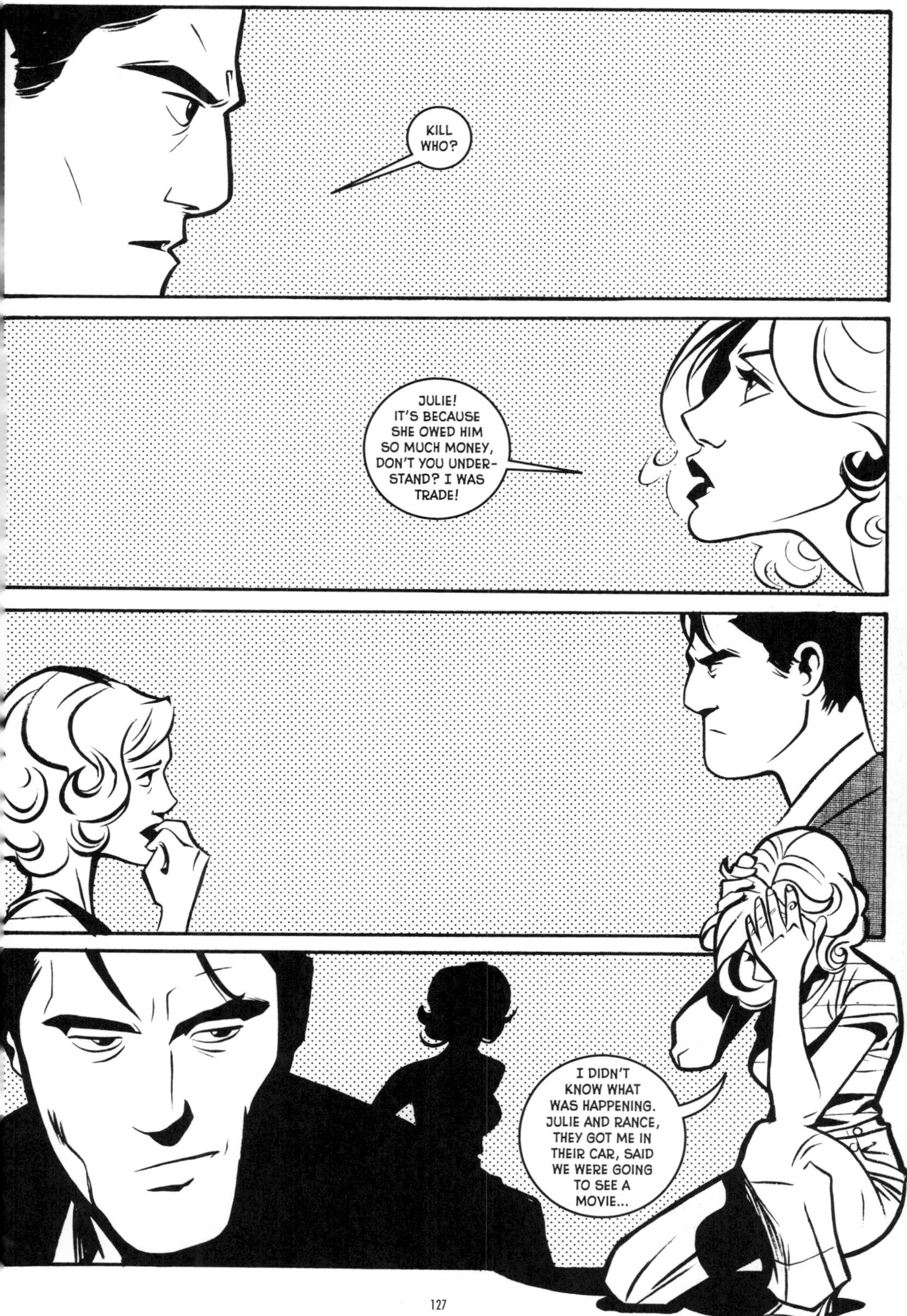
KILL WHO?
JULIE! IT'S BECAUSE SHE OWED HIM SO MUCH MONEY, DON'T YOU UNDER-STAND? I WAS TRADE!
I DIDN'T KNOW WHAT WAS HAPPENING. JULIE AND RANCE, THEY GOT ME IN THEIR CAR, SAID WE WERE GOING TO SEE A MOVIE...

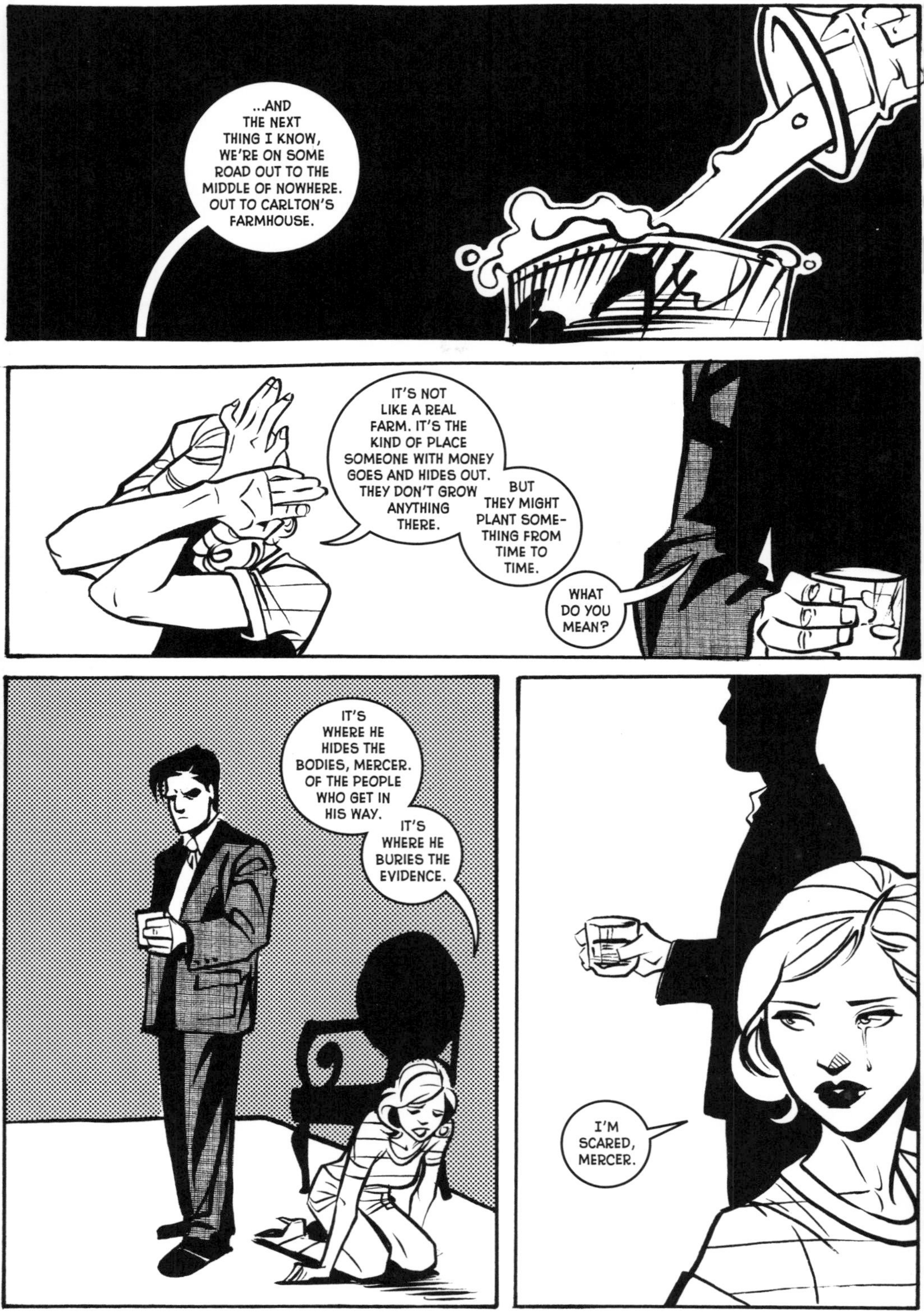
...AND THE NEXT THING I KNOW, WE'RE ON SOME ROAD OUT TO THE MIDDLE OF NOWHERE. OUT TO CARLTON'S FARMHOUSE.
IT'S NOT LIKE A REAL FARM. IT'S THE KIND OF PLACE SOMEONE WITH MONEY GOES AND HIDES OUT. THEY DON'T GROW ANYTHING THERE.
BUT THEY MIGHT PLANT SOME-THING FROM TIME TO TIME.
WHAT DO YOU MEAN?
IT'S WHERE HE HIDES THE BODIES, MERCER. OF THE PEOPLE WHO GET IN HIS WAY.
IT'S WHERE HE BURIES THE EVIDENCE.
I'M SCARED, MERCER.

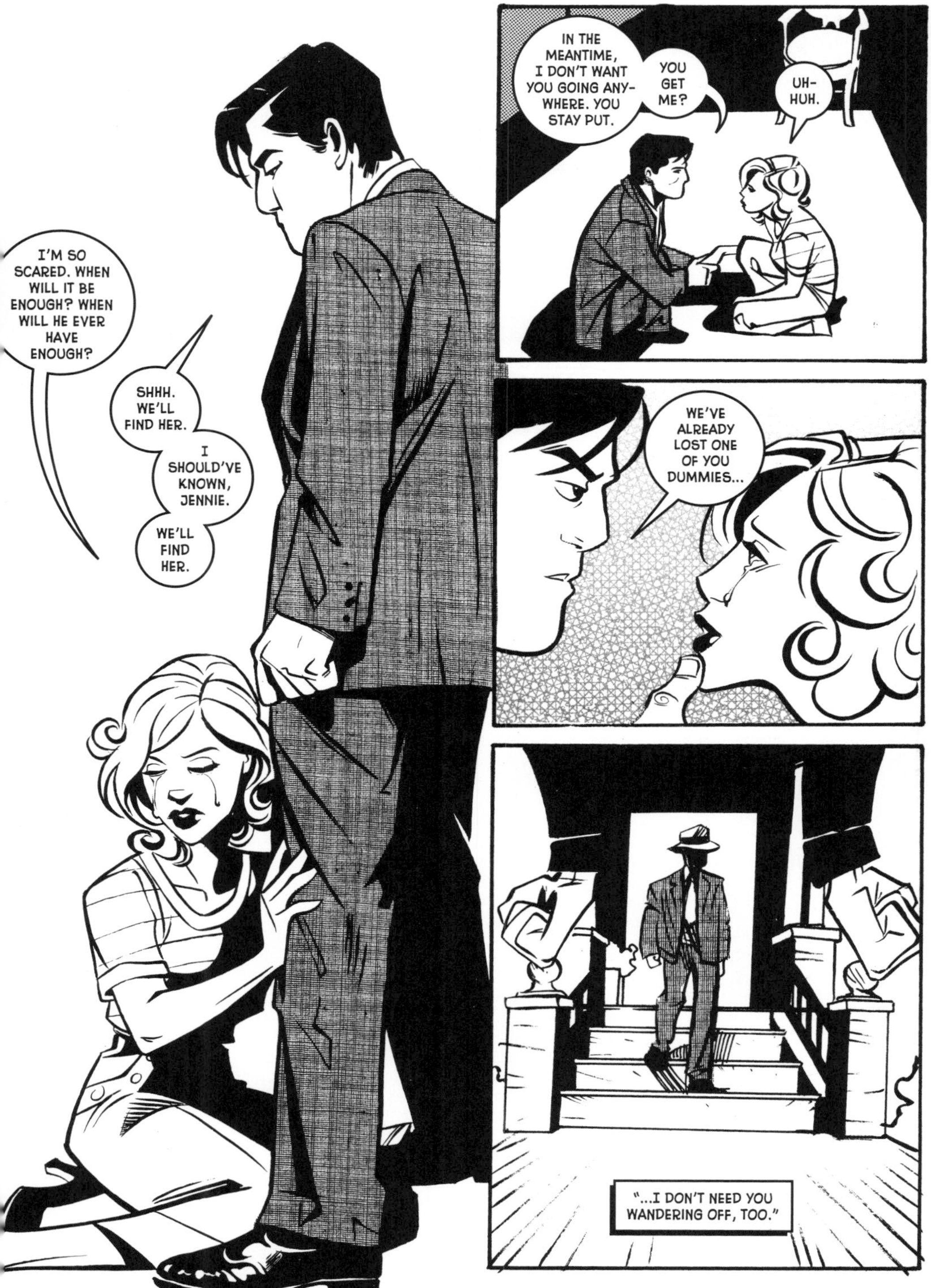
I'M SO SCARED. WHEN WILL IT BE ENOUGH? WHEN WILL HE EVER HAVE ENOUGH?
SHHH. WE'LL FIND HER.
I SHOULD'VE KNOWN, JENNIE.
WE'LL FIND HER.
IN THE MEANTIME, I DON'T WANT YOU GOING ANY-WHERE. YOU STAY PUT.
YOU GET ME?
UH-HUH.
WE'VE ALREADY LOST ONE OF YOU DUMMIES...
"...I DON'T NEED YOU WANDERING OFF, TOO."

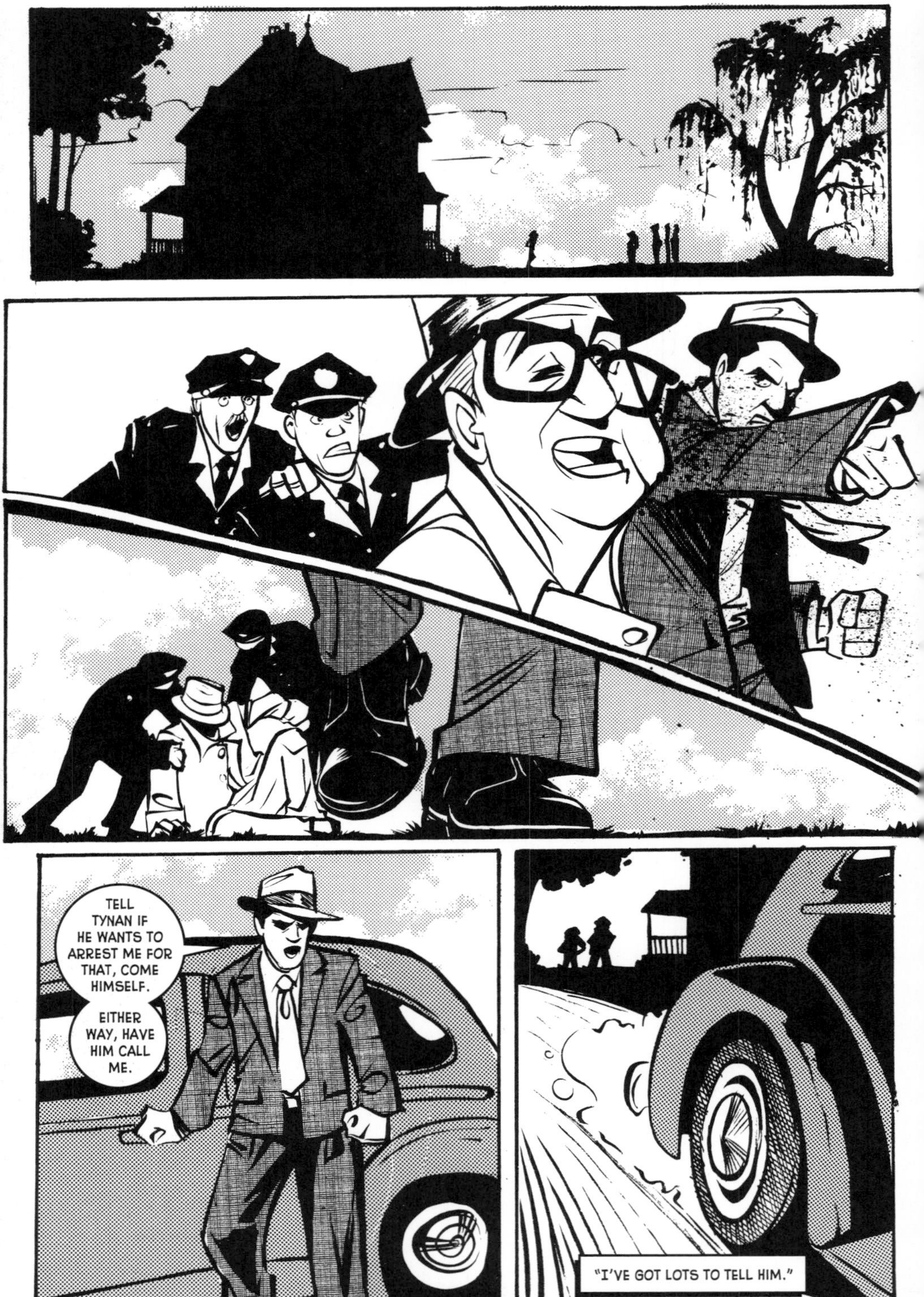
TELL TYNAN IF HE WANTS TO ARREST ME FOR THAT, COME HIMSELF.
EITHER WAY, HAVE HIM CALL ME.
"I'VE GOT LOTS TO TELL HIM."

CHAPTER 7

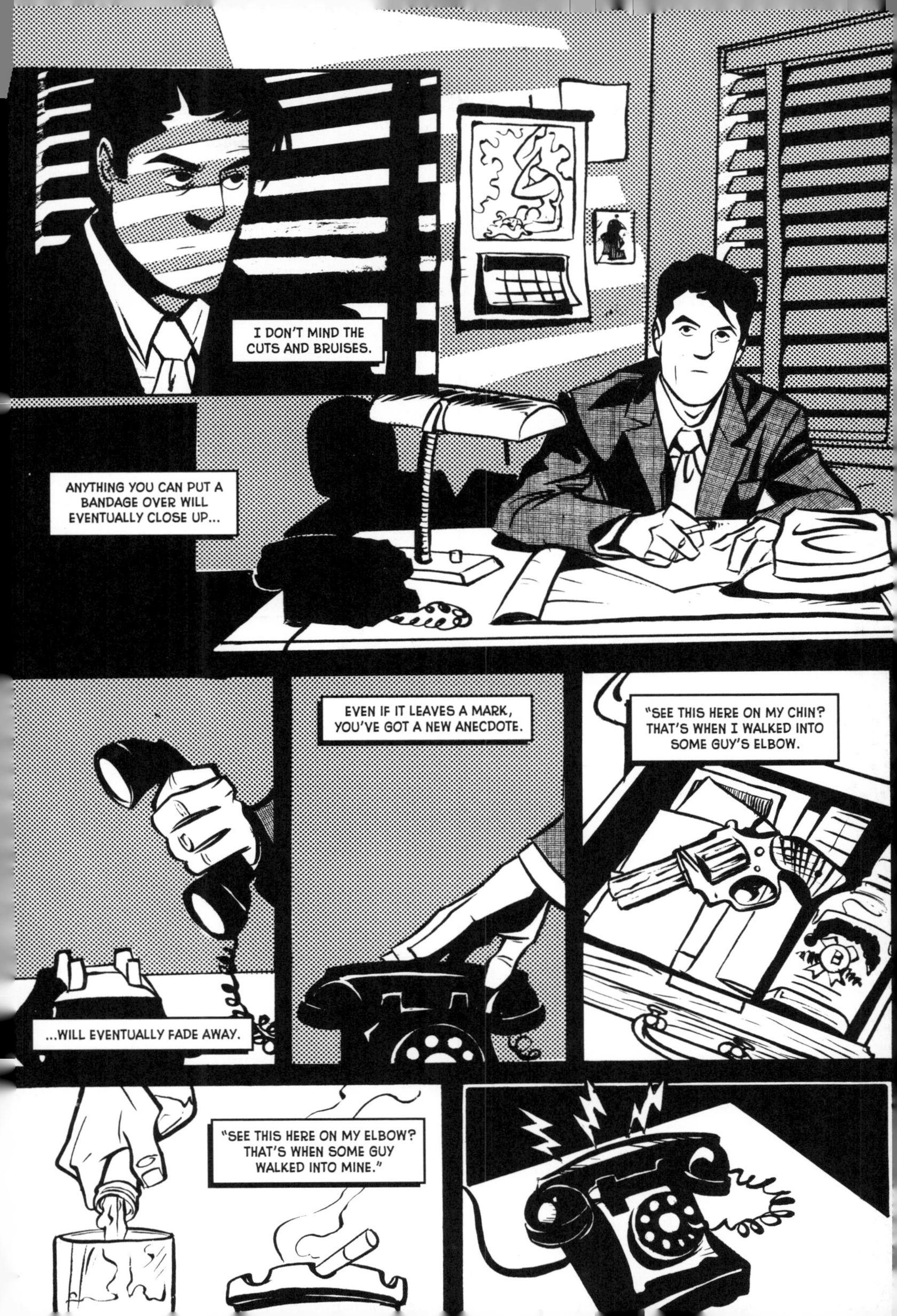
I DON'T MIND THE CUTS AND BRUISES.
ANYTHING YOU CAN PUT A BANDAGE OVER WILL EVENTUALLY CLOSE UP...
...WILL EVENTUALLY FADE AWAY.
EVEN IF IT LEAVES A MARK, YOU'VE GOT A NEW ANECDOTE.
"SEE THIS HERE ON MY CHIN? THAT'S WHEN I WALKED INTO SOME GUY'S ELBOW.
"SEE THIS HERE ON MY ELBOW? THAT'S WHEN SOME GUY WALKED INTO MINE."

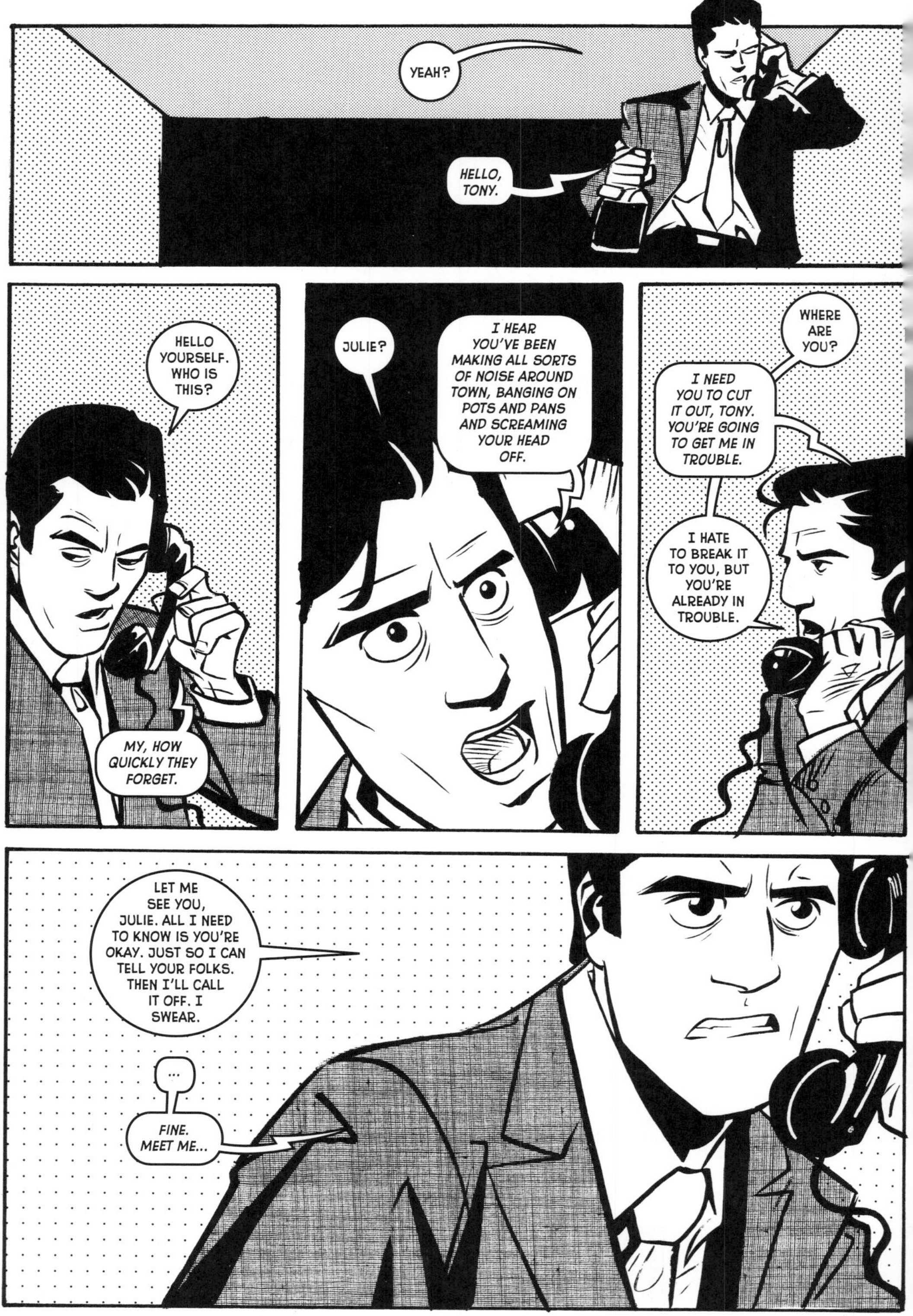
YEAH?
HELLO, TONY.
HELLO YOURSELF. WHO IS THIS?
MY, HOW QUICKLY THEY FORGET.
JULIE?
I HEAR YOU'VE BEEN MAKING ALL SORTS OF NOISE AROUND TOWN, BANGING ON POTS AND PANS AND SCREAMING YOUR HEAD OFF.
WHERE ARE YOU?
I NEED YOU TO CUT IT OUT, TONY. YOU'RE GOING TO GET ME IN TROUBLE.
I HATE TO BREAK IT TO YOU, BUT YOU'RE ALREADY IN TROUBLE.
LET ME SEE YOU, JULIE. ALL I NEED TO KNOW IS YOU'RE OKAY. JUST SO I CAN TELL YOUR FOLKS. THEN I'LL CALL IT OFF. I SWEAR.
...
FINE. MEET ME...

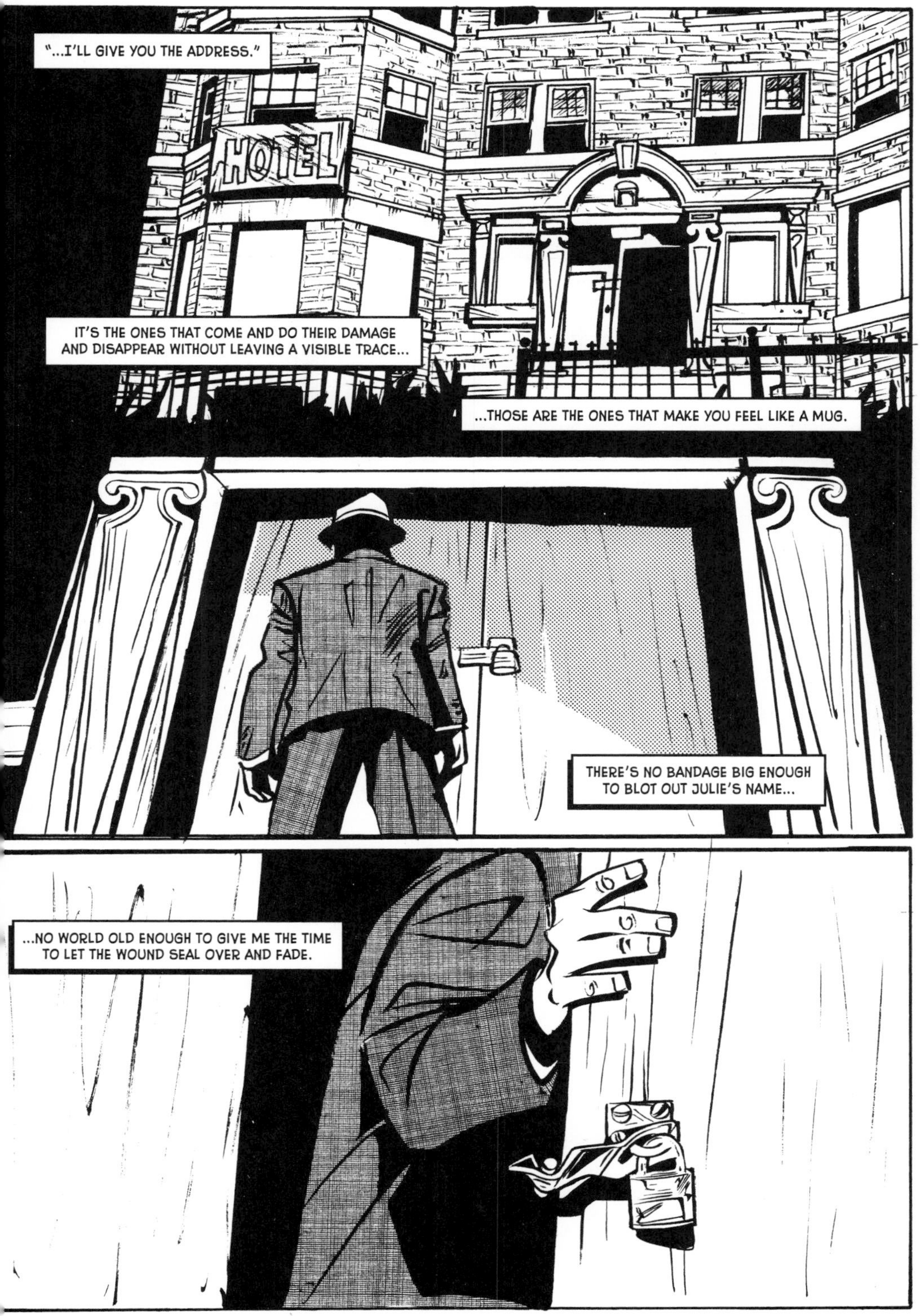
"...I'LL GIVE YOU THE ADDRESS."
HOTEL
IT'S THE ONES THAT COME AND DO THEIR DAMAGE AND DISAPPEAR WITHOUT LEAVING A VISIBLE TRACE...
...THOSE ARE THE ONES THAT MAKE YOU FEEL LIKE A MUG.
THERE'S NO BANDAGE BIG ENOUGH TO BLOT OUT JULIE'S NAME...
...NO WORLD OLD ENOUGH TO GIVE ME THE TIME TO LET THE WOUND SEAL OVER AND FADE.

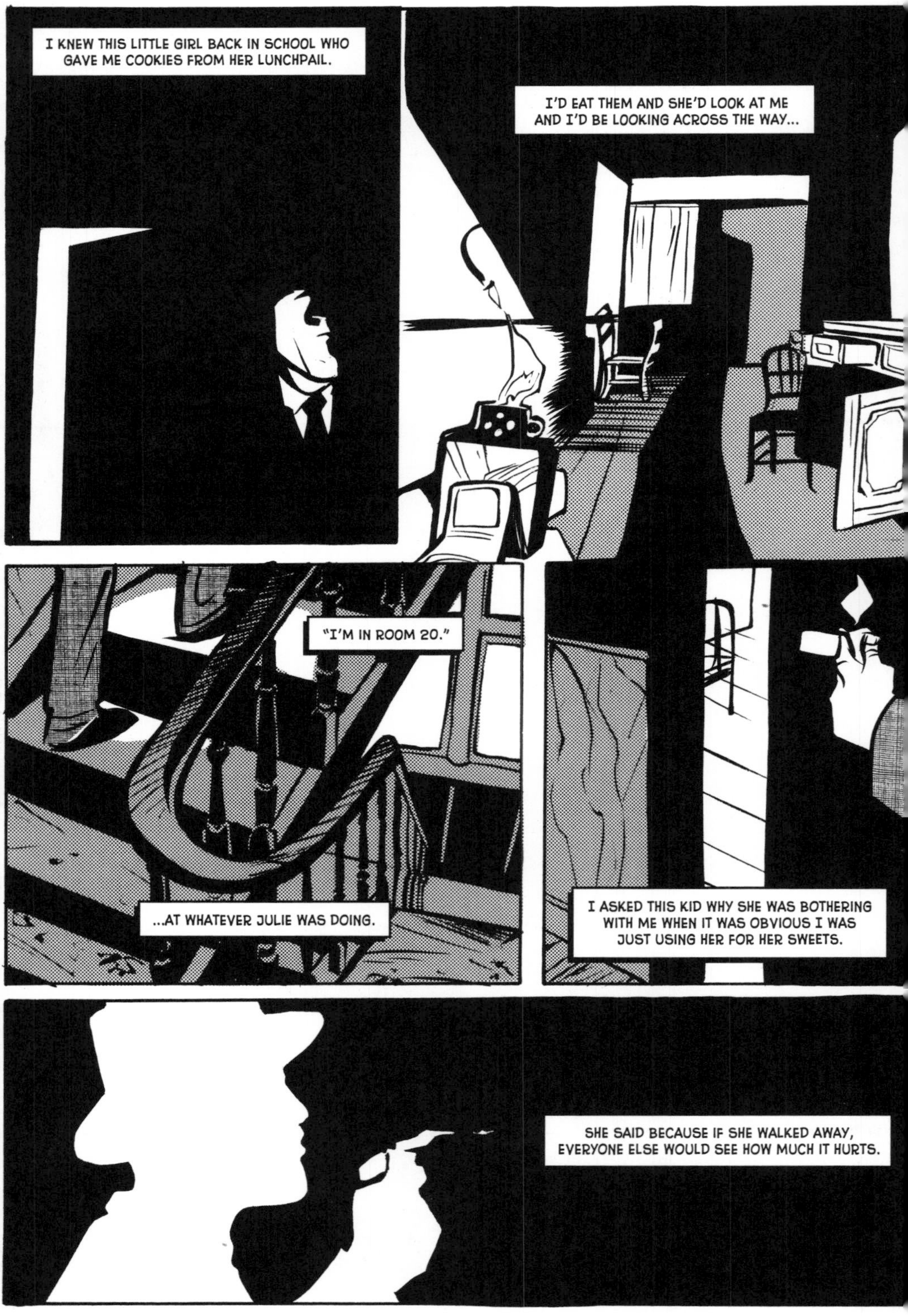
I KNEW THIS LITTLE GIRL BACK IN SCHOOL WHO GAVE ME COOKIES FROM HER LUNCHPAIL.
I'D EAT THEM AND SHE'D LOOK AT ME AND I'D BE LOOKING ACROSS THE WAY...
"I'M IN ROOM 20."
...AT WHATEVER JULIE WAS DOING.
I ASKED THIS KID WHY SHE WAS BOTHERING WITH ME WHEN IT WAS OBVIOUS I WAS JUST USING HER FOR HER SWEETS.
SHE SAID BECAUSE IF SHE WALKED AWAY, EVERYONE ELSE WOULD SEE HOW MUCH IT HURTS.

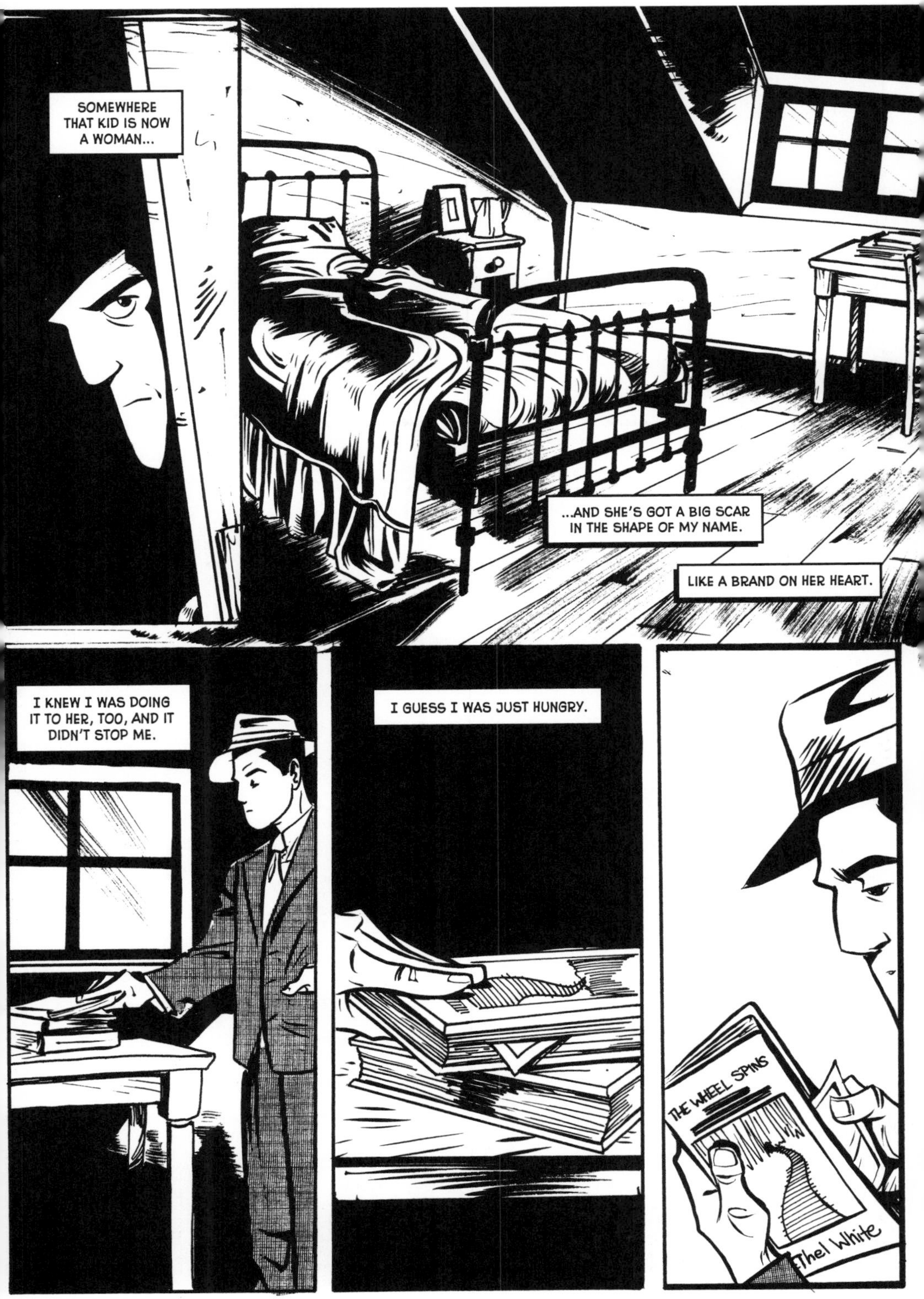
SOMEWHERE THAT KID IS NOW A WOMAN...
...AND SHE'S GOT A BIG SCAR IN THE SHAPE OF MY NAME.
LIKE A BRAND ON HER HEART.
I KNEW I WAS DOING IT TO HER, TOO, AND IT DIDN'T STOP ME.
I GUESS I WAS JUST HUNGRY.
THE WHEEL SPINS
Ethel White

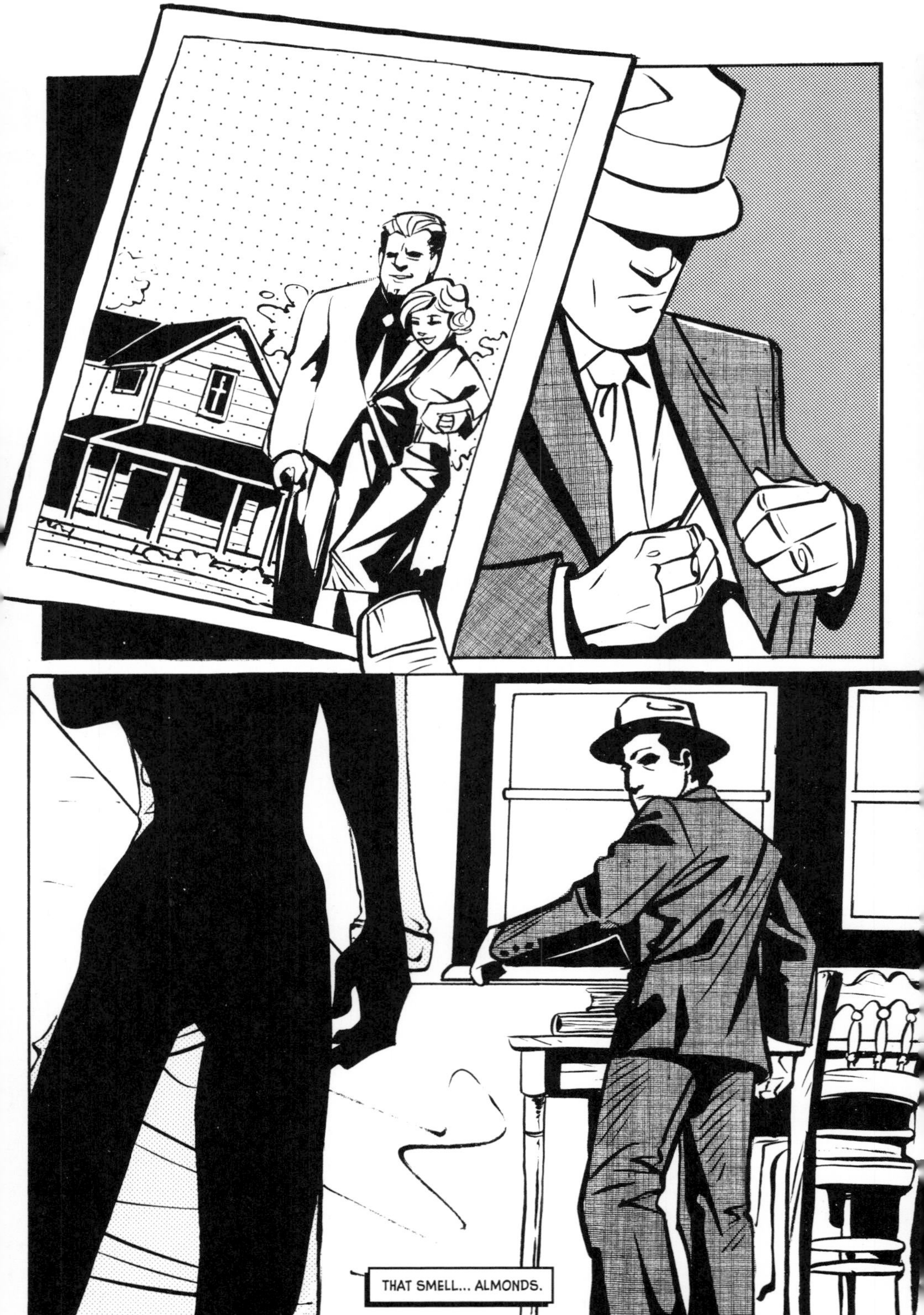
THAT SMELL... ALMONDS.

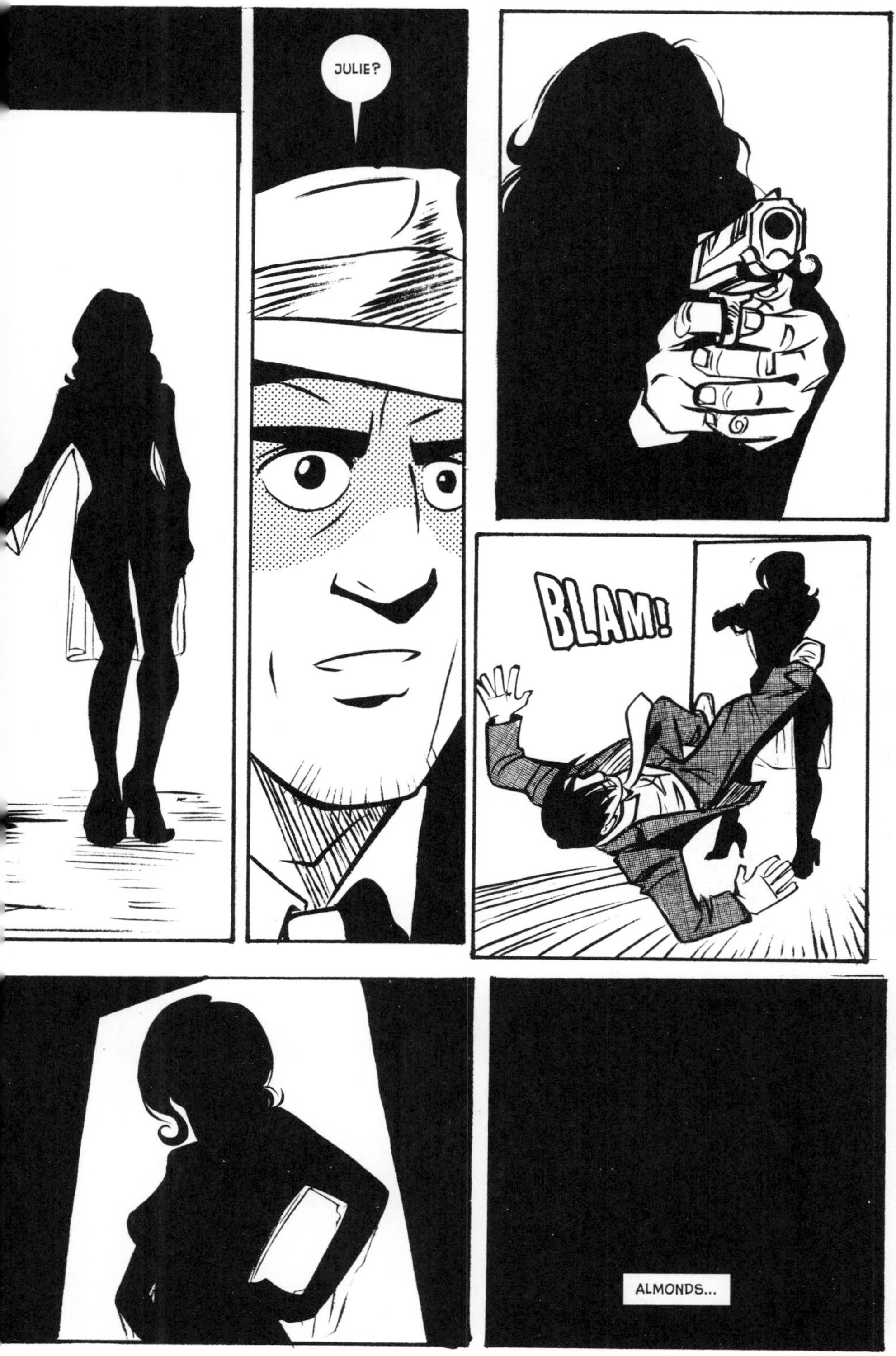
JULIE?
BLAM!
ALMONDS...

CHAPTER   8

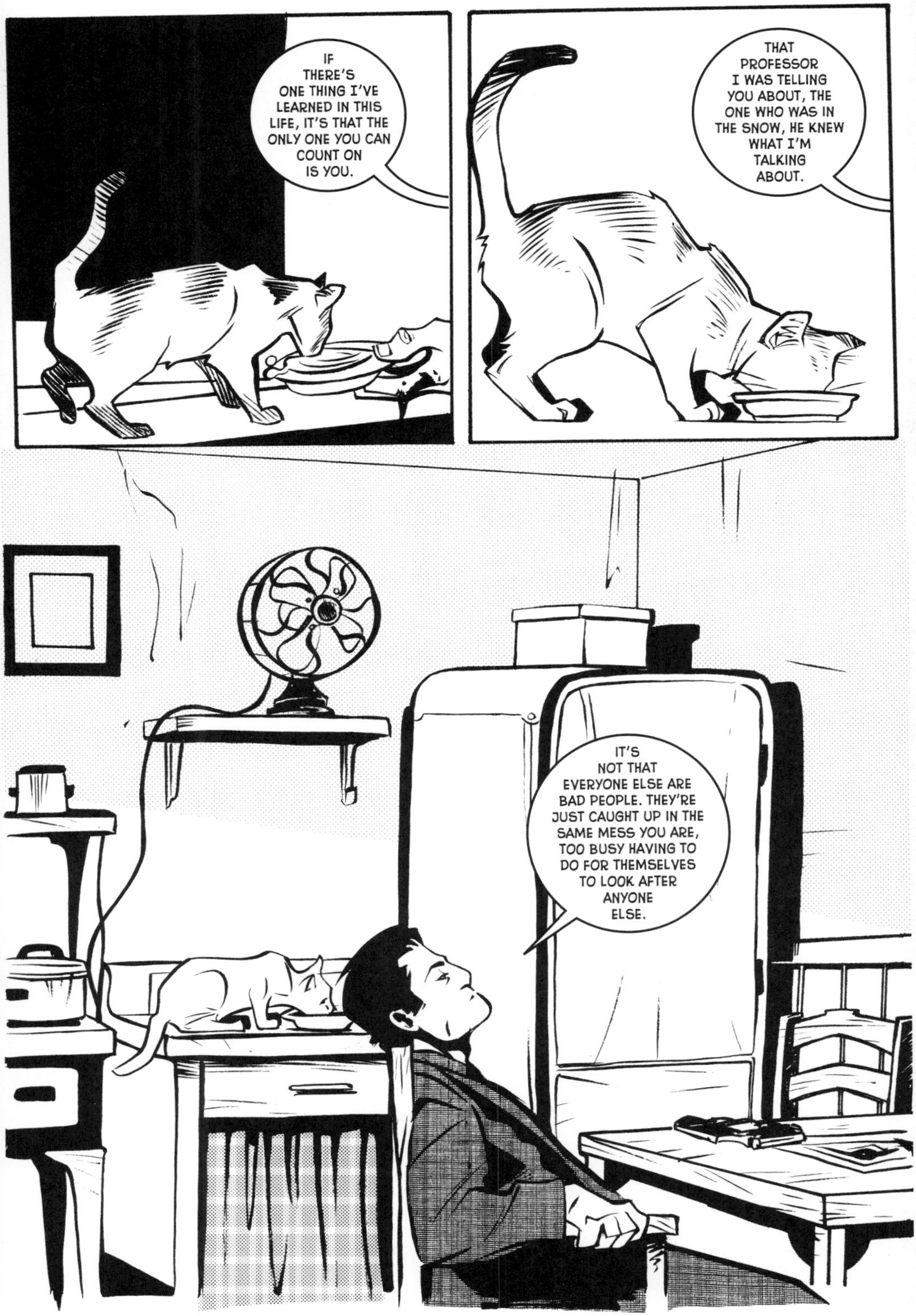
IF THERE'S ONE THING I'VE LEARNED IN THIS LIFE, IT'S THAT THE ONLY ONE YOU CAN COUNT ON IS YOU.
THAT PROFESSOR I WAS TELLING YOU ABOUT, THE ONE WHO WAS IN THE SNOW, HE KNEW WHAT I'M TALKING ABOUT.
IT'S NOT THAT EVERYONE ELSE ARE BAD PEOPLE. THEY'RE JUST CAUGHT UP IN THE SAME MESS YOU ARE, TOO BUSY HAVING TO DO FOR THEMSELVES TO LOOK AFTER ANYONE ELSE.

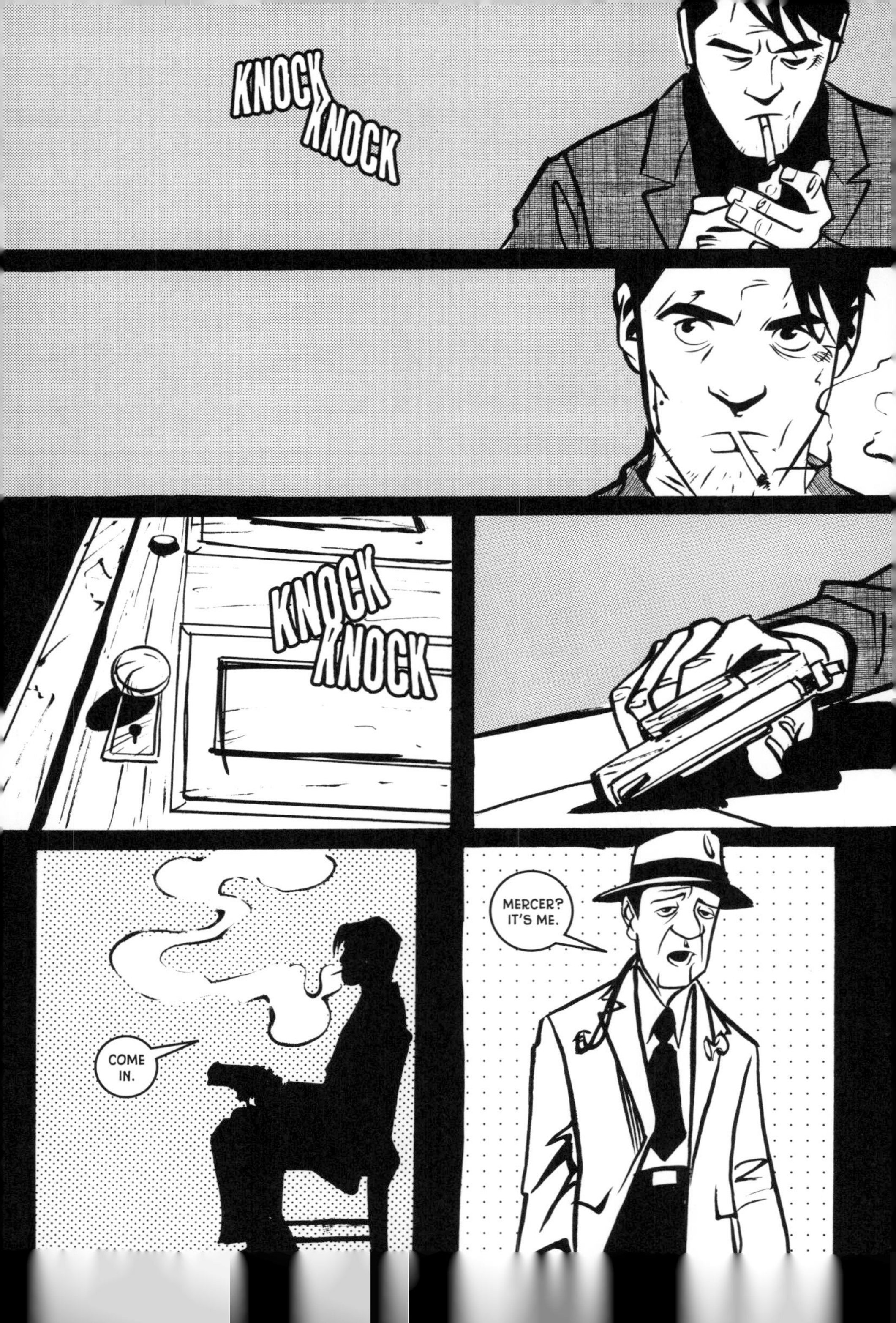
KNOCK KNOCK
KNOCK KNOCK
COME IN.
MERCER? IT'S ME.

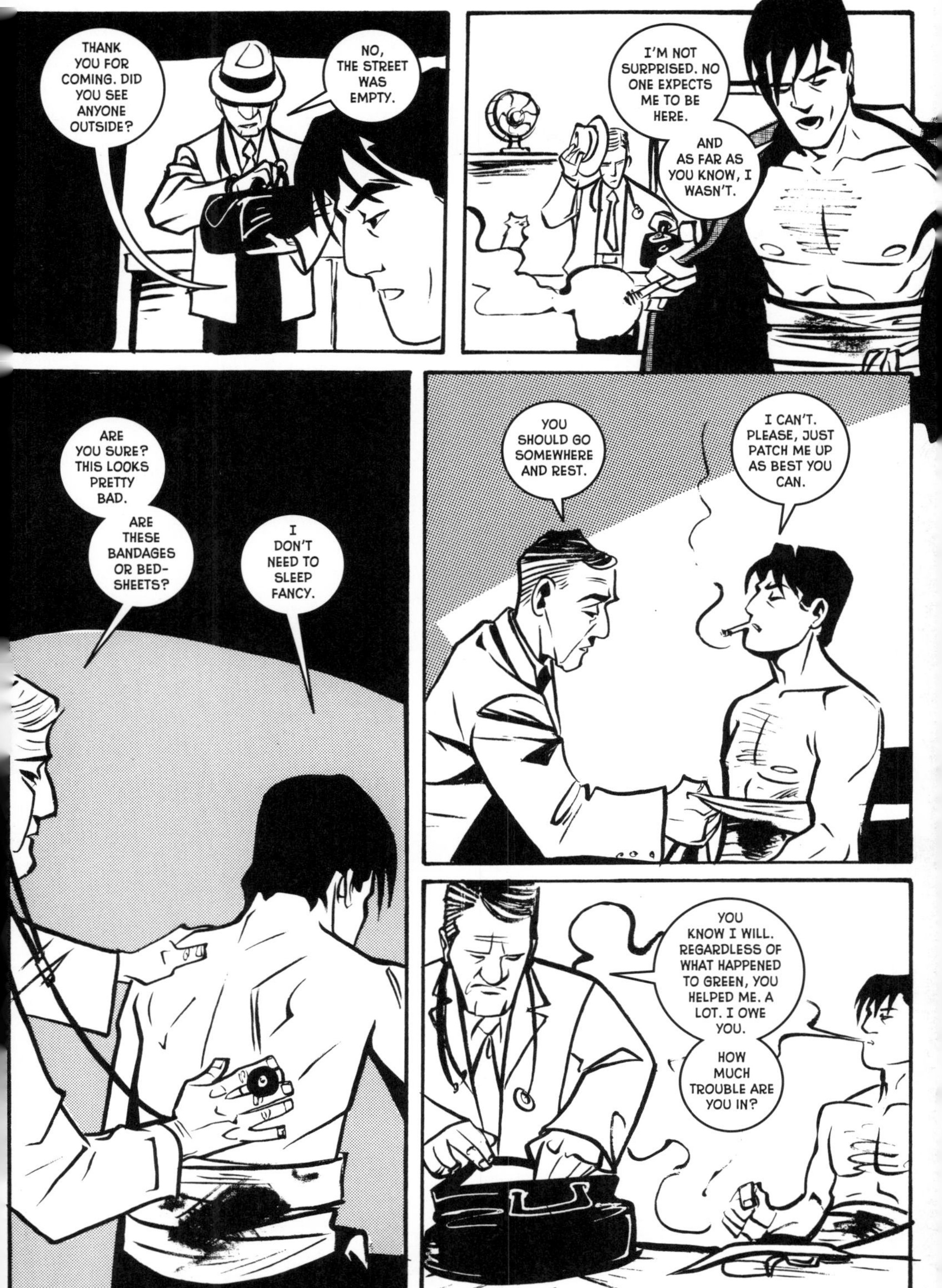
THANK YOU FOR COMING. DID YOU SEE ANYONE OUTSIDE?
NO, THE STREET WAS EMPTY.
I'M NOT SURPRISED. NO ONE EXPECTS ME TO BE HERE.
AND AS FAR AS YOU KNOW, I WASN'T.
ARE YOU SURE? THIS LOOKS PRETTY BAD.
ARE THESE BANDAGES OR BED-SHEETS?
I DON'T NEED TO SLEEP FANCY.
YOU SHOULD GO SOMEWHERE AND REST.
I CAN'T. PLEASE, JUST PATCH ME UP AS BEST YOU CAN.
YOU KNOW I WILL. REGARDLESS OF WHAT HAPPENED TO GREEN, YOU HELPED ME. A LOT. I OWE YOU.
HOW MUCH TROUBLE ARE YOU IN?

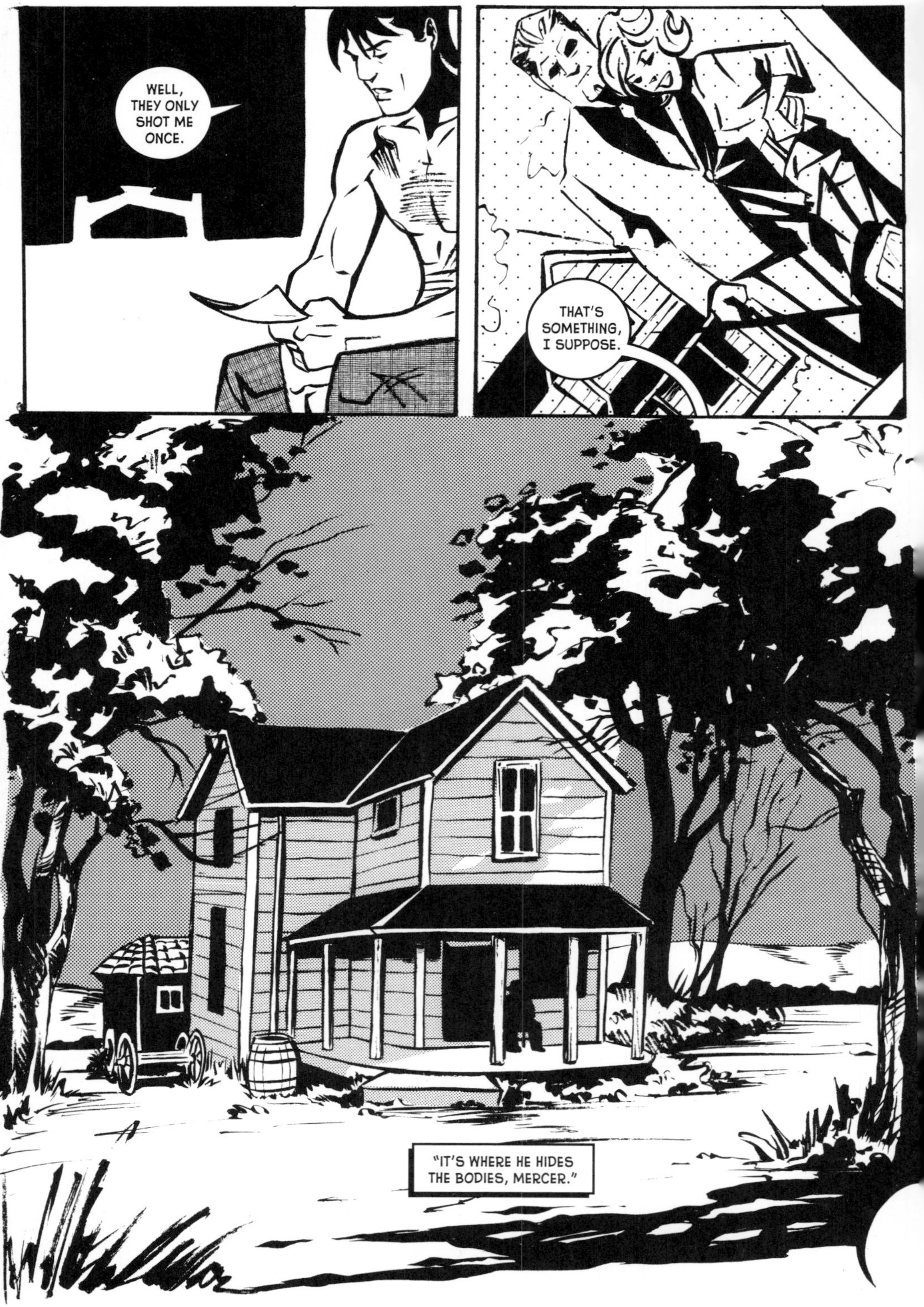
WELL, THEY ONLY SHOT ME ONCE.
THAT'S SOMETHING, I SUPPOSE.
"IT'S WHERE HE HIDES THE BODIES, MERCER."

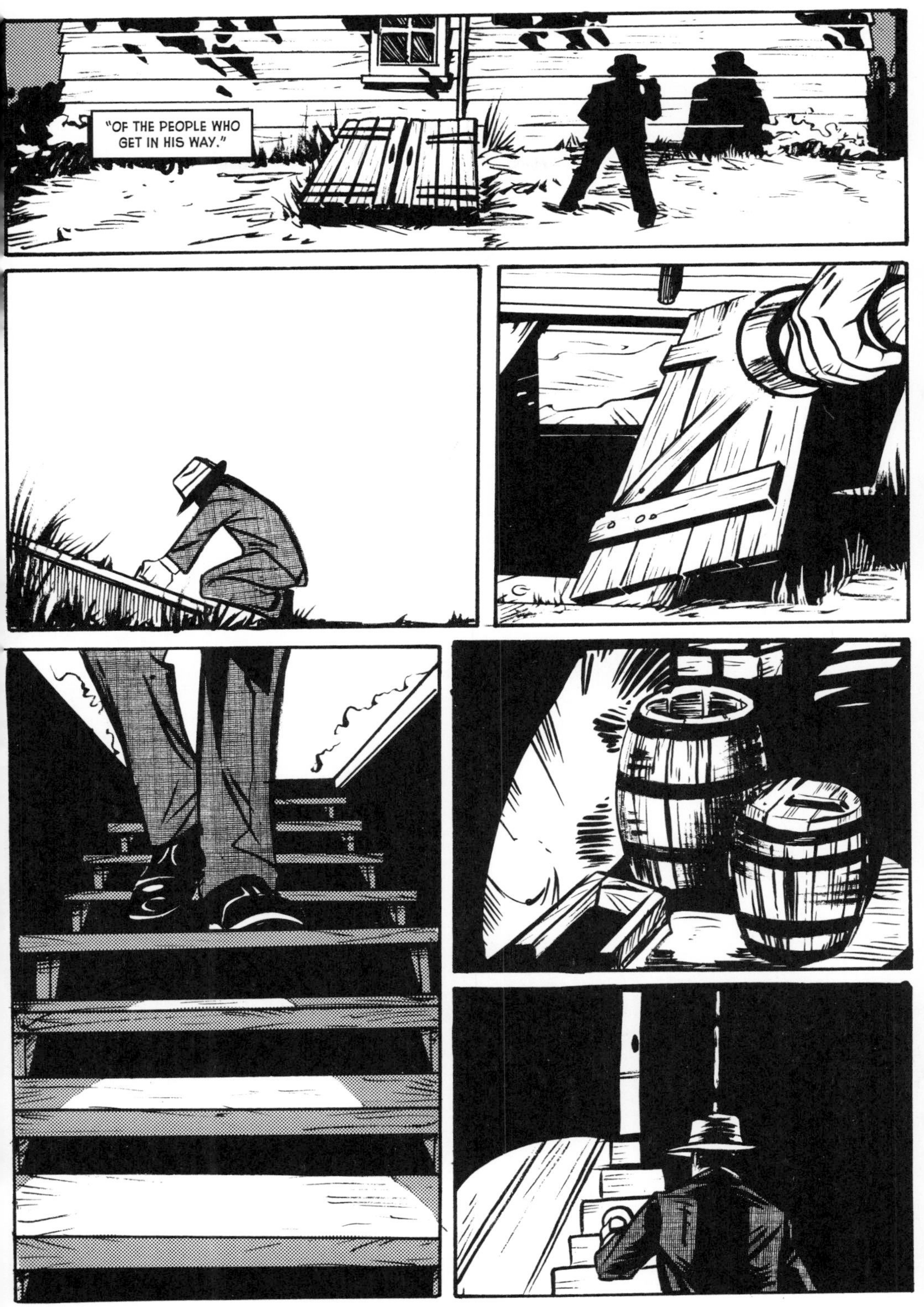
"OF THE PEOPLE WHO GET IN HIS WAY."

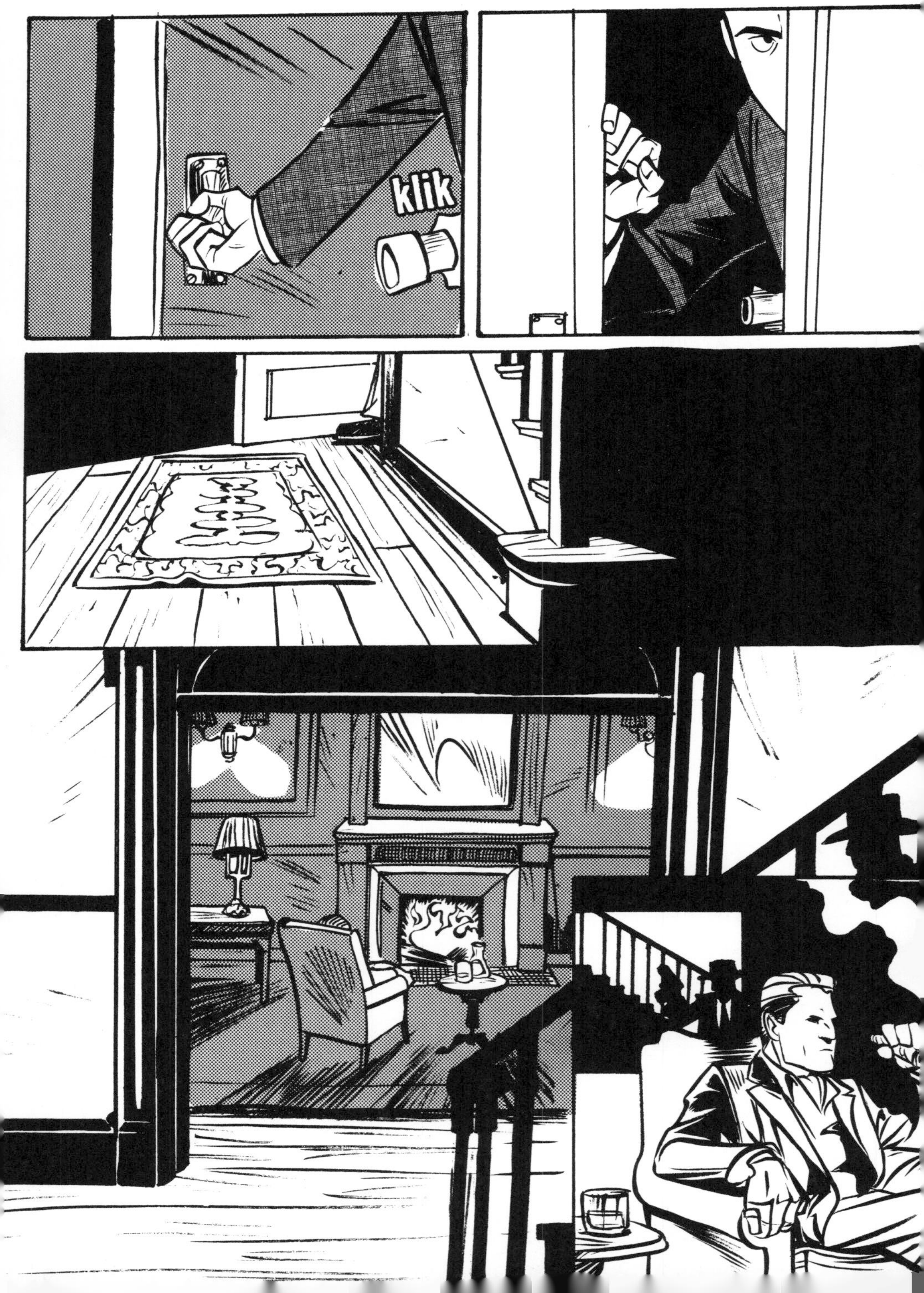
klik

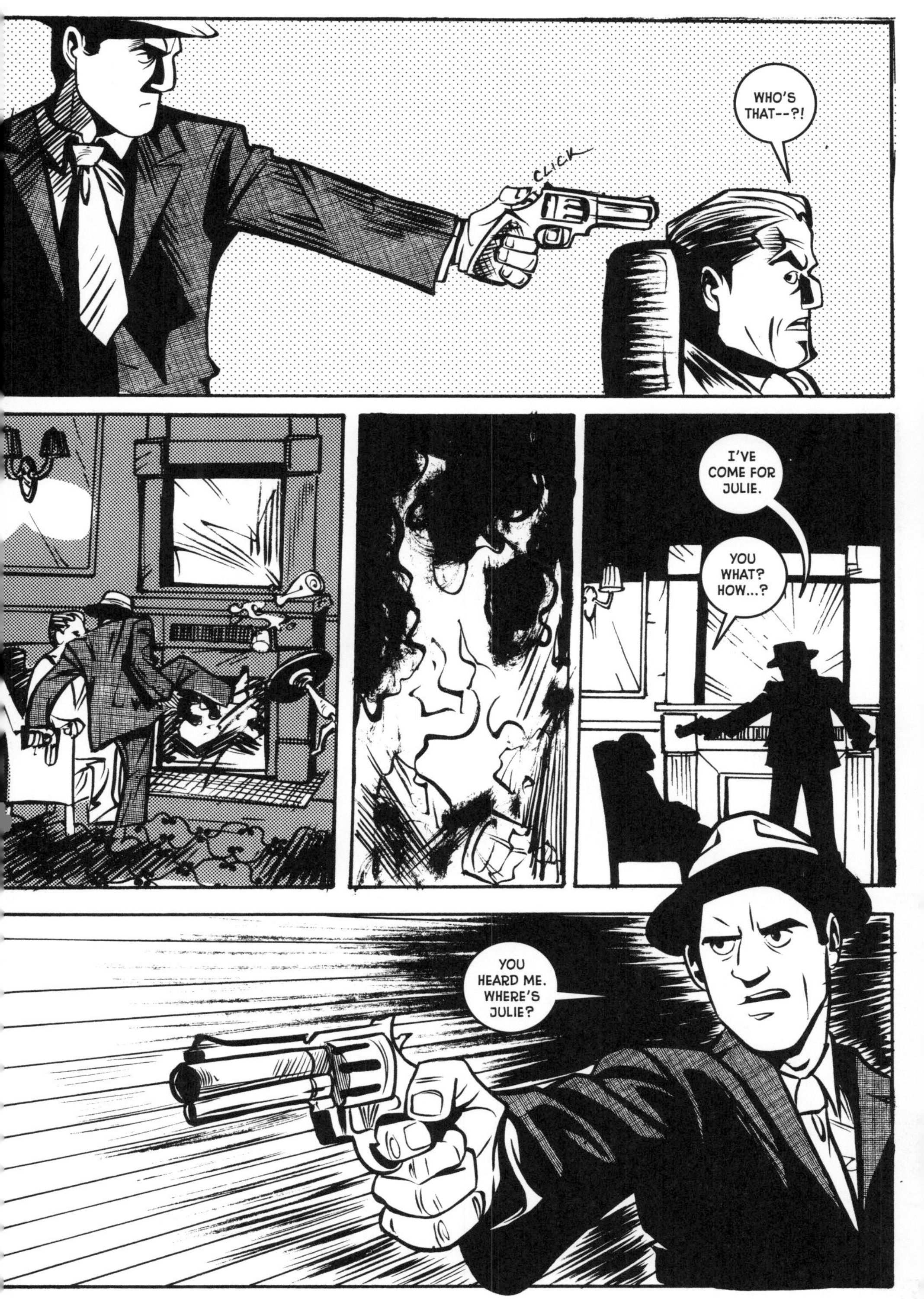
WHO'S THAT--?!
CLICK
I'VE COME FOR JULIE.
YOU WHAT? HOW...?
YOU HEARD ME. WHERE'S JULIE?

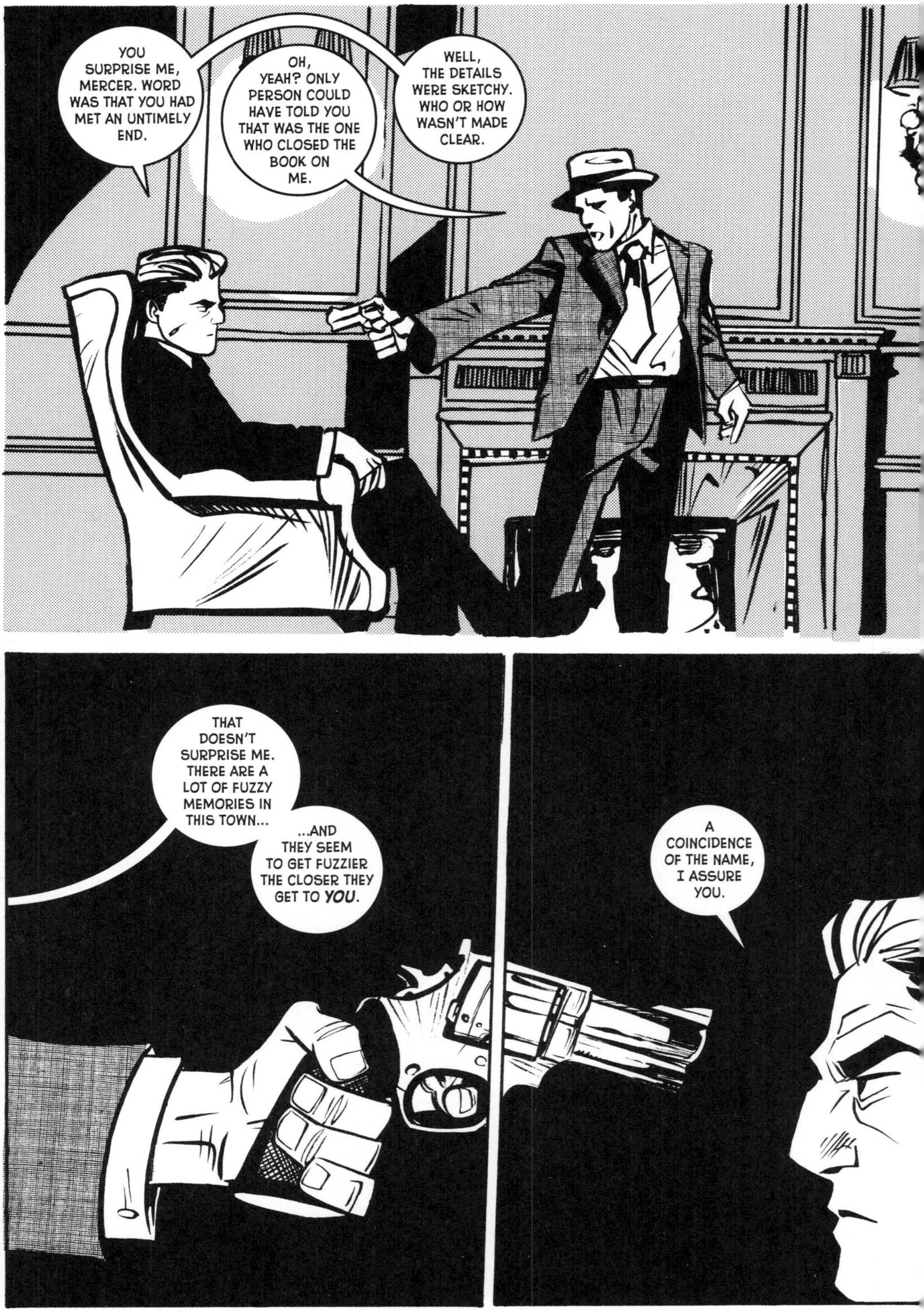
YOU SURPRISE ME, MERCER. WORD WAS THAT YOU HAD MET AN UNTIMELY END.
OH, YEAH? ONLY PERSON COULD HAVE TOLD YOU THAT WAS THE ONE WHO CLOSED THE BOOK ON ME.
WELL, THE DETAILS WERE SKETCHY. WHO OR HOW WASN'T MADE CLEAR.
THAT DOESN'T SURPRISE ME. THERE ARE A LOT OF FUZZY MEMORIES IN THIS TOWN...
...AND THEY SEEM TO GET FUZZIER THE CLOSER THEY GET TO *YOU*.
A COINCIDENCE OF THE NAME, I ASSURE YOU.

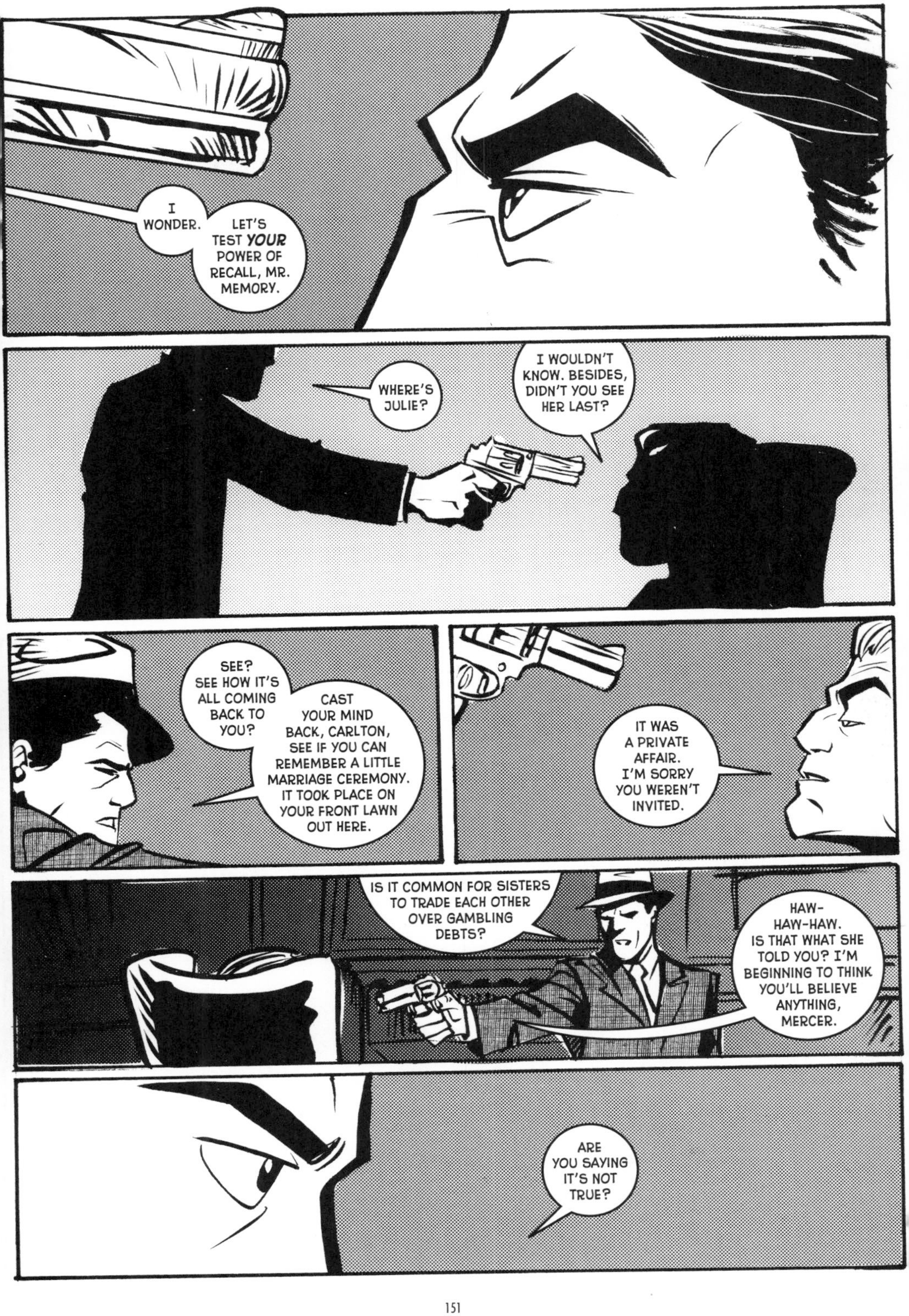
I WONDER.
LET'S TEST *YOUR* POWER OF RECALL, MR. MEMORY.
WHERE'S JULIE?
I WOULDN'T KNOW. BESIDES, DIDN'T YOU SEE HER LAST?
SEE? SEE HOW IT'S ALL COMING BACK TO YOU?
CAST YOUR MIND BACK, CARLTON, SEE IF YOU CAN REMEMBER A LITTLE MARRIAGE CEREMONY. IT TOOK PLACE ON YOUR FRONT LAWN OUT HERE.
IT WAS A PRIVATE AFFAIR. I'M SORRY YOU WEREN'T INVITED.
IS IT COMMON FOR SISTERS TO TRADE EACH OTHER OVER GAMBLING DEBTS?
HAW-HAW-HAW. IS THAT WHAT SHE TOLD YOU? I'M BEGINNING TO THINK YOU'LL BELIEVE ANYTHING, MERCER.
ARE YOU SAYING IT'S NOT TRUE?

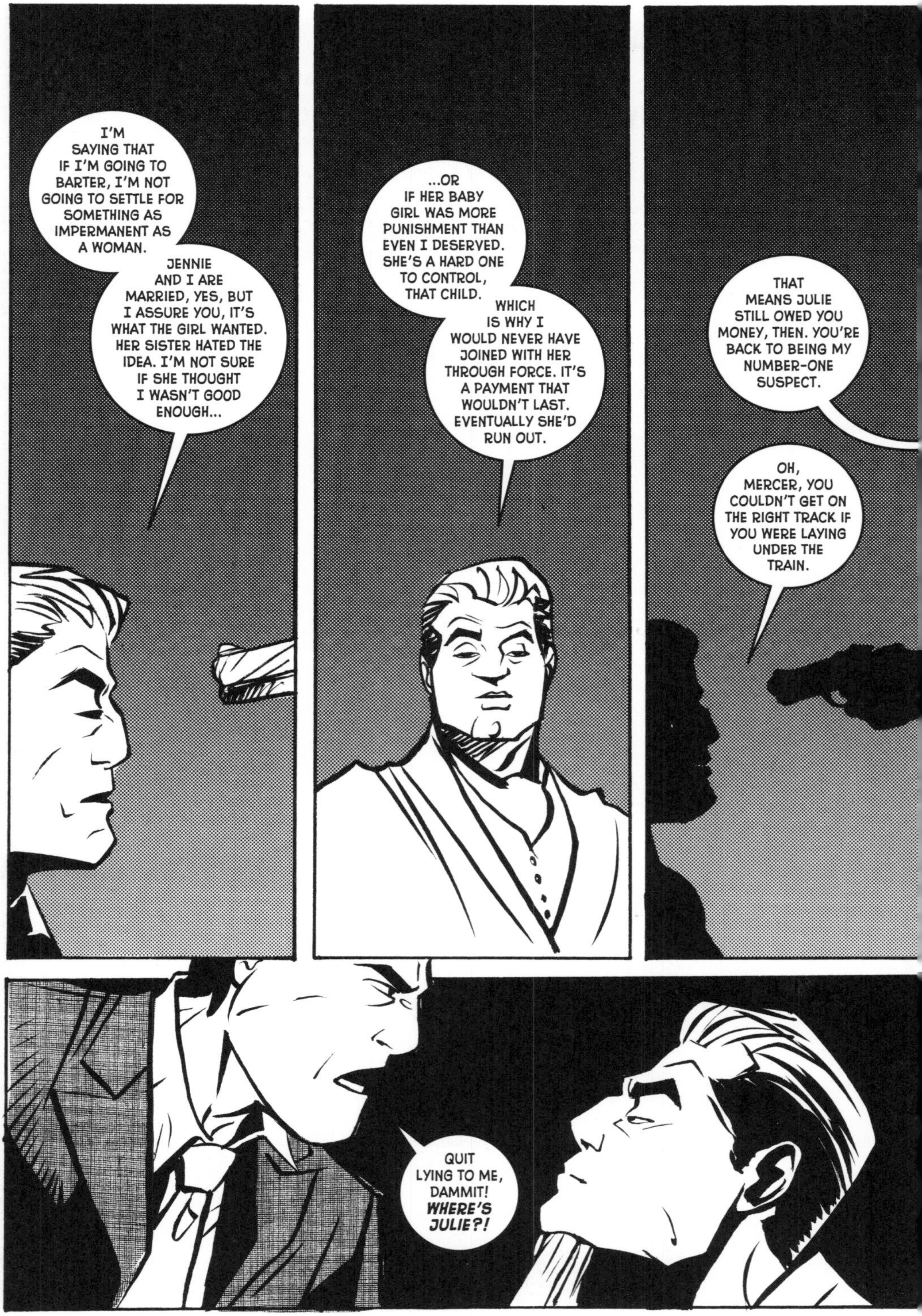
I'M SAYING THAT IF I'M GOING TO BARTER, I'M NOT GOING TO SETTLE FOR SOMETHING AS IMPERMANENT AS A WOMAN.
JENNIE AND I ARE MARRIED, YES, BUT I ASSURE YOU, IT'S WHAT THE GIRL WANTED. HER SISTER HATED THE IDEA. I'M NOT SURE IF SHE THOUGHT I WASN'T GOOD ENOUGH...
...OR IF HER BABY GIRL WAS MORE PUNISHMENT THAN EVEN I DESERVED. SHE'S A HARD ONE TO CONTROL, THAT CHILD.
WHICH IS WHY I WOULD NEVER HAVE JOINED WITH HER THROUGH FORCE. IT'S A PAYMENT THAT WOULDN'T LAST. EVENTUALLY SHE'D RUN OUT.
THAT MEANS JULIE STILL OWED YOU MONEY, THEN. YOU'RE BACK TO BEING MY NUMBER-ONE SUSPECT.
OH, MERCER, YOU COULDN'T GET ON THE RIGHT TRACK IF YOU WERE LAYING UNDER THE TRAIN.
QUIT LYING TO ME, DAMMIT! ***WHERE'S JULIE?!***

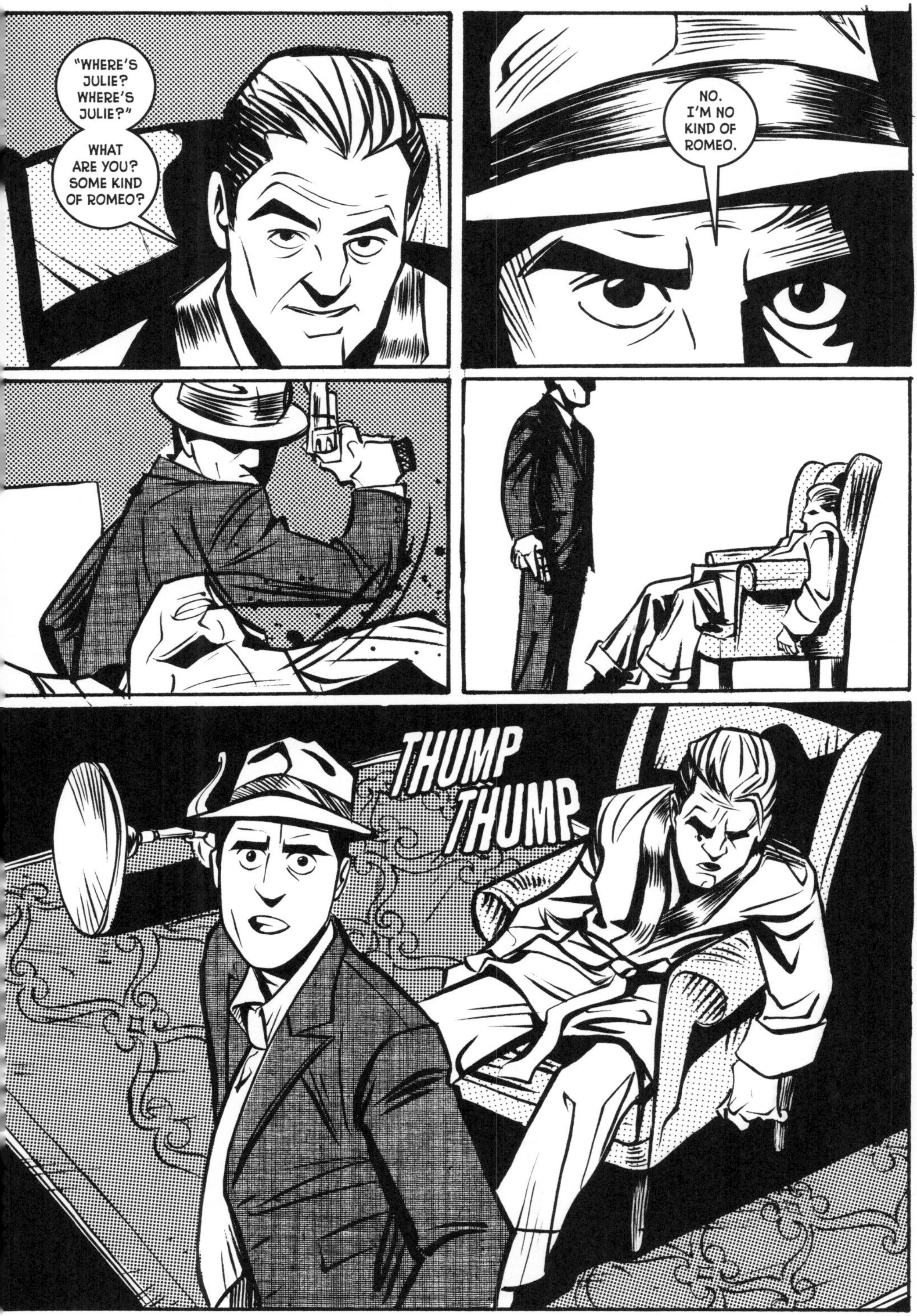
"WHERE'S JULIE? WHERE'S JULIE?"
WHAT ARE YOU? SOME KIND OF ROMEO?
NO. I'M NO KIND OF ROMEO.
THUMP
THUMP

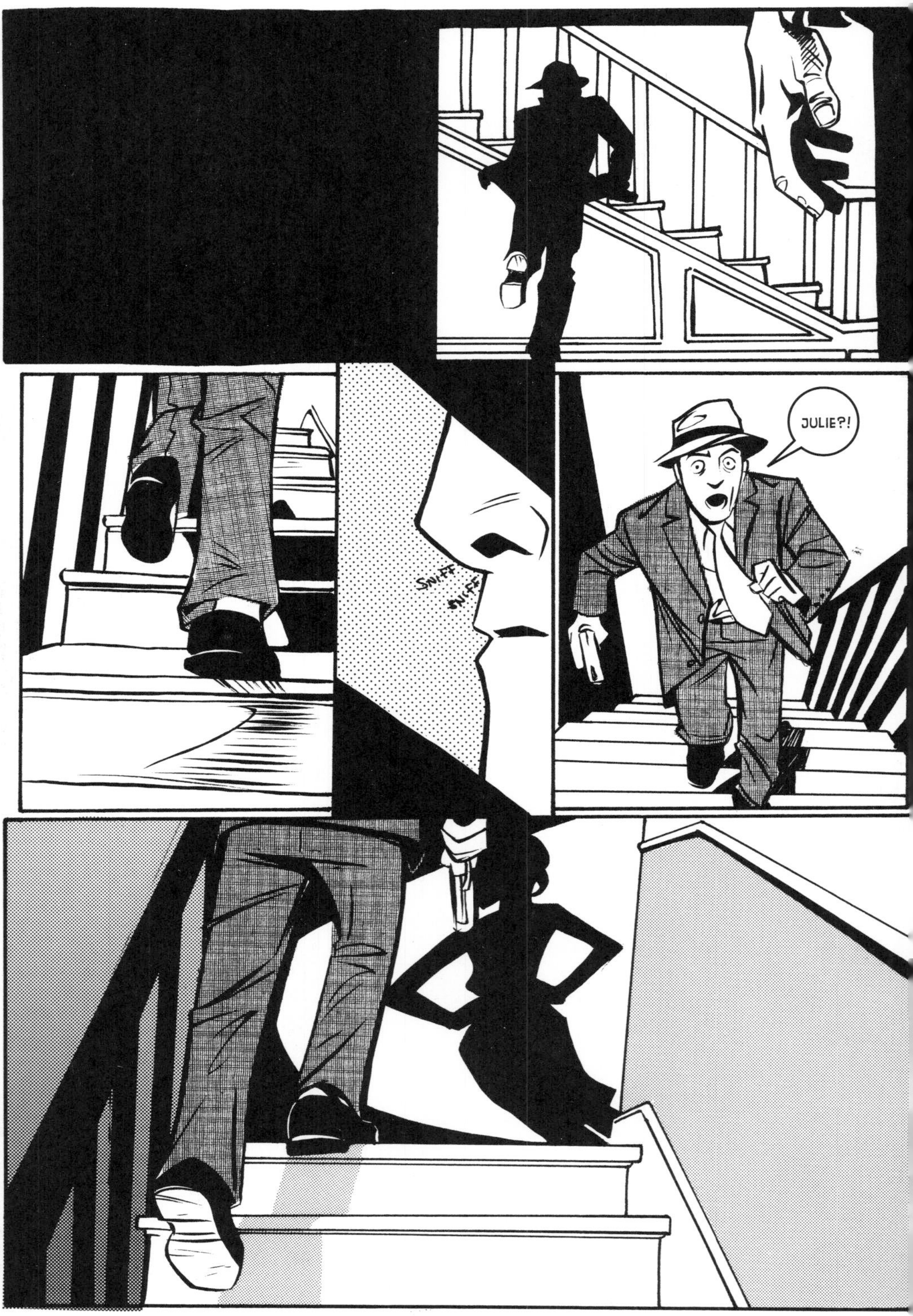
SNIFF
SNIFF
JULIE?!

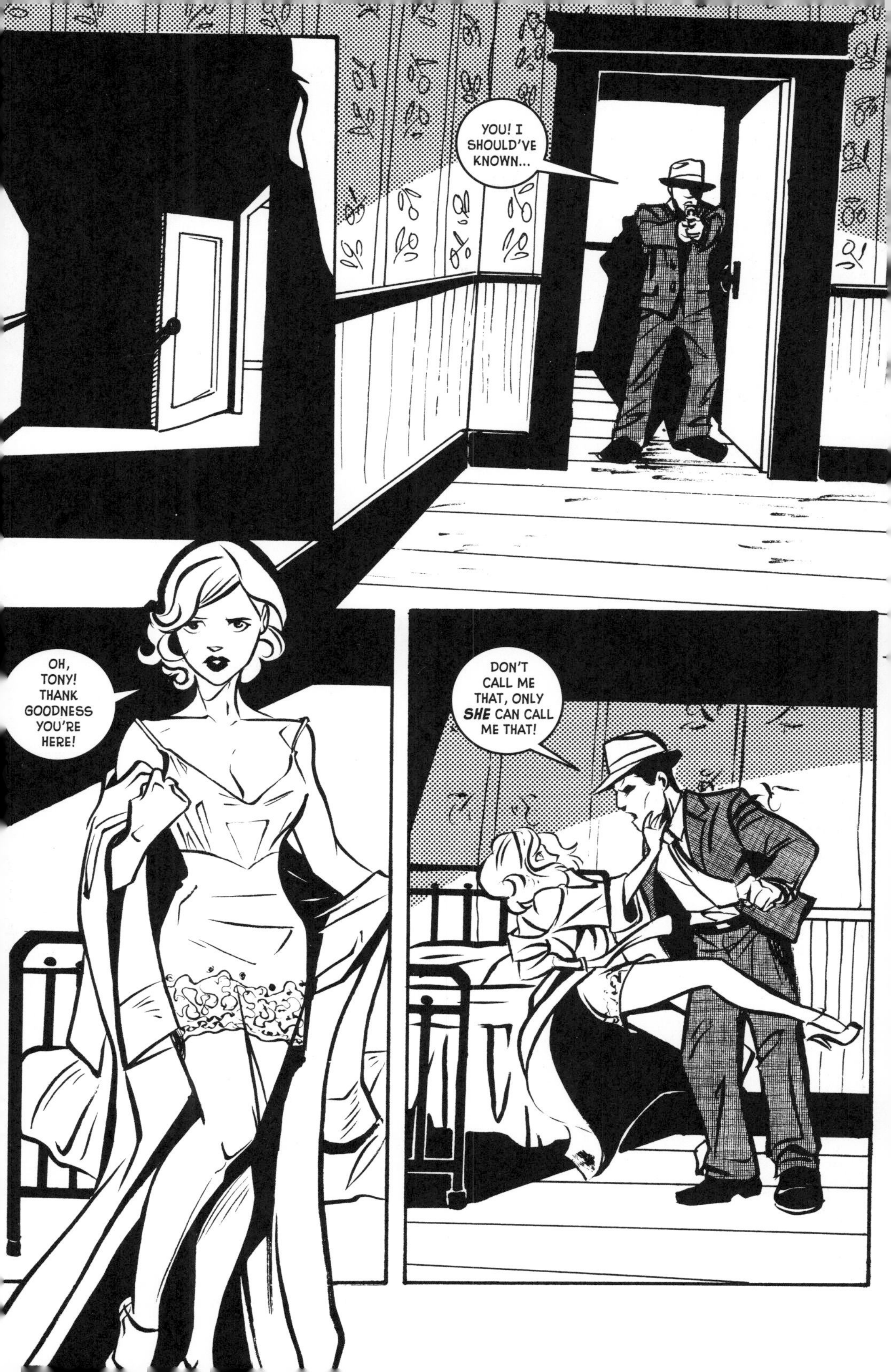
YOU! I SHOULD'VE KNOWN...
OH, TONY! THANK GOODNESS YOU'RE HERE!
DON'T CALL ME THAT, ONLY SHE CAN CALL ME THAT!

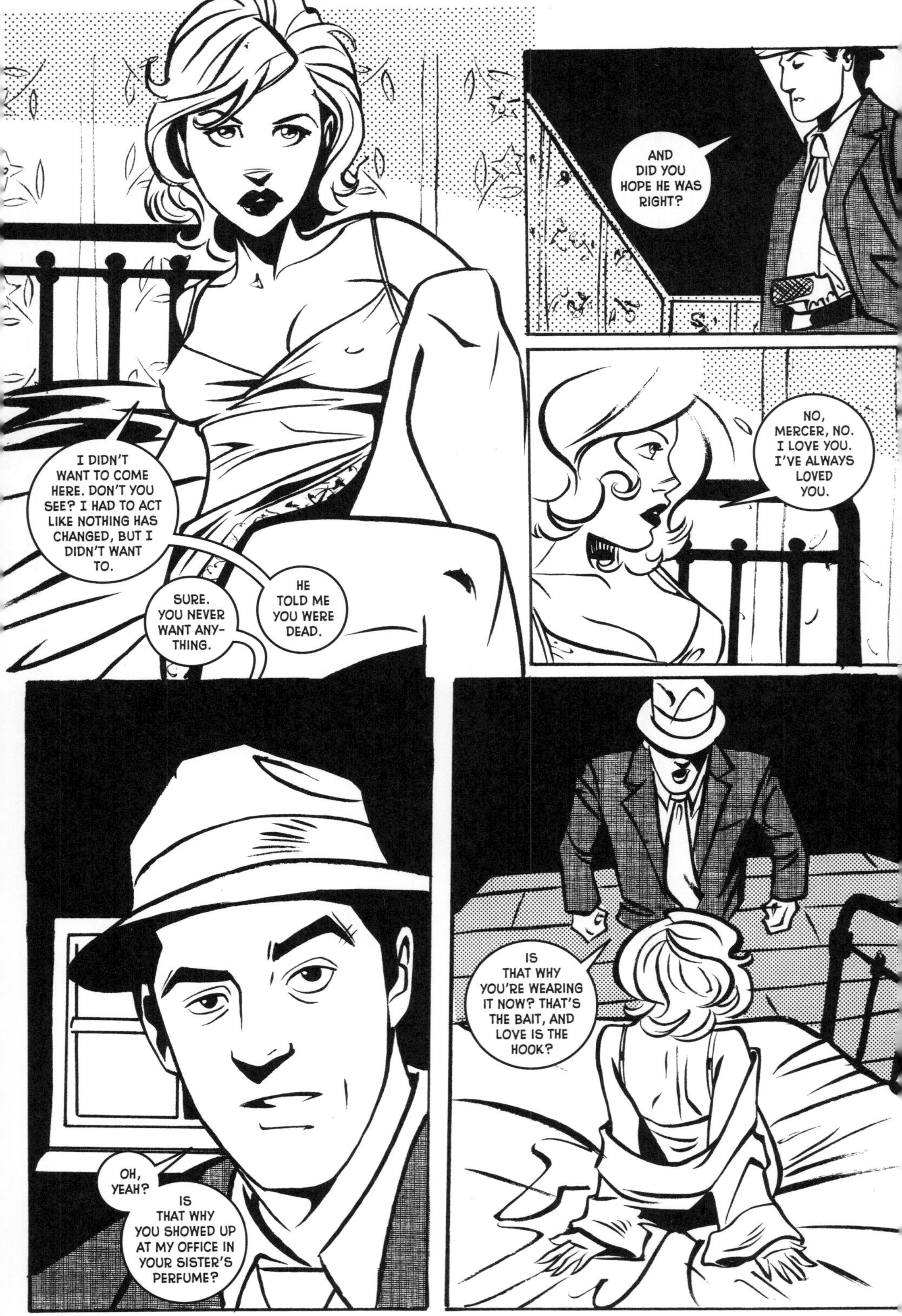
I DIDN'T WANT TO COME HERE. DON'T YOU SEE? I HAD TO ACT LIKE NOTHING HAS CHANGED, BUT I DIDN'T WANT TO.
SURE. YOU NEVER WANT ANY-THING.
HE TOLD ME YOU WERE DEAD.
AND DID YOU HOPE HE WAS RIGHT?
NO, MERCER, NO. I LOVE YOU. I'VE ALWAYS LOVED YOU.
OH, YEAH?
IS THAT WHY YOU SHOWED UP AT MY OFFICE IN YOUR SISTER'S PERFUME?
IS THAT WHY YOU'RE WEARING IT NOW? THAT'S THE BAIT, AND LOVE IS THE HOOK?

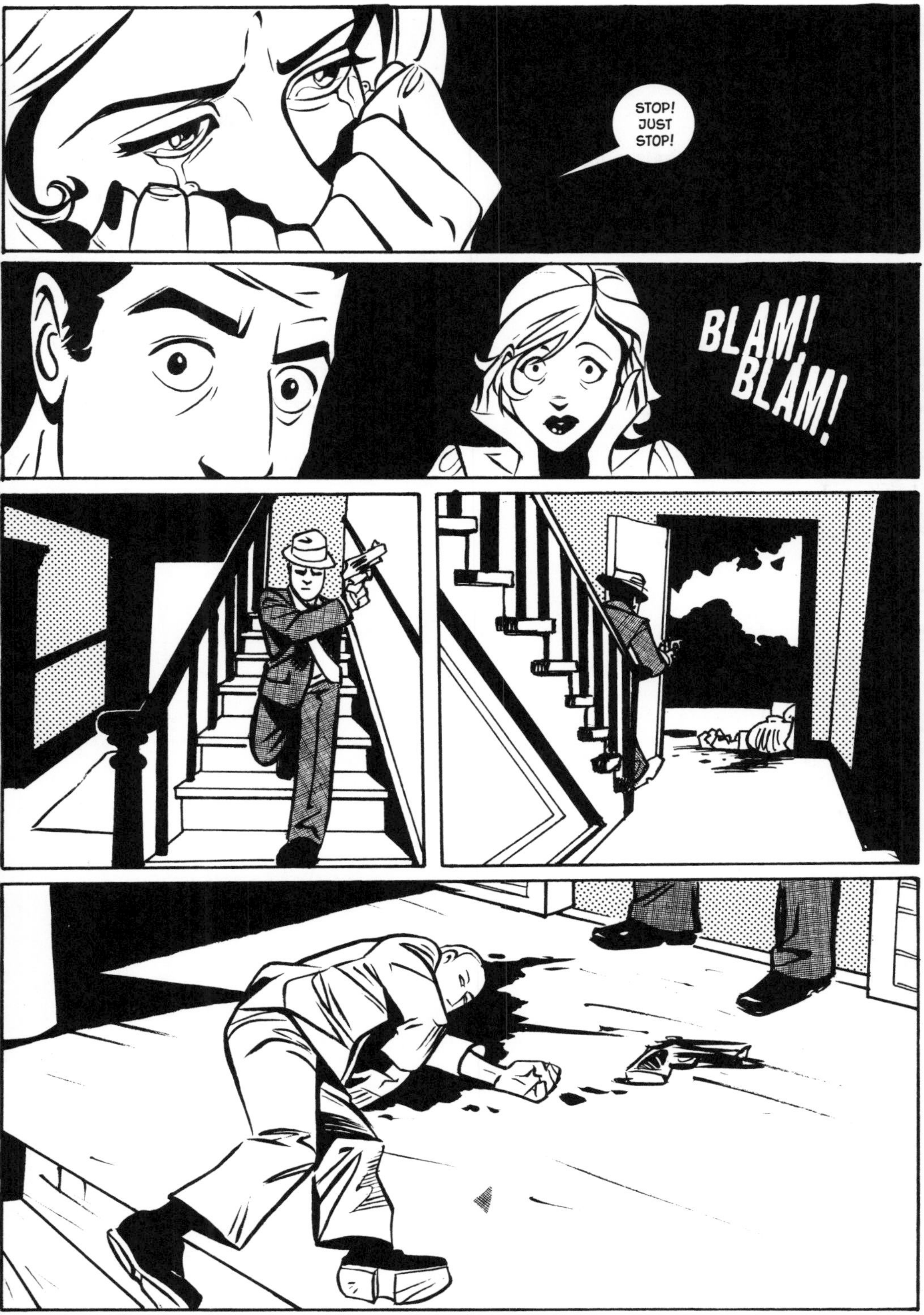
STOP! JUST STOP!
BLAM! BLAM!

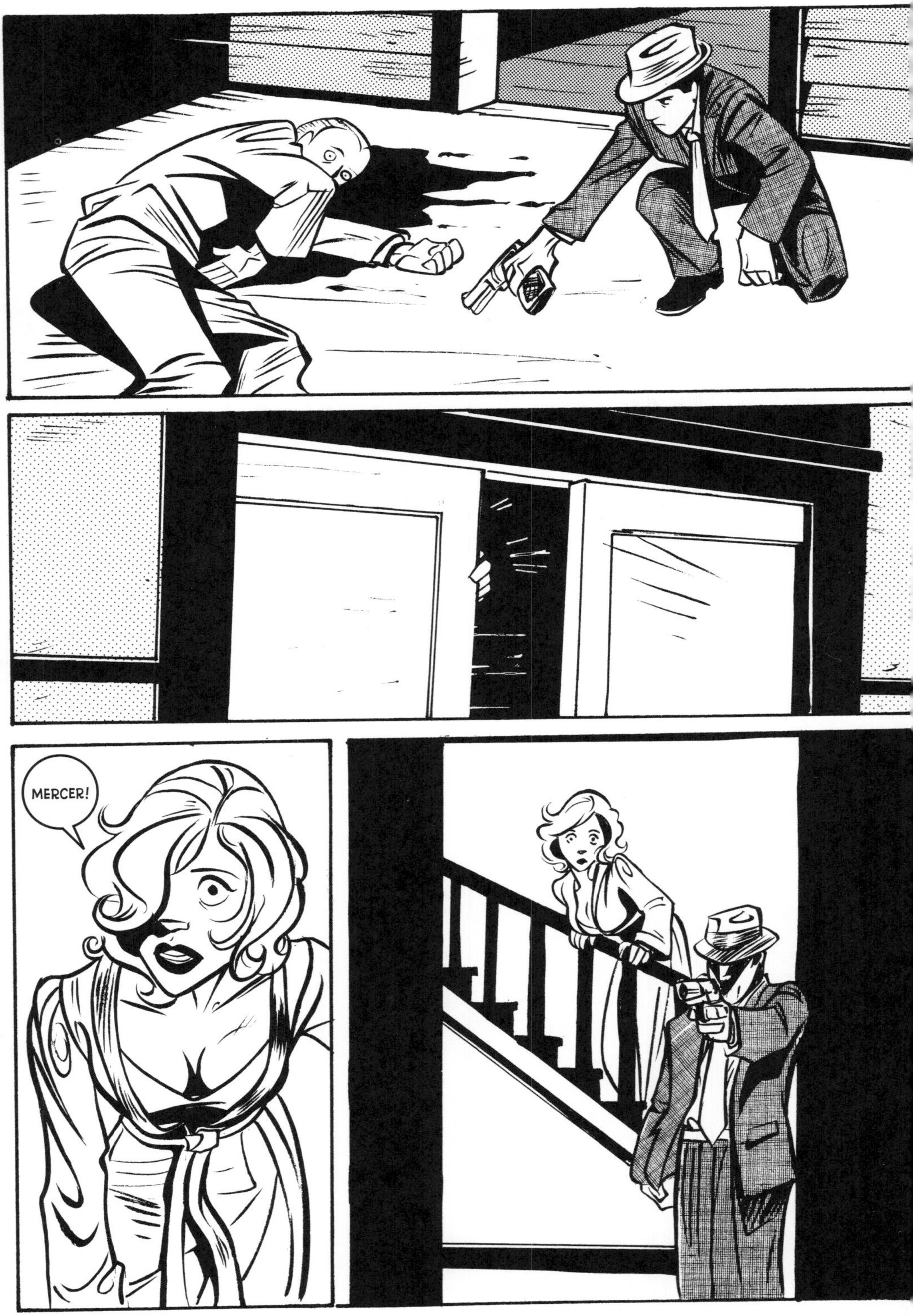
MERCER!

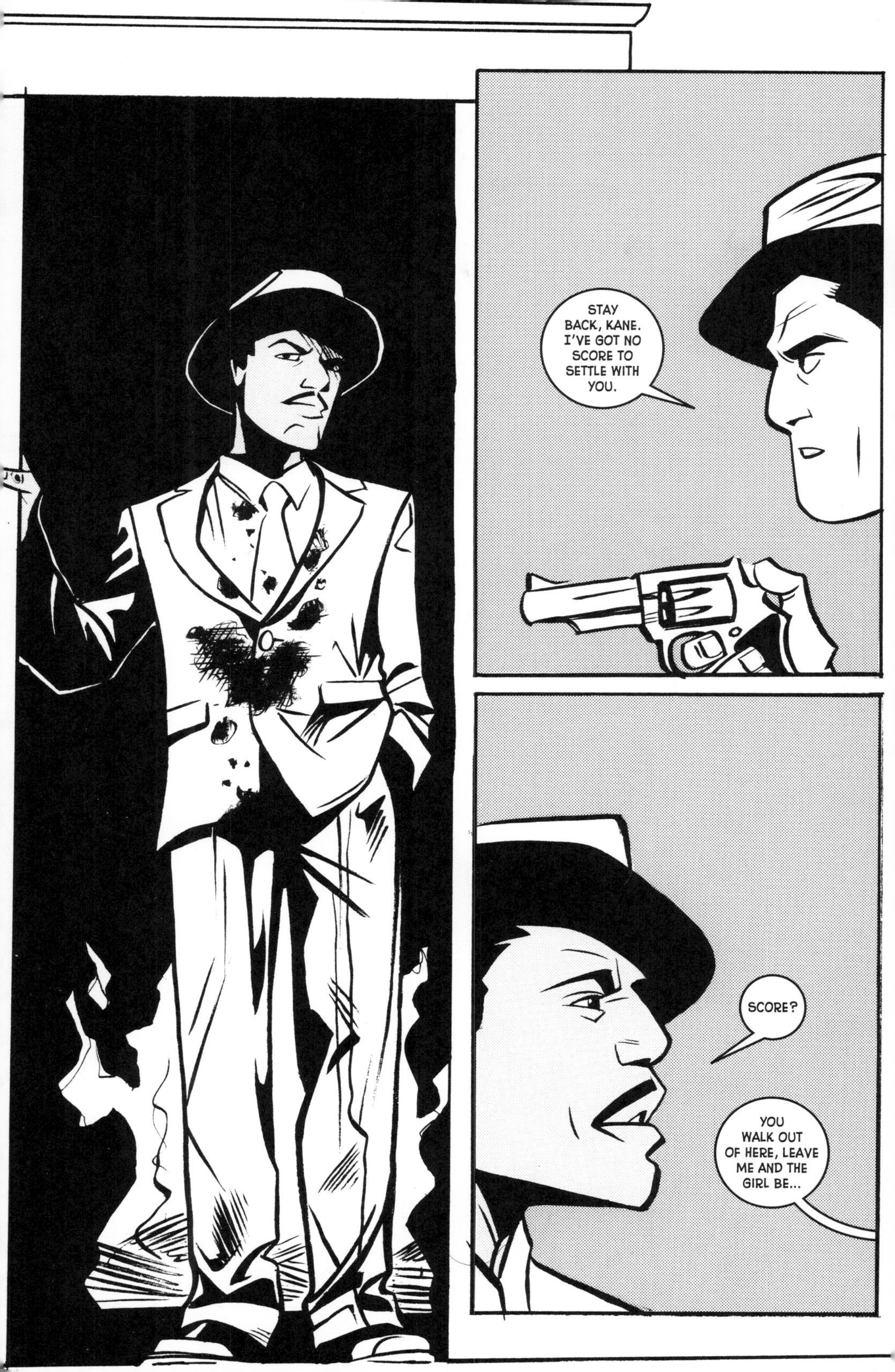
STAY BACK, KANE. I'VE GOT NO SCORE TO SETTLE WITH YOU.
SCORE?
YOU WALK OUT OF HERE, LEAVE ME AND THE GIRL BE...

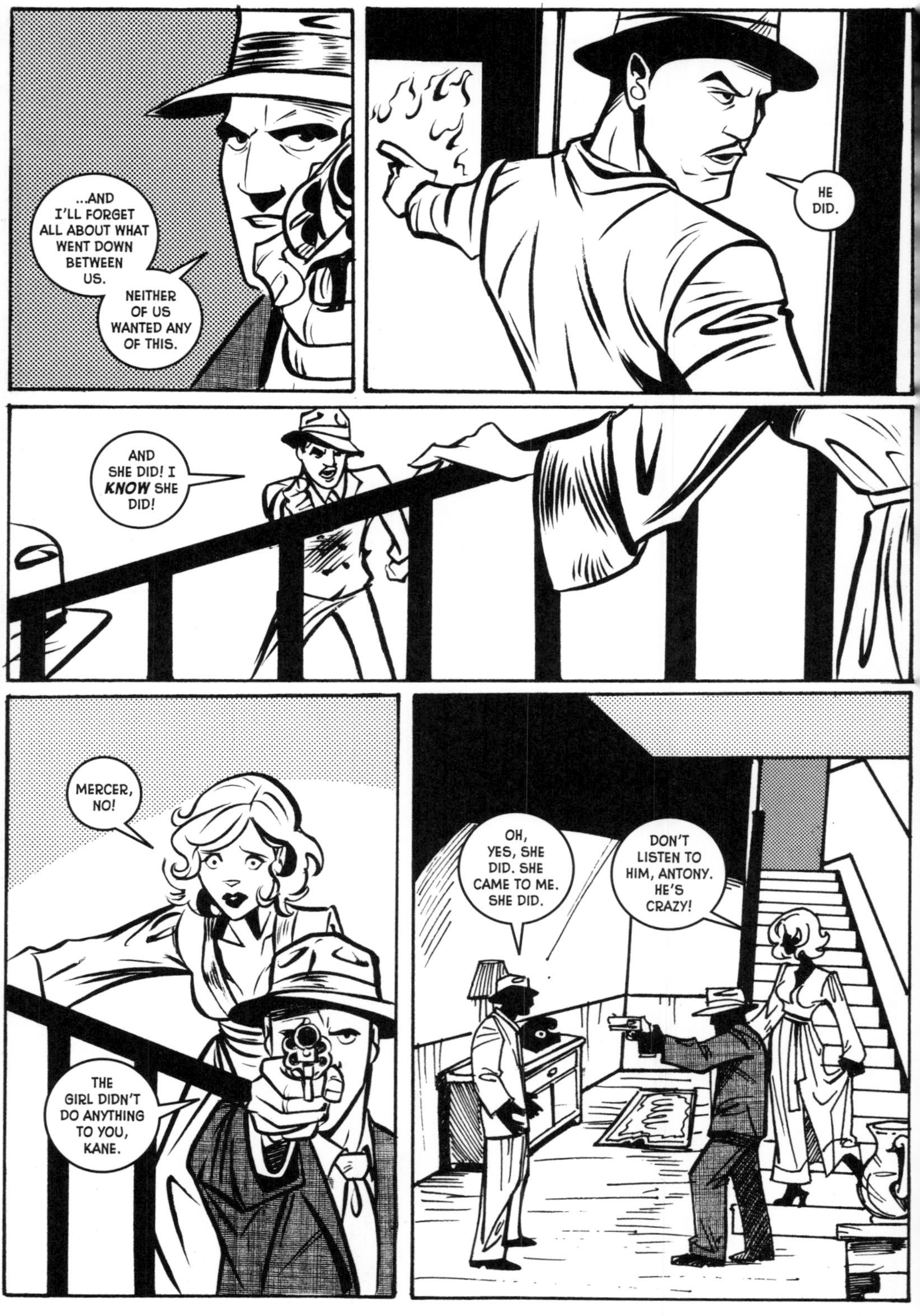
...AND I'LL FORGET ALL ABOUT WHAT WENT DOWN BETWEEN US.
NEITHER OF US WANTED ANY OF THIS.
HE DID.
AND SHE DID! I KNOW SHE DID!
MERCER, NO!
THE GIRL DIDN'T DO ANYTHING TO YOU, KANE.
OH, YES, SHE DID. SHE CAME TO ME. SHE DID.
DON'T LISTEN TO HIM, ANTONY. HE'S CRAZY!

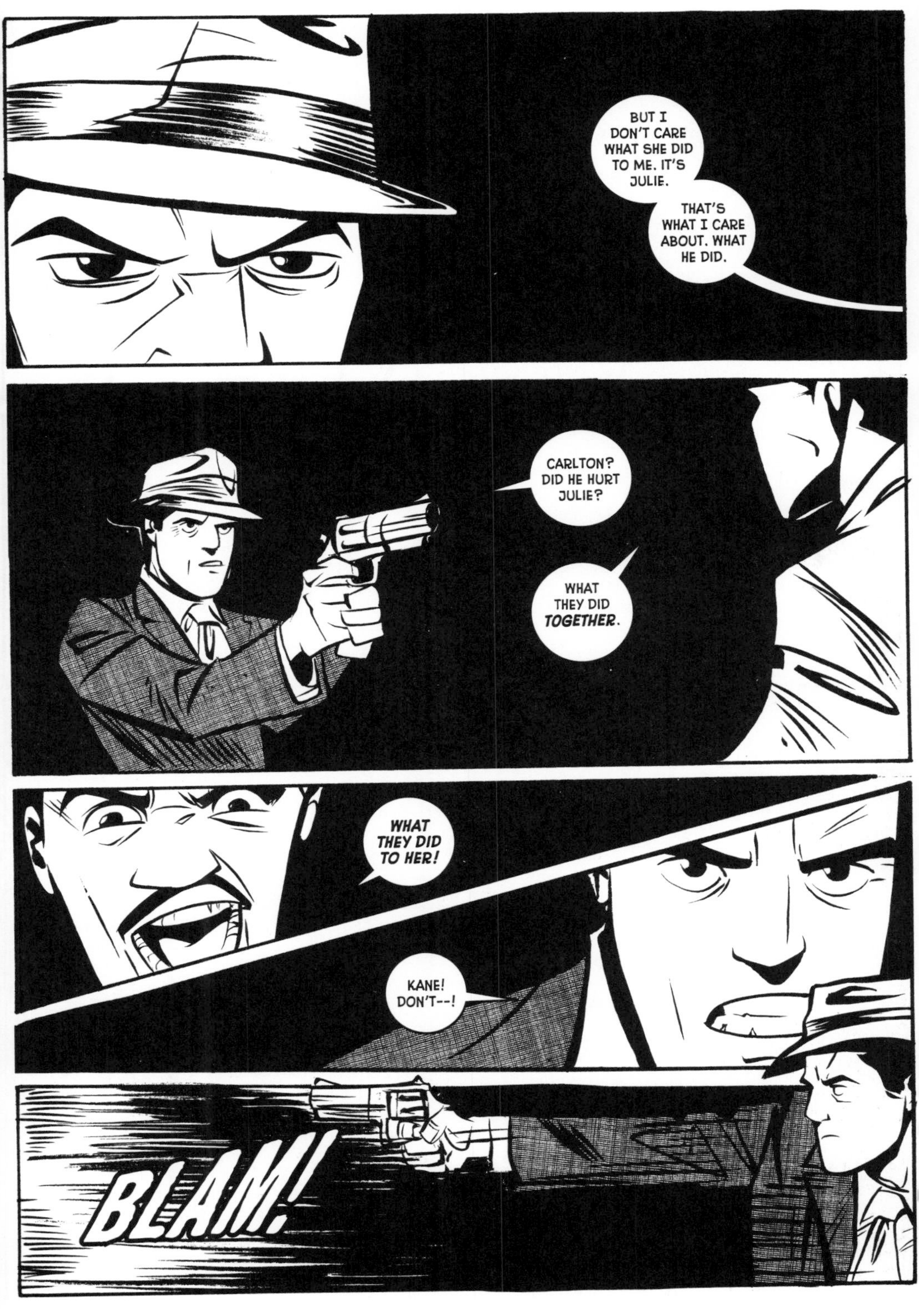
BUT I DON'T CARE WHAT SHE DID TO ME. IT'S JULIE.
THAT'S WHAT I CARE ABOUT. WHAT HE DID.
CARLTON? DID HE HURT JULIE?
WHAT THEY DID *TOGETHER*.
WHAT THEY DID TO HER!
KANE! DON'T--!
BLAM!

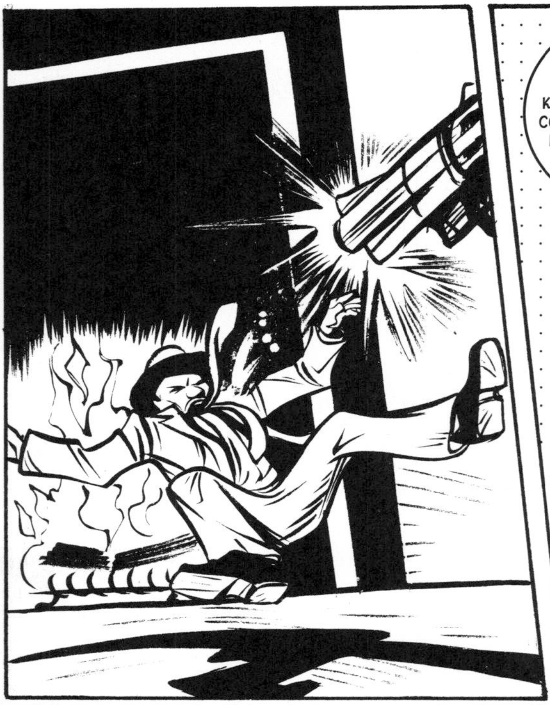

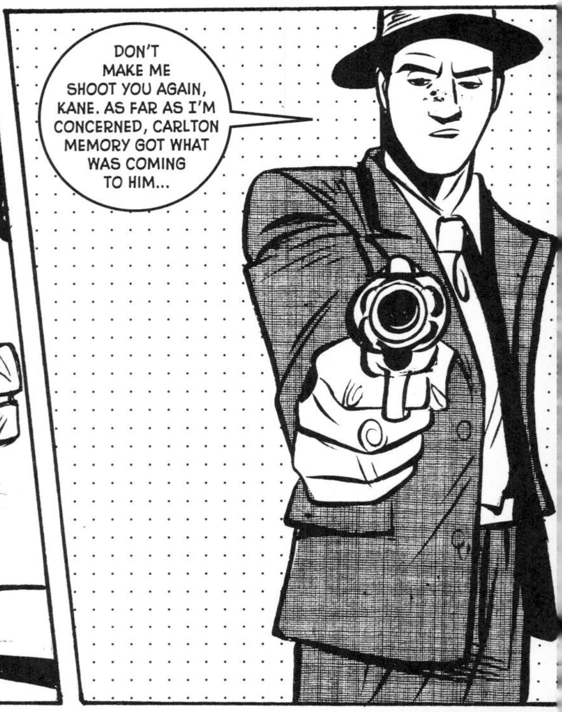
DON'T MAKE ME SHOOT YOU AGAIN, KANE. AS FAR AS I'M CONCERNED, CARLTON MEMORY GOT WHAT WAS COMING TO HIM...

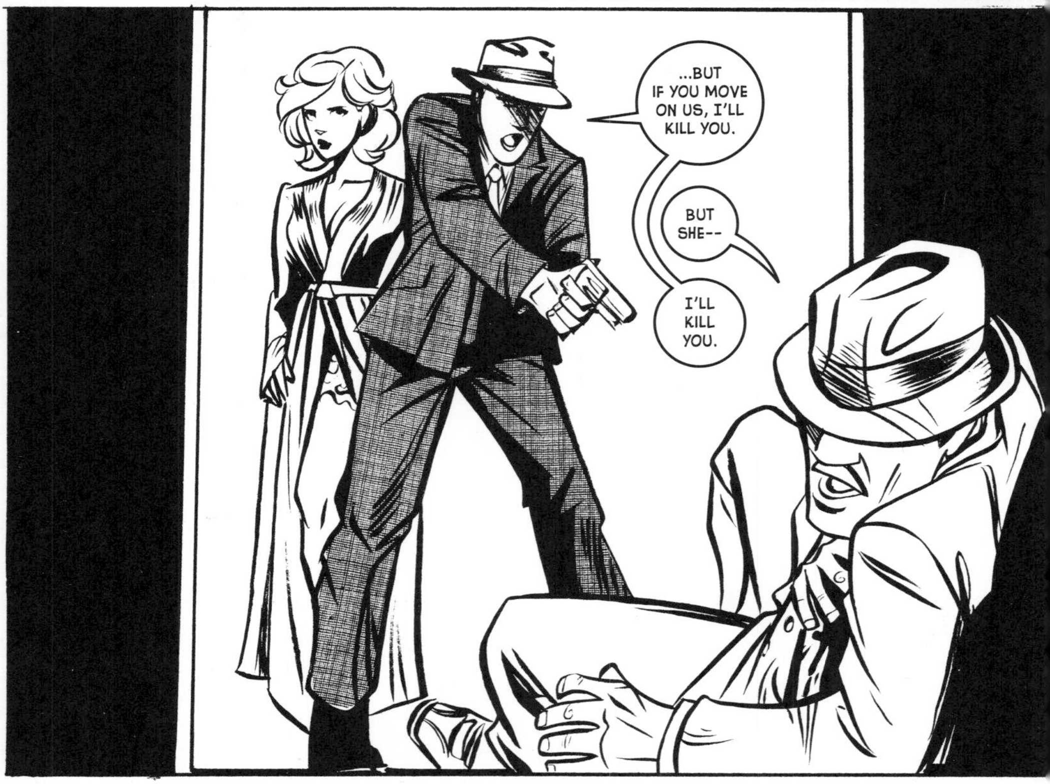
...BUT IF YOU MOVE ON US, I'LL KILL YOU.
BUT SHE--
I'LL KILL YOU.

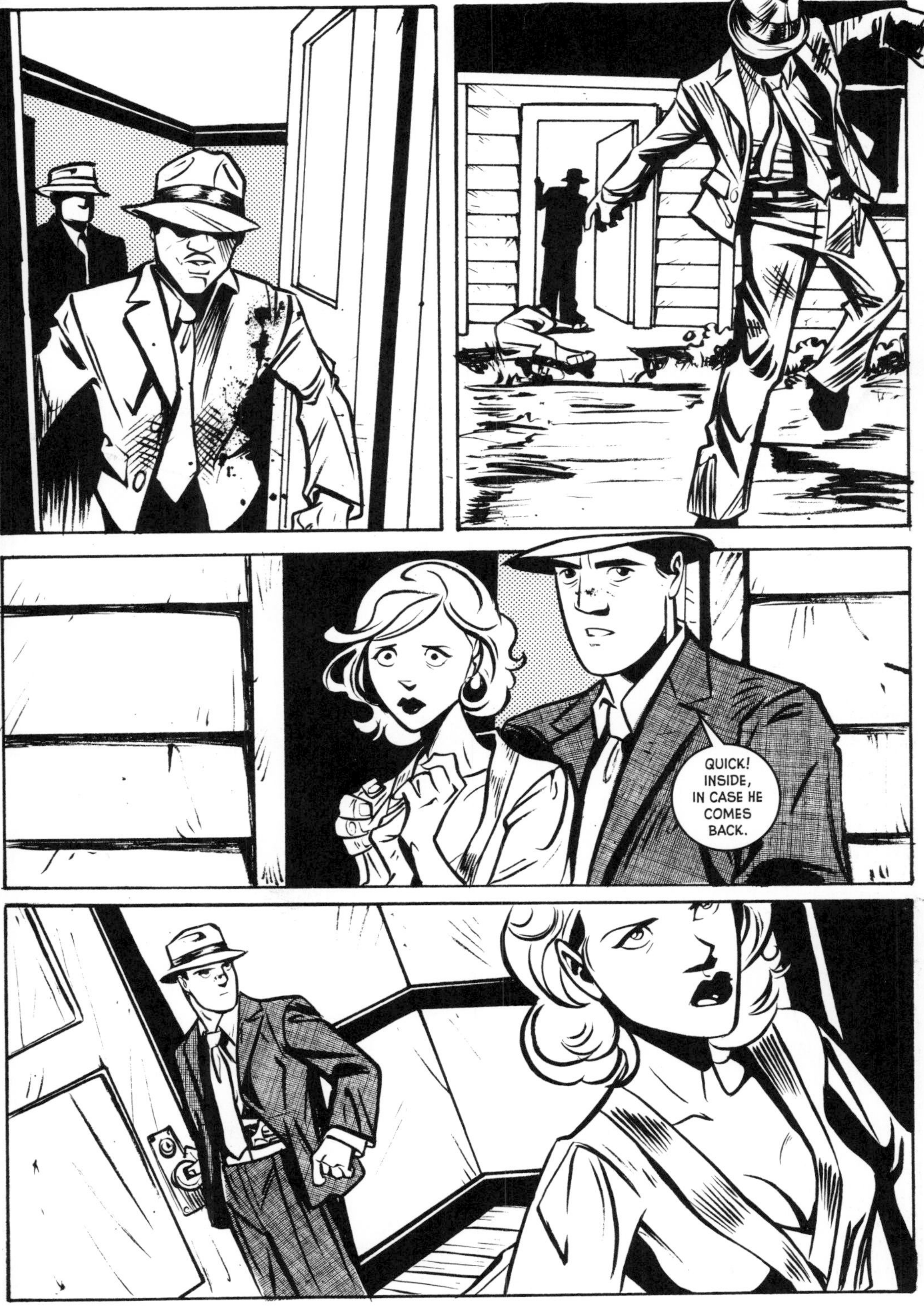
QUICK! INSIDE, IN CASE HE COMES BACK.

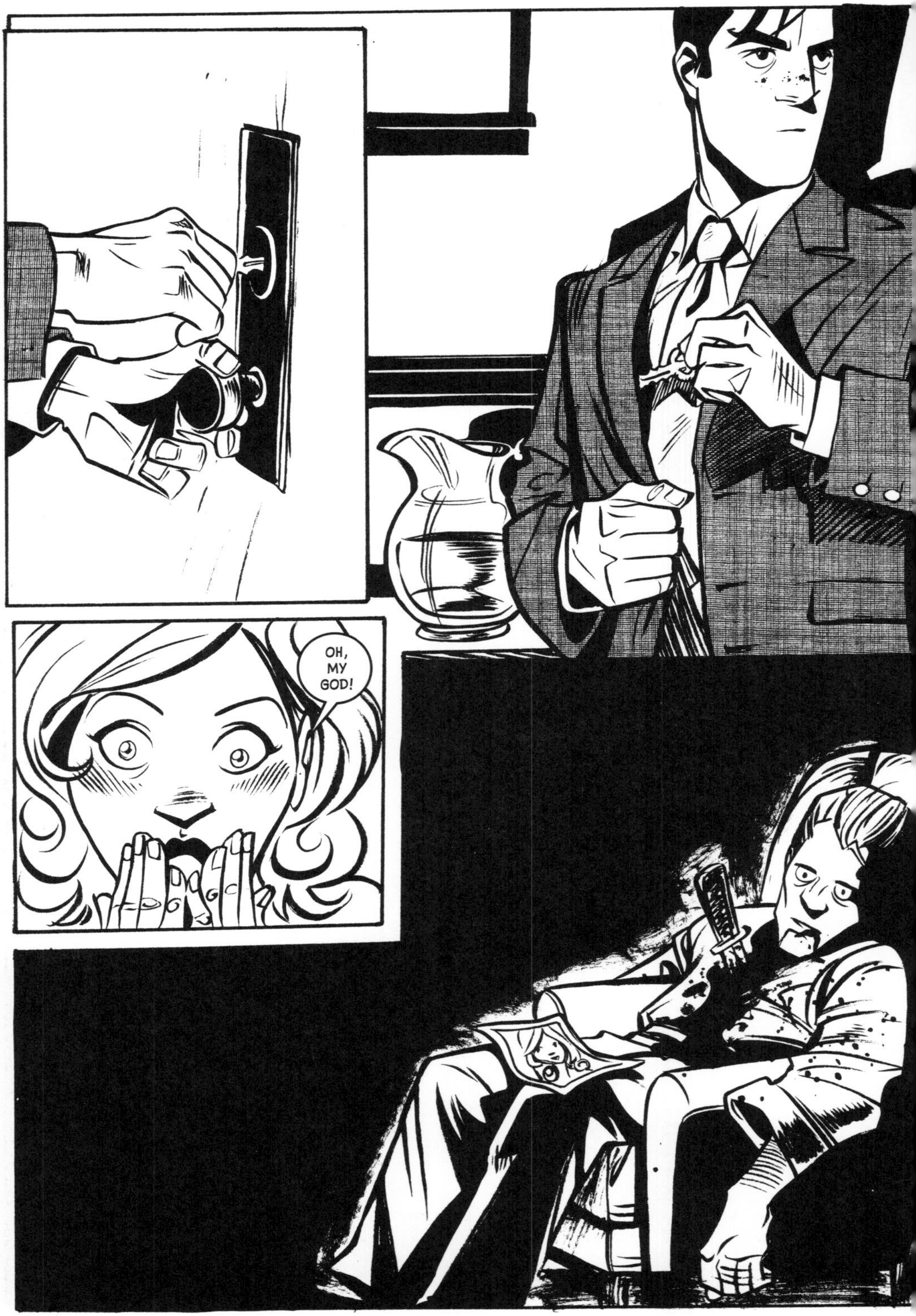
OH, MY GOD!

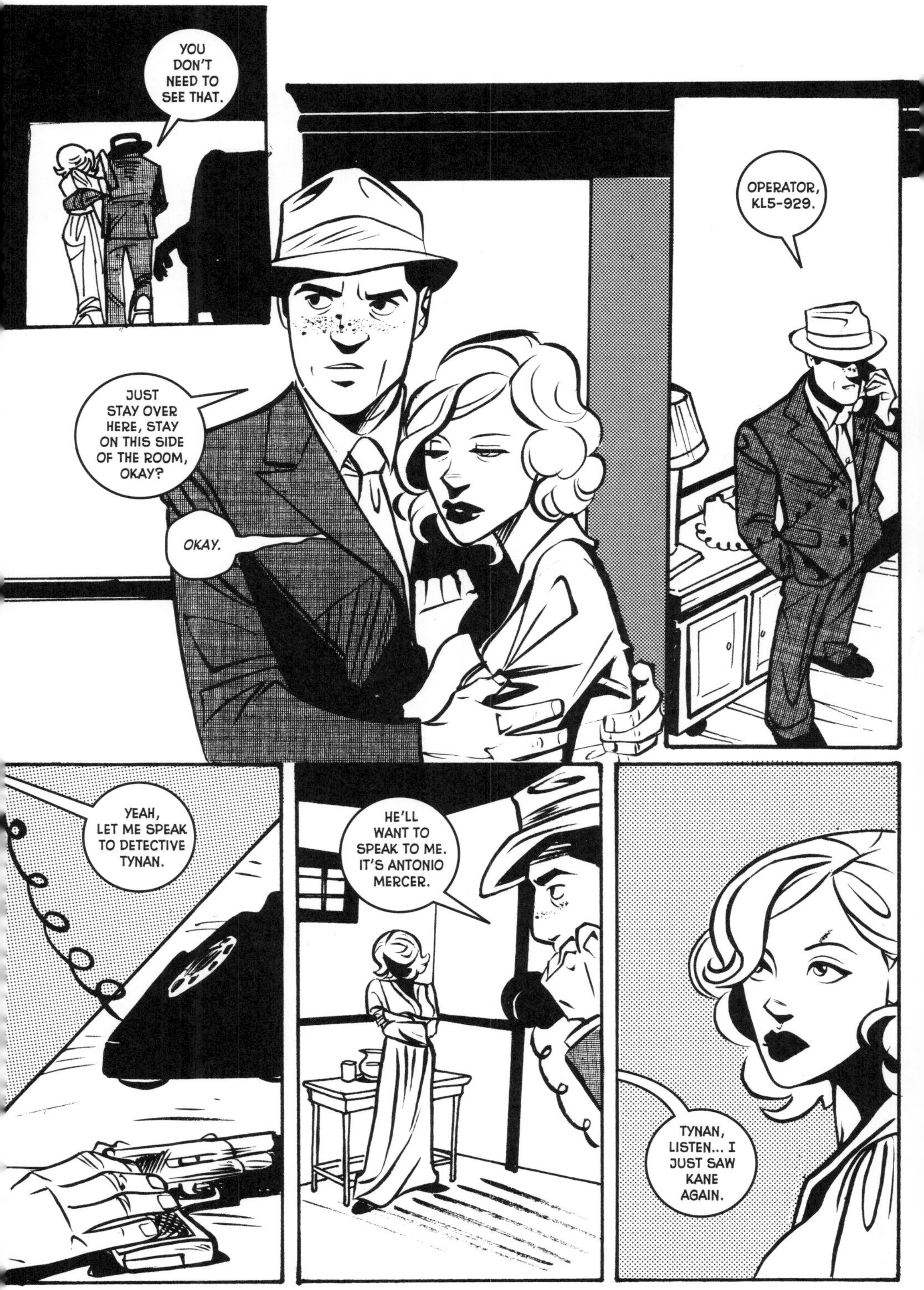
YOU DON'T NEED TO SEE THAT.
JUST STAY OVER HERE, STAY ON THIS SIDE OF THE ROOM, OKAY?
OKAY.
OPERATOR, KL5-929.
YEAH, LET ME SPEAK TO DETECTIVE TYNAN.
HE'LL WANT TO SPEAK TO ME. IT'S ANTONIO MERCER.
TYNAN, LISTEN... I JUST SAW KANE AGAIN.

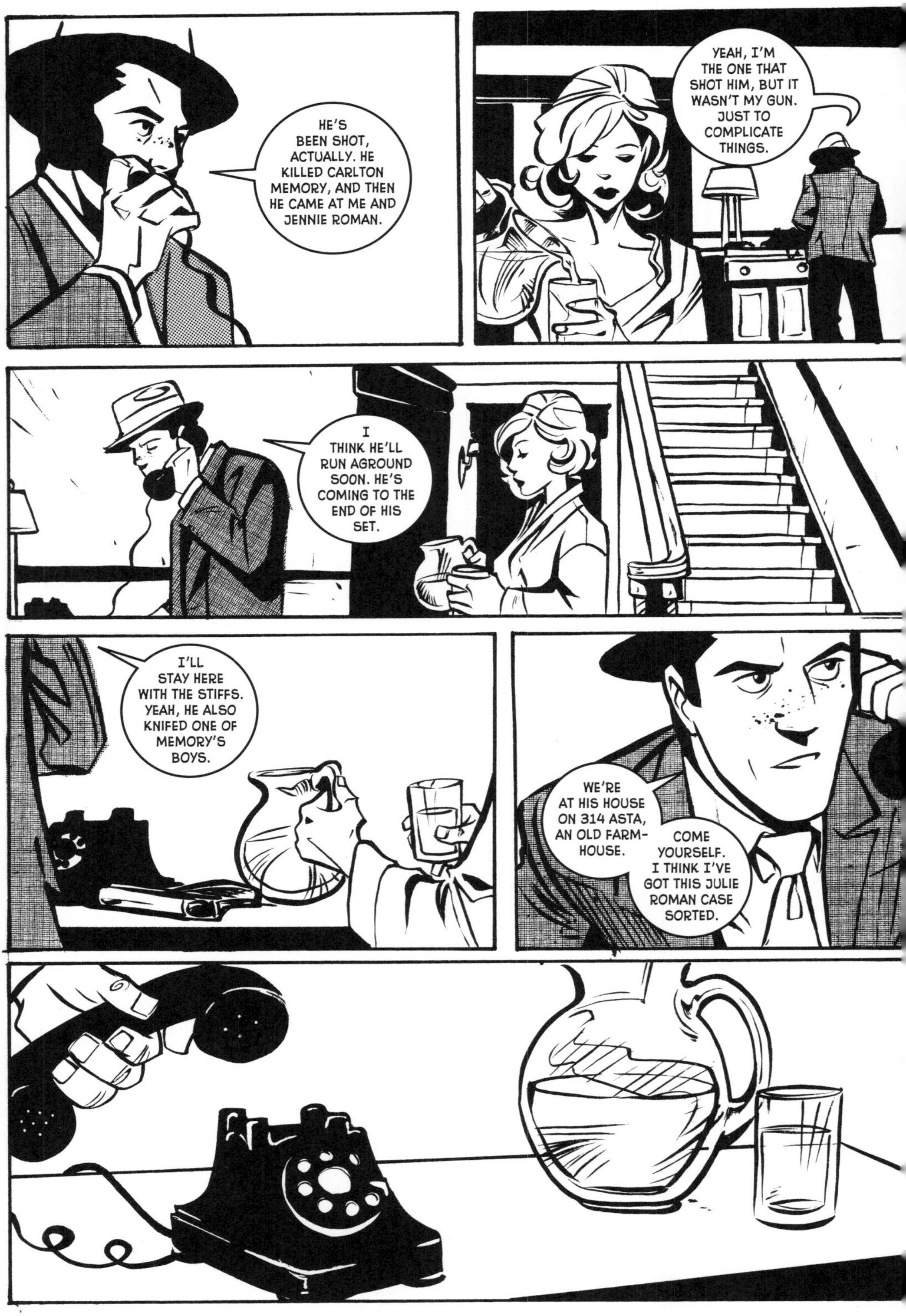

HE'S BEEN SHOT, ACTUALLY. HE KILLED CARLTON MEMORY, AND THEN HE CAME AT ME AND JENNIE ROMAN.
YEAH, I'M THE ONE THAT SHOT HIM, BUT IT WASN'T MY GUN. JUST TO COMPLICATE THINGS.
I THINK HE'LL RUN AGROUND SOON. HE'S COMING TO THE END OF HIS SET.
I'LL STAY HERE WITH THE STIFFS. YEAH, HE ALSO KNIFED ONE OF MEMORY'S BOYS.
WE'RE AT HIS HOUSE ON 314 ASTA, AN OLD FARM-HOUSE.
COME YOURSELF. I THINK I'VE GOT THIS JULIE ROMAN CASE SORTED.

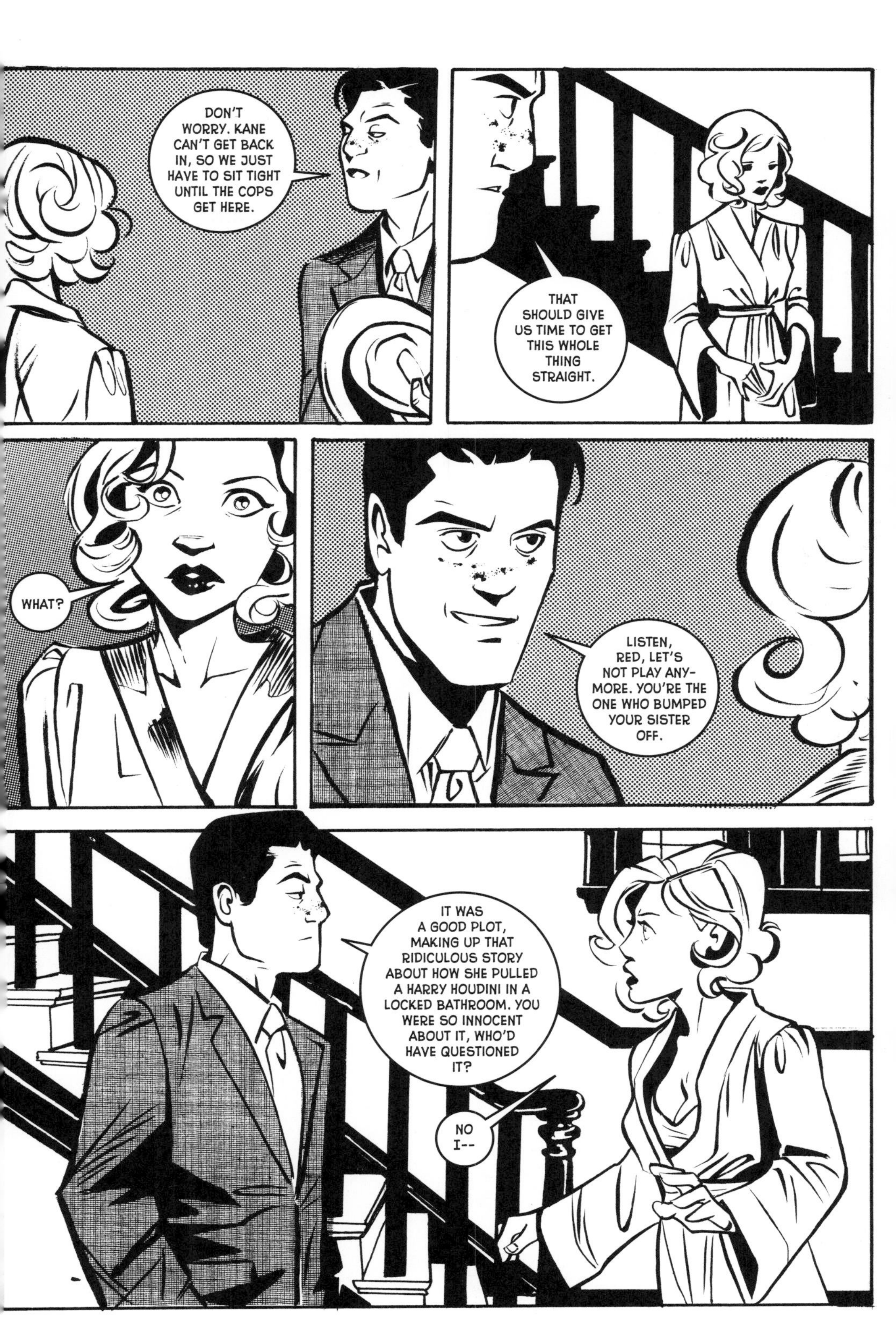
DON'T WORRY. KANE CAN'T GET BACK IN, SO WE JUST HAVE TO SIT TIGHT UNTIL THE COPS GET HERE.
THAT SHOULD GIVE US TIME TO GET THIS WHOLE THING STRAIGHT.
WHAT?
LISTEN, RED, LET'S NOT PLAY ANY-MORE. YOU'RE THE ONE WHO BUMPED YOUR SISTER OFF.
IT WAS A GOOD PLOT, MAKING UP THAT RIDICULOUS STORY ABOUT HOW SHE PULLED A HARRY HOUDINI IN A LOCKED BATHROOM. YOU WERE SO INNOCENT ABOUT IT, WHO'D HAVE QUESTIONED IT?
NO I--

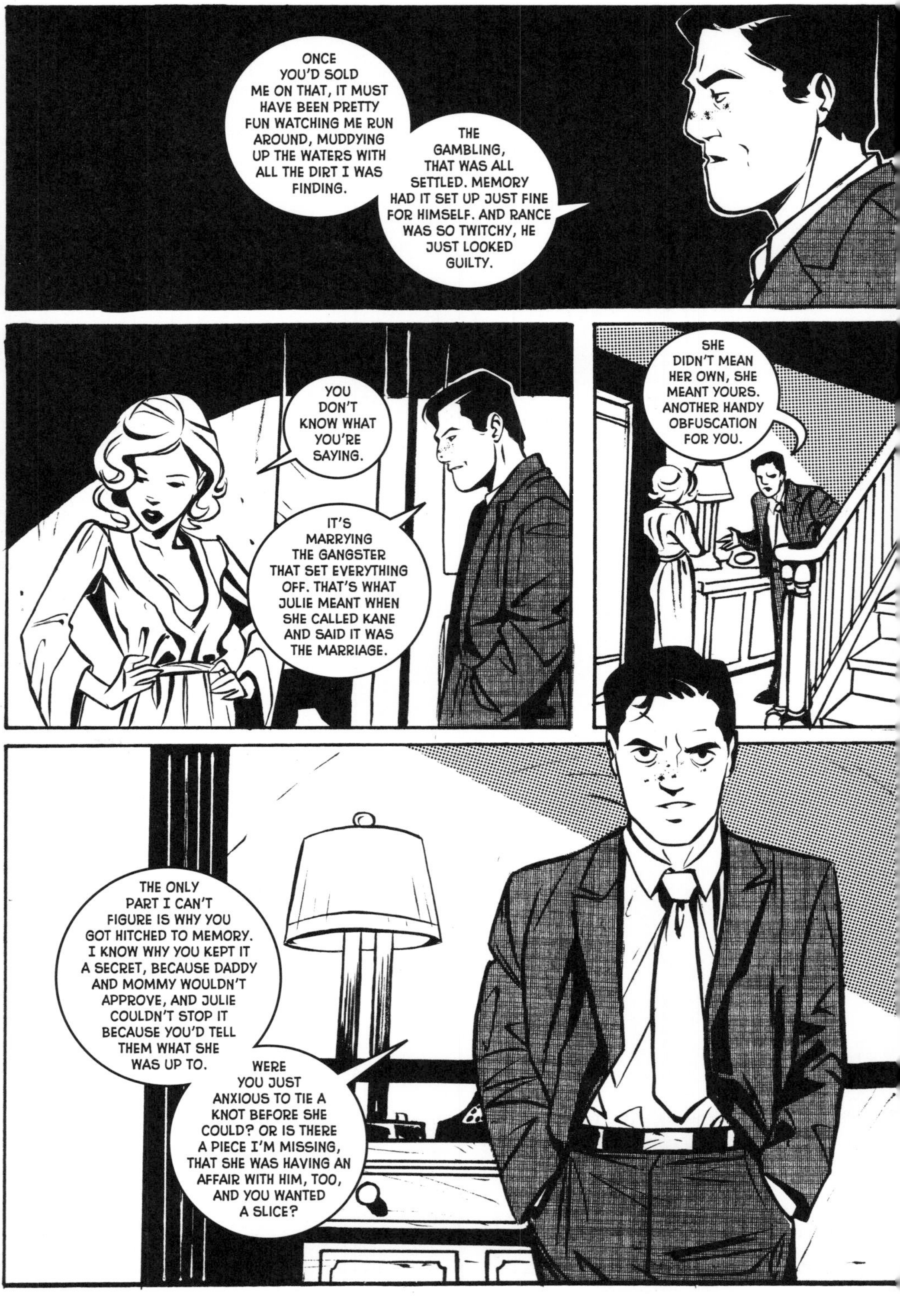
ONCE YOU'D SOLD ME ON THAT, IT MUST HAVE BEEN PRETTY FUN WATCHING ME RUN AROUND, MUDDYING UP THE WATERS WITH ALL THE DIRT I WAS FINDING.
THE GAMBLING, THAT WAS ALL SETTLED. MEMORY HAD IT SET UP JUST FINE FOR HIMSELF. AND RANCE WAS SO TWITCHY, HE JUST LOOKED GUILTY.
YOU DON'T KNOW WHAT YOU'RE SAYING.
IT'S MARRYING THE GANGSTER THAT SET EVERYTHING OFF. THAT'S WHAT JULIE MEANT WHEN SHE CALLED KANE AND SAID IT WAS THE MARRIAGE.
SHE DIDN'T MEAN HER OWN, SHE MEANT YOURS. ANOTHER HANDY OBFUSCATION FOR YOU.
THE ONLY PART I CAN'T FIGURE IS WHY YOU GOT HITCHED TO MEMORY. I KNOW WHY YOU KEPT IT A SECRET, BECAUSE DADDY AND MOMMY WOULDN'T APPROVE, AND JULIE COULDN'T STOP IT BECAUSE YOU'D TELL THEM WHAT SHE WAS UP TO.
WERE YOU JUST ANXIOUS TO TIE A KNOT BEFORE SHE COULD? OR IS THERE A PIECE I'M MISSING, THAT SHE WAS HAVING AN AFFAIR WITH HIM, TOO, AND YOU WANTED A SLICE?

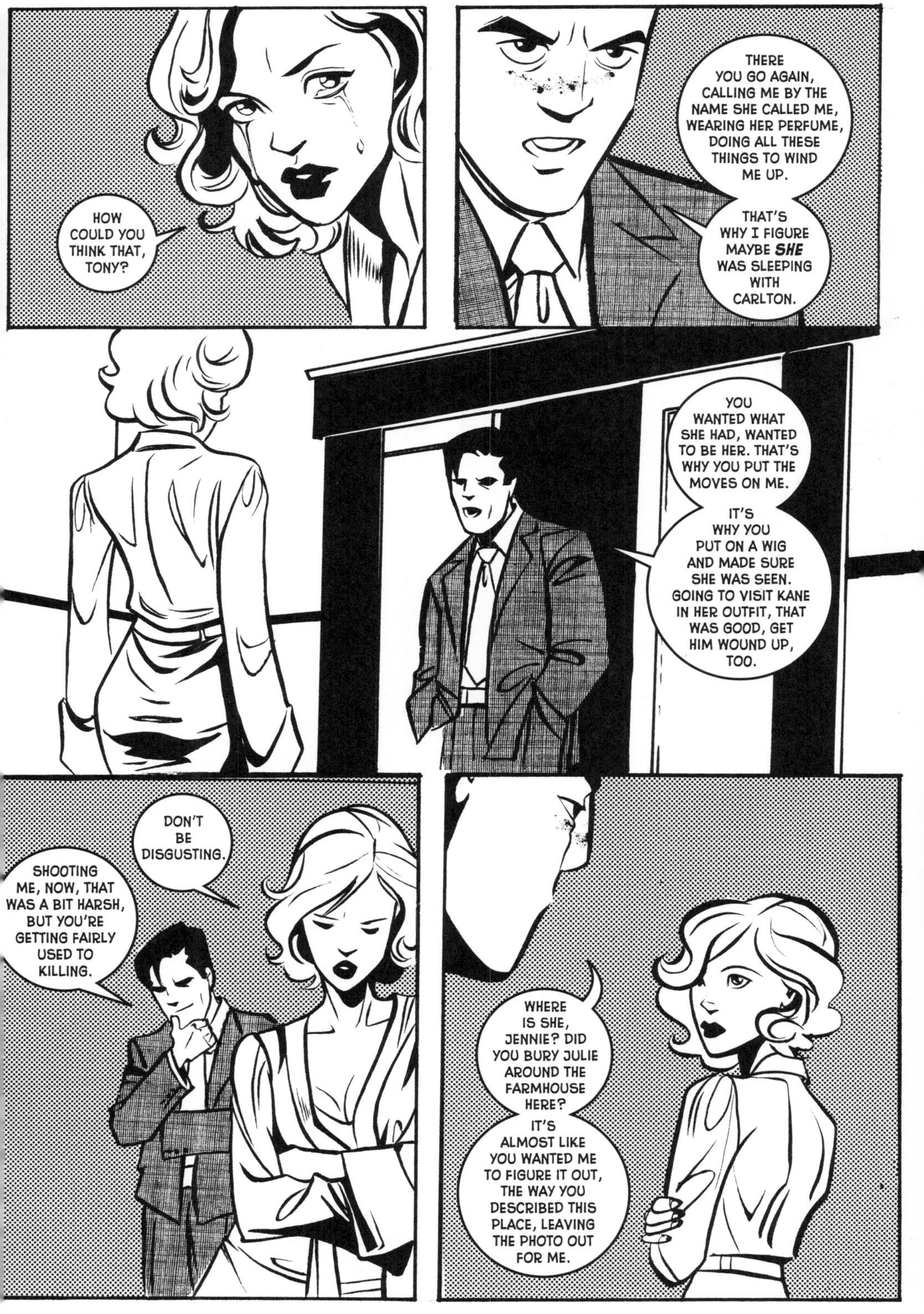
HOW COULD YOU THINK THAT, TONY?
THERE YOU GO AGAIN, CALLING ME BY THE NAME SHE CALLED ME, WEARING HER PERFUME, DOING ALL THESE THINGS TO WIND ME UP.
THAT'S WHY I FIGURE MAYBE *SHE* WAS SLEEPING WITH CARLTON.
YOU WANTED WHAT SHE HAD, WANTED TO BE HER. THAT'S WHY YOU PUT THE MOVES ON ME.
IT'S WHY YOU PUT ON A WIG AND MADE SURE SHE WAS SEEN. GOING TO VISIT KANE IN HER OUTFIT, THAT WAS GOOD, GET HIM WOUND UP, TOO.
SHOOTING ME, NOW, THAT WAS A BIT HARSH, BUT YOU'RE GETTING FAIRLY USED TO KILLING.
DON'T BE DISGUSTING.
WHERE IS SHE, JENNIE? DID YOU BURY JULIE AROUND THE FARMHOUSE HERE?
IT'S ALMOST LIKE YOU WANTED ME TO FIGURE IT OUT, THE WAY YOU DESCRIBED THIS PLACE, LEAVING THE PHOTO OUT FOR ME.

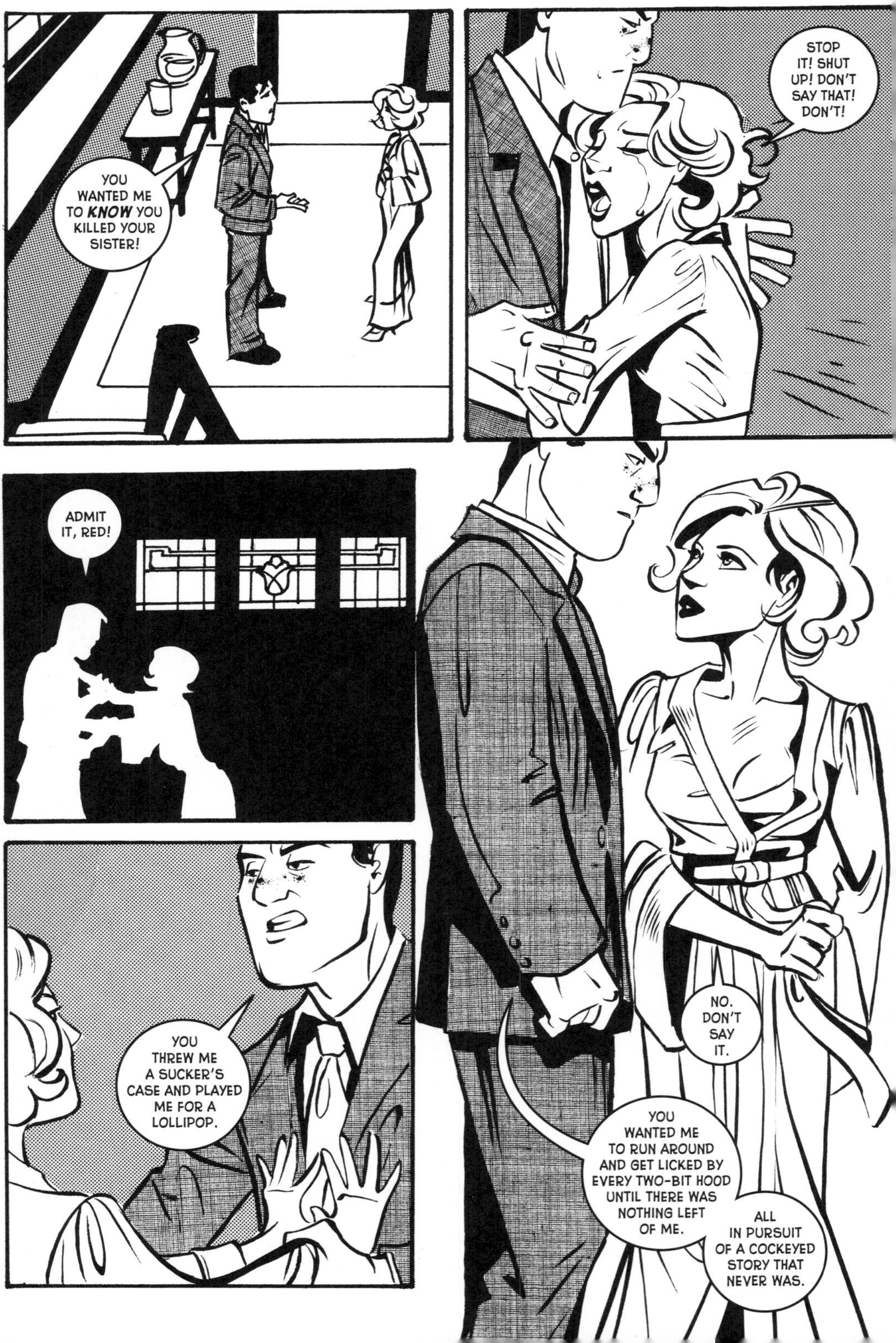
YOU WANTED ME TO ***KNOW*** YOU KILLED YOUR SISTER!
STOP IT! SHUT UP! DON'T SAY THAT! DON'T!
ADMIT IT, RED!
YOU THREW ME A SUCKER'S CASE AND PLAYED ME FOR A LOLLIPOP.
NO. DON'T SAY IT.
YOU WANTED ME TO RUN AROUND AND GET LICKED BY EVERY TWO-BIT HOOD UNTIL THERE WAS NOTHING LEFT OF ME.
ALL IN PURSUIT OF A COCKEYED STORY THAT NEVER WAS.

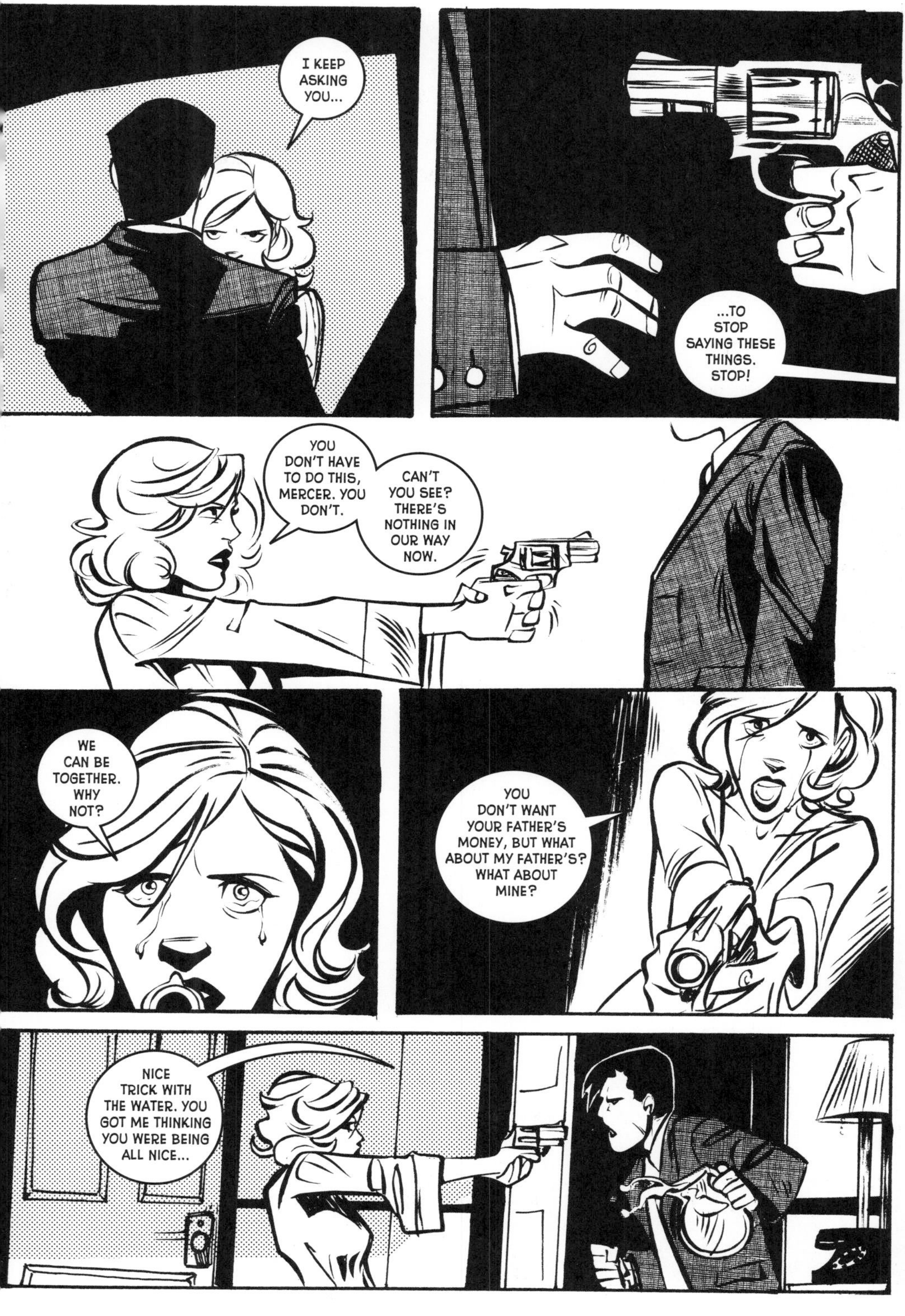
I KEEP ASKING YOU...
...TO STOP SAYING THESE THINGS. STOP!
YOU DON'T HAVE TO DO THIS, MERCER. YOU DON'T.
CAN'T YOU SEE? THERE'S NOTHING IN OUR WAY NOW.
WE CAN BE TOGETHER. WHY NOT?
YOU DON'T WANT YOUR FATHER'S MONEY, BUT WHAT ABOUT MY FATHER'S? WHAT ABOUT MINE?
NICE TRICK WITH THE WATER. YOU GOT ME THINKING YOU WERE BEING ALL NICE...

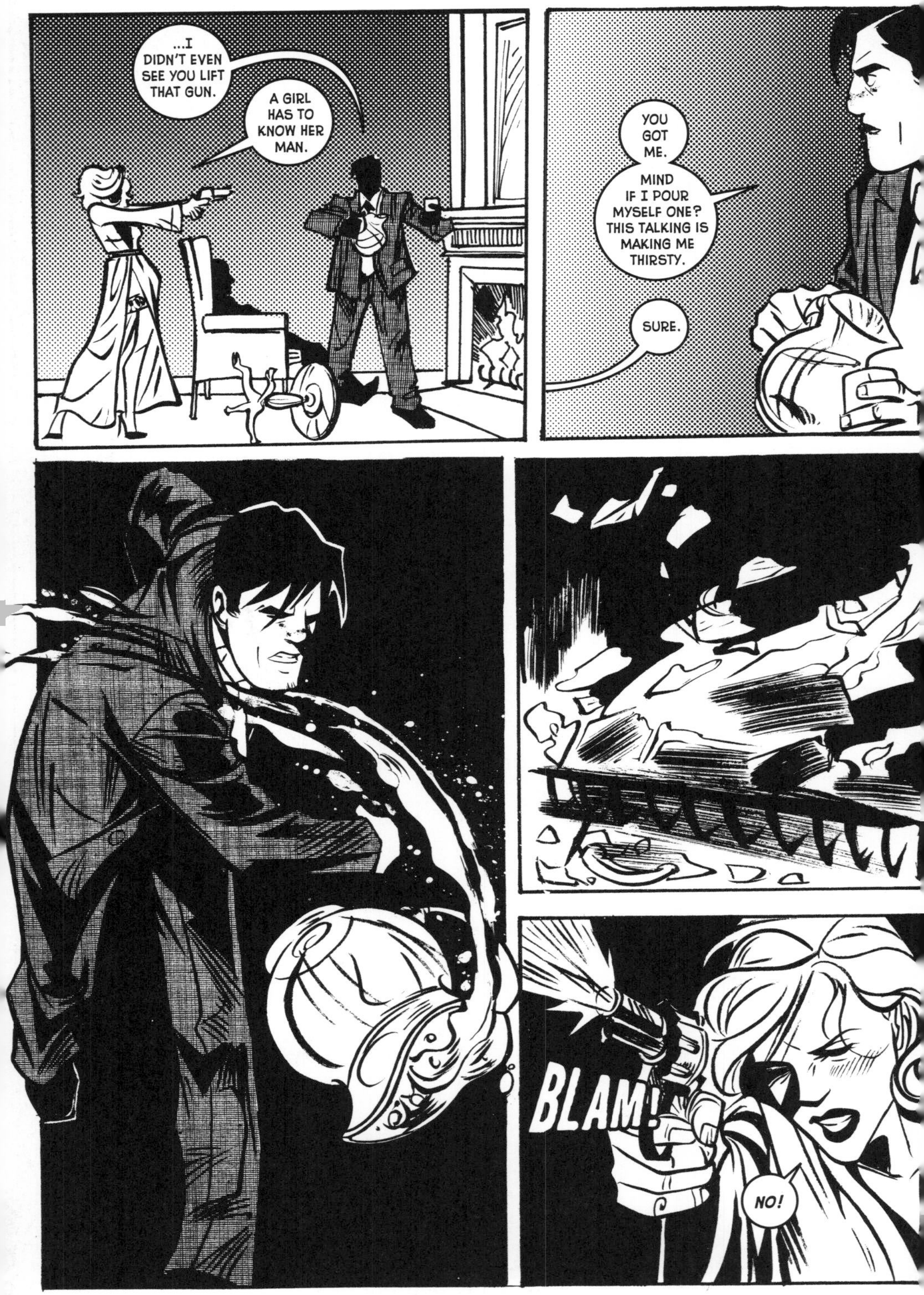
...I DIDN'T EVEN SEE YOU LIFT THAT GUN.
A GIRL HAS TO KNOW HER MAN.
YOU GOT ME.
MIND IF I POUR MYSELF ONE? THIS TALKING IS MAKING ME THIRSTY.
SURE.
BLAM!
NO!

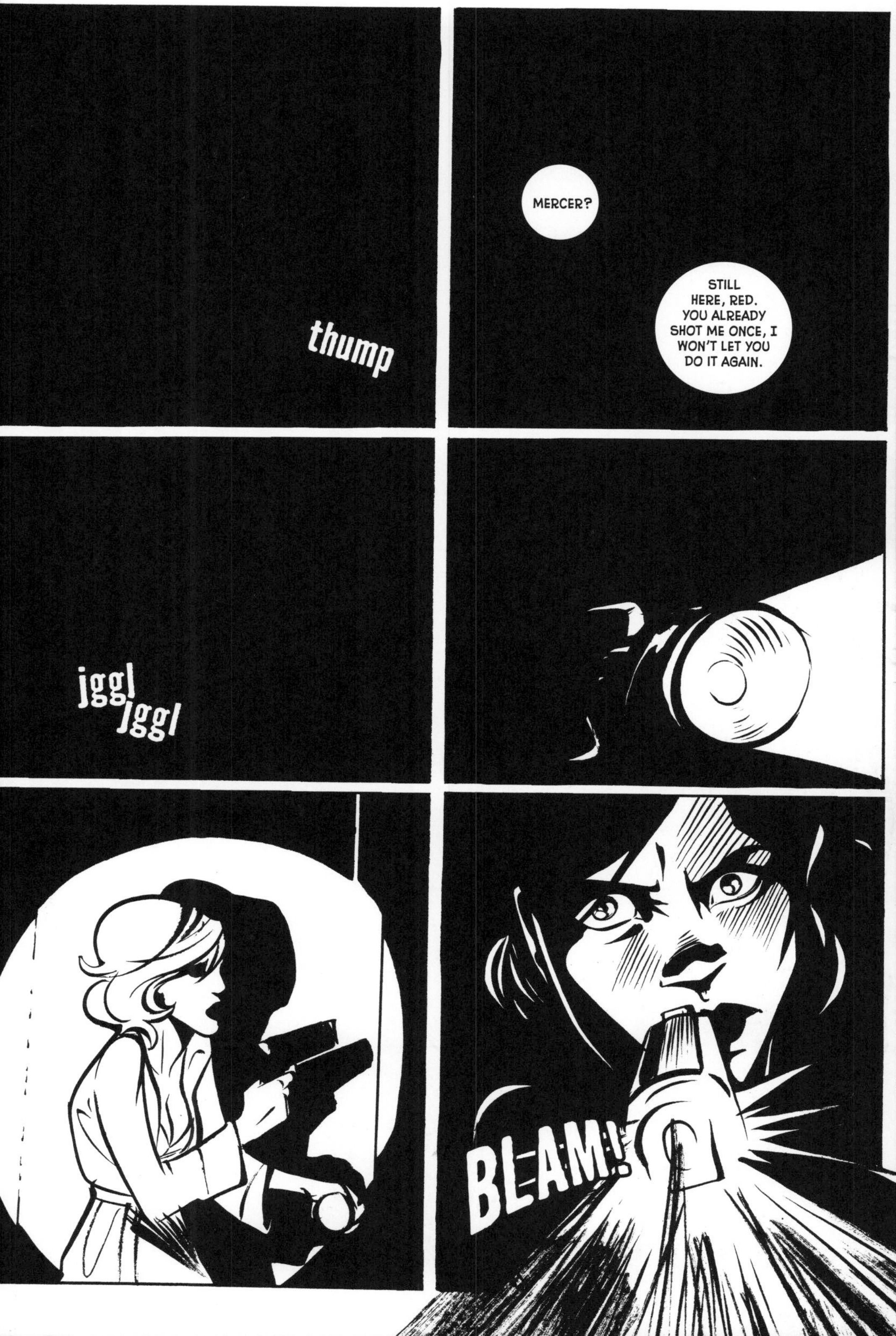
thump
MERCER?
STILL HERE, RED. YOU ALREADY SHOT ME ONCE, I WON'T LET YOU DO IT AGAIN.
jggl jggl
BLAM!

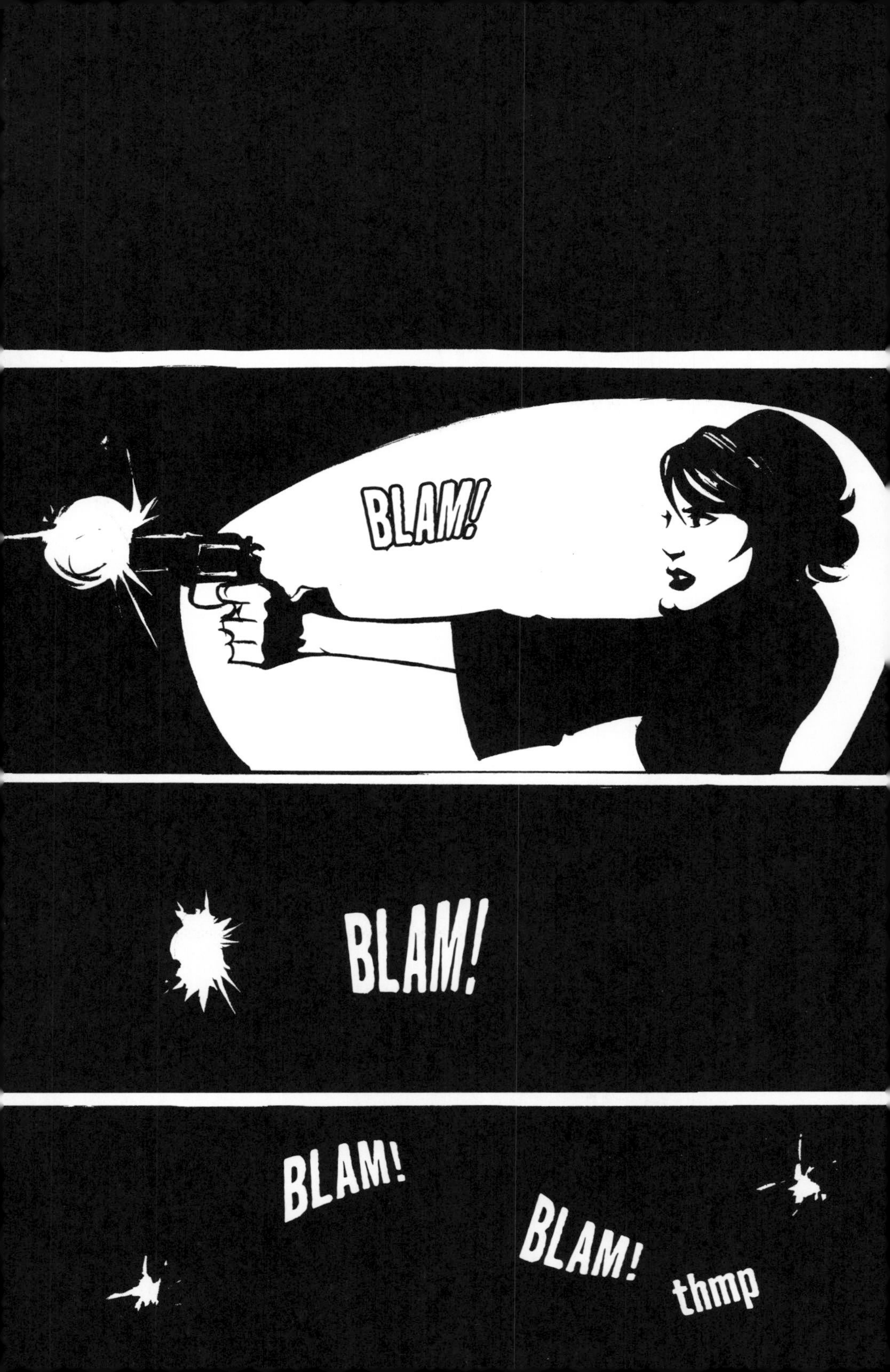
BLAM!
BLAM!
BLAM!
BLAM!
thmp

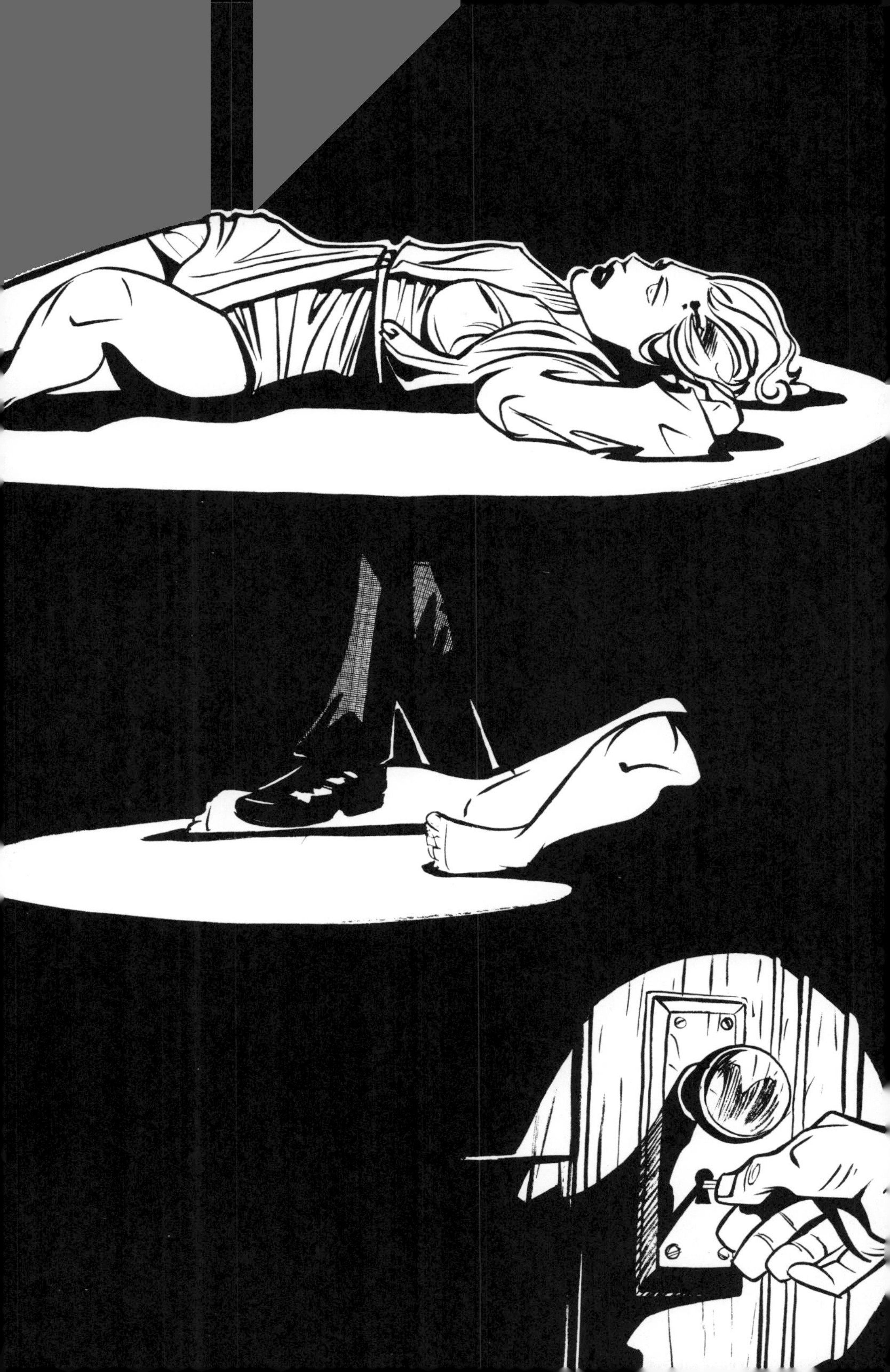

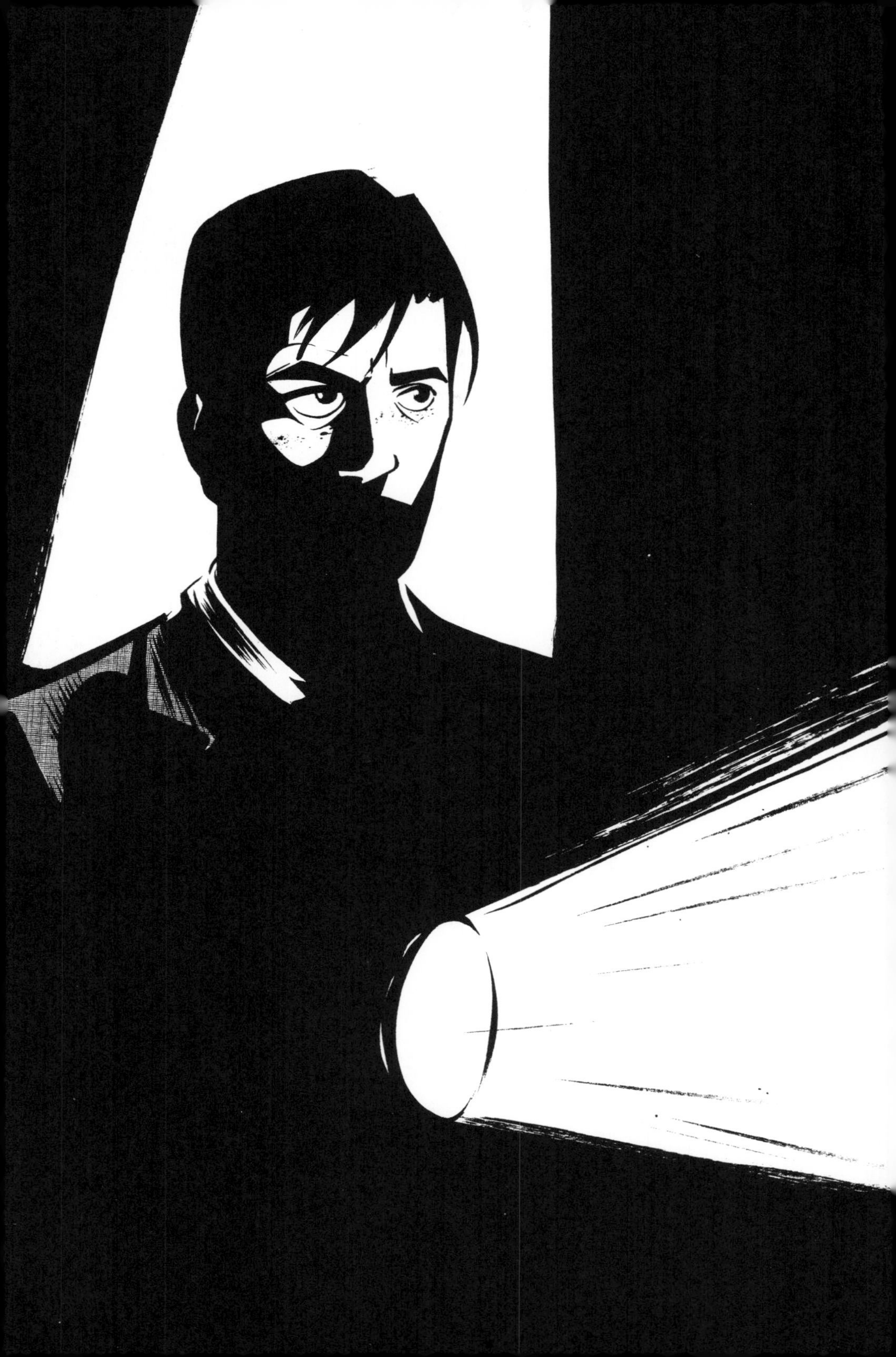

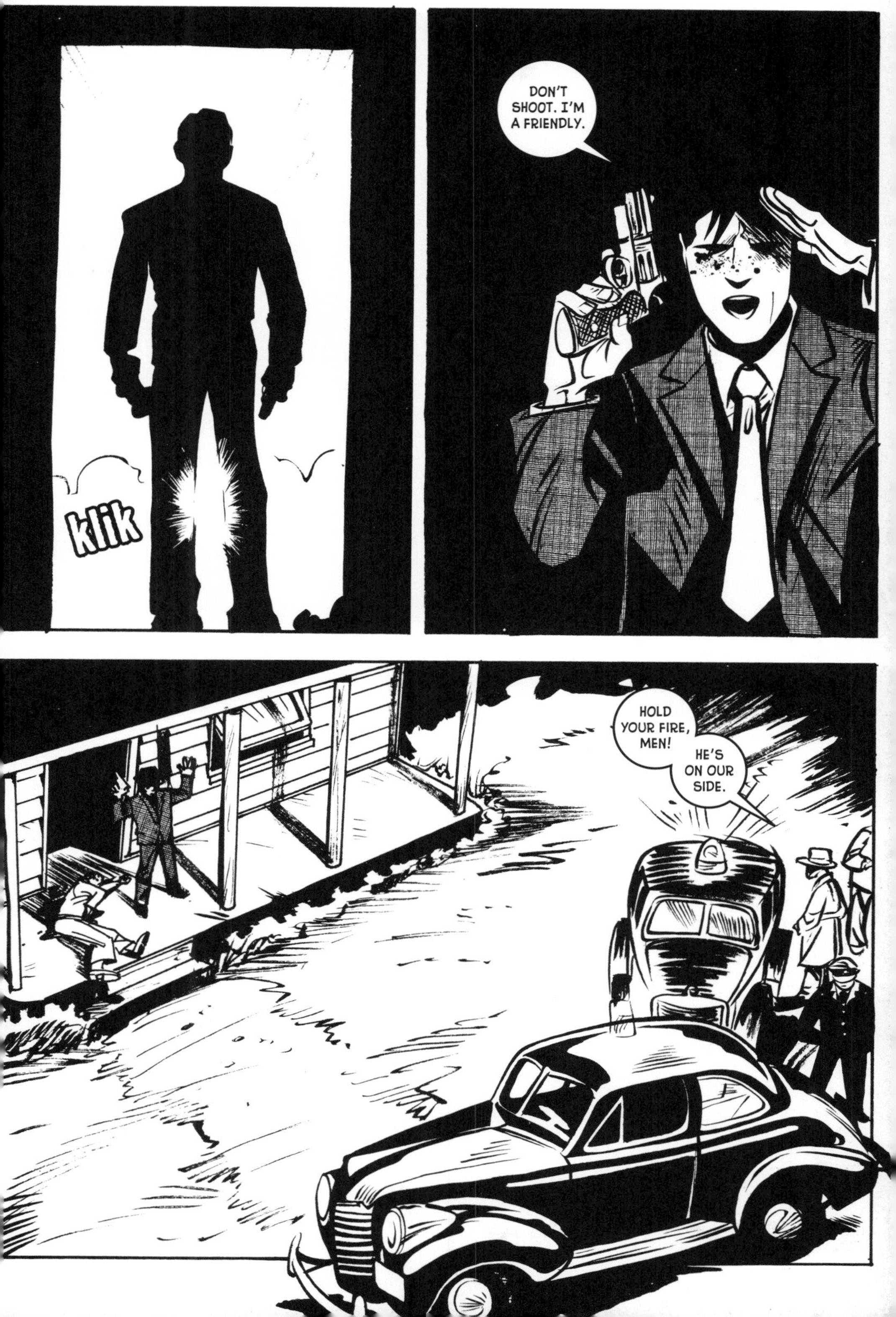
klik
DON'T SHOOT. I'M A FRIENDLY.
HOLD YOUR FIRE, MEN!
HE'S ON OUR SIDE.

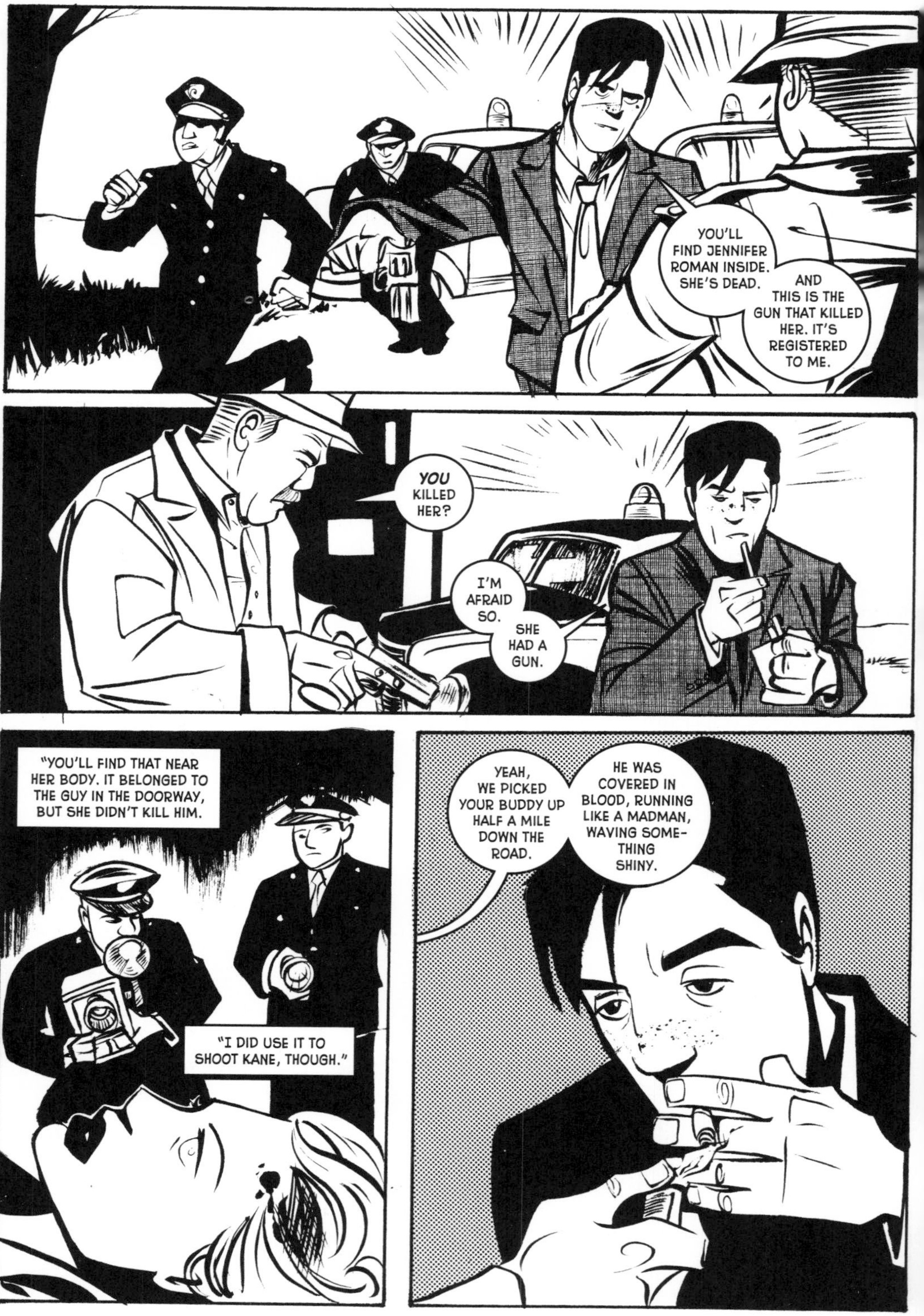
YOU'LL FIND JENNIFER ROMAN INSIDE. SHE'S DEAD.
AND THIS IS THE GUN THAT KILLED HER. IT'S REGISTERED TO ME.
YOU KILLED HER?
I'M AFRAID SO.
SHE HAD A GUN.
"YOU'LL FIND THAT NEAR HER BODY. IT BELONGED TO THE GUY IN THE DOORWAY, BUT SHE DIDN'T KILL HIM.
"I DID USE IT TO SHOOT KANE, THOUGH."
YEAH, WE PICKED YOUR BUDDY UP HALF A MILE DOWN THE ROAD.
HE WAS COVERED IN BLOOD, RUNNING LIKE A MADMAN, WAVING SOME-THING SHINY.

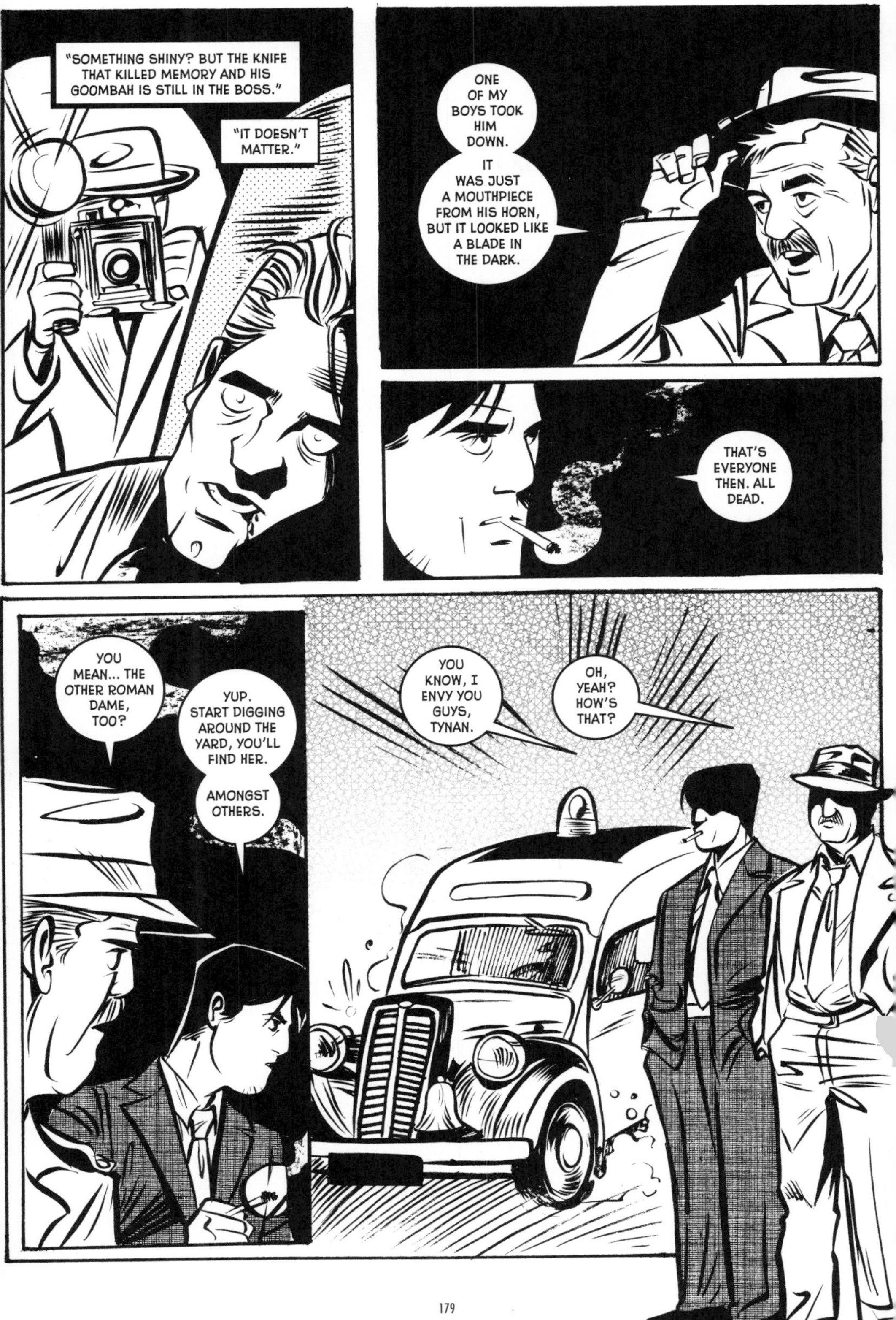
"SOMETHING SHINY? BUT THE KNIFE THAT KILLED MEMORY AND HIS GOOMBAH IS STILL IN THE BOSS."
"IT DOESN'T MATTER."
ONE OF MY BOYS TOOK HIM DOWN.
IT WAS JUST A MOUTHPIECE FROM HIS HORN, BUT IT LOOKED LIKE A BLADE IN THE DARK.
THAT'S EVERYONE THEN. ALL DEAD.
YOU MEAN... THE OTHER ROMAN DAME, TOO?
YUP. START DIGGING AROUND THE YARD, YOU'LL FIND HER.
AMONGST OTHERS.
YOU KNOW, I ENVY YOU GUYS, TYNAN.
OH, YEAH? HOW'S THAT?

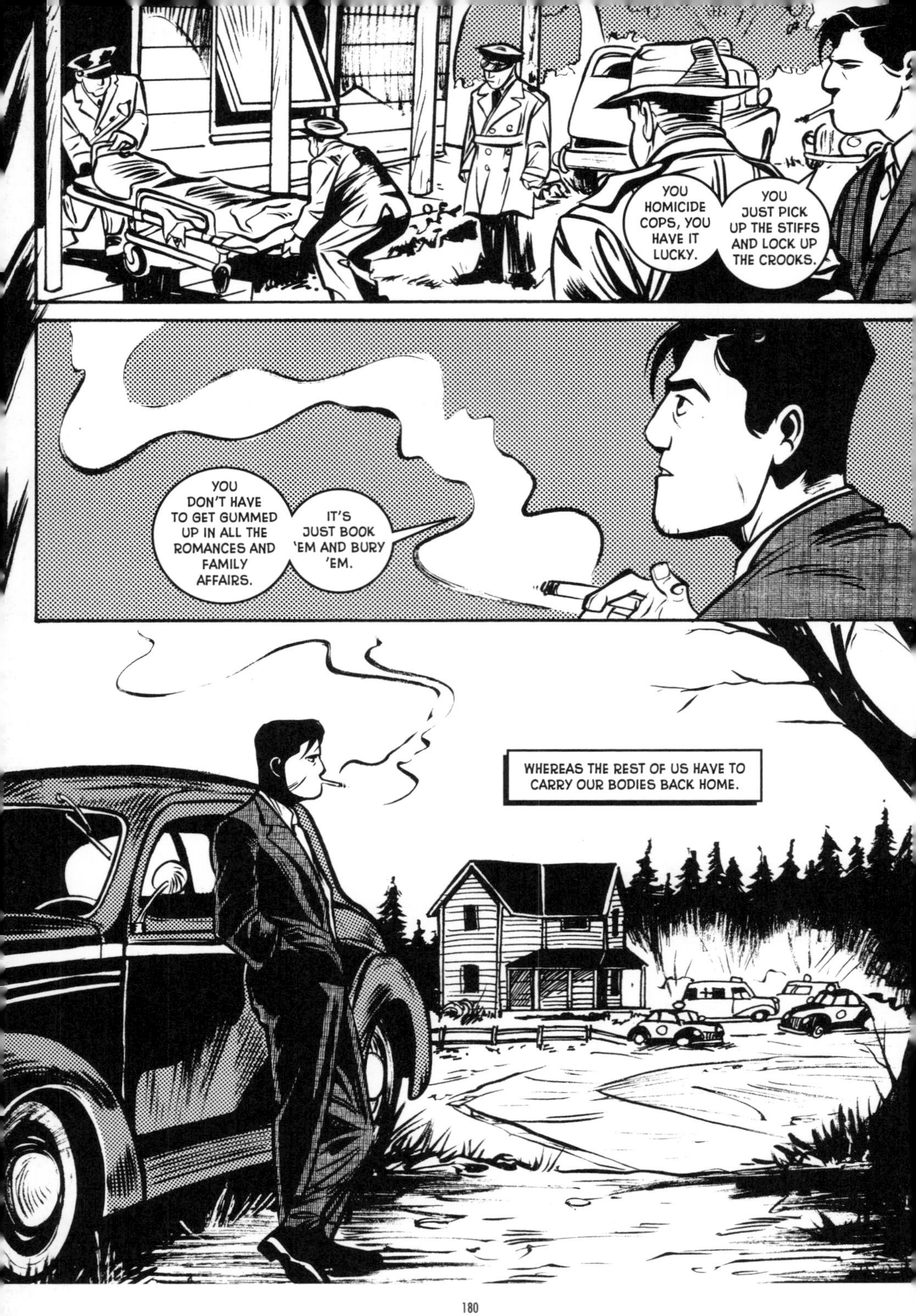
YOU HOMICIDE COPS, YOU HAVE IT LUCKY.
YOU JUST PICK UP THE STIFFS AND LOCK UP THE CROOKS.
YOU DON'T HAVE TO GET GUMMED UP IN ALL THE ROMANCES AND FAMILY AFFAIRS.
IT'S JUST BOOK 'EM AND BURY 'EM.
WHEREAS THE REST OF US HAVE TO CARRY OUR BODIES BACK HOME.

THE END

An Oni Press Production

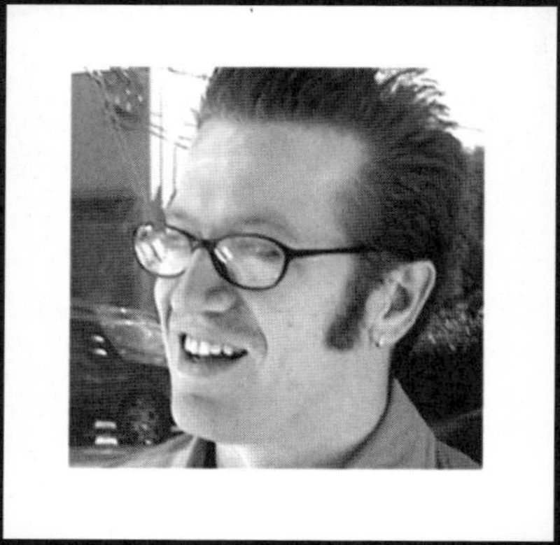

JAMIE S. RICH is an author and editor who began his career in the early 1990s at Dark Horse Comics before moving to Oni Press, where he was editor in chief from 1998 to 2004. Rich is best known for his collaborations with artist Joëlle Jones on the graphic novels *12 Reasons Why I Love Her* and *You Have Killed Me*. Their most recent and acclaimed collaboration has been *Lady Killer*. The series received four Eisner Award nominations in 2016.

Rich published his first prose novel, *Cut My Hair*, in 2000, and his first superhero comic book, *It Girl and the Atomics*, in 2012. In between, he has worked on multiple projects in both mediums. He has reviewed film for *The Oregonian* and *DVDTalk.com*, as well as hosting the comic book interview series *Back to the Gutters*.

Currently, Rich is a Group Editor at Vertigo, an imprint of DC Comics.

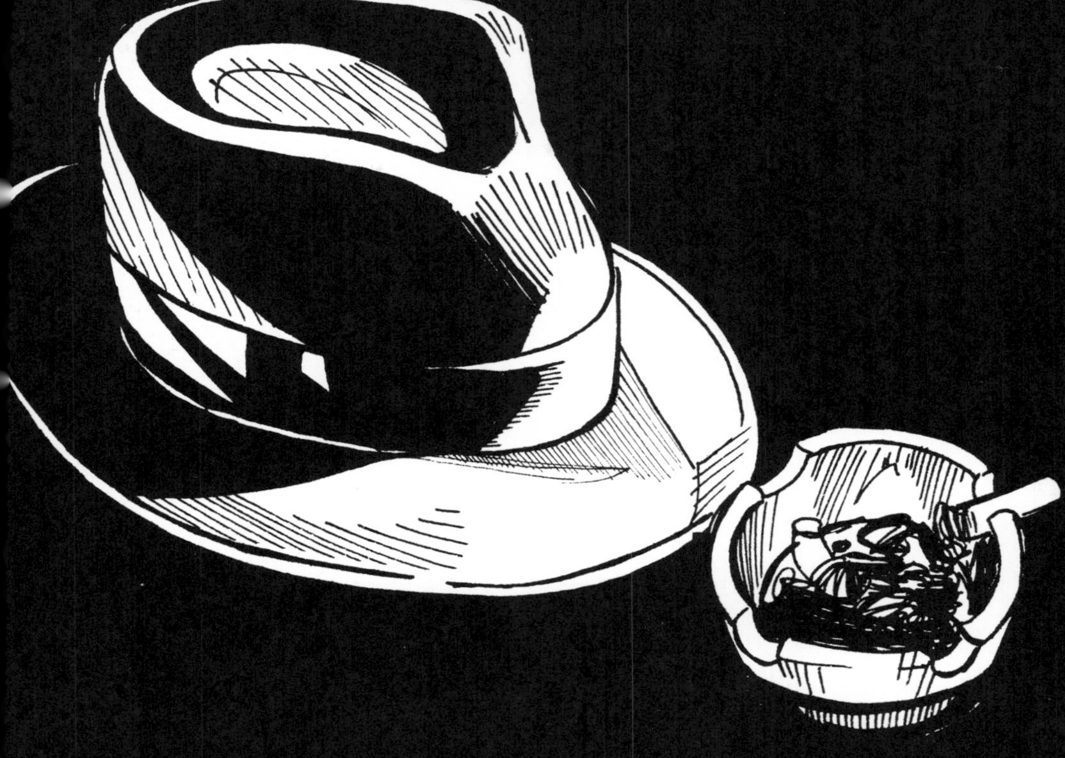

JOËLLE JONES is an Eisner-nominated artist currently living and working in Los Angeles, CA. Since attending PNCA in Portland, OR, she has contributed to a wide range of projects and has most recently begun writing and drawing her own series, *Lady Killer,* published by Dark Horse. Jones has also provided the art for *Superman: American Alien* (DC), *Helheim, Brides of Helheim* (Oni Press), and *Mockingbird* (Marvel). She's also done work for Boom! Studios, *The New York Times,* Vertigo and more! Joëlle will be taking on projects for DC and Marvel this year as well as continuing her series *Lady Killer.*

With best wishes,

Andrew McClellan

JUMBO
Marvel, Myth, and Mascot

Andrew McClellan

Tufts University

JUMBO: Marvel, Myth, and Mascot

By Andrew McClellan | Edited by Jane Bobko | Designed by Jeanne V. Koles
Printed by Hannaford & Dumas, Woburn, MA

Tufts

Library of Congress Cataloging-in-Publication Data

McClellan, Andrew.

 Jumbo : marvel, myth, and mascot / Andrew McClellan.

   pages cm

 ISBN 978-1-880593-12-7

1. Jumbo (Elephant) 2. Zoo animals--England--London--History--19th century. 3. Circus animals--United States--History--19th century. 4. Tufts College--Mascots. I. Title.

 GV1831.E4M36 2014

 791.3'2--dc23

             2014023221

COVER
Jumbo, The Children's Giant Pet, 1882

MAP, PRECEDING PAGE 1
Map of the world (detail) by D. Appleton & Co., New York, 1887

PAGE 5
Jumbo surrounded by London crowds, 1882

MAP, FOLLOWING PAGE 72
United States of North America (North Eastern Sheet) by W. & A. K. Johnston, London, ca. 1880

CONTENTS

ACKNOWLEDGMENTS

The author would like to thank the following people for their help with this book:

Michael Baker, Christopher Barbour, Ryan Belanger, Lori Birrell, Penelope Bodry-Sanders, Rosalie Bruno, Rocky Carzo, Carson Clarke-Magrab, Christine Connett, Don Cousens, Fred Dahlinger Jr., Samuel Evers, Bill Gehling, James Glaser, David Guss, Stuart Hicks, Eric Johnson, Darrin Lunde, Kathleen Maher, Barbara Mathé, James McClellan, Oliver McClellan, Anthony Monaco, Henry Nicholls, Dave Nuscher, Fred D. Pfenning III, Jennifer Lemmer Posey, Rosamond Purcell, Gabriel Quick, Jeffrey Quilter, Alexander Reid, Richard J. Reynolds III, Anne Sauer, Laurence Senelick, Christabelle Sethna, Peter Shrake, Adrienne St. Pierre, Deborah W. Walk, Melinda Wallington, Amy West, Mary Witkowski, and Matthew Wittmann.

A special thanks to Laura Beshears, Jane Bobko, Timothy Brooks, Christine Cavalier, Christa Clarke, Mrinalini Jaikumar, Jeanne Koles, Steve Peters, Christine Sanni, and the Tufts Association & Tufts Alumni Traditions Committee.

A number of the images in the final section, "Jumbo Comes to Tufts," were drawn from a photographic history of Tufts athletics mounted by Susanne Belovari at the Steve Tisch Sports and Fitness Center on the Medford campus.

For Christa Clarke and Steve Peters, Jumbomaniacs

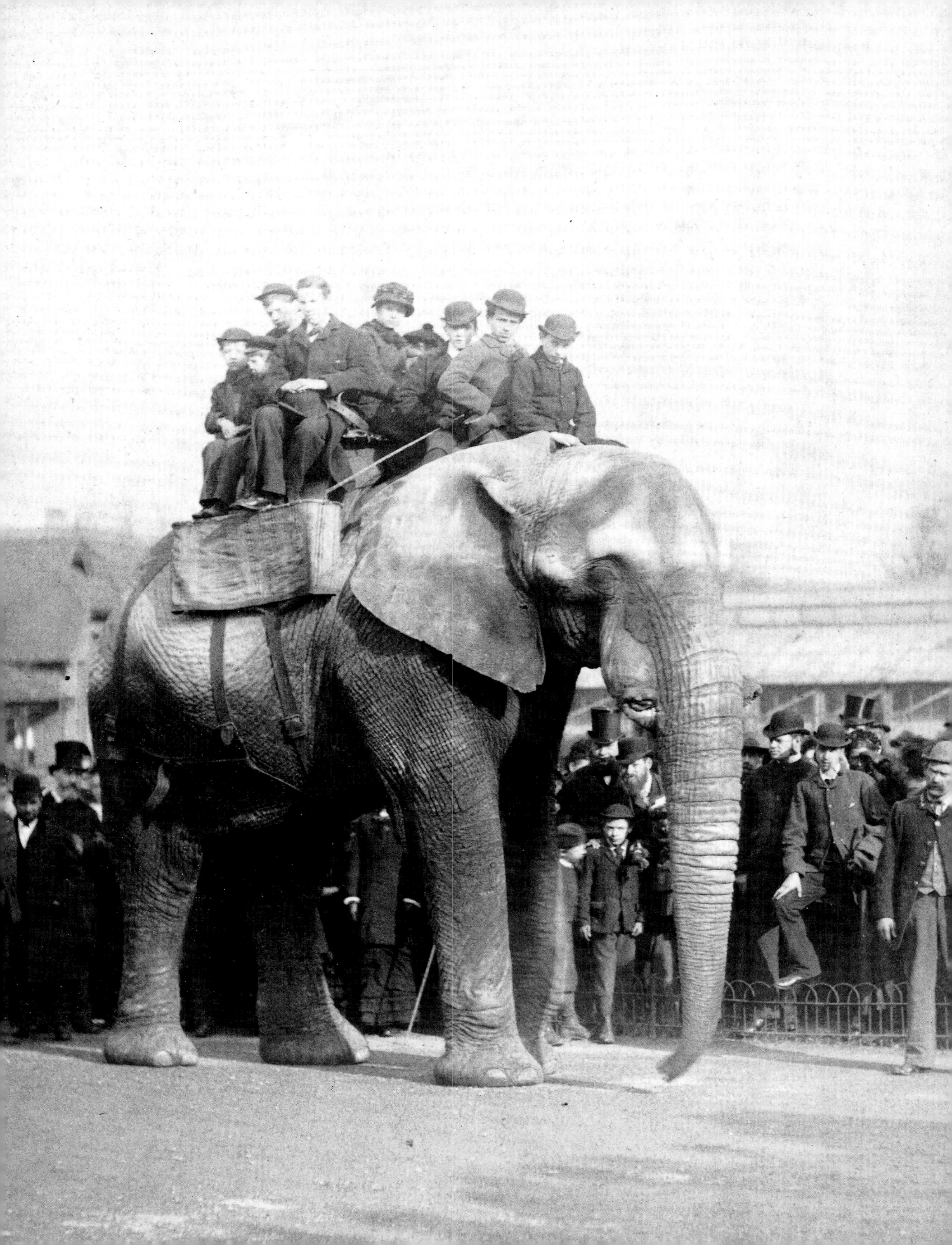

FACING PAGE, ABOVE

figure 1

Charles Eisenmann, *P. T. Barnum*, 1885.
This cabinet photograph shows Barnum, aged seventy-five, in the year of Jumbo's death.

FACING PAGE, BELOW

figure 2

Tufts students with Jumbo, ca. 1952

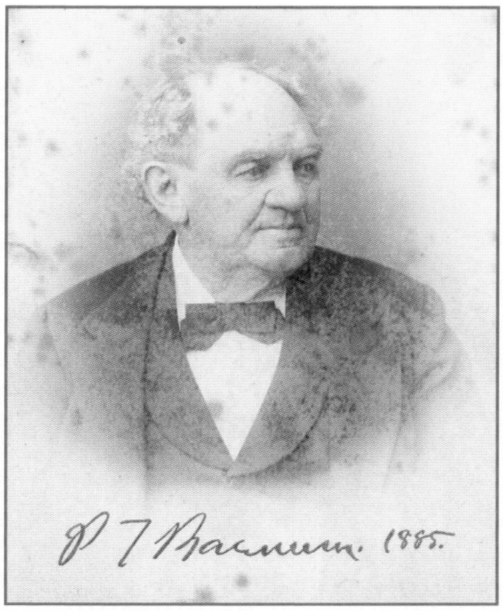
P T Barnum. 1885.

PREFACE

WHILE MOST COLLEGES AND UNIVERSITIES ANSWER to the call of a generic eagle, fierce feline, or knight in armor, Tufts is fortunate to have as its mascot a legendary elephant, Jumbo, who was once the most famous animal in the world. Jumbo (1861–1885) enjoyed (or, perhaps more accurately, endured) a remarkable life and afterlife, which took him from the plains of East Africa to captivity and fame in the zoos of Paris and London and P. T. Barnum's traveling American circus, to a fatal train accident in Canada, and, finally, to posthumous celebrity as a museum piece, college mascot, and byword for anything of great size.

Jumbo's story weaves together important strands of nineteenth-century history: the emergence of new vehicles of public education and entertainment—museums, zoos, and the circus—and the expansion of their exhibits in the wake of colonial exploration; the development of steamship travel and the railroad; the explosion of commercial products and advertising; the rise of American colleges and their mascots. At the center of Jumbo's tale is the great Barnum (fig. 1), showman extraordinaire, pioneer of popular culture, marketing genius, and philanthropist. Through his museums and circus, Barnum entertained more Americans than anyone else before the age of film and radio, and in the process made household names of Jumbo, Jenny Lind, Tom Thumb, and himself. By the time he died in 1891 he was known around the world, admired if also disparaged by some as the embodiment of the Yankee entrepreneur.

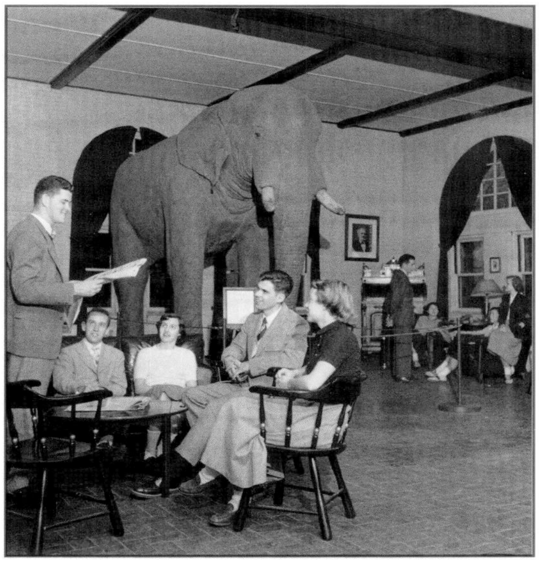

Jumbo came to Tufts as a gift from Barnum, who was a founding trustee and an early benefactor of the college. Barnum endowed the first science building at Tufts, which featured laboratories and a natural history museum whose chief exhibit was the stuffed hide of Jumbo (fig. 2). The mounted specimen perished in the fire that destroyed Barnum Hall in 1975, but Jumbo lives on as Tufts' mascot. Two thousand fourteen is the 125th anniversary of Jumbo's arrival on the Tufts campus, which is being commemorated by the erection of a new, life-size bronze statue and the publication of this book, which accompanies an exhibition of the same title at the Tufts University Art Gallery.

My interest in the story of Jumbo, Barnum, and Tufts stems from a broader interest in the history of museums and collecting. I was surprised to discover some years ago that little was known about the Barnum Museum on the Tufts campus. My research into the history of the museum expanded to encompass the development of lithography and popular culture, performance and spectacle, taxidermy and the representation of the animal kingdom in museums—and, more generally, the fraught interdependence of man and animals in the modern world. Jumbo's remarkable career is a vivid illustration of what the anthropologist Garry Marvin has poignantly described as the passages and journeys some wild animals make between the realms of nature and culture, traveling "from those spaces and conditions in which their lives are largely their own concerns and lived apart from us, to the differently configured spaces and conditions [of] our human 'cultural' world." While Jumbo's history has much to tell us about our evolving relationship with the natural world, it also belongs to Tufts. Drawing heavily on fabulous and too-little-known images, but also on new research, this book sheds fresh light on Jumbo's life and legend and seeks to underscore Tufts' claim to the most distinctive of college mascots.

—Andrew McClellan, Professor of Art History, Tufts University

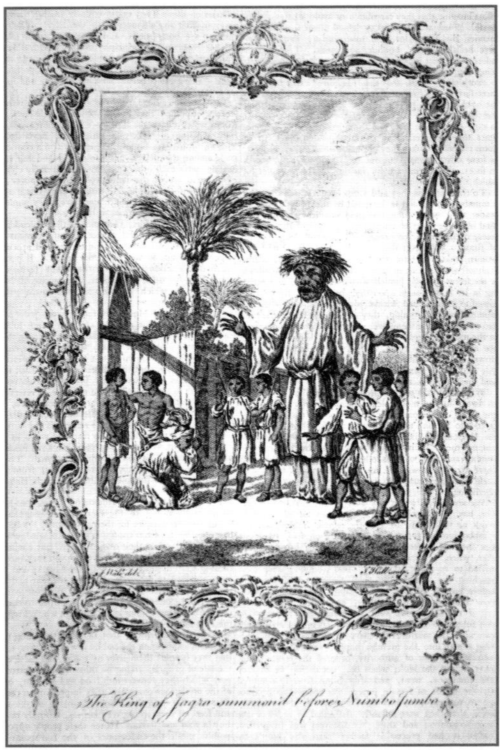
The King of Jagra summoned before Numbo Jumbo

ABOVE
figure 3
The King of Jagra Summoned before Numbo Jumbo, 1771. Some believe Jumbo may have been named after a West African holy man, Mumbo Jumbo (misspelled in this engraving).

BELOW
figure 4
Godefroy Engelmann, *View of the Rotonde . . . of the Jardin Royal des Plantes*, 1821. This early lithograph shows the structure built at the Paris zoo in 1804 to house elephants (and other large herbivores) brought to France following Napoléon Bonaparte's Egyptian campaign.

OUT OF AFRICA

JUMBO WAS CAPTURED IN THE REMOTE DESERT highlands near the border between Sudan and Eritrea (then Abyssinia; see map, preceding p. 1) early in 1862 by Hamran traders, nomadic hunters who dealt in ivory and hides but also secured live animals for Europe's thriving zoos and circuses. At the time of his capture, he was roughly a year old and stood about four feet tall. He was still but a calf, and the odds of his surviving separation from his mother and the arduous journey out of Africa were slim, but so rare and prized were African elephants in Europe that the rewards of delivering him safely to a zoo or traveling menagerie warranted the effort. Jumbo was not the first African elephant to reach European soil in modern times. Following Napoléon Bonaparte's Egyptian campaign (1798–1801), three African pachyderms were brought to the Jardin des Plantes in Paris, where the Rotonde (fig. 4) was built to house them and other large herbivores. None of them lived for long. Several others arrived at the Paris zoo in later decades, including one that survived for thirty years and another that died the year before Jumbo was captured. But none were living anywhere in Europe in 1862 when the dealer Lorenzo Casanova paid the Hamran handsomely for a live calf that would become the subject of our story.

From the banks of the Setit River the Hamran traders escorted their caravan of elephants, rhinos, giraffes, ostriches, and other animals to Kassala, where Casanova took over and supervised the grueling trek through the desert to the Red Sea port of Suakin, three hundred miles to the north. From Suakin a cargo ship moved the convoy farther north to Suez, where it was transferred to a train and taken overland to Alexandria. From Alexandria the animals sailed across the Mediterranean to Trieste in Italy, where they boarded another train for Dresden, Casanova's base of operations. Jumbo's fortitude was certainly tested by the 6,700-mile journey over sand and sea, in and out of dank ship holds and railway cars. Casanova sold his collection to a showman with a traveling menagerie, who in February 1863 sold Jumbo on to the Jardin des Plantes, which had been without an African elephant for the past two years. Within a year of arriving in Paris, Jumbo was joined by two more African elephant calves, purchased from the viceroy of Egypt. Dubbed Castor and Pollux, the playful pair quickly became popular with the public and rendered Jumbo a third wheel. In 1865 the London Zoological Society, seeking its first African elephant, negotiated with the Paris zoo to swap Jumbo for an Indian rhino, two dingoes, a pair of eagles, a possum, a jackal, and a kangaroo.

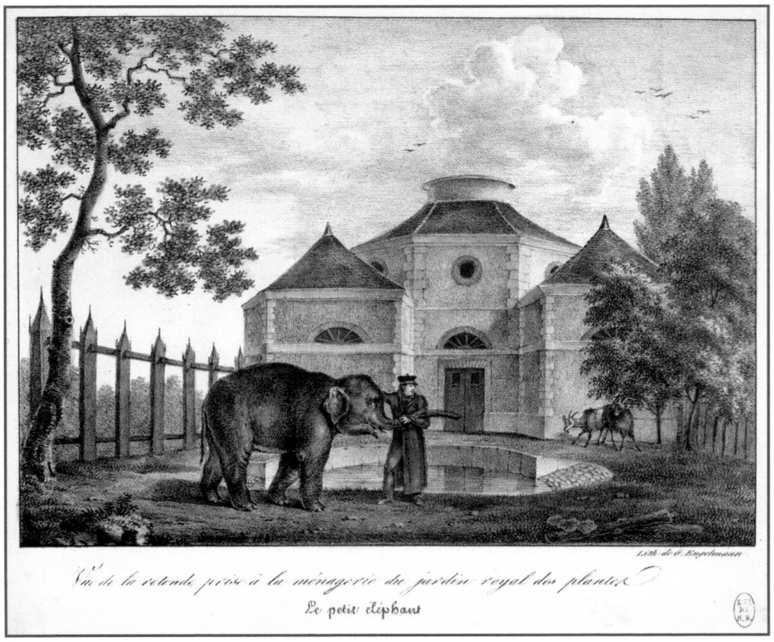
Le petit éléphant

RIGHT
figure 5
"The Newly-Imported African Elephant at the Gardens of the Zoological Society, Regent's Park," *Illustrated London News* (July 15, 1865). This is the earliest image of Jumbo, made shortly after he arrived in London.

MIDDLE
figure 6
Ernest Griset, *Elephants at London Zoo*, ca. 1865. Jumbo is at the left in this scene by one of the best-known animal artists of the Victorian era.

BELOW
figure 7
"Monday Afternoon at the Zoological Society's Gardens," *Illustrated London News* (September 23, 1871). Jumbo (rear) and Alice, his female companion at the zoo, are seen together, offering rides and accepting buns from children.

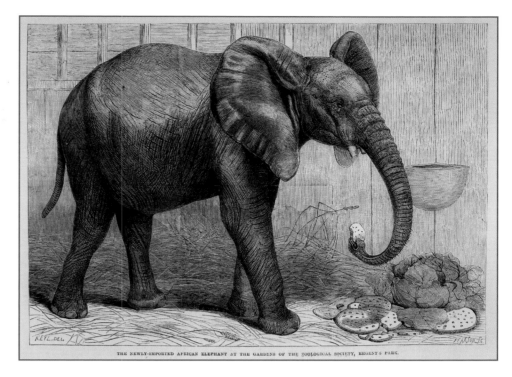

THE NEWLY-IMPORTED AFRICAN ELEPHANT AT THE GARDENS OF THE ZOOLOGICAL SOCIETY, REGENT'S PARK.

When Jumbo—acquired sight unseen—first arrived at London's zoo in Regent's Park in June 1865, zoo officials must have thought they had overpaid for the young pachyderm. The zoo's director, Abraham Bartlett, recalled in his memoirs: "At that date…he was in a filthy and miserable condition. … The first thing to do was to endeavor to remove the accumulated filth and dirt from his skin. … The poor beast's feet for want of attention had grown out of shape, but by scraping and rasping, together with a supply of good and nourishing food, his condition improved." One theory as to how Jumbo received his name is that his lamentable state upon arrival in London called to mind the disheveled appearance of a type of West African holy man, called Mumbo Jumbo, who was known through travelers' tales and engravings (fig. 3). Be that as it may, both the London *Times* and the *Illustrated London News* found the zoo's acquisition of its first African elephant worth reporting. The former instructed readers that the newcomer could be distinguished from an Indian elephant by the "enormous size of its ears," which are clearly depicted in the woodcut that appeared in the latter (fig. 5)—the earliest image we have of Jumbo. In a watercolor from around this time, the noted Victorian animal illustrator Ernest Griset captured a cheerful, big-eared Jumbo bringing up the rear of a parade of the zoo's three pachyderms (fig. 6). Both images may have exaggerated his health, as zoo records suggest a slow and uncertain recovery from various ailments.

But recover he did, and when we next encounter Jumbo—six years later, in a fine engraving in the *Illustrated London News*, dated September 1871 (fig. 7)—he has emerged from the shadow of his Indian housemates to become a top attraction at the zoo. We see Jumbo, accompanied by Alice, a

African Elephant.

Jumbo

Popular Series
African Elephant.

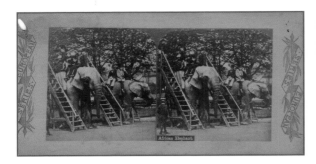

LEFT
figure 8
Frederick York, *Jumbo*, ca. 1870. Small carte-de-visite photographs were sold as souvenirs to zoo visitors.

FAR LEFT
figure 9
Frederick York, *African Elephant*, ca. 1872. Jumbo (nearest) and Alice stand at the mounting steps, near the refreshment house, at the London zoo.

LOWER LEFT
figure 10
Frederick York, *African Elephant*, ca. 1870. This twin image of Jumbo and his keeper, Matthew Scott, was made to be viewed through a stereoscope.

younger female African elephant who arrived at the zoo shortly after Jumbo, mobbed by children eager for a ride and proffering buns. In the foreground a boy receives the tuppenny fare from his father, who has taken a seat alongside other obliging parents. By this time, Jumbo measured approximately nine feet tall and weighed about three tons, and was fast approaching maturity. A ride on his back had become a must for children visiting the zoo.

Souvenir photographs in different formats—simple cartes de visite, larger cabinet photographs, and fancier stereoscopic images—testify to Jumbo's growing popularity and size (figs. 8–10). They also provide information omitted from the 1871 engraving. Double wooden stairs erected near the refreshment house allowed passengers to mount and dismount the elephants with ease and efficiency. Jumbo gave rides every afternoon between two and six o'clock, seven days a week, year round. Each ride lasted about fifteen minutes and took in the main pathways that led through the gardens (fig. 11). Though he could be restive at night, as we shall see, for well over a decade he calmly paraded children through the zoo by day without incident. According to Bartlett, "His docility and good temper rendered him the pet of thousands." Among the countless children said to have ridden on his back were Queen Victoria's son and daughter Prince Leopold and Princess Beatrice, Winston Churchill, and Theodore Roosevelt. When Jumbo was not touring the grounds, and during inclement weather, the public could visit him in the new Elephant House (figs. 12, 13), opened in 1869 and designed by the architect Anthony Salvin (the younger) as a row of gabled rustic cottages, which appear cozy in an early engraving in the *Illustrated London News*. Complete with paddock and pool, the new quarters obviated the need to walk the elephants down to the river Thames for an occasional bath, a spectacle whose passing must have been lamented by citizens of the great metropolis.

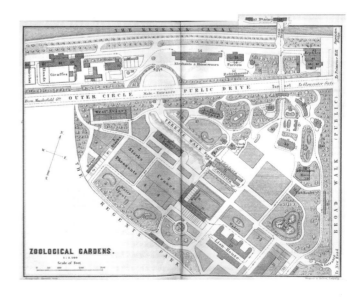

Absent from early engravings but conspicuous in virtually every photograph we have of Jumbo is his devoted companion and keeper, Matthew Scott. Jumbo was placed under Scott's supervision as soon as he arrived at Regent's Park. In Scott's anecdotal and self-serving biography, he described the strong bond formed between the two following the arrival of Jumbo, evidently in need of attention, and the elephant's near-fatal illness soon thereafter. "I watched him night and day with all the care and affection of a mother (if it were possible for a man to do such a thing)," he later

ZOOLOGICAL GARDENS.
OUTER CIRCLE
PUBLIC DRIVE
Giraffes
Elephants & Rhinoceroses
Parrots
Refreshments
West Aviary
Terrace Walk
Storks
Pheasants
Cranes
Lion House
BROAD WALK (PUBLIC)

ABOVE
figure 11
Plan of the London zoo, *Baedeker's Guide to London* (1894)

RIGHT
figure 12
The New Elephant-House in the Zoological Society's Gardens, Regent's Park, 1869. Jumbo lived in the gabled, cottage-style Elephant House from 1869 until 1882.

BELOW
figure 13
Interior of the new Elephant House at the London zoo, ca. 1895. A gallery inside the Elephant House allowed the public to visit Jumbo when he was not giving rides.

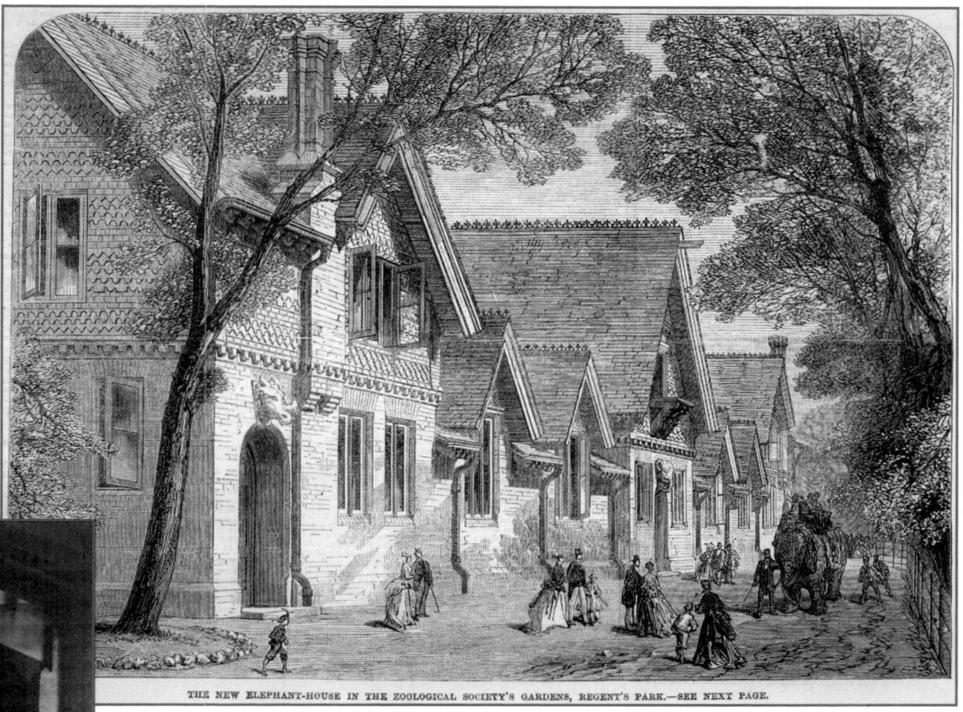
THE NEW ELEPHANT-HOUSE IN THE ZOOLOGICAL SOCIETY'S GARDENS, REGENT'S PARK.—SEE NEXT PAGE.

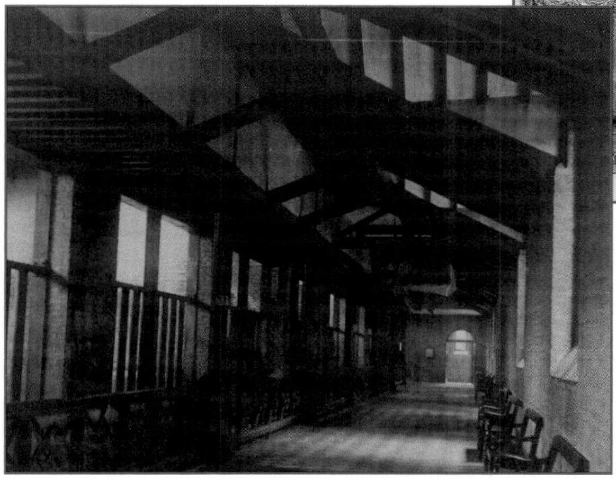

recalled. Unmarried and a loner, Scott rarely left Jumbo's side from that moment on, and he provided a buffer against harsher attendants and public curiosity. "Woe be to anyone who tries to come between us," he warned. In return for Scott's dedication, Jumbo would not take orders from anyone else. Scott was also permitted to keep the fee for rides on Jumbo, which earned him many times his annual salary as a keeper. His personal and financial attachment to the elephant helps to explain why he took fewer than five days off work in his sixteen years at the zoo, and why he remained with Jumbo until the end.

Scott had much to do with the anthropomorphization of his elephant friend, a contributing factor in Jumbo's rise to transatlantic celebrity. In Scott's book and also in his daily interactions with zoo visitors, he acted as Jumbo's interpreter and champion, ascribing endearingly human qualities to the pachyderm. Through Scott, we learn of Jumbo's compassion and courage, his aversion to rodents, his discriminating love of music (he preferred the Horse Guards bands to others that played in Regent's Park), his taste for a "medicinal" dram of whiskey, and his gallantry toward his "wife," Alice, who was also placed under Scott's care. Scott tells of a toddler who had wandered away from his parents on a busy day at the zoo and whom Jumbo gently lifted out of harm's way with his trunk—a story later replayed in the myth of Jumbo's saving a young elephant from the train crash that took his own life. Jumbo engaged the public with his sense of humor, pinching morsels of food and sips of tea, as well as Scott's derby from atop his head. We also learn of Jumbo's love for Alice. "Jumbo always showed the greatest respect for Alice, a good deal more so in fact than some young men show for their sweethearts in this or any other country," Scott writes. The two elephants were often seen together in public and widely referred to as husband and wife. On occasion they were even pictured with supposed offspring (fig. 14), though there is no evidence they ever consummated their relationship.

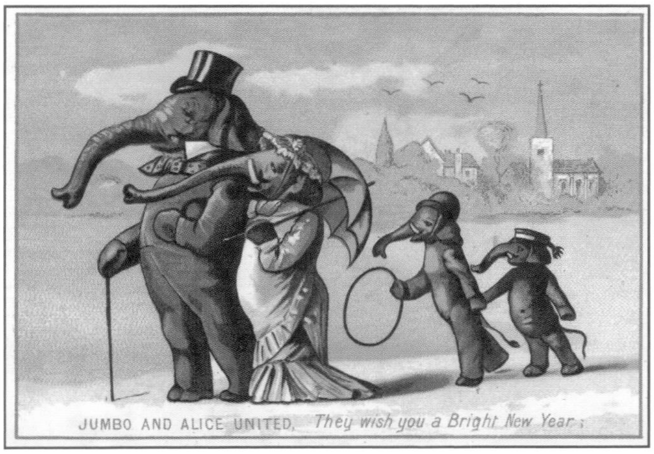
JUMBO AND ALICE UNITED. They wish you a Bright New Year.

ABOVE
figure 14
New Year's greeting card with Jumbo, Alice, and offspring, 1880s. This charming card imagines Jumbo and Alice as the contented Victorian parents of two young calves, out for a walk in the country.

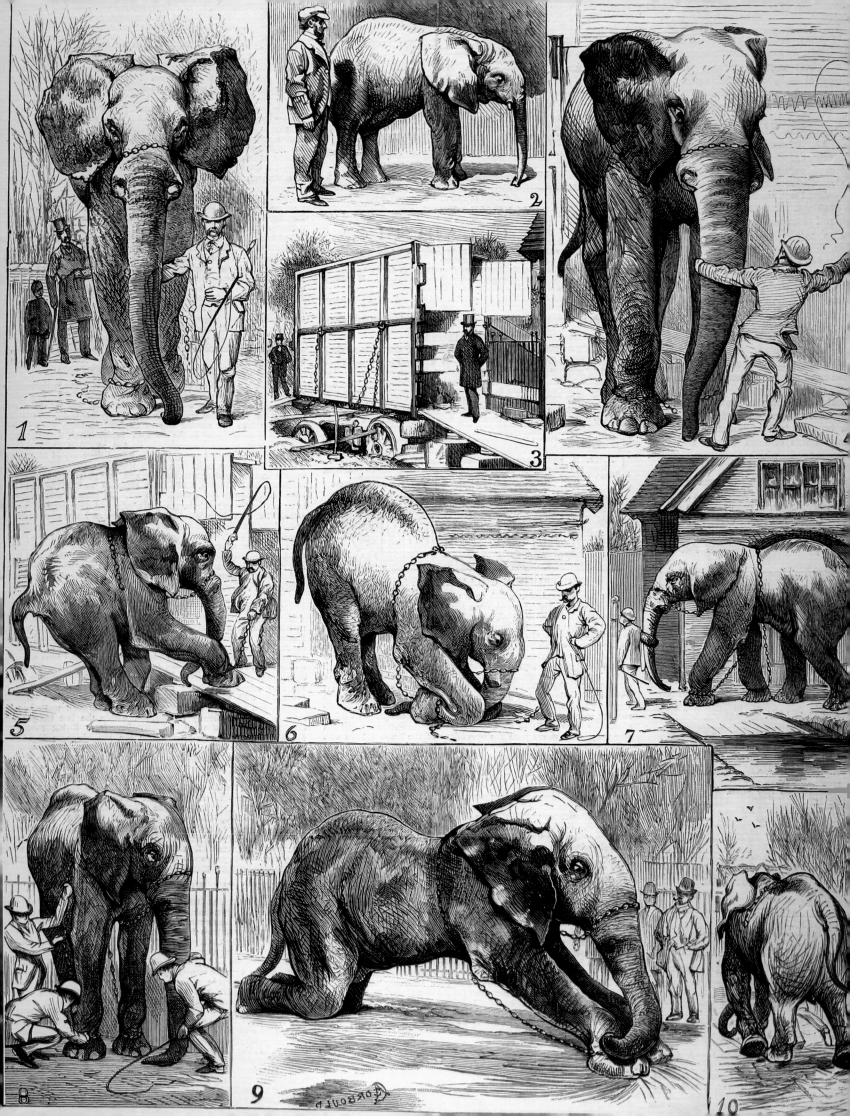

Scott's narrative fails to mention the extraordinary circumstances leading to Jumbo's departure from the zoo for America, most probably because events were beyond Scott's control. In 1881, Jumbo entered the elephant equivalent of puberty—a period in males known as "musth" that is accompanied by unpredictable and unruly behavior. Between June and November, Jumbo had over twenty violent nocturnal outbursts, battering his pen with head and tusks to the point of threatening the structural integrity of the Elephant House. Now close to eleven feet tall and weighing approximately five tons, he was bigger and stronger than any animal known to be in captivity and capable of compromising the sturdiest quarters the zoo's carpenters could devise. Zoo records note: "The door leading from the den into the open air is closed with massive beams of oak eight inches square; these are further strengthened by plates of stout sheet iron on both sides and are so heavy that two men can scarcely raise one of them from the ground. Nevertheless, these beams have not merely bent but positively broken through both iron and wood, by the muscular power of the animal. ... In spite of every precaution, the house is quickly being destroyed by the efforts of the animal during his fits of irritability." Not without reason, the zoo's director feared that Jumbo might one day become violent during visiting hours. Bartlett had heard of the "deaths of many persons ... killed from time to time by elephants while in this state." Anxiety was allayed somewhat by Matthew Scott's uncanny ability to calm Jumbo; nevertheless, Bartlett acquired a powerful rifle in case the elephant ran amok one day.

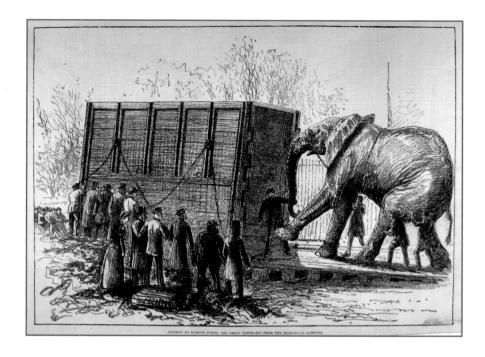

FACING PAGE

figure 15

"The Attempted Removal of 'Jumbo' from the Zoological Gardens," *Illustrated London News* (February 25, 1882). Jumbo vehemently refused to leave the zoo following his sale to P. T. Barnum.

ABOVE

figure 16

"Attempt to Remove Jumbo, the Great Elephant, from the Zoological Gardens," *Illustrated London News* (February 25, 1882)

BELOW

figure 17

Jumbo refuses to leave the zoo, 1882. Jumbo's defiant stand was followed closely in newspapers and drew the sympathy of patriotic animal lovers throughout Britain.

In December 1881, P. T. Barnum and his associates, who were always on the lookout for dazzling new acts, learned of the zoo's predicament and approached Bartlett with a solution he could never have anticipated and could not refuse. Reports of Jumbo's behavior prompted a telegram from the circus partners that got straight to the point: "What is the lowest price you can take for the large male African elephant?" Barnum, who knew Bartlett, followed up with a personal letter, hedging on the partners' level of interest in order to lower expectations, and the asking price, but when Bartlett proposed £2,000 (roughly $220,000 in today's money), plus the cost of transportation, no negotiations ensued and the deal was quickly sealed.

March 18, 1882.] PUNCH, OR THE LONDON CHARIVARI. 123

JUMBO IN CHANCERY.

to mind matters! This is certainly infamous! The provinces and their artistic aspirations be hanged! Here, if the Harleian MSS. are flying about all over the hedgerows of England, they can't so easily move the stuffed animals. You wanted to see the *Hippopotamus Africanus major*. I can at least show you that.

[*They once more dash off to South Kensington, and make for the National History Department, get a catalogue, and enter the Pachydermatous-room.*

Educational Enthusiast (*stopping in amazement opposite a misshapen specimen*). Why, what has happened to this creature! It is no more like a *hippopotamus* than I am. Here—what's the meaning of this?

Local Official. That bend in his legs, and the lump on the top of his back? Well, it does spoil the look of him; but you see, Sir, he went all the way to Cornwall, came back in an accident, was telescoped by the tender, and lost a good bit of his stuffing, to say nothing of the shape of his head. So we've made the best job we can of him, by filling him out with a couple of kitchen chairs and a bolster. Moving him about costs so much, that's all the department can do for him out of the grant this year. But, bless you, Sir, it isn't everybody that's so particular as you; for there's many likes him best with the lump and his legs curled; and I dare say when he goes to Weston-Super-Mare next spring they'll want to keep him there altogether, and run him on the end of the pier through the season along with the German Band.

[*Is continuing, when* Educational Enthusiast *dashes off with his Friend once more, this time to the Tower, to see the "Crown Jewels," and the "Block," but finding the former at Jersey and the latter at Rosherville, finishes the day in despair in Baker Street, invoking maledictions on the Provinces, in the midst of the only priceless and complete collection now left the Nation.*

A GENTLEMAN asked Mrs. RAMSBOTHAM if her friend the Professor hadn't "written a great deal?" "Ah! he *has!*" replied Mrs. R. "There's only one word to describe him, and that is Voluminious! He's a voluminious writer!"

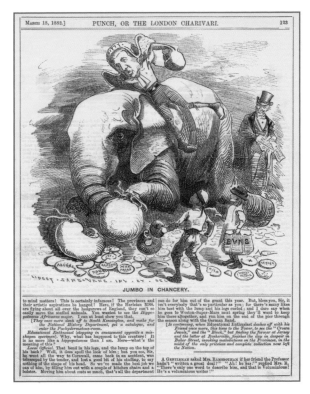

News of the sale, announced in the *Times* on January 25, 1882, produced little response. But when Barnum's men, including the trainer "Elephant Bill" Newman, arrived at the zoo in February to coordinate Jumbo's removal, newspapers picked up the story, the public took notice, and Bartlett had a late-breaking controversy on his hands. On February 18 the *Echo* gave a description of Jumbo's massive traveling crate—measuring twelve feet high, fourteen feet long, and eight feet wide, and weighing some eight tons—and opined that his departure from the zoo, set for the following day, a Saturday, promised to be "one of the most interesting scenes that has been witnessed at the Zoological Gardens for some years." Little did anyone know just how interesting the day would prove. The next morning, crowds gathered around the Elephant House to witness a remarkable sight: Jumbo stubbornly resisted every effort to move him into his box (figs. 15, 16). As the day unfolded and the number of curious onlookers increased, Scott's calm inducements gave way to Newman's use of heavy chains and force, but to no greater effect. Reporters were on hand to record events. The *Daily Telegraph* recounted that Jumbo's "loud trumpetings and fierce assaults upon his iron bonds told a tale

ABOVE
figure 18
Sir Joseph William Chitty, 1900. Justice Chitty presided over the court case that sought—unsuccessfully—to invalidate Jumbo's sale to Barnum.

MIDDLE
figure 19
"Jumbo in Chancery," *Punch* (March 18, 1882). The famous satirical magazine *Punch* followed the legal proceedings with interest.

LEFT
figure 20
Jumbo with Matthew Scott and "Elephant Bill" Newman, 1882. This photograph shows Jumbo being introduced to the massive moving crate that would take him from the London zoo and across the Atlantic to New York.

FACING PAGE
figure 21
"Jumbo's Journey to the Docks," *Illustrated London News* (April 1, 1882). Despite cold weather and the early hour, thousands lined the route from the zoo to the London docks to bid Jumbo farewell.

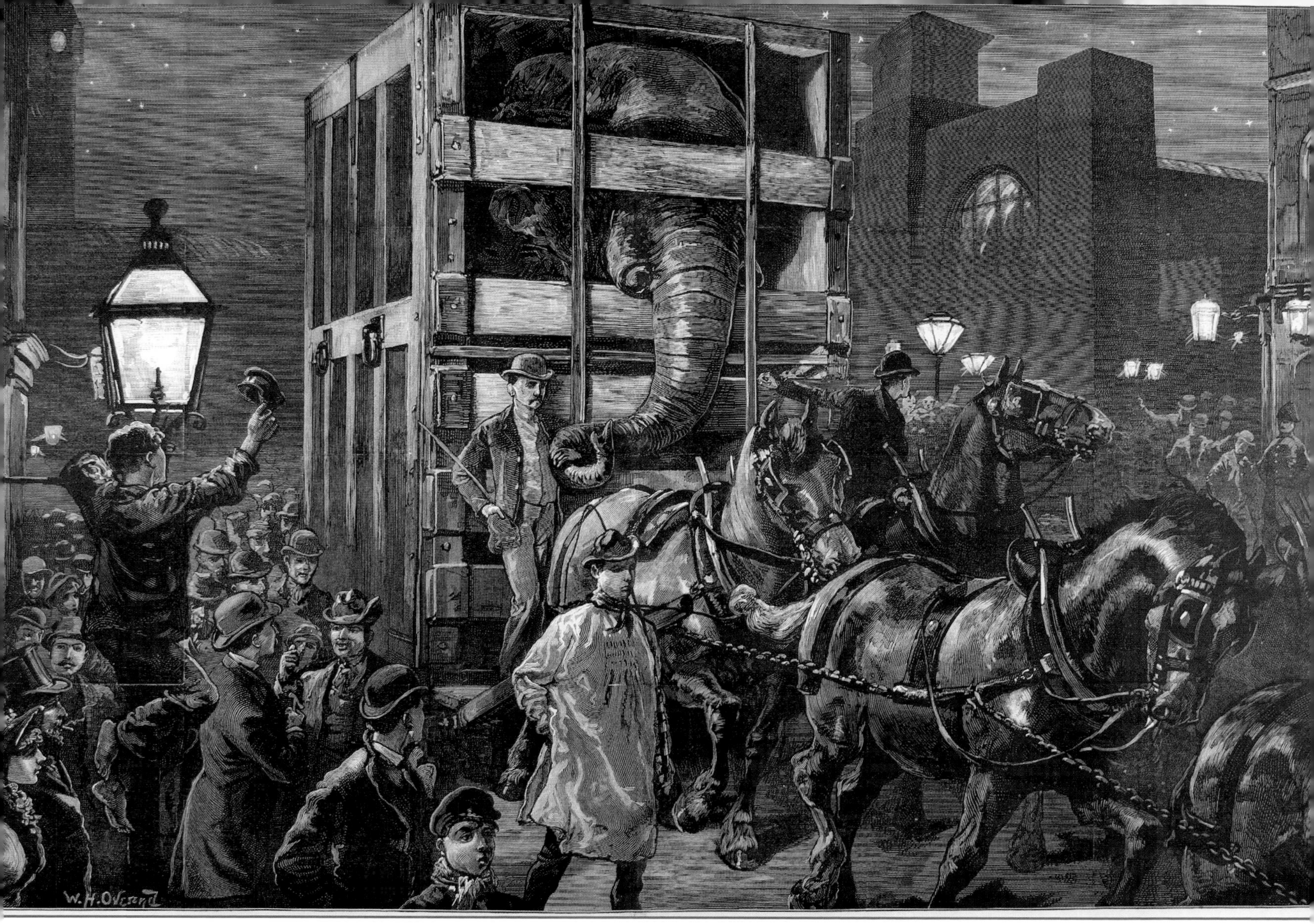
W. H. Overend

of something wrong to the elephants right and left of him. . . . The female elephant Alice, Jumbo's 'little wife,' as she is called, was most painfully agitated, and cried piteously in the cell next her lord's." At six in the evening, Scott tried one last time to coax Jumbo into his crate, still to no avail. By this point the crowd had swelled to twelve hundred, moved by Jumbo's plight and show of will. Overnight, Newman hatched a new plan. Instead of being crated at the zoo, Jumbo would be walked the eight miles from Regent's Park to Millwall Docks, where, exhausted and away from his mates, he would accept his fate and board the waiting steamship *Persian Monarch*, due to sail with the tide on Sunday afternoon.

Zoo employees assembled at dawn the next morning in their Sunday best to see Jumbo off, as did large crowds intrigued by news of Saturday's events. The *Daily Telegraph* offered the following account:

> Daybreak came, and the sagacious brute was once again brought out, and seemed docile enough as he walked sedately towards the wooden gate opposite the parrot house. Before emerging upon the road, Jumbo tried the ground, which differed in appearance from the accustomed paths of shingle, inside the grounds; and not being satisfied as to its security, refused to proceed. Then came one of the most pathetic scenes in which a "dumb animal" was ever the chief actor. The poor brute moaned sadly, and appealed in all but human words to his keeper, embracing the man with his trunk [fig. 17], and actually kneeling before him. Jumbo's cries were soon heard in the elephant house, where poor Alice was again seized with alarm and grief, so that every note of sorrow from the kneeling elephant in the road had its response within the gardens. At the sound of Alice's increasing lamentations, Jumbo became almost frantic, and flung himself down on his side.

THE GRAPHIC
AN ILLUSTRATED WEEKLY NEWSPAPER
No. 644—Vol. XXV. Regd. at General Post Office as a Newspaper
SATURDAY, APRIL 1, 1882
WITH EXTRA SUPPLEMENT
PRICE SIXPENCE Or by Post Sixpence Halfpenny
1. Through his Box at Last.—2. Visitors Inscribing Names on the Box as Having Called.—3. Jumbo Objects to the Irons.—4. At the Park Gates: Jumbo Drives *Himself*.—5. Albany Street: "Guard Turn Out"—6. *En Route*; "Jumbo's Old Lady."—7. Entering St. Katherine's Dock.—8. In Mid-Air: Being Lowered into the Barge.
THE REMOVAL OF JUMBO, I.—ON THE WAY TO THE DOCKS

LEFT
figure 22
"The Removal of Jumbo, I.—On the Way to the Docks," *Graphic* (April 1, 1882). Vignette engravings document the phases of Jumbo's removal from the London zoo.

MIDDLE
figure 23
Jumbo in his crate at Millwall Docks with Matthew Scott and "Elephant Bill" Newman, 1882

BELOW
figure 24
Loading Jumbo's crate onto the *Assyrian Monarch*, 1882. Souvenir photographs recorded Jumbo's departure from London.

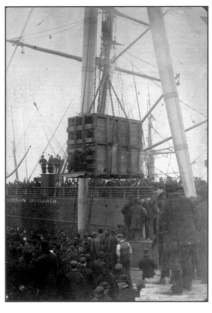

Jumbo would not be moved. Acknowledging defeat, the keepers led him back to his stall, much to the delight of a cheering public. The *Persian Monarch* left without Jumbo, and it would be two weeks before another ship with a hold big enough to contain his box set sail. The press and the public now turned on the zoo and its officials. Letters began pouring in to newspapers asking if something might be done to reverse the decision or change Barnum's mind. The *Standard* appealed to sentiment and patriotism, recalling that Jumbo's "afternoon promenade, laden with a swarm of liliputians, was to him a holiday" and asserting that his evident "love of London" would "farther endear him to the generation of children to whom he has been so long known as the most docile of playfellows." An editorial in the *Pall Mall Gazette* piled on: "Can nothing be done to rescue Jumbo? … Is this the way we recompense our oldest friends, those best benefactors who have given us the one boon which is without alloy—hearty and innocent enjoyment? … Is he to be turned out at last to tramp the world homeless and unbefriended, the mere chattel of a wandering showman?" Even the great art critic John Ruskin wrote a letter, reprinted in half a dozen papers, criticizing the zoo for its callous treatment of the children's

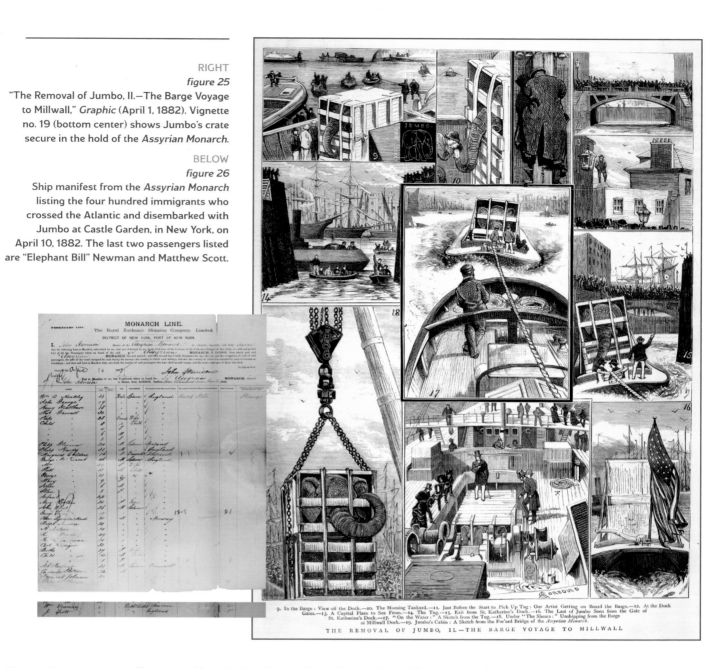

RIGHT

figure 25

"The Removal of Jumbo, II.—The Barge Voyage to Millwall," *Graphic* (April 1, 1882). Vignette no. 19 (bottom center) shows Jumbo's crate secure in the hold of the *Assyrian Monarch*.

BELOW

figure 26

Ship manifest from the *Assyrian Monarch* listing the four hundred immigrants who crossed the Atlantic and disembarked with Jumbo at Castle Garden, in New York, on April 10, 1882. The last two passengers listed are "Elephant Bill" Newman and Matthew Scott.

9. In the Barge: View off the Dock.—10. The Morning Tankard.—11. Just Before the Start to Pick Up Tug: Our Artist Getting on Board the Barge.—12. At the Dock Gates.—13. A Capital Place to See From.—14. The Tug.—15. Exit from St. Katherine's Dock.—16. The Last of Jumbo Seen from the Gate of St. Katherine's Dock.—17. "On the Water:" A Sketch from the Tug.—18. Under "The Shears:" Unshipping from the Barge at Millwall Dock.—19. Jumbo's Cabin: A Sketch from the For'ard Bridge of the *Assyrian Monarch*.
THE REMOVAL OF JUMBO, II.—THE BARGE VOYAGE TO MILLWALL

PASSENGERS' LIST.

MONARCH LINE.

The Royal Exchange Shipping Company, Limited.

DISTRICT OF NEW YORK, PORT OF NEW YORK.

pet. Queen Victoria reportedly received hundreds of letters from distraught children seeking her intervention. The matter was taken up in Parliament. Jumbo's delayed exit gave time for the pictorial weeklies the *Graphic* and the *Illustrated London News* to relay images of Jumbo's defiant last stand.

The wait between scheduled departures of ships of the *Monarch Line* created time for disgruntled members of the Zoological Society who had not been consulted about Jumbo's sale to try legal action to nullify the transaction. The journal *Vanity Fair* established a Jumbo Defence Fund to support the cause. At the High Court, Justice Joseph William Chitty (figs. 18, 19) granted an interim injunction to allow for a proper hearing of the case, which led to another missed departure and a further two-week postponement. Alarmed by this new development, Barnum wired his agents: "Employ best counsel in London. Spare no expense. We must have Jumbo. Have expended $30,000 for engraving, lithographs and colored posters representing the largest elephant in the world." In the end, on March 8, Justice Chitty declared the sale legal. The decision was carried in a special edition of the *Evening Standard* under the headline JUMBO IS TO GO.

With legal obstacles cleared, passage was booked on the *Assyrian Monarch* for the last week in March. Delays had given the zoo men and "Elephant Bill" time to ponder Jumbo's obstinacy and to wonder if Matthew Scott might have had something to do with it. The hunch proved correct. When Scott was threatened with permanent separation from his elephant friend, he pleaded for another chance and soon enough Jumbo cooperated. Scott was given leave to travel with Jumbo to America. A photograph of

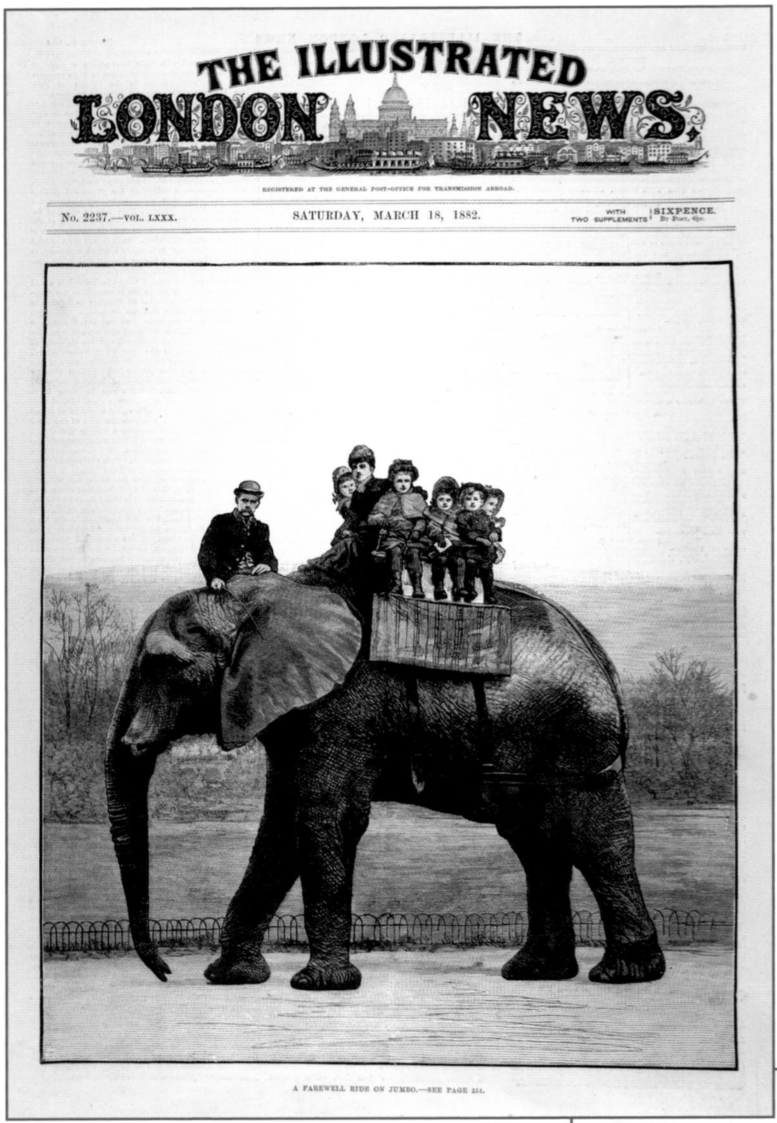
THE ILLUSTRATED LONDON NEWS,

REGISTERED AT THE GENERAL POST-OFFICE FOR TRANSMISSION ABROAD.

No. 2237.—VOL. LXXX. SATURDAY, MARCH 18, 1882. WITH TWO SUPPLEMENTS | SIXPENCE. By Post, 6½d.

A FAREWELL RIDE ON JUMBO.—SEE PAGE 254.

Newman and Scott alongside Jumbo in his box commemorated the new partnership (fig. 20).

Even with Scott's cooperation it took a full day to load Jumbo securely in his box and set the wheeled chassis in motion. At long last, in the early morning of March 23, 1882, the massive ten-ton carriage drawn by ten horses cleared the zoo gates. It took four hours to travel less than five miles to St. Katherine's docks, near the Tower of London. Despite the hour and the cold, thousands of people lined the route to bid farewell. Jumbo was transferred by crane to a barge that ferried him downriver to Millwall Docks, on the Isle of Dogs, where he was loaded the following day onto the *Assyrian Monarch*. Engravings and photographs documented each stage of the operation (figs. 21–25). A farewell luncheon was held on board for honored guests led by the United States consul general. Several toasts were offered, ending with one by Abraham Bartlett wishing Jumbo safe passage and a return visit to England one day. At five in the morning on Saturday, March 25, the *Assyrian Monarch* was towed downriver to Gravesend, attended by a flotilla of small boats laden with cheering sightseers. At Gravesend the ship was visited by Lady Burdett-Coutts, the richest woman in Britain and patroness of

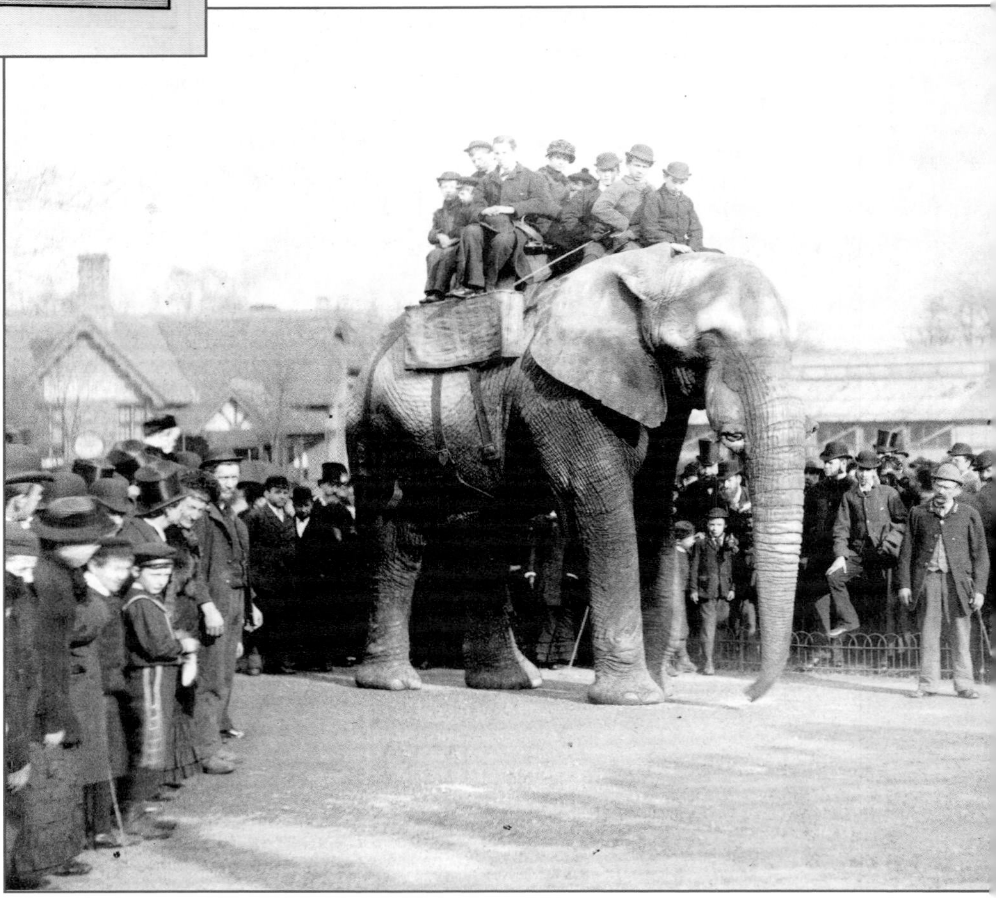

ABOVE
figure 27
"A Farewell Ride on Jumbo," *Illustrated London News* (March 18, 1882). During Jumbo's final weeks at the zoo, thousands came for a last ride on his back.

RIGHT
figure 28
Jumbo surrounded by London crowds, 1882

the Society for the Prevention of Cruelty to Animals, which had taken a close interest in Jumbo's sale and well-being. Burdett-Coutts inspected Jumbo's quarters and gave him a "parting feast of buns." The ship then set out to sea, its progress monitored until a final sighting off Lizard Point, the most southernmost tip of the English mainland. An American visitor in London wrote home: "It has been arranged for bulletins of Jumbo's health on the voyage to be enclosed in little rubber bags, which are to be thrown into the water, and may possibly drift to these shores." It seems no such communications were reported found, or perhaps were ever sent. One wonders what memories of the voyage were passed down from the four hundred emigrants from Britain, Germany, Scandanavia, and Russia who shared their crossing to the New World with Jumbo (fig. 26).

Throughout the Jumbo affair, Barnum reveled in the free publicity. Unconcerned about initial reports of Jumbo's intransigence, the showman responded, "Let him lie there for a week if he wants to. It is the best advertisement in the world." Barnum knew a good story when he saw one, and he had long ago learned how to use the press to his advantage. Renowned for hoaxes and preposterous exaggerations of all kinds, Barnum would consider any publicity stunt to inflate his business. In the decades before Jumbo, he contemplated offering to buy the cottage in which Shakespeare was born and Nelson's Column in Trafalgar Square. Of the latter he wrote to a friend: "I know they won't sell it, but no matter. All I want is a big advertisement." Barnum didn't simply revel in the media circus surrounding Jumbo; he contributed to it with his own letters to the press as well as one, which he was suspected of concocting,

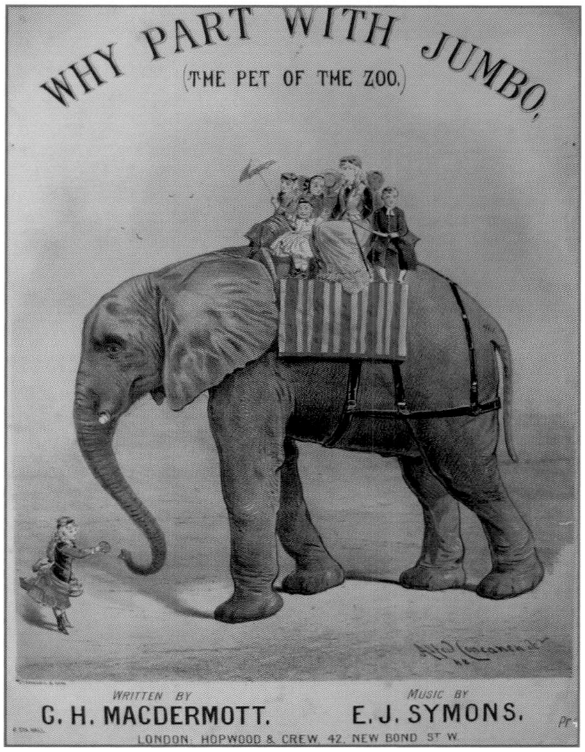
WHY PART WITH JUMBO,
(THE PET OF THE ZOO.)
WRITTEN BY
G. H. MACDERMOTT.
MUSIC BY
E. J. SYMONS.
LONDON: HOPWOOD & CREW, 42, NEW BOND ST W.

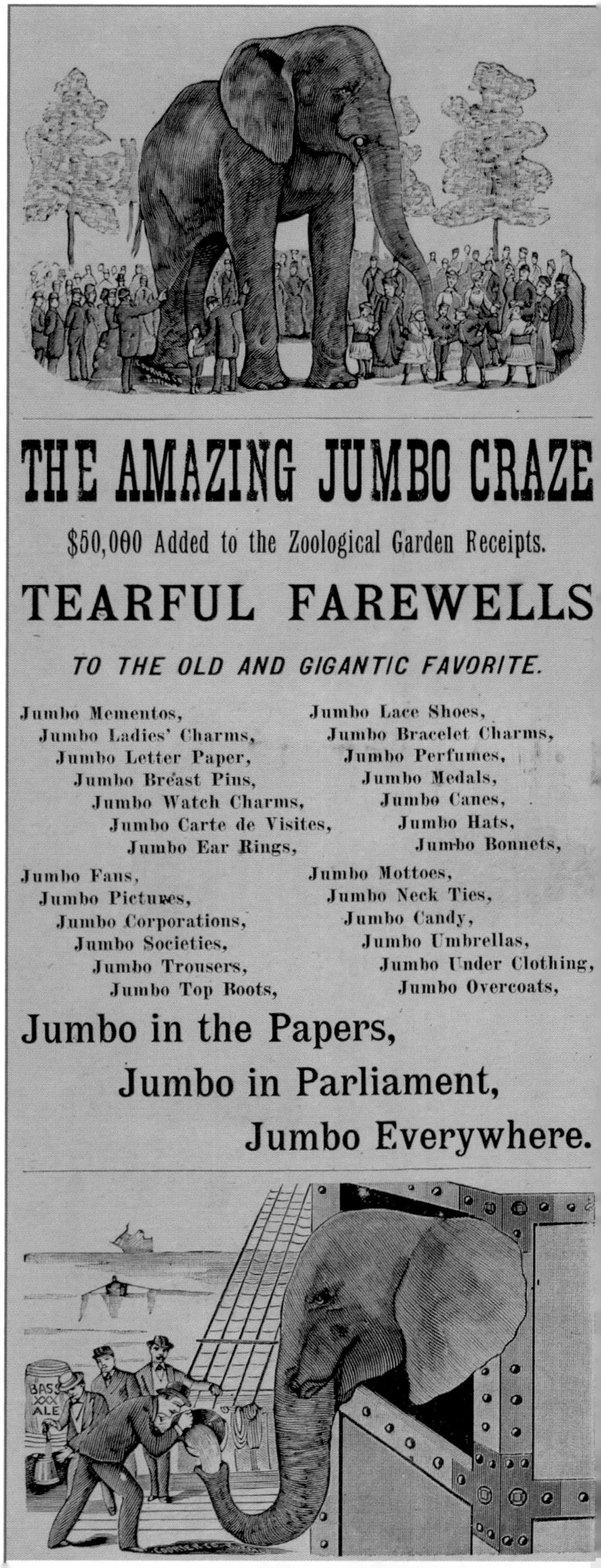
THE AMAZING JUMBO CRAZE
$50,000 Added to the Zoological Garden Receipts.
TEARFUL FAREWELLS
TO THE OLD AND GIGANTIC FAVORITE.
Jumbo Mementos,
Jumbo Ladies' Charms,
Jumbo Letter Paper,
Jumbo Breast Pins,
Jumbo Watch Charms,
Jumbo Carte de Visites,
Jumbo Ear Rings,
Jumbo Lace Shoes,
Jumbo Bracelet Charms,
Jumbo Perfumes,
Jumbo Medals,
Jumbo Canes,
Jumbo Hats,
Jumbo Bonnets,
Jumbo Fans,
Jumbo Pictures,
Jumbo Corporations,
Jumbo Societies,
Jumbo Trousers,
Jumbo Top Boots,
Jumbo Mottoes,
Jumbo Neck Ties,
Jumbo Candy,
Jumbo Umbrellas,
Jumbo Under Clothing,
Jumbo Overcoats,
Jumbo in the Papers,
Jumbo in Parliament,
Jumbo Everywhere.
BASS XXX ALE

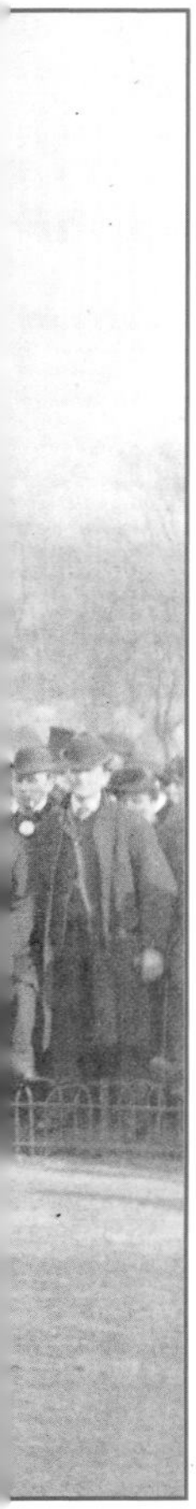

LEFT
figure 29
Sheet music for G. H. MacDermott and E. J. Symons, "Why Part with Jumbo, (The Pet of the Zoo)" (1882). A star of the Victorian music-hall stage, MacDermott was at the height of his fame when he wrote this popular song about Jumbo.

RIGHT
figure 30
"The Amazing Jumbo Craze," from *Book of Jumbo* (1882). The page lists souvenirs available at the height of Jumbomania in 1882.

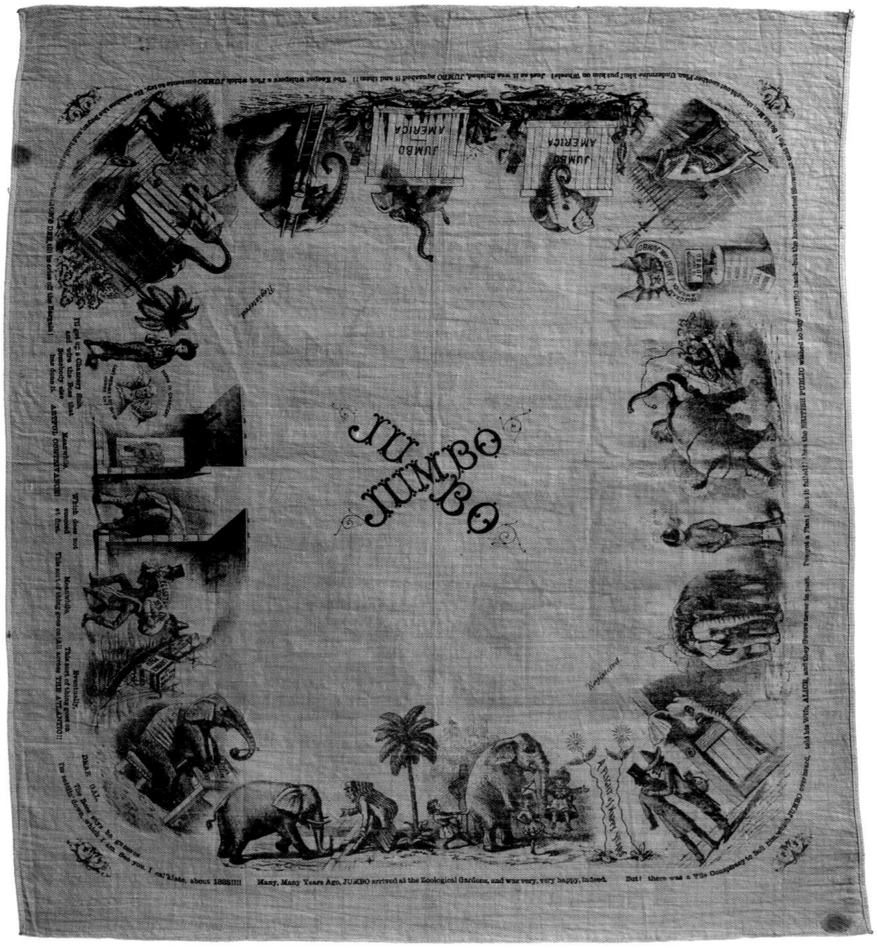
JUMBO
JUMBO

from a young English girl beseeching him to leave the great pachyderm in London.

Public pressure and legal complications notwithstanding, the zoo also benefited from the publicity. During Jumbo's final weeks attendance soared as people came for a farewell ride on his back (fig. 27). Weekly attendance rose from twelve thousand in late February to sixty thousand in the week before he left, yielding a visitor count for the month seven times higher than that for the corresponding period the previous year. Photographs from his last days show him swarmed by crowds (fig. 28). The zoo was also showered with edible presents for Jumbo—sweetmeats, cakes, and ale, even a pumpkin and a dozen oysters, spicing up his normal diet of straw and hay, bread and rice, beets and greens. Beyond press reports, Jumbo's fate became the talk of the town through popular song, including the ditties "Jumbo's Jinks" and "Why Part with Jumbo, (The Pet of the Zoo)," sung by the Great MacDermott (G. H. MacDermott), a star of the Victorian music-hall stage (fig. 29). The Jumbo craze generated a host of unlikely souvenirs, from Jumbo perfumes and bonnets to Jumbo umbrellas and undergarments, anticipating his use well into the twentieth century as an advertising tool for every product under the sun (fig. 30). The American visitor to London quoted above reported in late March:

> The great topic which has recently been on everyone's tongue is Jumbo. . . . There is Jumbo stationery, the Jumbo bracelet, the Jumbo pin and earrings, "Jumbo" is played in the theatre, and so on. . . . Thousands upon thousands of people have rushed to the gardens to see Jumbo and feed him on buns. A sewing machine was one of the articles sent to go towards the Jumbo Retention Fund; a bride sent him some of her wedding cake. . . . No description of the great Jumbo mania could be overdrawn. Every movement of the great animal has been chronicled and commented on. The recent attempted assassination of Victoria the noble Queen has not made one half the excitement.

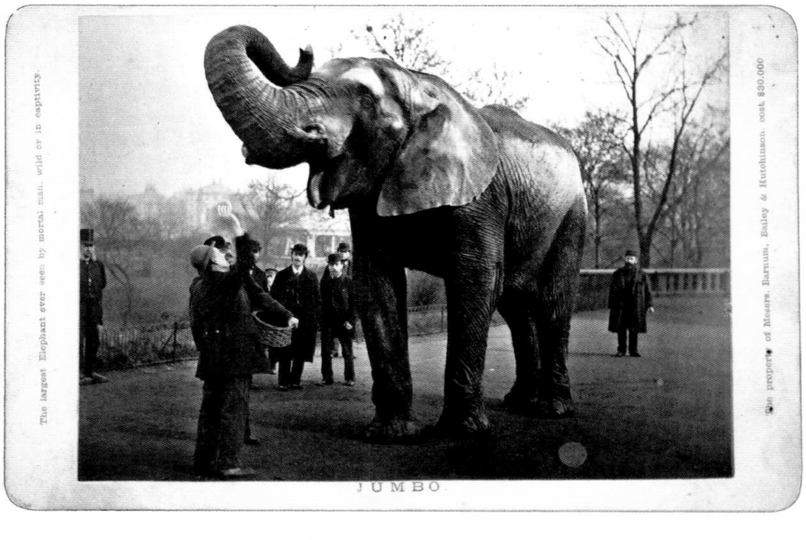
The largest Elephant ever seen by mortal man, wild or in captivity.
The property of Messrs. Barnum, Bailey & Hutchinson. cost $30,000
JUMBO

ABOVE
figure 31
Jumbo handkerchief, 1882. Text and images around the border narrate Jumbo's story in this rare surviving piece of ephemera.

LEFT
figure 32
E. Bierstadt, *Jumbo*, 1882. This popular photograph was taken at the London zoo during the Jumbo craze and sold at Barnum's circus following Jumbo's arrival in America. The text in the right border informed people what Jumbo had cost.

In addition to souvenir photographs, among the few mementos that have survived are a charming handkerchief decorated with vignettes of the Jumbo saga and a pair of illustrated booklets for children imagining his journey across the Atlantic (figs. 31–34). Perhaps also dating from this moment are a majolica pitcher and variants of a charming Staffordshire figurine (figs. 35, 36). Many more products bearing his image would soon follow. Barnum sent Abraham Bartlett a souvenir of his own in the form of an inscribed silver bowl and serving set (fig. 37).

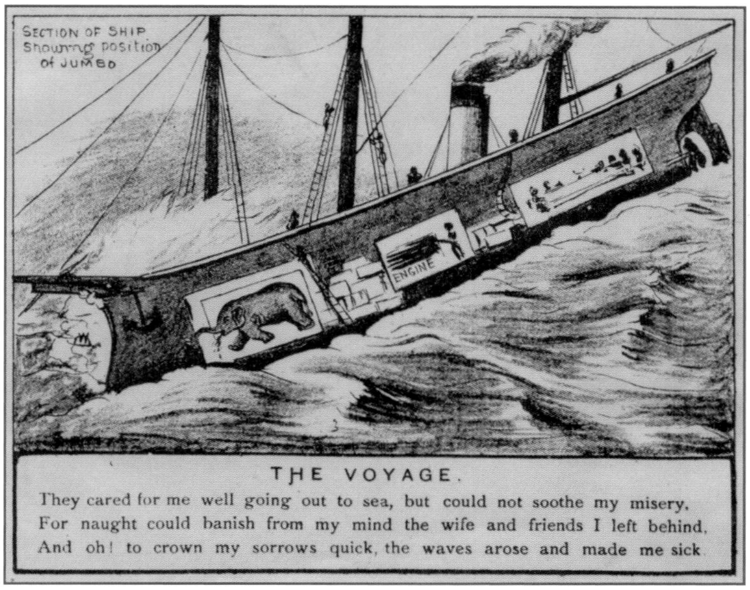
SECTION OF SHIP Showing position of JUMBO
ENGINE
THE VOYAGE.
They cared for me well going out to sea, but could not soothe my misery,
For naught could banish from my mind the wife and friends I left behind,
And oh! to crown my sorrows quick, the waves arose and made me sick.

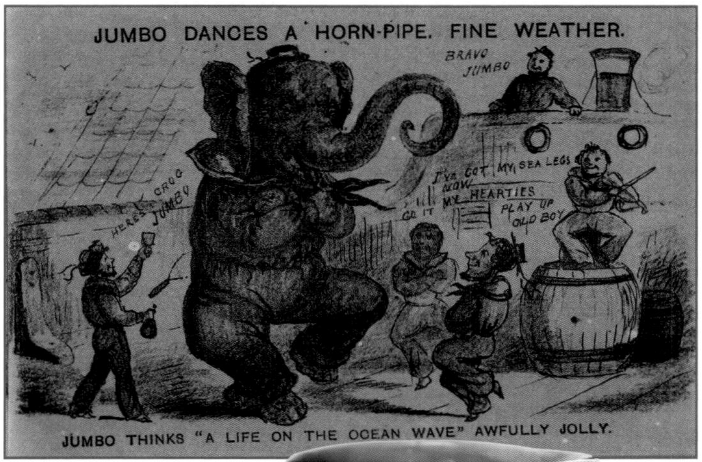
JUMBO DANCES A HORN-PIPE. FINE WEATHER.
BRAVO JUMBO
I'VE GOT MY SEA LEGS NOW
GO IT MY HEARTIES
PLAY UP OLD BOY
HERE'S GROG JUMBO
JUMBO THINKS "A LIFE ON THE OCEAN WAVE" AWFULLY JOLLY.

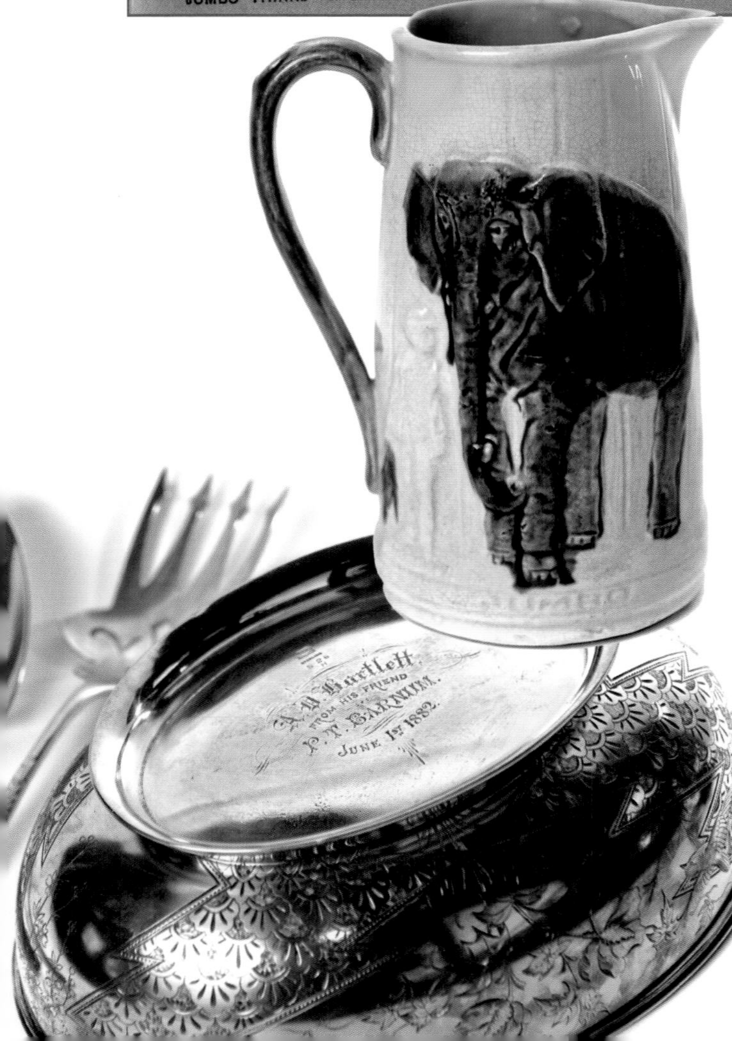
JUMBO
A.D. Bartlett
FROM HIS FRIEND
P.T. BARNUM.
JUNE 1st 1882.

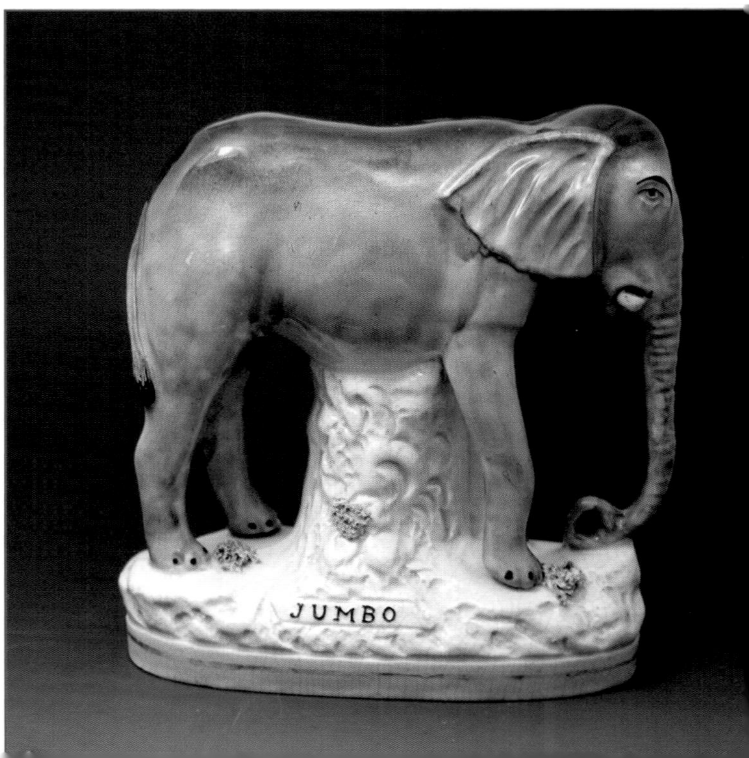
JUMBO

ABOVE
figure 33
"The Voyage," from *Jumbo's Farewell* (1882). Imagined scenes of Jumbo's voyage to the New World appeared in children's booklets.

ABOVE MIDDLE
figure 34
"Jumbo Dances a Horn-Pipe," from *The Arrival of the Zoo Pet* (1882). This illustration is from another children's booklet.

BELOW MIDDLE
figure 35
Jumbo majolica pitcher, ca. 1882. Household objects helped spread Jumbo's fame.

BELOW RIGHT
figure 36
Staffordshire pottery figure of Jumbo, ca. 1882

BELOW LEFT
figure 37
Silver salad bowl with matching fork and spoon, ca. 1882. Barnum gave this elegant serving set to the director of the London zoo, Abraham Bartlett, to thank him for his help in securing Jumbo for the circus.

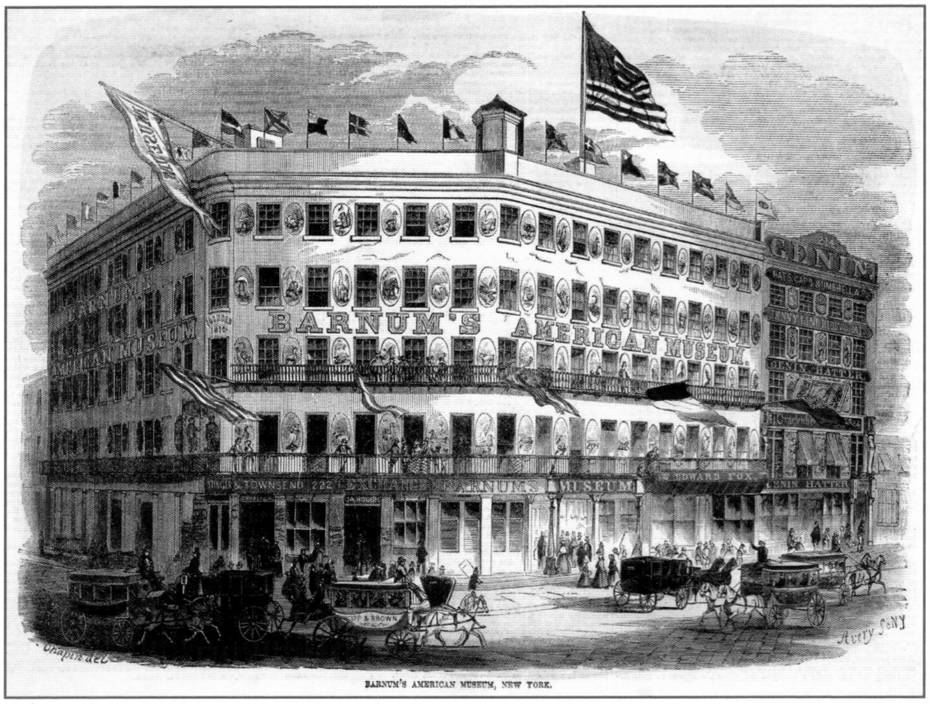
BARNUM'S AMERICAN MUSEUM.
BARNUM'S MUSEUM

BARNUM'S AMERICAN MUSEUM, NEW YORK.

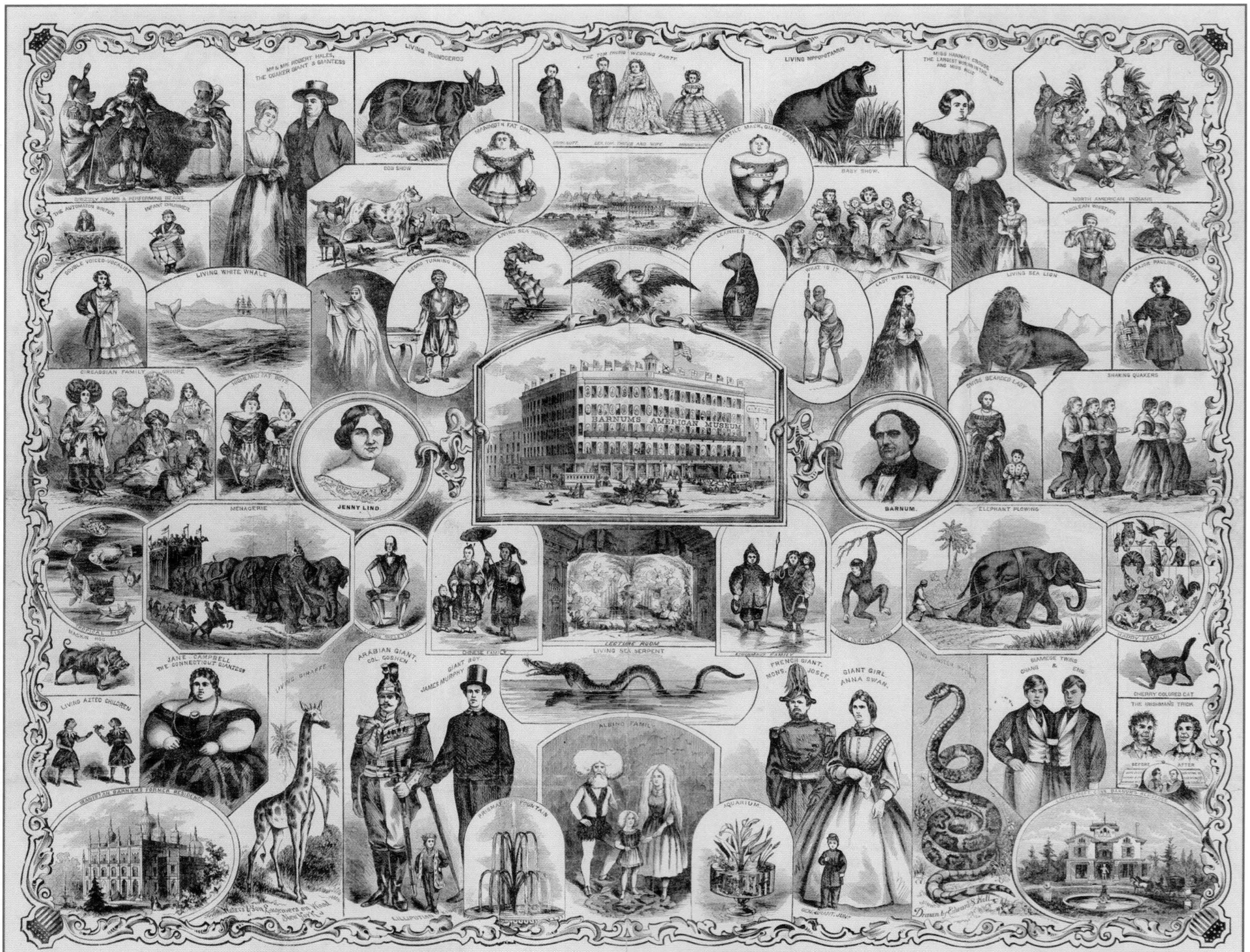
GRIZZLY ADAMS & PERFORMING BEARS
LIVING RHINOCEROS
LIVING HIPPOPOTAMUS
NORTH AMERICAN INDIANS
DOG SHOW
BABY SHOW
LIVING SEA HORSE
LEARNED SEAL
WHAT IS IT
LIVING WHITE WHALE
LIVING SEA LION
CIRCASSIAN FAMILY
SWISS BEARDED LADY
SHAKING QUAKERS
JENNY LIND
BARNUM
MENAGERIE
ELEPHANT PLOWING
LECTURE ROOM
LIVING SEA SERPENT
JANE CAMPBELL, THE CONNECTICUT GIANTESS
LIVING AZTEC CHILDREN
LIVING GIRAFFE
ARABIAN GIANT, COL. GOSHEN
GIANT BOY JAMES MURPHY
ALBINO FAMILY
FRENCH GIANT, MONS. JOSEF
GIANT GIRL ANNA SWAN
AQUARIUM
SIAMESE TWINS CHANG & ENG
CHERRY COLORED CAT
BARNUM'S COLLECTION OF CURIOSITIES.
Thos. McIlroy & Co., Printers, No. 10 Spruce St., New York.

P. T. BARNUM, SHOWMAN EXTRAORDINAIRE

WHY DID BARNUM AND HIS PARTNERS WANT JUMBO? AT THE HEIGHT OF A SUCCESSFUL career—over forty years in show business by 1882—Barnum well knew that staying on top entailed engaging only the biggest and the best. Jumbo was the biggest animal known to be in captivity and he was already famous across the Atlantic. The American public was eager to see him. Barnum and Jumbo were a match made in showmanship heaven; they would help make each other bigger celebrities than they already were.

Jumbo was merely the latest of a long line of amazing attractions and spectacles that had made Barnum the best-known purveyor of popular entertainment in the world. Born into a respectable but middling family in Bethel, Connecticut, in 1810, Phineas Taylor Barnum moved to New York City in search of opportunity and stimulation in 1835. Soon thereafter, with a confidence and bravado that would become his hallmark, he paid $1,000 in savings from previous speculations and mundane work in retail for the right to exhibit Joice Heth, a wizened slave who claimed to be 161 years old and the former nursemaid to the young George Washington. Though he would later become a staunch abolitionist and supporter of Abraham Lincoln, he had no qualms early in life about the institution of slavery into which Heth was born. He also chose not to question her preposterous story. After a successful stint in New York, Barnum took his "astonishing curiosity" on the road and pocketed a no less astounding $1,500 a week. As much as anything, the public paid to see if the claims of her age could possibly be true. When doubts about her authenticity began to spread, Barnum wrote an anonymous letter to the press claiming that Heth was in fact an automaton "made up of whalebone, India-rubber, and numberless springs," enticing many gawkers back for a second look. Heth fell ill the following year and passed away peacefully at the home of Barnum's brother in Bethel (where an autopsy revealed she was closer to half her purported age), but Barnum's enormously successful first foray into public entertainment demonstrated the money to be made from spectacles and curiosities, the more incredible the better.

Following Heth's death, Barnum managed other traveling acts before moving permanently into the business of show in 1841 with a bold decision to purchase John Scudder's American Museum, located at the corner of Broadway and Ann Street in lower Manhattan. Barnum replaced Scudder's name with his own and became a museum man. If today we think of museums as serious civic institutions dedicated to education and research, Barnum's American Museum was more in the mold of a dime museum, dedicated to "rational amusement" (what today is sometimes called "edutainment") and offering a dizzying array of natural and man-made objects of varying degrees of authenticity (figs. 38, 39).

Barnum invested heavily in new exhibits for his museum. Among the "million wonders" spread over five floors and four contiguous buildings were a menagerie of exotic animals, including large carnivorous cats and boa constrictors that fed on live rodents; porpoises, sharks, and beluga whales in saltwater tanks; trained bears and a sea lion, Old Neptune, that had been captured by the famous mountain man Grizzly Adams (fig. 42); a vitrine he labeled "Happy Family," full of natural enemies—rats and cats, mice and owls, eagles and rabbits—that had been trained to live in harmony; numerous mounted animal specimens, including the Grand Skeleton Chamber, containing the articulated mastodon bones Barnum bought from Charles Peale's natural history museum in Philadelphia; collections of insects, minerals, and shells; paintings; Roman and Native American artifacts; instruments,

FACING PAGE, ABOVE
figure 38
View of the American Museum, Broadway, New York, in the 1850s. Barnum's museum was one of New York's chief attractions during the middle decades of the nineteenth century.

FACING PAGE, BELOW
figure 39
Barnum's Collection of Curiosities, poster, ca. 1864–69

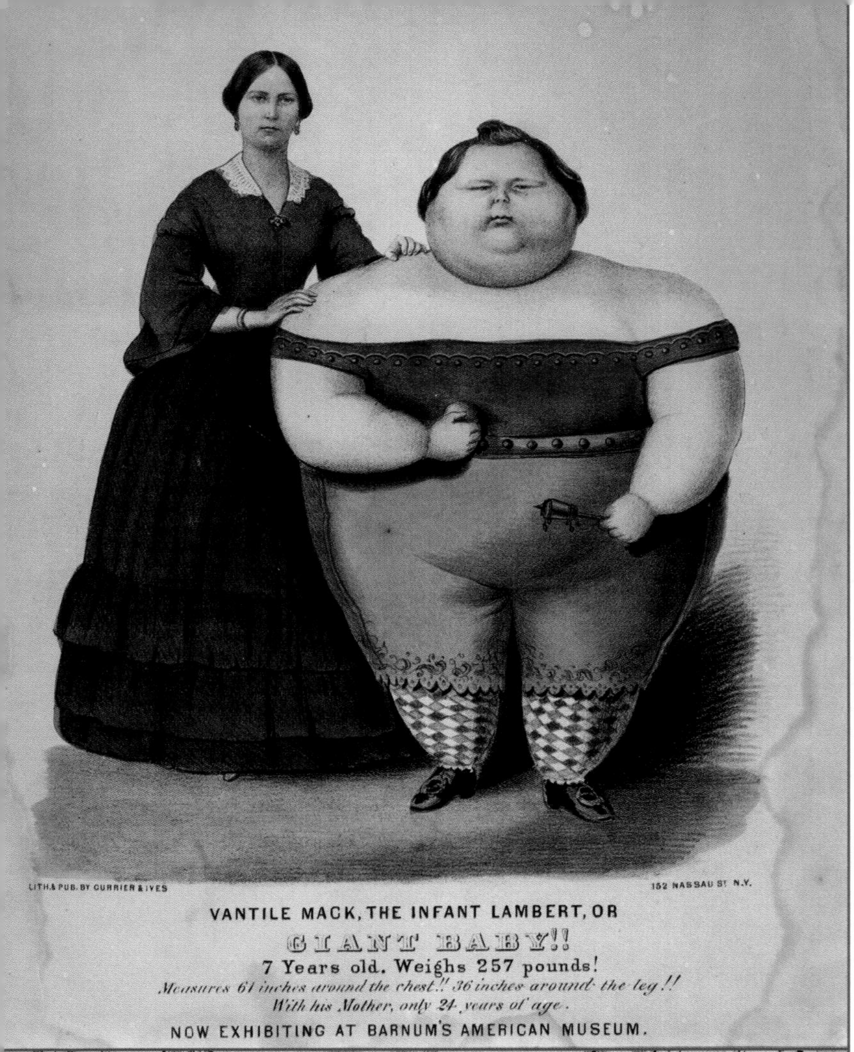

LITH.& PUB. BY CURRIER & IVES
152 NASSAU ST N.Y.
VANTILE MACK, THE INFANT LAMBERT, OR
GIANT BABY!!
7 Years old. Weighs 257 pounds!
Measures 61 inches around the chest!! 36 inches around the leg!!
With his Mother, only 24 years of age.
NOW EXHIBITING AT BARNUM'S AMERICAN MUSEUM.

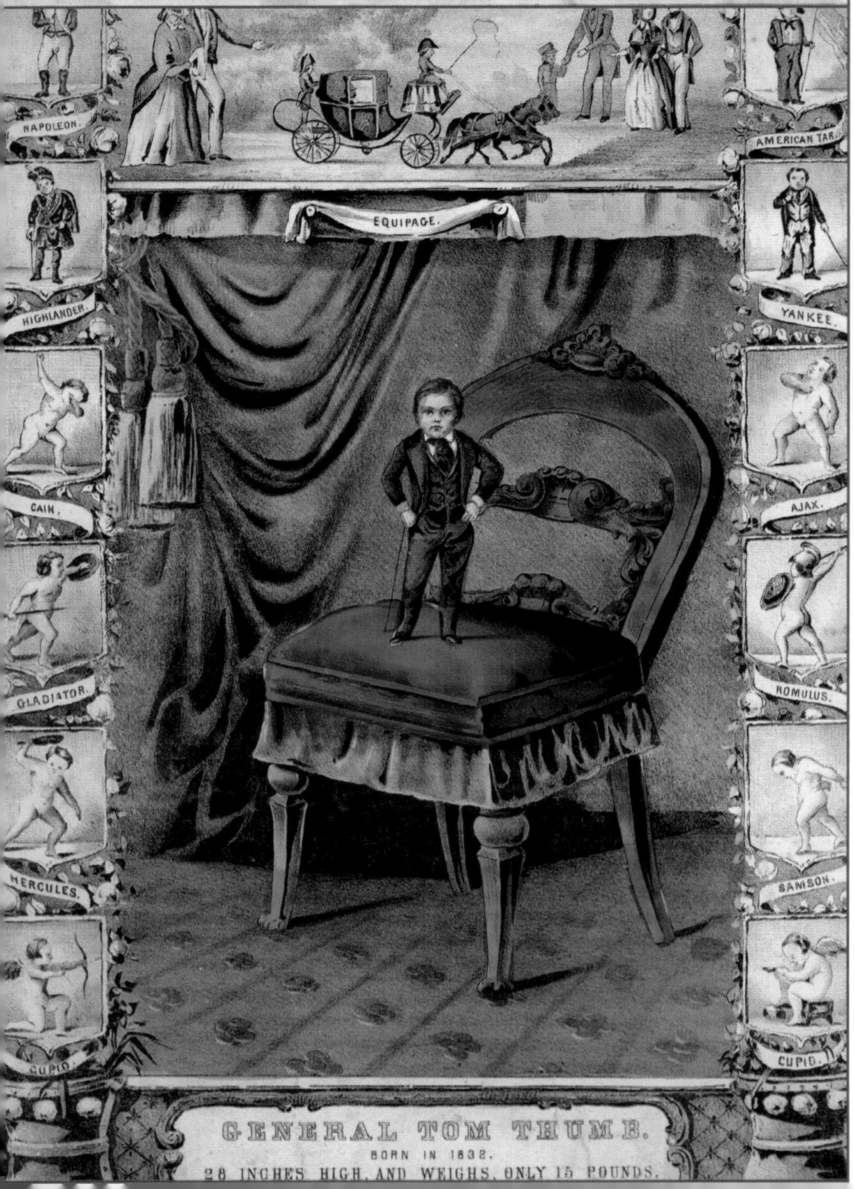

NAPOLEON.
EQUIPAGE.
AMERICAN TAR.
HIGHLANDER.
YANKEE.
CAIN.
AJAX.
GLADIATOR.
ROMULUS.
HERCULES.
SAMSON.
CUPID.
CUPID.
GENERAL TOM THUMB.
BORN IN 1832.
28 INCHES HIGH, AND WEIGHS, ONLY 15 POUNDS.

autographs, and suits of armor; wax effigies of famous people; a portrait gallery of the world's great criminals; dioramas of famous sites around the globe; a flea circus; a full-scale theater; a refreshment stand with ice cream, lemonade, and oysters; an amusement arcade; a rifle range; and a bowling alley. To attract repeat visitors, he advertised a never-ending variety of live acts: snake charmers and jugglers, dancing Native Americans, trained animals, serious theatrical dramas, and the country's first Punch-and-Judy show. Like other dime

ABOVE LEFT
figure 40
Currier & Ives, *Vantile Mack, The Infant Lambert, or Giant Baby!* ca. 1860. Size matters! Barnum shared and encouraged the public's fascination with people and things that were unusually big or small.

BELOW LEFT
figure 41
Currier & Ives, *General Tom Thumb*, ca. 1860. Under Barnum's management, Tom Thumb became one of the leading stars of the stage in the United States and Europe.

BELOW RIGHT
figure 42
Currier & Ives, *Old Neptune, The Great Black Sea Lion*, ca. 1860. Caught by the famous mountain man Grizzly Adams, Old Neptune appeared at Barnum's New York museum and would later reappear, as a stuffed specimen, at the Barnum Museum at Tufts.

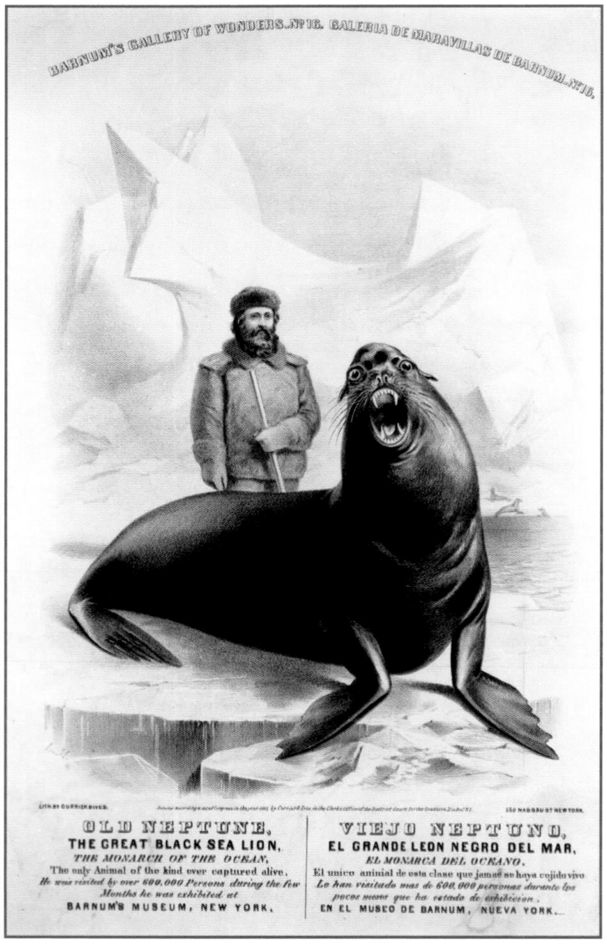

BARNUM'S GALLERY OF WONDERS. No 18. GALERIA DE MARAVILLAS DE BARNUM. No 18.
OLD NEPTUNE,
THE GREAT BLACK SEA LION,
THE MONARCH OF THE OCEAN,
The only Animal of the kind ever captured alive.
He was visited by over 600,000 Persons during the few Months he was exhibited at
BARNUM'S MUSEUM, NEW YORK.
VIEJO NEPTUNO,
EL GRANDE LEON NEGRO DEL MAR,
EL MONARCA DEL OCEANO.
El unico animal de esta clase que jamas se haya cojido vivo
Lo han visitado mas de 600,000 personas durante los pocos meses que ha estado de exhibicion.
EN EL MUSEO DE BARNUM, NUEVA YORK.

museums, Barnum's thrived on the display of human anomalies, or "freaks," as they were then called: obese children (fig. 40) and thin men, giants and dwarfs (fig. 41), albinos and bearded ladies—in sum, "all that is monstrous, scaley, strange and queer," as Barnum put it. A number of his chief attractions were featured in a series of lithographs, titled *Barnum's Gallery of Wonders*, by Currier & Ives, whose business was around the corner from the museum (fig. 42). Many more were photographed by Matthew Brady and others, whose studios were also nearby (figs. 43–45). Barnum spruced up the building's exterior with flags of the world, and the facade with oval paintings of dozens of exotic animals; he installed an early spotlight that raked Broadway by night, and opened a rooftop garden that hosted fireworks displays and aerial-balloon ascents. Musicians serenaded passersby from a first-floor balcony. All for an admission price of just twenty-five cents.

Open year round seven days a week, from sunrise until ten at night, and advertised through newspapers, handbills, and mobile "bulletin wagons," the American Museum became a must-see in New York City. In Barnum's autobiography, he records that during the museum's quarter-century existence it drew thirty-eight million visitors, a figure greater than the population of the United States at that time.

Unfortunately for Barnum, the American Museum burned to the ground on July 13, 1865 (fig. 46). The stage actors, human curiosities, and staff escaped, but virtually everything else was lost. The giantess Anna Swan (fig. 43), the "exceedingly tall and graceful specimen of longitude," as the *New York Times* described her, was hoisted to safety from a window by a makeshift derrick. Ned the Learned Seal, caught by a fireman and put in a tank at the Fulton Street fish market, was one of the few animals to survive. Once the smoke had cleared and the full extent of Barnum's loss was plain, his friend and prominent newspaperman Horace Greeley advised him: "Accept this fire as a notice to quit, and go a-fishing." But undaunted and far too restless to fish, the showman rebuilt his museum in a mere six weeks on a new site farther north on Broadway, above Canal Street. Smaller if no less varied in contents, the new museum survived just short of three years before it, too, was consumed by fire, on March 3, 1868. An overnight freeze following the conflagration turned the firemen's pump water into a wondrous winter spectacle, captured in prints and photographs (fig. 47).

BELOW
figure 43
E. & H. T. Anthony, *Anna Swan*, ca. 1860–65

BELOW
figure 45
D. Appleton, *The Belgian Giant and Commodore Nutt*, ca. 1860–65. Giants and dwarfs were a staple of Barnum's museum and circus.

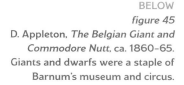

ABOVE
figure 44
Possibly Matthew Brady, *Living Curiosities at Barnum's Museum*, ca. 1865–68

Barnum's museum years were punctuated by a number of sensational exhibitions and acts that made him a household name beyond New York and even the United States. Among the captivating attractions he signed to refresh the museum was the so-called Feejee Mermaid (fig. 48), which Barnum co-owned with Moses Kimball, the proprietor of the Boston Museum and Gallery of Fine Arts, an institution comparable to Barnum's American Museum. Kimball had acquired the embalmed "mermaid" from a Boston sea captain who, it was claimed, found it at a market near Calcutta some years earlier. Though clearly fraudulent, it was well crafted and both showmen saw in it a curiosity that would draw. Dubbed by Barnum the Feejee Mermaid because nowhere seemed more exotic than those remote Pacific islands, the specimen made its debut in New York in August 1842. Thousands paid to see the marvel, their expectations raised by newspaper advertisements that promised a voluptuous seductress from the sea (fig. 49). But instead of a living, bare-breasted creature, half woman, half fish, the public was treated to a revolting, diminutive, and desiccated hoax.

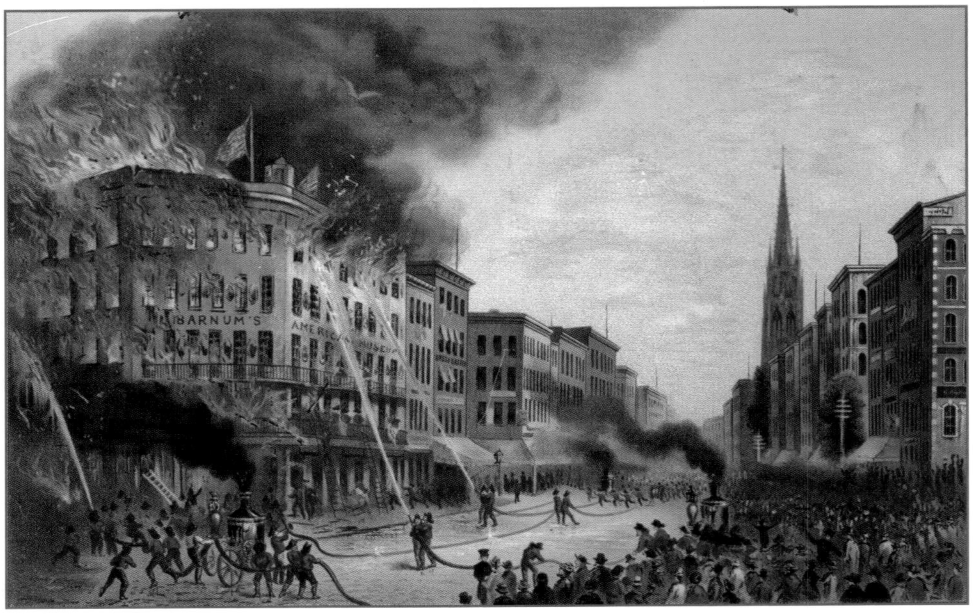
BARNUM'S

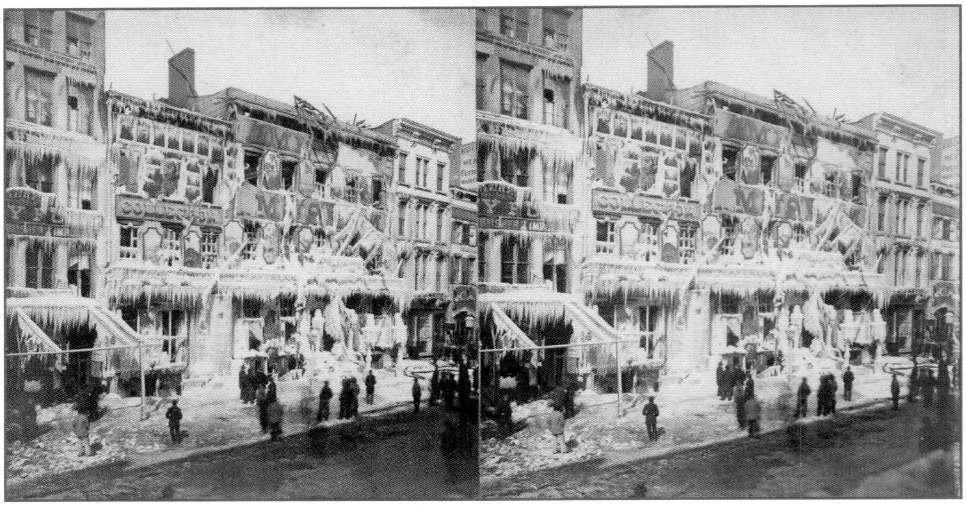

Barnum later conceded he may have gone too far in humbugging the public with the mermaid, but it was hardly the last time that he exploited the human fascination with the extraordinary or the still uncertain boundaries of the natural world. The nineteenth century was an age of astonishment and incredulity. Great leaps in technology, new inventions, and the routine discovery of previously unknown peoples, flora, and fauna, fueling reconsideration of the earth's history and fixity of species (Darwin's *Origin of Species* appeared in 1859), constantly tested the public's capacity for novelty and surprise. Why couldn't there be mermaids from Fiji or other Barnum favorites, such as "Wild Men of Borneo" or "missing links" between humans and animals? For Barnum there was profit and pleasure to be found in exploring the limits of what was possible. "I don't believe in 'duping the public,'" he wrote,

ABOVE
figure 46
Burning of Barnum's Museum, July 13, 1865, 1865. The dramatic fire destroyed the building and most of its contents. Barnum opened a new museum farther north on Broadway soon thereafter.

BELOW
figure 47
After the fire at Barnum's second museum, 1868. Barnum's second museum was also destroyed by fire. As shown in this stereoscopic photograph, an overnight freeze transformed the water used to douse the blaze into a ghostly palace of ice.

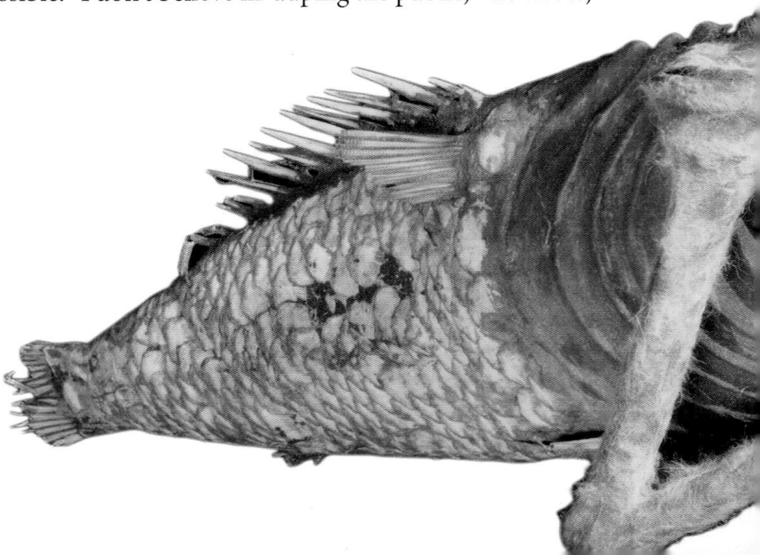

"but I believe in first attracting and then pleasing them." It would be truer to say that he believed the public enjoyed a hoax so long as it was well done and entertaining. No one understood or played to the public's desire for diversion better than Barnum, widely known as "the Prince of Humbugs."

Just as interest in the mermaid was winding down, Barnum stumbled upon a four-year-old, two-foot-tall, fifteen-pound son of a carpenter from Connecticut named Charles Stratton. Perfectly proportioned and naturally talented, Stratton was taken under wing by Barnum and dubbed General Tom Thumb (fig. 41); he quickly became the most sensational stage act of the day. Dwarfs were always a good draw, and Barnum's museum and circus were never without one, but what made Tom Thumb special was his charisma and stage presence. More than a diminutive human to be gawked at, Stratton was possessed of wit and confidence beyond his years, and he could sing and perform impersonations of a wide range of characters, from Greek gods to Napoléon Bonaparte. Tom Thumb was a big hit at the American Museum following his debut early in 1843, and his fame only grew when Barnum took him on tour in the United States and, a year later, to Europe, where he lured enormous crowds and enjoyed private audiences with crowned heads of state. So enamored was Queen Victoria that she summoned him to Buckingham Palace no fewer than three times. Key to the general's triumph was Barnum's mastery of publicity. As the historian Neil Harris observed, "As with so many other attractions, Barnum succeeded with Tom Thumb where others could have failed. He understood that even his most popular exhibits required extensive advertising." Late in life, Barnum wrote to his circus partner James A. Bailey: "I am indebted to the press … for almost every dollar which I possess and for every success as an amusement manager which I have ever achieved." He knew the power of verbal and visual seduction, and he had no qualms about exaggerating the size, age, good looks, or exotic origins of whatever he was promoting. In Tom Thumb's case, Barnum distributed thousands of copies of the general's fictionalized biography and lithographs in advance of tour stops. He was to do the same for Jumbo forty years later, and with no less success. Barnum's partnership with Tom Thumb endured off and on for many decades and made both men rich. Charles Stratton died in 1883, at the height of Jumbo's fame. According to Matthew Scott, Stratton thought Jumbo was a "bigger card" than himself, which Scott found amusing "coming from the smallest man" who yet had "the biggest record for sight-seeing on earth." Considered side by side as two of Barnum's most famous attractions, Jumbo and Tom Thumb underscore the abiding human fascination with size.

During the 1850s and 1860s, Barnum promoted other performers—notable among them, Jenny Lind, "the Swedish Nightingale," the giantess Anna Swan, Commodore Nutt (fig. 45), and the "Siamese" twins Chang and Eng—who further burnished his reputation as a showman. But the destruction of his second museum in 1868 set him back, at least temporarily. Rich despite his losses, Barnum retired to his estate in Connecticut to manage his extensive property holdings and invest more energy in local politics and the improvement of Bridgeport, his adopted home (from 1865 he served two terms in the state legislature and was briefly mayor of Bridgeport). He also spent time writing *Struggles and Triumphs* (1869), a revised version of an earlier autobiography and among the most successful books of the nineteenth century. Frequently reprinted and offered cheaply at circus stops, it sold over a million copies in Barnum's lifetime.

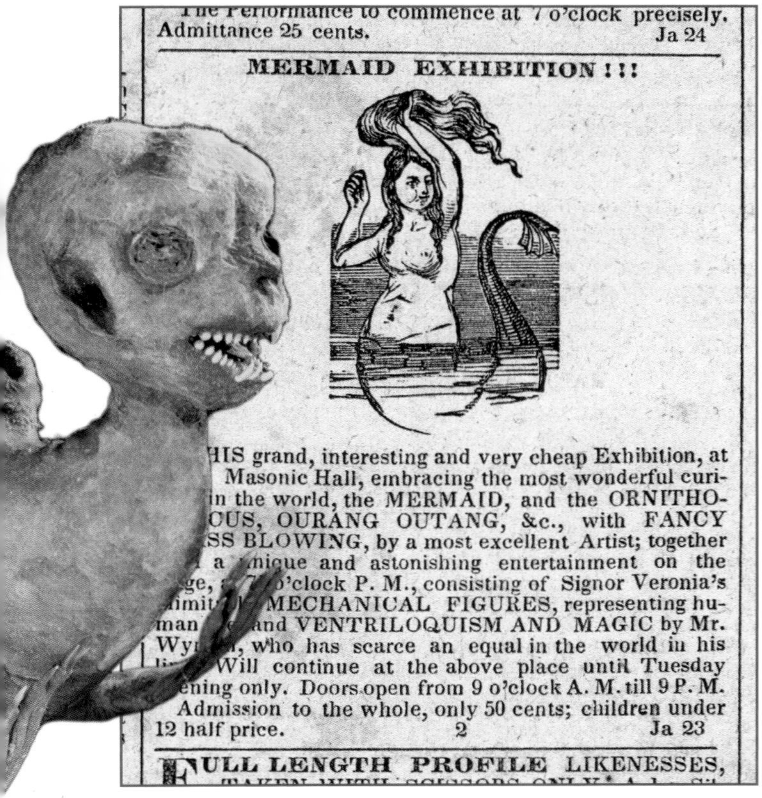

The Performance to commence at 7 o'clock precisely.
Admittance 25 cents. Ja 24

MERMAID EXHIBITION!!!

HIS grand, interesting and very cheap Exhibition, at Masonic Hall, embracing the most wonderful curi- in the world, the MERMAID, and the ORNITHO- CUS, OURANG OUTANG, &c., with FANCY SS BLOWING, by a most excellent Artist; together a nique and astonishing entertainment on the ge, o'clock P. M., consisting of Signor Veronia's imit MECHANICAL FIGURES, representing hu- man and VENTRILOQUISM AND MAGIC by Mr. Wy, who has scarce an equal in the world in his Will continue at the above place until Tuesday ening only. Doors open from 9 o'clock A. M. till 9 P. M. Admission to the whole, only 50 cents; children under 12 half price. 2 Ja 23

FULL LENGTH PROFILE LIKENESSES,

LEFT
figure 48
Feejee Mermaid, n.d. This "mermaid"—half monkey, half fish—came to Harvard University from Barnum's business associate Moses Kimball, which has led some to speculate it may have been the one Barnum exhibited in the 1840s.

RIGHT
figure 49
Advertisement for the Feejee Mermaid from the *Charleston Courier* (January 1843). The enticing mermaid image used in advance advertisements for Barnum's Feejee specimen led the public to expect something far different from what they found on exhibit.

P. T. BARNUM'S

New and Greatest Show on Earth coming by Four Special Trains.

LEFT

figure 50

P. T. Barnum's New and Greatest Show on Earth Coming by Four Special Trains, poster, n.d. The development of the railroad after the Civil War greatly increased the scale and geographical reach of the circus.

BELOW

figure 51

I Am Coming, ca. 1875–79. Barnum made heavy use of posters, handbills, and other media to announce the coming of his circus.

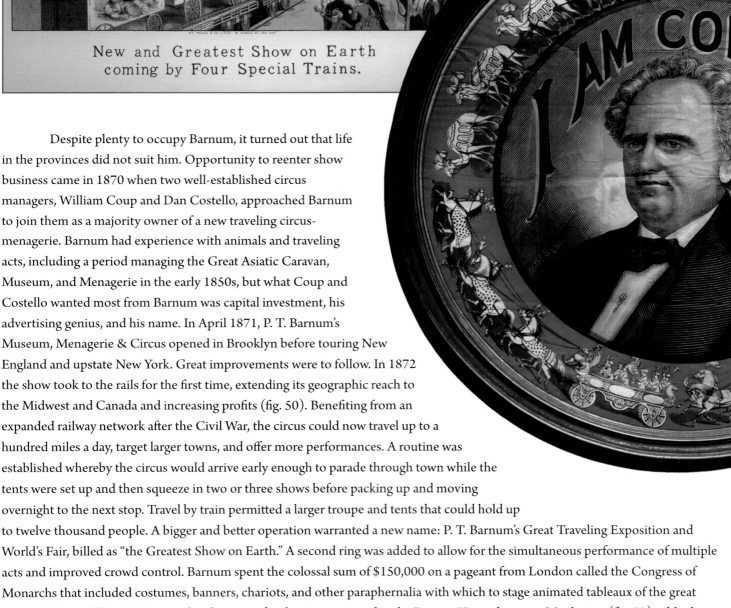

Despite plenty to occupy Barnum, it turned out that life in the provinces did not suit him. Opportunity to reenter show business came in 1870 when two well-established circus managers, William Coup and Dan Costello, approached Barnum to join them as a majority owner of a new traveling circus-menagerie. Barnum had experience with animals and traveling acts, including a period managing the Great Asiatic Caravan, Museum, and Menagerie in the early 1850s, but what Coup and Costello wanted most from Barnum was capital investment, his advertising genius, and his name. In April 1871, P. T. Barnum's Museum, Menagerie & Circus opened in Brooklyn before touring New England and upstate New York. Great improvements were to follow. In 1872 the show took to the rails for the first time, extending its geographic reach to the Midwest and Canada and increasing profits (fig. 50). Benefiting from an expanded railway network after the Civil War, the circus could now travel up to a hundred miles a day, target larger towns, and offer more performances. A routine was established whereby the circus would arrive early enough to parade through town while the tents were set up and then squeeze in two or three shows before packing up and moving overnight to the next stop. Travel by train permitted a larger troupe and tents that could hold up to twelve thousand people. A bigger and better operation warranted a new name: P. T. Barnum's Great Traveling Exposition and World's Fair, billed as "the Greatest Show on Earth." A second ring was added to allow for the simultaneous performance of multiple acts and improved crowd control. Barnum spent the colossal sum of $150,000 on a pageant from London called the Congress of Monarchs that included costumes, banners, chariots, and other paraphernalia with which to stage animated tableaux of the great rulers of the world. In 1874 a new headquarters for the circus opened at the Roman Hippodrome in Manhattan (fig. 52), a block-long building big enough to seat eight thousand and accommodate a circular track for horse and chariot races, staged buffalo hunts, and cowboy displays, as well as a museum, menagerie, and aquarium. The circus at its height was a grander, mobilized reincarnation of Barnum's earlier museums, with dazzling theatrical spectacles added in.

P. T. BARNUM'S
GREAT ROMAN
HIPPODROME.
The largest amusement building ever constructed, occupying the entire block bounded by Fourth and Madison Avenues and Twenty-Sixth and Twenty-Seventh Streets, New York.
Afternoon and Evening.
GRAND MENAGERIE of 500 rare Wild Beasts, open daily at 1:30 and 7:00 P.M.
The wonderful exhibition in the vast Amphitheatre, Roman Chariot Racing, Hurdle and Flat Races, Elephant, Camel, Pony, and Monkey Racing commences with the GRAND CONGRESS OF NATIONS, at 2:30 and 8:00 o'clock. Box Office open three days in advance.

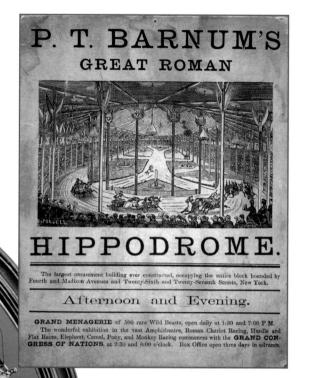

In charge of publicity as well as the major investor, Barnum became the face of the circus. His portrait was everywhere—on posters, handbills, railroad cars, newspaper ads, and booklets (figs. 51, 53). An engraving heralding the 1873 season shows Barnum in a cloud, summoning as if by magic the wonders of the world. A long train bearing Barnum's name snakes past an iceberg, Egyptian pyramids, and a fairy-tale city, with sailing ships in the distance. The foreground is littered with exotic creatures and peoples. To the left an image of his burning museum suggests that the traveling circus arose from its ashes. Building on advertising strategies devised for the American Museum, Barnum pioneered the circus "courier," a tabloid newspaper distributed in advance to tout the show's program and leading acts. He would soon take advantage of advances in chromolithography after the Civil War to produce striking posters that conveyed the color and vitality of the circus. Couriers, posters, and his publicity staff traveled in a well-appointed, dedicated railway car decorated on the outside with images of animals and the showman's portrait. Circuses were heavy users of advertising; for Barnum, who once declared: "Advertising—Advertising—nothing else. That is the sum and substance of the whole thing," it was the single largest cost associated with his traveling show.

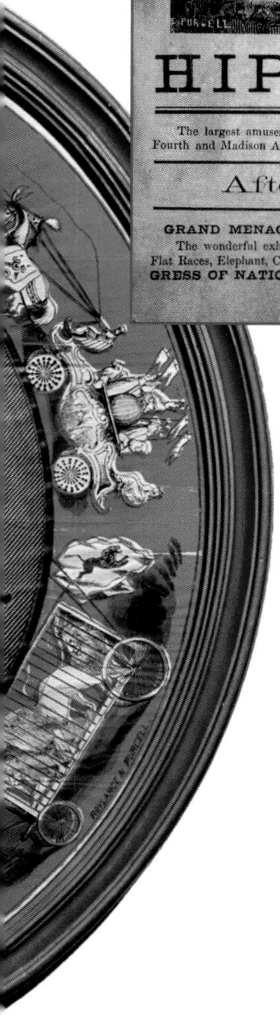

Barnum's Greatest Show on Earth carried on through the 1870s, with partners coming and going behind the scenes. In 1880 he formed a new alliance with the much younger James A. Bailey, manager of the rival London Circus. Bailey, bold and determined yet scrupulously attentive to detail, was a good match for the still ambitious but aging showman. Across his career, Barnum made his share of poor business investments (notably in unsuccessful fire extinguishers, shoe polish, and clocks), but when it came to show-business partners and performers he had excellent judgment. Barnum and Bailey, together with the latter's associate, James L. Hutchinson, formed a lasting partnership that produced the most celebrated of all circuses, P. T. Barnum's Greatest Show on Earth & Great London Circus, which is still in business (as the Ringling Bros. Barnum & Bailey Circus) and the source of Barnum's lasting fame.

P. T. BARNUM'S
THE WORLD IN CONTRIBUTION.
MUSEUM
CURIOSITIES ARRIVING.
GREAT TRAVELING WORLD'S FAIR FOR THE CAMPAIGN OF 1873.

ABOVE
figure 52
P. T. Barnum's Great Roman Hippodrome, placard, ca. 1874. The New York home of Barnum's Greatest Show on Earth was later replaced by the first incarnation of Madison Square Garden.

RIGHT
figure 53
"P. T. Barnum's Great Traveling World's Fair for the Campaign of 1873," *Harper's Weekly* (March 29, 1873)

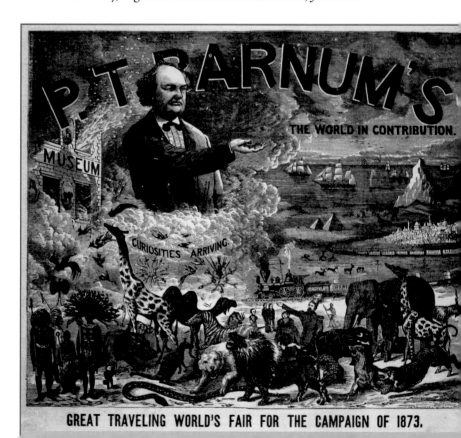

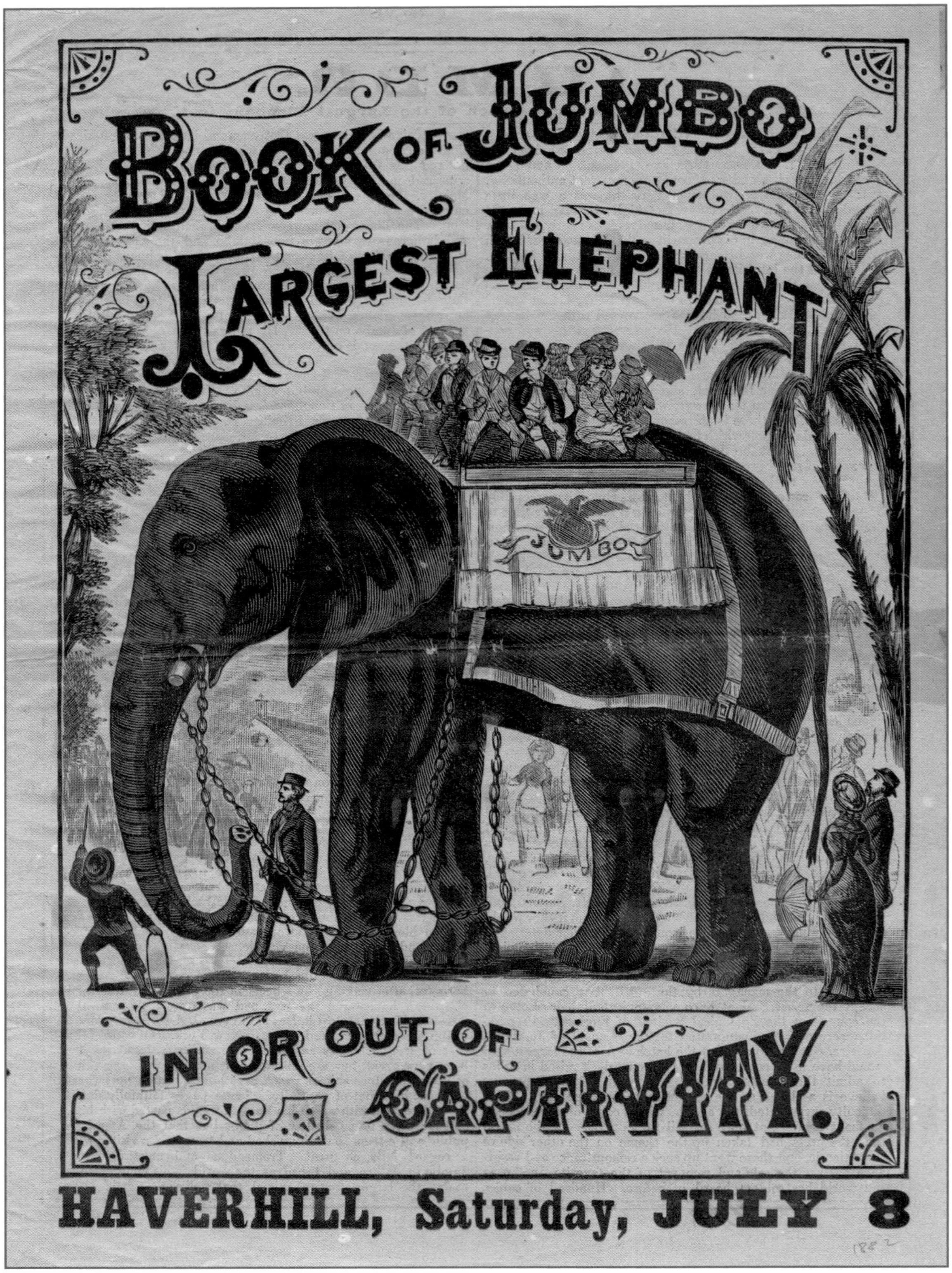
BOOK OF JUMBO
LARGEST ELEPHANT
JUMBO
IN OR OUT OF CAPTIVITY.
HAVERHILL, Saturday, JULY 8

ABOVE
figure 54
Book of Jumbo (1882). This well-illustrated booklet packaged Jumbo's story for the circus-going public.

FACING PAGE, ABOVE
figure 55
Jumbo, The Children's Giant Pet, 1882. This poster by the Hatch Company of New York was designed for display in shopwindows and rushed into production in time for Jumbo's arrival in April 1882.

FACING PAGE, BELOW
figure 56
"Jumbo's Arrival in America," *Leslie's Illustrated Family Almanac* (1883). Jumbo's arrival at Castle Garden in New York (the entry point for immigrants before Ellis Island) drew the largest crowds the city had seen to that date.

JUMBO JOINS THE CIRCUS

THE COMBINED FORCES OF Barnum and Bailey created a mammoth enterprise. In the 1880s the circus employed 620 people who, together with the animals and equipment, were transported by more than fifty railway cars and seventy-five wagons. There were more than 20 elephants, 20-odd camels, and 270 horses and ponies. The big-top tent, which now showcased three rings, measured 500 by 250 feet. A separate menagerie commanded a further 300 by 135 feet, and the museum another 215 by 135. Annual receipts during the decade averaged over $1 million, twice what Barnum's circuses had earned in the mid-1870s (profits after costs, which varied year to year, were between one-third and one-half of that amount, which in those days was still an enormous sum). Advertisements claimed the show represented an investment of $8 million. Greater revenues and profits meant there was more to invest in new attractions, the lifeblood of entertainment. Besides the public's insatiable demand for novelty, performers got injured or were lured away by rival outfits, and animals died. Barnum and Bailey depended on talent scouts to search the world for anything new and extraordinary. It was one such agent, Joseph Lee Warner, a former mayor of Lansing, Michigan, who first caught wind of the London zoo's problem with Jumbo. The partners quickly turned the zoo's predicament into their future profit—greatly assisted by the unexpected controversy Jumbo's sale provoked.

As soon as the deal for Jumbo was finalized, Barnum's publicity machine swung into action. Newspapers on both sides of the Atlantic carried details of his final days in London and arrival in New York on April 10, 1882. The *New York Times* estimated that ten thousand people turned out to welcome Jumbo, the largest crowd the city had ever witnessed (fig. 56). It took

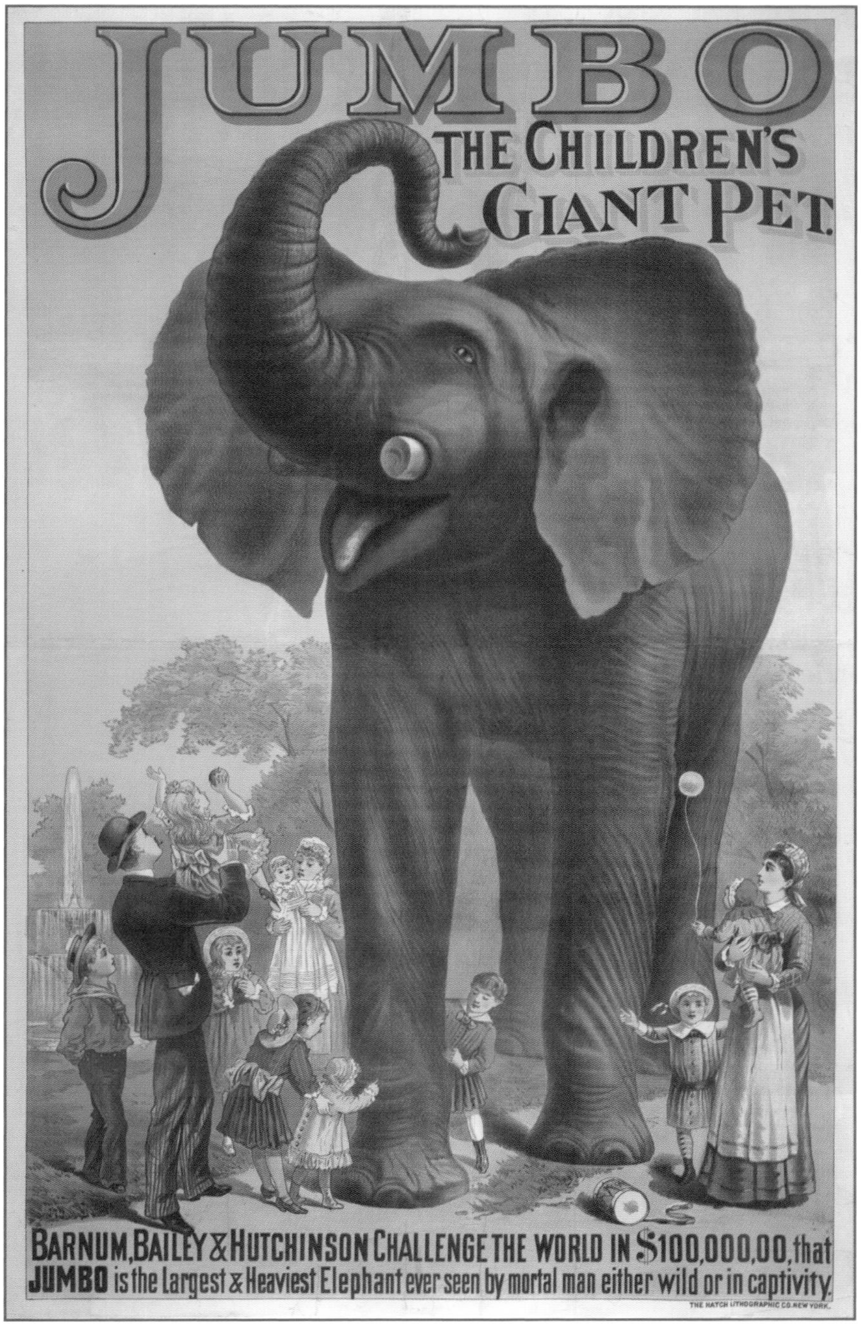
JUMBO
THE CHILDREN'S GIANT PET.
BARNUM, BAILEY & HUTCHINSON CHALLENGE THE WORLD IN $100,000,00, that JUMBO is the Largest & Heaviest Elephant ever seen by mortal man either wild or in captivity.
THE HATCH LITHOGRAPHIC CO. NEW YORK.

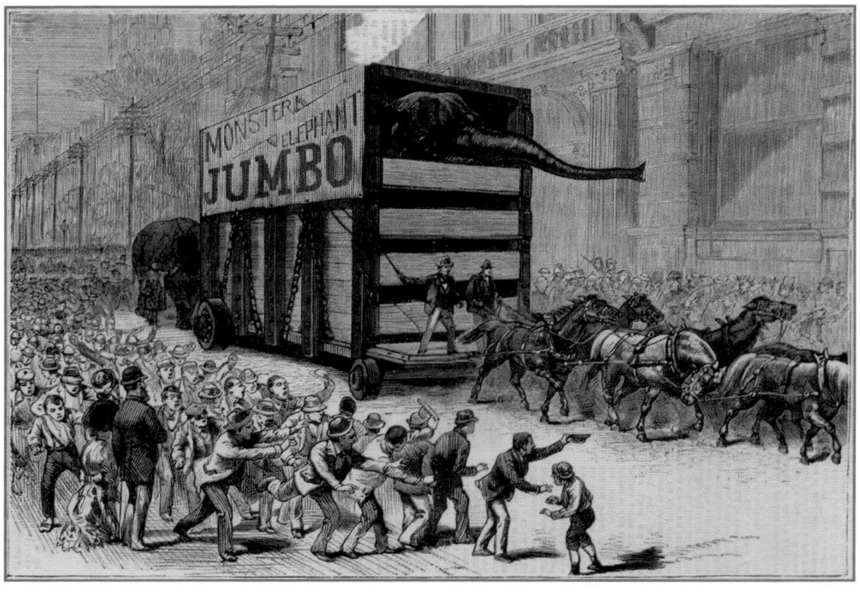
MONSTER ELEPHANT
JUMBO

eight horses and a pair of elephants to move Jumbo's crate from Battery Park to Madison Square Garden, the newly (1879) renamed site of the Roman Hippodrome, where the circus had opened a few weeks earlier. Heralding Jumbo's arrival were a magnificent chromolithograph poster by the Hatch company, which shows *Jumbo, The Children's Giant Pet* (fig. 55) towering over his human friends, and a booklet packed with every detail of the elephant's saga, titled *Book of Jumbo* (fig. 54).

Jumbo's financial value was broadly publicized. Everyone knew how much Jumbo had cost—$10,000 (twice the going price for a circus elephant), plus, Barnum claimed, another $20,000 in expenses for his protracted removal from England, legal fees, and promotional material. Photographs of Jumbo taken at the zoo at the height of Jumbomania (see fig. 32) conflated size and cost, having as their caption: "The largest Elephant ever seen by mortal man, wild or in captivity. Property of Messrs. Barnum, Bailey & Hutchinson. Cost $30,000." The investment was more than justified by the returns. Jumbo became the leading star of the Greatest Show on Earth. Matthew Scott claimed that people came to the circus just to see him: "The shouting at Jerusalem for the 'Son of Man,' when he rode triumphantly on an ass, could not have exceeded the shout that has gone up from the children of the United States, as they have watched and waited long hours to get a sight of Jumbo." Barnum boasted that within six weeks of joining the circus, Jumbo made in added gate receipts ten times what had been paid for him. Indeed, Jumbo's first two years under the big top recorded the biggest receipts and profits in the entire Barnum & Bailey era.

Jumbo joined, and even supplanted, Barnum as the icon of the circus, a relationship recognized in Thomas Nast's cartoon (fig. 57) depicting the showman cooing to Jumbo: "You are a humbug after my own heart. You have even beat me in advertising."

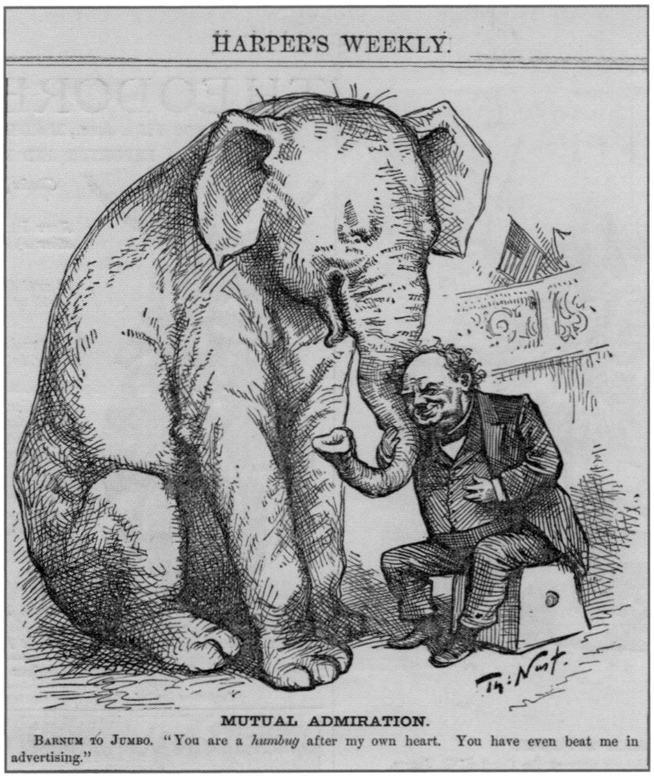
HARPER'S WEEKLY.
Th: Nast.
MUTUAL ADMIRATION.
Barnum to Jumbo. "You are a *humbug* after my own heart. You have even beat me in advertising."

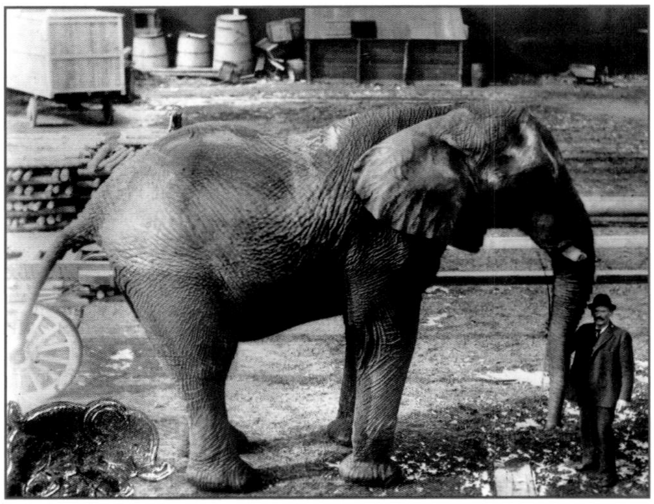

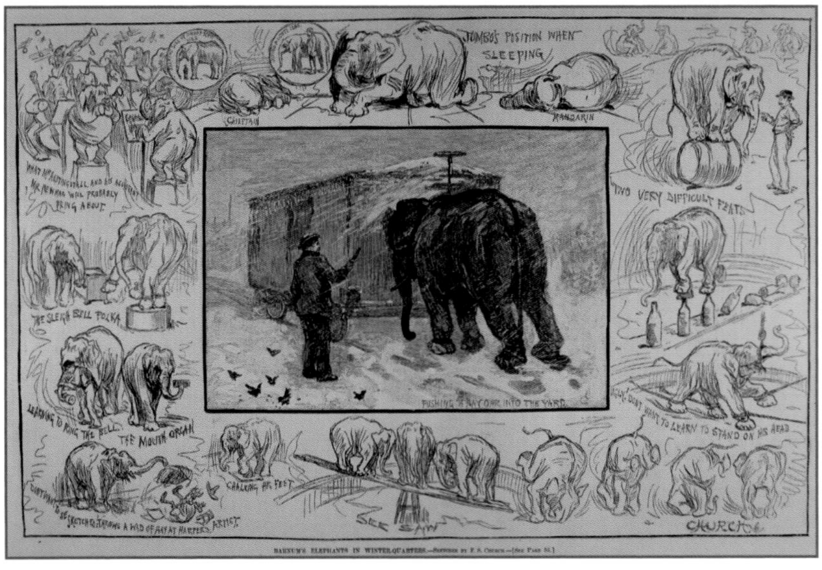
JUMBO'S POSITION WHEN SLEEPING
MANDARIN
TWO VERY DIFFICULT FEATS
SEE SAW
CHURCH

ABOVE
figure 57
Thomas Nast, "Mutual Admiration," *Harper's Weekly* (April 15, 1882). Nast's cartoon lampoons the enormously successful business partnership of Barnum and Jumbo.

BELOW
figure 58
Jumbo and Matthew Scott at Barnum's winter quarters, ca. 1882–84. Barnum prevented photography of Jumbo in order to keep his actual size a mystery. The tiny elephant design in the bottom left of this probably unsanctioned photo was added to hide Jumbo's excrement.

LEFT
figure 59
"Barnum's Elephants in Winter Quarters," *Harper's Weekly* (January 27, 1883). Jumbo's value to the circus was as a spectacle; during the off-season, while the Indian elephants learn new tricks, Jumbo is seen catching up on his sleep.

BELOW

figure 60

P. T. Barnum's Greatest Show on Earth . . . Jumbo, The Largest Living Beast, 1883. This poster was one of a few of Jumbo produced by the Strobridge Company of Cincinnati, the leading American poster makers of the day.

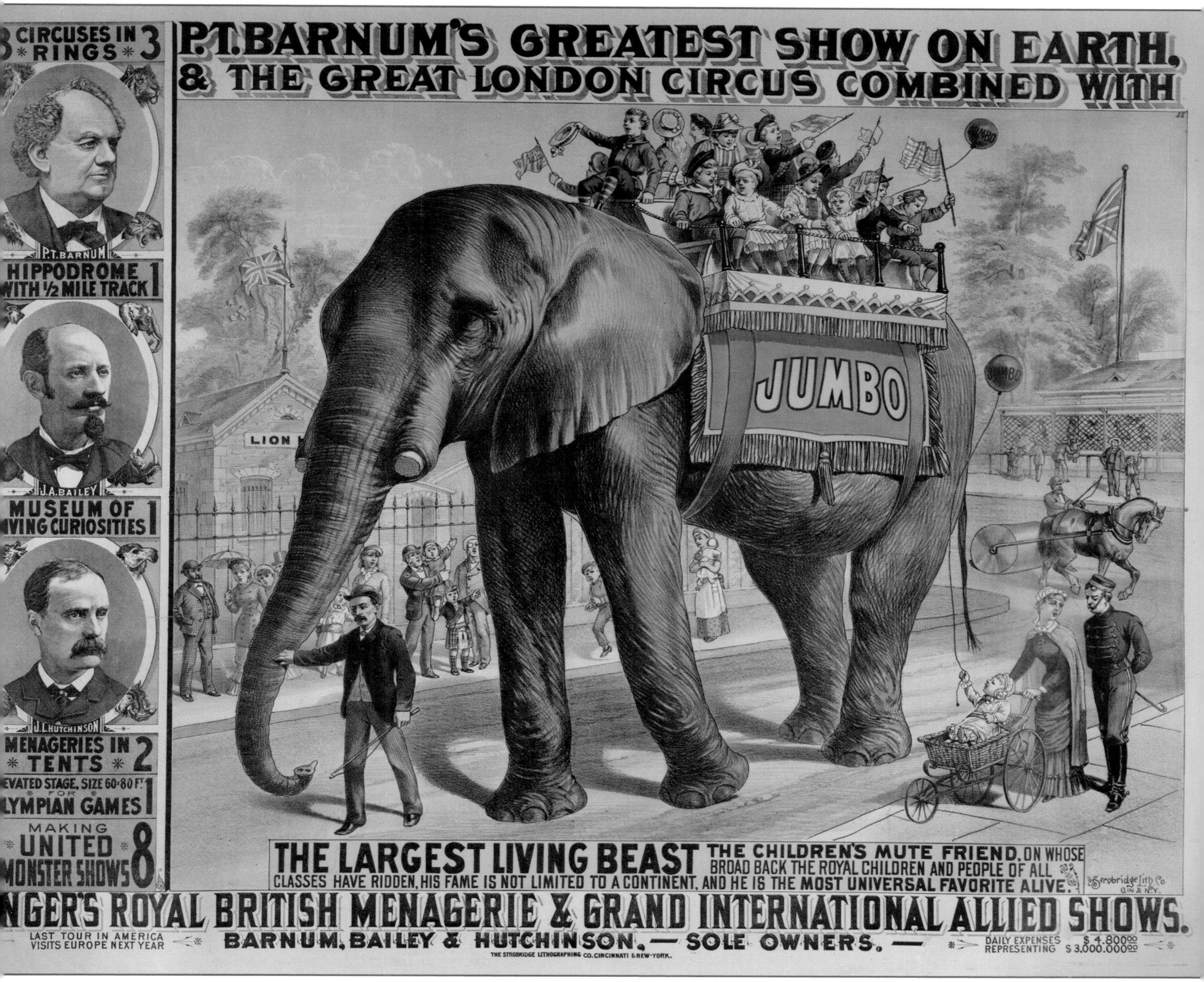

CIRCUSES IN RINGS 3
P.T. BARNUM'S GREATEST SHOW ON EARTH,
& THE GREAT LONDON CIRCUS COMBINED WITH
P.T.BARNUM
HIPPODROME WITH ½ MILE TRACK 1
J.A.BAILEY
MUSEUM OF LIVING CURIOSITIES 1
J.L.HUTCHINSON
MENAGERIES IN TENTS 2
ELEVATED STAGE, SIZE 60·80 FT FOR OLYMPIAN GAMES 1
MAKING UNITED MONSTER SHOWS 8
JUMBO
LION
THE LARGEST LIVING BEAST THE CHILDREN'S MUTE FRIEND, ON WHOSE BROAD BACK THE ROYAL CHILDREN AND PEOPLE OF ALL CLASSES HAVE RIDDEN, HIS FAME IS NOT LIMITED TO A CONTINENT, AND HE IS THE MOST UNIVERSAL FAVORITE ALIVE.
NGER'S ROYAL BRITISH MENAGERIE & GRAND INTERNATIONAL ALLIED SHOWS.
LAST TOUR IN AMERICA VISITS EUROPE NEXT YEAR
BARNUM, BAILEY & HUTCHINSON, — SOLE OWNERS. —
DAILY EXPENSES $ 4,800.00
REPRESENTING $ 3,000,000.00
THE STROBRIDGE LITHOGRAPHING CO. CINCINNATI & NEW-YORK.

But Barnum was happy to share the limelight. The remarkable money made from Jumbo demonstrated the showman's business acumen, a crucial part of his identity. Barnum had always played the Yankee—"clever, energetic, and flexible, always eager for a hard bargain," with an eye fixed "on the main chance," in the words of Neil Harris. The stereotypical Yankee was a self-made businessman, and profit was the measure of his ingenuity. Publicity about money served two purposes: listing the large sums paid for acts encouraged the public to think it was getting more than its money's worth, and disclosing how much those acts earned proved Barnum's savvy.

P.T. BARNUM'S GREATEST SHOW ON EARTH AND THE GREAT LONDON CIRCUS COMBINED WITH
JUMBO.
THE LARGEST ELEPHANT IN THE WORLD, AS COMPARED WITH THE SKELETON OF THE EXTINCT MASTODON.
AS LARGE AS ANY TWO ELEPHANTS IN EXISTENCE.
HIS EARS ARE AS LARGE AS FOLDING PARLOR DOORS
STROBRIDGE CO. CIN'TI & NY
JUMBO, THE ELEPHANT GIANT, WHOSE UPLIFTED TRUNK REACHES UPWARD 26 FEET.
SANGER'S ROYAL BRITISH MENAGERIE & GRAND INTERNATIONAL ALLIED SHOWS.
BARNUM, BAILEY & HUTCHINSON, SOLE OWNERS.

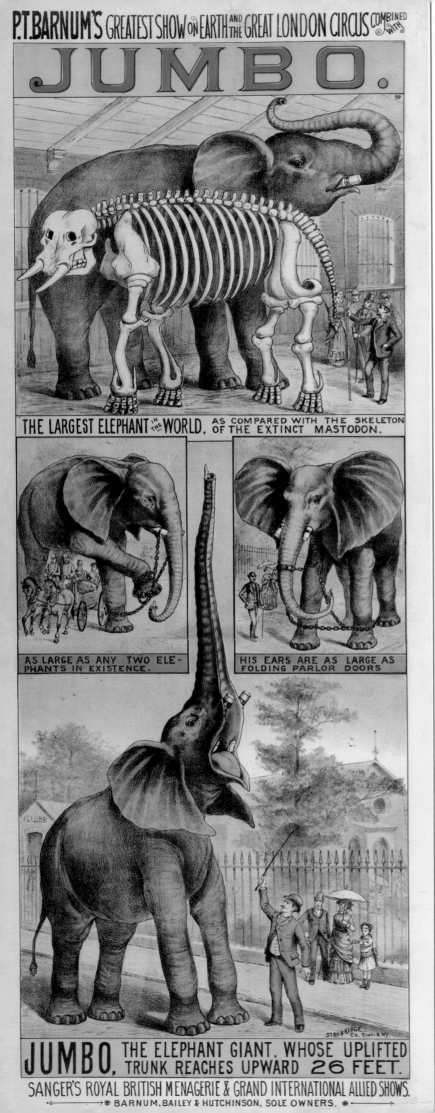

Jumbo's largely symbolic or ornamental role in the circus is reflected in how little was expected of him in the ring. Circus programs from the 1880s show that Jumbo was the first solo act seen by the public, but his act consisted merely in being paraded ahead of the other elephants and animals by his trusted keeper. Consistent with the general belief that Indian elephants could be taught tricks but their African cousins could not, Jumbo did very little to earn his keep; after an opening tour of the perimeter, his day was done. An amusing newspaper illustration (fig. 59) of the circus's winter quarters in Bridgeport shows the Indian elephants learning new tricks and pushing hay wagons through the snow while Jumbo catches up on his sleep. Jumbo's value was as a spectacle. Barnum's ad men clearly had fun coming up with new ways to celebrate his chief virtue—size—proclaiming him "Jumbo, The Prodigious Moving Mountain," "The Colossus of the Old and New World," "The Giant Monarch of his Mighty Race," "A Tremendous, Unexaggerated Prodigy, and Alone the Show of Shows," to list only a few epithets. Many of these lines were no doubt the work of Barnum's chief publicist, R. F. "Tody" Hamilton, known to his peers as a "verbal conjuror" who took phrasemaking to "the threshold of trembling tautology." Jumbo was further set apart by the special palace train car in which he traveled, brightly decorated and custom built to accommodate his height.

How big was Jumbo? Barnum took care to keep his actual size a mystery. He refused to allow Jumbo to be measured once he arrived in the United States. Abraham Bartlett recorded that he was 11 feet tall when he left the zoo. A furtive effort to measure him in 1883 by two circus performers using an acrobat's pole calculated his height at 10 feet 9 inches. Following Jumbo's death, the taxidermist Henry Ward listed him at 12 feet, based on a measurement taken when Jumbo was lying flat and limp on the ground. Modern estimates put his height at about 11 feet, from the base of his foot to his shoulder. He weighed between six and seven tons. Whatever his precise dimensions, he was a large African elephant, and certainly the largest animal known to be in captivity at that time. It seems that photographs

---

LEFT
figure 61
P. T. Barnum's Greatest Show on Earth . . . Jumbo, poster, 1882. Images produced for the circus invariably inflated Jumbo's size to mythic proportions.

were also not permitted, no doubt because they would give away his true size. The only photograph of Jumbo in the United States (fig. 58), taken from the side and from slightly above at the circus's winter quarters, and now known only from copies, has the feel of an unsanctioned image.

What we lack in the way of a photographic record of Jumbo during the Barnum years is made up for in a wealth of graphic images—posters, couriers, and advertisements—that enhanced his mythic size and character. In addition to the Hatch poster mentioned above, the circus commissioned striking posters from the Strobridge Lithographing Company of Cincinnati. In one, Jumbo ports a score of children rendered lilliputian by his stature (fig. 60), and in another he's presented as exceeding the dimensions of the extinct mastodon, with his trunk reaching twenty-six feet in the air (fig. 61). Shows of strength are balanced by his gentle embrace of children and his faithful keeper. Jumbo's colossal heft could also be suggested by association, as when Barnum, in an orchestrated publicity stunt, had Jumbo lead twenty circus elephants across the newly built Brooklyn Bridge as a test of its soundness—a scene comically recalled on the cover of the *New Yorker* magazine 120 years later (fig. 62).

PRICE $4.95
THE NEW YORKER
SEPT. 6, 2004

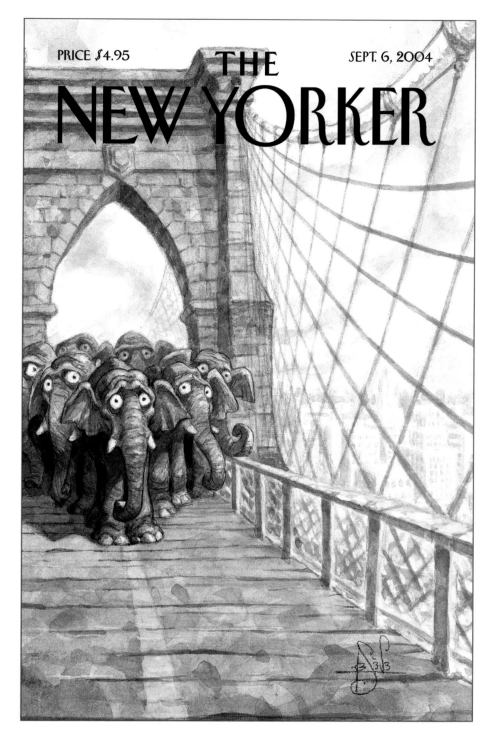

ABOVE
figure 62
The New Yorker (September 6, 2004). This amusing cover design recalls a publicity stunt organized by Barnum wherein Jumbo led the circus elephants across the Brooklyn Bridge, a year after it opened in 1883, to test its strength.

JUMBO WITH HIS NEW FRIENDS, MADISON SQUARE GARDEN, N.Y.
PINE STATE JAVA!
The above popular brand appears only on our very best grade of Roasted Java.
If you would have a good cup of coffee, always buy
PINE STATE JAVA.
TWITCHELL, CHAMPLIN & CO.,
Prop's Pine State Mills,
PORTLAND, ME

RIGHT
figure 63
Jumbo with His New Friends, Madison Square Garden, N.Y., Pine State Java Coffee, 1882. Jumbo's arrival in America coincided with the golden age of lithograph trade cards in commercial advertising. Jumbo was used to promote a wide range of products.

CLARK'S
TRADE
O.N.T.
MARK
SPOOL COTTON.
CASTLE GARDEN
MR JUMBO
LONDON, ENG.
JUMBO'S ARRIVAL.

USE R.W. BELL & CO'S
"PURE
SOAPS."
ICE WATER
500 GAL.
JUMBO'S VACATION.

CLARK'S
TRADE
O.N.T.
MARK
SPOOL COTTON.
JUMBO ÆSTHETIC.

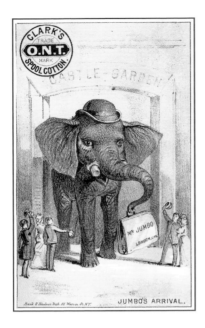

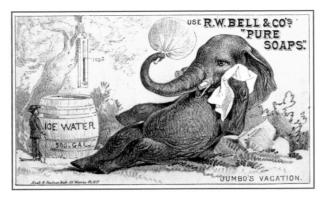

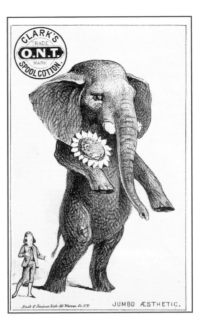

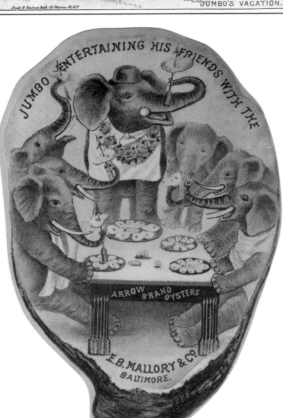

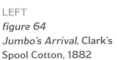

LEFT
figure 64
Jumbo's Arrival, Clark's Spool Cotton, 1882

MIDDLE
figure 65
Jumbo's Vacation, R. W. Bell & Co. "Pure Soaps," 1882

RIGHT
figure 66
Jumbo Aesthetic, Clark's Spool Cotton, 1882. Jumbo is seen imitating the dandified appearance and pose of Oscar Wilde, whose celebrated tour of the United States was underway when Jumbo arrived in New York.

JUMBO ENTERTAINING HIS FRIENDS WITH THE
ARROW BRAND OYSTERS
E.B. MALLORY & CO.
BALTIMORE.

LEFT
figure 67
Jumbo Entertaining His Friends with the Arrow Brand Oysters, E. B. Mallory & Co., ca. 1882

BELOW
figure 68
Trade card for Jumbo Paste Blacking, Wilson Yeast & Manufacturing Co., ca. 1882

PRODUCES AN INSTANTANEOUS, PERMANENT AND BRI
ON A
HOT OR COLD STOVE
NO DUST
JUMBO
PASTE
BLACKING
TRADE
MARK
MANUFACTURED
BY THE
WILSON YEAST & MANF'G CO. LIMI
WATERLOO, N.Y.

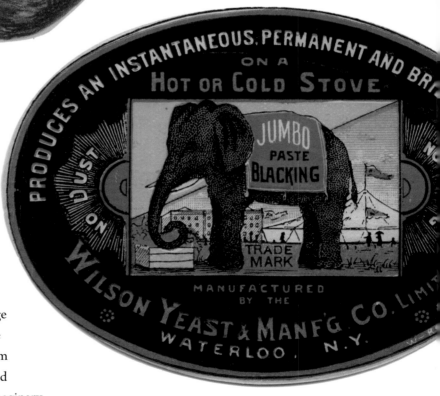

If Jumbo quickly became the face of the circus, his likeness was further imprinted on the American psyche through its appropriation by commercial advertising. Just as Barnum relied on Jumbo, the gentle giant and children's pet, to promote the circus as good family entertainment, so merchants in turn used Jumbo's universal appeal to men, women, and children of all social classes to sell products and services of every imaginable kind (figs. 63–73). Jumbo's years with the circus coincided with the explosion of mass advertising in the form of inexpensive trade cards. The simultaneous proliferation of eye-catching trade cards and circus posters was made possible by advances in chromolithographic printing, and Jumbo's image passed easily from one format to the other. During his brief life in America, Jumbo figured on cards advertising everything from sewing machines and laxatives to oysters, irons, suspenders, and thread. Especially popular were delightful scenes of Jumbo's imaginary

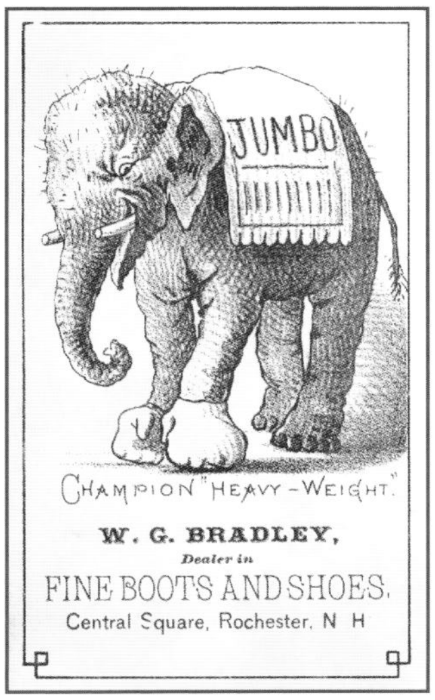
JUMBO
CHAMPION "HEAVY-WEIGHT."
W. G. BRADLEY,
Dealer in
FINE BOOTS AND SHOES.
Central Square, Rochester, N H

UPPER RIGHT
figure 69
Trade card for Mrs. Potts' Cold Handle Sad Irons, ca. 1882

UPPER MIDDLE RIGHT
figure 70
Jumbo Must Go, Willimantic Thread Co., 1882

LOWER MIDDLE RIGHT
figure 71
Barnum's Jumbo, Jackson Wagon Company, ca. 1882

BOTTOM RIGHT
figure 72
The Way Jumbo Was Suspended, Smith Clinch Back Suspenders, 1882. Lithograph trade card by Bufford

UPPER LEFT
figure 73
Jumbo Champion "Heavy-Weight," W. G. Bradley Fine Boots and Shoes, ca. 1882

BOTTOM LEFT
figure 74
Sheet music for J. A. Arneaux, "Jumbo (The Elephant King)" (1883). Jumbo was welcomed to America with a number of songs and marches.

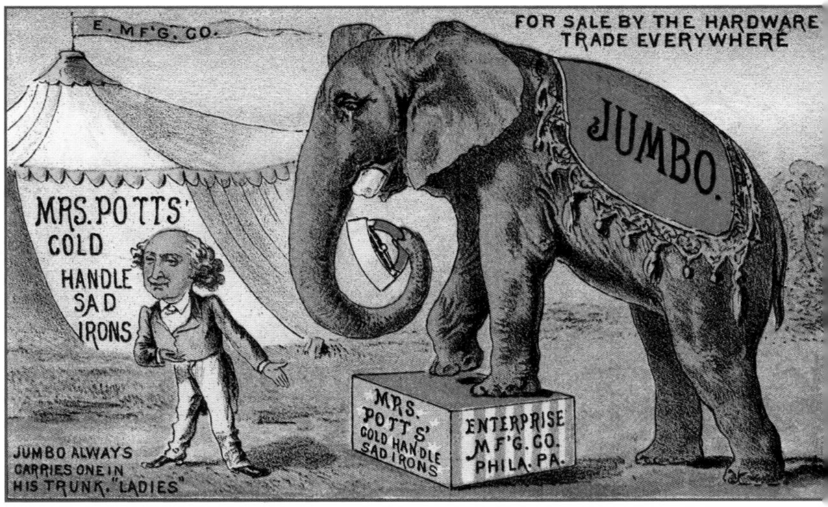
E. MF'G. CO.
FOR SALE BY THE HARDWARE TRADE EVERYWHERE
JUMBO.
MRS. POTTS' COLD HANDLE SAD IRONS
MRS. POTTS' COLD HANDLE SAD IRONS
ENTERPRISE M'F'G. CO. PHILA. PA.
JUMBO ALWAYS CARRIES ONE IN HIS TRUNK, "LADIES"

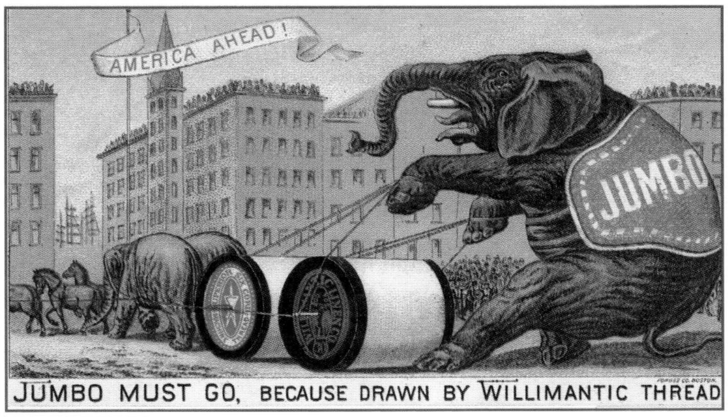
AMERICA AHEAD!
JUMBO
JUMBO MUST GO, BECAUSE DRAWN BY WILLIMANTIC THREAD

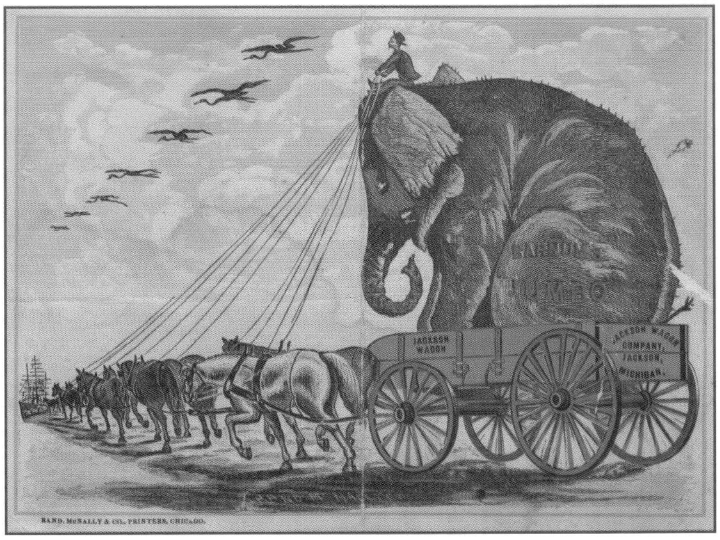
JACKSON WAGON
JACKSON WAGON COMPANY, JACKSON, MICHIGAN.

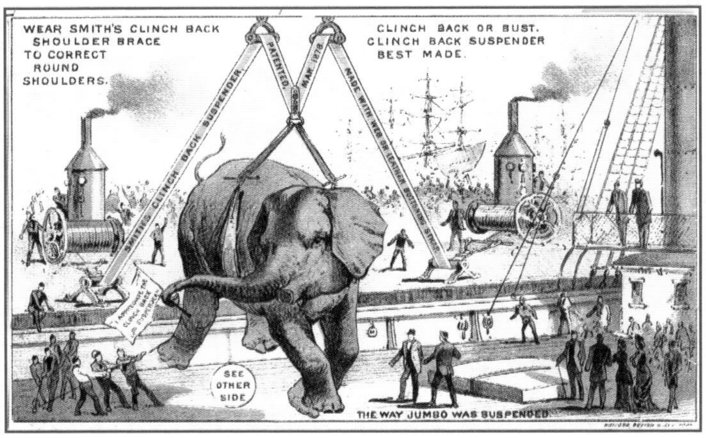
WEAR SMITH'S CLINCH BACK SHOULDER BRACE TO CORRECT ROUND SHOULDERS.
CLINCH BACK OR BUST. CLINCH BACK SUSPENDER BEST MADE.
SEE OTHER SIDE
THE WAY JUMBO WAS SUSPENDED

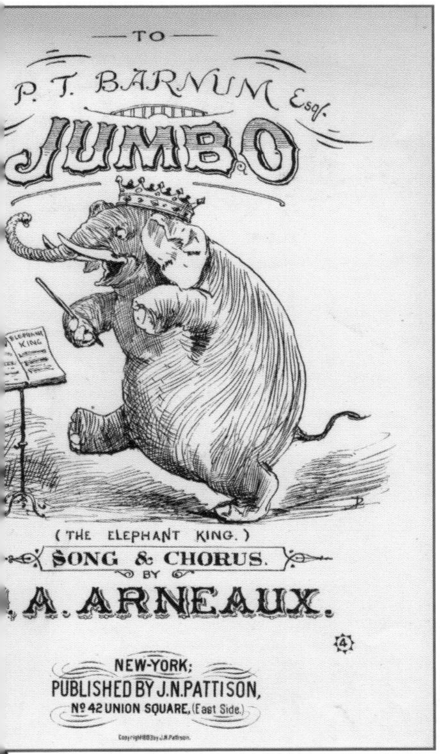
TO
P. T. BARNUM Esq.
JUMBO
(THE ELEPHANT KING.)
SONG & CHORUS.
BY
J. A. ARNEAUX.
NEW-YORK;
PUBLISHED BY J.N.PATTISON,
No 42 UNION SQUARE, (East Side.)

antics printed on stock cards, with blank space on front or back for individual advertisers to overprint details of whatever they were selling. J. H. Bufford and Sons' cards showing Jumbo's ocean crossing and reception in America were ubiquitous (figs. 63, 72); those by the New York firm of Buck and Lindner were less widely adopted but are unmatched in charm (figs. 64–66). The full series of the latter shows Jumbo bounding over the ocean and disembarking in New York sporting a derby; visiting the opera in coat and tails; downing a barrel of beer in a local bar; playing the violin and a game of cards; cooling off in the high summer and vacationing at Coney Island; and mimicking the pose and attire of Oscar Wilde, who toured the United States just ahead of Jumbo's arrival. Music publishers got in on the act by welcoming Jumbo to America with new parlor songs and marches (fig. 74).

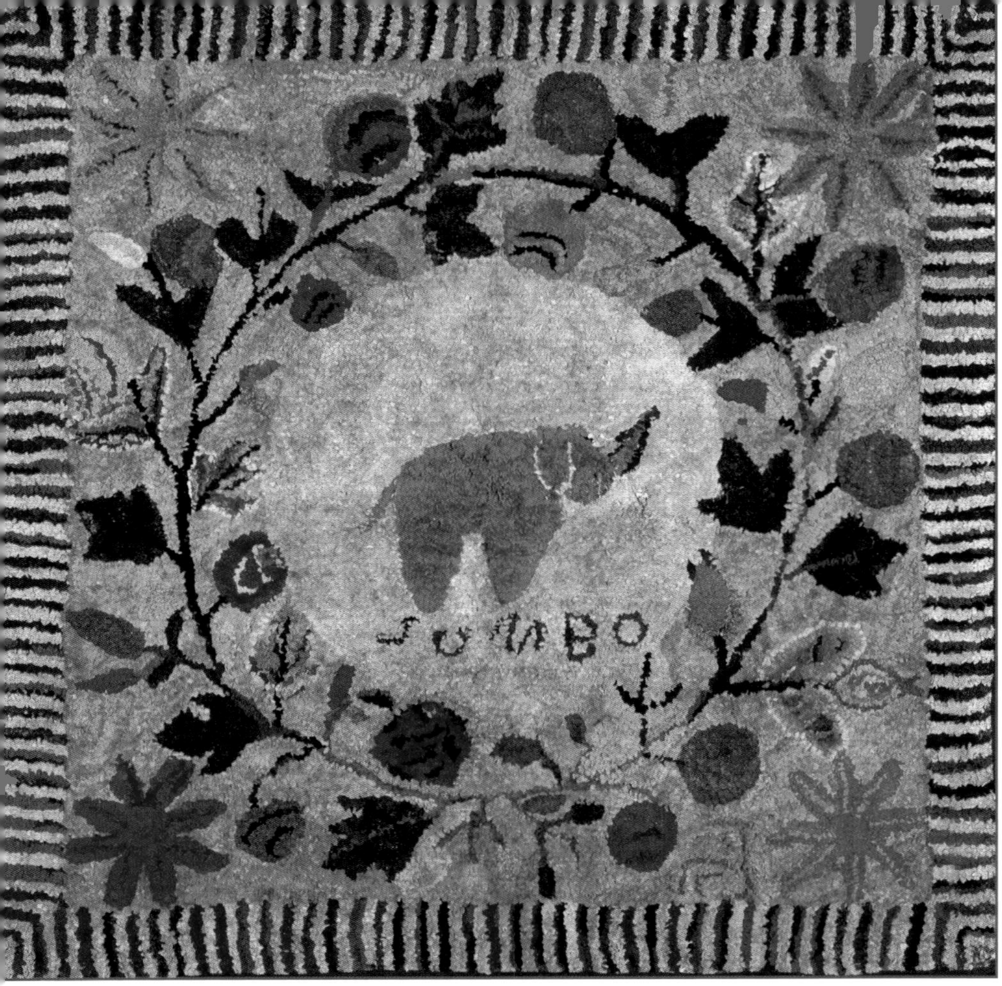
JUMBO

Jumbo's popularity was also manifested in the use of his likeness in products for the home and in nicknames given to a wide range of people and things. Jumbo's profile is the central motif of a homemade hooked rug and figures in the border of an equally charming crazy quilt (figs. 75, 76). People ate off Jumbo plates and the Canton Glass Company came out with a line of Jumbo ware (fig. 78). Thomas Edison named the massive steam dynamos designed to bring electrical service to Manhattan in 1882 after Jumbo (fig. 77). George Washington "Jumbo" McGinnis, an oversize pitcher for the St. Louis Browns, won over twenty games three years in a row in the early 1880s (fig. 82). The waiflike poet Emily Dickinson was affectionately called Jumbo by her friend (and lover?) Judge Otis Lord. A mountain in Montana and a redwood in Santa Cruz Grove, California, took his name (figs. 80, 81). Jumbo was a scale of reference, if not also the inspiration, for the once famous

ABOVE
figure 75
Jumbo rug, ca. 1882–85. Jumbo's popularity is reflected in handcrafted items for the home.

MIDDLE
figure 76
J. A. L.'s Crazy-patch Parlor Throw (detail), 1886

BELOW LEFT
figure 77
Thomas Edison's "Jumbo" dynamos at the Electric Lighting Station, Pearl Street, New York, ca. 1882. Edison's dynamos, which introduced electric service to New York City, were among various things and people nicknamed "Jumbo" following the elephant's arrival in America in 1882.

BELOW RIGHT
figure 78
Butter dish with lid in "Jumbo" pattern, Canton Glass Co., ca. 1882. This butter dish is part of a larger set of Jumbo tableware.

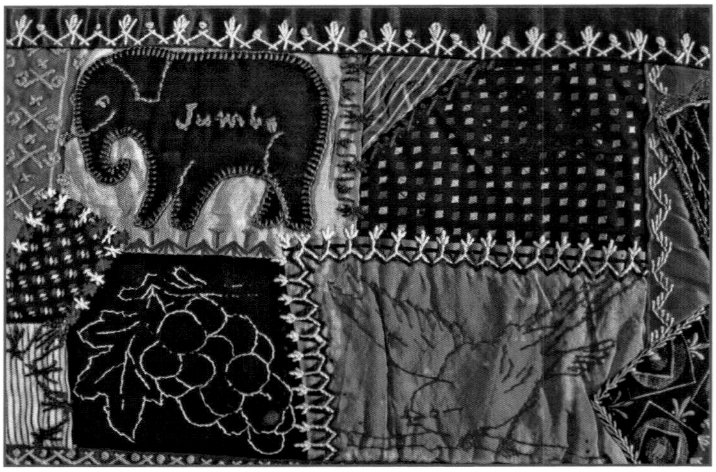
Jumbo

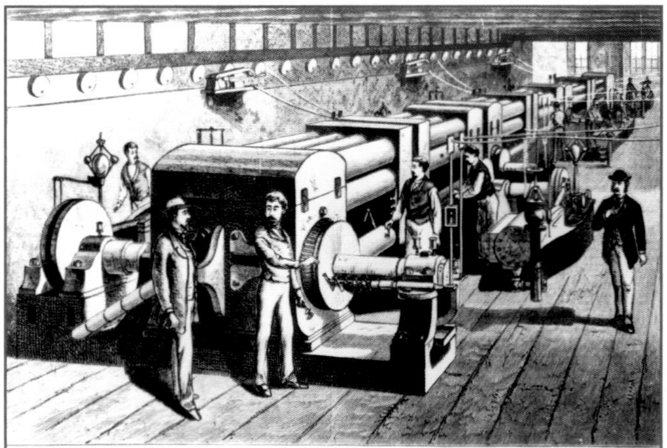
THE DYNAMO ROOM.
FIRST EDISON ELECTRIC LIGHTING STATION IN NEW YORK.

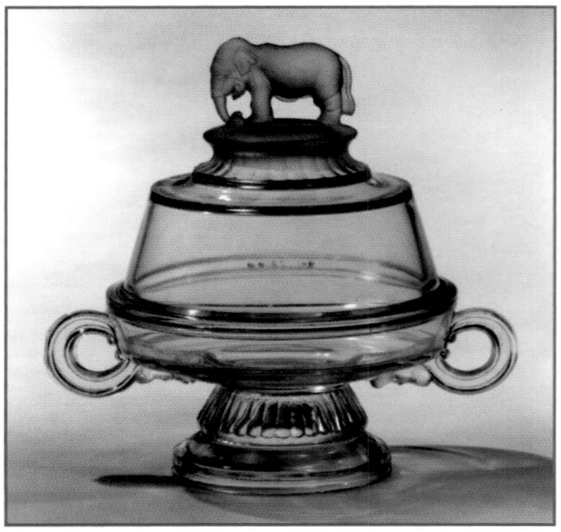

Colossal Elephant hotel at Coney Island, 150 feet long and 88 feet high, erected in 1885 (fig. 79). Thus was Jumbo associated with everything dear to American identity in the late nineteenth century—home and hearth, new technology and inventions, bountiful nature, and even baseball.

Jumbo's broad appeal led to the proliferation of his image across an astonishing range of product brands well into the twentieth century. His reputation as the "children's pet" fueled a long line of Jumbo toys, games, books, and crockery (figs. 83–89). Elephants' (mythic) fondness for peanuts made Jumbo a natural branding logo for nuts and peanut butter (fig. 92). For no obvious reason, various food and tobacco products and beers have sported his name over the years (figs. 91, 94–99). Anything that manufacturers wanted to seem bigger or stronger than competing products might be called "jumbo," from outsize soda bottles and tires to turpentine, roofing materials, spark plugs, and safety matches (figs. 93, 100, 101).

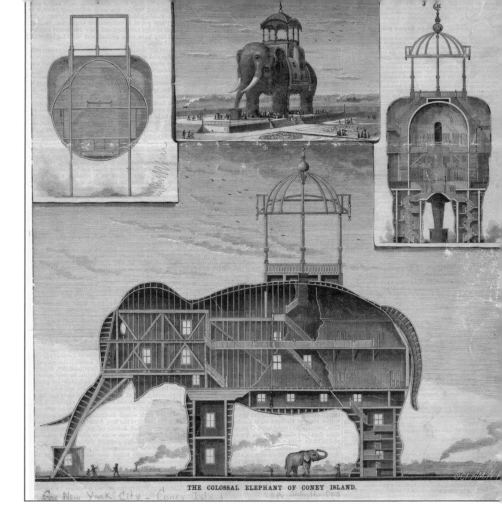

THE COLOSSAL ELEPHANT OF CONEY ISLAND.

Jumbo Mountain, in winter, Missoula, Mont.

ABOVE
figure 79
"The Colossal Elephant of Coney Island," *Scientific American* (July 11, 1885). Jumbo is seen at bottom, beneath the 150-foot-tall structure designed as a hotel by James Lafferty. The building burned down in 1896.

McGINNIS—CATCHER—ST. LOUIS.

ABOVE
figure 80
Postcard of Jumbo Mountain, Missoula, Montana, ca. 1910–20

RIGHT
figure 81
Postcard of "Jumbo" redwood, Santa Cruz Grove, California, ca. 1910–20

FAR RIGHT
figure 82
George Washington "Jumbo" McGinnis on Buchner Gold Coin baseball card, 1887. At five feet ten and 197 pounds, McGinnis was considered a large baseball player in his day.

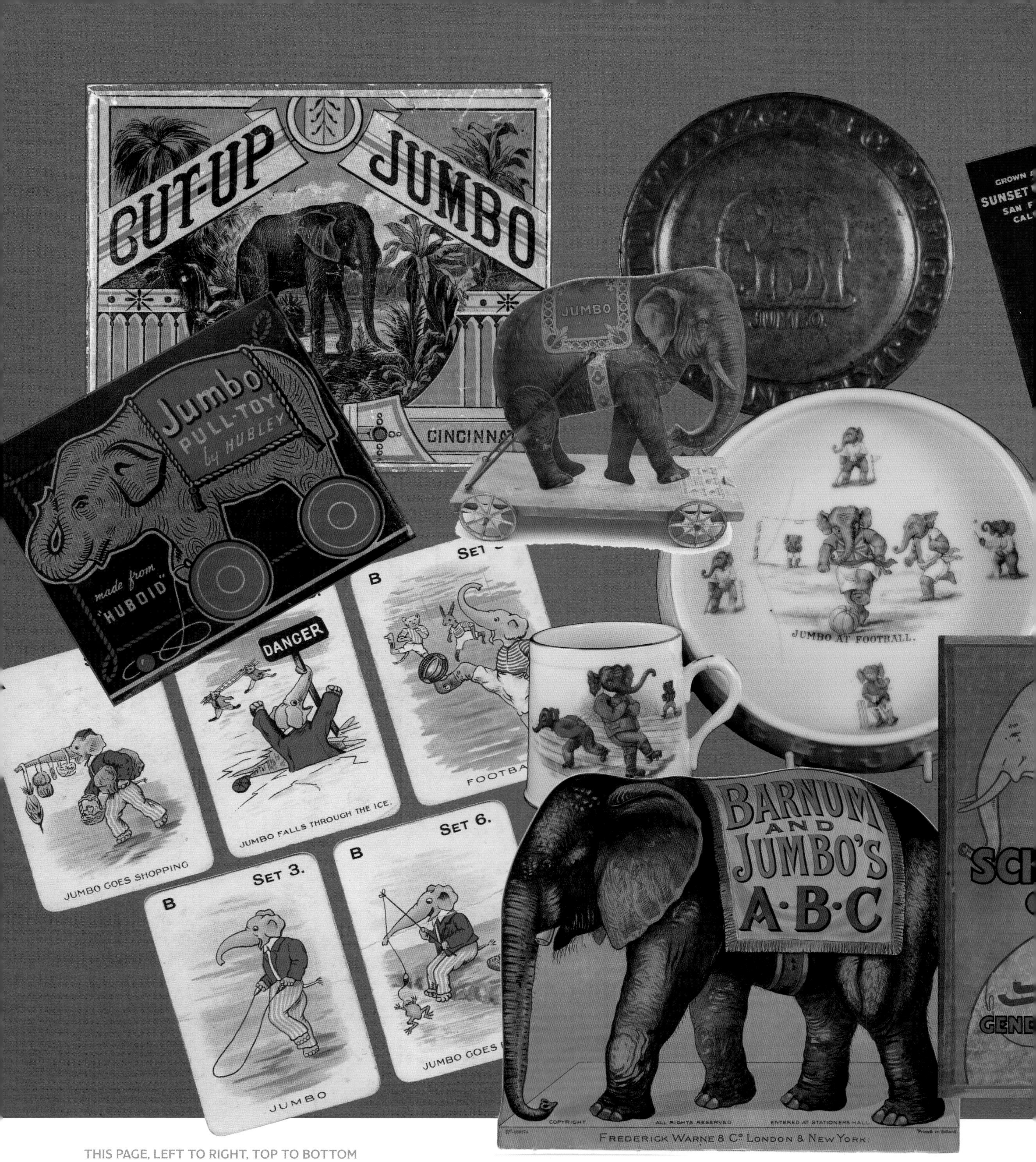
CUT-UP JUMBO
JUMBO
Jumbo PULL-TOY by HUBLEY
made from "HUBOID"
DANGER
JUMBO FALLS THROUGH THE ICE.
JUMBO GOES SHOPPING
SET 3.
SET 6.
JUMBO
JUMBO AT FOOTBALL.
BARNUM AND JUMBO'S A·B·C
COPYRIGHT
ALL RIGHTS RESERVED
ENTERED AT STATIONERS HALL
FREDERICK WARNE & C° LONDON & NEW YORK

THIS PAGE, LEFT TO RIGHT, TOP TO BOTTOM

figure 83: Cut-Up Jumbo jigsaw puzzle, Peter G. Thomson, 1885. Jumbo's popularity with children ensured a long line of toys, books, and games bearing his name and image. *figure 84:* Jumbo pull toy, Gibbs Manufacturing Co., ca. 1910–20; *figure 85:* Jumbo alphabet plate, ca. 1882–85; *figure 86:* Jumbo pull toy, Hubley Manufacturing Co., ca. 1940; *figure 87:* "Jumbo at Football" bowl, "Jumbo Rinking" cup, ca. 1910; *figure 88:* Jumbo playing cards, n.d.; *figure 89: Barnum and Jumbo's A-B-C* (ca. 1882–85); *figure 90:* Jumbo saddles, on the cover of *The Schoellkopf Company General Catalog No 25* (1924). Based in Dallas, the Schoellkopf Company was once the largest saddle and gun-leather producer in the United States.

FACING PAGE, LEFT TO RIGHT, TOP TO BOTTOM

figure 91: Jumbo Fruit label, Sunset Produce Co., 1940s; *figure 92:* Jumbo Peanut Butter jar and lid, Frank Tea & Spice Co., 1930s. Elephants' (mythic)

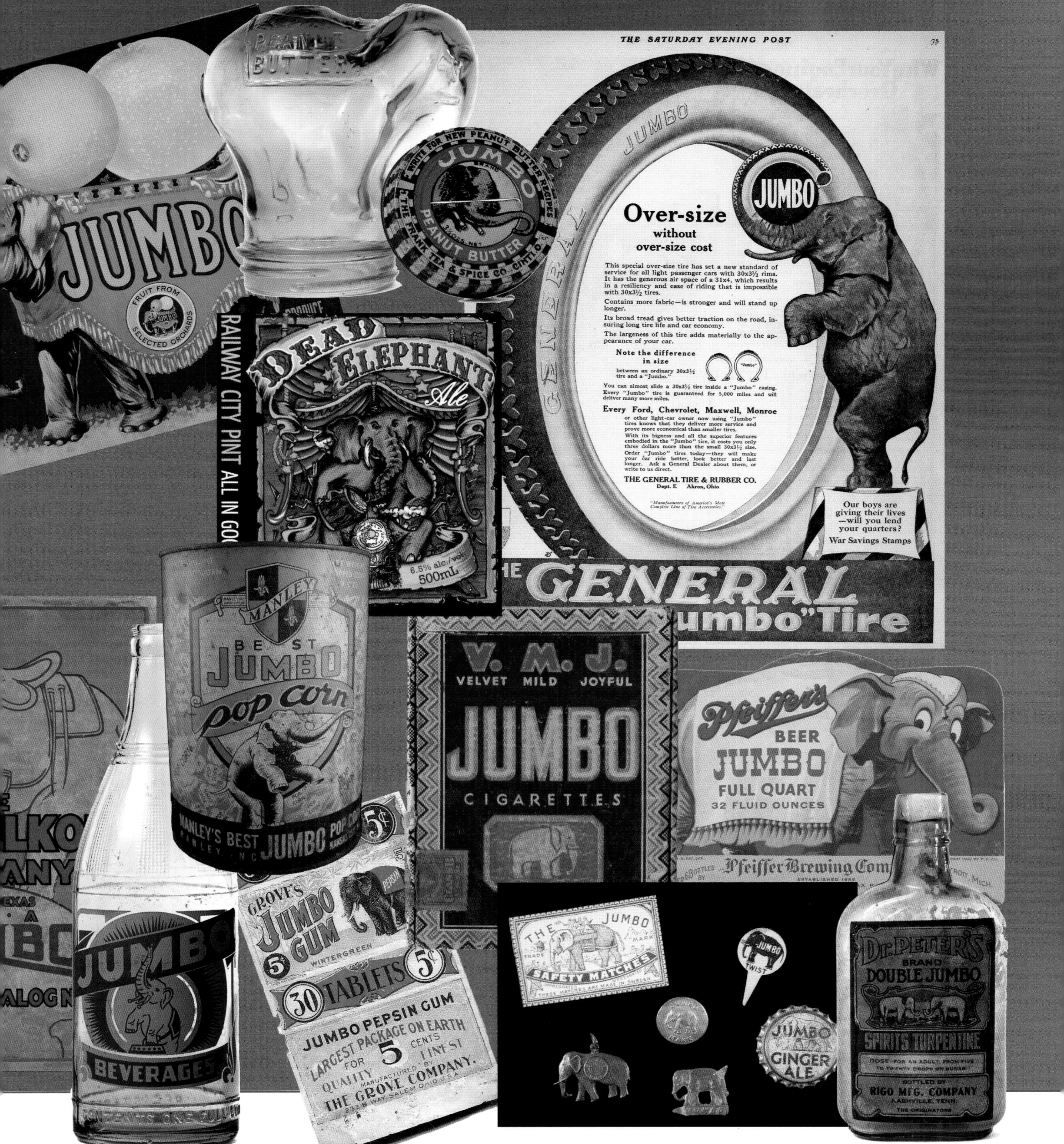
JUMBO
FRUIT FROM JUMBO SELECTED ORCHARDS
PEANUT BUTTER
WRITE FOR NEW PEANUT BUTTER RECIPES
JUMBO BRAND PEANUT BUTTER
THE FRANK TEA & SPICE CO. CIN'TI, O.
THE SATURDAY EVENING POST
JUMBO
Over-size
without
over-size cost
This special over-size tire has set a new standard of service for all light passenger cars with 30x3½ rims. It has the generous air space of a 31x4, which results in a resiliency and ease of riding that is impossible with 30x3½ tires.
Contains more fabric—is stronger and will stand up longer.
Its broad tread gives better traction on the road, insuring long tire life and car economy.
The largeness of this tire adds materially to the appearance of your car.
Note the difference in size
between an ordinary 30x3½ tire and a "Jumbo."
"Jumbo"
You can almost slide a 30x3½ tire inside a "Jumbo" casing. Every "Jumbo" tire is guaranteed for 5,000 miles and will deliver many more miles.
Every Ford, Chevrolet, Maxwell, Monroe
or other light-car owner now using "Jumbo" tires knows that they deliver more service and prove more economical than smaller tires.
With its bigness and all the superior features embodied in the "Jumbo" tire, it costs you only three dollars more than the small 30x3½ size.
Order "Jumbo" tires today—they will make your car ride better, look better and last longer. Ask a General Dealer about them, or write to us direct.
THE GENERAL TIRE & RUBBER CO.
Dept. E Akron, Ohio
"Manufacturers of America's Most Complete Line of Tire Accessories."
Our boys are giving their lives —will you lend your quarters?
War Savings Stamps
GENERAL
umbo" Tire
RAILWAY CITY PINT ALL IN GO
DEAD ELEPHANT Ale
6.5% alc./vol
500mL
MANLEY
BEST JUMBO
pop corn
MANLEY'S BEST JUMBO POP CORN
V. M. J.
VELVET MILD JOYFUL
JUMBO
CIGARETTES
Pfeiffer's
BEER
JUMBO
FULL QUART
32 FLUID OUNCES
Pfeiffer Brewing Com
GROVE'S JUMBO GUM
WINTERGREEN
5¢
30 TABLETS
JUMBO PEPSIN GUM
LARGEST PACKAGE ON EARTH
FOR 5 CENTS
QUALITY FINEST
MANUFACTURED BY
THE GROVE COMPANY.
JUMBO
BEVERAGES
THE JUMBO SAFETY MATCHES
JUMBO TWIST
JUMBO GINGER ALE
Dr. PETER'S
BRAND
DOUBLE JUMBO
SPIRITS TURPENTINE
RIGO MFG. COMPANY
NASHVILLE, TENN.
THE ORIGINATORS

fondness for peanuts led to Jumbo's association with peanut-butter products. *figure 93:* "The General 'Jumbo' Tire," *Saturday Evening Post* (July 15, 1918); *figure 94:* Dead Elephant Ale label, 2013. The Railway City Brewing Co. in St. Thomas, Ontario, where Jumbo was killed, produces a variety of Jumbo beers. *figure 95:* Jumbo Soda bottle, Nemo Bottling Co., n.d.; *figure 96:* Manley's Best Jumbo Pop Corn can, Manley Inc., 1940s; *figure 97:* Grove's Jumbo Gum wrapper, ca. 1905; *figure 98:* V. M. J. Jumbo Cigarettes box, ca. 1945; *figure 99:* Pfeiffer's Beer Jumbo Full Quart label, Pfeiffer Brewing Co., 1942; *figure 100:* Jumbo matches, Sinclair Oil charm, button, tobacco pins, bottle cap; *figure 101:* Dr. Peter's Brand Double Jumbo Spirits Turpentine, Rigo Manufacturing Co., n.d.

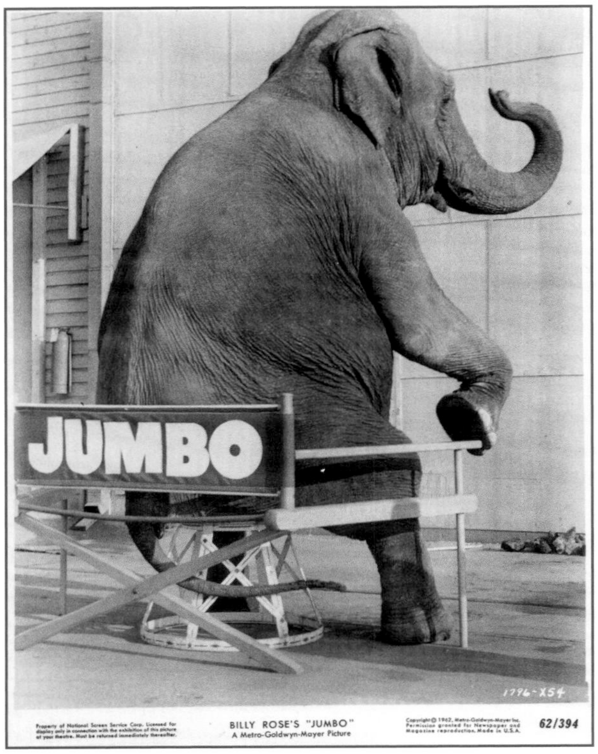
JUMBO
BILLY ROSE'S "JUMBO"
A Metro-Goldwyn-Mayer Picture
62/394

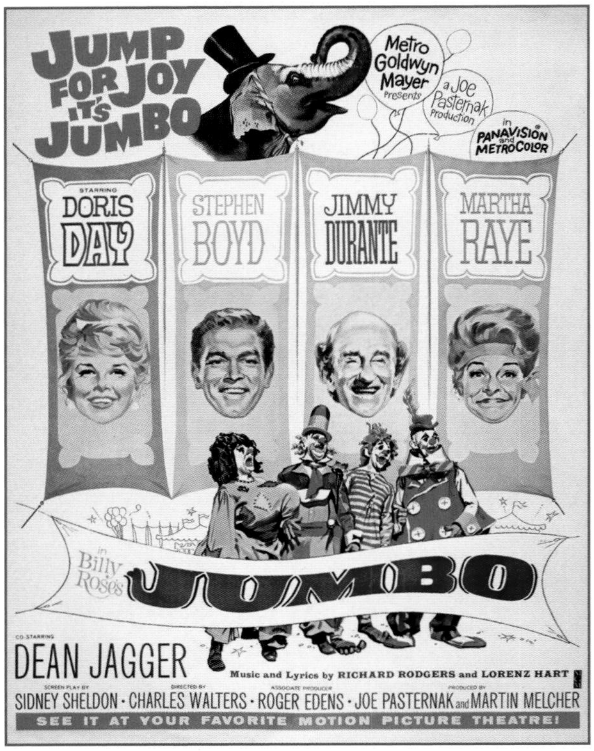
JUMP FOR JOY IT'S JUMBO
Metro Goldwyn Mayer presents
a Joe Pasternak Production
in PANAVISION and METROCOLOR
STARRING
DORIS DAY
STEPHEN BOYD
JIMMY DURANTE
MARTHA RAYE
Billy Rose's JUMBO
CO-STARRING
DEAN JAGGER
Music and Lyrics by RICHARD RODGERS and LORENZ HART
SIDNEY SHELDON · CHARLES WALTERS · ROGER EDENS · JOE PASTERNAK and MARTIN MELCHER
SEE IT AT YOUR FAVORITE MOTION PICTURE THEATRE!

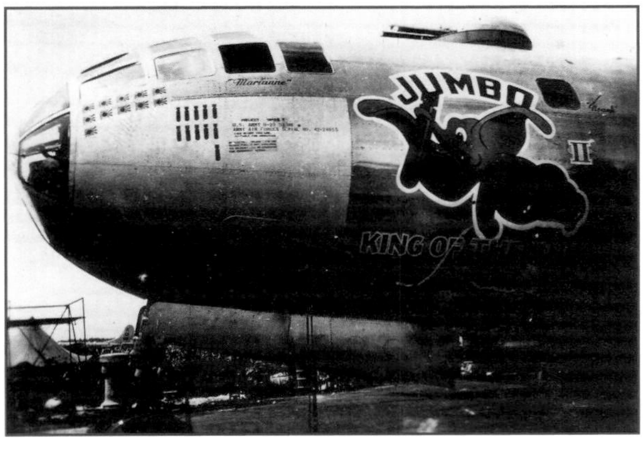

Of course today the historical derivation of "jumbo" is largely overlooked, as the word has come to be synonymous with "big" and entered common parlance teamed with other words, as in jumbo jet, jumbo shrimp, jumbo mortgage, jumbo guitar, and so on.

Jumbo's legacy endured in the popular imagination via stage and screen. In 1935 the producer Billy Rose's musical *Jumbo* opened on Broadway, starring Jimmy Durante and with a score by Rodgers and Hart (fig. 105). The musical was made into a movie in 1962, with Durante, Martha Raye, and Doris Day (figs. 102, 103). (Never mind that the elephant used in the film was clearly Asian.) Of course, Jumbo also lies behind the beloved Walt Disney character Dumbo, who in the animated film of the same name (1941) was named Jumbo Jr. at birth but cruelly nicknamed "Dumbo" by the other elephants in the circus. An interesting conflation of Jumbo and Dumbo occurred toward the end of World War II when an American B-29 bomber (fig. 104) flew above the Pacific emblazoned with Dumbo's image and the legend "Jumbo—King of the Show"—one of many examples of nose art for planes and ships painted by artists from Disney Studio during the war.

ABOVE
figure 102
Billy Rose's "Jumbo," 1962. This publicity photograph for the movie shows an Indian elephant in the starring role.

MIDDLE
figure 103
Flyer for *Billy Rose's "Jumbo,"* 1962. Though not a hit at the box office, the movie marked Doris Day's final appearance in a screen musical.

LEFT
figure 104
"Jumbo—King of the Show," B-29 bomber, 1945. This plane was lost over the Pacific toward the end of World War II.

FACING PAGE
figure 105
Program for *Billy Rose's "Jumbo,"* 1935. A comedic scene in the play involving the actor Jimmy Durante likely popularized the idiom "elephant in the room."

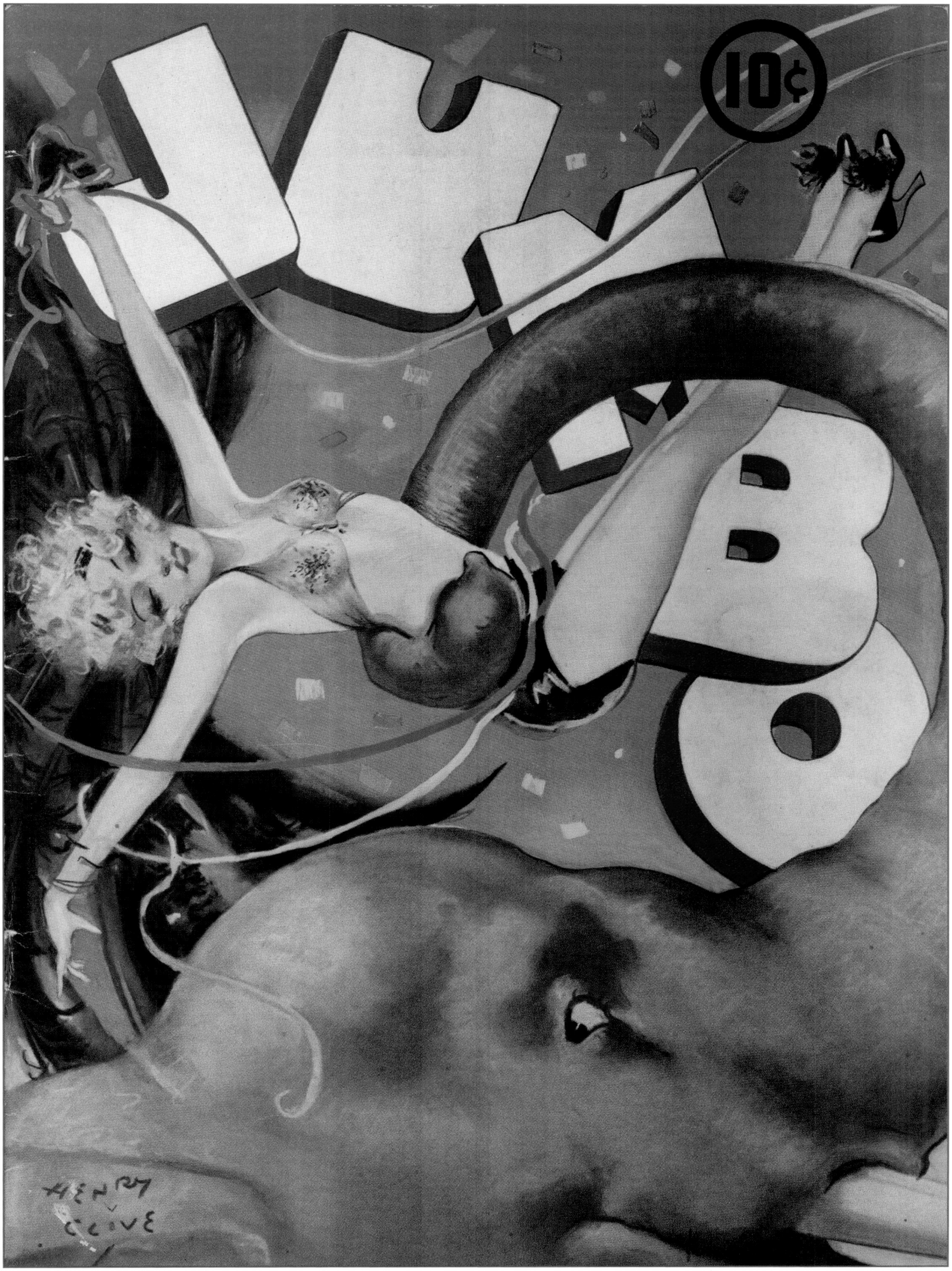
JUMBO
10¢
HENRY CLIVE

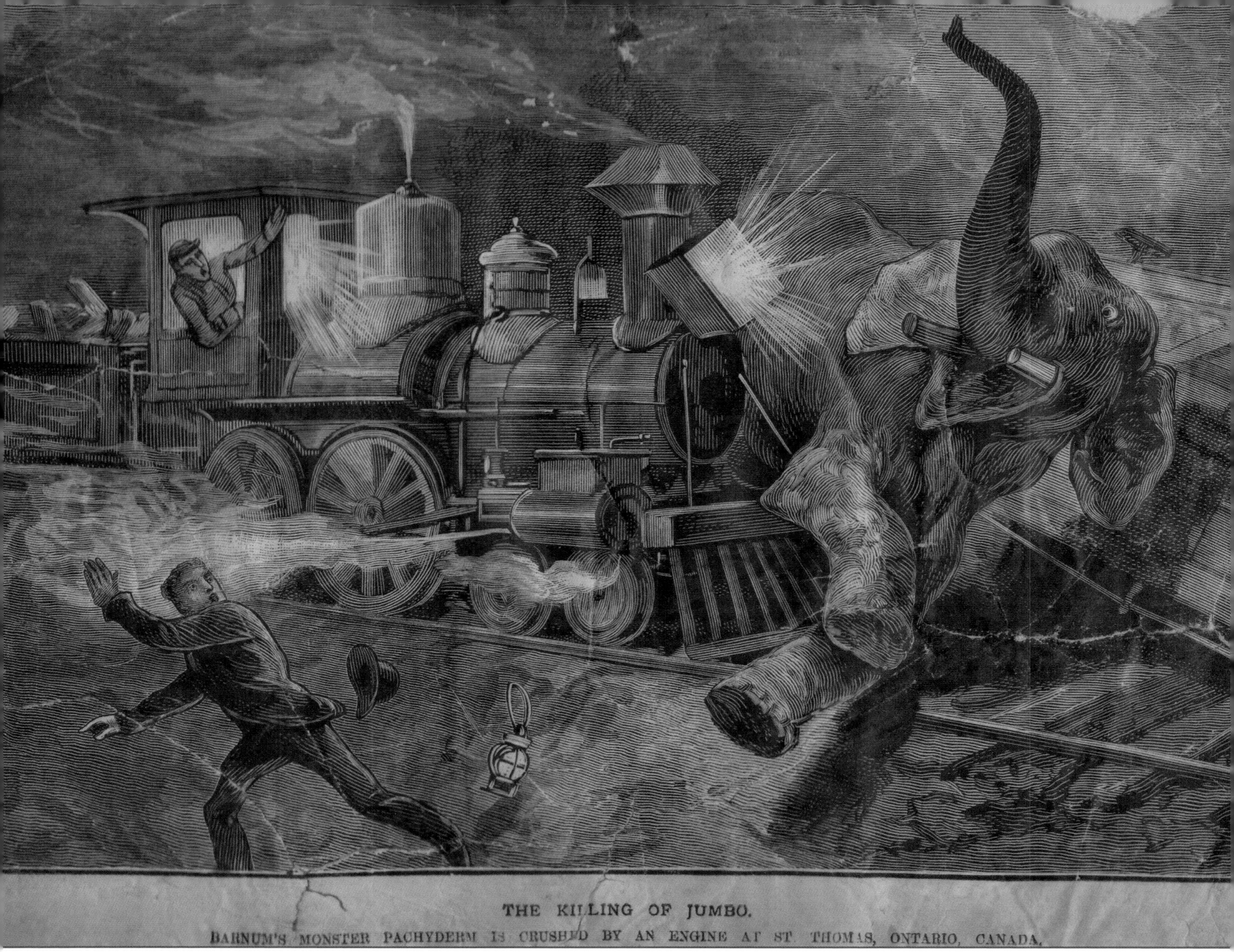
THE KILLING OF JUMBO.
BARNUM'S MONSTER PACHYDERM IS CRUSHED BY AN ENGINE AT ST. THOMAS, ONTARIO, CANADA.

ABOVE
figure 106
"The Killing of Jumbo," *National Police Gazette* (October 3, 1885). News of Jumbo's death was carried in newspapers and magazines across North America and beyond.

FACING PAGE, ABOVE
figure 107
Charles Eisenmann, *Dead Jumbo on the Embankment at St. Thomas*, 1885. This famous photograph, taken the morning after the accident, shows Matthew Scott standing by Jumbo's head, and Barnum's partner James Hutchinson leaning proprietarily against the elephant's belly.

FACING PAGE, BELOW
figure 108
Jumbo the Children's Friend Killed, 1885. This die-cut illustration is a rather gruesome children's memento.

JUMBO'S DEATH AND AFTERLIFE

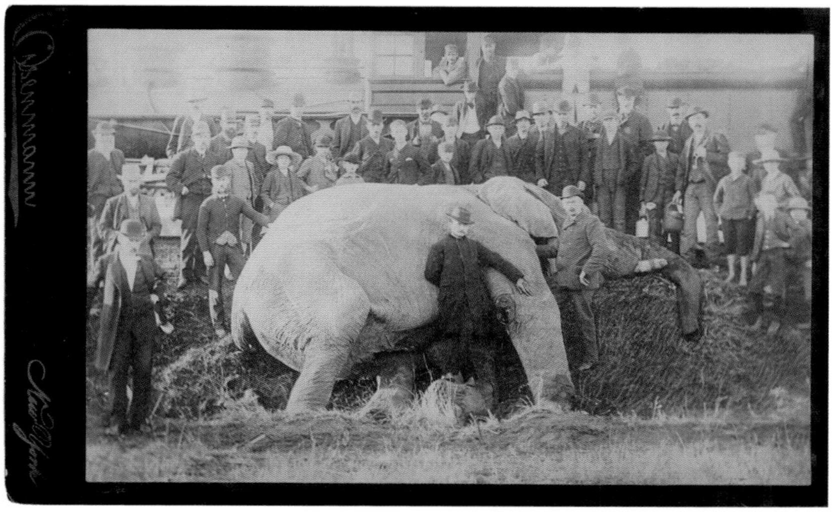

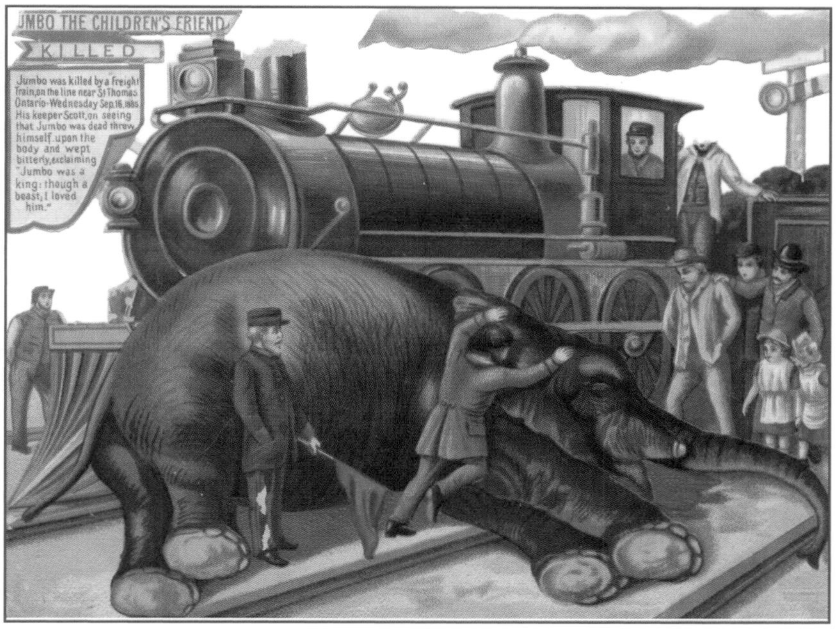

JMBO THE CHILDREN'S FRIEND
KILLED
Jumbo was killed by a Freight Train, on the line near St Thomas Ontario-Wednesday Sep.16.1885 His keeper Scott, on seeing that Jumbo was dead threw himself upon the body and wept bitterly, exclaiming "Jumbo was a king: though a beast, I loved him."

JUMBO'S DAYS WITH THE CIRCUS ended on September 15, 1885, when, toward the end of his fourth season, he was struck and killed by an unscheduled freight train in St. Thomas, Ontario (figs. 106–108). Several eyewitness accounts of the accident survive. Joseph T. McCaddon, James Bailey's brother-in-law and the assistant treasurer of the circus, wrote home to his sister the next day, offering what he imagined would be "a more correct account" of Jumbo's death than what would appear in the morning papers. In McCaddon's telling, the circus lot was some distance from the town and adjacent to the railway line, where the stock and elephant cars were parked on a switch. Toward the close of the evening show, the animals were being led along the track, all as usual, when, McCaddon wrote:

> A heavy freight train [unexpectedly] came in view over a heavy grade a short distance away. The animals were started to get them out of the way and with the exception of Jumbo, Queen and Tom the Clown Elephant they all descended the steep embankment. Queen was struck but escaped with a few scratches, little Tom was knocked under one of our flat cars, uninjured with the exception of his right hind leg which was broken. . . . Jumbo was the last on the track, he refused to go down the embankment, he ran down the track a short distance, head high in the air, trumpeting loudly, and lifting "Scotty" his keeper off his feet every step he made, Scott having hold of the strap he usually led him by. They came to an opening in the stationary train between the flat and the stock cars, which he started to enter and in a few seconds more would have been safe, but the engine struck his hind quarters knocking him on his side. The engine was derailed, cowcatcher completely demolished from the contact with the animal, and the train stopped. Jumbo's position was on his side, back to the freight train, two legs under one of the empty flats, and two on top. All the men were taken there at once, the cars removed out of the way, and every effort was made to assist Jumbo to his feet. He struggled for some time to raise himself, but died before the show was out. . . . His body was rolled off the track. Men were left to guard it until the proper disposition is made of it, and so ends the greatest attraction the show will, or has ever had.

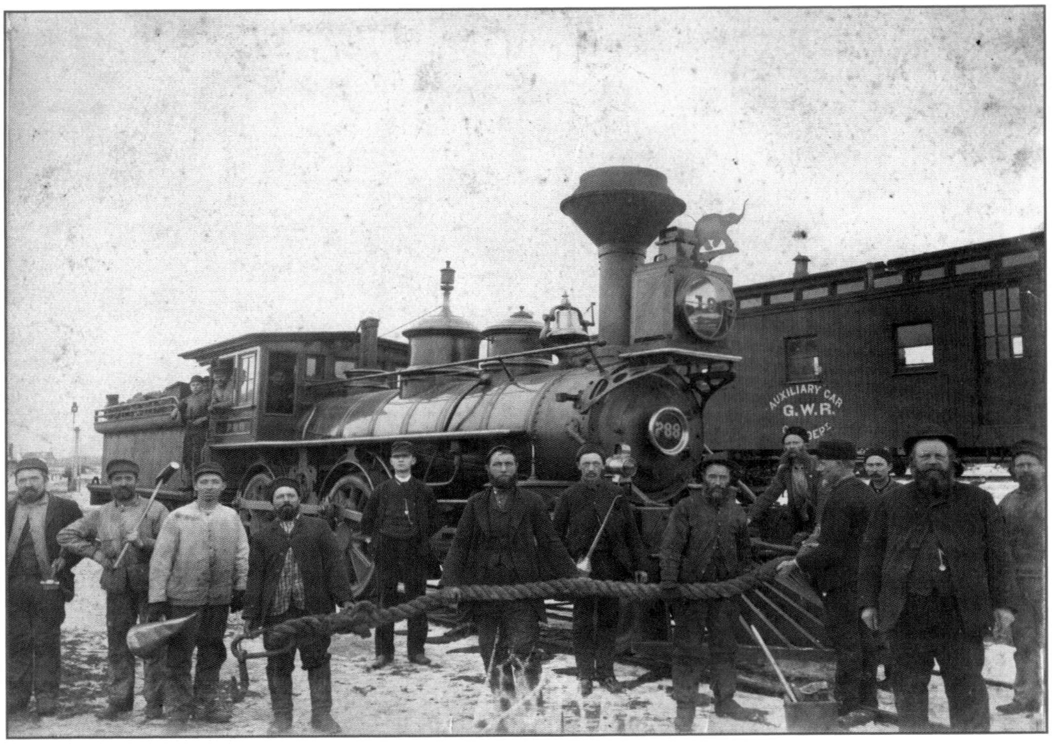
AUXILIARY CAR
G.W.R.
P89

By the time the train cleared the rise, and the engineer saw what was ahead and applied the brakes, it was too late. Jumbo died from internal injuries and a crushed skull. Curious onlookers gathered at the spot of the accident the next morning and were immortalized in the photograph of poor Jumbo lying dead against the embankment (fig. 107). James Hutchinson, the only partner traveling with the circus, leans proprietarily against the elephant's belly; Matthew Scott stands by Jumbo's head. The train crew was later photographed holding a thick rope used to drag Jumbo off the tracks (fig. 109; note the elephant cutout mounted on the engine headlight).

Hutchinson cabled Bailey the following morning with the crucial details. Later that day, having thought through the implications of the loss, he sent Bailey a second telegram:

> It is for your interest & mine that we both claim to all showmen & others we meet that the loss of Jumbo will not materially affect the drawing power of the show. That to build two enormous cages and exhibit him stuffed in one & skeleton in the other would prove a bigger card where he has been seen alive so often & would make him draw more than ever. You see the point. Keep confidential. Barnum consents that we keep him for that purpose and not give him away.

Back at home, Barnum swung into action to make the best of the catastrophe. Though the news had already been wired to newspapers around the world, he dispatched one of his publicity men to St. Thomas to spread an embroidered account of "heroic Jumbo" lifting the young elephant Tom Thumb out of harm's way and then defiantly charging the oncoming engine (fig. 111). On September 17 he telegrammed the prominent taxidermist Henry A. Ward of Rochester: "Go ahead, save skin and skeleton. I will pay you justly and honorably." Knowing that Jumbo would die sooner or later, Barnum had previously arranged with Ward to preserve his remains, but the idea of touring a "Double Jumbo" appears to have arisen on the spur of the moment in Canada. Having taken care of essential business, Barnum then wrote to Harper & Brothers publishers, suggesting that a well-illustrated "life history and

---

ABOVE
figure 109
Train and crew with rope used to haul Jumbo off the tracks, ca. 1885. The train's driver survived the collision with Jumbo, only to perish in the San Francisco earthquake of 1906.

FACING PAGE, ABOVE
figure 110
Objects found in Jumbo's stomach after his death. These objects were collected by the boy in a white hat standing by Jumbo's rump in figure 107.

FACING PAGE, BELOW
figure 111
"The Scene of Jumbo's Heroic Death," from *The Life and Death of Jumbo* (1886). Barnum fabricated the story of Jumbo's charging the train and saving the life of a dwarf elephant named Tom Thumb.

death of Jumbo" be prepared in time for the Christmas holidays. There would surely be an interest on both sides of the Atlantic, he wrote, since "millions of children and adults (myself included) are mourning the death of Jumbo."

Henry Ward arrived in St. Thomas on September 18, and with the help of six local butchers, salvaged Jumbo's skin and bones. Salted and packed for transport, the skin weighed 1,500 pounds, the bones another 2,400. Inside Jumbo's stomach, Ward discovered hundreds of coins, perhaps errant pennies from his days at the zoo. "Jumbo was a bank all by himself," he remarked. Several other odds and ends ingested by Jumbo over the years and retrieved by Ward were collected by a local boy (who, in the photograph of Jumbo's body, stands, wearing a large-brimmed, white hat, near the elephant's rump) and later donated to the Elgin County Museum, not far from the place of Jumbo's demise (fig. 110). Back at Ward's Natural Science Establishment in Rochester, the task of stuffing the hide and mounting the skeleton was given to two promising apprentices, Carl E. Akeley and J. William Critchley, both of whom were at the start of successful careers. Critchley

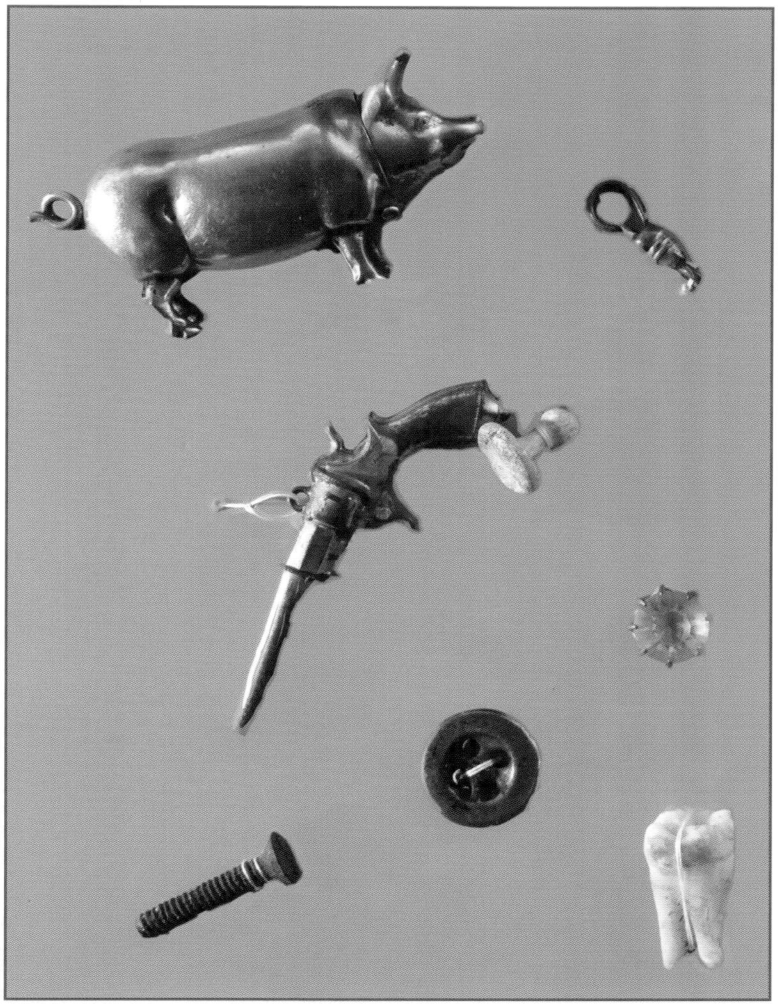

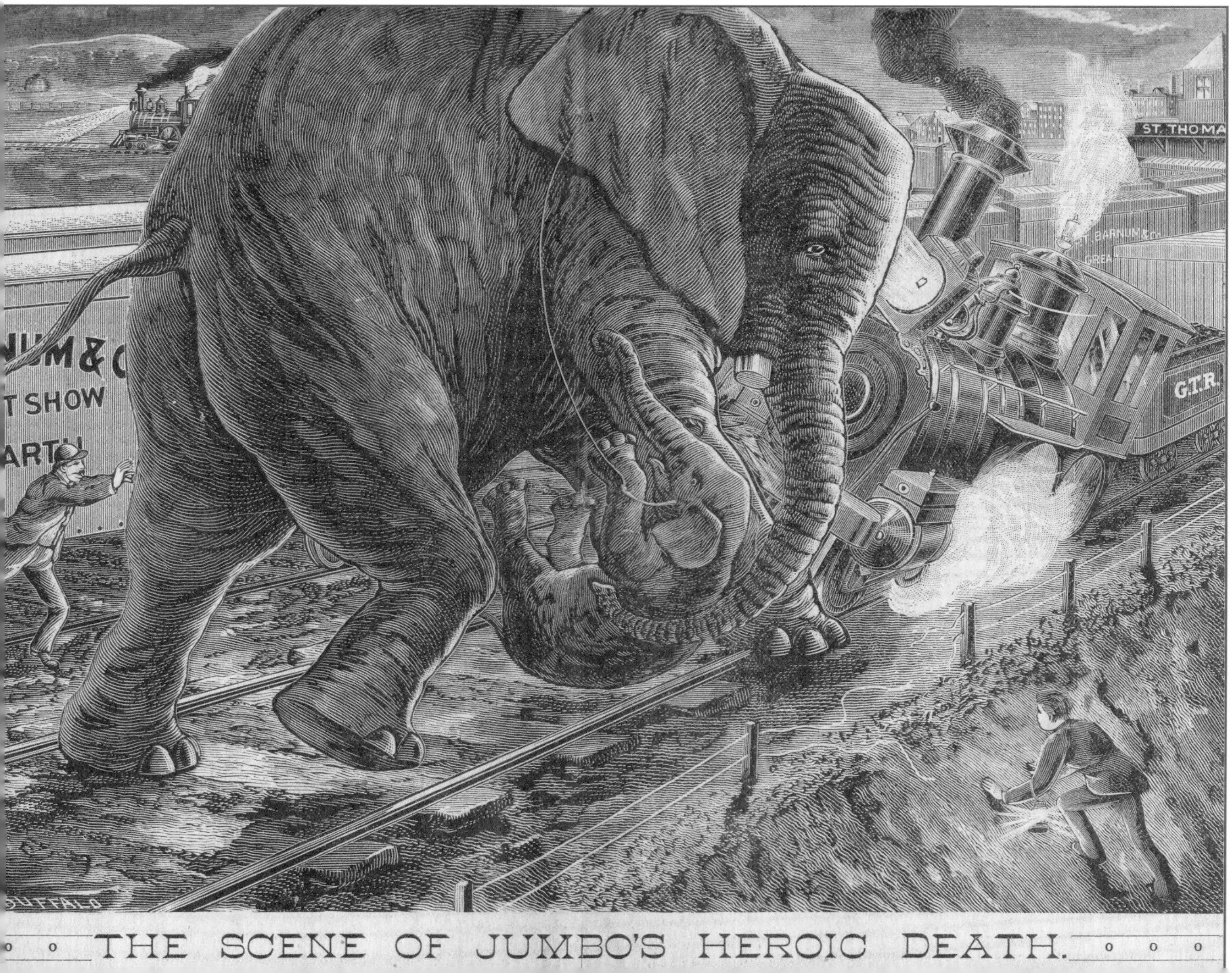
ST. THOMA
G.T.R.
T SHOW
THE SCENE OF JUMBO'S HEROIC DEATH.

ended up as chief taxidermist at the Brooklyn Institute of Arts and Sciences (predecessor of the Brooklyn Museum), while Akeley went on to become America's foremost taxidermist and animal modeler, remembered for his extraordinary elephant groups at the Field Museum of Natural History in Chicago and at the American Museum of Natural History in New York (see fig. 130).

During the winter of 1885–86, Ward and his young assistants created "Double Jumbo," finishing in time for the opening of the 1886 season. A pair of photographs shows the two models in Ward's studio ready for presentation. Akeley and Critchley pose next to the hide, while Ward and his cousin Frank A. Ward stand by the skeleton (figs. 112, 113). Akeley later recalled the primitive state of taxidermy at the time: "We used a method that was simplicity itself. Needless to say, the creatures resulting were awkward, stilted and unnatural." Steam-curved strips of basswood were attached to a wooden framework to give the appearance of musculature under Jumbo's skin, which was stretched tight over the armature and secured with 78,280 nails. The result was indeed stiff, but mounting an animal of that size was unprecedented and the model had to be made to endure the rigors of rail travel and the rough and tumble of circus exhibition. The skeleton, on the other hand, was ingeniously constructed to allow for quick assembly and transportation: the head is detachable, and the rib cage and vertebral column can easily be disconnected and lowered down the leg supports to rest on the base. To celebrate his achievement, Ward held a banquet for the press in late February; the pièce de résistance was a jelly dessert that had been fixed using finely ground powder from one of Jumbo's tusks. The *Buffalo Courier* reported: "The journalists of course sampled the unique dish, and some of Jumbo did they thus assimilate." Ward prepared a number of tusk souvenirs, including slices for the circus partners which he inscribed and decorated on the reverse with an adaptation of the British royal arms showing Jumbo, rather than the rampant lion, above the inscription "Jumbo et mon droit" (figs. 114, 115) Undecorated slices were presented to the Smithsonian Institution in Washington, D.C., and the British Museum in London. Smaller and simpler rectangular sections were also

JUMBO AFRICANUS, Mounted at Ward's Natural Science Estb Rochester N.Y.

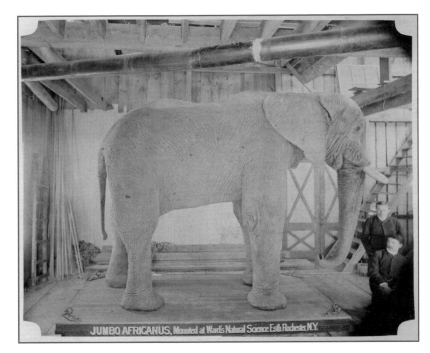

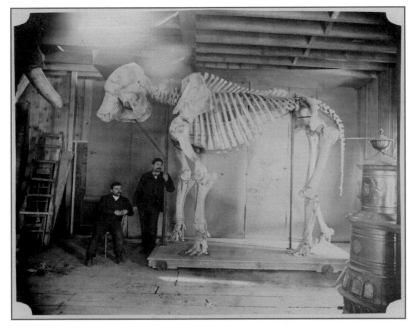

ABOVE
figure 112
Jumbo's stuffed hide at Ward's Natural Science Establishment, Rochester, New York, 1886. The taxidermists Carl E. Akeley (standing) and J. William Critchley are seen lower right.

BELOW
figure 113
Jumbo's skeleton at Ward's Natural Science Establishment, Rochester, New York, 1886. Henry A. Ward and another man (his cousin Frank A. Ward?) pose to the left of the skeleton.

FACING PAGE, ABOVE
figure 114
Cross section of Jumbo's tusk (front), 1885–86. This is one of five decorated slices prepared by Henry Ward as presentation pieces.

FACING PAGE, BELOW
figure 115
Cross section of Jumbo's tusk (back), 1885–86. The painted crest on the back is an amusing adaptation of the British royal coat of arms (pictured to its right), concocted at the height of Jumbomania in 1882.

given away. The circus hastily published a colorful booklet that detailed Ward's work and spread the embellished account of Jumbo's demise under the title *The Life and Death of Jumbo: An Illustrated History of the Greatest, Gentlest and Most Famous and Heroic Beast That Ever Lived* (figs. 116, 117).

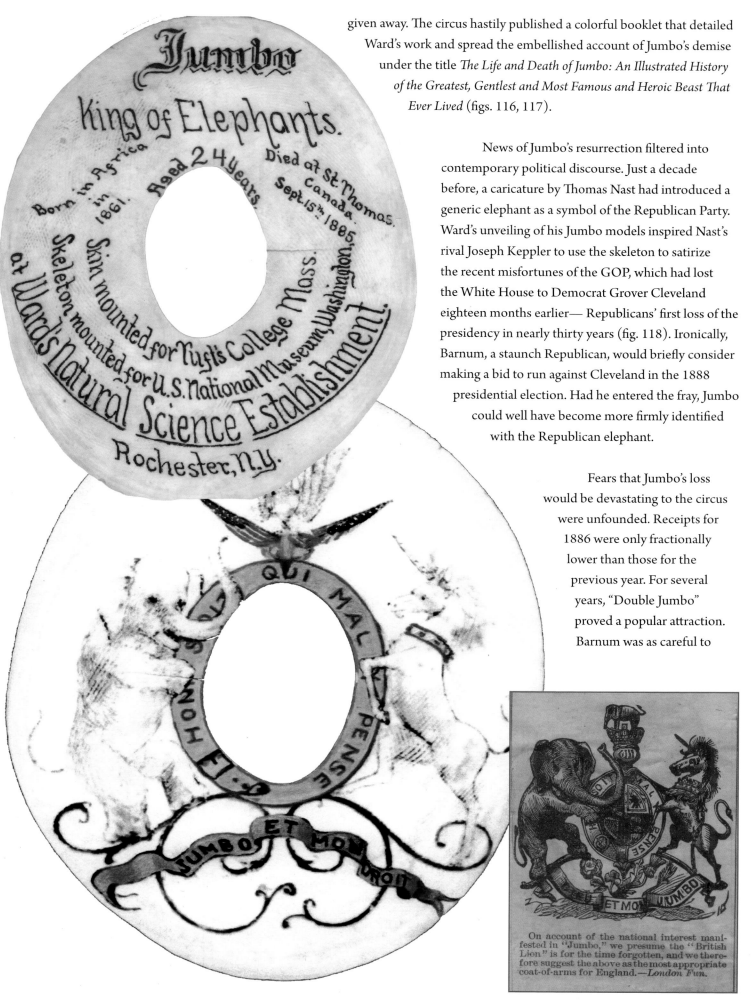

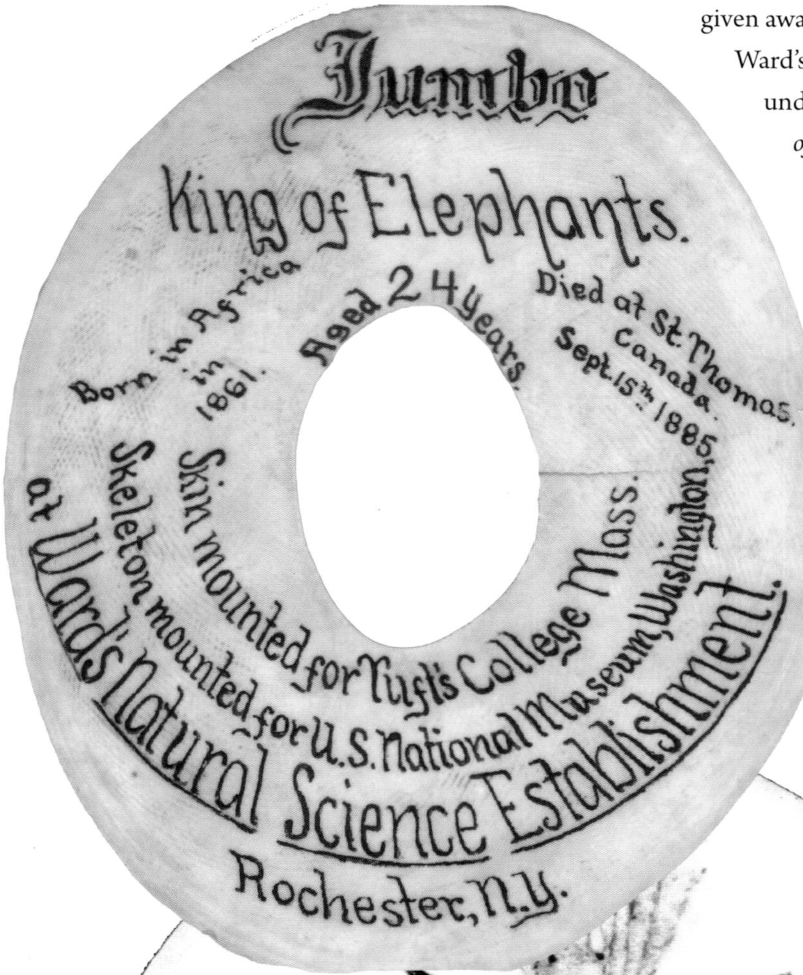
Jumbo
King of Elephants.
Born in Africa in 1861.
Aged 24 years.
Died at St. Thomas. Canada. Sept. 15th 1885.
Skin mounted for Tuft's College Mass.
Skeleton mounted for U.S. National Museum, Washington.
at Ward's Natural Science Establishment.
Rochester, N.Y.

News of Jumbo's resurrection filtered into contemporary political discourse. Just a decade before, a caricature by Thomas Nast had introduced a generic elephant as a symbol of the Republican Party. Ward's unveiling of his Jumbo models inspired Nast's rival Joseph Keppler to use the skeleton to satirize the recent misfortunes of the GOP, which had lost the White House to Democrat Grover Cleveland eighteen months earlier— Republicans' first loss of the presidency in nearly thirty years (fig. 118). Ironically, Barnum, a staunch Republican, would briefly consider making a bid to run against Cleveland in the 1888 presidential election. Had he entered the fray, Jumbo could well have become more firmly identified with the Republican elephant.

Fears that Jumbo's loss would be devastating to the circus were unfounded. Receipts for 1886 were only fractionally lower than those for the previous year. For several years, "Double Jumbo" proved a popular attraction. Barnum was as careful to

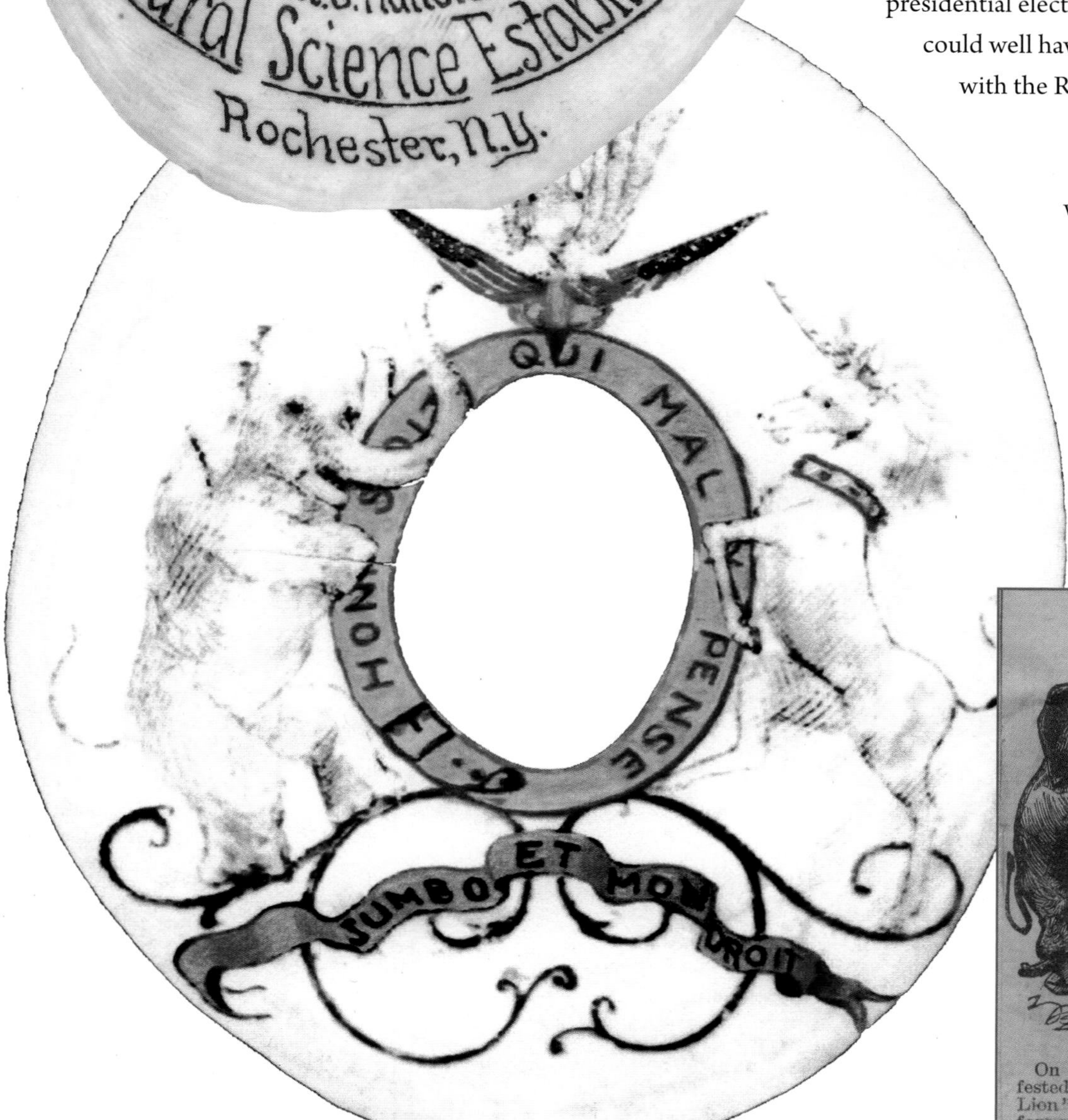
QUI MAL PENSE
HONI
ET
JUMBO ET MON DROIT

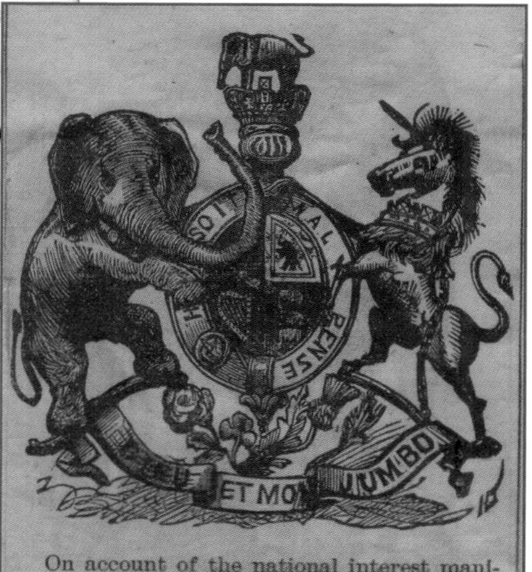

On account of the national interest manifested in "Jumbo," we presume the "British Lion" is for the time forgotten, and we therefore suggest the above as the most appropriate coat-of-arms for England.—*London Fun.*

control Jumbo's image in death as he had been in life. And once again size was at issue. Barnum had been delighted to learn during the mounting process that it was possible to stretch and enlarge the stuffed hide. He had written to Ward: "By all means let that show as large as possible. It will be a grand thing to take all advantage possible in this direction! Let him show like a mountain!" In the one surviving photograph of the two Jumbos on tour, the skeleton is displayed well away from the stuffed hide, to prevent the enhanced amplitude of the latter from being noticed (fig. 119). The two photographs taken at Ward's early in 1886 also show the two models in separate places. The last of the great Strobridge Jumbo posters depicts the skeleton rising off its base more than three times the height of the people who gaze up at it (fig. 120). Lingering behind the skeleton is Jumbo's old mate, Alice, whom Barnum had bought (without controversy) from the London zoo in time for the 1886 season. In a final act of sentimental anthropomorphization, the circus opened that year with stuffed Jumbo paraded around the ring followed by Alice and the elephant herd dabbing their eyes with giant, black-edged mourning handkerchiefs clutched in their trunks.

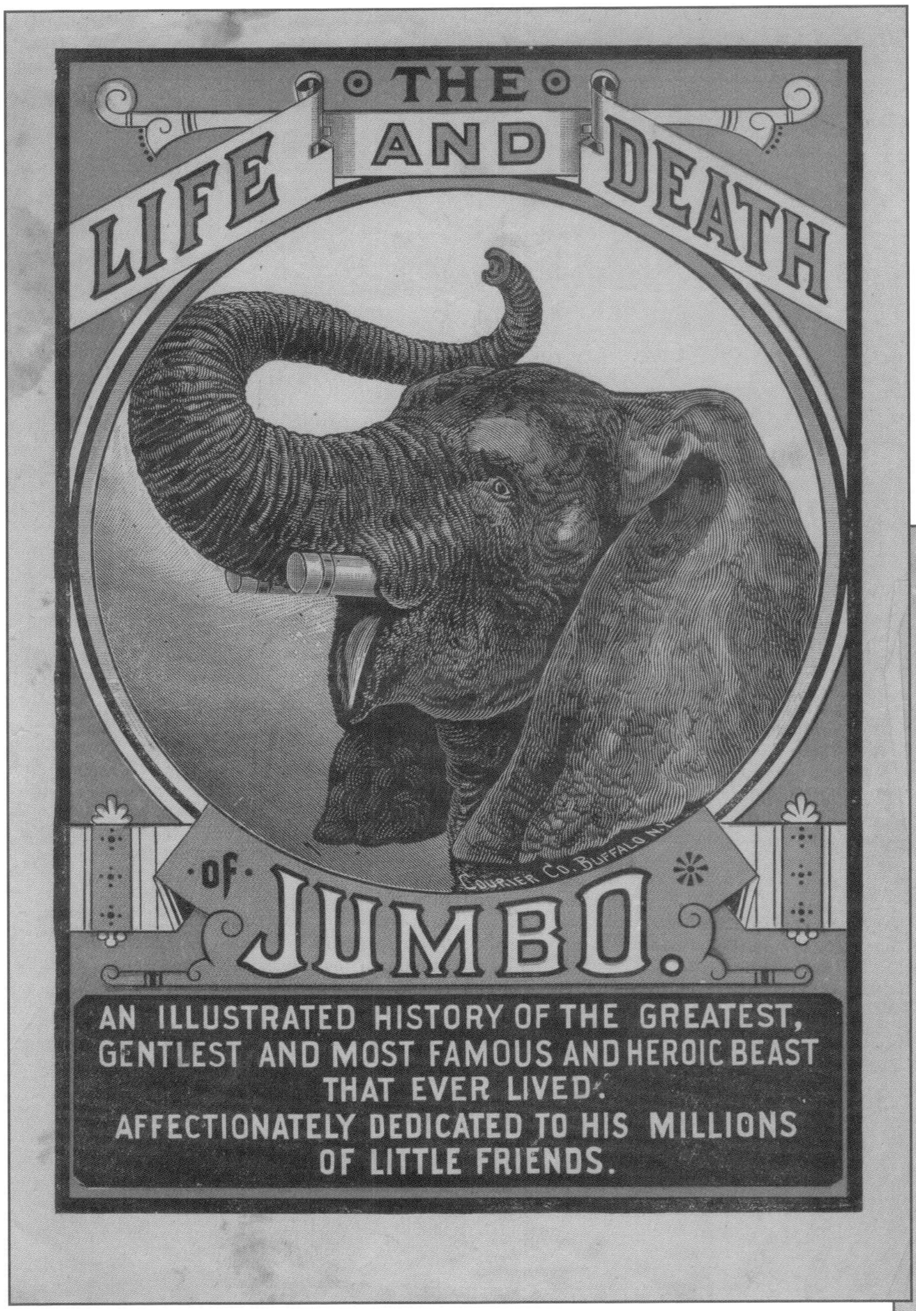
THE
LIFE AND DEATH
of JUMBO.
COURIER CO. BUFFALO N.Y.
AN ILLUSTRATED HISTORY OF THE GREATEST, GENTLEST AND MOST FAMOUS AND HEROIC BEAST THAT EVER LIVED.
AFFECTIONATELY DEDICATED TO HIS MILLIONS OF LITTLE FRIENDS.

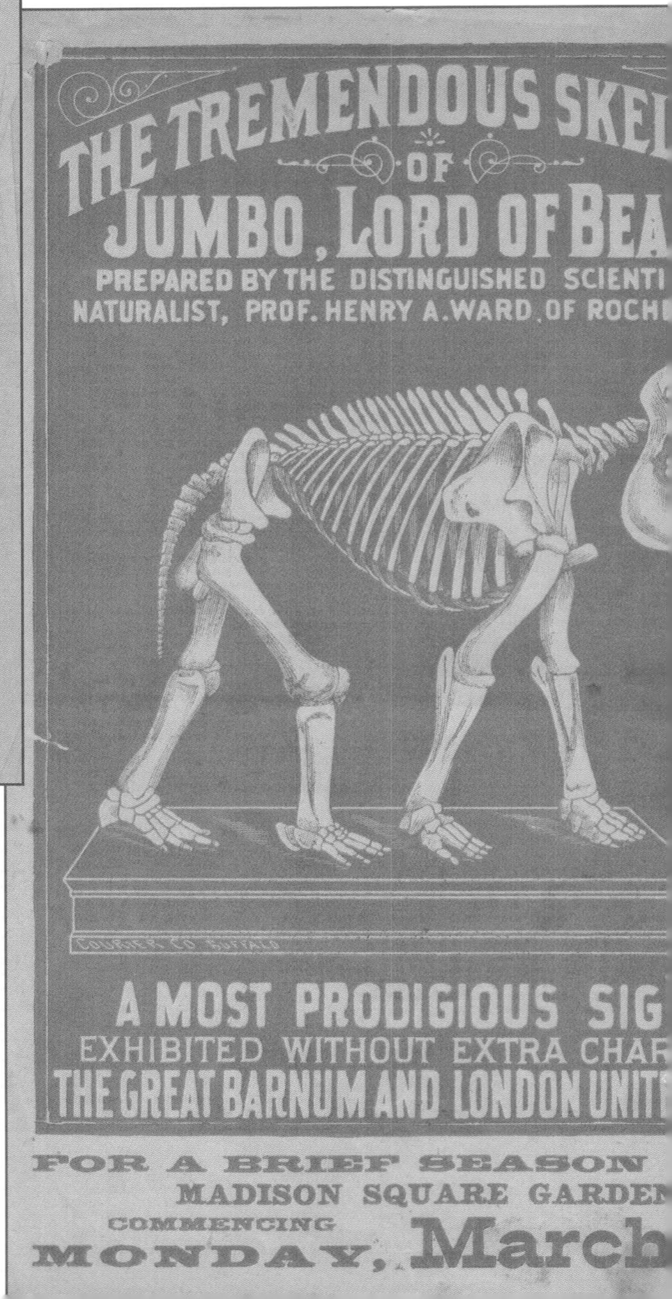
THE TREMENDOUS SKEL
OF
JUMBO, LORD OF BEA
PREPARED BY THE DISTINGUISHED SCIENTI
NATURALIST, PROF. HENRY A. WARD OF ROCH
A MOST PRODIGIOUS SIG
EXHIBITED WITHOUT EXTRA CHAR
THE GREAT BARNUM AND LONDON UNIT
FOR A BRIEF SEASON
MADISON SQUARE GARDE
COMMENCING
MONDAY, March

ABOVE
figure 116
Front cover of *The Life and Death of Jumbo* (1886). This booklet advertised the successful completion of the "Double Jumbo"—the stuffed hide and the mounted skeleton.

BELOW
figure 117
Back cover of *The Life and Death of Jumbo* (1886)

PUCK.
PRESTIGE
DAWES
J. KEPPLER.
"AS NATURAL AS LIFE."—PATCHING UP THE REPUBLICAN JUMBO FOR 1888.

P.T.BARNUM & CO'S GREATEST SHOW ON EARTH
& THE GREAT LONDON CIRCUS COMBINED WITH
GREAT JUMBO'S SKELETON
P.T.BARNUM
JUMBO
SANGER'S ROYAL BRITISH MENAGERIE & GRAND INTERNATIONAL SHOWS

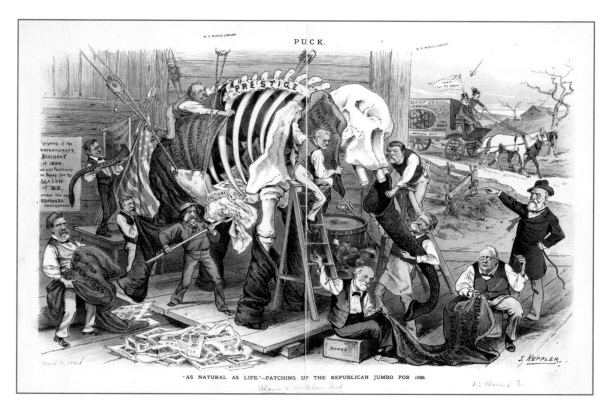

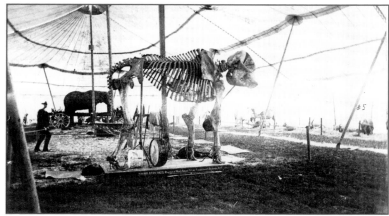

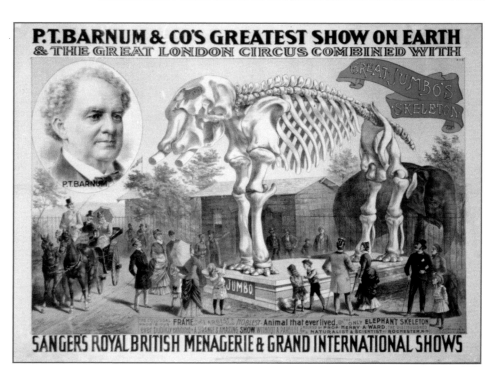

ABOVE
figure 118
Joseph Keppler, "'As Natural as Life.'—Patching Up the Republican Jumbo for 1888," *Puck* (March 31, 1886). This cartoon plays on the assembly of Jumbo's skeleton to satirize the misfortunes of the Republican Party, which had lost the White House in 1884 for the first time in thirty years.

MIDDLE
figure 119
Jumbo's skeleton and stuffed hide on tour with the circus, ca. 1886–88. "Double Jumbo" toured with the circus off and on between 1886 and 1888.

BELOW
figure 120
P. T. Barnum & Co.'s Greatest Show on Earth . . . Great Jumbo's Skeleton, 1888. The last of the great Strobridge posters shows Jumbo's skeleton towering over circus goers.

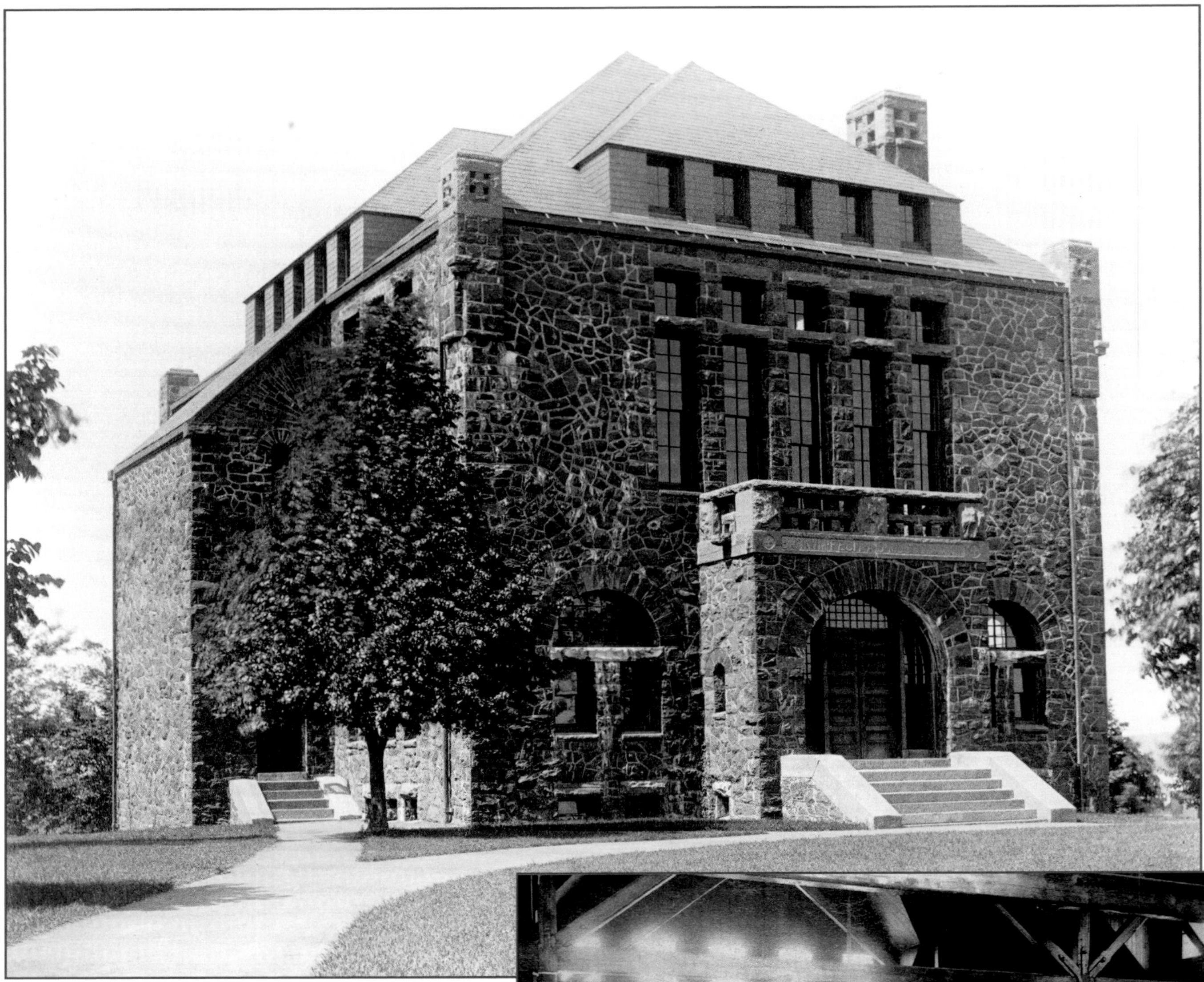

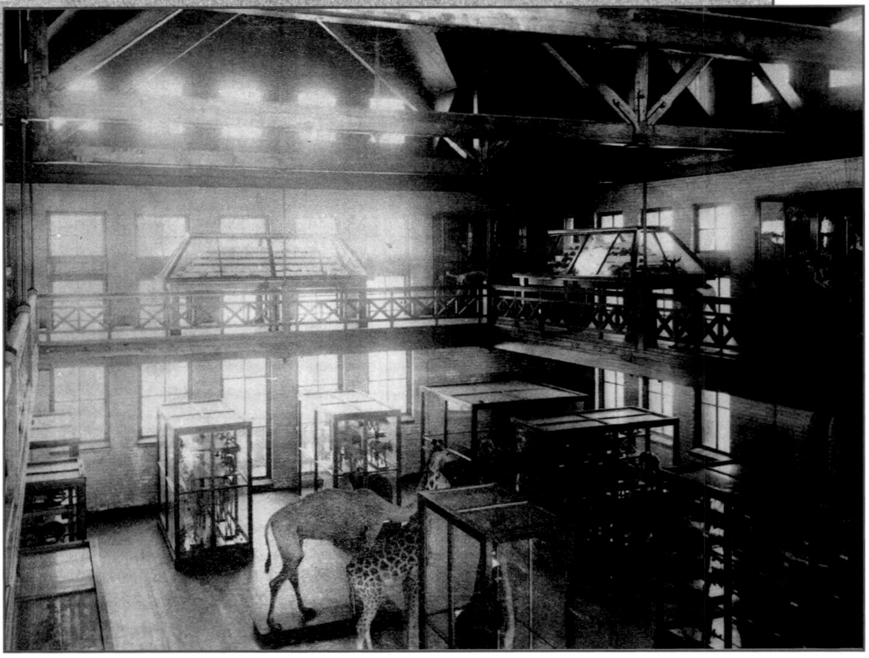

ABOVE
figure 121
Barnum Museum, Tufts College, 1887. The museum opened in 1884.

RIGHT
figure 122
Barnum Museum exhibits, Tufts College, 1930. Tufts boasted one of the best collections of mounted animal specimens on the East Coast until it was dispersed in the late 1930s.

FACING PAGE, ABOVE
figure 123
Reverend Elmer Hewitt Capen, president of Tufts College, ca. 1884. Capen persuaded Barnum to give money for a new science building as part of a campus-expansion campaign in the 1880s.

FACING PAGE, BELOW
figure 124
Specimen cases, Barnum Museum, ca. 1920

JUMBO COMES TO TUFTS

AS IT HAPPENED, BARNUM'S ASSOCIATION WITH MUSEUMS WAS NOT OVER. IN 1883 HE HAD agreed to pay for a new museum of natural history, complete with science facilities, at Tufts College in Medford, Massachusetts. Barnum's museum was conceived as part of a campaign to expand the Tufts campus during the transformational presidency of the Reverend Elmer Hewitt Capen, from 1875 to 1905 (fig. 123). When Tufts was founded in 1852, all functions—from library and lecture room to student dormitory and faculty offices—were concentrated in a single building on a hill offering a vista of downtown Boston. The gradual addition of new residence halls around a fledgling quadrangle allowed for growth in the student body, but core facilities were still lacking. Acknowledging an increasingly competitive educational environment, Capen told his trustees: "We must be progressive and aggressive if we expect Tufts College to maintain the rank it has gained among New England institutions." In his inaugural address in 1875, he identified a new library, gymnasium, chapel, and science building as top priorities, and he set out to find willing benefactors. In hopes of funding a new science building, Capen reached out to Barnum.

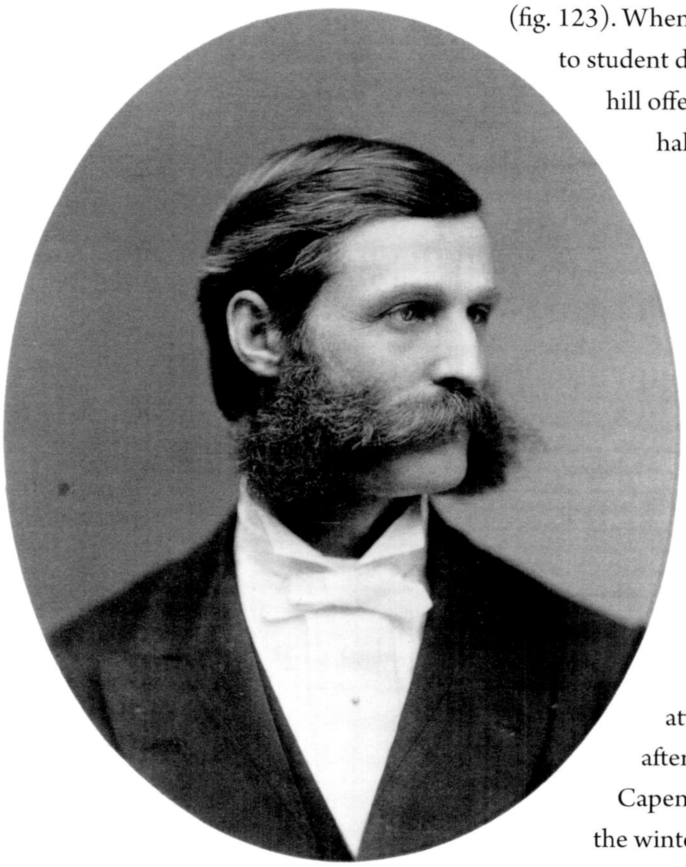

Barnum (see fig. 1) was an obvious target for Capen's capital campaign. A lifelong supporter of the Unitarian Universalist faith with which Tufts was affiliated, Barnum had agreed to be one of the college's founding trustees. Though his booming career prevented him from attending trustees' meetings and compelled him to resign from the board after five years of service, he continued to follow Tufts' progress with interest. Capen may also have known that Barnum had suffered a near-fatal illness during the winter of 1880–81 that left him feeling disposed to charitable giving. He confessed at the time that he "could hardly recall a benefit I had rendered to my fellow-man." Flushed with the nostalgia of advancing age and the desire to be remembered for good works, he bestowed an elaborate public fountain on Bethel, Connecticut, the town of his birth. Rumors about his will and net worth began circulating. Capen hoped the wealthy showman's generosity would extend to Tufts.

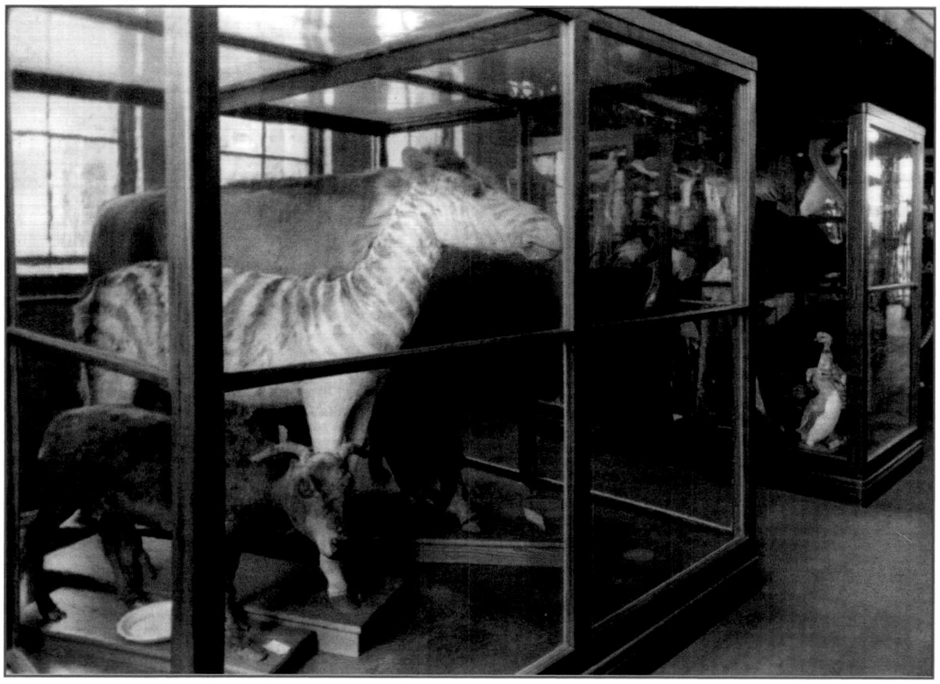

Capen's efforts were quickly rewarded. By May 1883, Barnum had committed to give $30,000 for a new building, on two conditions. First, fearing news of his gift would unleash ill feeling

ABOVE
figure 125
Professor John Marshall, 1879. Marshall was Tufts' first professor of geology and chemistry and served as curator of the Barnum Museum until his retirement from the faculty in 1898.

BELOW
figure 126
Letter from P. T. Barnum to John Marshall concerning the transfer of Jumbo to Tufts, dated March 27, 1889. In typical fashion, Barnum keeps open the possibility that he might want to borrow Jumbo again.

FACING PAGE
figure 127
Moving Jumbo into the Barnum Museum, 1889. When Jumbo arrived at the museum, he was too big to fit through the entrance, requiring the removal of the steps and dismantling of the stone arch.

THE WHOLE WORLD IN CONTRIBUTION. HONORABLY CONDUCTED. TRUTHFUL, MORAL, INSTRUCTIVE. ENTIRELY NEW, LARGER & BETTER THAN EVER BEFORE. HONESTLY PRESENTED.
P. T. BARNUM'S GREATEST SHOW ON EARTH. THE GREAT LONDON CIRCUS. BARNUM & BAILEY 15 UNITED SHOWS. SANGER'S ROYAL BRITISH MENAGERIES. INTERNATIONAL ALLIED SHOWS. PARIS OLYMPIA HIPPODROME.
3 CIRCUSES IN 3 RINGS. REMODELED ROMAN HIPPODROME. IMMENSE ELEVATED STAGE. MAMMOTH HORSE FAIR. RARE AQUATIC SPORTS. HUGE AQUARIUM. EXCITING ATHLETIC GAMES. MUSEUM OF MARVELOUS WONDERS. 2 MENAGERIES IN 2 TENTS. ALL KINDS OF THRILLING RACES. REALISTIC WILD WEST. EXTENSIVE AVIARY.
GRAND MONSTER WORLD'S FAIR. P. T. BARNUM, J. A. BAILEY, EQUAL OWNERS. GIGANTIC AGGREGATION OF LIVING CURIOSITIES.
40 SUPERNATURAL ILLUSIONS
AVERAGE DAILY EXPENSES $6,800. CAPITAL INVESTED $3,000,000.
640 People ~ 380 Horses ~ 64 Cars ~ 4 Trains.
Permanent Winter Quarters, BRIDGEPORT, CONN. LONDON OFFICE, 57 Charing Cross. BUSINESS OFFICES, Madison Square Garden, NEW YORK.

Murray Hill Hotel New York March 27 1889

Dear Prof Marshall — After "much tribulation" we have arranged with R. Roads, & Jumbo will reach North Somerville probably Friday 29th or Saturday. So please arrange to have him taken from car on arrival, so that our man can return with the car immediately. The Museum here holds the skeleton subject to our order — although I see that newspapers announce I have given it to them. This was without our knowledge, but perhaps it does no harm — I have it in writing that it is held subject to our order. The same must be done in regard to the Barnum Museum. We may never call for it — & yet we may possibly (though not probably) take our big show to England next fall & return following spring. In such an event we should want Jumbo's skin if only temporarily. In announcing that you have Jumbo, better let the "Barnum Museum of Natural History" stick out plainly & emphatically. Truly Yours P. T. Barnum

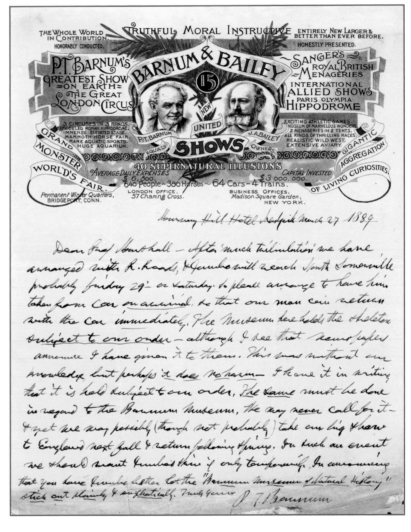

among heirs and "begging letters" from other good causes, he asked that the gift be kept secret, even from his wife, for as long as possible. Second, he insisted that once his identity as donor was disclosed, the building should "be forever called the Barnum Museum of Natural History." Perhaps realizing that his two wishes were somewhat inconsistent, he soon allowed self-promotion to trump discretion and asked that his name appear above the door, and his portrait at the entrance. "You see the passion for display is 'strong in death,'" he confessed. Mindful of his mortality, he pressed Capen for prompt action: "The quicker you get at it and the faster you drive it, the better I shall like it. Life is short."

Barnum was surely also mindful of his posthumous reputation. Sponsorship of a serious museum of natural history affiliated with a Universalist college compensated for a life in show business associated with hoaxes and mass entertainment. To be fair, Barnum had long demonstrated a genuine interest in natural history. He had always insisted that his early museum displays and menageries imparted "more valuable information in two hours than can be obtained from reading books on zoology in a year." He was an early supporter of, and contributor to, both the Smithsonian Institution in Washington, D.C. (founded 1846; National Museum opened 1881; National Zoo, 1889) and the American Museum of Natural History in New York (founded 1869). Both institutions relied on circuses and menageries as a chief source of exotic animal specimens for their taxidermy displays, and Barnum was especially generous. His generosity would continue with his new museum at Tufts.

Construction of the museum proceeded quickly once Barnum's gift was in hand. By June 1884 the building was ready for dedication (fig. 121). Designed by the architect John Philipp Rinn, the Barnum Museum rose two stories above a basement level fitted with a laboratory and lecture room. The ground floor included a library and vestibule, complete with Thomas Ball's marble bust of Barnum. The upper floor featured a well-lighted grand hall with mezzanine intended for the display of natural history specimens, mostly displayed in wood-and-glass cabinets (figs. 122, 124). On the eve of the building's completion, the university magazine asserted: "It will be equaled by few museums in the country either in point of size or elegance." Together with the new chapel, also designed by Rinn and built of local blue stone, the new museum flanked the original college building and gave the campus an increased sense of coherence and stature. Ill health prevented Barnum from attending commencement ceremonies in 1884, and from inaugurating his building in person, but he sent comments to be read, expressing hope that the museum would prove "another factor in the work of the College, helping it on its high career of usefulness."

Once the Barnum Museum was ready for occupation, attention turned to building the collection, under the supervision of John P. Marshall (1832–1901), Tufts' first professor of geology and chemistry (fig. 125). Following an approach taken at other American colleges, Marshall had been assembling an eclectic collection of minerals, fossils, and ethnological material since the 1850s, mostly through random gifts. Marshall's ambition for the new museum, supported by Barnum, was to amass a comprehensive display of natural history. In keeping with pre-Darwinian notions of science, an orderly arrangement of animals and plants would yield knowledge of and mastery over the natural world. It would also reveal, as Barnum himself put it, "the infinite wisdom and power of the Creator." In other words, nineteenth-century museums of natural history had both a scientific and a theological purpose, suited to the moral and intellectual formation of young men and women.

From the 1880s, Barnum gave Tufts first right of refusal on animals that had died in the circus. Those Tufts did not want were offered, as before, to the Smithsonian or the museum in New York on the condition that they give Tufts something in exchange, either another animal or a plaster cast of something valuable from their collection. Whatever the ultimate destination, all but a few of Barnum's dead animals were sent to Ward's Establishment in Rochester for preparation (he sent the occasional one to John Wallace in New York City in an attempt to keep Ward's prices down). Henry Ward supplied museums not only with stuffed animals but also with geologic samples, as well as glass models of plants and invertebrates made by Leopold and Rudolf Blaschka of Dresden (the creators of the famous glass-flower collection at Harvard). By his own account he assembled natural history collections for over two hundred American institutions, including numerous colleges and universities. One of Ward's important disciples, William T. Hornaday, said of him that he had done "more to inspire, to build up, and to fill up American museums than any other ten men of his time or since his time. But for him, our American museums would never have forged ahead as they did from 1870 to 1890." The bulk of the Tufts museum collection, totaling several hundred animals and more than a hundred shells, corrals, and Blaschka glass invertebrates, came from Ward.

As early as July 1883, Barnum had persuaded his partners to give Jumbo to Tufts once the elephant died. Whether Tufts would receive Jumbo's skin or skeleton he did not say—perhaps it had yet to occur to him that he might have two Jumbos to dispose of. A year later he wrote to Spencer Baird, secretary of the Smithsonian: "[We] think Jumbo's skin or skeleton should go to your Institution, you taking your choice, and then the 'Barnum' Museum at Tufts College take the other. … P.S. We hope however that Jumbo may yet live many years, but think it as well to decide now as ever where he shall be distributed when he ceases to breathe."

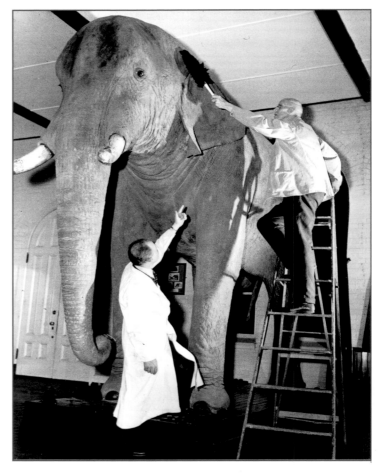

By the end of 1884, Barnum had made up his mind that the Smithsonian would get the skeleton, and Tufts the mounted hide. This was understood by John Marshall, who wrote to Henry Ward: "We fully expect to have the skin of Jumbo when he

ABOVE
figure 128
Jumbo on display at the Barnum Museum, 1889

BELOW
figure 129
Professor Russell L. Carpenter with unidentified man cleaning Jumbo, 1942. Carpenter joined the Tufts faculty in 1938, cleared Barnum Hall of the animal specimens, and created a student lounge dedicated to Jumbo and P. T. Barnum.

dies. ... I should not consider the Barnum Museum complete without this noble animal. It would be the greatest ornament that we could place in the Vestibule, near Mr. Barnum's bust." The showman's commitment to Tufts never wavered, but he was in no rush to deliver on his promise. As we have seen, he and his partners thought there was perhaps as much value in showing Jumbo dead as alive. Barnum estimated that the elephant was "worth $100,000 or more per year for exhibition in our show," and neither museum could expect delivery so long as Jumbo brought in good money. Finally, in the spring of 1889, after exhibiting Jumbo's hide for three seasons, Barnum was ready to part with it. On March 18 he wrote to Marshall: "If you and Pres't Capen think that the mounted skin of Jumbo put in Barnum Museum now—to remain till wanted—perhaps not for years and possibly never—will help the College—I will send it to you at my own expense ... if you will place it at once on exhibition in Museum, get it into Boston Newspapers and keep it clean and safe." After further correspondence Jumbo arrived at North Somerville station on April 3 and was taken by horse-drawn cart to the Tufts campus (fig. 126). The horse was unable to haul his load up the hill to the museum, and a group of some fifty professors, students, and neighborhood boys was quickly assembled to complete the job. When Jumbo arrived at the entrance to the museum it was discovered that he was too big to get through the door; the stone steps, brick flooring, and part of the door frame had to be removed (fig. 127). Barnum wrote to Marshall, saying he hoped "the trouble you have had in putting Jumbo in place will be more than compensated in the advertisement it will give Tufts College." No doubt much to Marshall's dismay, he added that the circus might need Jumbo again for its planned run in London later in the year. Sure enough, come autumn, Barnum called for Jumbo, and the bother of dismantling the entrance had to be repeated. He was returned to Tufts in March 1890, but again Barnum warned Marshall, "Glad you have Jumbo again. Perhaps he will remain always, but as he speaks all languages he may possibly in future years go around the world."

ABOVE
figure 130
Elephant group in Akeley Hall, American Museum of Natural History, New York, 2012. Carl Akeley's great career as a taxidermist began with Jumbo and culminated with the famous elephant group in the hall of mammals that bears his name.

BELOW
figure 131
Old Neptune on display at the New Bedford Whaling Museum, 2014. One of the few surviving stuffed animals from the Barnum Museum, Old Neptune appeared, as a live sea lion, at Barnum's American Museum in the 1860s.

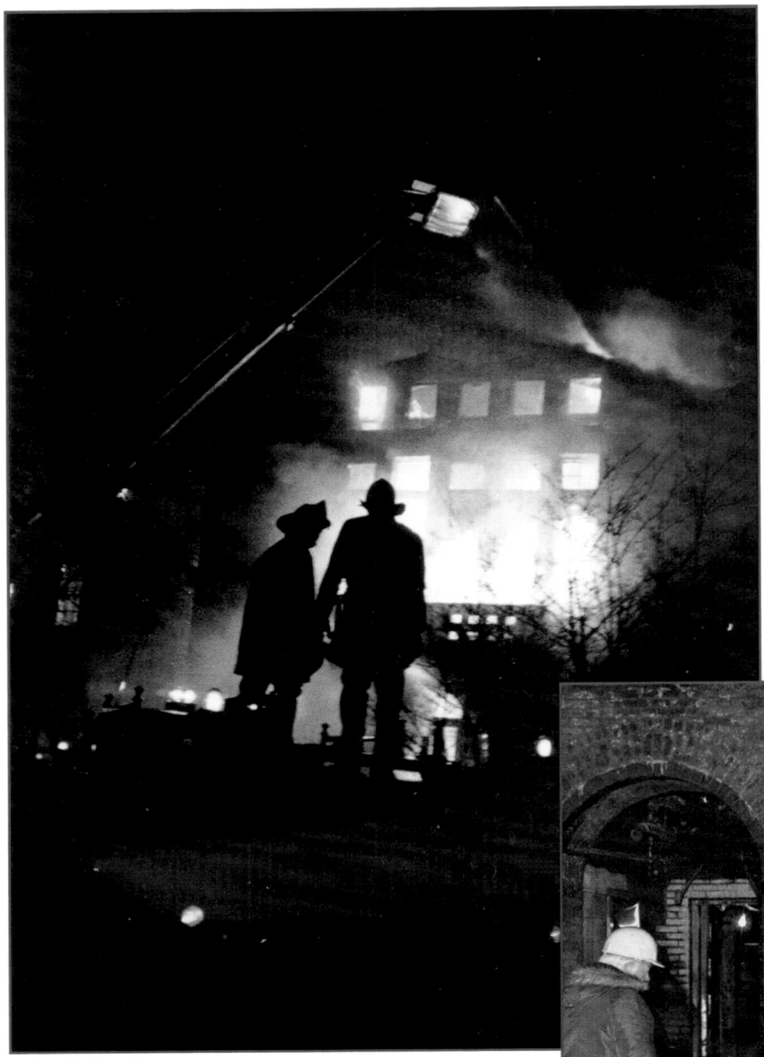

LEFT
figure 132
Barnum Hall on fire, 1975. An electrical malfunction caused the fire that gutted the building and destroyed Jumbo.

BELOW
figure 133
Jumbo's remains after the fire, 1975. On the day after the fire, an employee gathered some of Jumbo's ashes into an empty peanut-butter jar.

FACING PAGE, ABOVE
figure 134
Jumbo's ashes in a peanut-butter jar, Tufts University. The ashes are kept in the Athletics Department and occasionally summoned to bring good luck to Tufts sports teams.

FACING PAGE, BELOW
figure 135
Jumbo's tail. Repeatedly tugged by students, Jumbo's tail was removed for safekeeping and survived the fire in 1975.

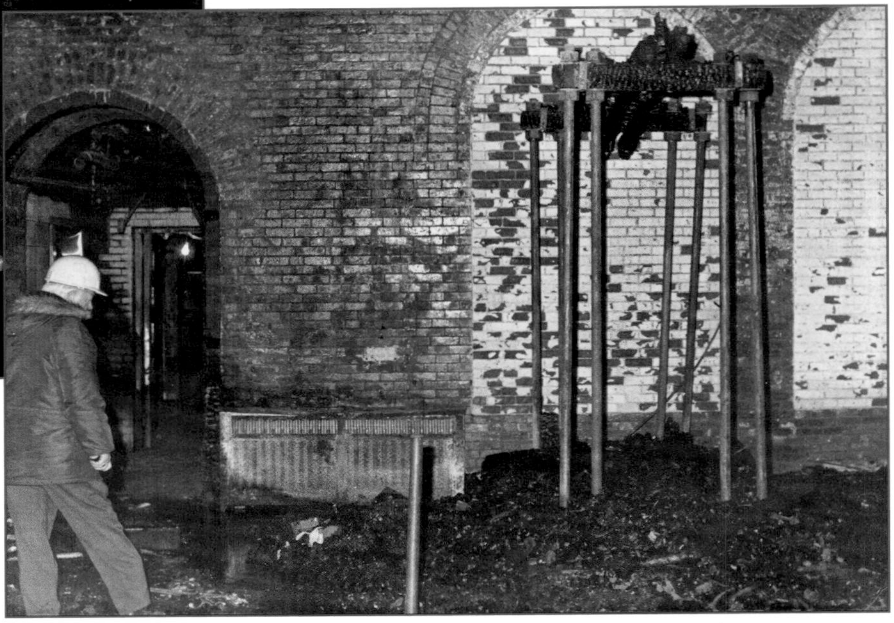

Jumbo's traveling days were indeed finally over, however, and he remained at Tufts (fig. 128). And whatever frustrations Marshall experienced dealing with Barnum, they were nothing compared to the tribulations endured by his counterparts in New York and Washington. From the beginning, Barnum had said that Jumbo's skeleton would go to the Smithsonian. The commitment was even inscribed on the tusk sections given to Secretary Henry and others (see figa. 114, 115). But relations between the showman and the Smithsonian deteriorated in the late 1880s, largely because the national museum repeatedly proved less generous than Barnum thought it should have been in providing materials to his museum at Tufts. His partners also preferred to see the skeleton go to New York, where the circus was based. In May 1887 he confided to John Marshall, "Entre-nous the Smithsonian has behaved so shabbily I hope Jumbo's skeleton will go to the NY Institution." In December he informed the American Museum of Natural History that the skeleton would come to it, and the exultant president of the museum invited Barnum to come and see it for himself: "I think you will be surprised & thoroughly pleased when you see his skeleton; it has been finely mounted, both as regards the body and the pedestal."

The museum at Tufts continued to prosper after Barnum's death in 1891. Barnum left the college a further $40,000 to build two new wings on to the museum, and new gifts were added to the collection. It continued to attract the public in healthy numbers—in the 1920s annual attendance was estimated at around 20,000. Over time, however, the collection of animal specimens aged and grew less vital to instruction in the life sciences as the discipline and its methodologies changed. Marshall's retirement in 1898 slowed further expansion, and his successors on the faculty came to the university with new and different priorities. The Barnum Museum was completed on the cusp of a revolution in scientific inquiry that, in the words of the historian Stephen Conn, "drew natural history into new areas of research, away from morphology and toward genetics, from whole organism biology into cellular biology," and consequently "from museum halls into university labs." At the Tufts museum, the two new wings Barnum intended for further specimens were instead used for classrooms and laboratories. Furthermore, as a museum display, the Tufts collection was gradually rendered old-fashioned by the evolution in taxidermy practice from static single specimens to dynamic habitat groups and dioramas. No one was more important in that development than Carl Akeley. The difference between his early work on Jumbo and his late masterpiece, the traveling elephant herd at the American Museum of Natural History (fig. 130), marks not only more advanced methods in taxidermy but also a shift in museum-based natural history from descriptive taxonomy to the study of animal behavior, habitat, and ecology.

In 1938, Russell L. Carpenter (fig. 129) joined the Tufts biology faculty and took over the museum. The museum had been closed to the public for some years, and Carpenter believed the space would better serve the needs of the university if it were converted to laboratories and classrooms. "Fifty years of sunlight, moths and the ravages of time have not dealt too kindly with some of the specimens," he wrote. "The lions have faded to a tawdry blondness, the zebra has stripes only on his shady side, and the giraffe split his seams some time ago. As a collection for public exhibition, it served its purpose for many years but I feel that its usefulness has passed." Some of the stuffed animals were given to Perry's Nut House in Maine, others were used as landfill in the new playing fields at Cousens Gym. One of the only specimens to survive, it seems, is the sea lion Old Neptune, who had once been exhibited, alive, at Barnum's American Museum (fig. 131). The Barnum Museum became Barnum Hall, and Carpenter redesigned the vestibule as a student lounge and shrine to Barnum and Jumbo. The mounted hide was restored and, freed of association with other natural history exhibits, gained a stronger profile as, in Carpenter's words, the "insignia and symbol of Tufts."

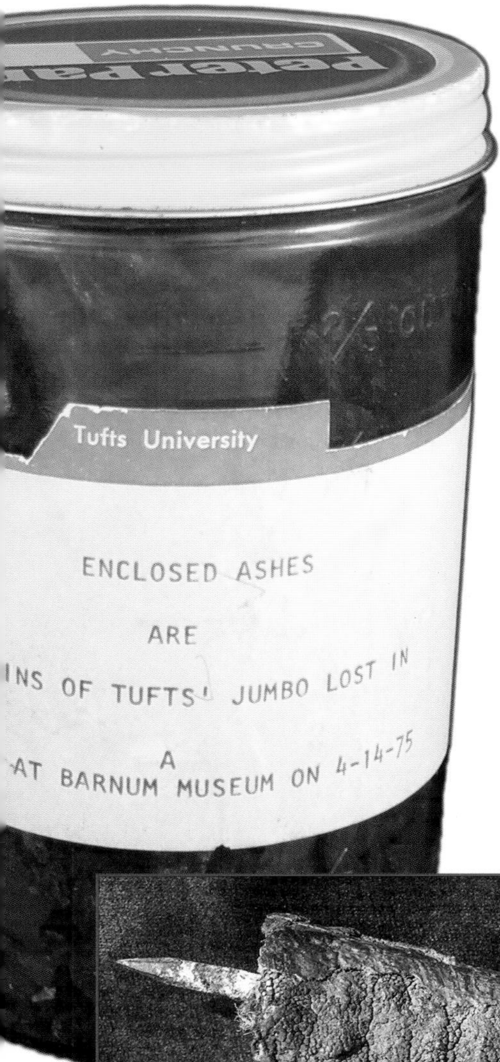
Tufts University
ENCLOSED ASHES
ARE
OF TUFTS' JUMBO LOST IN
A
AT BARNUM MUSEUM ON 4-14-75

Jumbo stood tall on the Tufts campus until, like the earlier museums, the last of Barnum's museums went up in flames: a fire destroyed the Barnum building and its contents on an April night in 1975 (figs. 132, 133). The morning after the fire, an employee entered the ruins and gathered some of Jumbo's ashes in an empty peanut-butter jar. Today, those ashes, kept in the Athletics Department and still in their makeshift urn, are brought out to inspire the Tufts sports teams that bear Jumbo's name (fig. 134). All that remains of Jumbo, apart from the ashes, is his tail, which had been removed for safekeeping many years before after being pulled one too many times by students seeking good luck in exams (fig. 135).

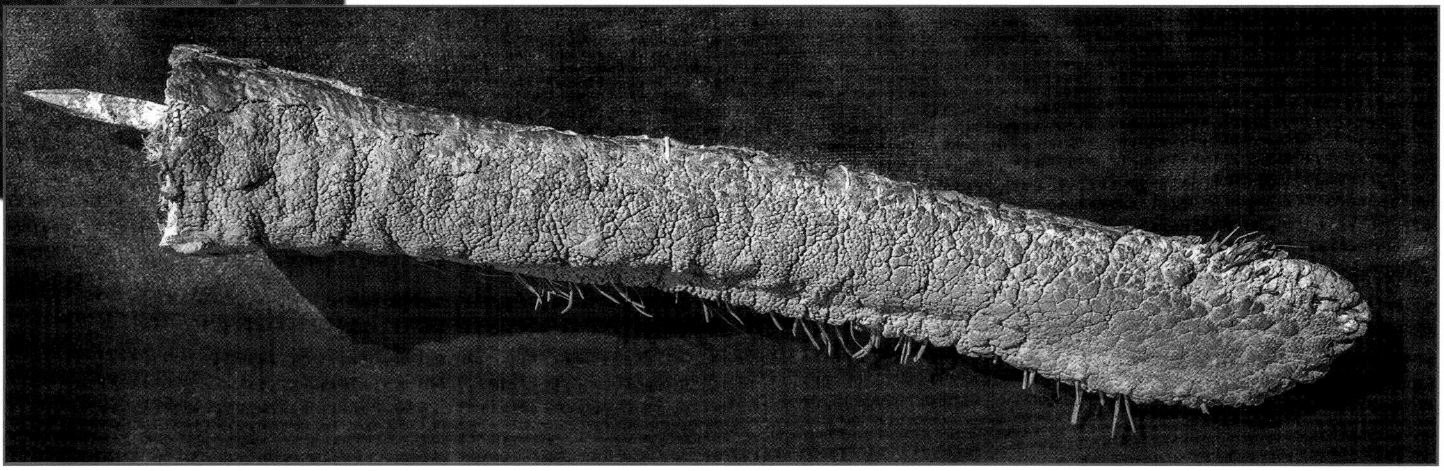

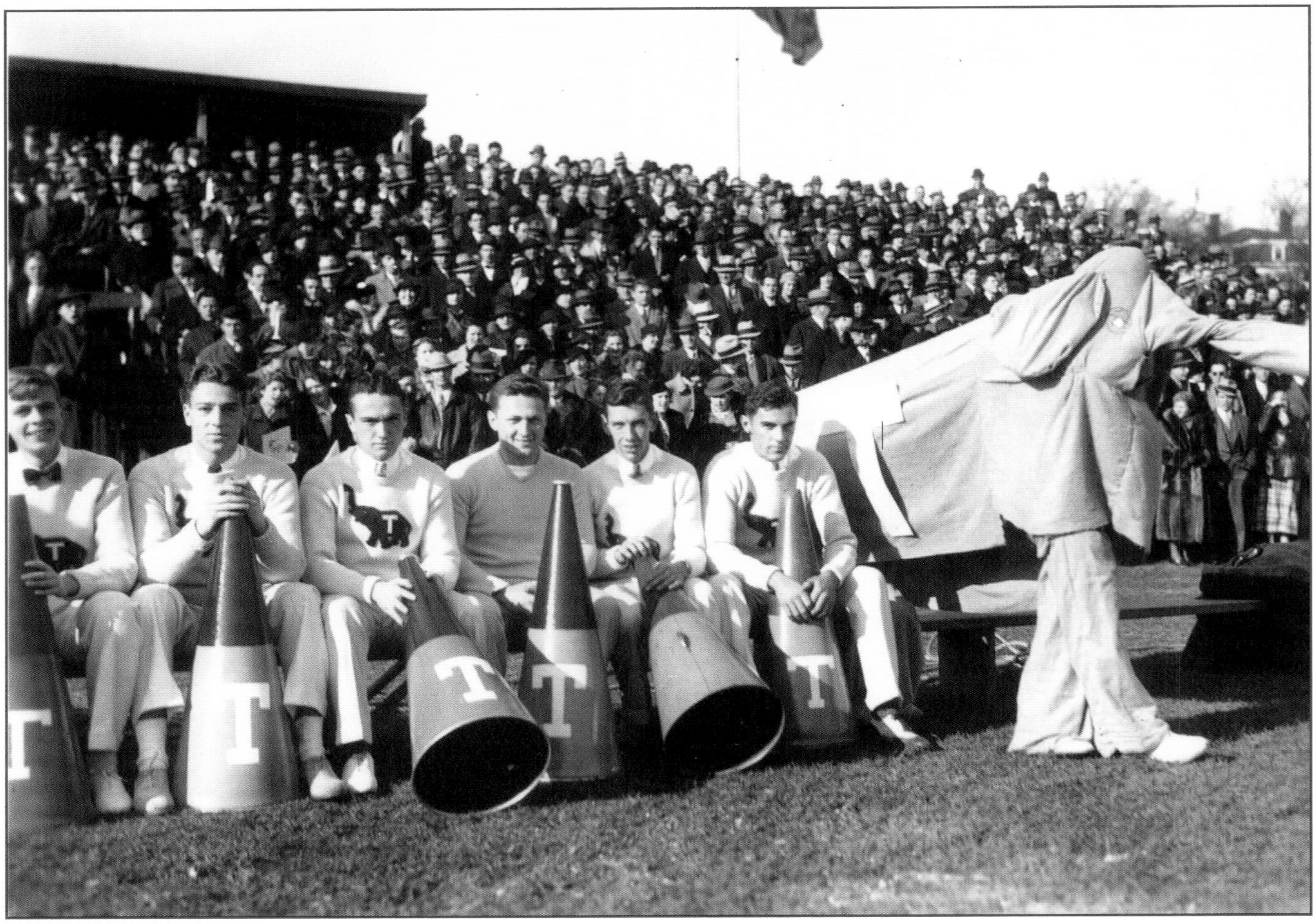

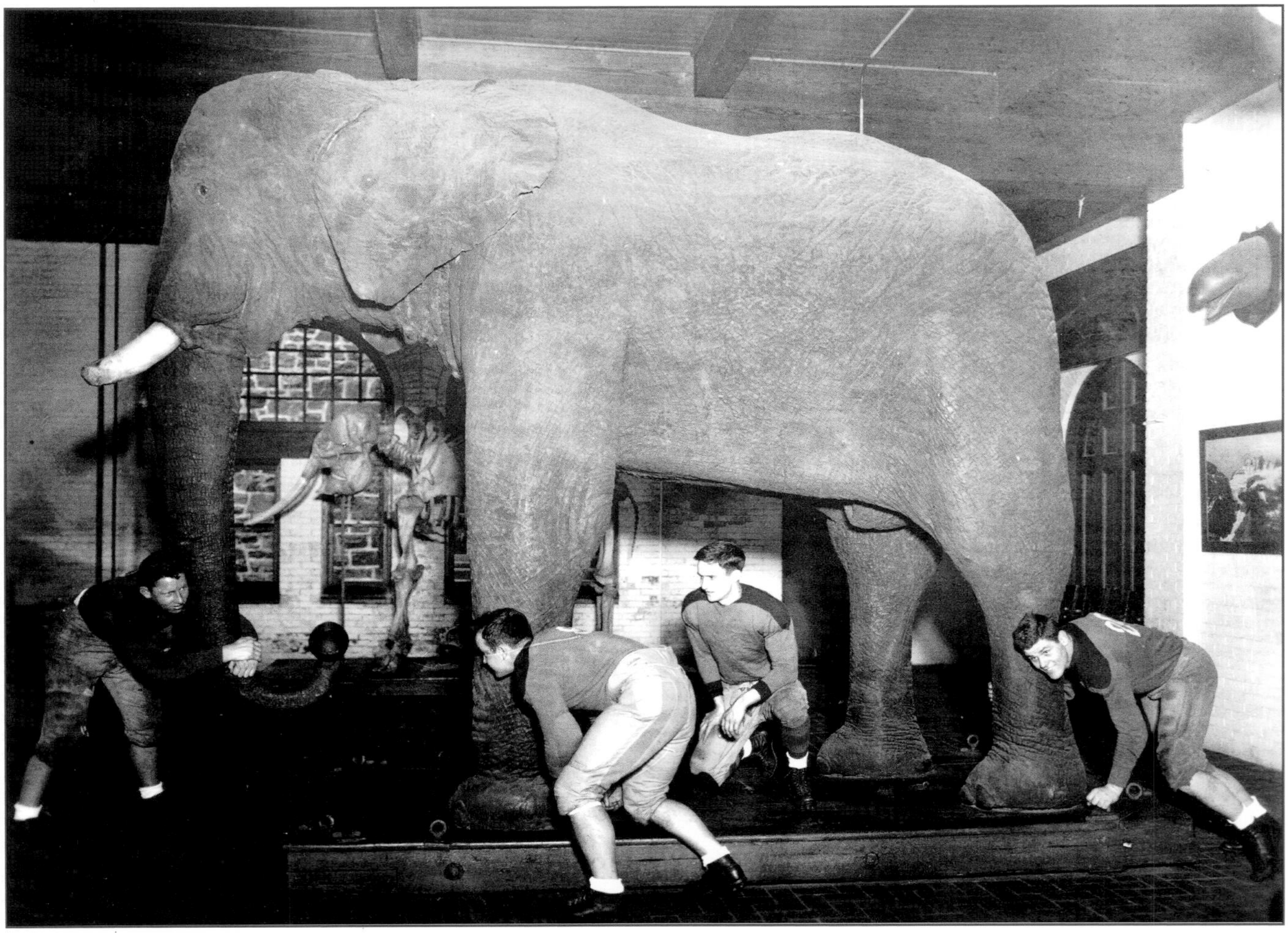

As was the case with mascots at other American colleges, Jumbo's emergence as a school symbol at Tufts was gradual, student-driven, and fueled by the growth of intercollegiate sports beginning in the late nineteenth century. Students were evidently delighted with the arrival of Jumbo's mounted hide—an early Tufts song, "The Jumbo Cantepic," by E. W. Newton, welcomed the famous pachyderm to campus in 1889–90 with the opening line: "Hail to the king of the elephants!" His presence in the Barnum Museum is noted in early yearbooks and chronicles of Tufts but without any mention of him as the college mascot. In a history of club sports at Tufts, Judge Edward Shea says that school teams were first known as the Medford Hillsiders.

Jumbo at Portland

Following Jumbo's arrival on campus in 1889, "teams were interchangeably known as the Hillsiders or the Jumbos until the early 20th century, when Jumbos became the preferred moniker." The usage was clearly informal, as team uniforms during the early decades sported merely a T, for Tufts, and Jumbo's name and image were nowhere to be seen. But around the field of play, if not on it, the elephant's identity as the team mascot soon acquired greater prominence. A photograph from 1913 (fig. 138) shows a pair of students in a Jumbo costume bound for Maine to support Tufts in a football match against Bowdoin College. Later photographs indicate that Jumbo's effigy became a regular fixture on the sidelines of football games by the 1920s, and his image drifted onto cheerleaders' apparel (fig. 136). In 1921 a Jumbo Cheer was printed for student use: "Jumbo Rah! Rah! / Jumbo Rah! Rah! / Y-e-e-e-h Bo / Tufts! Tufts! Tufts!" The 1935 football team posed with the real Jumbo as if he were a field-practice prop (fig. 137).

The women athletes of Jackson College (the women's college within Tufts) also adopted Jumbo's likeness as their

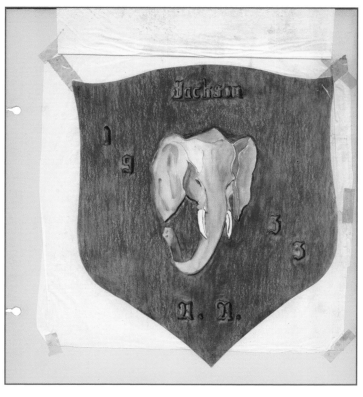

FACING PAGE, ABOVE
figure 136
The Whooperuppers and Jumbo at the Homecoming Day game, ca. 1930

FACING PAGE, BELOW
figure 137
Football players with Jumbo, 1935

THIS PAGE, ABOVE
figure 138
Students in a Jumbo costume accompanying the Tufts football team to a match against Bowdoin College in 1913. This photograph documents an early appearance of Jumbo as the Tufts mascot.

THIS PAGE, RIGHT
figure 139
Shield with Jumbo design for the Jackson College Athletic Association, 1933

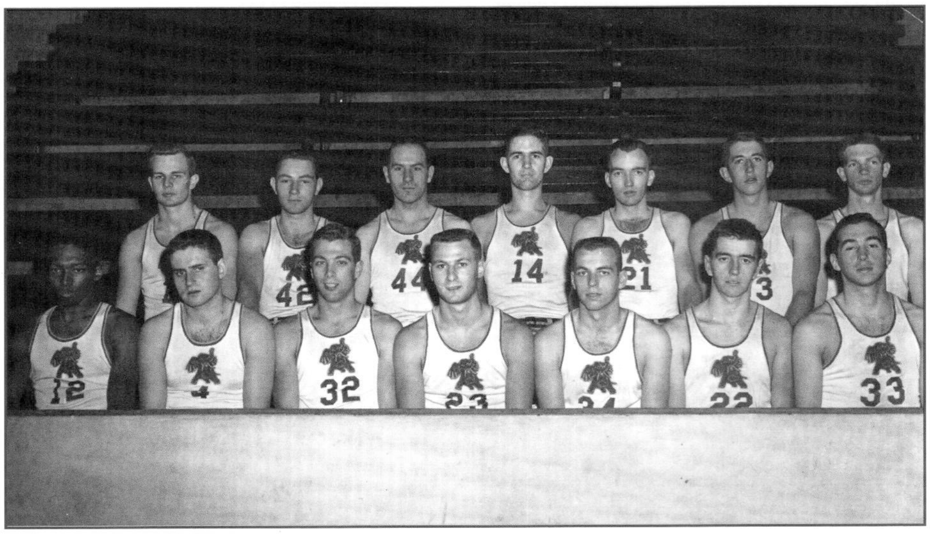

LEFT
figure 140
Tufts men's basketball team, ca. 1950. It seems this team was among the first to sport a Jumbo logo on its uniform.

BELOW LEFT
figure 141
Jumbo logo, 1985. The logo has been redesigned over the years in keeping with changing fashions.

BELOW RIGHT
figure 142
Jumbo logo, 1993

FACING PAGE, BELOW
figure 143
Jumbo logo, 2005. The newest logo was designed by NFL Properties, which designs all logos for teams in the National Football League.

symbol, as we see in a 1933 watercolor design for a shield or patch (fig. 139). When Jumbo's image first figured on a team uniform is unclear. By 1950 his head was on both the shorts and the shirts of the men's basketball team (fig. 140). Thereafter the Jumbo logo spread to other uniforms. Over the decades the logo has been redesigned in keeping with shifting fashions (figs. 141–143). Most recently, in 2005, thanks to alumni connections to the New England Patriots football team, the creative team at NFL Properties gave Jumbo a new and bolder look (fig. 143). This rebranding followed on the heels of belated official recognition of Jumbo as the mascot of the university, by unanimous vote of the trustees on May 28, 2004—a gesture that seems to have further encouraged the dissemination of his likeness across a wide range of Tufts products and venues beyond the playing fields in Medford.

Jumbo's identity as mascot was never exclusively associated with sports, however. The photographic record shows Jumbo's image and name being mobilized, from the first decades of twentieth century, in various settings and for different causes. In fact, the earliest photograph we have of his likeness deployed on campus is of a 1910 reunion of the Class of 1908, when the entrance to Goddard Gymnasium was draped in American-flag bunting in the shape of Jumbo's head to greet returning alumni (fig. 144).

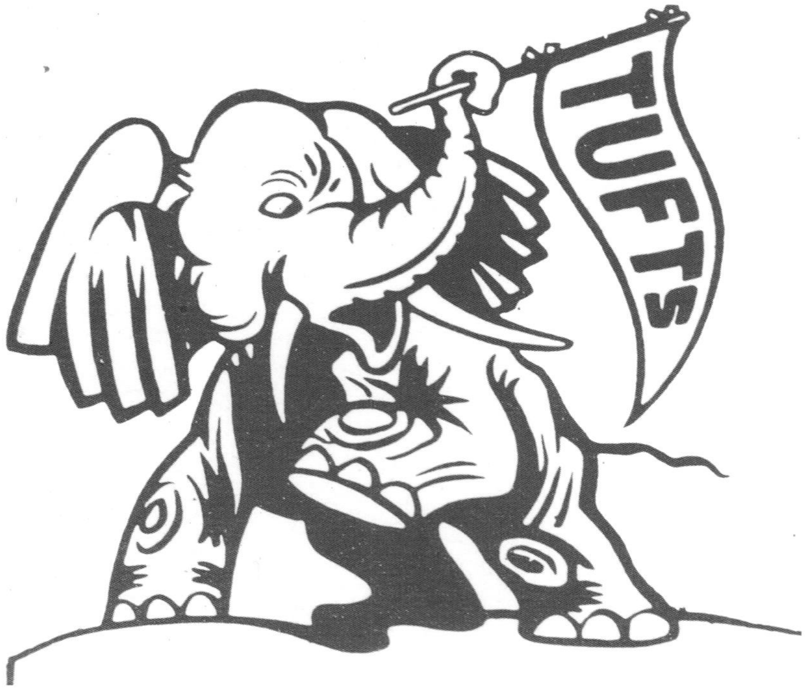
TUFTS

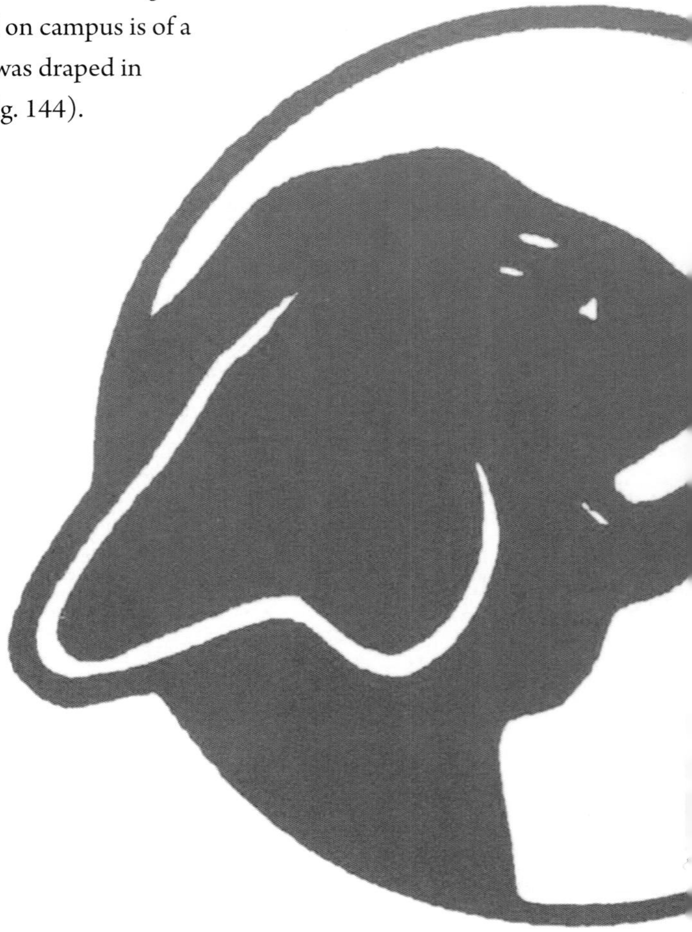

In 1917 students creatively referenced the publication of the yearbook, named *The Jumbo*, by positioning their bodies to form letters spelling out his name (figs. 145–150). Five years later, the Tufts administration appropriated his image to advertise a dance intended to raise money for the university's endowment (fig. 154). By this time (if not sooner) students had begun posing with stuffed Jumbo in ways that make it clear he was regarded as more than a museum specimen (fig. 152). In the mid-1920s the student jazz band, the Jumbonians, put the college mascot on their bass drum (fig. 153).

ABOVE
figure 144
Jumbo American-flag bunting decorating the entrance to Goddard Gymnasium, ca. 1910. This photograph records an early use of the mascot's image for festive purposes.

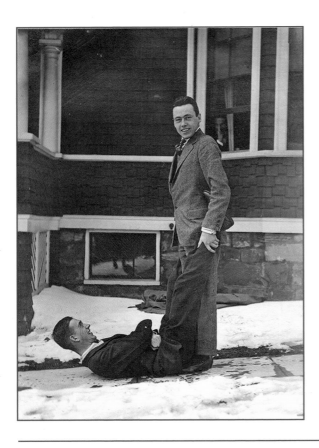

figures 145–150
Students pose as letters to spell out "Jumbo," to advertise the *Jumbo* yearbook, 1917

BELOW
figure 151
An unidentified woman holds a dedicatory plaque bearing Jumbo's image, made for the cargo ship SS *Tufts Victory*, 1945. The tusk piece on the plaque was taken from Jumbo's mounted hide in Ballou Hall.

As mentioned above, the clearing of the Barnum Museum around 1940 seems to have further cemented Jumbo's identity as Tufts' mascot. When the cargo ship SS *Tufts Victory* was launched in 1945 it carried a dedicatory plaque showing Jumbo in profile, complete with an ivory sliver taken from the mounted hide in Medford (fig. 151). After the war, the new lounge in Barnum Hall fashioned by Russell Carpenter became a popular meeting place for students; publicity photographs show students relaxing in the company of the motionless pachyderm (see fig. 2). The frequent disappearance of attractive Wedgwood Jumbo ashtrays made for the lounge reveals a desire for tangible souvenirs of the beloved mascot. Rituals involving the mounted hide—notably the placing of pennies in the trunk for good luck in exams (fig. 155)—developed into fond traditions (in the 1960s, according to at least one alum, pennies were offered for good fortune in love as well as in letters). In a sign of Jumbo's full adoption as cherished icon, fraternities represented the elephant as one of their own in the form of playfully irreverent snow sculptures (fig. 156).

Ephemeral student works and cuddly gridiron companions (fig. 157) fired school spirit and kept Jumbo as a mascot fresh for new generations of Tufts students. In recent decades, Jumbo's

FACING PAGE, LEFT
figure 152
Jackson students posing with Jumbo, November 25, 1933. From the 1920s, if not sooner, students began posing for photographs with Jumbo.

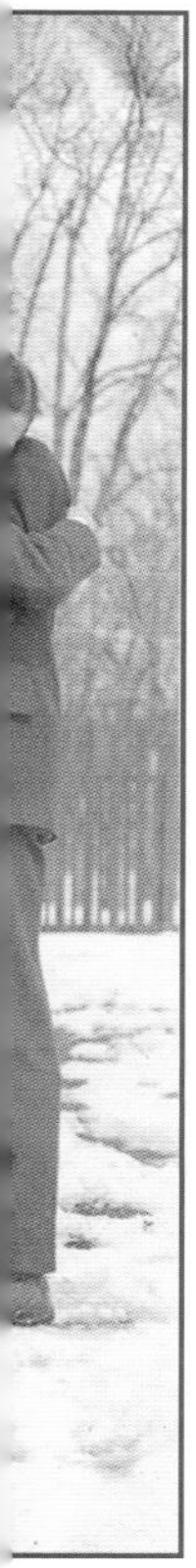

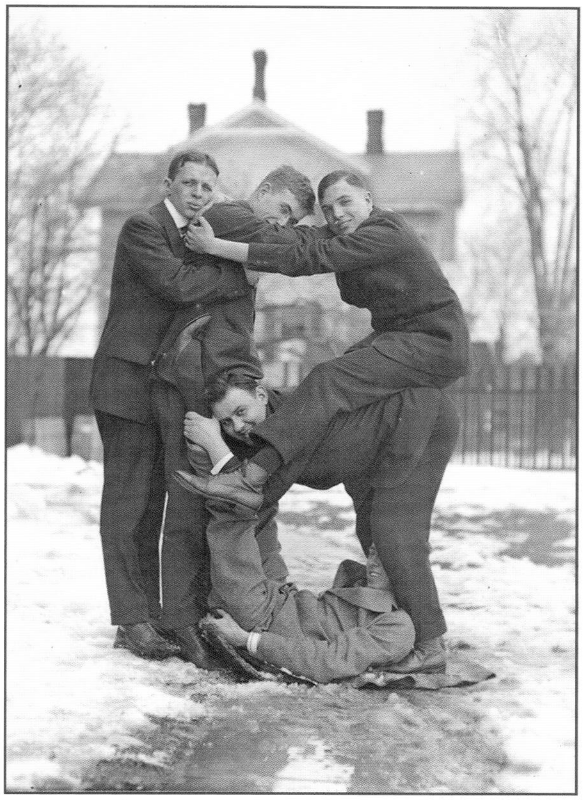

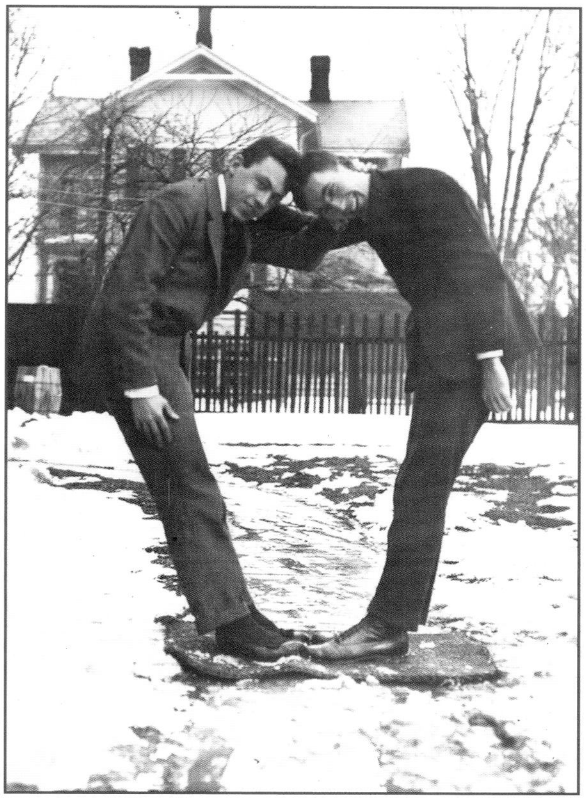

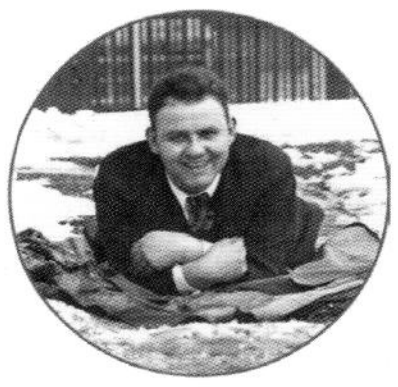

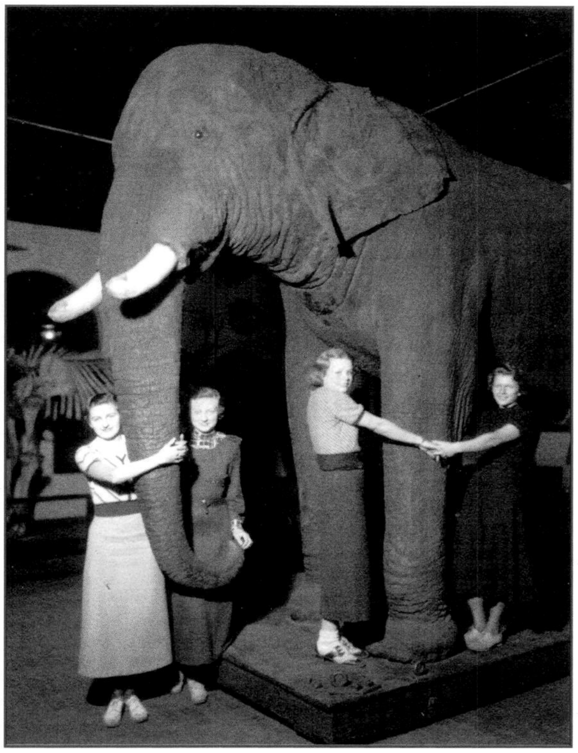

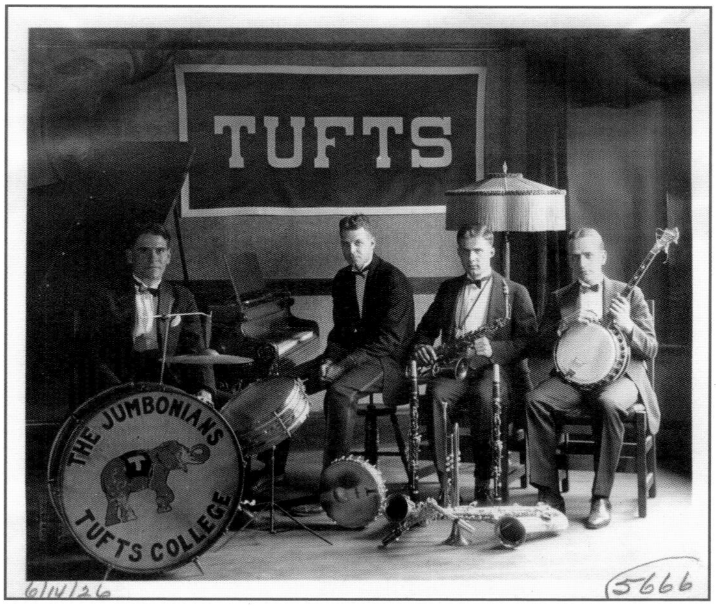
TUFTS
THE JUMBONIANS
TUFTS COLLEGE
6/14/26
5666

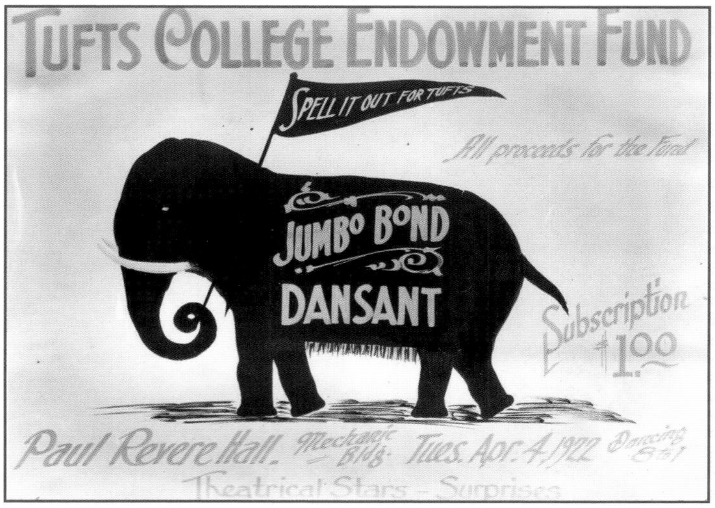
TUFTS COLLEGE ENDOWMENT FUND
SPELL IT OUT FOR TUFTS
All proceeds for the Fund
JUMBO BOND
DANSANT
Subscription $1.00
Paul Revere Hall. Mechanic
Tues. Apr. 4, 1922
Theatrical Stars - Surprises

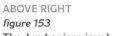

ABOVE RIGHT
figure 153
The Jumbonians jazz band, 1926

BELOW RIGHT
figure 154
Advertisement for a dance raising money for the Tufts endowment fund, 1922. Jumbo's popularity as the college mascot spread beyond the sphere of organized sports.

increasing prominence as a school symbol has been reflected in the addition of more permanent sculptures to the Medford campus. To commemorate its fiftieth reunion in 1965, the Class of 1915 gave a bronze elephant fountain by the Swedish artist Carl Milles to decorate the forecourt of the new Wessell (now Tisch) Library. In 1993 the Class of 1958 presented a cement elephant (demolished 2014) that had come from Benson's Wild Animal Farm, a private zoo and amusement park in New Hampshire. And, at the turn of the new millennium, the local artist Robert Shure created a full-tusked bronze elephant head for the entrance of Dowling Hall. Strangely, perhaps, none of these sculptures accurately represented Jumbo. To fill that void and to commemorate the 125th anniversary of Jumbo's arrival on the Tufts campus, the California-based artist Steven Whyte has created a life-size bronze portrait of the famous pachyderm (fig. 158), generously funded by the alumni Dick Reynolds (Class of '67) and Richard (Class of '53) and Sheila Asher. Whyte's sculpture, based on the popular 1882 photograph of Jumbo at the London zoo (see fig. 32), stands in front of Ballou Hall, just steps away from where the mounted hide inspired students for close to a century.

ABOVE LEFT

figure 155

Tufts students (Judy Tarentino, Linda Haarala [?], and Dorothy Campbell) with Jumbo, ca. 1954. Students placed pennies in Jumbo's trunk for good luck in exams.

ABOVE RIGHT

figure 156

Jumbo snow sculpture at the Zeta Psi fraternity on Professsor's Row, 1950

ABOVE

figure 157

Homecoming Queen Jean Harrison poses with Jumbo, October 23, 1965

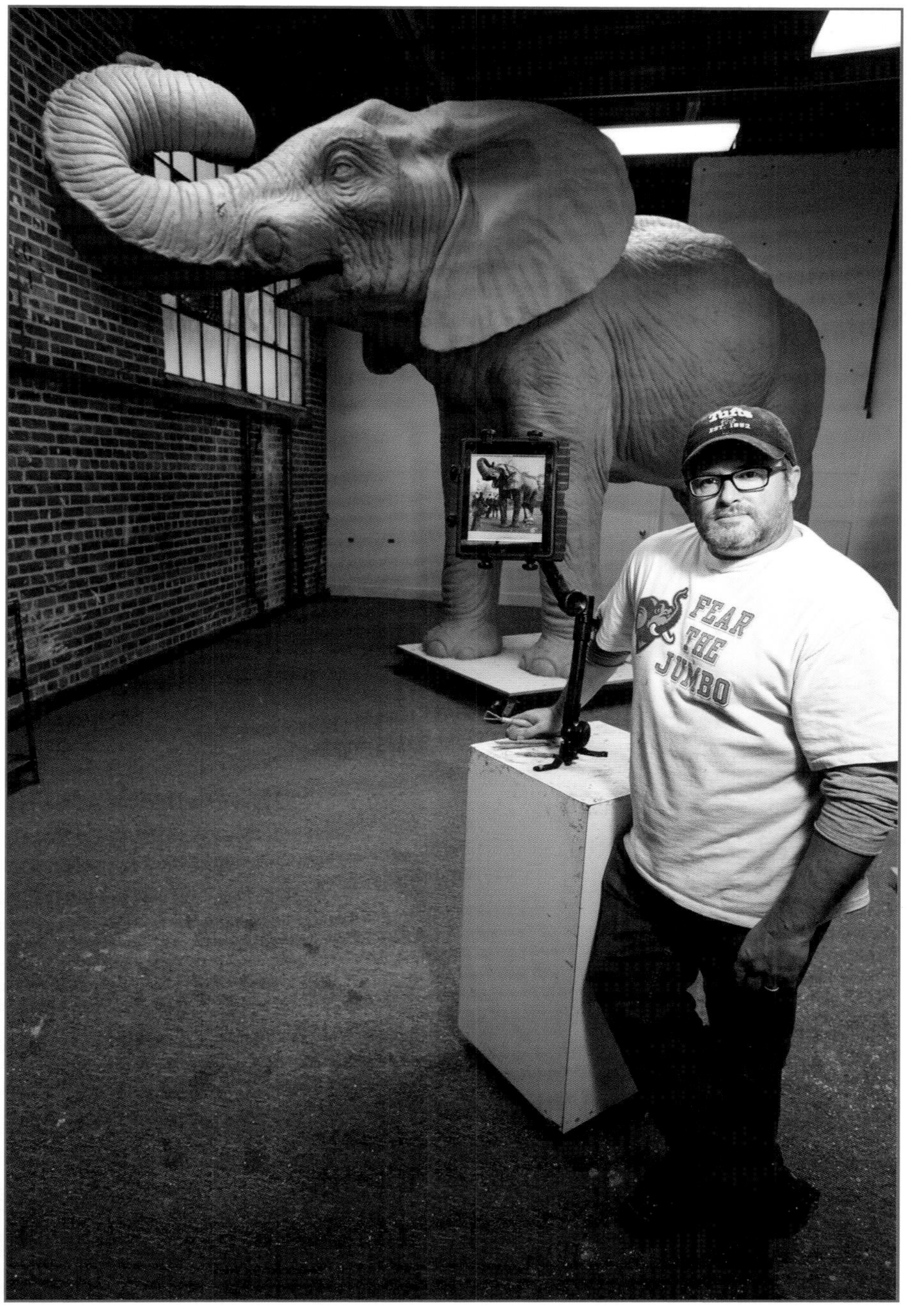
FEAR
THE
JUMBO

LEFT
figure 158
The sculptor Steven Whyte with the full-scale model of his Jumbo statue, 2013. The unveiling of the bronze cast of the model in fall 2014 commemorated the 125th anniversary of Jumbo's arrival on the Tufts campus.

INDEX OF FIGURES AND SOURCES

PAGE 22

figure 38: View of the American Museum, Broadway, New York, *Gleason's Pictorial Drawing-Room Companion* (January 29, 1853)
figure 39: Barnum's Collection of Curiosities, ca. 1864–69. Poster with woodcut illustrations, 20 x 20¾ in. © Shelburne Museum, Vermont

PAGE 24

figure 40: Currier & Ives, *Vantile Mack, The Infant Lambert, or Giant Baby!* ca. 1860. Hand-colored lithograph, 12 x 9 in. © Shelburne Museum, Vermont
figure 41: Currier & Ives, *General Tom Thumb*, ca. 1860. Hand-colored lithograph, 12 x 9 in. Laurence Senelick Collection
figure 42: Currier & Ives, *Old Neptune, The Great Black Sea Lion*, ca. 1860. Lithograph, 12 x 9 in. Collection of the New-York Historical Society

PAGE 25

figure 43: E. & H. T. Anthony, *Anna Swan*, ca. 1860–65. Photograph, 4 x 2½ in. Laurence Senelick Collection
figure 44: Possibly Matthew Brady, *Living Curiosities at Barnum's Museum*, ca. 1865–68. Photograph, 2½ x 4 in. Laurence Senelick Collection
figure 45: D. Appleton, *The Belgian Giant and Commodore Nutt*, ca. 1860–65. Photograph, 4 x 2½ in. Laurence Senelick Collection

PAGE 26

figure 46: Burning of Barnum's Museum, July 13, 1865, 1865. Chromolithograph after the original painting by C. P. Cranch, 6¼ x 10 in. Print Collection, Miriam and Ira D. Wallach Division of Art, Prints and Photographs, the New York Public Library, Astor, Lenox and Tilden Foundations
figure 47: After the fire at Barnum's second museum, 1868. Stereoscopic photograph, 3½ x 7 in. Laurence Senelick Collection

PAGE 27

figure 48: Feejee Mermaid, n.d., L. 15¼ in. © President and Fellows of Harvard College, Peabody Museum of Archaeology and Ethnology, Harvard University, PM#97-39-70/72853 (digital file #6-743308)
figure 49: Advertisement for the Feejee Mermaid from the *Charleston Courier* (January 1843). Photo: Charleston Library Society, South Carolina

PAGE 28

figure 50: P. T. Barnum's New and Greatest Show on Earth Coming by Four Special Trains, n.d. Color lithograph poster, 24½ x 25½ in. The John and Mable Ringling Museum of Art, Tibbals Digital Collection, ht2004438
figure 51: I Am Coming, ca. 1875–79. Framed poster with woodcut illustrations, Diam. 36 in. The Witte Museum, San Antonio, Texas

PAGE 29

figure 52: P. T. Barnum's Great Roman Hippodrome, ca. 1874. Cardboard, paper, 10 x 7½ in. Private collection
figure 53: "P. T. Barnum's Great Traveling World's Fair for the Campaign of 1873," *Harper's Weekly* (March 29, 1873)

PAGE 30

figure 54: Book of Jumbo (1882). 13¾ x 10¼ in. The John and Mable Ringling Museum of Art, Tibbals Digital Collection

PAGE 31

figure 55: Jumbo, The Children's Giant Pet, 1882. Color lithograph poster by the Hatch Lithographic Co., 48 x 30½ in. The John and Mable Ringling Museum of Art, Tibbals Digital Collection, ht2004500
figure 56: "Jumbo's Arrival in America," *Leslie's Illustrated Family Almanac* (1883). Picture Collection, Miriam and Ira D. Wallach Division of Art, Prints and Photographs, the New York Public Library, Astor, Lenox and Tilden Foundations

PAGE 32

figure 57: Thomas Nast, "Mutual Admiration," *Harper's Weekly* (April 15, 1882). Private collection
figure 58: Jumbo and Matthew Scott at Barnum's winter quarters, ca. 1882–84. Bridgeport Public Library, Connecticut
figure 59: "Barnum's Elephants in Winter Quarters," *Harper's Weekly* (January 27, 1883)

PAGE 33

figure 60: P. T. Barnum's Greatest Show on Earth . . . Jumbo, The Largest Living Beast, 1883. Color lithograph poster by the Strobridge Lithographing Co., 30½ x 40 in. The John and Mable Ringling Museum of Art, Tibbals Digital Collection, ht2004522

PAGE 34

figure 61: P. T. Barnum's Greatest Show on Earth . . . Jumbo, 1882. Color lithograph poster by the Strobridge Lithographing Co., 39 x 14¾ in. The John and Mable Ringling Museum of Art, Tibbals Digital Collection, ht2004514

PAGE 35

figure 62: The New Yorker (September 6, 2004) © New Yorker Magazine/Peter de Sève/Condé Nast
figure 63: Jumbo with His New Friends, Madison Square Garden, N.Y., Pine State Java Coffee, 1882. Lithograph trade card by J. H. Bufford & Sons, 6 x 4½ in. Private collection

PAGE 36

figure 64: Jumbo's Arrival, Clark's Spool Cotton, 1882. Lithograph trade card by Buck & Lindner, 4¾ x 3 in. Private collection
figure 65: Jumbo's Vacation, R. W. Bell & Co. "Pure Soaps," 1882. Lithograph trade card by Buck & Lindner, 3 x 4¾ in. Private collection
figure 66: Jumbo Aesthetic, Clark's Spool Cotton, 1882. Lithograph trade card by Buck & Lindner, 4¾ x 3 in. Private collection
figure 67: Jumbo Entertaining His Friends with the Arrow Brand Oysters, E. B. Mallory & Co., ca. 1882. Lithograph trade card, 5¼ x 3½ in. Steve Peters collection
figure 68: Jumbo Paste Blacking, Wilson Yeast & Manufacturing Co., ca. 1882. Lithograph trade card, 3 x 4 in. The John and Mable Ringling Museum of Art, Tibbals Digital Collection, ht5000281

PAGE 37

figure 69: Mrs. Potts' Cold Handle Sad Irons, ca. 1882. Lithograph trade card by Mayor, Merkel and Offman, 3 x 4 in. Steve Peters collection
figure 70: Jumbo Must Go, Willimantic Thread Co., 1882. Lithograph trade card by Forbes & Co., 3 x 5¾ in. Private collection
figure 71: Barnum's Jumbo, Jackson Wagon Company, ca. 1882. Lithograph trade card by Rand, McNally, 5¼ x 7 in. Steve Peters collection
figure 72: The Way Jumbo Was Suspended, Smith Clinch Back Suspenders, 1882. Lithograph trade card by Bufford, 3 x 5 in. Private collection
figure 73: Jumbo Champion "Heavy-Weight," W. G. Bradley Fine Boots and Shoes, ca. 1882. Lithograph trade card, 4 x 2½ in. Private collection
figure 74: J. A. Arneaux, "Jumbo (The Elephant King)" (1883). Sheet music, 14 x 10¾ in. Steve Peters collection

PAGE 38

figure 75: Jumbo rug, ca. 1882–85. Wool, linen, 38½ x 39 in. © Shelburne Museum, Vermont
figure 76: J. A. L.'s Crazy-patch Parlor Throw (detail), 1886. Quilt, 65 x 62 in. Archives Center, National Museum of American History, Smithsonian Institution, Washington, D.C.
figure 77: Thomas Edison's "Jumbo" dynamos at the Electric Lighting Station, Pearl Street, New York, ca. 1882. Engraving. Photo: Thomas Edison National Historical Park, New Jersey
figure 78: Butter dish with lid in "Jumbo" pattern, Canton Glass Co., ca. 1882. Glass, H. 7¼ in. Brooklyn Museum, New York

PAGE 39

figure 79: "The Colossal Elephant of Coney Island," *Scientific American* (July 11, 1885). Picture Collection, Miriam and Ira D. Wallach Division of Art, Prints and Photographs, the New York Public Library, Astor, Lenox and Tilden Foundations

figure 80: Jumbo Mountain, Missoula, Montana, ca. 1910–20. Postcard, 3½ x 5½ in. Private collection. Photo: Christine Cavalier

figure 81: "Jumbo" redwood, Santa Cruz Grove, California, ca. 1910–20. Postcard, 5½ x 3½ in. Private collection. Photo: Christine Cavalier

figure 82: George Washington "Jumbo" McGinnis on Buchner Gold Coin baseball card, 1887. Chromolithograph, 3 x 1¾ in. Private collection

PAGE 40

figure 83: Cut-Up Jumbo jigsaw puzzle, Peter G. Thomson, 1885. Chromolithograph box, 6½ x 5½ in. (top). Tufts University, Digital Collections and Archives, Phineas Taylor Barnum papers, 1818–1893, MS002.001.014.00001.00001

figure 84: Jumbo pull toy, Gibbs Manufacturing Co., ca. 1910–20. Wood, paper, W. 8½ in. Private collection

figure 85: Jumbo alphabet plate, ca. 1882–85. Metal, Diam. 6 in. Private collection. Photo: Christine Cavalier

figure 86: Jumbo pull toy, Hubley Manufacturing Co., ca. 1940. Painted metal, cardboard, W. 4 in. (box). Private collection

figure 87: "Jumbo at Football" bowl, "Jumbo Rinking" cup, ca. 1910. Ceramic, Diam. 7½ in. (bowl). Private collection. Photo: Christine Cavalier

figure 88: Jumbo playing cards, n.d. Paper, 3½ x 2½ in. (each). Private collection. Photo: Christine Cavalier

figure 89: Barnum and Jumbo's A-B-C (London, n.d.). Paperback book, 10 x 11½ in. The John and Mable Ringling Museum of Art, Tibbals Digital Collection

figure 90: Jumbo saddles, *The Schoellkopf Company General Catalog No. 25* (1924). Private collection

figure 91: Jumbo Fruit label, Sunset Produce Co., 1940s. Paper, 10 x 10¾ in. Private collection. Photo: Christine Cavalier

PAGE 41

figure 92: Jumbo Peanut Butter jar and lid, Frank Tea & Spice Co., 1930s. Glass, metal, W. 3 in. (jar). Steve Peters collection. Photo: Philip Bell

figure 93: "The General 'Jumbo' Tire," *Saturday Evening Post* (July 15, 1918)

figure 94: Dead Elephant Ale label, Railway City Brewing Co., 2013. Paper, W. 5 in. Private collection

figure 95: Jumbo Soda bottle, Nemo Bottling Co., n.d. Glass, H. 14 in. Steve Peters collection. Photo: Philip Bell

figure 96: Manley's Best Jumbo Pop Corn can, Manley Inc., 1940s. Metal, H. 9 in. Private collection. Photo: Christine Cavalier

figure 97: Grove's Jumbo Gum wrapper, ca. 1905. Paper, W. 3 in. Private collection

figure 98: V. M. J. Jumbo Cigarettes box, ca. 1945. Cardboard, paper, H. 5½ in. Private collection

figure 99: Pfeiffer's Beer Jumbo Full Quart label, Pfeiffer Brewing Co., 1942. Paper, W. 5 in. Private collection

figure 100: Jumbo matches, Sinclair Oil charm, button, tobacco pins, bottle cap. Matches, 1 x 2¼ in. Private collection. Photo: Christine Cavalier

figure 101: Dr. Peter's Brand Double Jumbo Spirits Turpentine, Rigo Manufacturing Co., n.d. Glass, paper, H. 6¾ in. Steve Peters collection. Photo: Philip Bell

PAGE 42

figure 102: Billy Rose's "Jumbo," 1962. Publicity photograph, 10 x 8 in. Private collection. Photo: Christine Cavalier

figure 103: Billy Rose's "Jumbo," 1962. Movie flyer, 13 x 10 in. Private collection. Photo: Christine Cavalier

figure 104: "Jumbo—King of the Show," B-29 bomber, 1945. Photograph, 3 x 5 in. Steve Peters collection

PAGE 43

figure 105: Billy Rose's "Jumbo," 1935. Theater program, 11¾ x 8½ in. Private collection

PAGE 44

figure 106: "The Killing of Jumbo," *National Police Gazette* (October 3, 1885)

PAGE 45

figure 107: Charles Eisenmann, *Dead Jumbo on the Embankment at St. Thomas*, 1885. Photograph, 4½ x 6½ in. Steve Peters collection

figure 108: Jumbo the Children's Friend Killed, 1885. Die-cut illustration, 4¾ x 6¼ in. Steve Peters collection

PAGE 46

figure 109: Train and crew with rope used to haul Jumbo off the tracks, ca. 1885. Photo: Elgin County Historical Society, Ontario

PAGE 47

figure 110: Objects found in Jumbo's stomach after his death. Elgin County Historical Society, Ontario

figure 111: "The Scene of Jumbo's Heroic Death," from *The Life and Death of Jumbo* (1886). Steve Peters collection

PAGE 48

figure 112: Jumbo's stuffed hide at Ward's Natural Science Establishment, Rochester, New York, 1886. Photo: Department of Rare Books and Special Collections, University of Rochester Library

figure 113: Jumbo's skeleton at Ward's Natural Science Establishment, Rochester, New York, 1886. Photo: Department of Rare Books and Special Collections, University of Rochester Library

PAGE 49

figure 114: Cross section of Jumbo's tusk (front), 1885–86. Ivory, ink, 5½ x 4½ in. Steve Peters collection

figure 115: Cross section of Jumbo's tusk (back), 1885–86. Steve Peters collection

PAGE 50

figure 116: The Life and Death of Jumbo (1886), front cover. Booklet, 10 x 7 in. Steve Peters collection

figure 117: The Life and Death of Jumbo (1886), back cover. Steve Peters collection

PAGE 51

figure 118: Joseph Keppler, "'As Natural as Life.'—Patching Up the Republican Jumbo for 1888," *Puck* (March 31, 1886). Print Collection, Miriam and Ira D. Wallach Division of Art, Prints and Photographs, the New York Public Library, Astor, Lenox and Tilden Foundations

figure 119: Jumbo's skeleton and stuffed hide on tour with the circus, ca. 1886–88. Photo: Circus World Museum, Baraboo, Wisconsin

figure 120: P. T. Barnum & Co.'s Greatest Show on Earth . . . Great Jumbo's Skeleton, 1888. Color lithograph poster by the Strobridge Lithographing Co., 30 x 40¼ in. Library of Congress Prints and Photographs Division, Washington, D. C.

PAGE 52

figure 121: Barnum Museum, Tufts College, 1887. Tufts University, Digital Collections and Archives, Phineas Taylor Barnum papers, 1818–1893, MS002.002.DO.00059

figure 122: Barnum Museum exhibits, 1930. Tufts University, Digital Collections and Archives, Edwin B. Rollins papers, 1860-1976, MS054.003.DO.02421. Photo: Edwin B. Rollins

PAGE 53

figure 123: Reverend Elmer Hewitt Capen, president of Tufts College, ca. 1884. Photograph, 6½ x 4½ in. Tufts University, Digital Collections and Archives, Office of the President records, 1828–2006, UA001.003.DO.00072

figure 124: Specimen cases, Barnum Museum, ca. 1920. Tufts University, Digital Collections and Archives, Historical materials collection, 1852–, UA136.002.DO.02851

PAGE 54

figure 125: Professor John Marshall, 1879. Photograph, 6½ x 4 in. Tufts University, Digital Collections and Archives, Historical materials collection, 1852–, UA136.002.DO.00602. Photo: Amory N. Hardy

figure 126: Letter from P. T. Barnum to John Marshall concerning the transfer of Jumbo to Tufts, March 27, 1889. Tufts University, Digital Collections and Archives, Phineas Taylor Barnum papers, 1818–1893, MS002.001.007.00001.00001

PAGE 55

figure 127: Moving Jumbo into the Barnum Museum, 1889. Tufts University, Digital Collections and Archives, Historical materials collection, 1852–, UA136.002.DO.00823

PAGE 56

figure 128: Jumbo on display at the Barnum Museum, 1889. Tufts University, Digital Collections and Archives, Facilities Management records, 1849–1994, UA021.001.003.00005.00003. Photo: N. L. Stebbins

figure 129: Professor Russell L. Carpenter with unidentified man cleaning Jumbo, 1942. Tufts University, Digital Collections and Archives, Phineas Taylor Barnum papers, 1818–1893, MS002.002.DO.00048

PAGE 57

figure 130: Elephant group in Akeley Hall, American Museum of Natural History, New York, 2012. Photo: Andrew McClellan

figure 131: Old Neptune on display at the New Bedford Whaling Museum, 2014. Photo: Herb Andrew

PAGE 58

figure 132: Barnum Hall on fire, 1975. Tufts University, Digital Collections and Archives, Phineas Taylor Barnum papers, 1818–1893, MS002.002.DO.00275. Photo: J. C. Baer

figure 133: Jumbo's remains after the fire, 1975. Tufts University, Digital Collections and Archives, Facilities Management records, 1849–1994, UA021.001.003.00005.00001. Photo: J. C. Baer

PAGE 59

figure 134: Jumbo's ashes in a peanut-butter jar, Tufts University. Photo: Christine Cavalier

figure 135: Jumbo's tail. L. 15 in. Tufts University, Digital Collections and Archives, Phineas Taylor Barnum papers, 1818–1893, MS002.001.008.00001. Photo: Rosamond Purcell

PAGE 60

figure 136: The Whooperuppers and Jumbo at the Homecoming Day game, ca. 1930. Tufts University, Digital Collections and Archives, Melville S. Munro papers, 1908–1945, MS036.008.022.00774. Photo: Melville S. Munro

figure 137: Football players with Jumbo, 1935. Tufts University, Digital Collections and Archives, Melville S. Munro papers, 1908–1945, MS036.011.DO.00019. Photo: Melville S. Munro

PAGE 61

figure 138: Students in a Jumbo costume accompanying the Tufts football team to a match against Bowdoin College in 1913. Tufts University, Digital Collections and Archives, MS036.001.001, vol. 1, p. 144

figure 139: Shield with Jumbo design for the Jackson College Athletic Association, 1933. Tufts University, Digital Collections and Archives, Jackson Athletic Association, 1942–1948

PAGE 62

figure 140: Tufts men's basketball team, ca. 1950. Tufts University, Digital Collections and Archives, UA46.003.DO.04487

figure 141: Jumbo logo, 1985. Tufts University, Digital Collections and Archives, UA046.007.073.00003.00001

figure 142: 1993–1994 basketball program cover, Tufts University, Digital Collections and Archives, 390900111161342

PAGE 63

figure 143: Jumbo logo, 2005. Tufts University, Marketing and Communications

figure 144: Jumbo American-flag bunting decorating the entrance to Goddard Gymnasium, ca. 1910. Tufts University, Digital Collections and Archives, MS054. 003.DO.2413

PAGES 64–65

figure 145: Students pose as letters to spell out "Jumbo," to advertise the *Jumbo* yearbook, 1917. Letter *J*. Tufts University, Digital Collections and Archives, MS036.001.002, vol. 1, p. 85

figure 146: Letter *U*. Tufts University, Digital Collections and Archives, MS036.001.002, vol. 1, p. 85

figure 147: Letter *M*. Tufts University, Digital Collections and Archives, MS036.001.002, vol. 1, p. 85

figure 148: Letter *B*. Tufts University, Digital Collections and Archives, MS036.001.002, vol. 1, p. 86

figure 149: Letter *O*. Tufts University, Digital Collections and Archives, MS036.001.002, vol. 1, p. 86

figure 150: Period. Tufts University, Digital Collections and Archives, MS036.001.002, vol. 1, p. 86

figure 151: An unidentified woman with Jumbo plaque for the SS *Tufts Victory*, 1945. Photo: Barnum Museum, Bridgeport, Connecticut

figure 152: Jackson students posing with Jumbo, November 25, 1933. Tufts University, Digital Collections and Archives, Melville S. Munro papers, 1908–1945, MS036. 001.055.00001.03344. Photo: Melville S. Munro

figure 153: The Jumbonians jazz band, 1926. Tufts University, Digital Collections and Archives, Munro scrapbooks, vol. 13, p. 16, MS036.001.007.00002

figure 154: Advertisement for a dance raising money for the Tufts endowment fund, 1922. Tufts University, Digital Collections and Archives, Munro scrapbooks, vol. 7, p. 19, MS036.001.007

PAGE 66

figure 155: Tufts students (Judy Tarentino, Linda Haarala [?], and Dorothy Campbell) with Jumbo, ca. 1954. Tufts University, Digital Collections and Archives, Melville S. Munro papers, 1908–1945, MS036.011.DO.00016. Photo: Melville S. Munro

figure 156: Snow sculpture of Jumbo for Zeta Psi, 1950. Tufts University, Digital Collections and Archives, Edwin B. Rollins papers, 1860–1976, MS054.003.DO.02521. Photo: Edwin B. Rollins

figure 157: Homecoming Queen Jean Harrison hugs Jumbo, October 23, 1965. Tufts University, Digital Collections and Archives, UA136.002.DO.01115

PAGE 67

figure 158: The sculptor Steven Whyte with the full-scale model of his Jumbo statue, 2013. Photo: Alonso Nichols

MAP, FOLLOWING PAGE 72

United States of North America (North Eastern Sheet) by W. & A. K. Johnston, London, ca. 1880, 12¾ x 16¾ in.

FURTHER READING

Alberti, Samuel J. M. M., ed. *The Afterlife of Animals*. Charlottesville: University of Virginia Press, 2011.

Barnum, P. T. *Selected Letters of P. T. Barnum*. Edited by A. H. Saxon. New York: Columbia University Press, 1983.

———. *Struggles and Triumphs; or, Sixty Years' Recollections*. Buffalo, NY: Courier, 1889.

Bartlett, A. D. *Wild Animals in Captivity*. Edited by Edward Bartlett. London: Chapman & Hall, 1899.

Bodry-Sanders, Penelope. *African Obsession: The Life and Legacy of Carl Akeley*. Jacksonville, FL: Batax Museum Publishing, 1998.

Bogdan, Robert. *Freak Show: Presenting Human Oddities for Amusement and Profit*. Chicago: University of Chicago Press, 1988.

Bondeson, Jan. *The Feejee Mermaid and Other Essays in Natural and Unnatural History*. Ithaca, NY: Cornell University Press, 1999.

Carzo, Rocco J., Karen Bailey, Linda Hall, and Paul Sweeney, eds. *Jumbo Footprints: A History of Tufts Athletics, 1852–1999*. Medford, MA: Tufts University, 2005.

Chalmers, Paul. *Jumbo: The Greatest Elephant in the World*. Hanover, NH: Steerforth Press, 2008.

Conn, Steven. *Museums and American Intellectual Life, 1876–1926*. Chicago: University of Chicago Press, 1998.

Dahlinger, Fred, Jr. "The Development of the Railroad Circus." *Bandwagon* 27, no. 6 (1983): 6–11; 28, no. 1 (1984): 16–27; 28, no. 2 (1984): 28–36; 28, no. 3 (1984): 29–36.

Daly, Michael. *Topsy: The Startling Story of the Crooked-Tailed Elephant, P. T. Barnum, and the American Wizard, Thomas Edison*. New York: Atlantic Monthly Press, 2013.

Davis, Janet M. *The Circus Age: Culture & Society under the American Big Top*. Chapel Hill: University of North Carolina Press, 2002.

Dennett, Andrea Stulman. *Weird & Wonderful: The Dime Museum in America*. New York: New York University Press, 1997.

Edwards, John. *London Zoo from Old Photographs, 1852–1914*. London: John Edwards, 2012.

Fox, Charles Philip, and Tom Parkinson. *Billers, Banners, and Bombast: The Story of Circus Advertising*. Boulder, CO: Pruett, 1985.

Harris, Neil. *Humbug: The Art of P. T. Barnum*. Chicago: University of Chicago Press, 1973.

Jay, Robert. *The Trade Card in Nineteenth-Century America*. Columbia: University of Missouri Press, 1987.

Jolly, W. P. *Jumbo*. London: Constable, 1976.

Kuhnhardt, Philip B., Jr., Philip B. Kuhnhardt III, and Peter W. Kuhnhardt. *P. T. Barnum: America's Greatest Showman*. New York: Alfred A. Knopf, 1995.

The Life and Death of Jumbo: An Illustrated History of the Greatest, Gentlest and Most Heroic Beast That Ever Lived. Philadelphia, 1886.

McClellan, Andrew. "P. T. Barnum, Jumbo the Elephant, and the Barnum Museum of Natural History at Tufts University." *Journal of the History of Collections* 24, no. 1 (2012): 45–62.

Miller, Russell E. *Light on the Hill: A History of Tufts College, 1852–1951*. Boston: Beacon Press, 1966.

Nance, Susan. *Entertaining Elephants: Animal Agency and the Business of the American Circus*. Baltimore: The Johns Hopkins University Press, 2013.

Poliquin, Rachel. *The Breathless Zoo: Taxidermy and the Cultures of Longing*. University Park: Pennsylvania State University Press, 2012.

Saxon, A. H. *P. T. Barnum: The Legend and the Man*. New York: Columbia University Press, 1989.

Scott, Matthew. *Autobiography of Matthew Scott, Jumbo's Keeper*. Bridgeport, CT: Trow's Printing, 1885.

Shoshoni, Sandra Lash, Jeheskel Shoshani, and Fred Dahlinger, Jr. "Jumbo: Origin of the Word, and History of the Elephant." *Elephant* 2, no. 2 (Fall 1986): 86–122.

Spangenberg, Kristin L., and Deborah W. Walk, eds. *The Amazing American Circus Poster: The Strobridge Lithographing Company*. Cincinnati: Cincinnati Art Museum, 2011.

Sutherland, John. *Jumbo: The Unauthorized Biography of a Victorian Sensation*. London: Aurum Press, 2014.

Weber, Susan, Kenneth L. Ames, and Matthew Wittmann, eds. *The American Circus*. New York: Bard Graduate Center, 2012 .

Wittmann, Matthew. *Circus and the City: New York, 1793–2010*. New York: Bard Graduate Center, 2012.

The letter quoted on pages 19–20 is from M. O. Hunter to Mrs. Rackliffe, dated March 28, 1882, and is among the Barnum papers in the Tufts archives. The letter from James McCaddon to his sisters (p. 45), the telegram from James Hutchinson to James Bailey (p. 46), and the letter from Barnum to Harper Brothers (p. 47) are at the Bridgeport Public Library. Henry Ward's correspondence about Jumbo's hide and skeleton can be found in the Henry Ward Papers, University of Rochester Library. All original material about Jumbo and Tufts is kept in the Digital Collections and Archives at Tufts. The reference to Emily Dickinson as Jumbo is in *The Letters of Emily Dickinson*, ed. Thomas H. Johnson (Cambridge, MA: Belknap Press, 1958), 3: 747. My thanks to Christopher Benfey for this reference.

BIOGRAPHICAL NOTE

Jumbo's trainer and faithful companion, Matthew Scott, died in obscurity at an almshouse in Bridgeport, Connecticut, on December 23, 1914. He was kept on by the Barnum & Bailey Circus as an animal keeper for many years after Jumbo's death. Alice, Jumbo's female companion at the London zoo, was killed in a fire at Barnum's winter quarters in November 1887.

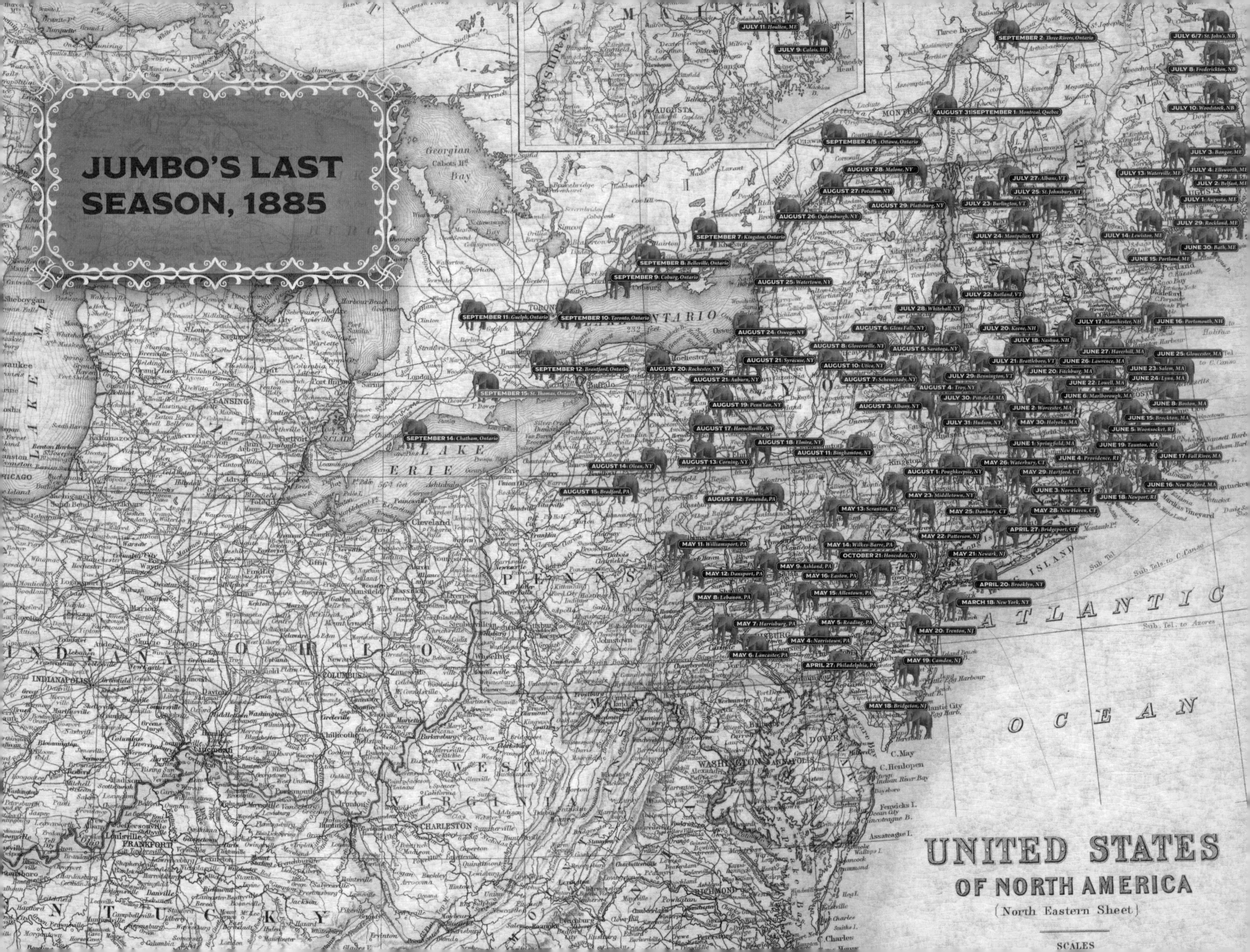
JUMBO'S LAST SEASON, 1885
UNITED STATES
OF NORTH AMERICA
(North Eastern Sheet)
SCALES
MARCH 18: New York, NY
APRIL 20: Brooklyn, NY
APRIL 27: Bridgeport, CT
APRIL 27: Philadelphia, PA
MAY 4: Norristown, PA
MAY 5: Reading, PA
MAY 6: Lancaster, PA
MAY 7: Harrisburg, PA
MAY 8: Lebanon, PA
MAY 9: Ashland, PA
MAY 11: Williamsport, PA
MAY 12: Dansport, PA
MAY 13: Scranton, PA
MAY 14: Wilkes-Barre, PA
MAY 15: Allentown, PA
MAY 16: Easton, PA
MAY 18: Bridgeton, NJ
MAY 19: Camden, NJ
MAY 20: Trenton, NJ
MAY 21: Newark, NJ
MAY 22: Patterson, NJ
MAY 23: Middletown, NY
MAY 25: Danbury, CT
MAY 26: Waterbury, CT
MAY 28: New Haven, CT
MAY 29: Hartford, CT
MAY 30: Holyoke, MA
JUNE 1: Springfield, MA
JUNE 2: Worcester, MA
JUNE 3: Norwich, CT
JUNE 4: Providence, RI
JUNE 5: Woonsocket, RI
JUNE 6: Marlborough, MA
JUNE 8: Boston, MA
JUNE 15: Brockton, MA
JUNE 16: New Bedford, MA
JUNE 17: Fall River, MA
JUNE 18: Newport, RI
JUNE 19: Taunton, MA
JUNE 20: Fitchburg, MA
JUNE 22: Lowell, MA
JUNE 23: Salem, MA
JUNE 24: Lynn, MA
JUNE 25: Gloucester, MA
JUNE 26: Lawrence, MA
JUNE 27: Haverhill, MA
JUNE 16: Portsmouth, NH
JUNE 15: Portland, ME
JUNE 30: Bath, ME
JULY 1: Augusta, ME
JULY 2: Belfast, ME
JULY 3: Bangor, ME
JULY 4: Ellsworth, ME
JULY 6/7: St. John's, NB
JULY 8: Fredericktion, NB
JULY 9: Calais, ME
JULY 10: Woodstock, NB
JULY 11: Houlten, ME
JULY 13: Waterville, ME
JULY 14: Lewiston, ME
JULY 29: Rockland, ME
JULY 17: Manchester, NH
JULY 18: Nashua, NH
JULY 20: Keene, NH
JULY 21: Brattleboro, VT
JULY 22: Rutland, VT
JULY 23: Burlington, VT
JULY 24: Montpelier, VT
JULY 25: St. Johnsbury, VT
JULY 27: Albans, VT
JULY 28: Whitehall, NY
JULY 29: Bennington, VT
JULY 30: Pittsfield, MA
JULY 31: Hudson, NY
AUGUST 1: Poughkeepsie, NY
AUGUST 3: Albany, NY
AUGUST 4: Troy, NY
AUGUST 5: Saratoga, NY
AUGUST 6: Glens Falls, NY
AUGUST 7: Schenectady, NY
AUGUST 8: Gloversville, NY
AUGUST 10: Utica, NY
AUGUST 11: Binghamton, NY
AUGUST 12: Towanda, PA
AUGUST 13: Corning, NY
AUGUST 14: Olean, NY
AUGUST 15: Bradford, PA
AUGUST 17: Hornellsville, NY
AUGUST 18: Elmira, NY
AUGUST 19: Penn Yan, NY
AUGUST 20: Rochester, NY
AUGUST 21: Auburn, NY
AUGUST 21: Syracuse, NY
AUGUST 24: Oswego, NY
AUGUST 25: Watertown, NY
AUGUST 26: Ogdensburgh, NY
AUGUST 27: Potsdam, NY
AUGUST 28: Malone, NY
AUGUST 29: Plattsburg, NY
AUGUST 31/SEPTEMBER 1: Montreal, Quebec
SEPTEMBER 2: Three Rivers, Ontario
SEPTEMBER 4/5: Ottawa, Ontario
SEPTEMBER 7: Kingston, Ontario
SEPTEMBER 8: Belleville, Ontario
SEPTEMBER 9: Coburg, Ontario
SEPTEMBER 10: Toronto, Ontario
SEPTEMBER 11: Guelph, Ontario
SEPTEMBER 12: Brantford, Ontario
SEPTEMBER 14: Chatham, Ontario
SEPTEMBER 15: St. Thomas, Ontario
OCTOBER 21: Honesdale, NJ
ATLANTIC OCEAN
LAKE ERIE
ONTARIO
Georgian Bay